the metapolis dictionary of advanced architecture

city, technology and society
in the information age

Authors

● MANUEL GAUSA
✖ VICENTE GUALLART
✚ WILLY MÜLLER
◆ FEDERICO SORIANO
▲ FERNANDO PORRAS
■ JOSÉ MORALES

Coordination

SUSANNA CROS

★ Contributions by

Iñaki Ábalos
& Juan Herreros, architects
Stan Allen, architect
Eduardo Arroyo, architect
Tom Avermaete, architect
Larraitz de Azumendi, architect
J. Alfonso Ballesteros, architect
Cecil Balmond, engineer
Ben van Berkel & Caroline Bos,
architects
Aaron Betsky, critic
Ole Bouman, critic
Marie-Ange Brayer, historian
Eduard Bru, architect
Karl S. Chu, architect
Xavier Costa, critic
Manuel Delgado, antropologist
Neil Denari, architect
María Luisa González, architect
Alain Guiheux, architect
José Miguel Iribas, sociologist
Francisco Jarauta, philosopher
Alexander Levi, architect
Duncan Lewis, architect
Greg Lynn, architect
Winy Maas, architect
Josep Lluís Mateo, architect
Frédéric Migayrou, philosopher-critic

Marcos Novak, architect
Ignacio Ontiveros, architect
Ignasi Pérez Arnal, architect
Salvador Pérez Arroyo, architect
José Pérez de Lama, architect
François Roche, architect
José Miguel Roldán, architect
Dominique Rouillard, architect
Andreas Ruby, architect-critic
Enric Ruiz-Geli, architect
Antonino Saggio, editor
Juan Carlos Sánchez Tappan, architect
Saskia Sassen, economist
Artur Serra, antropologist
Amanda Schachter, architect
Kelly Shannon, critic
Yorgos Simeoforidis, critic
José Antonio Sosa, architect
Lars Spuybroek, architect
Lars Teichmann, architect
Francisco Tolchinsky, mathematician
Roemer van Toorn, critic
Laura Vescina, architect
Jorge Wagensberg, physicist
Kris van Weert, architect
Mark Wigley, critic
Alejandro Zaera-Polo
& Farshid Moussavi, architects

PRESENTATION

The Metapolis Dictionary of Advanced Architecture was conceived, in its Spanish version, in June 2000, as a document-manifesto of action at *MET 2.0: Tráiler de ideas para una Arquitectura Avanzada*. On that occasion, fifty teams of Spanish architects met in Barcelona for the purpose of formulating a joint approach to strategic themes of the future regarding habitat, the city and the environment. The material gathered there led to the idea of creating a publication in a format which would permit crossing, overlapping and associating projects, themes and potentials, beyond individual conceptions and hermetic compartments.

We present the international version — more complete, extensive and diversified in its contents — which allows the themes initially adressed to be enriched and dealt with in greater detail. The intention with this edition is illustrate a more extensive and global territory of search defining what has come to be called 'Advanced Architecture,' and which brings together transverse attitudes, ideas, concepts, techniques, terms, scenarios and environments which — although addressed more and more frequently in a variety of ideological realms — are in need of an appropriate framework of reference.

The authors.

"Why am I an artist and not a philosopher?
Because I think by words and not by ideas."

ALBERT CAMUS

INTRODUCTION
"In an exquisite corpse what is important are the lines of connection..."

● Throughout these pages and in the format of a selective dictionary of crossed (and cross-referenced) terms (and voices), we seek to identify a new will in architecture. A will based upon a profound change in gazes, criteria, instruments, concepts and attitudes that brings together shared restless-mindedness and common objectives produced, beyond context, in diverse cultural spaces.

This is a network framework, defined today by a relating of searches and complicity in lines of action and research, rather than by a strict following of dogmas or models. A framework that seeks to foster other approaches to new (and old) problems.

Fostering — given the progressive complexity of new scenarios — environments and spatialities which are much more effective: by virtue of being at once precise and complex. Direct and flexible. Relational.

New, more open logics for new less stable scenarios. New actions and new organisations for new situations.

This is a will to revitalise what we have labelled 'advanced' for its innovative and anticipatory spirit.

A will to reactivate, that calls for a critical gaze — and action — alert to still incipient phenomena. Inquisitive. With a combined will for knowledge, relation and action.

Determined to grasp processes and decipher their parameters. Based upon the understanding of the nature of things as well as of the phenomena — and factors — that frame them. Through the assumption of the dynamic actions that determine them and their underlying heterogeneous logics. Seeking out, without inertias or bias, the data and the conditions of the environment itself and getting the most, in qualitative terms, out of their potentials; stretching the limits of new technological capacities; engendering new devices capable of favouring manifold interchange, at all levels. Through a recognition at once operative and tactical.

We have not sought to classify, like entomologists, species or types in closed categories; but rather to venture, like explorers, into still fresh, emergent and untamed territories; at times with intuitive curiosity, at times from an intellectual stance or following programmatic strategy.

The aim of the work presented is to establish a possible reference framework for the interpretation of the current projectual scenario, crossing voices and energies in special synergy.

Its objective: to propose a possible polyhedral definition of the architectural project "tuned into" the logics of the phenomena — and systems — that today define and articulate current understanding and approaches to our environment, and to its associated space and time.

▲ Our desks are being constantly invaded by flashes apparently far from our interests. Imported images which are introduced to our screens very easily: our projects change for the client before they are finished; our building programme changes during construction. For this reason, we just don't understand how there are those that think of architecture as a virtually closed discipline, dignified and serious. Not even how concepts such as context, material or application are visualised from a higher level, to others, which for us are more than the current ones. We have no alternative but to recognize that the interferences, the Browning movement of a drifting buoy, the transversal fracture of a mineral seam or a Ligetti score contain the expression of much of our changes, of many of our ideas. "*Science lets us see, little by little, how evolution is a continuous process of change of what we believe is fixed.*" Virilio *dixit*, that here and now we have no alternative but to accept certain premises in place of others which are presented to us as constants. The zero height of buildings has disappeared to occupy a site does not imply filling empty spaces. The elevations are not a problem of composition because they don't exist, cross-sections are not cuts, but states of mind for those that live in these spaces. So our environment is more a space open to an undisciplined approach than a site in which to exercise a disciplined work. And all this appears to us so obvious that it is not necessary to explain it further. We have referred in other places to new scenarios, new logics, new ways of working. More than new things, we have to say that they are our longings,which allow us the luxury of considering before they overcome us, and which, therefore, we cannot allow ourselves to continue listening to arguments from those who consider such parameters as contingent. For this reason, it is not a bad idea to articulate words and establish terminology. Terms which must be, above all, legible, convincing and which, in their entirety outline the state of the game, open, sensitive, changing, realistic and indisputable. And, consequently, whoever who pronounces such a word and explains it, establishes a link with which you can hear or you can understand, and as a consequence, this word appears to have been always there, bearing all the significance that it can, everything which makes us reflect about the present, a present made of glass which, each time we look at it, foresees for us what lies behind it.

■ The architecture or art that interests us now does not "speak" upon "being;" on the contrary, it proposes a singular syntax for architecture that elicits multiple sensibilities, both unable to be put together and unpredictable. All design attempts to convey meaning, but in the work we are discussing there exists an uncertain relation between form and meaning, that makes its exegesis or reasoning difficult. The affect, derived from this attempted design sense, is uncertain but supported by the phenomenological, so that the enjoyment of space and time is derived specifically from the outcome of the nearby and far-off, between reality and metaphor.
The work's meaning provokes the structuring of unexpected knowledge. Never more opportune, one can say that to design is to know. But this knowledge opens up new categories of "cubbyholes," demonstrating the possibilities of experience.
This project speaks of the construction of worlds, of composite realities. It is about opening possibilities, of constructing new worlds. Towards this

idea, we propose this vocabulary, one of whose intentions is, as Nelson Goodman explains: "*The best we can do is to specify the sort of terms, the vocabulary, [the observer] is to use, telling him to describe what he sees in perceptual or phenomenal rather than physical terms. Whether or not this yields different responses, it casts an entirely different light on what is happening. That the instruments to be used in fashioning the facts must be specified makes pointless any identification of the physical with the real and of the perceptual with the merely apparent.*" (GOODMAN, Nelson, *Ways of Worldmaking*, Indianapolis: Hackett, 1984)

We will try to make this dictionary a tool with which to reconstruct reality and invent worlds.

✚ To invent the format in which new ideas are expressed is to opt for a shift in the centre of gravity of architectural culture: a formatting job and change of operating system at once.

A dictionary (permanently incomplete) of advanced culture is a model of condensation of knowledge, a *zip* of images and words, where true meaning can only emerge from interchange between action and writing.

Only this language – rapid and direct, diagonal and polyglot – is effective and operative in the present, heretofore understanding that interpreting correctly a text is a special case of misinterpretation, according to a reading of *work in progress, of energy flow, of interaction. Knowledge, neither axiomatic nor reductionist, but rather understood as a new version. Knowledge 2.0.*

We need to recompose the arguments that tie us to things, among things, with ourselves, among ourselves: only then will we have anything new to say. A new culture of interchange recognises its images, it identifies them, it deciphers them. It informs us in the same moment as interaction occurs in the intelligent traffic of things and people. Instead of being everywhere at once, let us again occupy the centre of this energy in a new digital renaissance – where we stop being "I" in order to become Internet.

We are aware that to know a culture is to know its language, the words with which it expresses itself. The dictionary of this culture is a way of knowing of where it comes from.

We gather here the words of self-expression of an advanced culture; one that creates, reinvents and uses these words in order to know where it's going. Advancing rapidly, registering ideas® at the speed of the culture of our time.

● This approach, at once global and local, calls for efforts — and experiences — aimed at linking the critical diffusion of the facts (artistic or technical creation) with a cultural, holistic understanding of reality.

"*To know the nature of things in order to act upon them.*"

This is a question not only of exploring new territories but, above all, of proposing in, and for, them new definitions: discoverers, pioneers, adventurers — as well as scientists and philosophers and creators — constitute paradigms of the explorer destined not only to recognise reality, redrawing or replanning it, but also capable of reformulating it, founding new enclaves, locating points of tension, fostering intersections; marking it out — probing, signposting, demarcating — with other signs, with other codes, with other definitions, with other words or expressions ("with" and "in" other terms) those realities in need of new conceptions.

If, in fact, the emergence of the new is almost invariably a cause of uncertainty (precisely because we do not know how to label it, and thus the difficulty of isolating the signs that are its expression and identifying the relationships of those signs with the existing ones) this necessary conceptual reactivation (and redefinition) of language is indispensable for a prospective action that does not stop at establishing a collection of fixed (and all-encompassing) labels. This dictionary is aimed at constructing a hypothetical "basic" web (a matrix of terms, a mesh of codes) open to crossing and combination: aimed at favouring, in the last instance, the recognition of that other network of forces and mechanisms that, in turn, comprises contemporary reality today.

This work is not intended as a summary or compendium of isolated searches, but rather as a possible combined overall reformulation, recognising the conceptual foundation that inspired some of the newly tried paths, many of them parallel, simultaneous and coincident, despite, curiously, having come about in distinct realms. Its objective is to interlink those paths in order to construct a possible map of the contemporary project — and its scenario — from which in turn to select, relate, intersect and synthesise manifold internal stimuli, and impulses, grouped — according to the intensity of the movements that define them — in a format and a layout which are not necessarily linear in their development, reading or description.

Instead of the whole film, its minimal representation: a trailer.

◆ Contrary to conventions that attempt to construct official History, we offer other real stories:

We are witnessing the birth of the old Academy.

Bad omen.

Today, there are too many projects that are criticised as too modern for our time.

Bad sentiment.

We walk around in the dark, or, even worse, with the fixed idea of what is correct, of what one ought to do.

Bad times await us.

We believe ourselves to have prestige abroad, but it's not like that anymore.

Bad dream.

Cultural trends beyond our frontiers march on with strength, purposeful and young. They lack respect for the new tradition, as they believe themselves to be stronger. They have surpassed their teachers, trying to build a new paradigm. They have felt the need to reinvent the language of our architecture.

Words have been so manipulated, interpreted, or copied, that first we must forget them. And then go back and give them meaning. To understand what we know. We invent a word and then we need a concept to express. We read in Rorty: " *The world does not speak. Only we do.*" It continues: "*[the method consists in redescribing] lots and lots of things in new ways, until you have created a pattern of linguistic behaviour which will tempt a rising generation to adopt it, thereby causing them to look for appropriate new forms of non-linguistic behaviour.*" (RORTY, Richard, *Contingency, irony and solidarity*, Cambridge: Cambridge University Press, 1989)

But this dictionary has also been worked on backwards. From the dispersion of various people and media who know each other, but also work independently. Here, in this group of projects, texts, and works, there are many connections, references, and support, that have managed to reveal us with strength from early on.

So much happens by coincidence that we must be talking about the same thing. There is so much novelty that it would be unthinkable to give in to the temptation of doing what has been done before. We have such strength that it would be surprising not to depend on ourselves. We have so many projects that are worth building. We have so many words in hand that together they constitute a dictionary.

✖ We realise that we are now seeing the emergence of a new reality in which information technologies further a way of inhabiting a networked world, that requires a new approach to the conception of architecture and cities. We are now seeing the development of bases for the construction of 'intelligent realities' as a result of the interaction of persons, objects and spaces, in which architecture and its associated disciplines can be the integrators of processes and occurrences of this 'metareality.'

Faced with this new situation, architects cannot merely be passive problem-solvers; they have to accept a new active condition, like that of strategists who ask questions of their surroundings and anticipate lines of action. Whose form of procedure is based not on the application of a profession that is learned and mutually consented, but on innovation in planning processes and the application of the new techniques and materials that they help to develop.

This book has been written in the desire to relate to the multiple disciplines that have anticipated this advanced condition of reality to which we aim to respond from the field of architecture. With ideas and projects.

The scale of the architecture project therefore ranges 'from bits to geography.' From the software that interacts with places and projects them beyond their physical reality, to the flows and synergies running through the territory and organising the local action of the construction of new inhabited landscapes. An interaction between the natural, the artificial and the digital that draws up new rules for 'the art of dwelling'.

INSTRUCTIONS: PROTOCOL FOR USE

This *Metapolis Dictionary of Advanced Architecture* seeks to contribute to
the shaping of an overall — not necessarily absolute — vision of what manifests itself as an architectural action linked to what has been called "advanced culture," now present in many disciplines of contemporary art,
thought and technology.

In light of this and for the sake of synthesis, it was decided to define those
terms capable of reflecting the realm, the characteristics and impact, of an
architecture firmly inscribed in the information society and influenced by
the new technologies, the new economy, environmental awareness, interest in the individual, etc.
The decision to include a number of authors and special contributions should
be seen as a means of favouring the crossing and complicity of visions
and choices of like bent.

For the purpose of making the book more accessible to the reader, the dictionary offers various forms of entries for consultation:
— On one hand, a ideological dictionary (see the term 'ideological dictionary') located roughly in the centre contains analogical groups of words
related to a certain idea, ordered alphabetically according to their corresponding entry word.
The reader will find a possible path to follow in becoming familiar with and
verifying the elements of advanced architecture.
Not always do all those words that disciplinary tradition would lead one to
expect appear within a specific group. This is not normally due to an error of omission but rather to a purposeful, intentional decision: the value
and meaning of many of the common terms of traditional architecture have
changed (or are changing) in the new logic of advanced architecture. It is
expected that this terminological association will be one of the first paths
of consultation in using this dictionary.
Starting with the generic, the entries progress towards the particular.
— On the other hand, the dictionary is laid out in alphabetical order (from
the particular to the general), with the corresponding definitions following
the terms of the entry. As in all alphabetical dictionaries, this serves for
finding or pinpointing the meaning of a term.
At the front is found a list of codes which indicate the author of each entry, whether or not there are illustrations and other information of interest. Each definition, then, may include one or various interpretations in the
form of written "dialogue."
In addition, depending upon the scope of the term, at the beginning of each
definition there may be a list of links, that is, a series of words related to
that term, which may be consulted to find more information regarding the
topic at hand (this is the list in brackets headed by the sign →).
In certain cases, where the semantic relationship between terms is close

enough to be explained in the same manner, the definition of a word may consist only of a reference to another. This is indicated by "See" followed by the word to which the reader should refer.

The remaining text is essentially the written material necessary to understand the different elements and foundations of advanced architecture. Arranged alphabetically (like an easy-to-use manual), the manner in which the terms are explained allows the dictionary to be thought of not only as a tool for consultation, but also as a book for more conventional reading.
— A third dictionary (see 'synthetical') synthesises some of the key definitions of this work in short sentences, in the form of mottos or aphorisms of interest in themselves.
— At the end of the book there is the index, where the reader will find the list of all the architects, critics, engineers, designers, philosophers, etc. who appear on the dictionary, either with the projects either with the definitions (except the authors). It is a tool to understand what kind of architecture, which position or which themes everyone deals with.
— Finally, it should be pointed out that this is an illustrated dictionary and thus a word may bear satisfactory definition by means of an accompanying image. This does not mean that words appear without written definition, rather the illustrations facilitate quick consultation and explanation of the terms dealt with herein.

Most of the illustrations are from architectural projects and show the characteristics explained in the definition of the corresponding word. Otherwise the images are "snatches" which, although not specifically related to architectural projects, provide a definitive illustration of the desired explanation. Special mention should be made of those illustrations which, due to their size (one or two) and importance (projects representative of the most recent architecture) stand out notably from the rest of the dictionary. These are points of intensity which, as interruptions, focus the material that makes up the whole of the dictionary. This contributes to our insistence on the intention of conceiving the dictionary as a trailer-book for non-continuous and not necessarily linear reading, in addition to its intended use as tool for endeavouring to understand and define architecture — and, by extension, culture — implied in the shift from the notion of production to the idea of information, which here, contrary to classical or modern logic, we have chosen to call advanced.

KEY SIGNS

Authors:
- ● Manuel Gausa [MG]
- ✖ Vicente Guallart [VG]
- ✚ Willy Müller [WM]
- ◆ Federico Soriano [FS]
- ▲ Fernando Porras [FP]
- ■ José Morales [JM]

Collaborators:
- ★ Contributors [co]
  Citations [c]

Complements to definitions:
See= refer to an other definition
→ = associated terms
[i] Illustrations on another page

Meanings:
Some definitions include meanings in
smaller bold type.
These are referred to with the sign >.

A

✖ AA

[VG] Advanced architecture. See 'advanced>advanced architecture.'

★ abduction

→ 'criticism'

[co] The Latin American anthropologist Jesús Martín Barbero characterises new popular urban cultures by their use of knowledge and alternative action he calls abduction. Abduction, according to the Spanish language dictionary, denotes the epis-
temological action of taking a lateral exit in syllogism after the second premise,
rather then going forward to a conventional conclusion.
Understood as such, abduction is a form of resistance to the hegemony. In its best-
known contemporary use, related to stories of aliens, abduction denotes an irresistible attraction for something that is apparently aberrant.
The most effective criticisms of hegemonic concepts such as development, capitalist globalisation, democracy, town planning, market, architecture and education,
for example, are associated with the sphere of abduction. JOSÉ PÉREZ DE LAMA

■● abroad, etc.

→ 'action',
'Benidorm', 'field',
'foreigness', 'void'

[JM] Abroad is the sensation of subjects who are permanently "in transit." Today's
city is tied to the idea of the transit of its subjects. The city, more than a
sum of spaces, is the sum of time-actions. As a consequence, what are
relevant in a city are non-places, as Marc Augé has proposed.

[MG] See 'no-places (non-places).'

●◆ abstract

→ 'diagrams', 'global',
'maps', 'open'
'precision', 'synthetical'

[MG] Abstract is no longer essential, but synthetical. It is not refined (reduced
or extracted) information, but condensed information (compressed in order to be multiplied). Abstract meaning economic: diagrammatic.
Evolutionary (multi-layered) information, rather than minimalised (stripped)
information. Operative (dynamic) code, rather than substantial (static)
code. No longer "less is more," but "more from less."

[FS] Abstract is a quality defined and pursued by Modernity. Although there has
been a search to find relations and origins in Antiquity and Primitivism, the
Modernist 'abstract' invention is original and specific. Rather than representing nature as the only model of reality, technical and scientific advance
has made manifest another reality – removed from the concrete world and
whose image already does not correspond with nature. It does, however,
maintain a conceptual tie. The new reality of abstraction behaves as a model that substitutes the place of nature with a corresponding quality.
Today, these abstractions have recovered their role foreign to theoretical models and naturalist philosophies and are maintained as new realities and autonomous representations. They need not lose their condition to order the world.

[i] p. 22-23

Kazuyo SEJIMA,
Movements ideogram for
zig-zag typologies,
*Metropolitan Housing
Studio,* 1996.

Programmes on height

Ludwig MIES VAN
DER ROHE:

*Westmount Square
Building,* Montreal
(Canada), 1965-68.

*Seagram Office
Building,* New York,
1954-1958.

*Lake Shore Drive
Appartments,* Chicago
(USA), 1948-1951.

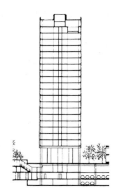

Educational facilities

Giuseppe TERRAGNI,
*Sant'Elia
Kindergarten,*
Como (Italy),
1936-1937.

Singular objects

LE CORBUSIER,
Ville Stein,
Garches (France),
1927.

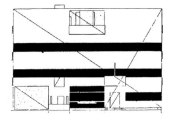

Public facilities

Ludwig MIES VAN
DER ROHE:
*Laboratory of chemistry
and metals* (IIT),
Chicago (USA), 1945.
National Gallery,
Berlin, 1967.

Multifunctional buildings

Louis I. KAHN,
*Brittish studies and art
centre,* Yale University,
New Haven (Connecticut,
USA), 1969-1977.

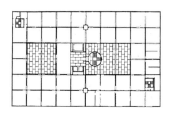

 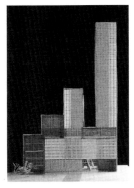

Programmes on height

S&Aa (SORIANO-
PALACIOS),
*Competition for
cultural centre
and auditorium,*
Benidorm (Alicante,
Spain), 1995.

Educational facilities

OMA, *Educatorium,*
Utrecht
(The Netherlands),
1997.

Singular objects

MVRDV, *Villa VPRO,*
Hilversum
(The Netherlands),
1997.

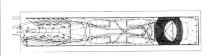 

Public facilities

FOA, *International
Port Terminal,*
Yokohama (Japan),
2002.

Multifunctional buildings

Toyo ITO,
Mediatheque, Sendai
(Japan), 2002.

● abstract and concrete

[MG] See 'abstract.'

The abstract is often opposed to the concrete and vice versa. Nonetheless, the architecture defined herein is at once of both natures: it responds to abstract logics and to concrete conditions. It does not resort to an ideal — refined, essential and Apollonian — purity, but rather emerges from a generic dimension only to deform, alter and bear influence, that is, to become enriched and inseminated with multiple layers of information provided by each of the different realities contemplated and addressed.

Eduardo ARROYO
(NO.mad
Arquitectura),
*Desierto
Square,* Barakaldo
(Vizcaya, Spain),
1999.

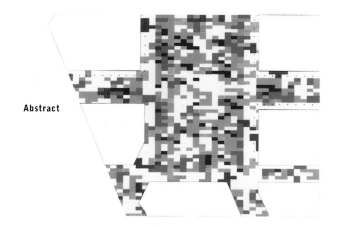

Abstract

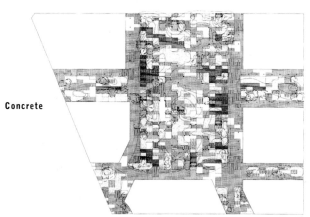

Concrete

★ abs-traction

[co] Abs-traction is a form of traction, a form of a-ttraction; something is abs-tract when it has attracted towards itself (or has removed for itself, drawing it away) another thing or things. All of the things that have been attracted in this way (drawn towards the abstract) are contained in the abstraction which is, therefore, a form of con-traction; the abs-tract is such because it contracts many things, because it is a con-tract (bringing together) of many things. Contemporary abstraction thus alludes to the compressive nature of publicness, by definition that of a space that is symbolic, absorbent, ambiguous, allusive, attractive, summarised and synthesised, schematic and imaginary. (PARDO, *Las formas de la exterioridad,* p. 241)
JOSÉ ALFONSO BALLESTEROS

● a-couplings

[MG] Traditionally, dualism illustrates the conceptual division of the world into categories: it is the exact recognition of a reality pointing to univocal, absolute classifications. This would be a "natural" tendency, rather than an intellectual or conscious effort – as Douglas R. Hofstadter has pointed out (HOFSTADTER, Douglas R., *Gödel, Escher, Bach: An Eternal Golden Braid,* New York: Basic Books, 1979) – which despite its apparent rational component occurs far below the upper strata of thought:

" *The essence of dualism is founded on language and consists fundamentally of words, mere words, articulated meanings meant to express an essential and intrinsically dichotomic "idea," since each word tends to represent as then a fixed category of meanings."*

Today, however, old substantive categories repeatedly clash with the undisciplined conditions of mixtures and slippages that, in all their manifestations, call for the brutal (and exciting at the same time) dissolution of the old *dichotomic* divisions which, for long years, were paradigms of our ideological and disciplinary baggage: *exterior/interior, natural/artificial, public/private, order/chaos, determinate/indeterminate, formal/informal, routine/extraordinary, domestic/universal, particular/general, discontinuous/linked, open/closed,* etc. All comprise of simultaneous voices and, therefore, mixed actions, and possible experiences. These "dual" voices are as ambiguous as they are explicit, born of unnatural couplings between formerly opposing terms which, nonetheless, are today fused in mongrel – bastardised. They are operations that provoke another type of more fertile situation creating new – and more intriguing – meanings; but also new – and more "uncodified" – principles associated with the capacity for hybridisation – and transfusion – of the contemporary project.

These fusions of former dichotomies do not seek to construct through contradiction compositions – or extravagances (the latter would be the Venturian option, more akin to aesthetic irony than to operative paradox) – but rather through interactions capable of reconciling – of making coexist – in the same hybrid framework twin – *coupled* – phenomena, the more paradoxical the more, apparently, impossible.

ULAY&Marina ABRAMOVICH, *Action and a-coupling.*

● act

[MG] See 'act-n.'

●✖★■ action

[MG] **architecture-action**

Architecture-action is an effect of expressing, operating, executing and doing. Requires energy, decision and capability. That is, disposition.

[VG] What we are interested in today is an 'action-architecture' defined by a desire to act, to (inter)act. That is, to activate, to generate, to produce, to express, to move, to exchange and to relate.

[MG] To 'agitate' events, spaces, concepts and inertias.
To promote interactions between things, rather than interventions on them.
Movements rather than positions. Actions rather than figurations.
Processes, rather than occurrences.

[co] We approach action as a generating mechanism, as a suggestion, as an alterer of stable awareness; that which is engaged in action remains in constant movement until it disappears. Action is an approach to the characteristics of architecture from unstable, shifting positions, not determined *a priori*, but rather dependent upon environmental factors, emotional factors, casual elements and other "interveners."
Action is a means of understanding architecture as an expression of reality more than as an evocation of the artificial systems with which man equips himself. As architects, we strive to respond to social events, but we answer with squares, circumferences and boxes. Moreover, the indisputable, absolute, irrefutable situations we create, we also seek to endure over time, such that they survive us, although the environment for which they were created constantly changes.
Academicism in behaviour is, in fact, not possible. Non-mechanical behaviour is natural to man because man's reactions naturally vary depending on his environment. While it is true that he establishes agreements for coexistence, they are never absolute in their execution; and when, in spite of it all, they hypertrophy, they produce splendidly comical scenes.
Actions are generators of attitudes. Attitude is a position shared with the object based upon which it is judged, possessed, used and altered.
Action is a category closely related to passion. Passion is the passive character of an action. Passion is the state in which something is affected by an action (as when something is broken by the action of destroying or when something is constructed by the action of constructing). It is not surprising, then, that architecture should stir passions only when it is the product of action, not of production. Generally speaking, the vestige of action is energy.
Passion is, therefore, also a vestige of action.
Action as such is ephemeral; it leaves only traces, passions. Watching the films of Gordon Matta Clark, one realises that the intervention is really the action and not what remains afterwards. The cutting, clearing away rubble and disassembling at the same time as the environment is modified – that is the true intervention.
Like the architecture contained in construction. All that remains in the aftermath is passion, understood as architecture insofar as there occurs inevitable alterations in use and time.
JOSÉ ALFONSO BALLESTEROS

[c] "*The decreasing importance of the production of objects, the taste for the ephemeral and for action, has permeated many of the last three decades' proposals which brought a critical approach to the connotations of language, value and aura running through art.*
Like in the architecture of the event, many of these experiences involved materialisation in a work, or representation by objects, rather than an experience of time and space (or an attempt to transform the public's perception or consciousness of the work of art by actions).
In this way, the object becomes the direct materialisation, with no mediation, of an idea which, as such, is unapprehensible, leaves no trace and cannot be subject to transaction. In addition to being, above all, an upheaval which aimes to destabilise art's commercial set-up, it shares an extremely transitory nature with certain forms of architectures: the end of the event also means the end of the architecture (or of the work).
From this point of view, a non-permanent architecture acts both inside and outside the system. Its ability to set itself up comfortably in the material, cultural world of our capitalist society and at the same time be an incisive critical instrument, neither adopting a posture of resistance nor letting itself be carried away by pure, unreflecting banality, is what makes it irresistibly attractive, thereby increasing its capacity for fascination."
(DÍAZ MORENO, Cristina; GARCÍA GRINDA, Efrén, "Impermanent architecture," *Quaderns* 224, 1999)

[JM] Action may begin when one speaks, but it can also be what interrupts discourse. From K. Schwitters to J. Pollock and from J. Beuys to F. Gehry, the concept of dissolution is what initiates work. Thus, it is also the reality base upon which one builds, in the sense that what remains after action are the traits, not completely articulate, of bodies making their way before a curtain, in landscapes or between the remains of earlier constructions. Language runs aground and meaning gives way before these actions define spaces in their own manner. A flood of words accompanies the excess of the working body, running and measuring itself against limits imposed by objects among, or by the rooms or landscapes in which we live.
To the phenomena that surround us, always closer to the subjects than to discourse, it superimposes pleats, disquieting noise or flattening silence.
These events, united in their interpretation of the pre-spatial quality of architecture, have come to surround the meaning of art and its works.

[co] Since the 1950's, architecture has consumed utopia. Utopia has become a negative novel, a negative utopia, the opposite of any project of mastery. Today's utopia is that of action upon the real: realising the architecture of utopia. We work only on material projects, materialist projects. There is an enormous need to do things on the limit-basis of this tense negotiation with the real, which we must infiltrate.
ALAIN GUIHEUX, DOMINIQUE ROUILLARD

Action in space-time
Toni GIRONÈS, *Installation "Throwing at Passanes*
Cadaqués (Girona, Spain), 1995.

Action and activity in public spaces
Temporary installations for ludic uses.
Xavier COSTA (curator), ÁBALOS & HERREROS, Vicente GUALLART, MVRDV,
RIEGLER & RIEWE, *Project "Fabrications,"* Barcelona, 1998.

[MG] **action, critical (explorations as opposed to chronicles)**

Like the bothersome – and mischievous – interloper in the Lumière brothers' film *Watering the Waterer* (*L'arroseur arrosé*, Paris, 1901), in an atmosphere vitiated with placidity or routine, a critical action truly committed to the advance of ideas is an element which is at once revitalising and transformative. A critical action is precise (intentional) and transgressive (undisciplined); a nasty but salutary shock *of* and *for* possible dormant scenarios, aimed at stimulating the present and arousing possible future spaces. It signifies alternative possibilities – anticipatory lines of research or decidedly innovative projects – and accepts, at the same time, the risk of all hazardous adventure that ends up involved in – and marked by – the action itself.

Active intrusiveness
LUMIÈRE Brothers,
L'arroseur arrosé,
Paris, 1901.

A critical action is geared more towards the quest for the emergent – the new, the "non-homologated" – than the description of the time-honoured, the "previously documented" (the merely notarial – and/or documental – activity of the mere chronicle, neutral – or fetishist – vis-à-vis the present, or erudite and nostalgic vis-à-vis a past now alien to our ambitions).

There are, nonetheless, other types of courses – more venturesome than prudent, more transverse than single-minded, more transdisciplinary than disciplinary – which in today's moment of technological changes and cultural transitions, receive impetus:

- concrete courses, in the form of action – with a certain accepted degree of belligerence – no longer aim at favouring the quantitative presentation of established discourses, but favour the qualitative anticipation of emergent potentials.

- concrete courses, in the form of reflection, aim at questioning the old time-honoured lessons, the mechanically accepted dogmas or those totemic images – and formulas – finished in themselves. Courses seek to examine new foci of interest, often clumsy – because they are incipient – but with sufficient vitality to recognise the birth of new landscapes of research and to stimulate the development of.alternative actions, which, though not wholly defined, are sufficiently sensed.

Explorations signal a will to propose, for the contemporary scenario, spaces of change approachable only from more open orders of definition, in accordance with the evolutionary potential of interchange and information; processes destined, in the last instance, to become further complicated and transformed beyond the old closed control of shape. Explorations as opposed to chronicles.

[co] **action or contemplation**

The possible positions – vis-à-vis our environment and, by extension, vis-à-vis our constructed environment – are action and contemplation. From contemplation we gain distance from the work, the supposed objectivity, what we already have and must accept as correct. From contemplation we obtain the pure delight of speculation. Contemplation takes pleasure in making suppositions, valuable in themselves, without any need to conform to the real.

The option to intervene, to manipulate, to superpose, to influence anything and everything within our reach is now almost a need that gives all that surrounds us the quality of variability. Architecture that modifies the world, that intervenes decisively in our environment, is an action – an action that leaves traces, objects subjects of action, passions. Architecture should leave in its wake an exciting world.
JOSÉ ALFONSO BALLESTEROS

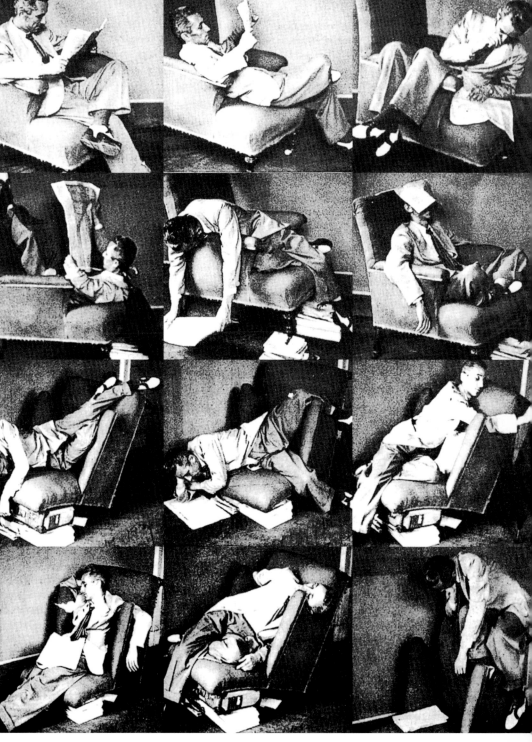

Critical action as a reagent
Bruno MUNARI, *Search for comfort in an uncomfortable armchair*, 1950, from *Fantasia*.

▲ activation

→ 'action>critical', 'act-n', 'avatar', 'client', 'context', 'decisions (and instructions) rather than designs', 'environment', 'field'

[FP] Activation is the action for excellence.

Activation proposes the most enriching reply to a request.

Activation may be endogenous or exogenous, both cases being equally positive.

Activation is always transforming, never inert or indifferent.

Activation is not only a direct response to an event or a provocation, but also something which implies commitment and results from the reaction, in the chemical meaning of the word, of transformation or progress.

Activation is classified as an indispensable quality of progressive architecture. The land is activated with the presence of the architecture; architecture operates through its use; use operates in relation to the new sensitivity to materials; materials are transformed in relation to the land which separates and unites us.

● activity

→ 'act-n', 'aformal', 'flexibility', 'function', 'infiltration', 'in-out', 'intelligence', 'multi', 'operative', 'plural', 'product', 'program'

[MG] See 'dynamism'.

[MG] A dynamic architecture is vitalising: it generates not only aesthetics – or shape – but also (above all) activity (not merely functional action, but as active materialisation of simultaneous actions and uses – as operative movements, generators of interchange operations between programmes, shapes, assiduous spaces, and events).

It is an architecture capable of favouring spaces that are more "unsettled," precisely by virtue of being active and activated: produced with a reactive (reactivating), flexible, plural and relational will, catalyst of possible (inter)actions between space(s), culture(s), information(s) and behaviours.

● act-n

→ 'action>critical', 'activation', 'activity', 'logic, direct', 'unrestrained (<un> factors)'

[MG] We the adopt the prefix ACT for its universal, plural and implicitly dynamic nature; implying active and activating at the same time.

It means, in fact, TO ACTIVATE (enliven, excite, accelerate).

But as well, TO ACT(UATE) (to put into action, exercise and undertake with determination).

It suggests ACTIVITY (that of a functional, or better said, operative action).

It implies ACT-TITUDE (a disposition of intentional spirit, a criterion for action).

It generates ACTUALITY (actual – in the sense of current, present – action, actuation, activity and attitude, effective in that which is real and anticipatory in that which is virtual).

● act-titude (attitude)

[MG] See 'act-n.'

● actuality

[MG] See 'act-n.'

● adaptation

[MG] See 'ad-herence / inheritance.' Adaptation is the flexible capacity of fitting and/or moulding a conceptual, abstract, strategy to specific, concrete, conditions.

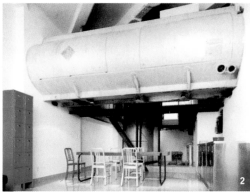

1. PÉRIPHÉRIQUES, *PinkGhost*, exhibition Place Furstemberg, Paris, 28 may-28 june 2002.
2. A body of a truck can be used for a dwelling. LOT/EK, *Morton Duplex*, New York, 1999.

+ adherence / inheritance

→ 'and', 'complicity', 'contract', 'flexibility', 'graft', 'infiltration', 'intelligence', 'interchange', 'strategy'

[WM] Adherence / inheritance is a script of greatest interest – that of its plot and that of its separation. Adherences follow from separating the genealogical package, and inheritance appears without warning in any operation of coupling, adaptation, grafting, superposition.

Adherences / inheritances are strategies of occupation, subtle and sibylline, amid some legality regarding consolidated territories altering radically meaning and bringing into crisis the model that sustains it.

It means that the previous model is dead, but not the inheritance.

This is the plot of separation. It is the *script*.

1. Willy MÜLLER + THB Consulting, *AD1 and AD2. Occupation structures*, Barcelona.

2. Santiago CIRUGEDA, *Inhabited scaffold*, Seville (Spain), 1999.

●◆▲✕ advanced

[MG] Advanced is moved, set forward or in the front. It may also be seen as innovative. To advance is, in fact, to move forward along a course or toward a terminus or goal; but also to further a cause or provide ahead of time. To thrust – or project – forward.

An action (an architecture) that is advanced is an action (an architecture) which is necessarily projective: propositive and anticipatory/anticipating.

An action (an architecture) with the capacity to connect with technological change (industry and technique), with cultural progress (thought and creation) and with scientific logic (research and development).

An action (an architecture) which values (ambitious) exploration, (rigorous) prospecting, (precise) application and (engaged) diffusion of potentially more qualitative — operative and complex — ideas.

An action (an architecture) that believes in the constant need to feed the system with energy. An action (an architecture) that works with interchange, relation, information and evolution.

An action (an architecture) which is "reinforming." precisely by virtue of being "informational."

advanced architecture

[FS] What advances, what progress! Walking architects as opposed to contemplative architects. Propositions as opposed to positions.

[FP] Advanced in the past used to mean a certain risk of disconnection (the vanguard could lose contact with the rest of the army). For us, to advance is to drag, to drive forward without leaving anyone behind.

[MG] There now seems to be a new architecture emerging on the horizon; beyond conventional iconography or the fixing of the object, it is an architecture positively bound to change: with events and the temporal and evolutionary dimension of processes. An architecture aware of the future importance of interchange and information. An architecture which, nevertheless, seeks to speak about the present, about day-to-day life. To provide expression, joy and freshness for a new emergent ordinariness and, consequently, dignity and stimulus for life. It is a path littered with traps (vanity, limelight-seeking behaviours, even cynicism, affectation and greed) but, today, it demands only a positivist and optimistic realism – marked by integrity, lack of restraint, joy and collaboration: between intuitions and investigations; between intentions and stimuli; between relationships and events – just as the reactive nature of the environment calls for.

Thus, we might ask ourselves whether this shared interest in these potentials does not define already a truly precise framework – as was the case in the 1930s and 50s – which lends itself transcending the traditional systems of disciplinary organisation and to the capacity for proposing new spatial dispositions, as precise and effective as they are open and exciting.

[VG]

• In order to build the future, it is necessary to accept the fact that major changes will be taking place in the near future, due to the information revolution, and that this revolution will affect every level of humanity.

• The advent of the digital world is a new possibility for humankind: for it to reinvent both itself and its environment.

• Digital culture may help humankind to advance in knowledge, to find answers to the old questions and to formulate new questions.

• The world is waiting to be built, innovation is the source of every project; we live in a state of permanent creation.

• The entire planet is a city; empty and full spaces must be planned with the same degree of interest.

• We think more in terms of landscape than of construction, of nature than of occupation, of integration than of superposition.

• The hybridisation of cultures, natures and processes, leads to greater complexity of proposals and opens up new lines of action.

• We are talking of processes, rather than occurrences; of open forms, rather than closed designs; of operating strategies, rather than finished pieces.

• Individuals are defined one by one, not as a mass.

• Where hierarchies exist, they are produced by knowledge, rather than norms.

• The world is built by the coming together of multiple individual persons; the traditional hierarchies of business and politics will disappear in coming years.

• People must be valued for their qualities, not for their quantities (years, money, etc.).

• A city is built inwards, it does not grow indefinitely; it is re-informed and protects its own environment.

• Sustainable development, on a global and a local scale, calls for urban and territorial ecosystems that must function for centuries.

• The digital world and the physical world will merge into a single interface that embraces everything, so the two have to be planned with the same intensity.

• We have to act locally and globally at the same time; cultures have to adopt dynamics of their own and interact.

• Education comes from within each individual, rather than from external systems. Learning requires training.

• Artificial intelligence will be one of the pillars of human and cybernetic activities in coming years, and this will change the way we work, the way we act.

1. Advanced architecture is to the digital society what modern architecture was to the industrial society: an architecture bound up with interchange and information. With the capacity for displacement and modification. With the dynamic evolution of processes and their associated spatial definition.

2. Advanced architecture is an architecture with a humanist bent, made by and for humankind. It is also positivist, with faith in its capacity to introduce positive energy into an environment qualified by the optimisation of those instruments, means and technologies developed by that same environment.

3. Advanced architecture is thus progressive and optimistic. It opts for a state of qualitative change produced through an effective combination of heterogeneous data, flows and bits of information. In an increasingly complex reality, it seeks to work with that complexity: not to limit its effects, but rather to multiply its potentials.

Accepting a greater degree of flexibility and mixedness in its actions. Creating more plural — and complex — scenarios in which to combine indetermination, interaction, innovation and information.

4. Advanced architecture occurs, in fact, as an outcome of a direct process of interchange; in synergy and flexible interaction with the environment in which it acts. It is an act of active ecology that interacts decidedly with the environment, whether natural, artificial or digital. Advanced architecture is, therefore, a reactivating architecture to the extent that it strives to react with reality in order to restimulate it. Innovating it: at once reinforming it and recycling it. Exchanging information with and within it.

5. Advanced architecture is a more relational architecture. It does not necessarily require hi-tech means, but rather supposes acting with coherency between means and ends. There is no first or third world advanced architecture, but rather situations of interchange that are diverse, plural and singular, although interlaced with a glocal logic aimed at favouring simultaneous events and activities: local and global.

6. Advanced architecture is an architecture which is more open: non-determinist; non-closed, unfinished and non-prefigured. Not limited in its movements. An architecture capable of expressing its own movements, but also the different demands that call for and shape it. Capable of working beyond the boundaries and the — traditional — dichotomies. With the context and beyond the context. With the place and with the city. With the city and with the geography. An architecture that is conceived as an operative system, rather than logic, as a closed design. As a processing logic rather than as a formal aesthetic. As a strategy, rather than as a composition.

7. Advanced architecture alludes to processes produced within and through the network.

Buildings and cities, spaces and activities, are defined as parts of a physical, operative system in constant interchange and interaction with the digital world. Crossings of forces in a "cybrid" environment.

An environment which suggests not formulas for universal action, but tactical criteria for recognition. Not disciplines, but transdisciplines. In this environment, architecture springs from the collaboration among manifold actors and events that collaborate in its construction in a process not of autistic imposition but of active co-participation. A process bound up with the dynamical, diverse and uninhibited conditions of its time.

> **8.** Advanced architecture is, in fact, decidedly dynamic. It proposes the development of processes, rather than the definition and the limiting of occurrences. It thus operates with dynamic geometries and organisations, closer to fractal differential orders than to absolute Euclidian orders. Closer to adaptable, elastic topologies than to universal, rigid reticules. Closer to digital logics than to analogical models.

9. Advanced architecture articulates diversity because it is developed within multicity: in a "city of cities" conceived as a "hyperplace:" a "place of places," the more positive and stimulating the more specific and interlinked. A metacity in which priority is afforded to global links and local singularities.

A metapolis that would unfold on the territory as a flexible mesh of diverse landscapes, of spaces and interspaces. Grids, matrixes, topographies or fabrics conceived through the active optimisation of their potentials.

A menu of opportunities for an architecture capable of producing menus of results. An architecture aimed at combining individual and heterogeneous situations in new plural scenarios.

A architecture that would work, at the same time, with the individual and the plural.

> **10.** Advanced architecture is, thus, an architecture more uninhibited and spontaneous in its manifestations: unsettled, expansive. Extrovert by virtue of being dynamical. Informal by virtue of being informational. Joyful in its movements.
>
> Therefore, it is an architecture that seeks to be more explicit, direct and expressive. That is, more ludic and unrestrained. Colourful, rather than austere. Eloquent, rather than elegant. Bold, rather than resistant.
>
> A more communicative architecture. Prepared to favour the cultural signs and expressions of its time: hybridisations, transfusions, mixtures and influences. New natures produced through new marriages for an architecture that seeks to project the individual in more stimulating landscapes: interfaces between the individual and his or her own world.

● advertisements

→ 'advertising',
'marks'

[MG] A reading of press advertisements and messages extracted from the *media* around the world – as Yago Conde and Bea Goller once proposed with the exhibition and catalogue *International Property* (CONDE, Yago; GOLLER, Bea, International Property, Barcelona: Ed. COAC, 1995) – permits us to posit a reflection upon the real-estate phenomenon and its impact upon the construction of territory. Accordingly, housing manifests itself as the standard product par excellence. It is a market commodity fully thrust into the mechanisms of consumer society and, as such, subject to commercial inertias largely tending towards generalisation – and trivialisation – of messages. Its common patterns tend towards universality (nostalgia for the rural, the caricature of well-being, the evocation of the atemporal, etc.) and therefore, its codes are directed towards the more rooted, stable and permanent part of the collective imagination. Surprisingly, the shared codes of housing for a nebulous "middle class," at the planetary scale, has converted its desires into an *"elemental and abstract system of ideologies, as acritical as they are mediatically accepted."*

[MG] Some advertisements are only "commercial-universal-trivial." Others are "commercial-singular-original;" at the "origin" – advance, foretaste – of something new and, thus, unexpected. These are advanced.

Real state advertisements

Bea GOLLER, Yago CONDE,
International Property, Barcelona, 1995.

● + advertising

[MG] **(medium)**

Contemporary interest in the imaginative capacity of advertising – and of cinema, as stimulus rather than as evocation – lies in its capacity for generating "extreme images." These "extreme images," often transgressions or anticipated heterodoxies, bring into confluence and into simultaneity – sometimes unnaturally – different elements, situations, references, codes and energies that increase their effectiveness precisely through the enhancement of the idea of paradoxical crossroads (images "on the edge" of things and of events).

Direct expressions of explicit messages (powerful hooks or uppercuts) proclaim the explicit and astute effectiveness of advertising language, the expressive force of cinema and television, or the assembling capacity of the new media of contemporary animation and communication.

[WM] **(signs)**

Tenant architecture is that which is adapted or adhered to the empty surfaces of the city with the aim of introducing architecture from the place that appropriates its inexistence: advertising.

Until now, the possibility of architecture was linked to the existence of property. However, the promotional installation is covering all available urban surfaces under a legal formula of pre-architectural occupation. We should create structures of occupation that would provide the promotional surface with a certain thickness, appropriating an existent legality: vertical ground, adding the movement and the volume inside the advertisement, *plus informing instead of announcing*.

The mutant urban or ad-hered landscape of metacities could stand at the antipodes of pollution. It is an intelligent dialogue among administrators, entrepreneurs and creators.

1. Willy MÜLLER + THB Consulting, *AD2. Occupation structures*, Barcelona.

2. Advertising in an Asian city.

✘ ◆ aformal

[VG] The state of maximum freedom of architecture is that in which form, rather than being sought, appears as the result of a process. The aformal is weightless, profound, mysterious black.

[FS] Why without form? One character of modern architecture is precisely its indetermination. Better said, the inconsistency of its determination, since even the initial phase also must suffer lack of definition. Architecture whose base consists principally in formal processes as the agents of architecture's structure can not resist the change of one of its parts without losing its whole identity. Architecture without form allows the reform, restoration and change of its image without evident change of form, and as such, the object remains. It can spontaneously absorb additions, subtractions and technical modifications without disturbing its sense of order. This constancy allows the coherence of the unit without falling into the extreme chaotic superimposition of fragments.

✘ agriculture

[VG] For centuries, man has colonised territory by means of agriculture, creating irrigation systems and planting crops according to the laws of geometry. He has denaturalised natural spaces by planting natural elements. The distance left between the various trees and plants depends both on the size of the actual crops and on the systems used to harvest them.

Each crop produces a texture and a colour on the territory. On mountainous terrain, the slopes have been converted into finite elements by the construction of terraces.

In aggressive climates, greenhouses can be used to overcome the specific conditions of place, creating light-weight constructions that contain microclimates imported from other latitudes. Agriculture is being industrialised. The landscape is being urbanised.

The spectacle of nature and that of the city are now comparable.

Naturartificial
Vicente GUALLART,
Willy MÜLLER, Enric
RUIZ-GELI, *Scape
House, Territorial
sprawl*, 1998.

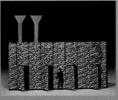

ÁBALOS & HERREROS, *AH Houses, Industrial Prototypes,* 1996.

★ AH houses

→ 'catalogue', 'combination', component', 'diversity', domestic', 'house, the', housing', 'kits', 'object', production, intelligent', rurban life', 'stampings'

[co] The AH houses or its surprised version "¡ah! houses" are the result of a consultation carried out for a group of businessmen interested in producing a line of industrialized housing aimed, in principle, at an extremely wide market: public housing, holiday homes, young people, civil defence, etc. The assignment posed a double problem: how to differentiate itself from similar things on offer — and to make these dwellings also capable of competing with conventional housing — and how to think of the house as a total abstraction, without a context, with no parameter other than generic and universal efficiency.

This openness and indetermination induce, as basic criterion, the systematisation of reduction: of variables, constructional complexity, surface, glazed areas, particularities, of operations *in situ.* A reduction from which one endeavours to extract a poetics in syntony with the rationalisation and simplification implicit in industrialisation (and equally to avoid a badly understood and restrictive moralizing severity: here to reduce is, or aspires to be, to intensify, to lend intensity to the work and to the experience of living in these houses). It is the production with air, with volume, a space of *déjà-vu,* never associated with the 'cheap' or 'functional,' yet of tremendous subjective importance in the house.

Neither the scale, form nor the materials maintain a relation with traditional figuration. The proposed strategy is to switch the associations towards two esthetic references: the 'magic box' and the 'techno artefact,' in seeking positive generic accords with the landscape and with the idea of living.

Awakening curiosity, contrasting inner and outer, offering mystery: the domestic as game. Developing superficial finishes of extreme density and coloring, we endeavour to make use of the possibilities implicit in the material of the panelling, PVF2, whose finish is capable of taking impressions of a serigraphic kind or similar. So, we try to differentiate the product from prefabricated houses of wood and from the caravans/mobile homes on offer, in producing an alternative image, with another potential market. The system also includes a series of optional extras which make personalization of the house. AH houses are to the traditional house what the Swatch is to the pendulum clock: not only or not so much a technological change as the verification of a change in habits, of the way of relating oneself to things. A product of contemporary material culture. And based upon a modification of the concept of durability associated with that of economy in industrial production: the introduction of a product invested with cultural trustworthiness in the logic of consumerism.

IÑAKI ÁBALOS & JUAN HERREROS

★✕ AI, Artificial Intelligence

[c]   "AI, a system modeled after the brain, would not be guided by top-down procedures. It would make connections from the bottom up, as the brain's neurons are thought to do. So the system could learn by a large number of different connections. In this sense, the system would be unpredictable and nondeterministic. So the intelligence emerges not from rules, but from experience and from "fuzzy" processes.
The assertion that mind could not be represented as rules made connectionism began to present the computer as though it were an evolving biological organism. And it thus suggested that traditional distinctions between the natural and artificial, the real and simulated, might dissolve."
(TURKLE, Sherry, *Life on the Screen. Identity in the Age of the Internet*, New York: Touchstone, 1997)

[VG] See 'arkitektor.'

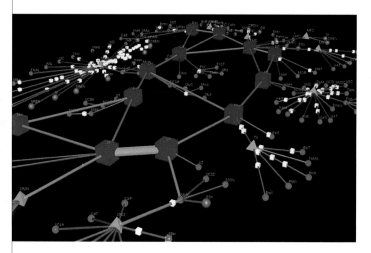

Jeff BROWN
(MOAT, National
Laboratory for
Applied Network
Research), screenshot
of a 3D model
of the vBNS network
which connects
universities
and laboratories
in the USA.

★ algorithm

→ 'mathematics',
'sequence and series'

[co] Algorithms are a series of symbols for operating procedures and for the relations between these groups of signs and operating procedures.
Processes of artificial relation that determine modes of 'relaction' and enable their proliferation. The algorithm is a tool in any system for operating in a way that is open and directed – that is, intentional – and, in most of the cases that interest us, factitious.
" *The term algorithm comes from the Latin transliteration of the name of the Arab mathematician Al-Kwarismi (ninth century). By algorithm we understand the precise rule governing the execution of a given system of operations, in a specific order, in such a way that all problems of a given kind are solved. We use algorithms whenever we master the procedures for solving a problem in its general aspect — that is, for a whole class of its variable terms. Given that the algorithm, as a system of rules, possesses a formal nature, it can be taken as a basis for a programme of operations for a calculating machine by means of which to solve the problem."* (*Diccionario soviético de filosofía*, Montevideo: Ediciones Pueblos Unidos, 1965, translated from Spanish)
JOSÉ ALFONSO BALLESTEROS

[co] An algorithm is a repeating rule that is mathematical or geometrical. In numbers, a famous algorithm is that of the Fibonacci series where each number is the sum of the previous two e.g. 1 1 2 3 5 8 13 21 34 , etc. This growth pattern is often found in nature – in snails' shells, in the arrangement of sunflower seeds, on pineapple skins and in growth patterns where exponential increase is controlled by discrete jumps. In geometry, a pattern motif that repeats on itself in feedback can lead to a fractal, a pattern that has non-integer dimensions.
CECIL BALMOND

[co] Algorithm, stemmed from the word Al Khwarizme, nickname of the mathematician Muhamed Ibn Musa (9th century) born in Khwarizem, Uzbekistan. An algorithm is a finite series of ordered instructions or rules that applied to a set of data carries out a procedure or solves a problem in a finite time period.
The above formulas are algorithms that applied to the set of the Complex Numbers solve the problem $AX_- + BX + C = 0$.
FRANCISCO TOLCHINSKY

$$X = \frac{-B+\sqrt{B^2\ 4AC}}{2A} \quad \text{and} \quad X = \frac{B\ \sqrt{B^2\ 4AC}}{2A}$$

★ alienation (and estrangement)

→ 'armadillo', 'criss-crossing', 'infiltration', 'rootlessness', 'suspense', 'tourism'

[c] See 'de-location' and 'foreigness.'

" *We talk about alienation and anomaly. As a reaffirmation of a possible spatial delocation, similar to what De Certeau calls the "tactics of the weak," closer to the instrumental reorientation of places than to their actual production. Rather than obeying the laws of place, being identified with it, these tactics appropriate and manipulate its laws, using them transversely and ingeniously. This host architecture is a product of the appearance of an anomaly – temporary, in this case – within a system, of something from the outside, of an architecture alienated from its traditional durability. The provisional nature of these host artefacts accords it a veil of displacement which bursts into the stability of the events like a stranger; the object becomes an alien.*" (DÍAZ MORENO, Cristina; GARCÍA GRINDA Efrén, "Impermanent architecture," *Quaderns* 224, 1999)

● alienism

[MG] See 'de-location,' 'alienation (and estrangement)' and 'foreignness.'

● allegory

→ 'abstract', 'action> critical', 'archaeology', 'collage', 'criteria', 'erudition', 'event', 'goodbye to the metaphor', 'innovation', 'logic, direct', 'meaning', 'past', 'positioning','transversality'

[MG] Allegories are not what we need now.

" *The allegory seeks (as Juan Delcán, citing Walter Benjamin, recalled) to recover that which tends to die out. And the allegory acquires greater presence when a culture feels threatened, when a civilisation is transformed and when certain historical forms fade. The allegory expresses the lament – the nostalgia – for this loss and has come to produce a whole series of aesthetic strategies which slow that loss or which, at the very least, maintain alive and present in another form that which, or the image of that which, is being lost.*"
(DELCÁN, Juan, "Arquitectura en la era de la electrónica," *BAU* 016, 1997.)

● ambiguity (and ambivalence)

[MG] See 'hybrid' and 'intermediate places.'

[MG] Univocal space now yields to a space decidedly ambivalent in its physical and virtual manifestations. Not only because it is functionally non-prede-termined, but also substantively hybrid. Categorically ambiguous.

In a multifaceted, polyphase, definitively non-essential reality, architecture can create spaces that are more plural, by virtue, precisely, of being inde-terminate. Implicitly changing and (in)formal. Multiple. Multiplied and mul-tiplicative. What certain authors would understand as the definitive hu-miliation of the object – its loss of substantiveness or category — in fact, favours plurality and intrigue (a thing, an action, a scenario as "one" and "many" at the same time, as "one" and possible "others"). Different lev-els of overlapped information, interpretation and reading are combined, re-sulting in different layers of meaning and relationship.

The old notion of identity becomes more ambiguous and, accordingly, more complex and rich in events.

A building can be a garden. A garden, a building.

NL, *Booster*, Amsterdam, Zeeburger Eiland, 2002.

● ambushments

[MG] Partial concealment – camouflage – of certain devices for an operation of foresting // Slippage – or infiltration – among the trunks or the branches of to forest or grove // Cleverness in occupation of a landscape by flexible ruse: "between."

1. ACTAR ARQUITECTURA, *M'House Houses*, 1997.

2. Cristina DÍAZ MORENO, Efrèn GARCÍA GRINDA, *Europan 6: Housing in Jyväskylä*, Suomi (Finland), 2001- (First Prize), from *El Croquis* 106/107, 2001.

3. ROCHE, DSV&SIE, *Landscaping project*, Maïdo, Reunion Island (France), 1997.

4. Edouard FRANÇOIS&Duncan LEWIS, *Rural houses*, Jupilles (Compiègne, France), 1997.

5. Anne LACATON & Jean-Philippe VASSAL, *House in Cap Ferret*, Lege Cap Ferret (Bordeaux, France), 1998.

★ American pragmatism

→ 'action>critical',
'criteria', 'essayist
knowledge', 'positioning'

[co] While it is true that most practitioners would identify with pragmatism in its every-day, small p. sense (useful in dealing with clients, engineers, building inspectors and the like), there is an alternative notion of pragmatism: a progressive philo-sophical tradition that looks for verification not in abstract universals, but in con-crete things and their consequences in the world. The writings of the American Pragmatists – John Dewey, Charles Sanders Pierce and William James – outline a pragmatic realism that is more austere, thoughtful and tough-minded, and at the same time, more generous and optimistic. These thinkers find a philosophical rich-ness in the texture of the world itself: "No ideas but in things" as William Carlos Williams has famously remarked.

Pragmatism, understood this way, would suggest that architecture is a practice and not a discourse; it recognizes that architecture has never been particularly effec-tive as a vehicle of criticism. It is, on the contrary, insistently affirmative. Architectural practice does not comment on the world, it operates in and on the world. It pro-duces ideas and effects through the volatile medium of artifacts, short-circuiting the established pathways of theory and discourse. This is architecture's attraction: its source of creativity, operational power and – not the least – pleasure.

Pragmatism, in this sense, has little to do with the easy acquiescence to existing norms and conventions. Pragmatism is instead persistently skeptical and contrary. It is a stubborn practice that consists in holding up those generic norms to strict performative criteria, and leaving them behind when they fall short. Unlike con-ventional practice, pragmatism cannot depend on stable rules and conventions. Tethered to a fast moving reality, pragmatism needs to be agile and responsive, which often requires that it leave behind some of the weighty baggage of received ideas. But pragmatism is not simple relativism. In as much as it works in and among the world of things, governed by the hard logic of matter and forces, prag-matism cannot be arbitrary or capricious.

Pragmatism respects the verifiable laws that govern matter and forces, but it is al-so attentive to the fact that these laws operate without regard to consistency or the established conventions of rational expression. This attention to the gaps and in-consistencies in theory's fit to reality is, as T. S. Kuhn has pointed out, a tremendous source of invention and creativity. It is precisely when practice and experimentation turn up inconsistencies in the "normal science" that new theories are produced. The practice of architecture is messy and inconsistent because it has to negotiate a re-ality that is itself messy and inconsistent. But often, that mess is more interesting than the stiff formulations of theory. "Pragmatism," William James has written, "unstiffens all our theories, limbers them up and sets each one at work." See: Things in the Making: The Pragmatist Imagination" Museum of Modern Art Conference, Fall 2000, publication forthcoming. STAN ALLEN

Alex S. MACLEAN,
"The American City",
in KOOLHAAS,
Rem; *et al*, *Mutations*,
Barcelona: ACTAR,
Bordeaux: Arc
en rêve, 2000).

★ amphibious

[co] Amphibious living bridges the dynamic threshold between solid (stable) and liquid (ephemeral and indeterminate) landscapes. Mobile allotments, floating agriculture and water-based living work with a tidal urbanism – inextricably tied to the ebb and flow of water ecology, climatic influences and seasonal cycles.

CanTho, Vietnam.

★ anarchitecture

[co] See also 'self-urbanism.'

Anarchitecture is a term that was introduced by Gordon Matta Clark in New York in 1973. It refers to a constructional practice in confrontation with the conventions of Architecture (capitalised). Also, and in the same sense, it can refer to an anarchist architectural practice.

JOSÉ PÉREZ DE LAMA

■ and

[JM] To keep focusing on the "and." In other words, to fasten ourselves to the particulars that can unite thoughts, traces and the boldness of a project. To try to avoid paralysis – the permanent invasion towards the outside. To break the border of the All-One. To break the limits of a project trapped by figures of the past or of the already known.

It is a project that swims in the intermediaries; perhaps here is where it is liberated from its fastenings. Where it navigates best, appropriating the events really useful to the project. This project-thought of the copulating "and." Of the union of the relation of the outside (M. Blanchot.) But it is also the project of the spacing, the interval.

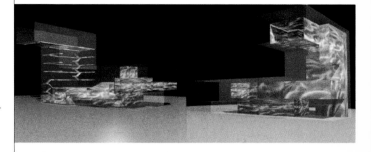

José MORALES,
Sara GILES,
Juan GONZÁLEZ,
Theatre, Nijar
(Almeria, Spain),
1998.

● ★ animation

[MG] Animation suggests a term definitively linked to the dynamic: to movement. Yet whereas movement implies transfer and action, animation suggests animalism, animism, evolution, growth, actuation, vitality and virtuality. It is based upon an inform(ation)al – informatised and informalised – logic. A topological relationship, of transformation, of mutation and of change, more flexible and fluid, produced through more elastic, deformable structures and geometries. More "formless," that is.

[co] In order to deny the transcendence of the static form architecture must begin to describe the particular characteristics of the unfinished, refused until now by the rigid exactitude of pure geometry and strict symmetry of proportions; it must recuperate the animate value of evolutive configurations.

An animation model of time and motion would resist the separation of form from the forces that animate it.

Form can be conceived in a space of virtual movement and force rather than within an ideal equilibrium space of stasis.

For example, discrete fixed point coordinates define an object in ideal static space. The trajectory relative to other objects, forces, motion fields and flows defines an object immersed in an active space of forces.

The shift from a passive space of inert coordinates to an active space of interactions implies a global move which does not refuse any contextual specificity.

GREG LYNN

Greg LYNN, *Henie onstad installation design*, in LYNN, Greg, *Animate form*, New York: Princeton Architectural Press, 1998.

Animate Form

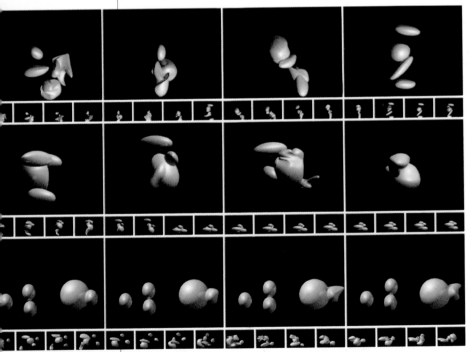

■ anonymity

→ 'abroad, etc.',
'foreigness', 'no-place',
'space'

[JM] Anonymity is the experience we habitually feel in large commercial areas, in airports or in transit along the periphery of big cities.

● anonymous

→ 'bored', 'client', 'hotel',
'joy (*alegria*)'

[MG] See 'open,' 'expression' and 'extroversion: <ex> factors of form.'

We propose, instead of the insubstantiality of the anonymous (the timid, the prudent, the "invisible," the "integrated," the unnoticed, the discrete, the bored/boring, etc.), a more extrovert architecture. Expressive. Not expressionist (forcing the gesture), but rather explicit (expressing movement). An architecture capable of communicating the dynamic logic – and tensions – that shape it (its topology) and of reacting vis-à-vis the exterior stimuli that solicit it.

This is not to suggest opposing the anonymous with the "d'auteur" (stardom-seeking) or the "gestural" (aestheticism), but rather with the relational. Rather than the rhetorical, the eloquent.

★ antigravity

→ 'environment', 'field',
'holograms', 'inflatable',
'lightness'

[co] Antigravity is a potential state of advanced architecture.

Necessary question. In an electronic – digital – medium, matter loses its gravity; the space becomes subaquatic, free-fall speed, free.

The three dimensions acquire their complete importance and there is no hierarchy between floor and walls; all are equally important, equally useful surfaces.

Putting the three dimensions into equilibrium, we place greater importance on the fourth dimension: time. ENRIC RUIZ-GELI

Situations of work and rest in environments of no gravity

International Spatial Station Project (ISS), in *El Pais semanal*, 15/XI/1998.

1. Karl S. CHU (XKavya), $Ad9GrBel5^7. OSa314.$

2. SPILLER FARMER Architects (with SIXTEEN, Makers), *Hot Desk*, London.

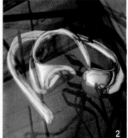

3. OOSTERHUIS Associates, *Salt Water Pavilion*, Neeltje Jans (The Netherlands), 1997.

Antitype. *Flight-Fancy,* in *I.D.,* March-April 1994.

● antitypes

[MG] See 'a-couplings.'

[MG] A surprising image shows a car coupled to an aeroplane flying through the air. The car wishes to run; the aeroplane can fly. The new object wants to – and can – run and fly.

This is not, however, an univocal object, purpose built to perform both functions, but rather a dual object, born of the melding of two individual parts, each one destined to perform a non-specific function but whose union, potentially, permits it to perform both.

It is not then a typological design, but rather an a-typological mechanism; an antitype.

Run+fly = AEROPLANE-CAR. Not aerocar, nor autoplane, but rather AERO-PLANE-CAR!: a explicit grafting, without nuances or transitions.

An unnatural, hybrid contract capable of combining in a single project codes of different a order, which alludes, in fact, to the very unlinking of the parts of the contemporary project. Meldings, cuttings, grafts; recent – anticompositive – mechanisms translate the will to conceive more expressive and unbiased shapes and structures in harmony with their interpretation of a space – the current one. Antitypes are capable of being effectively represented only through the superposition of diverse and differentiated layers and networks (as happens in scanner readings or in the GIS computer-generated maps with interlinked, though not necessarily symbiotic, data and information).

Antitypes are effective in dealing with scenarios which definitively lack formal typification. Antitypes in which – as in the contemporary scenario itself – diverse objectives and interests overlap, not in harmonious and coherent bodies, but rather in simultaneous landscapes made up of structures, shapes and identities in shared commensalist coexistence.

★ appropiation strategies

[c] "*All realities manifest themselves with a gradient of variable factors. The paths we have to pursue to understand them cannot reproduce the paths of conventional urban planning, as the invisible, mutant structures which interact in the urban space create a complex fabric which makes the idea of global, closed planning inconceivable. The speed at which changes take place in urban space suggests specific places and given epochs, so the design and construction of this space constantly require regenerating mechanisms which address the particular factors of the various places and their interaction with global changes and systems. For institutions, the idea of a global process is an attempt to simplify and control all possible forms of behaviour and action. My proposal consists of perpetually redefining global systems (urban planning and legislation), looking out for possible loopholes and uncertainties which allow the various human groups freedom of action. Spanish urban planning acts on the placing of skips in urban space define exactly what these skips should be like: measurements, the material they are made of, their position... but they do not define what they are for, because a skip, of course, is for disposing of rubble and rubbish, isn't it? So the design works in different ways, because people pay the local government for their permit, and can then do what they want —or what they need— with it: an urban reserve, breathing space, a meeting point, a children's playground, a tree plantation... In the case of regulations on scaffolding, you can obtain a permit to install one because you 'need' to paint the facade of the building you wish to contaminate. (You can always produce this need by scribbling some eye-catching graffiti on it.) You then install your scaffolding and build your new space, your own private refuge, your architecture of silence, with whatever materials, style and measurements you decide. And the duration is up to you, because the architecture of silence ought to be provisional and variable, because these are the conditions which the other architecture (the regular sort) does not have. In the same way, there are other loopholes or 'new definitions' we can employ to remind the institution of its inability to deal with plural reality, and to point up people's ability —and their need— to take part in urban drift.*"

(CIRUGEDA, Santiago, "Strategies for subversive occupation", *Quaderns* 224, 1999)

Santiago CIRUGEDA,
*Dwelling inmersed
in a housing block*,
Seville (Spain), 2000.

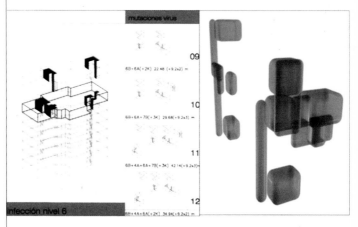

■●✖ archaeology

[JM] Archaeology is a science that identifies or hides unexpectedly, but that also recomposes, resuscitates or localizes again what once was. Its labour is realized through fragments of history, of those agreed upon after having imagined them in the place of discovery, separating them from real space, from what was already formulated. Discontinuous archaeology, abandoning those discoveries that had already become homogeneous, starts anew as heterogeneous. What metaphorical images come to mind about research when we see an archaeological dig! The researcher's task is that which needs, in effect, discontinuities in space and time in order to obtain reasons and ideas about what we were and what we are. Space, time, life.

[MG] **archaeology (Past and Present)**

There are times when the hidden past suddenly reappears, like the corpses emerging from the pool in *Poltergeist*. We might find ourselves trapped in its (their) claws; we might observe it (them) – paralysed – from a prudent distance; or we might simply play with its (their) bones.

[VG] **advanced archaeology**

The best way of protecting heritage is to increase it. Traditional archaeology has studied, catalogued and exhibited the remains of the past as inert matter. From a physical point of view, a 'fragment of a wall' is a ruin. But seen as reactivated 'information' it can, once again, be a living (and active) urban element. That same wall, converted into an 'urban document,' can issue information about the history of the city by ordering the genetic traces of our forefathers. Traces that need to be conserved, transmitted and integrated into the city's cultural-museumistic-touristic activity.

An on-line 'urban editor' could, then, act as an intelligent agent – an interface – that would help to show and order a considered route around historical environments. The new constructions should also use foundation techniques that are able to conserve most of the remains on which they rest, by means of partially glazed floors with underlighting. The multilayer city would, in this way, highlight its multistrata nature.

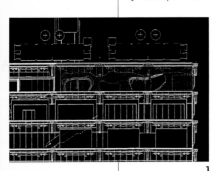 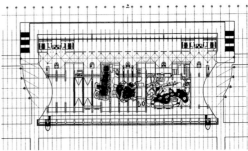

1   2

Archaeology in recent heritage
1. Dominique JAKOB, Brendan MACFARLANE, *Restaurant Le Georges*, Centre Pompidou, Paris, 2000. **2.** S&Aa (SORIANO-PALACIOS), *Cyberauditorium and Museum of Children. Intervention in the Museum of Sciencies*, Valencia (Spain), 1998.

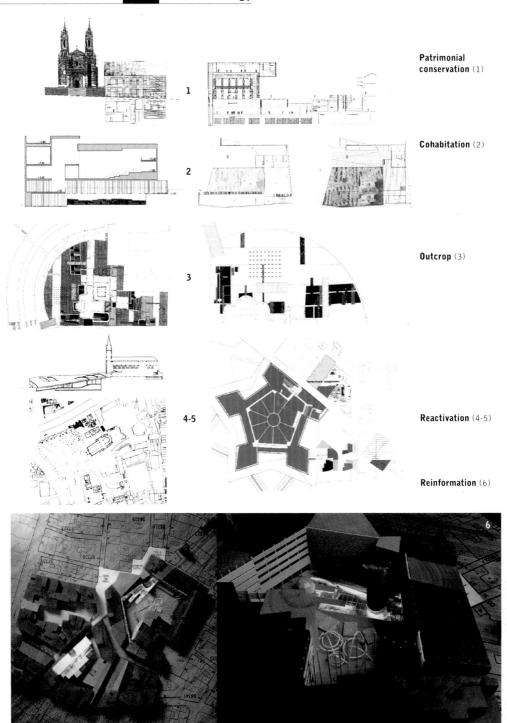

Patrimonial
conservation (1)

Cohabitation (2)

Outcrop (3)

Reactivation (4-5)

Reinformation (6)

1. Alberto MARTÍNEZ CASTILLO, Beatriz MATOS, *International Competition for the enlargement of Prado Museum*, Madrid, 1998. **2.** José MORALES, Sara GILES, Juan GONZÁLEZ, *Competition for the new headquarters of the Assembly of Extremadura*, Mérida (Spain), 1999. **3.** ACTAR ARQUITECTURA, *Project of restoration and public space in Sant Pau del Camp*, Barcelona, 1996. **4.** FOA, *Reorganization of the cathedral of Myeong-Dong*, Seoul (Korea), 1995. **5.** Willy MÜLLER, *Competition for auditorium and conference centre*, Pamplona (Spain), 1998. **6.** Vicente GUALLART, *Rehabilitation of the Arab ramparts of eleventh century*, Valencia, Oficina RIVA, 1998-.

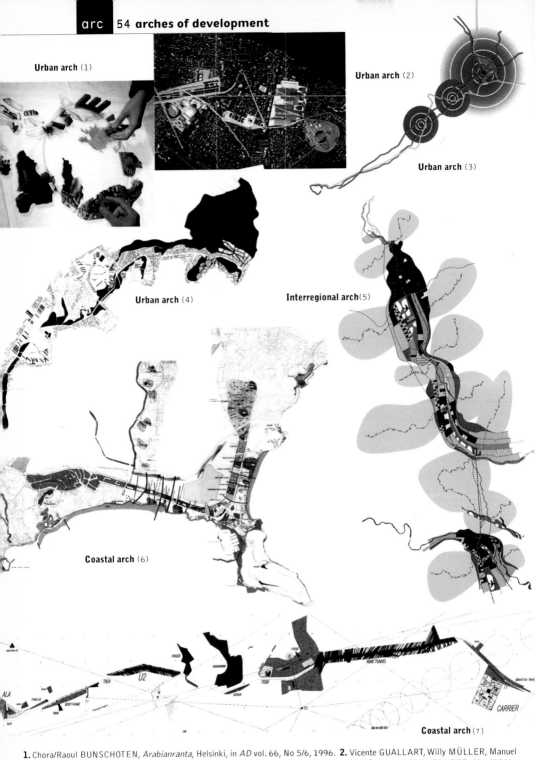

Urban arch (1)

Urban arch (2)

Urban arch (3)

Urban arch (4)

Interregional arch(5)

Coastal arch (6)

Coastal arch (7)

1. Chora/Raoul BUNSCHOTEN, *Arabianranta*, Helsinki, in *AD* vol. 66, No 5/6, 1996. **2.** Vicente GUALLART, Willy MÜLLER, Manuel GAUSA, ACTAR ARQUITECTURA, *Competition ARC OUEST*, Thessalonica (Greece), 1997. **3.** Susan NIGRA SNYDER, Alex WALL, *After Expo*, Seville (Spain), in *Quaderns* 198, 1993. **4.** José MORALES, Juan GONZÁLEZ, Felipe PALOMINO, *Competition ARC OUEST*, Thessalonica (Greece), 1997. **5.** ACTAR ARQUITECTURA, *Graz-Maribor Corridor*, (Austria), 1999. **6.** ACTAR ARQUI-TECTURA, *Arch of mixed activities*, Calpe (Alicante, Spain), 1998. **7.** Manuel J. FEO, Juan RAMÍREZ GUEDES (TWA, TWICE ARCHITECTURE), *Eyeliners: proposal for the walk of Chil*, Las Palmas de Gran Canaria (Spain), 1999.

● arches of development

→ 'in-between fingers,
in-between links',
'land links', 'places',
'program', 'self-urbanism',
'strategy', 'territory'

[MG] Certain processes of urban (re)definition and development might be applied to nuclear attractor schemes, aimed at articulating evolutionary strategies, in the short, medium and long term, based upon sequences between foci/areas of activity, discontinuous, interconnected by linkage and routing channels. These sequences form "arches of development:" they are not in themselves continuous axes or lengths, but rather circuits of interaction, syncopated and intermittent, between "bound landscapes" (understanding the term 'landscape' in its more plural sense, at once a place/scenario and field of activity).

Their effective planning allows us to define basic operative trajectories as "horizons of certainty" or "islands of consensus," localised in the global territorial system under consideration.

OMA, *Competition for the new city,* Melun-Sénart (France), 1987.

★ ● ArchiLab

[co] ArchiLab designates the International Architectural Meetings in Orléans, France. This event was created in 1999, at the request of the municipality, which wished to create a festival devoted to architecture. The proposal originated in the existence of the collection at the FRAC Centre (Regional Endowment for Contemporary Art, Centre region) in Orléans, directed by Marie-Ange Brayer, who since 1991 has been collecting emblematic architectural research projects dating from the 1950s to the present. Today, the FRAC Centre collection has perhaps become the most important collection, from the historical viewpoint, of utopian or "radical" architecture.

Conceived by Marie-Ange Brayer and Frédéric Migayrou, chief curator of architecture and design at the Pompidou Center in Paris, ArchiLab is currently organized by Marie-Ange Brayer and Béatrice Simonot. Since 1999, ArchiLab has offered itself as a platform for meetings and exchanges between French and international architects, and between architects and clients, with a focus on the most innovative dimensions in architecture. Thus, ArchiLab has become the annual rendezvous of future-oriented architecture on the international level.

In the space of four years, some 140 different architectural teams have been exhibited; more than 300 architects and critics have come to Orléans to participate in the meetings. From 2002 onward, these architectural meetings will be mirrored by a new rendezvous of architectural criticism, initially in the form of an symposium. ArchiLab 1999 raised the question of the mutation of the architect's trade. ArchiLab 2000 explored the new urban phenomena on a global scale, with the UrbaLab symposium. ArchiLab 2001 inquired into the dimension of habitat, into the new ways of inhabiting, between individualization and phenomena of standardization. ArchiLab 2002 turns toward the problematic of the "environment," understood in all its dimensions: natural and urban, digital and informational, cultural and political.

ArchiLab wishes to contribute to the promotion and development of emerging experiments in architectural creation and reflection, offering a platform on which people can take a principled stand, maintain a forward-looking attitude, and assert a position which is at once critical and effective.

MARIE-ANGE BRAYER

[MG] See 'action>critical' and 'Think Tank.'

ArchiLab is the Orléans meeting point. International observatory of emergent actions, positive energies and global interactions. Advanced think tank.

●★◆✕+■▲ architecture

"*To know the nature of things in order to act upon reality. Thus begins architecture,*" suggested Vicente Guallart.

The value of architecture no longer results from creating shapes in space, but rather from fostering relationships within it. Combined relationships and actions – reactions – in (and *for*) a definitively "open" and non-predetermined reality; the more qualitative, the more potentially interactive. In positive synergy with the environment.

This points to a latent change in the figure of the architect, no longer formulable only in terms of a "designer of objects," but rather in that of a "strategist of processes."

The methodological gaze of standard practice (based upon formulas, models and disciplines) thus yields to a tactical gaze: that of an alert – and conscious – explorer capable of synthesising multiple bits of information – ever more indeterminate, and uncertain – in effective devices, as precise (direct) as they are complex (implicitly synthetic).

Devices/criteria to "reinform" (restructure with new bits of information) reality.

To propose an advanced architecture is to immerse oneself in this strategic will orientated towards an effective disposition and restructuring of the city, of the territory and of the networks that articulate it, of the fabrics generated throughout them and of the new relational spaces that have infiltrated them. Advanced architecture also strives towards the conception of new logics for colonising operations which affect the habitat – environment and technology – and which call for the reuse and recycling of the pre-existences and for reflection upon the frictional boundaries between disciplines, techniques, types of knowledge and actions.

If one of the greatest responsibilities traditionally placed upon the figure of the architect is this capacity for synthetic action between the conditions of reality and a vision of the world, it is in this sense that prospective "recognition" of new definitions of our environment acquires special importance, not as a shaping, recreation or reproduction of reality itself, but rather as a prospective reformulating 'disposition' vis-à-vis that reality.

"*To recognise reality is to begin to transform it.*"

Our chief mission as architects still resides precisely in this capacity for articulating a propositive mediation between the forces of production (economic, political, social, cultural and other powers) and the conditions of those scenarios (physical, processal, technological, cultural, etc.) to which the latter are associated. Hence is derived the capacity to "PROJECTISE," that is, to KNOW, CONCEIVE and PRODUCE; to RELATE (explore, associate, deduce, imply, etc.); to PROPOSE (imagine, foresee, anticipate, invent); and to CREATE (build, structure, organise, coordinate, etc.).

A mediation, aimed at equipping the productive and cultural structures of each moment with an appropriate spatial organisation, capable of syntonising with the "environmental conditions" (of the global), and which today allude to a progressively hybridised and multifaceted – diverse and heterogeneous – dimension of reality. A reality with accumulate fluctuations and mutations, layers of reality (realities) and layers of (bits of) information. Thus, this situation (and the capacity for intervention in it) points to the conditions of a hypothetical "battlefield;" a battlefield illustrative of the dynamic, uncertain and operative dimension of the contemporary project. Advanced architecture is capable of synthesising different moments and situations of recognition and representation (cartography), of tactics and of relationship (strategies), of manoeuvre and handling (logistics), of order and formation (disposition), in possible associated trajectories, structures, schemes and devices and articulates new (more qualitatively directed) proposals and new natures associated with the relational capacity of a truly resolvent – and advanced – (reactive, and reactivating) architecture.

[co] Nowadays, architecture is obliged to deal with the problem of sovereignty, identity and legitimacy. It must win back its area of activity. It must redefine the conditions in which it stays close to the real and become interventionist in every area involved by the industrial production of the building, from which it has been bit by bit excluded. The very conditions formulating this issue of identity define both the challenge and the deadlocks in which the cultural, social and political positioning of architecture is entangled. All our mainly western conceptions of architecture, and the way it has become a discipline and an area of learning and knowledge, have been adapted to an identity-related conception where the principle of foundation had to be defined at some distance from the real, at some distance from the complexity of the world conceived as an intolerable tower of Babel-like process. The architecture that is now happening is plural, pluralist and multifaceted; it intermingles discourses, practices and techniques. It is efficient and embraces the industrial world like an inexhaustible register of materials and procedures, from which it is necessary to draw in order to regenerate our relationships with the limitless urban sphere that looms ahead.
FRÉDÉRIC MIGAYROU

[FS] "*Real Architecture is always in the least likely place. Where nobody is thinking of him and no one pronounces his name. [Architecture] detests being recognized and saluted by name. He immediately slips away. [Architecture] loves to pass incognito. When he is discovered and pointed to, he escapes, leaving in his place a praised figure that carries a large banner on its shoulders that reads [ARCHITECTURE] and to all that are hasty to sprinkle champagne, and to those lecturers passing from one city to another with a ring pinned from their noses. This is the false man Mr. [Architecture.] And as it is he that wears the laurels and carries the banner, this is the one recognized by the public. There is no worry that the real Architecture will parade with banners! And as such, no one recognizes him. He passes by everywhere, every one has crossed his path and pushed him twenty times a day turning the corner, but to no one has it occurred to think that this could be the selfsame Mr. Architecture, whom so many appreciate. And all because he does not seem anything like him. Understand me, the false Architecture is real and the real one is who least seems so. And this provokes confusion; what a big confusion!*"
(Modification of DUBUFFET, Jean, "El arte bruto frente a las artes culturales")

[VG] Can architecture be digital?

Architecture is the process by which the organisation of activities in space is defined. Physical or virtual.

The architect and architecture have traditionally operated by manipulating material in order to define the limits of spaces to allow for activities. From a physical point of view, the aims of traditional architecture are clear. The gravity of the physical world always works in the same direction.

Now, the digital material created using information, intangible, without gravity and mutable in time, leads us to reflect upon the essence of architecture: how much of architecture is material and how much is information?

Cultural, functional, aesthetic, economic, physical, energy information.

Information that becomes saturated in time and space, defining a solid, visual, tactile fact.

Producing architecture is an abstract process that relates information to material, in space and in time. This is the task of the architect. Architecture is the process, not the result.

Buildings, parks, objects are all results of architecture.

Therefore, certain buildings that have remained unbuilt physically are also the result of architecture as a process. Many of the best buildings in history were never built (this does not contradict the fact that architecture has, on many occasions, been produced by the sublimation of construction processes, with given materials, at a given moment in history).

In fact, in most cases, buildings are more beautiful during the construction process than when complete, because they represent the staging of a process of construction of ideas.

The ideal state of a building would be one of constant construction, supporting human activities.

The project for a motorway in a territory covering five thousand kilometres, the construction of a reservoir, a chair design or the soundproofing of a city – all are Architecture. Even, in spite of the economic logic that prevails in our world, the project for a building of dwellings ought to emerge from an architectural process. Specialisation and the complexity of processes have, on most occasions, forced the architect to forgo designing large infrastructures built on the territory, as well as objects that contain space, be they fixed or moving.

Defining virtual reality, places of transit, meeting places, how we access information by means of a spatial code, using virtual material (noughts and ones), with a result that – whether or not it is similar to the constructions of the physical world – is an activity proper to architecture. Up until now, architecture has operated principally with space, because building meant finishing a process. Now, in the digital world, time too belongs to architecture. New architecture organises what has come to be referred to as 'heightened reality,' where the physical and the digital relate. Buildings and spaces also begin to more actively include time and its self-transformation. Architecture is, then, the creator of processes, rather than of finite events. As a process, it can be digital because it does not require material.

[WM] **(advanced) architecture x 7**

1. The digital age is to advanced architecture what the industrial revolution was to modern architecture. The greatest innovations in the history of housing were possible due to the industrial revolution. The current digital revolution should engender changes of equal scope.

2. Distances do not exist. We have a greater interest in knowing with whom and for whom, than from where. The whole world is a terminal. The concern is not to be near, but to be connected: new technologies renew the concept of proximity in a broader context. Doors, windows...

3. The three-dimensional representation permitted by new technologies makes observation a direct experience. As soon as he can place himself inside an artificial reality, the observer splits his experience. We are living a digital neo-renaissance: while having another self in virtual space, the observer occupies (once again) the centre of control. The computer-generated model of the world centres on the observer.

4. Scale belongs to the past. Advanced architecture works with virtual models at real scale. The chip transforms intelligent commerce among people and objects in the context of an advanced culture, disintegrating established levels and scales.

5. Energy is a new transforming concept of structure, form, function and space itself. As our capacity to store information about things grows, we become increasingly capable of modulating its energy, using it and transforming it. The buildings of the future will be distinguished by the type of energy they generate, receive or use.

6. The intelligence of construction follows in the footsteps of the chip: material is incorporated in the same measure that its power increases. Technique is giving way to science in all spheres of construction.

7. All advanced culture is contained in the speed of movement: the fate of the world is determined by how three words (departure, journey and arrival) will be reduced to two: the journey will be seen as no more than inertia, constantly approaching the speed of light, or zero. Travelling by the Internet will condition the idea of the city and of territory: as a time-space relationship, the latter have ceased to exist.

[JM] In the first place "to architecture" is about identifying the work of architecture, the project as "a making." The term "to architecture," has to do with this – getting to know something that previously had no pre-established path with and from which to be obtained.

[FP] *"Architectue is already submerged in another metadiscipline: Geography."* (Ricardo Sanchez Lampreave)

★ areas of impunity

→ 'criteria', 'hybrid', 'program', 'spaces> vector space'

[co] We call areas of impunity those sites in where vectorial space can unfold. Areas of impunity are opportunities for developing programs free of restrictions and hierarchies, centers or rhetorical figures; they are opportunities and programs (to be invented, for the most part) in which the modes and practices of the new social subject can be developed: activities that enable a tangent topology to unfold.

They operate neither through reform nor criticism; they coalesce through the varied use of contemporary techniques, in contexts and with a physicality different from traditional one. They seek to isolate within the system of social regulation prevailing today, which produces the new subject and his practices, fields that are free from domination, new political spaces selected from the hybridization of culture, production and leisure.

IÑAKI ÁBALOS & JUAN HERREROS

ÁBALOS & HERREROS, *Comtetition for the river Guadalhorce*, Málaga (Spain), 1994.

◆ areas of opportunity

→ 'field'

[FS] See 'areas of impunity.'

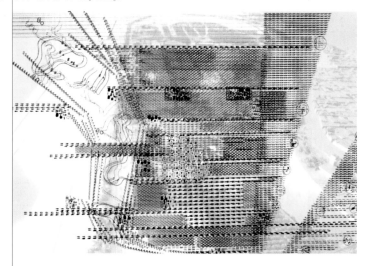

Yago CONDE, Bea GOLLER, Cartuja'93

✱ arkitektor

→ 'advanced> advanced achitecture', 'architecture', 'artificial', 'logic, digital'

[VG] The artificial intelligence that, as explained by Ray Kurzweil in his book *The Age of Spiritual Machines* (Texere Publishing, 2001), will become an everyday reality when a standard computer has the same processing capacity as a human brain (set for 2020), suggests that the coming years will bring computer programs that can produce architecture projects.

'Starting with a fixed site, with specific requirements, respecting legislation, the ARKITEKTOR program will be capable of offering different solutions to clients all over the world, who will be able to receive as many projects as they wish (and pay for) for their site, with an explanation of their advantages and drawbacks. The program will subsequently draw up the executive project, include the construction details of the geographic area of the world in question, calculate the structure and apply for building permission. And it will be built, using artisan or industrial means.'

This reduction to the absurd shows how the architect either brings added value to the process of the conception and construction of a building, or ceases to be necessary in the drawing up of projects.

– Architect: We're going to create a program that produces architecture projects so we need to find the genetic laws necessary to develop it.

– Programmer: Yes, that is quite possible.

– Architect: Just like *Deep Blue*, that knows all the principal chess matches in history and applies them as required, we will have to analyse history's foremost buildings and extract their basic principles.

– Programmer: Perfect.

– Architect: Producing buildings as Le Corbusier did, or like Gothic palaces, can't be difficult.

– Programmer: Of course not.

– Architect: Still, we have to think that someone might want a house in the style of Le Corbusier with Gothic windows. That ought to be more expensive, because the program will have more thinking to do. Or perhaps it should crash…

– Programmer: As far as programming is concerned, everything is possible. Both a strict definition of patterns and orders that, when logically applied, generate coherent buildings, and the absolute freedom of kitsch. To produce 'new buildings' we'll have to define laws of innovation, if they exist. It's your job to define the rules of play for the ARKITEKTOR.

– Architect: That's what we'll do.

Producciones NewMedia, *Scape Model* for Vicente GUALLART, Willy MÜLLER, Enric RUIZ-GELI, *Scape House*, El Penedès (Barcelona), 1996.

● armadillo

→ 'fuselages',
'(inter)weavings
and inter(plots)',
'skeleton', 'strategy'

[MG]

1

2

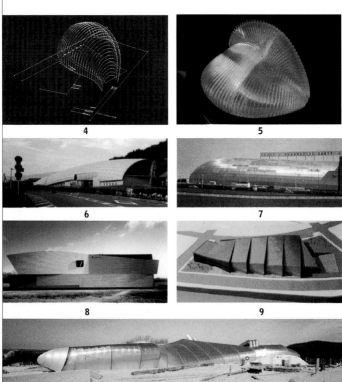

3

1. Car-armadillo, in *Quaderns* 218, 1997.
2. Armadillo, in *Quaderns* 199, 1993.
3. *Armadillidium*, in *Quaderns* 199, 1993.
4. Vicente SARRABLO (with H. Jala), *Air Inflated System, Inflatable prototypes for sport facilities,* (Engineering: Javier Marcipar – CIMNE), 1999.
5. Greg LYNN, *Embryological House,* 2000.
6. Toyo ITO, *Museum of Shimosuwa,* Nagano (Japan), 1993.
7. Renzo PIANO, *Shopping centre Bercy II,* París, 1990.
8. Ben VAN BERKEL & Caroline BOS (UN-Studio), *Karbouw Building,* Amersfoort (The Netherlands), 1992.
9. Javier FRESNEDA, Javier PEÑA, Javier SANJUÁN, *Covered swimming-pool,* Totana (Murcia, Spain), 1999.
10. NOX; OOSTER-HUIS ASSOCIATES, *Water Pavilion,* Neeltje Jans (The Netherlands), 1997.

'Armadillo' is the common name for a mammal whose back is covered in bony plates, and that, when faced with danger, rolls itself up into a ball. There is also an invertebrate of the isopoda order, the *armadillidium*, which, when disturbed, contracts its body, normally long and narrow, into a hard and segmented sphere.

In both cases, response to a conflictive environment lies not in adaptation and camouflage (common mechanisms in other species), but rather in inhibition and withdrawal from a suddenly hostile reality behind a shield of retractile plates. In this reaction, the "natural" organic shapes, due to a reflexive, rolling-up movement, transform rapidly into autonomous geometric elements: spheres, spirals, disks, etc.

This mechanism inherently resorts to formulas, which though not necessarily sceptical, are indeed reserved, with a particular (dis)position vis-à-vis reality that causes the appearance of strange and astonishing – winding – bodies; hard coils, prosthetic shells or retractile foldbacks. Armadillo and armadillidium represent acontextual objects, dynamic only in the braid that they generate, and explicitly artificial, whose expressive force, rather than in loquacity, resides in enigma; rather than in communion with an exterior, often hostile or decharacterised landscape, in the concise gesture of an intense, simultaneous movement of contortion, contraction and retraction. Resistant rather than reactive (reactivating) responses.

4

5

6

7

8

9

10

Mariko MORI, *Empty Dream*, 1995, in *Parkett* 54, 1998/99.

★✗◆ artificial

→ 'abstract', 'a-couplings', 'agriculture', 'camouflage', 'countermarks', 'criss-crossing', 'cuts' 'eco->ecomonumentality', 'ecology, active', 'globalization', 'land-arch', 'landscapes, operative', 'landstrategy', 'mountain', 'natuficio', 'naturartificial', 'nature', 'reliefs', 'rurban', 'synthetical', 'terraces', 'topographies, operative', 'trays'

[CO] "We will not be able to see what is artificial and what is real. So we will call artificial what does not rely to us," Sonja Bettel.
XAVIER COSTA

[VG] Natural nature ceased to exist when humankind left the planet and we were able to see ourselves from the outside. Everything is artificial.

[FS] The artificial-natural duality has disappeared. Its boundaries have blurred, confusing traditional fields and arriving at a common definition: naturartifical. The landscapes of nature can be as natural (untouched) as artificial: environmental destruction is absorbed and transformed. Urban landscapes have an artificial or natural character. Naturartificial is a new form of designing; a transformation of the concept of place. Before, the natural background was to artificial constructions – the modern mechanism of figure-ground. Today, the background is of primary interest, as much (if not more so) as the pieces that can disappear. In the same way, figure-ground has disappeared in the mechanisms of tangram, moiré or felt. Natural and artificial are not permanently united to landscape and city respectively. A place is not only a landscape. A place is a drawing of a place. Place is a construction. Place is artificial.

● artificial reactivity (or artificial complicity)

[MG] See 'artificial,' 'alienation (and estrangement),' 'reactive,' 'complicity,' 'ambiguity (and ambivalence),' 'naturartificial.'
Non subordinated complicity. Artificialisation and reactivation of the context, which are sensitive to its (unexpected) requests.

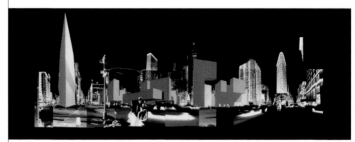

Buildings / Gardens

WEST 8, *Project 1:00 PM Square*, New York, 1996.

●■ a-scalarity (scalar ambiguity)

[MG] Scale it is neither measure nor dimension (both univocal), but capacity for relation (ambivalent). The dynamic systems which govern our universe (and the complex geometries of the structures associated with them) give rise to possible relations of "a-scalar" zoom among themselves (like recursive – and enjambed – phenomena of growth and development). In the same way, of interest here are those open configurations (or dispositions) that do not conform to any scale. Or better yet, those configurations that alter the idea of scale – of scale, not of size, as Federico Soriano pointed out – referring, thus, to the diffuse nature of contemporary environment(s) resonating flexibly and unbiasedly with and among its surprising – and ambiguous – manifestations.

[JM] A-scalarity is action and effect of an architecture that does not distinguish limits, that dissolves. All space of this architecture would be intermediate space, "between."

b&k+, *Telematische-landschaft*, project for Expo 2000, Hannover (Germany), 2000.

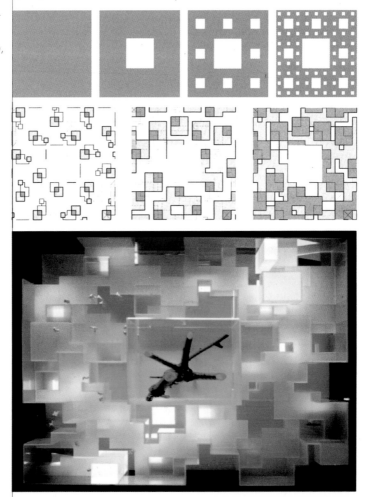

★ aspiration

[co] A building can be a selective "aspiration" of the context. It can grow by capillary sucking up, according to the print of the pre-existent buildings.
FRANÇOIS ROCHE

ROCHE, DSV & SIE,
*Cultural Centre
(extension of the
School of
Architecture)*, Venice
(Italy), 1998.

■● assembly

→ 'associate, overlap,
connect', 'collage',
'component', 'construction,
intelligent', 'geometry',
'recycling', 'transversality'

NJIRIC+NJIRIC, *Think Pad*, New
Library for the School of
Architecture, UPC, Barcelona, 2000.

[JM] **(union of the diverse)**
See 'collaging.'
We assist a dyslexic use of language that involuntarily incorporates strangeness. The mechanism of this incorporation is not realized on the basis of kitsch, but on the ensemble. The means of these operations is not brought to head from syntaxes: that which is before and after, but rather many operations are realized by adding bits and pieces. Ingredients derived from the huge information of heterogeneous functional programs, forces of the city and also by the actual mechanisms of the standardised.

(joining of components)
Assembly is the joining of pieces by fitting projecting parts of one into the cavitary parts of the other. Dovetailing. Preferably dry construction. Construction based upon paired or overlapping materials and components. Truly or virtually dismountable creation.

■ associate, overlap, connect

→ 'a-couplings',
'action>critical',
'assembly', 'collaging',
'criteria', 'hybrid',
'relationships, transitive',
'strategy', 'transversality'

[JM] Since reality leads us, the project is about relating, associating, overlapping, connecting, tensing and a whole series of actions related to manufacture. It is about work that leans on something—that needs excuses to extend, unfold and become seen. Once these links are open, the game is open and in each play, possibilities are opened anew. But for the game to not end, architecture should not implant decisions, and constrictions, but indetermination and incertitude.

◆● attractors

[FS] *"...the most important property of a dynamical system is its long-term behaviour. This selects a much simpler set of movements from among all those of the complete system. For example, in the above system a starting point vanishes outside the figure, stays where it is or else converges on the limit cycle and orbits and orbits more. Of all the possible movements, long-term behaviour selects precisely those characteristics that we have deemed especially noteworthy.*

Engineers speak in similar way. They speak of "transitories" when the system switches on, in comparison to what happens if we wait a bit... but, for an overall vision of the general nature of the system, not of the fine details, "transitories" can be ignored.

So, what does a general dynamical system do in the long term? It stabilises in an attractor. An attractor is defined as anything in which something stabilises. The essence of an attractor is that some portion of the phase space is such that any point that begins to move in its vicinity increasing approaches it." (STEWART, Ian, *Does God play dice?*, Oxford: Basil Blackwell, 1989)

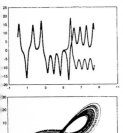

**Visualisations
of trajectory**

Computer graphic of the
equations of Lorenz:
dx/dt = -10x+10y; dy/dt =
28x-y-xz; dz/dt = -
(8/3)x+xy. Above: x-t.
Below: y-x.
In *AD* vol 67 No 9/10,
1997.

One property of fractals is that they do not have a dimension that can be expressed by a complete number. Their dimension is found between the lines and the drawing, between areas and volumes. They are, in a certain way, more efficient in occupying space than their Euclidean equivalents. They are denser than lines, but without amassing into a drawing; or bodies made up of many drawings of infinite area, but whose total volume is null, like a compact house of cards. To represent their dimension, one must use fractions. A second characteristic of fractals is that their irregularity, or physiognomy, remains constant at various scales. The object has the same form, in the general sense of the word, as the amplified detail of itself. A minimal fragment can generate and configure the whole. As opposed to other generative groupings in nature, there is no difference between the detail and the whole because there is no reference to size. And as scale does not exist, a fractal is merely an infinite series in which we do not know its origin or which parts are amplifications of a totality. Which, by the way, is impossible to learn. Detail and whole share the same rank.

[MG] While the evolution and reproduction of dynamic systems refers largely to fluctuating and uncertain – indeterminate – trajectories, their movements may be condensed in certain figures of consensus – called "strange attractors" – of largely fractal geometry.

The movements – open, multiple and unpredictable – of the system tend to coil and evolve around these basic trajectories of *complex geometries* that identify a sort of relatively precise internal code – or nuclear movement – ascribable to basic stimulatory criteria.

Therefore, the attractor is – according to the mathematician Ivar Ekeland – an "extreme element." If the curves of the system are infinite, their movements may create a finite, quasi-synthetical, extreme representation (that which any of the trajectories would describe if we were to allow it to continue indefinitely).

This permits the identification of similarities between the representation of the process and the process itself, that is, between synthetical diagrammed and dynamic movement, which alludes to the compressive capacity of the evolutionary organisms in elemental data.

The generic properties of the system permit the condensing of the manifold movements that generate its changes in surprising – disconcerting, the mathematician Ivar Ekeland would say – virtual trajectories of synthesis.

The attractor expresses, according to biologist Mae-Wan Ho, an ideal state of basic determinism, of coherence and stability, that the system ideally tends to recover (like that retractile movement of the armadillo in situations of disturbance or defence). However, the dynamic nature of the system removes it from this stabilised state: its entropy is generated proportionally to the incoherence of the actions.

In either case, the final outcome is a virtual coiling of the system around itself, as in the movement of a spiral that condenses all the information – diverse and infinite – in this "trajectory of consensus" (this sort of internal criterion or basic initial disposition) diagrammable in basic data as abstract – synthetical – as they are concrete, or explicit.

(EKELAND, Ivar, *Le Chaos*, Paris: Dominos, 1995).

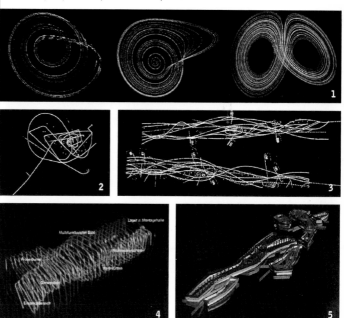

Geometrical definition by approximation of fluctuating trajectories.
1. Attractors of Lorenz, in *Quaderns* 222, 1999. **2.** Enric MIRALLES, Benedetta TAGLIABUE, *Maretas Museum*, Lanzarote (Spain), 1999. **3.** Cristina DÍAZ MORENO, Guillermo FERNÁNDEZ PARDO, *Competition Sharaku's House*, Tokyo, 1996. **4.** Ben VAN BERKEL & Caroline BOS (UN-Studio), *Competition for the Music Theatre*, Graz (Austria), 1998. **5.** José Alfonso BALLESTEROS, *Office Building Complex Ressort*, La Habana (Cuba), 1998.

● a-typ-I-call (atypical)

[MG] The old idea of typological classification, with its corollary "form=function," leaves its way to a shared search which gives power to an almost "typo-graphical" action. This action is associated to the research of "genotypes" that can synthesize strategies of tactical hybridisation between conditions or natures, programmes or uses. It combines synthetical processes of development rather than pure functions-figurations.

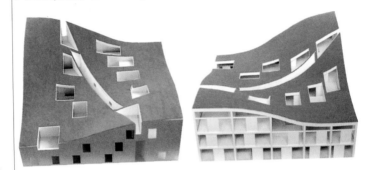

NL, *Het Funen, 10 individual houses,* Amsterdam, 1999-.

● audacity

→ 'AA', 'action> critical', 'advanced> advanced architecture', 'architecture', 'competition', 'critical pragmatism', 'ecology, active', 'form', 'ideas', 'innovation', 'intelligence', 'memory', 'precision', 'recycling', 'Think Tank'

[MG] Audacity is no gratuitous temerity or imprudence, but calculated innovation and risk: at once precise and determined.

Audacity is daring, in the positive sense: higher stakes, for higher gain.

Audacity is not to save, but rather to give energy.

Instead of a speculative, or restorative, conservative, or evocative (that is, paralysed/paralysing: timid, sceptical, suspicious, anachronistic or simply nostalgic) action, we propose a more audacious action, that is, more innovative.

Those terms heretofore preserving – conservationist (whether they are called ecology or memory, structure or discipline) – thus yield to more propositive and revitalising proposals. Audacious: more qualitative; more daring.

[MG] Audacity is boldness. Projection.

Projective capacity subject to chance (and fortune).

"*Audaces fortuna Juvat.*"

(Pliny the Younger)

NL, *Oefenfabriek,* Hoogvliet, satellite town of Rotterdam (The Netherlands), 2002.

● auditoriums

→ 'competition',
'field', 'program'

[MG] Auditoriums are not morgues.

Certain official culture, however, has confused terms.

The decisions of competitions held in recent years demonstrate this.

– When boxes (closed figures) win over trajectories (open movements);
– crosses (as literal lines) over crosses (as abstract interchanges);
– monuments over "fields;"
– static geometries over dynamical geometries;
– typologies over topologies;
– rhetorical spaces over reactive spaces;
– closed elementalities over interactive complexities;
– anachronistic architectures over advanced architectures.

The time has come to rethink certain conditions of the old disciplinary culture with the aim of fostering another type of operative – more singular, dynamic, plural and qualified – systems for programmes now simultaneously ambiguous, multifaceted, mixed and renewable at the same time.

[i] p. 70-71

NEUTELINGS
RIEDIJK Architecten,
Concert Hall, Bruges
(Belgium), 1998
(Price Winning
Competition Entry).

● authenticity

[MG] See 'crossbreeding' and 'hybrid.'

[MG] *"This is a time of hybridisation. There is no place for authenticity because we do not know any more what authenticity means. We do not have examples nor definitions. We only know it by the books of history.*

This is a time of crossbreeding, as enrichment we can get from the combination, sum and multiplication of elements. We do not search the pure and rational, but the impure and emotional. People are not pure, exact or perfect, nor is architecture.

In a world that is changing every second, we should not simplify and reduce to authenticity, but we need to work with systems, processes, mechanisms of evolution that allow us to join all information and processing it into a complex piece of architecture.

In this sense, architecture becomes the context where technological advances and social needs meet without any filters, appearing as a multi-layered object." (Susanna Cros)

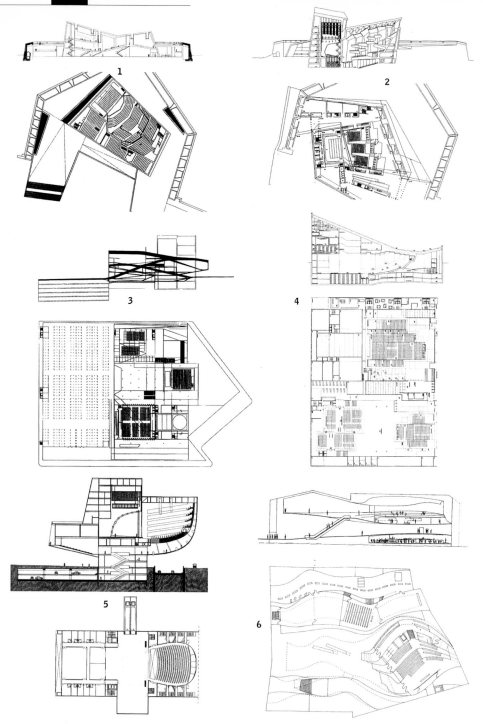

1. Alberto MARTÍNEZ CASTILLO, Beatriz MATOS, *Competition for conference centre* (3rd prize), Badajoz (Spain), 1999.
2. María José ARANGUREN LÓPEZ, José GONZÁLEZ GALLEGOS, *Auditorium*, Badajoz (Spain), 1995. **3.** Vicente GUALLART (with Max SANJULIÁN), *Competition for auditorium and conference centre*, Pamplona (Spain), 1998. **4.** Eduardo ARROYO (NO.mad Arquitectura), *Competition for auditorium and conference centre* (finalist), Pamplona (Spain), 1998. **5.** NEUTELINGS RIEDIJK Architecten, *Concert Hall*, Bruges (Belgium), 1998 (Price Winning Competition Entry). **6.** ROCHE, DSV & SIE, *Cultural Centre* (extension of the School of Architecture), Venice (Italy), 1998.

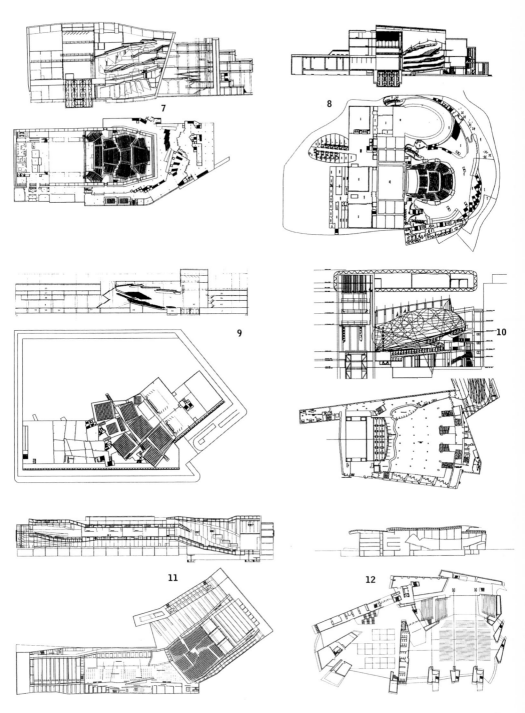

7. S&Aa (SORIANO-PALACIOS), *Euskalduna Hall*, Bilbao, 1991-1998. **8.** S&Aa (SORIANO-PALACIOS), *Competition for the National Opera House*, Oslo (Norway), 2000. **9.** S&Aa (SORIANO-PALACIOS), *Competition for auditorium and conference centre*, Pamplona (Spain), 1998. **10.** S&Aa (SORIANO-PALACIOS), *Fleta Theatre*, Zaragoza (Spain), 2001. **11.** Ginés GARRIDO, Ricardo SÁNCHEZ LAMPREAVE, Fernando PORRAS, *Competition for auditorium and conference centre*, Pamplona (Spain), 1998. **12.** AMP (ARTENGO-MENIS-PASTRANA), *Conference centre Tenerife Sur*, Playa de las Américas, Costa Adeje (Tenerife, Spain), 1998-.

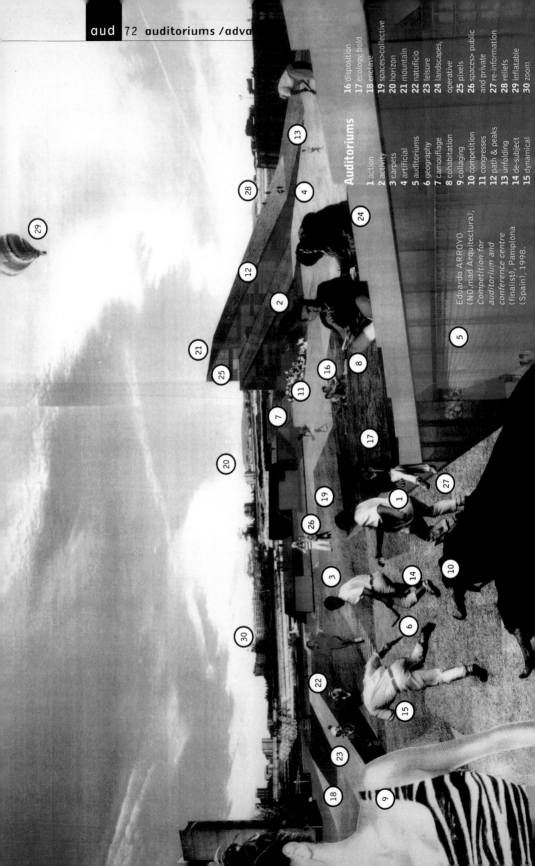

Auditoriums

1 action
2 activity
3 carpets
4 artificial
5 auditoriums
6 geography
7 camouflage
8 cohabitation
9 collaging
10 competition
11 congresses
12 path & peaks
13 unfolding
14 de-subject
15 dynamical
16 disposition
17 ecology, bold
18 enclave
19 spaces>collective
20 horizon
21 mountain
22 natuficio
23 leisure
24 landscapes, operative
25 pixels
26 spaces> public and private
27 re-information
28 reliefs
29 inflatable
30 zoom

Eduardo ARROYO
(NO.mad Arquitectura),
Competition for
auditorium and
conference centre
(finalist), Pamplona
(Spain), 1998.

×● avatar

[VG] Avatar is the virtual personality of a physical entity. An avatar of a person may be a three-dimensional model of that person or any other form that represents him or her.

[MG] 'Avatar' is, in the romantic spirit, an adventure subject to the whims of chance: an uncertain experience, subject to a fortuitous series of unforeseen events. It also describes each of the incarnations of the god Vishnu.
In contemporary language, an avatar is a virtual figure, animated and dynamic, capable of simultaneously evolving and mutating (real and virtual). This sort of illusion or incarnation – this avatar – possesses no univocal and substantial (deterministic) essence, no nature or category: it can transform and alter itself – mutate or hybridise — fusing (and processing) conditions and bits of information. It is, then, rather than a image, an open-ended trajectory that responds to a "logic of programming," to a basic evolutionary criterion, which, however, alters and conforms tactically (like the "cyborg-avatar" in Terminator) thus acquiring different degrees of complexity and identity: a dog sounds, therefore, like a piano, a dinosaur is a door, a pavement contracts like a face, a face flattens into a landscape, a flower cracks open a mountain, a tree is a lamp post.
Despite its seemingly virtual – digital – definition this sort of fortuitous mutation, as unexpected as it is uncertain, alludes to the capacity for transfusion, for coupling and hybridisation, of the contemporary project, as well as to its dynamic capacity for processing bits of information and for evolving through stimulatory logics. As in an open adventure: as accidental as it is vocationally unfinished (indeterminate: non-determinate but, also, non-terminated).

MOOG, Simulations of a virtual body as an evolutionary meshed structure.

[VG] **urban avatar**

If in the virtual world there are representations of physical beings that are not pure mimesis of that which is represented, the physical world can construct elements whose forms differ substantially from those that are traditionally attributed to them. It would be unthinkable to place a musical instrument (a piano or a synthesiser) as an item of urban furniture beside a fountain in a children's play area. But sound instruments could be designed for public space that react, with sound, to human activity. Musical series produced by man's interaction with space and with other men. Instruments produced with natural or artificial forms. A tree, a rock, a cylinder. A world behind another world.

ARCHIKUBIK,
Bit landscapes.

Vicente GUALLART
(with Max
SANJULIÁN),
*Project for the
urbanization of
Cristóbal
de Moura street,
Barcelona, 1999.*

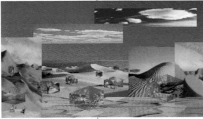

Natural Avatar

Urban Avatar

B

●★ bank & beach

[MG] Bank is an arrangement of objects in a lineal pattern. Bank & beach is an arrangement of objects in a non-lineal system.

[co] **beach**

The beach is the scene of the most celebrated and inexhaustible synthesis between nature (sea) and culture (city), the best and cheapest urban park, the most frequented and sought after place, the setting for countless games and joys, the birthplace and feeding ground of one of the most important modern economic activities. The chief point of reference for the most important recent construction process of a space (the touristic), the beach continues, after so many years, to hold the power to evoke in our imagination all sorts of sequences and uses. Transitory space between sea and city, the beach is the most accessible representation of the four natural elements of the Greeks (Empedocles) and the host-place for the most elementary and pleasurable behaviours: relating, play, laughter and desire. Three considerations should feature in our reflection on beaches: their exceptional and singular character (the tourism of the warm Mediterranean coast is sustained on just a few million square metres, less than an average ski area); their capacity for endlessly synthesising liturgies and spontaneities in a renewed/renewing manner; and, last of all, the manner in which they resolve the apparent contradiction between a superhuman scale and a routine and ritual use, graspable and naturally proximate to the domain of the users.

Beaches are the most consistent, lasting, appreciated and popular theme park (without being afflicted with problems of recurrence and obsolescence or any need for exceptional investment), and they are the cornerstone of the most successful tourist industries. Not requiring any energy consumption, they are the cheapest and most efficient attraction. And they never boring, because the user writes his own script – as opposed to the most sophisticated apparatuses at amusement parks, and even more so at theme parks, where the true protagonist is the gadget. So, being so complex and beneficial, why does intellectual negligence disregard beaches and reduce them to a strictly mechanical and technical perception? In less periphrastic terms, why do they continue to be the exclusive domain of so often deplorable engineering?

JOSÉ MIGUEL IRIBAS

Beach in Benidorm (Spain).

BCN Metápolis, *Land Grid* (digital image), in GAUSA, Manuel; GUALLART, Vicente; MÜLLER, Willy, *Met 1.0. Barcelona Metápolis*, Barcelona: ACTAR, 1998.

● Barcelona Metapolis

→ 'islands', 'm. city',
'maps (to map)',
'Metapolis', 'multicity',
'place of places'

[MG] Barcelona has been for years a city of lyrical profiles, rather than epic movements. Wedged into the restricted ambit defined by its geographical boundaries (the sea to the south, Collserola ridge to the north and its larger rivers – the Besòs and the Llobregat – to the east and west), the physical space over which the city has spread has come to be characterised by a closed and limited position defined by its natural boundaries, its vertical flows and the "agoraphobic" use of its scarce land resources.

The construction of territorial infrastructures (ring-roads, tunnels and by-passes) suddenly materialised a large-scale change in just a few short years: that of a "multi-Barcelona" which today spreads like an irregular patchwork over the territory with barely any strategic contracts for the future. While the old model of a episodic micro-urbanism of static concepts ("light" monumentalisation) and of ad hoc "darning," may have been decisive in its day for repairing and regenerating the city of the transition, it no longer suffices for dealing with the new demands of the city we are likely to see in the future.

Present-day Barcelona is no longer a single space or a single, more or less ideal model, but rather a city of cities: a place of places. A kaleidoscope – or a menu – of opportunities.

What is called for is no longer regeneration, but rather revitalisation: re-activation of this polyphase scenario promoting diverse, combined and interactive experiences, energies and relationships, stimulating the coexistence of co-participative situations and information, rather than the homogeneity of aesthetics which lead nowhere. Barcelona is today a multi-city which must accept itself as such: bolstering its diversity, developing the differences, articulating the specificities. Not in order to reproduce them, but rather to recognise them and be able to act qualitatively with them.

In its day, with this ambition, was proposed the programme "Barcelona Metapolis." It had the goal of detecting strategic questions and situations in a complex and dynamic system and synthesised five diagrams for action as a

strips

nodes

wedges

fingers

hot points

BCN Metápolis, 5
ideograms for
Barcelona multilayer,
in GAUSA, Manuel;
GUALLART, Vicente;
MÜLLER, Willy,
Met 1.0. Barcelona
Metápolis, Barcelona:
ACTAR, 1998.

translation of an equal number of possible layers of a(n) (re)active city.

1- Strips: Is a new relationship with the territory possible? The force of the metropolis drives the territory, but the greater equilibrium of the territory affects Barcelona. A new interterritorial logic is called for, one that might permit concerted development based upon effective empty-full sequences in accordance with the infrastructural scheme: a large-scale "landscape-architectural" grid.

2- Nodes: Is a mixed exploitation of infrastructures possible? The visualisation of a Barcelona of flows and transferences allows for a fresh reflection upon the spaces of transference and interconnection, no longer as mere monofunctional structures, but rather as mixed programmatic supports: areas of interchange and interchange conceivable as new "gateways to the city."

3- Wedges: Is an implosive, and not explosive, movement possible for the city? Beyond territorial thrust, Barcelona must think about "growing within," reinforming its existent structures through determined operations of restructuring, rather than of cosmetic change. Reimploding its limits through intrusions, rather than extrusions.

4- Fingers: Is a new seafront possible for the city? Barcelona needs urgently to look not only towards the sea but also to penetrate it. To been seen from the sea. Not only timidly or clandestinely, but also decisively and ambitiously. The sea as a new territory.

5- Hot Points: Is it possible to detect sequences of systematic intervention in the city? Barcelona presents "clonic" points susceptible to reappropriation through new models of intervention, in an action as extrapolable as it is intermittent and discontinuous. Tactically reconvertible, that is, technological, functional, ludic and/or temporal "lands."

Barcelona must today learn how to strengthen these new situations, not through bureaucratic structures, but rather through manifold research: Barcelona should be a permanent observatory of international urbanism; it should create structures for R+3D (research, development, education, diffusion) that demand new ambitions in their course of action.

BARCELONA
METÁPOLIS,
Producciones
NewMedia, Interactive
model for the Biennale
di Venezia, 2000.

● beaches

[MG] See 'bank & beach.'

● beacons (maps as beacons)

→ 'cartographies',
'diagrams', 'dictionary',
'geomancy', 'language',
'maps (to map)',
'name', 'networks'

[MG] In the years prior to the First World War, the geographer Haldford J. MacKinder (1861-1947) established a possible correlation between "geographical maps" and "mental maps."

His definition is not as relevant to the psychological realm as it is to the strategic, that is, to decision-making. MacKinder showed how the notion of a map appeared to be associated with the capacity for forming, deforming and informing visions of the world: a map not only implied recognising established boundaries, but also recognising potential opportunities for altering them.

This allowed for a translation of the idea of a map not only as static representation of reality, but also as a marking-out – an anticipatory mental scheme – of possible movements, implying not only a capacity for representing (with an alert gaze) new territories, but also for proposing new definitions within them.

Instrumentalising this interaction requires, in fact, crossing paths, signalling agreements, marking confluences, discovering intersections, fostering crosses and exploring limits. Ultimately, required is a marking out fields and mapping links, through an action based upon the exploration – and the proposition – of "atopical" relationships rather than upon the recording and documentation of accepted "models."

Hence, maps are understood as "tactically operative," rather than as static drawings – or descriptions – rely upon this positive and propositive qualities of an intentional recognition of reality, as a restructuring – thus manipulative – action of the basic data. A manipulation that would allude to the "exploration-manipulation-fórmulation" process implicit in any projectual marker.

[MG] *"We might ask ourselves how the Inuit can orientate themselves in kilometres of frozen ice. In fact, these referents – these markers – these traces are not made up of objects or true points, but rather of relationships: relationships between, for example, the cleanness and precision of edges, the quality of the snow, the force of the wind and the density of the air or the size of the cracks."*

(HALL, Edward T., *La dimension cacheé*, Paris: Editions du Seuil, 1971. Translated from Spanish.)

Ove ARUP, Jannuzzi
SMITH in BALMOND,
Cecil, *informal*,
Munich: Prestel, 2002.

★ beauty (the latent garden)

[co] The word beauty remains proscribed in modern professional debate today only as a vestige of puritanism. The attraction of constructing a new notion of beauty is practically the only thing that gives meaning to our profession (if we want it to continue to be understood as such) in conceiving an effective programme of action, avoiding the traps that we so meticulously lay for ourselves. If one accepts this proposition, work itself becomes notes in a private travel log, with which it constructs a mental atlas, an imaginary geography capable of illuminating every place through projection (inverting the traditional contextualism) and shaping, step by step, a latent garden. This vision perhaps points to the colourful lode, a string names – Uvedale Price, Frederick Lan Olmsted, Le Corbusier, Bruno Taut, Roberto Burle-Marx, Lina Bo Bardí, Robert Smithson, Archigram, Cedric Price and others – like an underground seam which survives to the present. The fusion of nature and artifice, the blurring of disciplinary boundaries between architecture, art, garden and thought, the organisation of experience as narrative sequences, the predominance of the visual and movement, as well in the immaterial and invisible, the construction of a public space and architecture reflecting new sensitivities, etc. These ingredients lead to a new garden that is seen or unseen, yet without which there is no new architecture but rather, at best, variations.

We who imagine such draw not only on abstract statements and proper names; we must construct another – parallel – cartography that illuminates our projects conquering new formal references, new symbols, words and technologies that permit us to let go of the old ones, now lacking in necessary appeal. And we must reconstruct our interlocutor; the world we address. The log is thus made up of sketches (works and projects), footnotes, borrowed and original ideas, names, addresses and personal contacts, images, conversations; manifold materials that gaze upon themselves and recompose our own gaze. The work of the architect approximates that of the gardener: clearing the plot, preparing the terrain, choosing the species and sowing them in an orderly manner and then ensuring that the passage of time makes the work bear fruit.

IÑAKI ÁBALOS & JUAN HERREROS

● bends and (un)bendings

→ 'form', 'geometry', 'roll-ups', 'topographies, operative'

[MG] See 'braids,' 'circuits,' 'coilings,' 'contortionisms,' 'fold,' 'folding' and 'fold (unfold-refold).'

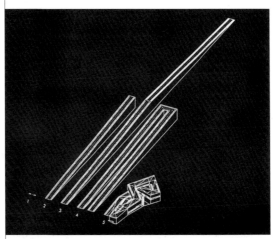

NL ARCHITECTS,
*Parkhouse Carstadt
Project*, Amsterdam,
1996.

● Benidorm

[MG] "Benidorm is Las Vegas," according to a well-known image by Vicente Guallart. Benidorm is B.B. (Big & Bold). Benidorm is S.S.S. (Sun, Sea & Sex). Benidorm is an icon: that of the tourist megalopolis as a new paradigm of the Mediterranean coast. An extreme "scenario," scorned by the discipline. An icon rejected in favour of other, imported icons.

A direct and uninhibited space, for use, consumption and fun: informally functional, rather than formally ritual. The more unbiased the more unrestrained. Produced through the open superposition of autonomous, discontinuous and spaced events. An open process, in constant mutation, definitively "beyond" the harmonious continuity of the traditional city.

From afar, Benidorm possesses the epicness of a bold skyline: an immense cluster of vertical and intermittent sprouts and outcrops emerging from a desert on the sea. By night, Benidorm is a constellation, a focus of energy, a glitter of messages and slogans, of lights and activities. Suddenly, Benidorm is an advertisement: a graphic icon, an mediatic action, a ludic promise of action and/or pleasure. "Funitron." Up close, Benidorm is a potential, a hope and a promise — all broken. Because it is clumsy, (merely) accumulative, ad hoc, and often as episodic as it is vulgar.

It is, however, an organism with the capacity to grow upon itself, endlessly — and unstoppably — recasting itself, an organism that cries out for restructuring based upon exploration of its own attributes: drawing upon this and improving upon that. Giving rise to more relational spaces as in-between experiences – "exotic" interior landscapes or operative topographies – but also mixed accumulations – formations, sprouts and meldings — made up of programmes which are definitively hybrid because they are overlapped. Synthetic antitypes for a scenario that exploit its decidedly artificial nature.

Night Benidorm

1. Nuria DÍAZ, Vicente GUALLART, *Benidorm is Las Vegas*, digital image, 1992.

2. S&Aa (SORIANO-PALACIOS), *Competition for cultural centre and auditorium*, Benidorm (Alicante, Spain), 1995.

Benidorm / biodiversity / black holes

1 action
2 event
3 concentration devices
4 areas of impunity
5 buds
6 datascape
7 artificial reactivity
8 conservation
9 unrestrained (<un> factors)
10 direct
11 global

12 sea
13 bank & beach
14 decisions (and
 instructions) rather
 than designs
15 mountain
16 multimedia, urban
17 challenge
18 optimism
19 blunt
20 glocal

21 original and replica
22 inhabit
23 extrusion
24 crossings
25 fish
26 bluntings
27 reactive
28 just do it
29 devices
30 housing
31 ....

32 skyscrapers
33 España
34 density
35 imagine
36 tourism
37 Yeti
38 interaction
39 vertigo
40 XL
41 hotel
42 re-direction

MVRDV, *Densifying Benidorm*, in MVRDV,
Costa Ibérica, Barcelona: ACTAR, 2000

◆ big glass

[FS] Marcel Duchamp. Big glass is the only myth, or contemporary metaphor, sufficiently complex to reflect the new complexity of relations in the metropolis.

● Bilbao effect

[MG] See 'franchise'.

Bilbao: outline from the estuary

S&Aa (SORIANO-PALACIOS), *Europan 5* (mention), Barakaldo (Vizcaya, Spain), 1998.

ÁBALOS & HERREROS, *Abandoibarra planning*, Bilbao (Spain), 1994.

▲ biodiversity

→ 'and', 'diversity', 'economy', 'environment', 'field', 'multi', 'plural'

[FP] Let us look at the new stupefying economies which depend on intangible factors (information, entertainment, communications). These values fluctuate in the market as real consumable products, their quoted prices changing at speeds never before reached. But it is not the only commercial novelty of the present. Each time the capacity of countries to offer biological elements with specific properties achieves greater importance, amongst which we can single out those with the potential to be transgenically active, they transform themselves into biological models à la carte. As on many occasions, certain entities of advanced technological design cast their shadow over these products (almost always natural, not cultivated) to obtain miraculous results (probably not shared with the producer countries). In summary, vegetable species which always had their place, are classified, immediately treated and mutated genetically, substituting synthetic elements at much higher cost. The euphemistic term that has been attached to these groups of species is biodiversity.

Let us stop for a moment to consider an optimistic reading of this dubious practice: the elements so highly-esteemed were always in the same place, and the laboratories, in order to increase their opportunities, are able to get profit from them, that is to say, it is the eye which moves the thoughts which has to enhance them so that what we contemplate in the future acquires a new meaning. On the other hand, the principal contribution of these agents consists of the introduction of parameters which are nothing but strategies for future development. By being strategies, they don't operate in order to get immediate results, but, just the opposite – they operate trusting in their own internal (genetic) mechanisms to be those which in the process contribute to producing the desired effects. Translating this to architecture, we can design by reviving those matters which we bring into our hands, increasing our capacity for new discoveries. We can design as strategic planners, with open and self-generating processes. We can design by saving energy, when we rediscover within fixed parameters a conjoint of new and changing possibilities.

●✕black holes

→ 'action>critical',
'attractors', 'energy',
'light', 'm. city',
'no-places', 'time'

[MG] "*When a star has shrunk to a certain critical radius, the gravitational field at the surface becomes so strong that the light cones are bent inwards so much that the light can no longer escape. According to the theory of relativity, nothing can travel faster than light. Thus, if light cannot escape, neither can anything else; everything is dragged back by the gravitational field. So one has a set of events, a region of space-time, from which it is not possible to escape to reach the distant observer. The region is what we now call a black hole. Its boundary is called the event horizon and in coincides with the paths of light rays that just fail to escape from the black hole. [...] One could well say of the event horizon what the poet Dante said of the entrance to Hell: "All hope abandon, ye who enter here." Anything or anyone who falls through the event horizon will soon reach the region of infinite density and the end of time.*"
(HAWKING, Stephen W., *A Brief History of Time: From the Big Bang to Black Holes*, London: Bantam, 1988)

[MG] "*Nothing can escape a black hole once it has fallen under its power, not even light. Not even Clare Light. Then —he thought—, that Theseus Hadesovich must be a kind of human black hole. How many kinds of black hole must there be in the Universe? Perhaps there are places and people on this very planet who operate like that. That was what he was thinking the day he had the attack and he felt close to death.*" (COVADLO, Lázaro, *Agujeros negros*, Barcelona: Ediciones Altera, 1997. Translated from Spanish)

[VG] Cities, organisations, are centres that accumulate informational energy. They can be stars. Environments in which the attitude of the governors has the effect of one idea being amplified by another, producing a chain reaction that illuminates its environment. Or they can be black holes. Places with great potential due to their infrastructure, places that receive large amounts of information, places that attract activity and energy, though they overload their interior. That nothing comes out of. Their energy can be felt around them. And sometimes cause fear...

Black holes

1. Black hole Sagittarius A. Milky Way: galactic longitude/ latitude: 0°/0°; distance from the Earth: about 30000 light years; estimated mass: five million times the mass of the Sun. In *Newton* 8, December 1998.

2. Black hole Cygnus X-1. galactic longitude/ latitude: 71,3°/3,1°; distance from the Earth: about 8000 light years. In *Newton* 8, December 1998.

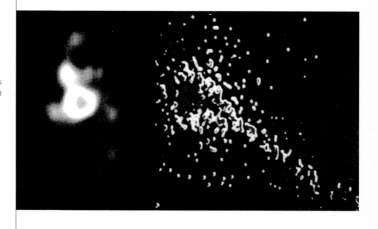

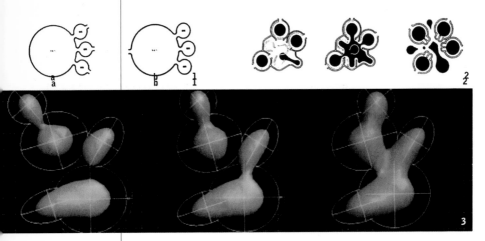

1. Yamamoto's sketches of a dwelling nLDK: a: individual rooms with exterior access; b: communitary space with exterior access, in *Fisuras* 6, 1998. **2**. Transformation of the wife's space in the dwelling, in *Fisuras* 6, 1998. **3**. Greg LYNN, Blobs, in *Fisuras* 3 1/3, 1995.

● ★ blobs

[MG] According to Webster's Encyclopedic Unabridged Dictionary of the English Language, a blob is *"a globule of liquid; a bubble; a small lump, drop, splotch, or daub."*

Recently, a class of topological geometric types for modeling complex aggregates that exhibit the qualities of multiplicity and singularity has been developed. The most interesting example is the development of "isomorphic poly-surfaces" or what in the special effects and animation industry is referred to as "meta-clay," "meta-ball" or "blob" models. The explanation of the organisation of these topological geometries actually outlines a working schema for a new typology for complexity.

In a software program by Wavefront Technologies, Inc. called Metaballs in their Explorer 3Design program, it is possible to geometrically model an organisation whose singular characteristics are defined by an assemblage of interacting local forces.

Unlike a conventional geometric primitive such as a sphere, these objects are defined with a centre, a surface area, a mass relative to other objects and importantly by two types of fields of influence. These meta-ball primitives are surrounded by halos of influence.

The inner volume defines a zone within which the meta-ball will connect with another meta-ball to form a single surface. The outer volume defines a zone within which other meta-ball objects can influence and inflect the surface of the meta-ball object.

The surfaces are surrounded by two halos of relational influence, one defining a zone of fusion the other defining a zone of inflection. When two or more meta-ball objects are related to one another, given the appropriate proximity of their halos, they can either mutually redefine their respective surfaces based on their particular gravitational properties or they can actually fuse into one contiguous surface that is defined, not by the summation or average of their surfaces and gravities, but instead by the interactions of their respective centres and zones of inflection and fusion.

A meta-ball aggregate is defined as a single surface whose contours result from the interaction and assemblage of the multiple internal fields which define it. In this sense, an aggregate geometric object such as this is a multiplicity; it is simultaneously singular in its continuity and multiplicitous in its internal differentiation. From the perspective of the unified surface, it is a singularity (as it is contiguous but not reducible to a single order) and from the perspective of the constituent components, it is a multiplicity (as it is composed of disparate components that are put into a complex relation).

Temporal development manifests as both subtle and catastrophic movements and fluctuations within and between interacting components results in varying degrees of singularity in more global or large scale structures. In the case of the isomorphic polysurfaces, a low number of interacting components and/or a stable relationship of those components over time leads to a global form that is more simple and stable and less complex and unstable.

A high number of components and/or a gradual or abrupt change in relative position of those components, over time, leads to a global form that is more complex and unstable and less simple and stable.

In this schema, there is no essential difference between a more or less spherical formation and a blob. The sphere and its provisional symmetries are merely the index of a rather low level of interactions where the blob is an index of a high degree of information in the form of differentiation between components in time. In this regard, even what seems to be a sphere is actually a blob without influence; an anexact form that merely masquerades as an exact form because it is isolated from adjacent forces.

Yet, like the blob that it is, it is capable of fluid and continuous differentiation based on interactions with neighboring forces with which it can be either inflected or fused to form higher degrees of singularity and multiplicity simultaneously. Complexity is not only always present as potential in even the most simple or primitive of forms, moreso, it is measured by the degree of both continuity and difference that are copresent at any moment. This measure of complexity (the index of which is continuity and differentiation) might best be described as the degree to which a system behaves as a blob.

GREG LYNN

★ blondels
[co] **(factors for a possible philosophy of action)**

According to Maurice Blondel, action is not a principle, but rather a necessity, a movement that cannot be stopped, as opposed to what occurs in speculative activity. Action has no principles; it does not conform to suppositions. Action does not understand anything as agreed, neither in that which concerns facts, nor principles, nor obligations. Action is not based upon postulates, nor even morals. For Blondel, action can be understood in three ways:

1. Action as an indicator of the impetus of the living, the living as fertile, productive.

2. Action designates the continual series of the means employed.

3. Action as result attained. Result considered less as object than as creation, which, real or not, remains as a combination of the powers of action.

The pragmatists (Pierce, James, Dewey, Mead) consider man to be a true agent that acts in the world and among his fellows, being, in the literal sense, an artifice. They consider thought to be action only insofar as it is a sizing-up of existence, an experiment that inevitably leads to the achievement of a relationship with reality.

NL, *Sky Cemetery NT.*

● blunt

→ 'competition',
'direct'

[MG] See 'logic, direct' and 'uppercut.'

● bluntings

→ 'devices',
'sequences'

[MG] We call bluntings (or sprouts) those deployments which are built upwards, freely developed through strategic use of the vertical dimension. These are dynamic eruptions of constructed mass: arrhythmic extrusions aimed at fractalising dense processes of local volumetric accumulation, favouring movements of irregular segmentation and decompression. Devices that value an irregular treatment of the edifice not as a unitary tectonic mass – compact edificial presence – but rather as a peaked vibration, that is, as a "notched sequence" of multi-scalar events ("between the small and the large").

Schemes are conceived as discontinuous growths, but also as functional mutations, of differing heights, drawing upon an operative and virtually fortuitous variation of the building outline, rather than upon a specific formal regularity. Spurts, extrusions, "protuberances" of the edifice itself – and of the uses the latter articulates – are called upon to structure profiled masses on lower bases; abscesses (emergences) of vertical impulse that break up their actions in complex sections, composed of independent strata, variable heights and/or mixed programmes.

Developments intended to yield evolutionary processes adapted to movements of growth and trimming; sudden shifts and inflections between full and empty – between constructed and non-constructed – produced by means of the combination, in height, of programmes not rigidly separate, but rather mixed in hybrid organisms, in complex cohabitation.

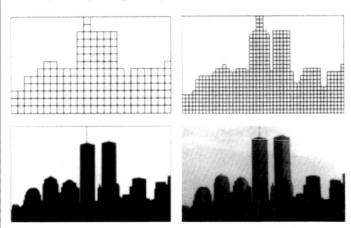

Manhattan skyline,
in *AD* vol 67
n. 9/10, 1997.

1. S&Aa (SORIANO-PALACIOS), *Competition for cultural centre and auditorium*, Benidorm (Alicante,Spain), 1995. **2.** ÁBALOS & HERREROS, *El Mirador, Mixed tower*, Cádiz (Spain), 2000. **3.** ARANGUREN-GALLEGOS, *Europan 4* (1st prize), Cartagena (Murcia, Spain), 1996. **4.** Eduardo ARROYO (NO.MAD Arquitectos), *New Urban Centre Marijin Dvor*, Sarajevo (Bosnia-Herzegovina), 2000. **5.** Eduard BRU, E. SERRA, L. VIVES, J. CARTAGENA, *Poblenou's seafront*, Barcelona, 1995.

★ blur

[co] Blur is a state of the gaze; tool that permits the joining of the analogical and the synthetic world; bonding agent between the virtual and the real (see Star Wars). Blur is a sensitivity that gives rise to doubt and that turns visual architecture into something impermanent. Blur, Ltd. New material in the building industry that permits the construction of air.
ENRIC RUIZ-GELI

Vicente GUALLART,
*Glass, Vapour,
Water, Iceberg,*
Barcelona Port, 2000.

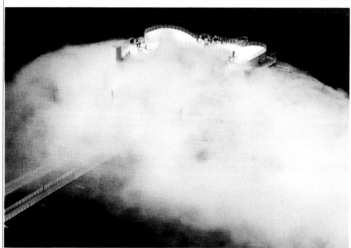

DILLER & SCOFIDIO,
Blur Building,
Yverdon-les-bains
(Switzerland), 2002.

★ blurring

[co] Blurring is working with a material layer of immaterial feelings, a floating jelly-fish in trees, a metaphoric filter of pollution.
FRANÇOIS ROCHE

ROCHE, DSV & SIE,
La Baïse (France),
1997.

1. NOX (Lars Spuybroek with Chris Seung-Woo Yoo, Kris Mun, Florent Rougemont and Ludovica Tramontin), *SoftOffice*, United Kingdom, 2000-2005. 2. Vicente SARRABLO (with H. Jala), *Air Inflated System, Proto-types for inflatable sport facilities* (Engineering: Javier Marcipar – CIMNE), 1999. 3. Enric MIRALLES, Benedetta TAGLIABUE, *Moore Farm*, Lancashire (United Kingdom), 1999-.

●■▲ body

→ 'inflatable',
'interfaces', 'prosthesis',
'skin', 'synthetical',
'trajectory'

[MG] Formerly, the body was a head, torso, two upper extremities and two lower extremities. Now, it is n-heads, n-torsos, n-extremities (upper and lower) and n-accessories.

[JM] The body is not only surrounded by things or faced with their phenomena, but is immersed in them. It is the body that has put itself inside objects.

[FP] The body is a place (which we can find today in different locations on the planet at the same time).

★ book

→ 'action>critical',
'dictionary',
'essayist knowledge',
'knowledge', 'name'

[co] A book is "an object that contains about a day or two worth of reading material. Just as a paragraph means a group of sentences on the same topic. It won't be a word associated with the definition of a particular physical object," David Small. XAVIER COSTA

●◆ bored

→ 'action>critical', 'joy
(*alegria*)', 'conventional',
'expression', 'reactive'

[MG] See 'anonymous.'
He was never bored because he always imagined (himself in) other situations. Other conditions. Other (possible) actions.

[FS] We do not want architects seated, but walking. Looking, seeing, absorbing, and perhaps even stealing. We are not moved by being alone. We have been told that the earth is flat. But we peep onto the other side. We work in situations that appear normal. But we ask new questions. We question the limits of things. There is no need to do the contrary. We are not original, but extraordinary in the most banal way. We have to practice smiling.

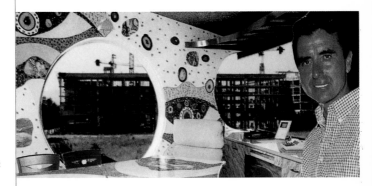

Bored or kitsch?

Collage, in VVAA,
*Met 1.0. Barcelona
Metápolis*, Barcelona:
ACTAR, 1998.

● braids

The notion of the braid translates to the elastic and undisciplined – at the same time as disconcerting – characteristic of dynamic systems, capable of favouring topological actions of "folding, unfolding and foldback." Braids are coiling movements among phenomena, processes and structures which are compressed and expanded, concentrated and dilated, interlaced and wound, in new and unwonted combinations.

Braids are spatial loops: transgressive trajectories; nodes and crosses; virtual bonds and links of movements, but also superposed messages; attractors of activity tending to provoke strange situations of intrigue (apparently impossible unions suddenly wrought possible) in spatial arrangements at once open and closed. Not aesthetic images, but rather unusual formulations in the system: as braids of movements, but also of principles. "Operative paradoxes."

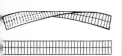

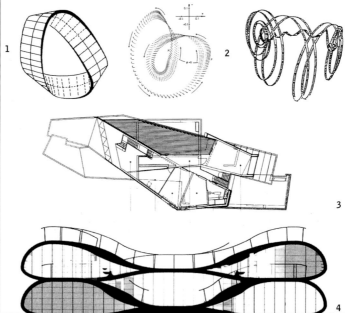

1. Folding and unfolding Moebius band, in *Arch+* 117, 1993.

2. Movement in a double closing torus, in *El Croquis* 72, 1995.

3. Ben VAN BERKEL & Caroline BOS (UN-Studio), *Moebius House*, Het Gooi (The Netherlands), 1997.

4. FOA, *Virtual House*, 1997.

5. MVRDV, *Shopping mall Loop Project*.

6. NL ARCHITECTS, *Parkhouse Carstadt Project*, Amsterdam, 1996.

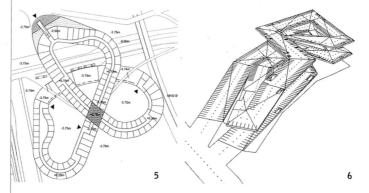

● branchial

→ 'armadillo', 'elastic',
'fissures', 'fold',
'geometry', 'grids', 'land',
'membrane', 'topological'

[MG] See 'devices' and 'system.'

Branchial refers to branchiae. Certain elastic surfaces of variable geometry dilate at strategic points by means of incisions or folds – gills – to facilitate the access of exterior fluids – or flows. The topology of the whole
permits such local dilations – and slashes – as part of the deformational
capacity of the system.

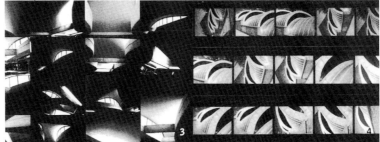

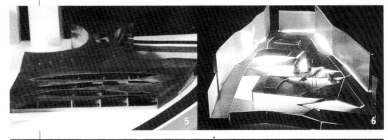

1. Gills. **2.** FOA, *Glass Centre*, Sunderland (United Kingdom), 1994. **3.** Josep MIÀS, *Parc-king, square
and parking of the bus and train station*, Girona (Spain), 1999. **4.** FOA, *Belgo Restaurant*, London, 1999.
5. Javier FRESNEDA, Javier PEÑA, Javier SANJUÁN, *Metal Technological Centre*, Murcia (Spain),
1998. **6.** ACTAR ARQUITECTURA, *Alfaro Cine Square*, Cehegín (Murcia, Spain), 1998. **7.** OMA, *Housing*, Fukuoka (Japan), 1991.

✦ breakwater

[WM] The metapolis is no longer a unit. Creating another city, within the city, is no longer a problem of scale or size, but of social reading, functional complexity and interaction of layers of use. A part of the city is another city, just as movement, cabling and the underground trains create other cities within the city. A jetty attached to a port (that of Barcelona, for example) is a breakwater, an unclassifiable place of manifold interchange between a domesticated sea and the natural one, an urban spur jutting into the unconstructed half of the city: the sea. The breakwater is a potential void for thinking about a city, not about a building: buildings can be cities, in fact, depending on the amount of information they contain.

Willy MÜLLER
+ THB Consulting,
*Breakwater. Project
on the dock*, Port
of Barcelona, 1997.

● bridge(s)

[MG] See 'link,' 'platforms' and 'landstrategy.'

A bridge is a factory or device – usually a platform – used to connect two separate territories // To build a bridge: to create a physical or virtual relationship. Of articulation or complicity. To effect a link. To link.

1. Carme PINÓS, *Pedestrian footbridge*, Petrer (Alicante, Spain), 1999. **2.** MAX, *30 bridges*, Leidsche Rijn (The Netherlands). **3.** FOA, *Dock planning*, Santa Cruz de Tenerife (Spain), 1998. **4.** UN STUDIO, *Barranco de la Ballena pedestrian bridge*, Las Palmas de Gran Canaria (Spain), 2002.

◆ brocades

[FS] See 'plaits.'

+ bubbles

→ 'abroad,etc.',
'animation', 'holes',
'geometry',
'inflatable', 'topology'

[WM] Like holes, bubbles are "non-box" agents (to use Federico Soriano's term), but more qualified: they add air, increase in volume, cause gravitation. They modify the relationship between weight and the sensation of weightlessness. Bubbles, in themselves, are an archetype of a future architecture: devoid of joints, single volume, spatial continuity and in-form. Box vs. Bowls, it's a war. Bubbles, after infiltrating and subverting, want to have it all.

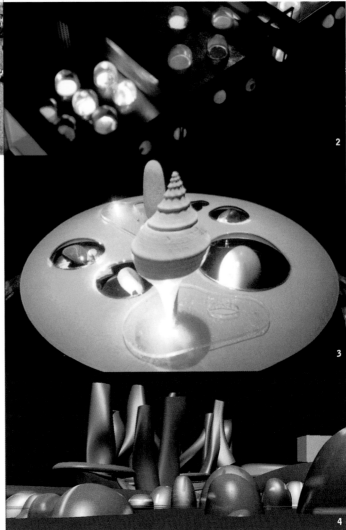

1. Boiling mud in Beppu (Japan), in VVAA, *Història Natural*, Barcelona: Ed. Océano-Institut Gallach, 1990, vol. 6.

2. Willy MÜLLER + THB Consulting, *Industrial building*, Sant Andreu (Barcelona), 1998.

3. Vicente GUALLART, Enric RUIZ-GELI, *La Beauté à la nature*, Avignon (France), 2000.

4. NOX (Lars Spuybroek with Kris Mun, Ludovica Tramontin, Florent Rougemont and Chris Seung-woo Yoo), *ParisBRAIN, a transurban scheme for the area west of La Défense*, Paris, 2001.

● buds

[MG] See 'bluntings.'

C

●+★ camouflage

[MG] The term 'camouflage' is of relevance for its sense of reinterpretation – and of reformulation – rather than of obscuring.

As with certain military artifices – paint, patterns, coverings or fabrics – camouflage is generally achieved through an intentional manipulation of reality: a synthetical diagramming of its most apparent, or literal, patterns converted into abstract schemes capable of interacting with the environment, rather than of changing colour with it: dissolution, rather than dilution. Appropriating its most elemental features, compressing them.

This alludes to a tactical dissolution of the object based upon the blurring of its silhouettes and the dissolution of its former solemn presence. This should not, however, be confused with a possible tendency towards passive invisibility – produced through obscuring or concealment, in sum through desertion of shape. On the contrary, it should be interpreted as faith in an active impurity, in a "straddle" (non-absolute, but also vague, indefinite, mongrel, contingent) transvestism ultimately aimed at responding to concrete local demands through ambiguous mechanisms of fusion and transfusion. The idea of camouflage is accepted: for its sense of "tactical mechanism" (abstract, generic and vibratile scheme in synergy with a landscape) – a mechanism of "recodification" (for the proposal of new codes) and "uncodification" (redefinition of old ones); that is, of interchange and of multiplication (relational and semantic) through which things eventually become – or may become – other things at the same time.

1. Camouflage
of the British army [WM]
"chillie" (trimmings
of sewed clothes
in a net), in NEWARK,
Quentin, *Book
of Camouflage*.

2. Kubelwagen type 82,
1940, in FUTURE
SYSTEMS, *For
inspiration only*,
Londres: Academy
Editions, 1996.

Most of the advanced instruments that we know, such as Internet, have been conceived for military intelligence, for military ends. It is important to recognise how the threat of war tends to gear up the mechanisms of innovation and production for new strategies, which may be offensive or defensive in nature. Camouflage is a spontaneous defensive strategy, present in certain natural intelligence (from animals to plants), one which military intelligence does not fail to capitalise on. It artificially interprets this natural condition, turning it into a logotype. If there is anything that truly characterises the military image it is camouflage ("smart weapons" notwithstanding). It speaks of the invisible and of the selective. Camouflage is, then, the mark that the army invented.

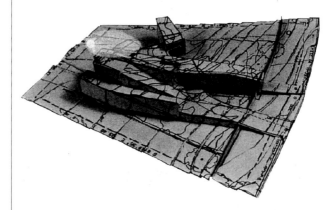

Douglas GAROFALO,
Camouflage House,
Chicago (USA), 1991.

[c] "*In the animal world, predators' skins tend to be opaque in colour, or have markings which make them blend in with their surroundings. This fact has historically been used by local hunters as a way of hiding themselves. In the same way, animals which are the target of predators, usually herbivores, have markings which blur their outline so that they blend in with the rest of the herd, making it difficult to select the prey. The average, typical organism of the population became more and more adept at the art of survival.*

All the markings of camouflage are based on one principle: to erase, blur, the silhouette, make the outline disappear, disguise the envelope."

(URZAIZ, Pedro; PÉREZ PLA, Carlos, "Camouflage. 3 extracts", *Quaderns* 224, 1999)

[co] See 'digitonature.'

Camouflage is the contemporary attitude of architecture that acquires intelligence and learns visually from the territory, from the site, from the cosmos it inhabits. There exists, therefore, a syntony between container and content.

The second skin of the content reads the container and reacts.

Architecture enters into symbiosis with the container producing a common will for a single image, as well as a single speed in the changing image.

Attitude opposed to the struggle against the landscape. State prior to digitonature architecture. The process of camouflage, taken to the limit, will make architecture invisible.

ENRIC RUIZ-GELI

[c] "*The contemporary project deals with the oscillation between what is natural and what is constructed, through a permanent exchange of matter and form; neither of them is ever above the other. One cannot talk about a camouflage of architecture by nature or landscape, nor of an instrumentalisation of nature by architecture. The project attempts to establish a dialogue between naturalisation phenomena (nature and its biological, repetitive, cyclical sense) and the separation processes of this naturalisation.*"

(LEWIS, Duncan; POTIN, Hervé, "Reflection on walls, space, materials...", *a+t* 15, 2000)

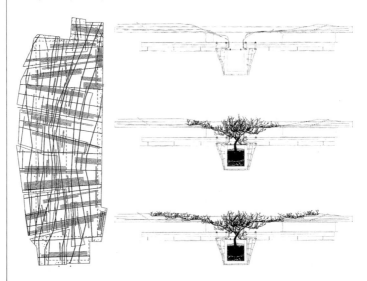

LEWIS, POTIN et LEWIS, *Civic Centre*, Sant Quirze de Safaja (Barcelona), 1999.

Vegetal

Weavings and stampings

1. Toni GIRONÈS, *Rehabilitation of a factory as a civic centre*, Sant Quirze de Safaja (Barcelona), 1999. **2.** Enric RUIZ-GELI, *Competition for auditorium and conference centre*, Pamplona (Navarra, Spain), 1998. **3.** FRANÇOIS & LEWIS, *Rural houses*, Jupilles (Compiègne, France), 1997. **4.** ROCHE, DSV&SIE P., *Project for landscape development*, Maïdo, Reunion Island (France), 1997. **5.** Pedro URZAIZ, Carlos PÉREZ-PLA, *Rehabilitation of a factory as a civic centre*, Sant Quirze de Safaja (Barcelona), 1999. **6.** Eduardo ARROYO (NO.mad Arquitectura), S&Aa (SORIANO-PALACIOS), *Competition for administrative building*, Bolzano (Italy), 1999. **7.** FOA, *Virtual House*, 1997.

●+ cantilevers

→ 'fragile',
'impermanences',
'in/unstable',
'lightness'

[MG]

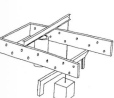

OMA / Rem
KOOLHAAS, *Singular
house*, Bordeaux
(France), 1997.

The old zeal for anchorage and permanence yields to proposals based upon unstable situations of tension and imbalance that have recourse to a reality which is progressively changing, mutable, detached. Cantilevers are architectures that have in common a desire to dislocate, to separate themselves from the land or from those existing edifices upon which they operate, and so suspend their volumes, avoiding as much as possible any subjugation to specific territories. They are singular projects – corbels – that demonstrate their expressive force by emphasising a forward impulse: a voluntary flight produced by the use of constructional or technical devices imported from larger scales and which resolve conventional programmes by means of extreme procedures, exploring the functional and expressive potency, sometimes almost eccentrically, to the boundaries of places and spaces. Leaps into the void.

[WM] There is a field of application of such structures that makes corbels potentially interesting. It involves the consequences of land use. If land is as well the history of property – with its rules, rights and obligations, with owner and value – certain structures are especially subversive, intrusive, defiant, not only in their technical condition, but also in their political condition. Certain structures of occupation can be corbels intruding on the (air) space of the other. Corbels are the opposite of foundations.

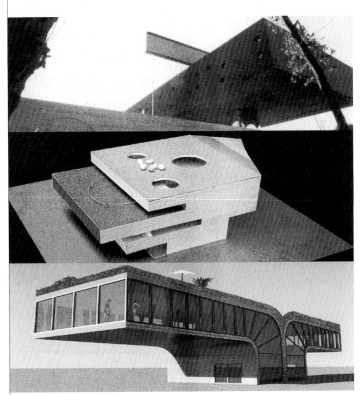

OMA / Rem
KOOLHAAS, *Singular
house*, Bordeaux
(France), 1997.

WMA Willy Müller
Arquitectos,
*Competition for the
Navarra library*,
Pamplona (Spain),
2001.

NL, *Bendover,
singular house*,
Bloemendaal
(The Netherlands),
2000.

▲ ● carbon fibre

→ 'matter',
'technique, the'

[FP] Carbon fibre is the colloquial name of the latest generation of composite materials, broadly used in aeronautics, that basically have the following characteristics: maximum continuity in their configuration and in their intermolecular space, reasonable resistance of their chemical links and very light components.

What do we get by having all these virtues together? Minimum weight with maximum resistance.

This resistance applies especially to specific situations, caused by external non-permanent phenomena, that are neither topical, nor directly related to the activity developed by the objects constructed by these materials (for example, in the case of carbon fibre, wind friction, the moment produced by the large wavelengths of certain elements in corbel, the torsion that appears in aerial movement, etc.).

Until the emergence of this family of materials, aeroplanes were manufactured using two complementary materials: a structure of lines (ribs) with more or less complete qualities (from wood to titanium) and a more or less flexible layer in which they were wrapped in (from the canvas to the aluminium).

With these two systems, could be constructed an habitable fuselage and its various flying components (wings, rudders, stabilisers, etc.) This duality has disappeared with the emergence of composite materials. Now, one membrane is capable of both providing resistance and compartmentalising.

The manufacturing of this type of material largely depends on the smelting process carried out with successive adhesion of superimposed fibres, which allows one to control the direction of the chemical links and alienate them to improve the elastic module.

Amazingly, the impact of these new procedures has not yet been enough to change the shape of aeroplanes and their components. The industry has not developed this due to the necessity of not underestimating the real life experience accumulated in many unexpected events and situations, which are the main source of data to step-by-step improve aeronautical designs.

Changing the shape of aeroplanes without taking into account the records of aerial accidents would represent a real revolution with the impossible assumed risk of accumulating immense economic losses. In architecture, we could look at things in exactly the opposite way.

The in-formal/in-formational evolution followed by the buildings we think about nowadays, is conceived according to the accumulation of data, the flexibility of the representation systems or the trans-disciplinary integration.

This represents an acceptable frame in which to apply more active materials, which transcends the archaic linear or superficial (surface) systems of support and enclosure.

[MG] See 'production, intelligent.'

● carpets (advanced landscaping)

[MG]

See 'land(s) in lands.'

If we imagine the surfaces of a territory as the floors of certain great rooms, scattered with colourful carpets of diverse motifs, we might then also imagine, rolled out over the landscape, possible "architectures" conceived, in turn, as virtual *operative carpets*.

A dwelling space might be conceived today as a large void – to be habilitated – strategically marked out with equipped clusters – amassed services. In the same way, the structuring of certain landscapes can also be formulated preserving their "vacant" qualities through the tactical location of scattered programmatic mats – spots – not camouflaged but rather slid into and over the landscape: Land(s) in lands.

[MG]

"*All ideas were instantly embodied in a welter of forms and colour; all those forms in turn triggered new ideas. This method of reconstructing reality, which cocked a snook at all manner of accepted ideas and all manner of conventions, this very open-minded combination [...] was a way of being, and would consequently take on a conceptual mantle, no more no less. And the rare in this approach is the fact that it surmounts particularly well the difficulty of putting things together in view of the dual nature of landscape: at once the thing and its representation.*"

(AURICOSTE, Isabelle, "Yves Brunier, narrator," *Quaderns* 217, 1998)

Yves BRUNIER,
Waterloo, 1989,
in *Yves Brunier
(1962-1991)*,
Bordeaux: Arc en
rêve, 1993.

Vegetal carpets BCQ (BAENA, CASAMOR, QUERA), *Forest fringe planning,* Viladecans (Barcelona), 1998.

Vegetal carpets Arturo FREDIANI (with SOB Arquitectes), *Torrent Ballester park,* Viladecans (Barcelona), 1996-1997.

Textile carpets Carpet market in Tunis, in *Rutas del Mundo* 53, 1994.

x ● cartographies

→ 'beacons', 'geography', [VG]
'geomancy', 'layers',
'maps', 'places', 'stains,
ink', 'trailers', 'trip'

[VG] 'To represent a reality is to begin to transform it.'

[MG] José Antonio Sosa, paraphrasing Deleuze, suggested that *"each system of representation should be assigned a different capacity for organising the world."*

If perspective representation (pre)supposed a hierarchical structuring of the world, if modern planimetry counterposed the latter to the relativity of its own fragmented and self-referential organisations, then today we sense the passage from what had been, in both cases, a deterministic cartography (univocal, total, exact and literal in its referent, but also in its procedures and in its outlines) to a cartography which is increasingly 'indeterminate' (open, versatile, abstract) and, therefore, also more evolutionary in its trajectories. The classical observer and the modern *flâneur* are thus succeeded by the contemporary *explorer*.

Indeed, to the classical observer, the term 'space' is translated into a static and permanent concept; an absolute framework, exact and literal in its manifestations, but always observed "from without," with an apparently stable framing, which would present at its vanishing point – in its relationship with the human eye – its maximum reference.

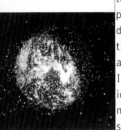

Distribution map
of satellites.

Modernity, on the contrary, enhances the notion of "relative position." The compact (and cohesive) idea of hierarchical, absolute, genuine, classical space has thus yielded to a more atonal vision, of discontinuous experiences in "correlative positions;" a discontinuous surveying of fixed, though fragmented, figurations; fundamentally static in their conception, though incipiently dynamic in their objectual perception; pertaining to a vision that still trusts in autonomous scenarios (or grids) – panoramas – of codes as predetermined as they are exact and univocal.

Today, however, the contemporary *explorer* – at once navigator, hunter and "soldier" – confronts a progressively multiphase – complex and heterogeneous – space. A multiplied, physical – and not always physical – space in a constant situation of latent flux and of simultaneousness between different messages and scales in which the traditional distinctions between *city*, *nature* and *territory* have increasingly lost their traditional meanings, blurred in progressively equivocal and overlapped geographies.

Plural, undisciplined scenarios – increasingly less "domesticable" – physically identify a structure which becomes more ungraspable and invisible in its globality, and from which emerges only a field of projections and displacements, simultaneous and intersected, hardly adaptable to the traditional – and static – parameters of traditional perception and representation.

By the same token, their representation can no longer remain a simple question of figuration or grid, but rather of an operation that should necessarily draw upon a multilayered set of bits of "n-dimensional" information (open and elastic maps) intended to recognise the web of manifold hidden relationships which develop simultaneously within it over time and whose shape defies exact definition.

The old idea of representation is now complemented – in this new intelligent cartography – by the capacity for projection, combination and modification provided by new interscalar logics and instruments of recognition based upon a sophisticated organisation of an information, captured no longer (only) in the place, but remotely (via satellite), proper to present-day digital technologies.

Logics aimed at articulating the superposition and the crossing of data, of currents, of flows and of forces. Logics that introduce the temporal variable, modification and alteration. Logics emerging from abstract processes rather than from literal figurations.

Synthetic, evolutionary and a-figurative matrixes (capable of compressing – synthesising – information) rather than predetermined forms – or models. Search structures conceived based upon diagrammatic formats – graphics, grids, webs, etc. – aimed at recording and processing multiple data: parameters of incidence assimilable in synthetic signs – or trajectories – (points, lines, surfaces) which would subsequently undergo specific appropriate alterations and/or manipulations in indeterminate processes of concretion and, therefore, a movement from the abstract to the singular in situations as uncertain as they are specific.

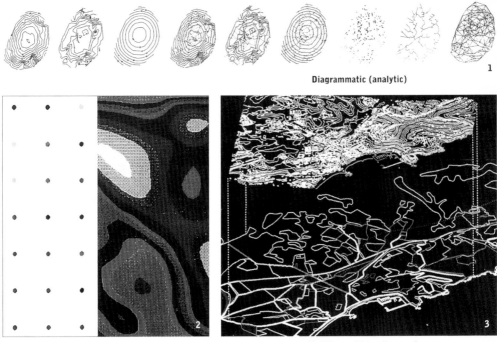

Diagrammatic (analytic)

1

Matrix (evolutionary)   **Multilayered (simultaneous)**

1. System of paths on a topographic surface, in *Arch+* 121, 1994. **2.** Strategic codifications and visualizations on a map, in GAUSA, Manuel, *Housing. New alternatives, new systems*, Barcelona: ACTAR, 1998. **3.** Thematic maps of land régime and planning sectors with topographic projection (Direcció General d'Urbanisme, Generalitat de Catalunya), GAUSA, Manuel, *Housing. New alternatives, new systems*, Barcelona: ACTAR, 1998.

●+ **catalogue**

→ 'combination',
'component', 'diversity',
'product', 'production',
intelligent', 'prototypes',
'system'

[MG] See 'kits.'

[WM] A new society that organises itself around the idea of options – that exchanges the idea of consumption for that of use, that interacts while it chooses – is a society of catalogues: catalogues in constant preparation, endlessly in construction, permanently re-establishing the contents that delimit it.

Ideas cannot remain apart from this trend. IKEA is a paradigm of our time of catalogues: it is not an ethical model, yet it is an aesthetic model of social behaviour.

We are progressing towards ideas à la carte, also going beyond the idea of general catalogue in favour of particular catalogues, like our DNA. Our studios invest a major part of their time in establishing options of choice, according to different parameters. Ideas are, in fact, catalogues, introducing different levels of the Architecture chain into our potential for impact.

[i] p.105 Users, industries, ourselves, users, financing, ourselves, advertising, the user, etc.

● **catastrophe**

→ 'catalogue',
'container',
'emergency', 'fleeting',
'house, the',
'precarious(ly)',
'reversible',
'self-organization',
'self-urbanism'

[MG] We are continuously faced with spontaneous manifestations of self-organisation in unexpected situations of catastrophe or civil emergency (earthquakes, volcanic eruptions, floods, fires, war, etc.) which generate rapid and unplanned responses from voluntary groups seeking to make up for the ineffectiveness of official mechanisms which are often paralysed by lack of foresight.

Catastrophes are situations that require serious contemplation regarding their urban consequences. Catastrophes demand more effective solutions for the transfer, relocation and rapid housing of populations largely in transit. Alternative habitat systems need be sufficiently decent and qualified to ensure new residential settlements in areas of more or less temporary occupation.

[MG] In all cases, there arises the importance of working with a possible "ephemeral colonisation" of the landscape, associated with the possibility of conceiving reversible systems of construction and land occupation.

1. ACTAR ARQUITECTURA, *M'House modules*, 1999.
2. Shigeru BAN, *Paper log houses for refugees*, Nagata-ku (Kobe, Japan), 1995.

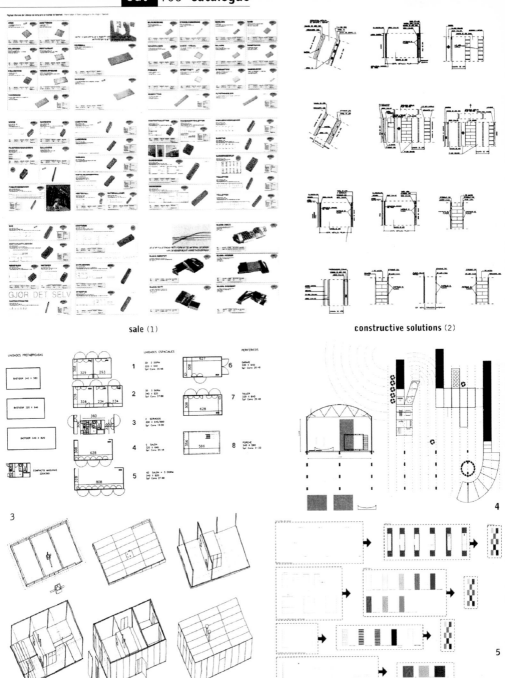

sale (1)

constructive solutions (2)

residential modules (3, 4, 5)

1. Eduardo ARROYO (NO.mad Arquitectura), *Competition for municipal sports complexes in Denmark*, Naestved (Denmark), 1999. **2.** S&Aa (SORIANO-PALACIOS), *Euskalduna Hall*, Bilbao (Spain), 1998. **3.** ÁBALOS & HERREROS, *AH houses. Industrial prototypes*, 1996. **4.** Vicente GUALLART, Willy MÜLLER, Enric RUIZ-GELI, *Scape House*, El Penedès (Barcelona), 1996. **5.**ACTAR ARQUITECTURA, *M'House houses*, 1998.

● catches

→ 'interchange', 'transversality', 'trip'

[MG] See 'collaging.

"As we speak, some things are consumed and new ones arise: advancing, moving on from one theme to another, describing trajectories, taking journeys through the mind. There is such an architecture, made up of snatches – in the language of Soriano, another sophist – instantaneous mixtures, patches, shreds; explosive mixtures, above all mixtures never perceived by the professional commentator (commentary is the opposite of conversation)."

(ÁBALOS, Iñaki; HERREROS, Juan, "Una conversación," *CIRCO* 9, 1993)

◆ cephalia

[FS] See 'hypertrophy.'

● chains

→ 'buds', 'city?', 'cultivations', 'genetics', 'geometry', 'one is many', 'sequences'

[MG] An architecture produced through combinatorial formal systems (dispositions and evolutions) favours the emergence of chains of superposed events. These are flexible – and alterable – sequences of variation and transformation produced through the mutation of certain generative rules – nuclear logics or criteria.

Such chains, also called combinatorial protocols or theorems, are virtually infinite and their development, though interrupted, manifest themselves as virtually unfinished.

They permit the recognition of generative action, the genome or that elemental trajectory of which they are composed, and usually respond to ascalar mechanisms of linkage between generic nuclear diagrammed – or "instruction" – and contingent result, favouring the appearance of concatenated and recursive processes at all scales – from a formation to a city – that involve different combinations between points (occupations), surfaces (separations) and lines (linkages) in meshed and/or normed complexes that en-

[i] p.108   gage individual occurrences and global distributions.

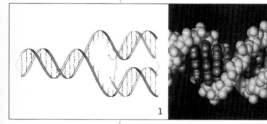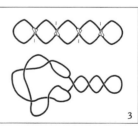

1. ADN sequence, in VVAA, *Met 1.0. Barcelona Metápolis,* Barcelona: ACTAR, 1998. **2.** Infographic image of an ADN molecule. **3.** Double helix of ADN rolled in itself.

◆ challenge

→ 'audacity', 'ideas', 'unrestrained (<un> factors)'

[FS] *"If you leave me alone // And you go by the beaten path // With words that no longer have power // That the demon carries you // To the hell that you have chosen // Because you condemn me to your oblivion // I condemn you to my loneliness."* (AUSERÓN, Santiago, "If you leave me alone," 1990)

■▲● chance

[JM] Chance is the meeting between all things and other objects.

[FP] Today, more than ever, when we think of lack of control, of disorder, we think of chance and chaos. We find it convenient to produce ideas imbued with this form of organising things. Chance is, therefore, instead of an un-desired aspect, an adequate environment with which to make commitments. Nevertheless, it is necessary to confirm Popper's conception that chance is no more than a compendium of instructions which lead to this or that re-sult, in principle unpredictable, and whose rationalisation is not possible only because we lack the instruments with which to classify or understand it. Thus, chance becomes an inexpugnable field of possibilities and poten-tial information. Chance stops being a factor identifiable only as a means for gathering statistics and probable collections and reveals itself as a con-tainer which we must explore, devoid of whatever paralysing restraints.

[FP] Chance is no more than a digest of instructions, in theory unpredictable, which achieves results.

[MG] Chance is uncertainty (or luck) which is "projected" (programmed and trans-ferred). A logic sensitive to the contingent, the possible, the fortuitous. Sys-tem and distortion. Determinate indeterminism. Open intentionality. Undisci-plined. Flexible. *Alea jacta est*. Beyond certainty. Beyond limits. Beyond Rubicon.

●◆ chaos

→ 'chance', 'complexity', 'creation', 'dynamism', 'evolutionary', 'glocal', 'indetermination', 'inform(ation)al', 'in/unstable', 'multi', 'open', 'order', 'time'

[MG] "*Potentially profitable state.*" (Susanna Cros)

[FS] See 'entropy.'

[MG] The recent study of dynamic systems, related to theories of chaos and quan-tum mechanics, has advanced progressively over the last fifty years due to the technological capacity for computer simulation (and calculation) of trajectories of complex geometry and random definition.
Dynamic simulation has replaced traditional exact formulation: the scien-tist records situations, becomes involved in processes and verifies results, but does not prefigure the total "writing" of phenomena and is often sur-prised by the results. He or she can only take note of protocols of experi-ence, that is, combinations of results pointing to basic criteria for action. Indeed, the mathematical term 'chaos' does not, in fact, imply absolute dis-order. Its properties do not emerge from random, totally disconnected ac-cumulations. They rather emerge from what has come to be called "deter-ministic chaos" – a determinate indeterminism –: a marriage of apparently contradictory concepts which explains the terms in which certain undisci-plined – yet not necessarily lacking in certain internal generic logic – phe-nomena are produced.
Chaos – that is, the indetermination of trajectories – emerges because the sys-tem is sensitive to variation, to the incidence of local individual – particular

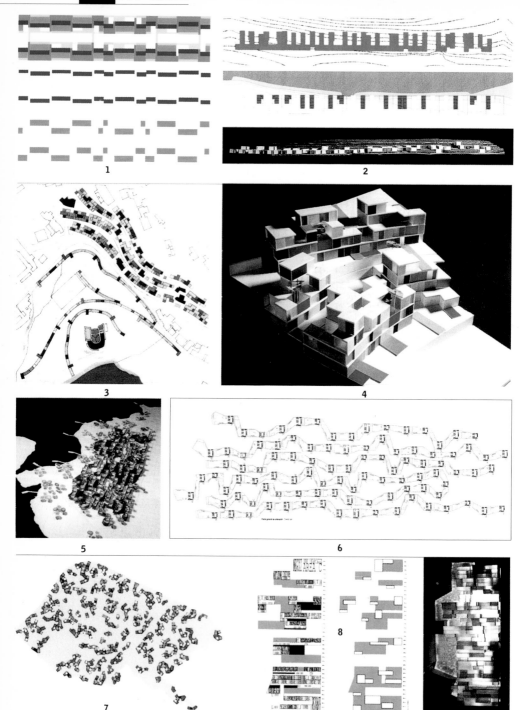

1. & 2. José MORALES, Sara GILES, Juan GONZÁLEZ, *Studies for housing of variable typologies*, Jaén and Guadalcanal (Spain), 1997 and 1998. **3. - 4.** ACTAR ARQUITECTURA, *Europan: 400 dwellings*, Ceuta (Spain), 1999. **5. - 6.** Cristina DÍAZ MORENO, Efrén GARCÍA GRINDA, *Europan 6: Housing in Jyväskylä*, Suomi (Finland), 2001- (First Prize). **7.** Eduardo ARROYO (NO.mad Arquitectura), *Europan 5: hibridisation process 001* (First Prize), Barakaldo (Vizcaya, Spain), 1999. **8.** Eduardo ARROYO (NO.mad Arquitectura), S&Aa (SORIANO-PALACIOS), *Competition for administrative building*, Bolzano (Italy), 1999.

in all senses – actions that end up disturbing and altering the globality. The contribution of chaos theory is the suggestion of a pseudo-deterministic model leaving room for chance, a dimension for the unpredictable, for randomness. Though the system, globally speaking, refers to hairpin-shaped movements or more-or-less recurrent trajectories – strange attractors – its particular movement (each of the infinite combinations that define it) defies the prefigured and stabilised. Thus, each protocol is at once independent and generic. The system itself is, in fact, what appears different but always synthesised and compressed.

★ chromatisms

→ 'colours'

[co] The fusion of colours, ambiences, temperatures, light, atmospheres, surfaces, the volumes, their faces and perspective: colours are not matter, but chromatisms: chromatic spectrum. You exist for me because my sensitive retina receives reflections of your chromatism, matter called flesh when light reflects off it.
ENRIC RUIZ-GELI

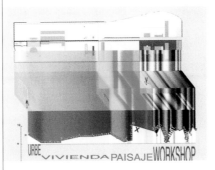

Enric RUIZ-GELI,
Lifescan plothouse,
Barcelona, 1999.

+ *Chrysler Voyager*

→ 'advertising',
'catalogue', 'form',
'house, the'

[WM] Lee Iacocca, father of the Mustang, is a design freak and the creator of the best-selling van in the world, the *Chrysler Voyager*. He has demonstrated a much more resolute passion for design – and for bold design – than his colleagues. But not all success stories are due to design: *Renault* created the *Espace* twenty years ago, but at the time they failed to popularise the concept. Why? They failed to define the scale of the product of as clearly as *Chrysler* did: a man standing on top of his car, as if it were the roof of a house. It is the image of a change in the way of perceiving size, a factor that hadn't been previously taken into consideration in automobile advertising. An express intent of marketing or simply a foreseeable consequence? Never has the house been so close to another industry. Is it not intriguing to see the extent to which the car, perhaps the most emblematic product of the 20th century, has become architectural not only in its forms, but also in the form in which presented to us as a consumer good? What next?

Chrysler Voyager
advertisement.

★ chunking

→ 'associate, overlap,
connect', 'combination',
'game', 'knowledge'

[co] Chunking is a chess term. An operation in which information is grouped in sequences. Chunking enlarges the memory, increases processing, stimulates association.
JOSÉ MIGUEL ROLDÁN

● circuits

[MG] (1) Looped device enclosed within a flexible perimeter // Path – webbed, threaded or tracked – intended to favour the movements of certain dynamical systems of occupation and spatial-temporal definition // Line – or field – that defines certain inductor conductors in which an energy flow oscillates // Traffic – or round – of people, vehicles or flows.

(2) We call "evolutionary circuits" those devices conceived as virtual tracks of movement: their paths (i.e., those of the processes of spatial organisation that define them) define intertwined virtual routes corresponding to preferentially infrastructural arrangements. Underlying in them, in effect, is a basic movement, meshed and/or tracked (unfolding) or winding and/or interlaced (foldback) a well as a condition of linkage, that is, of infrastructural connection, routing, access, artery (and support), of grid or network.

Certain properties of infrastructural networks, such as "connectability," and "connectivity," flexibility and nodality, appear to be particularly pertinent, given that they underlie the systematic character of the circuits.

LINKS

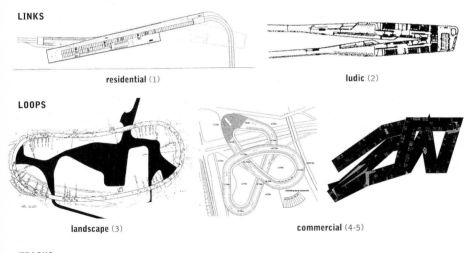

residential (1)   ludic (2)

LOOPS

landscape (3)   commercial (4-5)

TRACKS

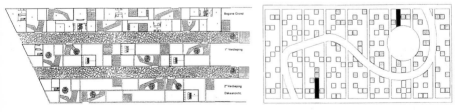

residential (6-7)

1. Alberto NICOLAU, Montse DOMÍNGUEZ, *Europan 5* (First Prize), Almere (The Netherlands), 1999. **2.** Cristina DÍAZ MORENO, Efrén GARCÍA GRINDA, *International competition of ideas: Mar artificial* (First Prize ex aequo), Super-south M-40 intersection (Madrid), 1998. **3.** ACTAR ARQUITECTURA, Intervention at the circuit of Sitges, Sitges (Barcelona), 1998. **4.** MVRDV, *Shopping mall Loop project.* **5.** NL Architects, *Parkhouse Carstadt project*, Amsterdam, 1996. **6.** ROAGNA-EHRENSPERGER CELLINI, *Europan III*, Yverdon-les-bains (Switzerland), 1992. **7.** KAZUYO SEJIMA&ASSOCIATES, *Housing studies.*

★ citilab (community laboratory)

→ 'hypercontext',
'incubator',
'inter-community',
'link', 'R+3D',
'telecentre'

[co] Citilabs are new centres of R+D open to the whole community.

As we enter an age of knowledge, this activity can be extended to the community: thus citilabs, new cultural centres in cities and town, and an evolution of telecentres, are where the community learns the notions of research and development.

Innovative activity, in the professional sense of the word, in the industrial age reduced to a minority activity (universities and a few companies), can now extend to a growing sector of the population, who in Internet have already found a distributed system of R+D. See P2P projects,

Seti@Home <mailto:Seti@Home> or Clickworkers, http://clickworkers.arc.nasa.gov/top. See Dutch Science Shops or Community Based Research, http://www.loka.org/crn/pubs/comreprt.htm

ARTUR SERRA

◆ city?

[FS] An old word. See 'm. city (or multicity).'

✗ + ● client

→ 'bored', 'complicity',
'contract', 'conventional',
'flexibility', 'game',
'I/(my)self', 'ideas',
'interactivity', 'logic,
fuzzy', 'moral', 'negotiate',
'relationships, transitive',
'stimulus'

[VG] Client: I'd like to have a big house. When I was little, I lived in a conventional house, with an L-shaped living room and a little bedroom where I could always hear the television. Now I'd like to be able to enjoy a large, high space, with lots of light and not very much furniture. The bedroom will be on the top floor overlooking the mountains.

Architect: That sounds good.

Client: I'd also like a garden, with trees and flowers, a tennis court and a swimming pool, but I don't want to have to look after it, like my father did in his allotment.

Architect: We'll make it all artificial. Astroturf, iron trees, artificial mountains with the earth dug away, flowers with coloured lights inside them... It won't be a 'consolation' project.

Client: But I've only got a very low budget.

Architect: Achieving the highest quality at low cost is a good challenge. We'll construct a noble building out of simple materials.

Client: How will you manage it?

Architect: The house will be hard and comfortable; abstract and natural, all at once.

"I'd rather have the customer come and say: 'Wow, I've never seen that before,' then, 'Wow, look how they've changed that,'"
B. Gilbert.

"The customer is a rearview mirror, not a guide to the future,"
G. Colony.

"Our job is to give the customer what he never dreamed he wanted,"
D. Lasdon.

Accomplice to whom one should never speak as Groucho Marx once did:
"*I never forget a face, but in your case I'll make an exception.*"

1. Vicente GUALLART, *Dwelling at the limit of the town,* Llíria (Valencia, Spain), 1995.
2. R&Sie (François ROCHE, Stephanie LAVAUX), *Barak House,* Sommières (France), 2001.

S&Aa (SORIANO-PALACIOS), *Extension of Fleta Theatre*, Zaragoza (Spain), 2001.

▲● cloning

→ 'dual(ity)', 'genetics', [FP] What is the real interest in cloning? Deviation. After engendering two ge-
'genetics of form', 'hybrid' netically identical organisms, they begin to accumulate different experiences and they change, change and change. Without this reality of "diver-
gent clones," the question of cloning would not be so amazing.

[G] Cloning is not serialisation. It is not a repeated product, but rather a generated process. Combining the generic and the specific, the immanent and
the altered. Cloning is type-information influenced by the contingent, the
indeterminate.

◆ cloud

[FS] See 'fish.'

★ cloud9

→ 'optimism' [co] Cloud9 is a feeling of extreme happiness or elation: *That boy's on cloud 9.* This expression shows that, besides looking like things, being drawings of real things,
clouds have numbers: the ninth, the tenth, the twenty-fifth, cloud 89… Cloud 9 is
translated in German as *Wolke sieben*: therefore, in German culture, the good cloud
is the seventh. Conclusion: pick a number and get on your cloud.
ENRIC RUIZ-GELI

★ + code

→ 'catalogue', 'chains', [co] **codes**
'component', 'culture',
'decalogue', 'language', In the English language, code is the word one uses both for the underlying math-
'logic', 'mathematics', ematical equations on which computer language (and any mode of communica-
'name', 'networks', tion) is based, and for the rules one must follow in the construction of buildings.
'patterned distributions', The latter includes both life and safety codes and the restrictions imposed by mu-
'patterns', 'slogans', nicipalities and other agencies to make the building respond to its context. In
'synthetical', 'system' addition, the term "code" also can apply to how one behaves or appears as a
person. The confluence of these three meanings indicates the current place of architecture: it is the translation of computer programs and obscure architectural
canons into form according to the norms acceptable to society. It is up to the architect to allow for another reading through her or his coding of the project. In
addition, there exists another form of code which is taking on a more and more
important place in the making of architecture: the codes of financing and returns,
which are "value engineering" all other considerations out of the code books of
architects. AARON BETSKY

[co] A code is the "same as now – instructions to be interpreted by a machine,"
Paul Haeberli. XAVIER COSTA

[WM] **(bar) code**

The definition of a bar code can be reduced to the formula:
$A=2.5B$, under the condition of the continual alteration of full following upon empty.

It is also a schematic definition of the forest, of the image in the train window, of the illusion of film, of the rhythms and cadences of a decision or camouflage.

[co] No norm, no precept. Code as a system, rather than a rule.

That which is codified behaves according to a series of relations that vary in accordance with each event. The code is sensible to surrounding conditions, to the natural exterior, to the transformations prior (memory) to the simultaneous, and can assimilate groups of behaviours on the basis of which to estimate predictable relations. The codified can self-transform, self-modify, suit itself to each condition in the best way possible, adapt to or subvert conditions in order to transform itself at each instant into what it wishes.

The codified is an artificial system of relations and objects capable of mutating in accordance with the conditions of the system itself at that instant.

The codified takes many forms. It can be algorithmic, or rather the superposition of algorithms; it can be intuitive, it can adopt the simplest forms of linearity or comprise so much superposition of conditions that it defies synthesis.

The code is to a large extent dependent on its protocol, which may be implicit in it, or be a further transformation of the same.

JOSÉ ALFONSO BALLESTEROS, IGNACIO ONTIVEROS, LARRAITZ DE AZUMENDI

1. & 5.
NJIRIC+NJIRIC,
*Leisure Centre
Lago Veritá*, Locarno
(Switzerland), 1999.

2. José Alfonso
BALLESTEROS,
*Project for railway
station*, Castelló de la
Plana (Spain), 2000.

3. José MORALES,
Juan GONZÁLEZ,
Town Hall, Chiclana
(Spain), 1998.

4. Manuel J. FEO, Juan
RAMÍREZ GUEDES
(TWA, TWICE
ARCHITECTURE),
*Eyeliners: proposal
for Chil Walk*,
Las Palmas de Gran
Canaria (Spain), 1999.

6. Willy
MÜLLER+THB
Consulting, *Treatment
of the facade of
Mercabarna*,
Barcelona, 2000.

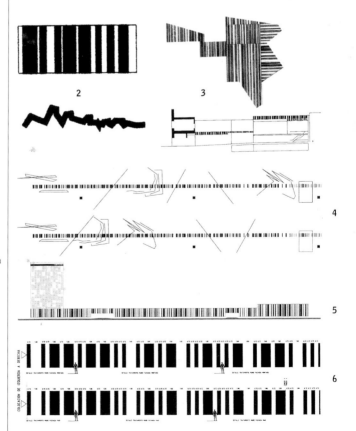

● cohabitation

[MG] Cohabitation is to inhabit together. It represents a contract of non-adherent coexistence; a contingent complicity of interests that implies sharing of (real or metaphorical) spaces of influence. Cohabitation is a plural and heterogeneous architecture, based upon diversity and simultaneity, alluding to constant arrangements and negotiations of cohabitation between its parts.

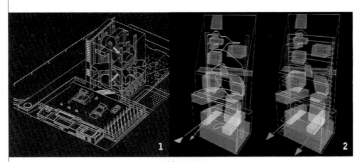

Spatial cohabitation

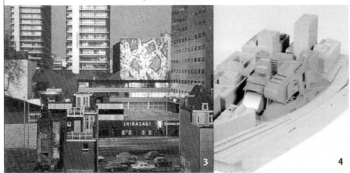

Urban cohabitation

1. OMA, *Competition Très Grande Bibliothèque*, Paris, 1989. **2.** MVRDV, *Media Galaxy (Competition concept for the new Eyebeam Institute)*, New York, 2001, 2nd prize. Tour and fire emergency routing. **3.** OMA, *Dance Theatre*, Den Haag (The Netherlands), 1987. **4.** Neil DENARI Architects, *Tokyo International Forum*, Tokyo, 1992, project.

●coilings

[MG] See 'braids,' 'contortionisms,' 'bends and (un)bendings,' 'strategy,' 'geometry,' 'fold,' 'fold (unfold-refold),' 'topological' and 'trajectory.'

Alberto NICOLAU,
Montse DOMÍNGUEZ,
Europan 5
(1st prize), Almere
(The Netherlands),
1999.

1. NL ARCHITECTS,
*Parkhouse Carstadt
project*, Amsterdam, 1996.

2. Ben VAN BERKEL,
Caroline BOS (UN Studio),
Moebius house, Het Gooi
(The Netherlands), 1997.

3. Arturo FREDIANI,
Business Centre,
Port of Barcelona, 1997.

4. Luís ROJO,
Ángel VERDASCO,
Begoña FERNÁNDEZ-
SHAW, *Auditorium*,
Guadalajara (Spain),
1999.

5. José MORALES,
Sara GILES, Juan
GONZÁLEZ, *Theatre*,
Níjar (Almería, Spain),
1999.

6. María José
ARANGUREN LÓPEZ,
José GONZÁLEZ
GALLEGOS, *Competition
for auditorium and
conference centre*,
Pamplona (Navarra,
Spain), 1998.

7. PÉRIPHÉRIQUES,
*Competition for Canal+
Headquarters*,
Loupveciennes (France),
2002.

8. NOWHERE,
Music Centre, Helsinki,
1998, competition.

9. Blai PÉREZ, *Clara
Torres house*, Viladecans
(Barcelona), 2002-.

◆ collage

→ 'a-couplings',
'action>critical',
'allegory', 'assembly',
'associate, overlap,
connect', 'catches',
'hybrid', 'interchange',
'recycling',
'tergiversation'

[FS] "*Collage and consciousness of the architect, collage as a technique and collage as a state of mind: Lévy-Strauss speaks of how the intermittent mode of collages, originating when folk-art was dying, cannot be more than the transfer of bricolage to the domains of contemplation.*

If the 20th-century architect has done quite the opposite of wishing to imagine himself as a bricoleur, that is exactly the context in which we should situate his coolness towards the great discovery of the 20th century. The collage seemed to lack sincerity, to represent a corruption of moral principles, an adulteration. One thinks of Picasso's Still Life with Chair Caning, from 1911-12, his first collage, and begins to understand why. In his analysis, Alfred Barr speaks of "the section of chair caning, which is neither real nor painted; rather it is, in reality, a bit of facsimile on oilcloth stuck to the canvas and partly painted. Here, in a painting, Picasso plays with reality and abstraction in two means and at four different levels or relations. If we stop to think about which is the more real, we find ourselves shifting from aesthetic to metaphysical contemplation, since what looks most real is the more false, and what seems most removed from everyday reality is perhaps the most real, given that it is less imitation."

And the facsimile of chair caning on oilcloth, an objet trouvé snatched from the underworld of low culture and catapulted into the superior world of high art, might illustrate the architect's dilemma. The collage is at once innocent and torturous.

In fact, among architects only that great amalgamator, Le Corbusier, sometimes hedgehog and sometimes fox, has demonstrated any sympathy for this sort of things. His buildings, though not his urban plans, are replete with the results of a process that we might consider more or less equivalent to that of the collage. Objects and episodes are meddlesome imports and, although they conserve the nuances of their source and origin, they also obtain an entirely new impact founded in their change of context. At the Ozenfant studio, for example, we find ourselves with a mass of allusions and references that all seem to come together by means of the collage." (Paraphrasing ROWE, Colin; KOETTER, Fred, *Collage City*, Cambridge (Mass.): The MIT Press, 1973

◆●collaging

→ 'a-couplings',
'action>critical',
'allegory', 'assembly',
'associate, overlap,
connect', 'catches',
'hybrid', 'interchange',
'recycling',
'tergiversation'

[FS] 1. Method of representing space.
2. Method of producing space.
3. Action and effect of using the technique of collage to imagine a space or architectonic object. A substitute for sketches or working models.

[FS] [MG] To collage is to superimpose intentionally and make uncohesively simultaneous.
1. Method of representation: superimposing images.
2. Method of production: superimposing shots.
3. Method of design: superimposing program and events.

Representation method

1. Willy MÜLLER + THB Consulting (with Margareth AVELAR), *Factory,* Sant Andreu (Barcelona), 1998.
2. Ricardo SÁNCHEZ LAMPREAVE, *Office building,* Madrid, 1999.
3. Juan DOMINGO SANTOS, *Renovation of the old factory of San Isidro as a culture and leisure centre,* Granada (Spain), 1999.

Production method

4. S&Aa (SORIANO-PALACIOS), *Europan 4,* Bilbao (Spain), 1996.
5. ÁBALOS & HERREROS, *Intervention on the Guadalhorce River,* Málaga (Spain), 1994.
6. ACTAR ARQUITECTURA, *Bit Park,* Mallorca (Spain), 1995.

Projection method

7. PÉRIPHÉRIQUES, *Café Musiques,* Savigny-le-Temple (France), 1999.
8. S&Aa (SORIANO-PALACIOS), *Euskalduna Hall,* Bilbao (Spain), 1998.

● colours

→ 'camouflage', 'joy (*alegria*)', 'printings', 'stampings', 'unrestrained (<un> factors)'

[MG] Quality of matter that allows it to reflect or let pass certain rays of light and absorb others, producing in the eye a specific chromatic sensation // Combinatorial effect of pixelled grids // Joy and expression.

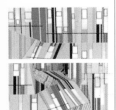

Enric MIRALLES & Benedetta TAGLIABUE, *Music school*, Hamburg (Germany), 2000.

José M. TORRES NADAL, *Public library*, Murcia (Spain), 1994.

SAUERBRUCH-HUTTON, *Photonics Centre laboratories*, Berlin, 1998.

OOSTERHUIS Associates, *Dancing facades*, Groningen (The Netherlands), 1995.

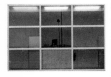

PÉRIPHÉRIQUES, *Café Musiques*, Savigny-le-Temple (France), 1999.

Josep Lluís MATEO
(MAP Arquitectes),
Housing, Den Haag
(The Netherlands),
1993.

● combination (combinatorial)

[MG] The combinatorial capacity of the contemporary device interests us for its multiplicative character in relation with the idea of change and diversity. Combination, in effect, is the "possibility of simultaneous existences," but also the "possibility of a given series of events."

The combinatorial disposition is the narrator at each moment of space-time (all the superimposed realities); a simultaneous space-time based upon the interaction and superposition of changing sequences and/or events. The combinatorial parameter refers, in effect, to the capacity of the system to generate evolutionary processes, of interchange and interaction, among different and simultaneous situations – or elements. A type of structure in which all the component-points represent "significant moments" not joined hierarchically, but rather differentially arranged.

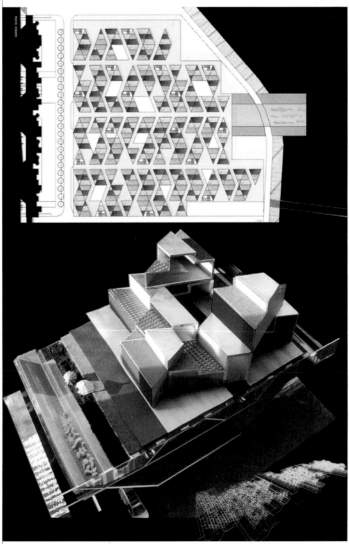

WMA Willy Müller
Arquitectos, *Europan
6*, Barakaldo (Vizcaya,
Spain), 2001.

● commensalism

→ 'ad-herence',
'appropiation strategies',
'graft', 'meldings'

[MG] See also 'antitypes,' 'enjambements,' 'cuttings' and 'hybrid.'

By commensal we mean a sort of freeloader, a person – guest, kin or dependent – who lives in the home of another at the latter's expense.

This tacit dependence is common among certain animals, with different types of commensalist relationships that involve mutual benefits and interchanges.

This cohabitation alludes to a contractual arrangement which is neither adhesive nor cohesive, but rather is in appearance – and nature – contingent.

The superior organism ensures the sustenance and the inferior provides certain services not covered by the operative capacity of the former.

This implies a sort of parasitism or patronage system, not necessarily negative – nor even definitively binding – but rather more effective the more individual – independent – are the two positions.

These situations may resemble, then, operations of melding, cuttings, couplings – or grafting – between different codes of information, inserted – or simply arranged – one atop another larger one.

1. Rhinoceros and bird, in *Zoo Animals*, London: Warne&Co Ltd, 1972. **2.** Eduard BRU/OAS, *Proposal for housing complex*, Cerdanyola (Barcelona). **3.** Willem Jan NEUTELINGS, *Prinsenhoek housing*, Sittard (The Netherlands), 1995 (Photograph: Kim Zwarts). **4.** Steven HOLL, *Makuhari housing*, Chiba (Japan), 1996.

★ communication

[CO] "About the same as now, but with higher access charges," Bill Gaver.
XAVIER COSTA

★● community

→ 'hypercontext',
'intercommunity',
'networks'

[CO] "I can only answer with a dream, not with a forecast: it will be a set of complex organisms integrated at different scales, from very small to global, supporting the exchange of experiences and the everyday's social practices. Physical and material local communities, enhanced by digital networking," Marco Susani.
XAVIER COSTA

[CO] **community networking**
Community networking is a new type of non-governmental association set up by the community itself in order to promote Internet use among the whole society. Unlike online associations, community networks are Internet associations, born to promote its use by the rest of the community. They are the new NGOs of the digital age.
Normally local, community networks may also be coordinated regionally, nationally and globally. They emerged in the 1980s in the US and Canada under the name of freenets or community technology centers (www.ctcnet.org <http://www.ctcnet.org>). In Latin America they are known as telecentros (Ecuador), redes comunitarias (Chile), etc. Common to all is their status as community associations offering access services, computer literacy and support for the creation of new enterprises and jobs. See, http://www.globalcnpartnership.org
ARTUR SERRA

[MG] See 'globalisation' and 'glocal.'

◆ compact

[FS] See 'no-box' and 'refold.'
End in disuse.

+● companies

→ 'advertisements',
'advertising', 'economy',
'incubator', 'marks',
'product'

[WM] "In this company you'll be fired for not making mistakes."
Steve Ross, former president of Time Warner.
"In the digital age, as we move into quicker and quicker changes of information, more and more intricate technology, and reinventions of the world of work, our organizations and our careers in action will become more and more aligned with the jazz ensemble. We will find ourselves improvising with greater and greater confidence and fearing less and less the imaginative powers of the individual committed to enrich the whole."
Stanley Crouch, Forbes social commentator. "Who runs the companies? Answer: the customers." Tom Peters, The Circle of Innovation.
(Translated from Spanish.)
I propose: Who runs the construction companies? We do!!!

[MG] The Apple Computer slogan: "Think different."

◆ ● competition

→ 'advanced> advanced
architecture', 'audacity',
'innovation', 'moral'

[FS] A competition is an empirical method of distinguishing an advanced architect. A frame of mind to participate in a competition: the participant never tries to check whether what s/he is doing is correct. The jury: in a competition, the jury is really the one being judged.

[MG] **competition / concurrence**

Meeting (excessive) of efforts.

Existence (accumulative) of diverse (and different) ideas, wills or occurrences.

Wasting (generous) of energies.

Help (ignored) in achieving an end.

Excuse (surprisingly habitual) for not facing or following up on decisions.

(Paraphrasing *concurso* in CASARES, Julio, *Diccionario Ideológico de la Lengua Española*, Barcelona: Gustavo Gili, 1966)

★ complex system

→ 'emergence',
'self-organization',
'system'

[co] A complex system emerges from the interaction of its components in such a way that the system is not reducible to the simple sum of its parts.

Liquid water can be seen as a complex system, in that it is much more than the simple sum of Oxygen and Hydrogen.

Although complex systems may emerge as chaotic, patterns are frequently found, thus self-organization occurs.

Cities can be thought as self-organized complex systems.

FRANCISCO TOLCHINSKY

★ ● complexity

→ 'avatar', 'chance',
'chaos', 'contract',
'diversity','event', 'form',
'fractal', 'multi', 'plural',
'poly', 'program',
'simultaneity',
'standardisation'

[co] The complexity of a real object is measured by the wealth and variety of the parts that make it up and by the wealth and variety of the different states it can take on.

Glass, made up solely of sodium chloride atoms, is a homogeneous object of low complexity. A watch is an object of greater complexity. And a bit of living matter is an object of extreme complexity.

Accordingly, a farm is less complex than a tract of forest and a tract of forest, less than a zoo.

How is complexity acquired, maintained and altered?

Answering that question presupposes the existence general laws of nature that regulate these processes. It is one of the great challenges to science today: to come up with something worthy of being called a General Theory of Complexity. In the evolution of the architecture of Gaudí, for example, we can trace a clear growth in complexity.

JORGE WAGENSBERG

[co] In order to develop a theory of complexity that is not founded on the contradiction of differences it is necessary to reconceptualize identity as neither reducing toward primitives nor emerging towards wholes. A theory of complexity that abandons either the single or the multiple in favor of a series of continuous multiplicities and singularities is one way of escaping the definition of identity through dialectic contradiction.

In other contexts I have argued for the development of theories of multiplicitous organizations that are neither attributable as one or many. Likewise, one approach to a theory of complexity might be to develop a notion of the composite or the assemblage which is understood as neither multiple nor single, neither internally contradictory nor a unified. Complexity involves the fusion of multiple and different systems into an assemblage which behaves as a singularity while remaining irreducible to any single simple organization. Such a state of organization would have to be distinguished from the merely contradictory or complicated as it is organized as a singularity, yet it would be distinguished from the wholistic by its internal multiplicity.

The terms multiplicity and singularity are linked as an assemblage of discrete components into a provisional composition that exhibits a collective identity can be understood as a singularity, and a provisionally unified composition that exhibits its own internal diversification and difference can be understood as a multiplicity.

Singularities and multiplicities are linked terms depending on the perspective of the either; the one that is internally multiple (multiplicity) or the many that are aggregated into an assemblage (singularity).
GREG LYNN

[MG] Complexity is the capacity for combining manifold, simultaneous and not always harmonious layers of information.

The traditional single and essential meaning of things thus yields to more ambivalent and multivalent definitions, less defined, more diffuse (polyhedral and polyfaceted).

The latter translates the ubiquitous and split (multiplied) character of reality itself; a reality that calls for an approach to events that is not only formal but also infrastructural (relational and strategic), associated with an apparently or virtually chaotic understanding of the idea of complexity.

In the order of the complex there is neither total all-embracing hierarchy nor episodic abandonment, but rather tactical focusing and/or alteration of a flexible initial vector such that different bits of information and energies reveal themselves, interact and mutate in importance, according to the case, or cohabitate — coordinated and interlinked — in different roles, at once individual and intertwined: combined, their force multiplies in a way which is neither regular nor homogeneous, but rather indeterminate: as open as it is plural.

● complicity

[MG] Complicity is not only capacity for dialogue – or for adhesion – but also for synergy; interaction between energies at once different and empathetic, harmonised in a single contingent field – situation, place or context – of action and vibration.

Concurring individual interests and common objectives: diversity and whole.

Internal logics and external demands.

Abstract criteria and concrete situations.

Alienness and influence.

Autonomy and resonance.

Affirmation of the self and a nod to – or calling upon – the whole.

Singularity and plurality.

Never isotropy or integration.

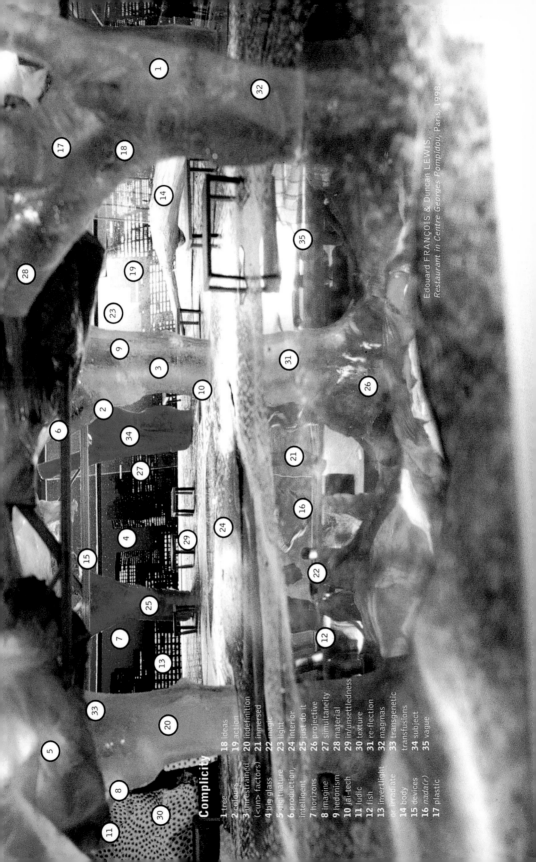

Edouard FRANÇOIS & Duncan LEWIS,
Restaurant in Centre Georges Pompidou, Paris, 1998.

Complicity

1 tree
2 colours
3 (mrestrained
    (<un> factors>
4 big glass
5 nightnature
6 production,
    intelligent
7 horizons
8 imagine
9 hedonism
10 jef-tech
11 ludic
12 fish
13 invertlight
    or irradiate
14 body
15 devices
16 *nada(r)*
17 plastic

18 ideas
19 action
20 indefinition
21 immersed
22 magic
23 light
24 interior
25 just do it
26 projective
27 simultaneity
28 material
29 in/unsettledness
30 texture
31 re-flection
32 magmas
33 transgenetic
    transfusions
34 subject
35 vague

+■ component

[WM] An example of an advanced-process architecture is the idea of the component: it would be an error not to grasp the literalness of its meaning. As in chemical or physical combinations, the elements become components of other new elements, transforming their purity or impurity into another purity or impurity, altering properties, cancelling out or promoting reactions. A new materiality is a product of the tactical or strategic orientation of the components, which are agents within an idea, with chain effects that are delayed or disseminated

Any other way of understanding components has frankly fallen into disuse. In the digital age, the industrial parts of a whole are no longer formally divisible..

Industrial components are to analogue technology what advanced components are to digital technology.

Components instead of composing (or I am a component).

[JM] **(mobile)**

Mobile is not about dressing this description up in a new metaphor, but rather making manifest the reality of an architecture and a city that obliges us to recalculate an adequate tactic for a project and the city. Maneuvers that make us think, given the pre-linguistic atmosphere in which we move, in the phenomenology that is found and developed in these places, and to attend more than ever to the economic and collective processes that take place in these realities.

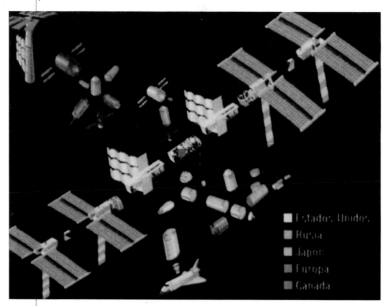

Project for International Spatial Station (ISS), in *El País semanal*, 15/XI/1998.

● concentration devices

[MG] See 'stack (stacks)', 'tornadoes (or twisters)', 'bluntings', 'buds'.

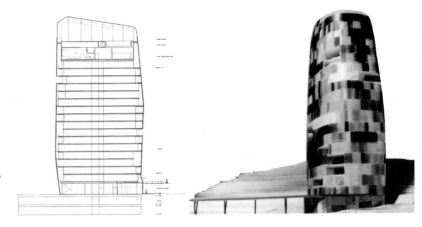

Cristina DÍAZ
MORENO, Efrén
GARCÍA GRINDA,
Tower in Las Vegas,
Corvera de Asturias
(Spain), 2000,
competition.

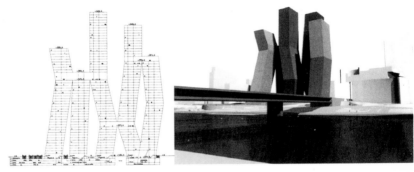

MVRDV, *Donau
City (Kissing
Towers),* Viena,
2002, competition,
2nd Prize.

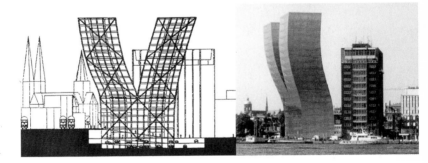

NL, *Y Building,
Flower Tower,*
Amsterdam, 1999.

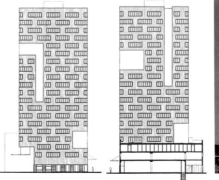

NEUTELINGS-
RIEDIJK,
*Java Eiland
Apartments,*
Amsterdam, 1998.

★ concept

[co] Concept is a widely applicable tool. What interests us most of all is naturally its capacity for synthesis. It is a question not of attempting to break down an object or complex residue in order to discover elements, or components, or characters (not unitary but heterogeneous too), but of attaining an element, producing an element of 'relaction' by means of generalisation. It is also a procedure of synthesis, involving not isolation but conjunction. It is a nominal form of united bodies, of complete, recognisable systems. JOSÉ ALFONSO BALLESTEROS

● concise

→ 'blunt', 'criteria', 'direct', 'economy', 'logic, direct', 'new vision', 'precision', 'production, intelligent', 'synthetical'

[MG] To be concise is to be strategic and tactical. Precise, economic and synthetic. Direct and diagrammatic. Also abstract – but not necessarily purified – in the conceptual. And in the instrumental.

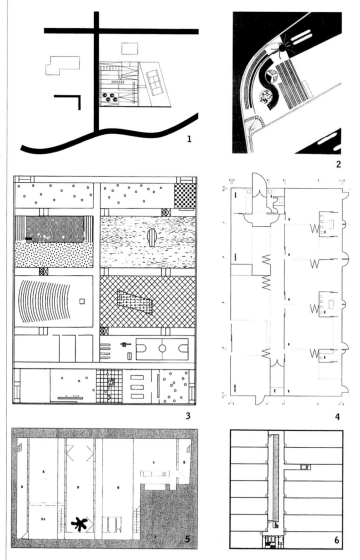

1. Vicente GUALLART, *Dwelling at the limit of the town*, Llíria (Valencia, Spain), 1995.

2. OMA, *Project for ferries terminal*, Zeebrugge (Belgium), 1989.

3. OMA, *Competition Très Grande Bibliothèque*, Paris, 1989.

4. Eduardo ARROYO (NO.mad Arquitectura), *Kindergarten*, Sondika (Vizcaya, Spain), 1997.

5. Kazuyo SEJIMA, *M-house*, Tokyo, 1997, in RILEY, Terence, *The Un-Private House*, New York: MOMA, 1999.

6. NEUTELINGS & RIEDIJK, *NAA, Nederlands Audiovisueel Archief*, Hilversum (The Netherlands), 2001-.

✶ congresses

→ 'auditoriums', 'knowledge', 'mixed-use', 'program'

[VG] Congress centres are the meeting places of information society. A suitable setting not only for the issuing of contents, but also for the interaction of people.

Two at a time, four at a time, ten at a time, a hundred, five hundred, a thousand…

In the face of the Virtual Reality that is advancing and conquering moments of human relation, congress centres are the place of Real Space.

● consequent

→ 'criteria', 'logic, direct', 'optimism'

[MG] Better to be consequent than coherent.

Consequence implies a will to achieve – action.

Coherence implies a will to cohere – resistance.

Better active intentionality than resistant compactness.

✶■● conservation

→ 'audacity'

[VG] The best way of conserving something is to increase its number. The best way of conserving heritage is to increase it.

(patrimonial intervention)

[JM] Work with landmarks recalls the past, but demands of the present come with it. One could say that it is this solicitation that characterizes design work. It is this articulation between the past and the design process from which one can understand an idea of the modern as something that, occurs, yet, decays, and that in the making, nonetheless, crumbles and that in taking shape, distorts and becomes muddled.

[MG] See 'archaeology' and 'history.'

José M. TORRES NADAL, *Intervention on the ramparts*, Cartagena (Spain), 1996.

Eduard BRU, *New accesses to the Alhambra*, Granada (Spain), 1991.

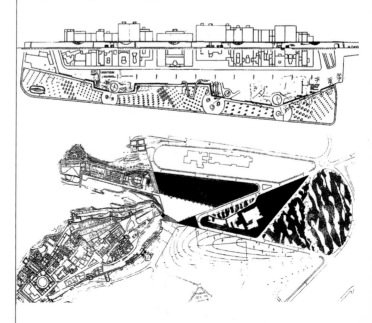

+●× construction, intelligent

→ 'component',
'devices', 'genetics of
form', 'kits', 'process',
'system'

[WM] The growing possibility of building discrete elements in series, linked to a growing importance of strategy in formal decisions, and above all the appearance of material intelligence, are relegating the idea of the container, as we conceive it today, to the history dustbin.

The greater indifference of function is linked to the rise of the container-box; the appearance of strategy as informative of shape is linked to its decline as a contemporary concept.

The idea of the container is basic to the ideas of industrialisation of architectural products.

Mass production, the possibility of guarantees of behaviour and formal inexpressiveness, all contributed to the appearance of the concept in a number of industrial processes with different ends. We might reflect on the importance of the fact that it has been understood and absorbed massively as a contemporary concept.

Today the idea of containers of knowledge could be as effective as it is synthetic for communicating new ideas in the global village.

[MG] See 'catalogue' and 'flexibility.'

In answer to the oft advocated adaptation of cumbersome production methods and unfavourable profit margins to quasi-artisanal modes and technologies, it has become increasingly necessary to stimulate research and integration of industrial processes, techniques, materials and products capable of favouring greater precision, versatility and efficiency into construction processes:

- On one hand, it is worth considering the growing importance of systems based upon semi-prefabricates (not a "hard" prefabrication oriented towards the repetition of complete cellular modules, but rather a "tactical" prefabrication). These systems, based upon combinable components, are usable in both structure – pre-stressed slab walls, floors and roofs – and in the definition of installations and fittings, based upon compact technical solutions or those "equipped walls" that, combined with engineered floors and ceilings, permit manifold spatial approaches.

- The progressive substitution of traditional weighty enclosures – based upon massive wet wall systems – with lighter enclosures made with dry materials (sandwich or multilayer panels and composites) is also worth considering. In this respect, treating the façade as a double-filter layer allows for the presence of a lightweight exterior membrane, replacing the traditional weightiness and edificial aggressiveness with a less aggressive, evanescent image in the landscape.

- By the same token, research into sustainable climate-control systems should also take into account the expressive integration of collectors and the incorporation of new high-inertia materials in thermal sections of façade. Here should be borne in mind the growing importance of the notion of recycling: non-aggressive products, reuse of means, low-impact construction, reversibility, etc.

Finally, the growing importance not of mass (repetitive), but rather of "informatised" (processal, evolutionary and diversifying) industrial production permits the conception of a new field of action in the realm of intelligent production system design.

These are some the many paths yet to be explored and that nonetheless suggest an approach to construction much more in accordance with the current demands of the environment.

[VG] See 'production, intelligent.'

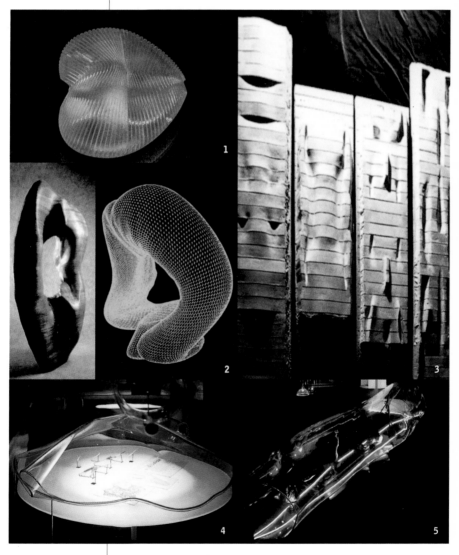

1. Greg LYNN, *Embryological House*, 2000. **2.** OBJECTILE, *Project for ArchiLab*, 1999. **3.** FOA, *International Port Terminal*, Yokohama (Japan), 2002. **4. & 5.** Vicente GUALLART, Enric RUIZ-GELI, *La Beauté à la nature*, Avignon (France), 2000.

● container

[MG] " *The container is a neutral protective receptacle into which fit multiple shapes and a great diversity of objects arranged in its interior. Its exterior shape – cubical, cylindrical or otherwise – has its own laws for stacking or abutment with other containers, but never that of explaining the object and shape contained therein.*" (ARANGUREN, María José; GONZÁLEZ GALLEGOS, José, "Habitar la caja," unpublished)

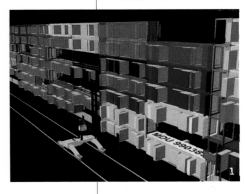 

1. LOT/EK, *MDU, Mobile Dwelling Unit*, 1999.
2. JONES&PARTNERS, *Arias Tsang Residence*, Brisbane (USA), 2000.

◆● contemporary

[FS] See 'advanced.'

[MG] Advanced (in architecture).
Beyond the classical or the modern, we speak of an advanced time, space, order or shape; advanced, meaning contemporary: simultaneously present and "protological." Advanced vis-à-vis a point in time and, as well, a logic, both now and future.

●◆ context

[MG] Formerly context, now field or environment.

[FS] The context of a project – the place, its environment – is much larger than the city or piece of earth upon which it will sit. It is greater than the historic discipline, larger than the traditional composite methodology. For us, there exists an amplified concept of context, in the same way that we understand that a work of architecture is not only found in its construction. A text, a critique, or a magazine are solid objects, tangibles, a project analysed in the studio as if it were another real program. We begin, as editors, to travel across borders through the limits of architecture. This border keeps getting further away from the academic discipline and has entered readings and interferences in apparently foreign areas. There is no point in proposing readings within the same tradition. History, common and assumed forms, and distributions that can not regenerate themselves, become reborn and sprightly.

● contortionisms

→ 'braids', 'coilings', 'fold', 'geometry', 'roll-ups', 'trajectory'

[MG] Contortionisms or curls. Configurations and structures, twisted or coiled around themselves.

Irregular and – at times – swirling movements.

More or less convulsive foldbacks.

[MG] **doublings**

See 'fold (unfold-refold).'

Doublings are parts of a body that crease or fold up, but also devices or tricks produced through (un)creasing.

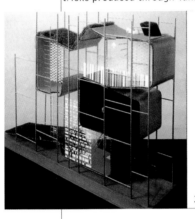
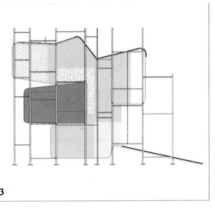

1. MVRDV, *Conceptual image for Parkhouse/Carstadt*, Amsterdam, 1995. **2.** Freestyle wrestling combat. **3.** ACTAR Arquitectura, *Paraloop: project for interactive habitat*, 2000 (Photograph: Giovanni Zanzi).

★ contours

Neil DENARI Architects, *Details Design Studio*, New York, 1993.

[co] From terrain and surface mapping to repetitive structural logics, contours are the physical surfaces and systems that govern both the data and the intuition of the work. They are the manifold conditions of the physical, static, and cultural forces at play. NEIL DENARI

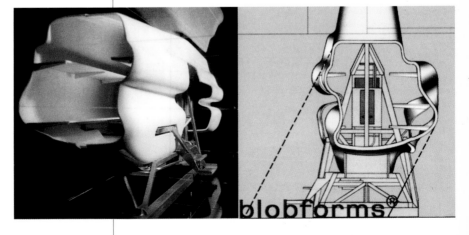

● contract

[MG] A contract is an agreement, arrangement or negotiated pact, of temporary – or virtually temporary – duration that implies neither adhesion nor syntony, but rather mutual interchange of bits of information, services or interests among different and not necessarily harmonious individual situations.

★ contraction and extrusion

[co] There can be two kinds of infiltration in nature. On one hand, contraction, a geometrical distortion which multiplicates the effect of the building's reflections amongst the trees. On the other hand, extrusion, a subcutaneous piercing including dwelling surfaces, in a pure stealth and food building.
FRANÇOIS ROCHE

ROCHE, DSV & SIE,
Salasie Crater,
Reunion Island
(France), 1996.

◆ conventional

[FS] Advanced architecture wagers as a value, more for convention than for originality, in that it is a language and not an object. Rather than an impediment, the appropriation of convention and the deep awareness of the basic rules of the market are the most radical instruments for surprise, innovation and originality.

★ cosmos

[co] The cosmos is the place constructed beforehand so that things can happen. The terrain is the site of the cosmos and the cosmos is the site of the architecture. The setting is the site of the cosmos and the cosmos is the site of the action. It is necessary to survey, measure, photograph, mark contours, visualise, render, model and then intervene, change scale, distort, transgress and create another world of the site in order finally to turn it into a cosmos. Your cosmos: particles that surround concentrically the vision of an author. An author sees absolutely everything in a unique way.
ENRIC RUIZ-GELI

● countermarks: craters and basins

→ 'cuts', 'ecology,
active', 'landscapes,
operative', 'land(s) in
lands', 'landstrategy',
'places', 'reliefs', 'terraces',
'topographies, operative'

[MG] Countermarks – craters and basins – are active landscapes in the shape of a vessel or central cavity.

Architectural manipulations of the topography in depression or depth.

Holes of activity.

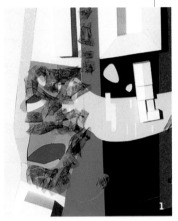

1. ACTAR ARQUITECTURA, *Pau Picasso square*, Montornés del Vallès (Barcelona), 1999. **2.** Vicente GUALLART, Willy MÜLLER, Manuel GAUSA, ACTAR ARQUITECTURA, *Competiion ARC OUEST*, TesaloniKa (Greece), 1997. **3.** Duncan LEWIS, SCAPE ARCHITECTURE + BLOCK and H. Potin, *Primary & Nursery School*, Trelaze (France), 2002. **4.** AMP (ARTENGO-MENIS-PASTRANA), *Competition for athletics stadium* (1st prize), Santa Cruz de Tenerife (Spain), 1997. **5.** Eduard BRU, *North campus of Universitat Autònoma de Barcelona*, Beliaterra (Spain), 1997. **6.** Enric MIRALLES, Benedetta TAGLIABUE, *Colours park*, Mollet del Vallès (Barcelona), 2001.

● cover (covering)

[MG] Formerly, 'to cover' was, architecturally speaking, to hide, to cap, to protect or to dissimulate one thing with another. Now it is, once again, "to join in order to generate." A meaning that speaks of the possibility of uniting, of coupling energies and genres. But also, in another sense, of understanding the act of covering. Creating covers not only as shelters, but also as new natures. Landscapes.

José MORALES, Juan GONZÁLEZ, *International competition for the extension of Prado Museum*, Madrid, 1998.

Enric MIRALLES, Benedetta TAGLIABUE, *Rehabilitation Santa Caterina Market*, Barcelona, 1999-.

S&Aa (SORIANO-PALACIOS), *Multipurpose centre in the old Concepción Hospital*, Burgos (Spain), 1997.

+ crash test

[WM] Linked to the production of prototypes, crash tests are one of the auto-motive industry's great successes for two reasons: the realisation of these tests and their use in advertising. Their use has proved vital in the design process of any automobile. We verify their behaviour under real circum-stances and we reapply the data obtained in the design process. Why not do the same thing with houses?

At the 1999 Barcelona Automobile Show, the Mercedes-Benz stand dis-played the prototype used in the crash test for the Class A.

The criticisms of its design and, above all, the fact that in the experimen-tal phase it had failed the "moose test" led advertising executives to think that displaying the test model – an utter wreck, all dents and sensors – was preferable to showing the model itself.

Crash tests themselves have become a mainstay in advertising: an advert for Renault suggested that the dummies used to measure personal injuries from impacts had enough intelligence and reasons not to perform the test, instead driving off with the car.

1. OMA, *Housing,* Fukuoka (Japan), 1991. **2.** Enric MIRALLES, Carme PINÓS, *Archery facilities,* Barcelona, 1991. **3.** NJIRIC+NJIRIC, *Baumaxx Supermarket,* Maribor (Slovenja), 1998. **4.** MVRDV, *New Office of the Ministry of Agriculture,* The Hague (The Netherlands), 2000, study (3rd proposal).

■● creation

[JM] If this architecture does not understand hierarchy, nor known worlds, if this thought needs conjunction and connection to continue, articulation and particularity, these architecture-thoughts are allied with chaos.

They do not begin from clichés, and, of course, have nothing to do with stereotypes. Everything seems new, new thought – architecture of creation, disappearance of determination, construction from the new and not from examination.

What is important for this thought-architecture is the happening. This event must construct its own tools to investigate reasoning and content. This project requires machines, tools to measure its discoveries.

What's important is that there is something to tell, something unknown.

[MG] The musicologist Jorge Fernández Guerra called "the hour of talent" the present moment of "proneoists" explorations, a moment made up of both unencumberance and uninhibitedness as well as disinterestedness and "disdisciplines:"

"*Timidly and embryonically, there begins to emerge a resistance to the habitual submission to the "tried-and-true," the accepted. Perhaps it is time to declare that modernity, under attack from an elitist snobbism that has virtually destroyed its immune system, has breathed its last.*

"*It might be that the present historical and social conditions encumber the initial development of this new emergent situation, but the creator is learning, the hard way, that there is nothing to be gained in repeating a situation characterised by exhaustion and insignificance.*

"*Innovation and freedom are the natural territory of talent. It is to them that the present hour belongs.*"

(FERNÁNDEZ GUERRA, Jorge, "Veinte años sin imagen", *12 Notas* 1, 1997)

[MG] See 'audacity.'

✗● creators

→ 'creation'

[VG] "*The talent wore a bottle-green velvet suit and immaculate suede wingtips. [...] He was scarcely taller than Kumiko, and something was skewed in his back or hip, so that he walked with a pronounced limp that heightened an overall impression of asymmetry.*"

(GIBSON, William, *Mona Lisa Overdrive*, London: Gollancz, 1988)

[MG] Creators will be necessary to create systems and to assess results. Only those who add value to the chain of knowledge shall have a place in the production system.

● crest

[MG] See 'bluntings' and 'mountain.'
Crest is the summit of a mountain, top of a wave.
Fractal profile.

criss-crossing (environmental conditions)

[MG] Artificialisation, simultaneity, dynamism, evanescence, instability, dispersion: these are a few of the many variables that we today sense as characteristics associated with what we might call new "conditions of our environment." These conditions of change are related to the transformation of new scenarios, but also to the transformations that may be glimpsed in behaviours sensitive to the current superposition and heterogeneity of social, cultural and spatial realities; conditions which allude to a diffuse and paradoxical time of coexistences and interlinkings, of relationships and alienations, of mixtures and slippages between the universal and the particular, the substantial and the anecdotal, the domestic and the collective, the local and the global – between the routine and the extraordinary, in sum — that tends increasingly to articulate situations and experiences, inherent and removed, and to which contribute decisively the prominent role of the new technologies, informatics and telematics, and of the realms of movement and communication, in current life at work and in the home.

Willem Jan
NEUTELINGS,
"De Ringcultuur",
Vlees en Beton 10,
1998.

[MG] Events produced in situations of collision and displacement. Of crossing and intersection. Criss-crossings.

ACTAR ARQUITECTURA, *In the infrastructures, a new nature*, 2000.

● × criteria

[MG] [VG] The orientation of a universe that is multiplied by communication and information requires a precise selection of the operating data that can be processed with a view to action. Exploration then becomes 'tactical intentionality,' capable of formulating criteria, rather than following models. At once, diagnoses, hypotheses and predictions of movements are able to connect physical data and strategic information; generic conditions and specific responses; ideas and materials. Criteria as positionings, as formulations that are both flexible and precise, directly related to the idea of disposition. We prefer the terms 'positioning' and 'disposition' to that of 'position:' both designate an elastic situation; a contingent, unstable action, rather than a position that is fixed or stabilised (whether by dogma, conquest or permanence). Strategic criteria for the global and tactical criteria for the local. Criteria of relation and action. They are, then, operating criteria – that is, 'active machinations.'

★ critical object

[co] In his book *Only an Illusion*, Ilya Prigogine explains how Werner Heisemberg was strolling with Niels Böhr in the environs of Kromberg castle, and Böhr commented: 'Isn't it strange how this castle changes when you think that Hamlet lived there? Nothing should change by reason of this fact, but suddenly the walls and battlements speak another language... After all, all we know about Hamlet is that his name figures in a thirteenth-century chronicle... but everyone knows the questions Shakespeare attributes to him, the secrets of human nature he explains by way of his character....'

In the case of Kronberg castle, imagined history is superposed on the real attributed place, and the castle certainly loses its condition as a fortress to some extent and inclines towards configuration as an idealised model, as the setting for the myth. Seen in its full scope as a critical object, it is more like an imagined castle than a real fortress.

How, in what way, a constructed object is understood and known can become more important than its physical reality. A constructed object is not completed within itself, in its own physical limits, but by countless factors that complement it so that we can consider as a complete work that which is formed by the built work itself and how it is considered.

We are faced, then, by the inverse case in which it is not architecture that excites criticism, but criticism that excites some factor of architecture. To go along with Oscar Wilde's well-known comment on criticism, we might think of creation in the exercise of criticism, with the substantial alteration of the built object seen from the viewpoint of the subject who is looking at or imagining it. Thus, the critical object also feeds on what is thought about it, which in turn completes it and makes it the object of further considerations.

JOSÉ ALFONSO BALLESTEROS

★ critical pragmatism

→ 'AA', 'advanced, architecture', 'architecture', 'audacity', 'Metapolis', 'positioning', 'X-architecture'

[co] Critical pragmatism is a phrase used to describe a movement, largely Dutch in origin, in which the architect becomes a surfer on the tides of modern economic and social systems. She or he must try to maintain a balance, catch the latest waves of fashion and open a space in which a human being can live in the sea of commercially produced structures that makes up our modern landscape. The image was devised by Ole Bouman in his *Invisible Architecture* (with Roemer van Toorn, 1998) and was further popularised by critics such as Bart Lootsma. It found resonance in the United States because of the reference to "pragmatism," a philosophical movement of the late 19th and early 20th century that sought to replace faith- and reason-based systems with experimental, intuitive, and contingent methods of decision making. The star of Critical Pragmatism, the man who has surfed the Biggest Waves, is Rem Koolhaas.

AARON BETSKY

● cristicism

[MG] **(referring to a capacity to judge or criterion)**
See 'action>critical.'

[MG] **(referring to mistrust, grumbling or censorship)**
"*It reminds one of certain smalls animals that lack any real aggressiveness but fake it because they have learnt that such a pose looks daunting. Until the elephant comes along and squashes them simply because he doesn't see them...*" (Paraphrasing McCULLOUGH, Colleen, *César*, Barcelona: Planeta, 1999)

crossbreeding

[MG] Crossbreeding is the "*combination of elements the result of which multiplies the mere sum of its components.*" (Susanna Cros)

crossing

[MG] Action of crossing (or advancing) paths/trajectories // Hybridisation. Mixture, coupling, melding, cutting // Strategic space in which different flows, grids and/or structures end, meet and interlink – and interchange. (Inter)meshed linkage, tie, node, braid or loop.

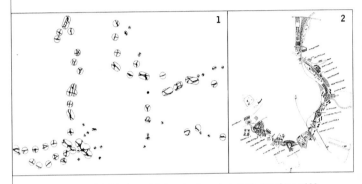

1. ACTAR ARQUITECTURA, *Around Collserola, Preparks systems*, Barcelona, 1998.
2. Willem Jan NEUTELINGS, *The Ring Cultur,* Antwerpen (Belgium), 1990.

cultivate

[MG] "*The little society, one and all, entered into this laudable design and set themselves to exert their different talents. The little piece of ground yielded them a plentiful crop. [...] Pangloss used now and then to say to Candide: 'There is a concatenation of all events in the best of possible worlds.' 'Excellently observed, "answered Candide; "but let us cultivate our garden.'*" (VOLTAIRE, *Candide ou l´Optimisme, in Romans, Contes et Mélanges*, Paris: Ed. Le livre of poche, 1972)

cultivations

[MG] See 'chains.
Cultivations are the evolutionary fostering of organic (and/or mineral) growths and their environment.

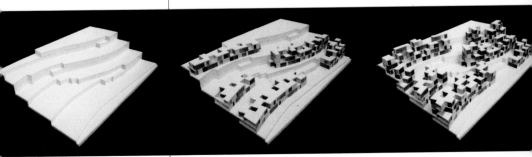

ACTAR ARQUITECTURA, *Europan: 400 housing* (finalist), Ceuta (Spain), 1999.

●✷ culture

[MG][VG] The construction of the city environment is a cultural problem, taking culture in the broadest sense of the word – that is, the focus of intervention for economy, art, science, thought, etc. Culture is a driving force of the economy: creating products according to guidelines of the advertising market, directing them at the right people at the right time and in the right place and selling them at the highest admissible price (having invested what was needed for their production). Architecture is a product of our time. And the only way to be timeless is to be absolutely of a time: for buildings to reflect the hour and the minute in which they were designed and constructed.

✷ culture, advanced

[VG] 1. In advanced culture, the ultimate aim is the increased quality of life of the individual, seen as an independent entity that participates in a collective. In the industrial world, the masses come first, followed by the individual.
2. Information and communication technologies amplify creative actions. Advanced culture aims to achieve active interaction between sustainable development and the integration of new technologies with a view towards achieving increased quality of life.
3. Advanced culture arises from the interaction between all humankind's activities and information and communication technologies.
4. In advanced culture, information technologies are not just an instrument for carrying out the same activities as always, but more efficiently (as in the case of electronic mail), they actually transform the very base of the activity they affect.
5. Advanced culture sees the reappearance of optimism in the construction of a future that is foreseen as differing from the conditions in which we live today: more intelligent buildings, sustainable cities, large quantities of information that can be accessed from anywhere, much more leisure time, etc.

★ customisation

[c] "*Customisation is the act of modifying, diverting, embellishing, in short of appropriating the standard productions.*
Originally this popular practice (derived from do-it-yourself) focused on cars: widened sides, lowered ceilings, personalized colors, a whole arsenal of diversions that made it possible to transform this standard product into so many playful and provocative personal creations.
Consumption, across all fields, imposes standardised products, leveled out to target the customers most effectively.
By extension, today this standardisation reaches all the fields of the production of space: from design to town planning, from construction to cultural concept. Facing this reality, where culture and consumption have concluded a strategic alliance, the rebel alternative approaches must intensify themselves. For us customisation is an interesting strategy because it takes reality as basis for turning away and embellishing: this attitude is at once fatalistic and subversive."
(PÉRIPHÉRIQUES, *IN-EX* 02, 2001)

◆cut-outs

[FS] See 'origami' and 'papyroflexy.'

Cut-outs are a mechanism of spatial and volumetric generation. They are differentiated from origami in that they produces cuts and ruptures in the original. These discontinuities do not impede that the resultant space is defined as unique and derivable.

1. Lygia CLARK, *Caminhando*, 1964 (Photograph: Beto FELÍCIO), in *Lápiz* 134-135, 1997.

2. Isamu NOGUCHI, Models in paper, 1958, in *Fisuras* 3 1/3, 1995.

3. Federico SORIANO, Ricardo SÁNCHEZ LAMPREAVE, *Competition for cultural centre in the old factory of Cervezas El Águila*, Madrid, 1994.

◆cuts

[FS] See 'manipulate' and 'landstrategy.'

●cuttings (and slips)

→ 'ad-herence', 'cohabitation', 'commensalism', 'graft', 'hybrid', 'meldings', 'prosthesis', 'reversible', 'unbuilding'

[MG] Cuttings and slips are operations of grafting, of hybridisation, which consist, fundamentally, in the interaction between a structure of flexible support and the couplings – or assemblies – of another hypothetical structure inserted within it. The support structure "feeds" them and the new cuttings improve upon the initial conditions. This is, then, an alliance or beneficial and – virtually – reversible or precarious contract (the inputs can be replaced without altering the sustaining organism) implicit in all hybrid nature. A contract of "individual experiences," arranged and diverse, rather than a single – cohesive – "collective experience." Because in the hybrid – melding or cutting – each part is known as itself. And as a part of others at once manifold and multiplied.

Cutting or graft.

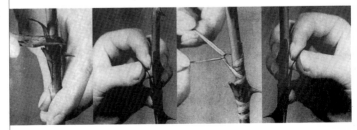

★ cyber_punk

→ 'cyberspace',
'Gibson's sprawl',
'hacker', 'hackitecture'

[co] Cyber_punk is a subgenre of [19]80s science fiction. Cyber_punk is characterised by its interest in technology, daily life, the media, urban change and the multiplicity of forms of resistance. Marc Dery considers cyber_punk an heir to the Californian countercultures of the 20th century: the beat generation, Merry Pranksters, YIPs, Black Panthers, punk, etc.
Martin Dodge and Rob Kitchin, authors of Mapping Cyberspace, state that "reading authors such as William Gibson and Neal Stephenson gives us a much clearer understanding of contemporary urban processes than studying Castells or Sassen."
Nonetheless, according to Deleuze and Guattari, cyber_punk does not so much propose an interpretation of reality, as the creation of a new unconscious, new desires, imagining new habitats; producing rhizomes, in sum.
In recent years, the term cyber_punk has been employed pejoratively to describe the anticorporate and antigovernmental activities of hackers and hacktivists. But as J. M. Parreño writes: "we know we're doing art when the police come after us."
JOSÉ PÉREZ DE LAMA

●×★ cyberspace

→ 'abroad, etc.',
'environment', 'Gibson's
sprawl', 'limit', 'logic,
digital', 'virtual'

[MG] *"Cyberspace. A consensual hallucination experienced daily by billions of legitimate operators, in every nation. [...] A graphic representation of data abstracted from the banks of every computer in the human system. Unthinkable complexity. Lines of light ranged in the non-space of the mind, clusters and constellations of data."*
(GIBSON, William, *Neuromancer*, London: Grafton, 1986)

"There's no there, there. They taught that to children, explaining cyberspace. She remembered a smiling tutor's lecture in the arcology's executive crèche, images shifting on a screen: pilots in enormous helmets and clumsy-looking gloves, the neuroèlectronically primitive "virtual world" technology linking them more effectively with their planes, pairs of miniature video terminals pumping them a computer-generated flood of combat data, the vibrotactile feedback gloves providing a touch-world of studs and triggers... As the technology evolved, the helmets shrank, the video terminals atrophied...
She leaned forward and picked up the trode-set, shook it to free its leads from the tangle. No there, there.
She spread the elastic headband and settled the trodes across her temples: one of the world's characteristic human gestures, but one she seldom performed. She tapped the Ono-Sendai's battery-test stud.
Green for go. She touched the power stud and the bedroom vanished behind a colorless wall of sensory static. Her head filled with a torrent of white sound.
Her fingers found a random second stud and she was catapulted through the static wall, into cluttered vastness, the notional void of cyberspace, the bright grid of the matrix ranged around her like an infinite cage."
(GIBSON, William, *Mona Lisa Overdrive*, London: Gollancz, 1988)

[co] Cyberspace as a whole, and networked virtual environments in particular, allow us not only to theorise about potential architectures informed by the best of current thought, but to actually construct such spaces for human inhabitation in a completely new kind of public realm. This does not imply a lack of constraint, but rather a substitution of one kind of rigour for another. When bricks become pixels, the tectonics of architecture become informational. City planning becomes data structure design, construction costs become computational costs, accessibility becomes transmissibility, proximity is measured in numbers of required links and available bandwith. Everything changes, but architecture remains.
MARCOS NOVAK

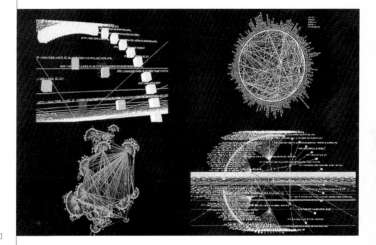

Maps of the cyberspace, in DODGE, Martin; KITCHIN, Rob, *Atlas of Cyberspace*, 2001

★ cyberspace architecture

[co] Cyberspace architecture would be an architecture designed as much in time as in space, changing interactively as a function of duration, use, and external influence; it would be described in a compact, coded notation, allowing efficient transmission; it would allow different renditions under disparate fundamental geometries; and it would be designed using the most advanced concepts, tools, and processes. Emphatically non-linear and non local, its preferred modes of narration would inherently involve distributedness, multiplicity, emergence, and open-endedness. MARCOS NOVAK

★ cybertect

[co] The cybertect's job is to create reliable pathways and useful environments in cyberspace and between cyberspace and real space. The words "connected architecture" bring the two realms together and define the area of specialization that is required to deal formally with them together.

To the extent that architecture deals with building places for people in face-to-face presence, connected architecture deals with structuring connections, designing forms and patterns of telepresence and collaboration in the networks between such places.

While formal architecture was the response to space expanding in perspective, connected architecture is the response to the electronic implosion of space, time and architecture.

ANTONINO SAGGIO

★ cyborg architecture

→ 'AI, Artificial
Intelligence', 'energy',
'networks'

[CO] Cyborg architecture is an architectural practice that applies the ideas of cyborg identity, as suggested by Donna Haraway (A *Cyborg Manifesto,* 1991). It is made up of elements and systems organised in network, analogous to that of information and communication systems. Cyborg components may be autonomously designed, produced, fitted and replaced: resilient structure, energy, fittings, information and communications systems, façades, enclosures, roofs, "wet areas," partitions, finishes, furnishings, maintenance systems, etc.

The cyborg architect forms part of a network of horizontal and flexible production that replaces the old/modern pyramidal structure theoretically culminated by the Architect. Drawing on Haraway, the slogan of this form of architecture would be: "I'd rather be a cyborg than a goddess."

JOSÉ PÉREZ DE LAMA

✗ cybrid

[VG] Cybrid is an object or an environment produced by the interaction between cyberspace and the physical world. It is the state in which we permanently operate when nanotechnology is widespread throughout the physical world.

● cyclops

→ 'cephalia', 'eye',
'hypertrophy'

[MG] Cyclops are giants with a single eye on their foreheads.

Certain architectures appear to wish to scan the horizon: they crane their necks or look out from the heights. They are "Polyphemi." They possess observant heads, like corbels with (one) great open eye(s).

1. Javier PEÑA, MTM Arquitectos, *Competition for a housing building,* Corvera (Asturias, Spain), 2001 (1st prize). **2.** J.L. ESTEBAN PENELAS, *Housing competition,* E.M.V. Madrid, 2002. **3.** Eduardo ARROYO (NO.MAD Arquitectos), *New Lasesarre Football Stadium,* Barakaldo (Basque Country, Spain), 1999-.

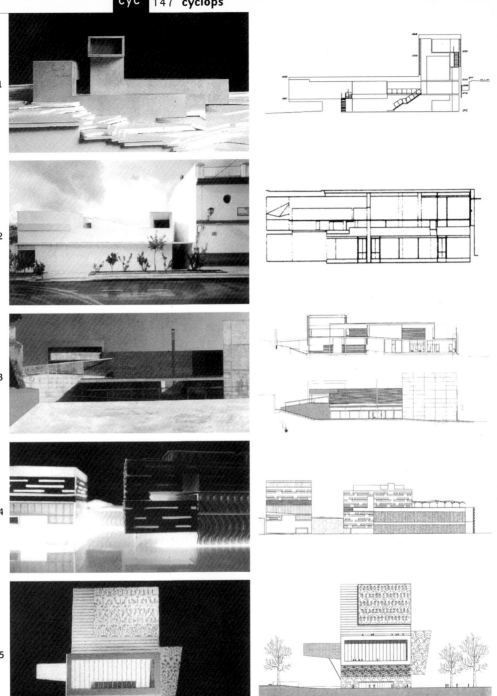

1. José MORALES, Sara GILES, Juan GONZÁLEZ, *Theatre*, Níjar (Almería, Spain), 1999. **2.** José MORALES, Juan GONZÁLEZ, *Town Hall*, Coripe (Seville, Spain), 1995. **3.** R+B (José Miguel ROLDÁN, Mercè BERENGUÉ), *Extension and rehabilitation of the school "El Pi"*, Sant Pere de Ribes (Barcelona), 1996. **4.** Arantxa LA CASTA, Fernando PORRAS-ISLA, Gemma MONTÁÑEZ, *Headquarters and Industry and Commerce Council*, Palma de Mallorca (Spain), 2000. **5.** NEUTELINGS RIEDIJK Architecten, *Concert Hall*, Bruges (Belgium), 1998 (Price Winning Competition Entry).

D

■ data (data and/or reality)

[JM] The architectures that we are talking about construct landscapes that conform to reality and are informed by functional, social and economic programs. These programs do not translate necessarily into organigrams (organizational diagrams), but into statistical calculations, whose relation, at times improbable, can result in a suggestive project – a project that shows us the paradoxes of reality. This is one of its most interesting, as well as controversial, aspects. The problem of space as a concept, according to some examples, is about being in agreement with design viability that could be deduced by the bringing together, almost impossibly, of an amalgam of numbers that, conveniently worked out, end up sketching an unseen image at the beginning of the process. It is about a behaviour undetermined by form or figure, but literally dependent upon the conditions of the game. The project is determined by the circularity of reason and the permanent reflection of programs translated by statistics. A. Giddens, mentor of the latest neo-liberalist theories, bases his theory of modern economic order on the concept of reflexibility.

We can deduce that architecture and its space is the result of a re-elaboration in function of reality and its data. This work of reality on reality, program, etc. leads to an idea of space that is much denser, more compact and alienated from ideas of composite and spatial hierarchies.

Dynamic diagrams of spatial organization, spaces vectory organized, incidence ofconsiderations about space not necessarily stable and the introduction of what has come to be called "data landscape" (with a progressive character in the attainment of a result, and not only informative) rethinks the relation between space and architecture.

agua	2142 m2	13.7%
piedra	3170 m2	20.3%
asfalto	0252 m2	01.8%
arena	1378 m2	08.8%
verde	4938 m2	31.7%
bosque	2796 m2	17.9%
acero	0268 m2	01.8%
madera	0631 m2	04.0%

distribución del material

territorio   materiales   paisaje

Eduardo ARROYO (NO.mad Arquitectura), *Desierto Square*, Barakaldo (Vizcaya, Spain), 1999.

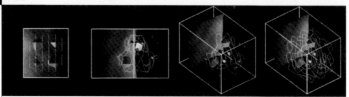

Marcos NOVAK,
Data-Driven Forms,
1997-98.

★ data-driven forms

[co] The data-driven forms are the result of deriving forms from fields of found data. As spatial models, the forms explore two concepts: the delamination of passage from one data set to another and arbitrary cross-fade (between data sets). An algorithmic function extracts from linked Web pages as two sets of points in the three dimensional matrix. Using spline-based interpolation, two sets of curves are generated. From further functions, the two sets of interwined surfaces, or "lamina", are formed. A series of crossing links (cross-fades) are then enframed between the conjoined surface-forms, producing a rich enmeshing of distorted frames and surface modulations.

MARCOS NOVAK

★ datascape

→ 'cartographies',
'diagrams', 'economy',
'interchange', 'logic,
digital', 'maps (to map)',
'synthetical'

[co] Under maximized circumstances, every demand, rule or logic is manifested in pure and unexpected forms that go beyond artistic intuition or known geometry and replace it with 'research'. Form becomes the result of such an extrapolation or assumption as a 'datascape' of the demands behind it. It shows the demands and norms, balancing between ridicule and critique, sublimizing pragmatics. It connects the moral with the normal. Having found the opportunity to criticize the norm and the moral behind it, it constructs a possible 'argument'. Artistic intuition is replaced by 'research': hypotheses that observe, extrapolate, analyse and criticize our behaviour.

WINY MAAS

Penelope DEAN /
MVRDV, *Noise scape*
(Datascape), 1997.

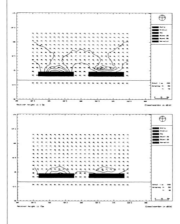

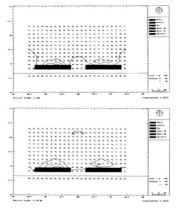

●✗+▲ decalogue

[MG] [VG] [WM] Synthetic mottoes. See 'slogan' and 'synthetical.'

[MG] [VG] [WM] Action (uninhibited), rather than prudence (timid).

[FP] See "Decalogue II of the modern house" in 'housing.'

Action [uninhibited]
 rather than caution [shy]

Idea [projective]
 rather than analysis [erudite]

Strategy [operative]
 rather than planning [conservationist]

Map [prospective]
 rather than representation [literal]

System [open]
 rather than composition [closed]

Process [evolutionary]
 rather than figuration [regulatory]

Superposition [multilayered]
 rather than aggregation [linear]

Diversity [mongrel]
 rather than homogeneity [harmonious]

Flexibility [structural]
 rather than permanence [monumental]

[Construction of] landscapes
 rather than [construction of] geometries

(VARIOUS AUTHORS, *Met 1.0-Barcelona Metápolis*, Barcelona: ACTAR, 1998)

● decisions (and instructions) rather than designs

→ 'cartographies',
'client', 'distribution',
'form', 'geometry',
'maps, battle',
'maps (to map)',
'negotiate', 'no-form',
'projective'

[MG] Decisions rather than designs are, in effect, the issue: dispositions – as configurations (distributions or deployments) but, also, as decisions (resolvent logics). Dynamic dispositions – more open and flexible systems and structures – produced through a purposeful reading of overlapped bits of information aimed at generating linked events; variable, manifold and heterogeneous.
Decisions rather than designs.
Configurations rather than figurations.
Strategic and tactical – operative – criteria but, at the same time, (infra)structural – reactive – mechanisms (rather than (pre)determined responses).
Thus, rather than predetermined forms or formulas, to foster , criteria for action: "battle maps," effective, precise and vectorised and, at the same time, necessarily receptive and open to the unforeseen. The contingent.

★ de-countrified (wastelands)

[co] Dissolution of the natural-artificial opposition can be seen on every scale and involves a programme which is nothing other than the rediscovery, through architecture, of the contemporary human position in the world. The "areas of impunity" are precisely zones where this ambiguous condition, whose definition – as public or natural spaces – is imprecise, is exceptional. The gaze of the new social subjects and their practices has endowed places hitherto negative with a new urbanity. Let us look at the empty fields in the outskirts, let us see how almost all the emerging forms of socialisation have been constructed on those wastelands although, or precisely because, they are deregulated territories. One senses the temptation to ask oneself whether they may not contain a metaphoric model, a near.model, or whether there is room to think of its complement, the de-edified, as the term 'de-countrified' itself embodies a fascinating concept: countryside that has lost its attributes as the city approaches, sterilising it before proceeding with the occupation, but also giving it a transcendental role on its new context. We ask ourselves whether an architecture could be constructed in the same way.
IÑAKI ÁBALOS & JUAN HERREROS

◆ ★ deleuznable

→ 'fold'

[FS] Given that the intensive use of the term 'deleuznable' in various media, in very little time, it has accumulated diverse meanings, although all of them have a similar root (from the Castilian deleznable or fragile). An object of inconstant thought, unattainable by convention, used as a general characteristic of the group of ideas in arguing and developing architectural themes, and of other arts, as a basic support for diverse contemporary compositions.// That evades and slides easily.// What is a candidate as little durable in its actual state, susceptible, at any moment, of becoming something else in narrow dependency of its environs.// Inconsistent, of difficult definition of its parts, these being equally susceptible of indiscriminately changing function and configuration depending on the necessities of each moment.// Of little resistance.// When it is opposed in architecture for being unknown, by being difficult to obtain by the dogma and inflexible conventions: the laws.// What is not appreciated in architecture, for having lost the memory of its reason; what is rejected, for having mistakes and imperfections.

[co] How are we to interpret the global fascination with contemporary French philosophy where it would seem impossible to read any university or critical text without seeing quotations from Jacques Derrida, Gilles Deleuze and Michel Foucault spread serial-like in it? What a paradox to see what was set up like some vast critical undertaking of identity-related forms of discourse turning back into an unfathomable lack of understanding, into a perhaps authoritative discourse eager to renew an ultimate dimension of the modern, new spaces, new technologies and new hermeneutics. French philosophy itself, still permeated by phenomenology, has incidentally been nurtured by a boundless register of spatial metaphors broadly taken up by architectural criticism. The current fortunes of these topological metaphors respond to the difficulty in challenging discourses of foundation, often in a misinterpretation about their use. FRÉDÉRIC MIGAYROU

■ de-location

→ 'abroad, etc.',
'criss-crossing',
'foreigness',
'globalisation',
'no-place', 'strategy',
'telepolis', 'tourism',
'unrestrained
(<un> factors)'

[JM] De-location, not being locatable, characterizes the relation between man and the city. This dislocation causes the sensation of being lost in the larger sense. It is possible to think that things were better in the past. However, to live without place, with the feeling of loss, is a good situation in which to propose the relation between the subject and the city, and the configuration from which to suggest another relation between public space, architecture, and subjects.

◆ delynniate

→ 'animation',
'blobs', 'dynamism',
'topological'

[FS] " [To delynniate is to] challenge traditional ideas about architectural design methods. [....] through animations and the moving section. In its search for systems that can simulate the appearance of life, the special effects and animation industry has developed a useful set of tools [...] utiliz[ing] a combination of deformable surfaces and physical forces. The convergence of computer aided technological processes and biological models of growth, development and transformation can be investigated using animation, rather than conventional architectural design software. Rather than being designed as stationary inert forms, space is highly plastic, flexible, and mutable in its dynamic evolution through motion and transformation. In animation simulations, form is not only defined by its internal parameters, as it is also effected by a mosaic of other fluctuating external, invisible forces and gradients including: gravity, wind, turbulence, magnetism and swarms of moving particles. ·These gradient field effects are used as abstract analogies for pedestrian and automotive movement, environmental forces such as wind and sun, urban views and alignments, and intensities of use and occupation in time. [...] To initiate transformation and mutation, external constraints are exerted on these internally regulated prototypes. The result of this interaction between a generalized flexible organization and particular external constraints is a design process that has an undecided outcome. This process of increasing novelty through the incorporation of external constraints mandates an improvisational design attitude. This shift from determinism to directed indeterminacy is central to the development of a dynamic design method. The use of topological geometries that are capable of being bent, twisted, deformed and differentiated while maintaining their continuity is also necessary." (From the brief of the online exhibition of Greg Lynn FORM at Artists Space designed by Ed Keller for basilisk/straylight imaging and design)

● de-materialization

tar Trek, Paramount Pictures.

[MG] "*If cathedrals sought to narrate the virtual tale of the celestial Jerusalem and skyscrapers posited the virtual construction of Nietzsche's magic mountain, then today's world of networks, virtual spaces, simulation, animation and projections constitute active expansions of reality through practically intangible material supports. Accordingly, research into physically constructed architectures, even apparently conventional, are capable of producing, through their own interventions, effects of spatial-temporal dilatation, leads to actions of urban dematerialisation: architectures of immaterials.*" (DE SOLÀ MORALES, Ignasi, "Architecture des immatériaux", in GUIHEUX, Alain, *Architecture Instantanée*, Paris: Ed. Centre G. Pompidou, 2000. Translated from Spanish.)

[MG] "*Today we are covered in two different natural bodies: the primitive physical being and the virtual being. Our present challenge is how to accommodate and integrate these two bodies; architecture and contemporary urban space face similar challenges. That of making real this space of virtuality. There is a gaping void between virtual space and the physical space of reality. When virtual space finds the mechanisms to make itself substantial there will be no more than one reality, once and for all. The attempts to create a "dematerialised" space — a gravitational space that is perceived as a space of null gravity — and a real space founded on virtual images, are, for me, the only endeavours that can supply us with a new reality.*" (Paraphrasing ITO, Toyo, "Architecture in a simulated city", *Architectural Monographs* n. 41, Academy Editions)

Toyo ITO, *Mediathèque*, Sendai (Japan), 2000.

★ de-militarization

[co] September 11th proved conventional warfare obsolete. Across the globe, pre 9-11 military installations are becoming vacant and require deployment of new programs. Nonetheless, there exists an innate drive for man to engage in combat — only now the enemy is within society's own civilized beast. Urban terrorism, war games and simulations replace war as it was once known. Current urban reality is a fantasy-reality of urban guerrilla warfare and freedom is traded for 'safety.' KELLY SHANNON / TOM AVERMAETE

urbADS (T. Avermaete, J. Juhasz, K. Shannon), *Deployment of urban warriors in the real-life war games of the Rocky Arsenal*, Colorado (USA).

✖ + demolish

→ 'appropiation strategies', 'associate, overlap, connect', 'strategy'

[VG] To demolish is an action carried out when architecture is worth less than the space it occupies.

[WM] There is a reflection to be made on the theme of demolition: when an advertisement doesn't work (is not accepted, lacks appeal, doesn't sell, lacks interest, is annoying, irritating, offensive, ignored, etc.) is it immediately withdrawn.

It is evident that architecture is not comparable, but that leads us to two clear conclusions: first, that its immediate impact must be far more carefully studied than that of any other creative endeavour which means a capacity to interact prior to its construction (among the functions of virtual reality would be to test: the resulting opinion would be clearly binding on developers, architects and politicians) and second, that we should avail ourselves of corrective mechanisms, tools of operative criticism, channels of diffusion and opinion polls.

This is to understand architecture as a process.

That architecture should increasingly realise that if it doesn't work it is more expensive to continue a mistake than to demolish it.

On the other hand, a way should be found to peg land values in city centres to the value of architecture that occupies it. Were it directly related to the quality of the architecture that it will finally receive, we might better understand the tremendous speculation on land.

There exists another vision that I would defend: there are strategic demolitions in which the value of the operation is measured by the future projection of the result. This type of operation is measured, not for what is lost, but for what is gained.

In destructive operations there is always a Manichaean game that must be unmasked: it's like the difference between the atom bomb and hydrogen bomb. One destroys everything, the other only life.

There are buildings like bombs, snuffing out all (existent or possible) life around them. Demolition is sometimes as destructive as building.

MVRDV, *Deconstructing Cambrils*, 2000.

●★✘ den**s**ity

→ 'diversity', 'form', [MG]
'geometry', 'information',
'layers', 'multi', 'stack',
'stenosis'

Density is the quantity and quality of simultaneous and/or mixed space(s) – and use(s) – available per person.

[c] "*The proportionately high development density expresses the concentration of urban life, satisfying the legitimate claim to urbanity, experiental value, intimacy and attractiveness. Density is the city's third dimension. Density is a critical tool, linked as much to the dimensions and disposition of the urban plan as to the traffic flows evoked by the untold relations between parts of the city. By processing density, the city is shaped in plan and section and its areas and individual buildings fixed.*"

(TILMAN, Harm, "When dense, when lite?", in MVRDV, *Farmax. Excursions on density*, Rotterdam: 010 Publishers, 1998)

(density and scale)

The historic city also exists in the 'place supply' that is a metapolitan city. The differential value of each of these cities in the city is its scale. Urban scale is the relation between humankind and the spaces offered by the city (streets, squares, etc.). For this reason, scale, the relation between the size of things, is always more important than the form of the things themselves. Formal mimesis produces grotesque situations in the city that merely undermine originals. Spatial mimesis, in the traditional places of the city, differentiates the historical part of the city from others. This is why the regular interventions of demolishing buildings produces decompressed spaces in historic centres and thereby dispossess them of one of their differential qualities.

Something quite different is the discovery of new spaces for and in the city, where it is possible to innovate. In built-up environments, roof tops are places to be conquered. They are places that enjoy the conditions of light, ventilation and views that are characteristic of environments further from the centre. The dwelling is, however, a contrast in this urban density. The large spaces of traditional constructions (large houses, very high ceilings) make for good climatic conditions and are generous in terms of space. New dwellings ought to recover this a-dimensional condition of generous spaces. Strategically situated tunnels would also enable vehicle access to dwellings and commercial areas a potential operative use of a new reinterpretation of density.

1. The densest block in the world, Hak Nam, in Hong Kong.
2. Benidorm.
3. MVRDV, "The world of the extreme Floor Area Ratio", in MVRDV, *Farmax. Excursions on density*, Rotterdam: 010 Publishers, 1998.
4. Eduardo ARROYO (NO.mad Arquitectura), S&Aa (Federico SORIANO, Dolores PALACIOS), *Competition for administrative building*, Bolzano (Italy), 1999.

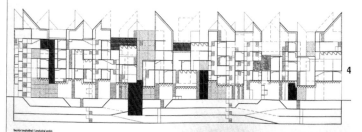

● *déployé(r)*

[MG] See 'fold,' 'fold (unfold-refold),' 'refold,' 'unfolding.'

To unfold materials, wefts, densities, programmes and energies as dynamic and elastic trajectories in the space.

FOA, *World Trade Centre*, New York, 2002.

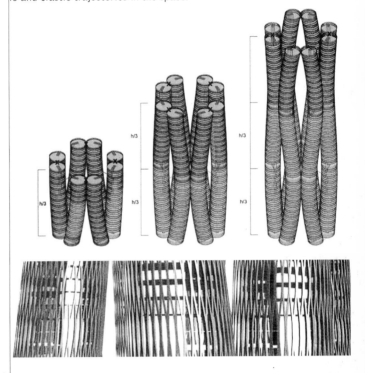

★ **desire**

[co] Desire is the triggering off of action and of the action of transformation. Imbalance that forms the intention. We are interested in desire as an inevitable form of inclination towards an option. We are interested in desire as a leaning that makes us prefer one of the options for no apparent reason, which in most cases proceeds from a succession of previous choices, which is a consequence of prior decisions. Desire also as a directed act, as pretension, as aspiration with no conscious diversion to a marked-out and in most cases very specific and defined object.
JOSÉ ALFONSO BALLESTEROS

■ **de-subject**

→ 'de-location', 'extend', 'extroversion: <ex> factors of form', 'open', 'unrestrained (<un> factors)', 'unfolding'

[JM] To de-subject is to make the subject not subject to anything.

[JM] To propose better environments (spatial and urban) for the subject implies work on relationships and locations. However, another approach involves making the most of mobility and dislocation of the being in a medium, wherein the subject manages to un-subject himself.

● *détournement*

[MG] See 'alienation (and estrangement),' 'de-location,' 'alienism,' 'rootlessness' and 'foreignness.'

Jordi BERNADÔ, in DASKALAKIS, Georgia; WALDHEIM, Charles; YOUNG, Jason, *Stalking Detroit*, Barcelona: ACTAR, 2001.

★ Detroit

→ 'Disneyification',
'McDonaldization'

[co] Detroit, unequivocally associated with the rise and nightmarish fall of twentieth century 'Fordist' urbanism, represents an exaggerated paradigm for all American cities. Its singular devotion to the idea of profitable industrial production has rendered it not a place, but a product – incessantly reinvented in the form of the latest production ideas. Urbanism of the 'Motor City' has proved to be a globally replicable model of optimising profit from speculative capital through industrialized production. The form and function of modern cities have been driven by innovation and implementation of techniques of mass production, the fabrication of desire and demand for consumption in mass-markets, the decentralization of both production and consumption through transportation and communications infrastructures. Yet, as the model is internationally replicated, the prototype – the city of Detroit itself – persists in a spontaneous evolution of aggressive dismantling, a process of de-urbanization. Obscuring the fact of the city's ongoing demolition is an on-going annexation of the city by its own suburbs. In the devastating wake of the city's disappearance are a series of extraordinary landscapes and an increasingly indeterminate urbanism. (See also DASKALAKIS, Georgia; WALDHEIM, Charles; YOUNG, Jason, *Stalking Detroit*, Barcelona: ACTAR, 2001)
KELLY SHANNON

★ developing

→ 'precarious(ly)'

[co] Developing replaced 'Third World' as the term used for the poorer countries of Africa, Asia and Latin America. The most recent politically-correct terminology is 'the South.' Of late, the developing South has become a fashionable 'site' for progressive Western architects/urbanists to research and occasionally intervene. Notably, a number of leading educational institutions in the field (Harvard, Sci-Arc, Berlage Institute, Architectural Association, etc.) has recently incorporated the study of cities in the South into their normal curricula. The favelas of Rio de Janeiro, canal-side squatter settlements in Ho Chi Minh City, informal housing communities of Nairobi and gecekondu in Istanbul are documented, analysed and to a certain degree romanticized. 'Experts' from the richer world are regularly flying the globe to assist 'developing' countries; yet the gap between rich and poor, developed and developing, North and South continues to widen.
KELLY SHANNON

★ ◆ deviation

→ 'chance', 'evolutionary', 'knowledge', *quidam*, 'trajectory', 'trip', 'vector'

[CO] See 'flexibilisation.'

From Poe's strolls round London, from Baudelaire and Aragón round Paris, from Benjamin's errancies round Berlin, is born a manner — somewhere between casual and random — of wandering round and living the city. The situationists subsequently systemised it and called it deviation.

Deviation requires certain estrangement (hence the use of city maps in another, quite different manner) in order to see, for the first time, the city as a given, as nature.

This is the first vindication of the active role of "background". Through deviation, object and background become elements of shared code. A form of nature.

Let us not confuse deviation with a possible meaning we might also suggest: the detour: i.e., that which takes us off our course or perhaps suggests another one, maybe better. "Detours" should be accepted in architecture so as not to work always with predetermined forms, but with processes in permanent revision. EDUARD BRU

[FS] Deviation is a "*mode of experimental behaviour tied to the conditions of urban society: technique of the fugitive step through diverse situations. It is used also and more particularly, to designate the duration of a continuous exercise of this experience.*" (*International Situationist* 1, 1958)

★ ● devices

→ 'beacons', 'braids', 'buds', 'carpets', 'collaging', 'decisions (and instructions) rather than designs', 'evolutionary', 'field', 'figure-background', 'fold', 'housys', 'interfaces', '(inter)weavings and inter(plots)', 'livrid', 'maps, battle', 'occupation structures', 'open', 'operative', 'order', 'paradoxes', 'prototypes', 'reversible', 'strategy', 'system', 'topographies, operative', 'X-Architecture'

[CO] See '*dispositif* (device).' ALAIN GUINEUX

[MG] *Dispositif* (device): "*that which disposes or arranges in a particular order.*" (CASARES, Julio, *Diccionario ideológico de la lengua española*, Barcelona: GG, 1966)

A device is a system, mechanism, criterion, logic, norm, strategy, map or diagram. Our challenge as architects is to produce new devices of action which are adapted to — and in recurrence with — the stimuli of the new global order in a constant state of suspense.

New devices — systems, mechanisms, logics and strategies on all scales capable of dealing with the casual and infrastructural (informal) are dimensions of our environment and, at the same time, enter into empathic synergy with it. We prefer, in fact, the term '*dispositif* (device)' to that of 'system.' '*Dispositif*' as a tool of a new "dispositional" logic.

It is not a question of creating binding frameworks — or structures — as productive and globalising machines, but rather relational and generative logics. Flexible programmes are adapted to global — abstract — principles and to particular — concrete — demands and are capable of stimulating, inducing and producing any number of global trajectories in space, in turn, transformed into a single local, specific and unique trajectory. The operative system is thus conceived as an "open device," simultaneously a vehicle of information, global and local response and operative instrument. *Dispositifs* (devices) (open and evolutionary), rather than design (closed and exact). *Dispositifs* (devices) are posited from the viewpoint of and as a virtual battle map: as a map of movements, that is, as an active scheme: a synthetic diagram (processor of situations and programmer of actions). At the same time, however, the device is a strategic and tactical criterion, operative logic — or programme —organisational (infrastructural) norm, (formal) system and, finally, mechanism of reaction: reactive vis-à-vis place.

● devoid of complexes

[MG] See 'unrestrained (<un>factors).'

◆ ■ diagonalisation

→ 'holes', 'landstrategy', 'section', 'surface', 'ubiquity'

[FS] **(as a spatial link)**

On the modern volume, one must apply diagonalisation, a process by which space runs continuously through the section. The interior is understood at once in its totality and in its diverse levels. A space is diagonalised when we produce a connection between its distinct levels through voids that flow, connect and link topologically or sequentially. Patios and openings at various heights do not necessarily produce this effect if they are not accompanied by the conjunction or confluence of the various floors in a single comprehensible unit. They must, as such, lose the sensation of superimposed floors to be lived as single place. Origami exercises or "folded paper" are attempts to transform a plane by its diagonalisation, by ramps that connect and develop in the volume.

Diagonalisation comes as a consequence of the one dimensional readings of Modern space – the abstract, infinite space that developed continuously between the floor and the roof. According to Colin Rowe, this is no different conceptually from classical space, only its elements that materialize the spatial definition have been rotated –before the walls, now the ground.

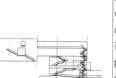

S&Aa (SORIANO-PALACIOS),
University School of Infirmary, Cádiz (Spain), competition, 1999.

[JM] **(as excited space)**

Proximity and distance – the means for constructing many images of modern architecture – are being substituted by all that connects and implicates works with the "excited landscape" in which it lives. The most evident consequence of this living together, at times difficult, is the space that architecture subverts, tricks, amplifies and shows unseen possibilities.

Now, we apply tricks on space that explain certain design manipulations such as those understood by folding, flow, and that, in a general sense, are included in the geographical analogies of Serres, or in the theories of fractals of Mandelbrot.

At times, these tricks of space are translated into the dissolution between interior and exterior, and serve as images for the configuration of space as a landscape and vice versa. It is not an accident that many of these landscapes or spaces come from virtual reality.

The glance, as an interpretation of reality but as a separation from it, makes way for a vectorised vision that crosses spaces, that opens up through objects or between bodies. This vectorisation makes space indiscreet or endangers the necessary stability to be interpreted from reposed contemplation. To this we add an agitation provoked by the impossible restitution of a geometry that makes us understand what our role is in this place.

S&Aa (SORIANO-PALACIOS),
Administrative building for the Community of Madrid, Carretas (Madrid), 1998.

These place-landscapes seem to make time gain over space, and as such deal with unstable places and almost always suggesting a multitude of possibilities for the subject. The goal could be to conquer a space that is within the reach of the eye. Space, thus imagined and designed, is a field of possible actions and unexpected experiences.

1. MVRDV, *Villa VPRO*, Hilversum (The Netherlands), 1997. **2.** OMA, *Euralille: Centre international d'affaires*, Lille (France), 1996. **3.** Enric MIRALLES, Carme PINÓS, *La Mina civic centre*, Sant Adrià del Besòs (Barcelona), 1992. **4.** MVRDV, *Media Galaxy (Competition concept for the new Eyebeam Institute)*, New York, 2001, 2nd prize. **5.** NOX (Lars Spuybroek with Chris Seung-Woo Yoo, Kris Mun, Florent Rougemont and Ludovica Tramontin), *SoftOffice*, United Kingdom, 2000-2005.

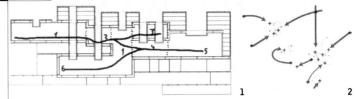

1. S&Aa (SORIANO-PALACIOS), *MZMK (Bolzano Museum of Modern Art)*, Italy, 2001.
2. NOX (Lars Spuybroek with Kris Mun, Ludovica Tramontin, Florent Rougemont and Chris Seung-woo Yoo), *ParisBRAIN, a transurban scheme for the area west of La Défense*, Paris, 2001.

★ ● diagrams

→ 'abstract', 'beacons', [CO]
'concise', 'criteria',
'direct', 'dual(ity)',
'extroversion: <ex> factors
of form', 'knowledge',
'logic, digital', 'maps,
battle', 'no-form',
'recursiveness',
'synthetical', 'trajectory'

Although diagrams can serve an explanatory function, clarifying form, structure or program to the designer, and notations map program in time and space, the diagram's primary utility is as an abstract means of producing new models of organization. The variables in an organisational diagram include both formal and programmatic configurations: space and event, force and resistance, density, distribution and direction. In an architectural context, organisation implies both program and its distribution in space, bypassing conventional dichotomies of function versus form or form versus content. Multiple functions and action over time are implicit in the diagram. The configurations it develops are momentary clusters of matter in space, subject to continual modification. A diagram is therefore not a thing in itself, but a description of potential relationships among elements; not only an abstract model of the way things behave in the world, but a map of possible worlds.

A diagram is a graphic assemblage that specifies relationships between activity and form, organising the structure and distribution of functions. As such, diagrams are architecture's best means to engage the complexity of the real. The diagram does not point inward, towards architecture's interior history as a discipline, but rather turns outward, signaling possible relations of matter and information. But since nothing can enter architecture without having been first converted into graphic form, the actual mechanism of graphic conversion is fundamental. The diagram may be the channel through which any communication with architecture's outside must travel, but the flow of information along these channels will never be smooth and faultless. The resistance of each medium – in its most literal sense – needs to be taken into account.

Unlike classical theories based on imitation, diagrams do not map or represent already existing objects or systems but anticipate new organizations and specify yet to be realized relationships. The diagram is not simply a reduction from an existing order. Its abstraction is instrumental, and not an end in itself. Content is not embedded or embodied, but outlined and multiplied. Simplified and highly graphic, diagrams support multiple interpretations. Diagrams are not schemas, types, formal paradigms, or other regulating devices, but simply place-holders, instructions for action, or contingent descriptions of possible formal configurations. They work as abstract machines and do not resemble what they produce.
STAN ALLEN

[MG] **(as "compressions of information")**

Here we refer to the notion of the diagram as a map – or cartography – of movements. Accordingly, a diagram is a graphic representation of a dynamic process synthesised through compression, abstraction and simulation. It thus supplements other techniques of representation and calculation through the formulation of selective figures: concentrated trajectories that, as economically as possible, permit ordering, transmission and processing of information.

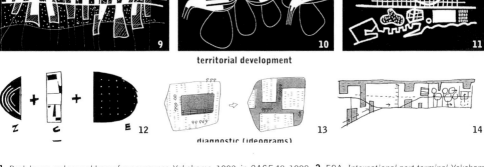

1. Peak hours and assemblage of programmes, Yokohama, 1992, in *OASE* 48, 1998. **2.** FOA, *International port terminal,* Yokohama (Japan), 2002. **3.** MVRDV, *Villa KBWW,* Utrecht (The Netherlands), 1997. **4.** Vicente GUALLART, *Seven peaks house,* La Pobla de Vallbona (Spain), 1998. **5.** Vicente GUALLART, Willy MÜLLER, *Justice city,* Valencia (Spain), 1998. **6.** Eduardo AR-ROYO (NO.mad Arquitectura), *Kindergarten,* Sondika (Spain), 1997. **7.** ACTAR Arquitectura, *Rail system, slippings diagram,* 1996. **8.** Vicente GUALLART, *Camping enlargement,* La Pola de Gordón (Spain), 1999. **9.** ACTAR Arquitectura, *Barcelona Land Grid,* 1998. **10.** ACTAR Arquitectura, *Graz-Maribor corridor,* 2000. **11.** Willem Jan NEUTELINGS, *New boomerang outline,* Barcelona, 1990. **12.** OMA, *Euralille international centre,* Lille (France), 1996. **13.** NJIRIC+NJIRIC, *Baumaxx supermarket,* Maribor (Slovenia), 1998. **14.** NJIRIC+NJIRIC, *International Port Terminal,* Yokohama (Japan), 1996.

1

2

3

1. Transformation of the space for the wife in a dwelling.

2. Computation diagram.

3. Frank DRAKE, Fragment of a message sent to any alien civilisation from the radiotelescope of Arecibo in Puerto Rico, in BECKMANN, John (ed.), *The Virtual Dimension*, New York: Princeton Architectural Press, 1998.

[co]

It is precisely in this economic – synthetic – property that their true expressive and operative value resides. Their being almost instantaneous reproductions of complex factors renders them capable – despite their high degree of reduction – of (re)producing and expressing a "suggestion of the whole."

As a medium, the diagram plays a dual role. It is a manner of notation (of analysis, of recognition and of reflection) but also a machine of action (generative, synthetic and productive). Diagnosis and response. Map and trajectory.

This projective condition alludes to the operative nature of the diagram as an *abstract machine* – as Gilles Deleuze would call it – in turn capable of spurring – and channelling – processes and actions.

It is abstract by virtue of being its being conceptual and ontologically different from material reality. However, at the same time, it is machine by virtue of being functional, because recognisable are possible assemblies, connections, internal and external organisations, deployments and dispositions. The diagram thus becomes the essential bit of action. A synthesis of evolutionary forces, vectors and – possible – events. It is this "hypothesis of conductivity" that permits these machines – these diagrams – to appear as "being-made," a being, stimulating and synthesising dynamic processes within other larger systems, in turn synthesised: "*In them* – as Sanford Kwinter pointed out – *the selected information permits the transfer of effects and occurrences towards other dimensions and scales.*" (Translated from Spanish.)

The diagram explains a "logic of action," that is, a "tactic inherent to the system."

Such intentionality of the system (or criterion for nuclear action) permits reference of possible movements (their combinations) to vectorised/vectorising schemes – diagrams – as genetic and generic stimuli of the processes unleashed and as synthetical codes of possible ascalar relationships (isomorphisms and recursivities).

Diagrams, then, are compressions of the proposed operative system, but also of the superior "meta-system" (compressions of their potential dynamics and of their most operative bits of information) produced – programmed – around certain trajectories of synthesis. The latter permits simulation and compression not only of the nodal criteria – the operative nucleus – that underlies them, but also their manifold transformations and evolutions.

"The place of the diagram corresponds to an operational, intersubjective field, which is put together over a given period of time, where meanings are formed and deformed in an interactive way" (Ben van Berkel and Caroline Bos). Form itself is no longer the receptacle of intuition, it loses its unity, it is constituted in movement and in permanent interrelation. "More than an entity formed just by its inner definition, topological surfaces and forms are arranged in interaction with the field which forms them" (Greg Lynn). Architects are in the process of weaving the framework of a new horizon of objectives, and they are doing this, without references, by openly side-stepping all logical forms of the modern sphere.

FRÉDÉRIC MIGAYROU

● dictionary

→ 'action>critical',
'beacons', 'cartographies',
'essayist knowledge',
'holistic', 'ideological
dictionary', 'language',
'maps (to map)',
'synthetical',
'transversality'

[MG] We propose here a "transversalising dictionary."

It is not intended to establish a collection of hermetic and absolute labels, but rather to construct a "basic" web (a matrix of terms, a mesh of keys) open to crossing and combination, and aimed at favouring recognition in that other web of forces and mechanisms that constitutes today, in turn, the big city.

The work we seek to promote is not so much an attempt at a summary or compendium of such searches as a quest for "combined global redevelopment" (in a new conceptual corpus) of some of the reflections formulated, handled (and merely sensed) and combined with new ones aimed at structuring and filling out the theoretical framework to be constructed.

1. Jeffrey SHAW,
The Legible City,
1990, in *AD* 11/12,
1994.

2. NEUTELINGS
RIEDIJK Architecten,
Veenman Printers,
Ede (The Netherlands),
1997.

3. PÉRIPHÉRIQUES
with MVRDV,
*Quai Branly Museum
of Arts and
Civilisations,* Paris,
1999.

4. NJIRIC+NJIRIC,
*MSU, Museum
of Contemporary Art,*
Zagreb (Croatia),
1999.

5. S&Aa (SORIANO-
PALACIOS),
*MZMK (Bolzano
Museum of Modern
Art),* Italy, 2001.

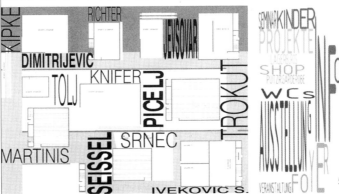

3

5

● dichotomies

[MG] Old dichotomies, for years paradigms of our disciplinary baggage (exterior/interior, artificial/natural, public/private, order/chaos, geometric/shapeless, abstract/concrete, global/local, routine/extraordinary, urban/territorial, unity/diversity, part/whole, small/large, open/closed, above/below, figure/background, etc.), have suddenly lost their strict limits and yield new and effective binomials in interaction.

Mixed, "coupled" realities, generated through unexpected associations and transversalities.

These are possible protocols that underlie the dynamic definition of the systems contemplated, alluding to the flexible character of their associated shape and order, as well as their own – and implicit – possibility of alteration and transgression.

Herein resides the force of their paradoxical nature: in formulating possible trajectories based upon principles born of apparently impossible unions (above and below, within and without, figure and background, volume and surface, etc.).

■ difference

[JM] The difference: what is not the same or universal.

● × ★ digital

[MG] Technological advances permit, ever more rapidly, not only the simulation of growth processes, but also the animation of structures, anticipation of interactive processes and generation of more heterogeneous – and heterodox – shapes defined with basic programmes and messages incorporated in simultaneous, not always harmonious, stable or cohesive complex wholes.

The digital world announces – still tentatively – a space abounding in barely embryonic possibilities; a space more open to new programmes, to systems and to devices capable of syntonising, reacting and mutating with reality: at once capable of receiving and acting.

This heralds a new period of architecture that will likely imply concepts heretofore unsuspected in all that refers to the static nature – and to the perception itself – of space; to the fluid continuity; to the dematerialisation of structures; to variation – real – of shape and of the programming of its movements; to the changing expression of the exterior and interior image and to its connection with a possible processing of data transformed in real time.

Programmed mutations based upon processed bits of information.

The future holds the possibility of thinking, in effect, about a more abstract nature of shape and of the processes that develop it, made up of real experiences and of virtual simulations produced in a universe of appropriately vectoral digital data.

It is a new digital logic, related to the application of animation programmes aimed at exploring the potential of dynamic – in all senses of the term – systems and of the inform(ation)al order that concerns us here.

[VG] New technologies make it possible to transform data flow to the point of creating authentic landscapes.

Spaces with or without limits.

Spaces with or without gravity.

The paradigms and the physical laws of the real world are not necessarily applicable to the virtual world.

But this virtual world could be a clone of a real world, or generate infinite possible spaces, like a world with infinite times and therefore infinite possible, parallel histories.

Quasi-real spaces.

An acoustic space: a music room.

A fractal trajectory.

A mountain of infinite dimensions.

A cloudy dawn: a city.

Settings for virtual meeting and real use.

Spaces and computer programs accessible from an intermediate space that can lead into a virtual world full of real content.

[co] The digital tool is not the instrument of abstraction, of a final transcendence of the design; it simply increases the register of an exploration of dimensional changes as well as perceptual and visual changes. Nothing must be frozen as principles, everything remains within a convention that is expressed by words which seem to halt what is common, shared by everyone, fluidity, hybridisation, complexity, morphogenesis... We will stand on the threshold of these exchanges at the moment when it is architecture itself that is becoming generic, regaining a fully-fledged capacity for indication and intervention, at the very moment when the architecture is becoming a distinct figure, proposing solutions which no other professional body can henceforth snatch from him. (From "Generic Architectures", *Archilab Catalog*) FRÉDÉRIC MIGAYROU

[VG] **digital world**

The digital world is like a stratum superposed upon an existing human geography. A geography formed by cultural, social, technological, economic strata, and so on, which are, in turn, all constantly interacting. A stratum that issues digital material, like radioactive rain that soaks the layers through which it seeps, transforming old substances and creating new chemistries.

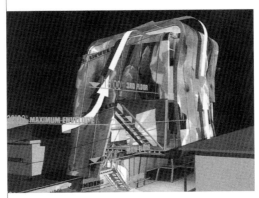

Neil DENARI,
Vertical Smooth House,
Beverly Hills
(California, USA), 1999.

★ digitnature

[CO] Nature is a point of reference in architecture that seeks, observes, camouflages and constructs another architecture that is natural; an architectural nature.

There is another process: digitonature. Natural effects occur according to natural laws. Laws that can be studied, measured and constructed. A cloud is reconstructable. A sea wave is reconstructable. A tornado is very reconstructable and, in addition, redirectable reactivatible and controllable. If the representation exists, so does the construction. The control of the constructed, the modelled, makes the digital malleable and means that its existence can be controlled. It is a "digito" power because we return to the power of touch, of the fingers, capable of moving and activating natural effects.

While the new technologies draw, study and construct digitally or analogically the reality of nature, the architect of *The Truman Show* says: "Bring on the Sun." And it happens. ENRIC RUIZ-GELI

Digitonatural
Enric RUIZ-GELI,
Olga SUBIRÒS,
Conference centre and auditorium,
Pamplona (Spain),
1999.

■ dimension

[JM] This "looking upwards" peruses the sky and stays, however, below, on the earth. This looking measures the "between" the sky and the earth. This "between that" is assigned as a measure of inhabiting. To this transversal measure, assigned to man, between the sky and the earth, we will now name: dimension.

Walter DE MARÍA, *10 milles* (steel bars on the ground), 1968.

• direct

→ 'blunt', 'essayist knowledge', 'open', 'yes!'

[MG]   See 'logic, direct' and 'uppercut.'

Explicit and expeditious. Prompt.

Steven SPIELBERG, *Raiders of the Lost Ark*, Paramount Pictures, 1981.

★ dirty details

→ 'expression', '*millefeuilles*', 'puff pastry', 'reality', 'society of the and, the'

[CO]   Architecture, art, film, philosophy and economics all seek to achieve new insights by delving into the dirty reality of the artificially urbanized landscape of our corporate globalized world.

The new architecture which results from this is relational; it consists of the interpersonal experiences it generates and it makes the visitor into a spectator, a conversation partner and a neighbour.

This new architecture does not try to restore contact with the user and spectator by means of passive experience, but by means of active participation. It seems to attempt fusion with the dirtiness of reality. This is not so much an aspiration to abolish the profession, as an emancipation from the institutional/representative structures, from the adulation of autonomy and from the tradition of the critical margin. It is a plea for dealings, experience and doing. It expresses a longing to establish a link with time and reality, which are to be understood as fragmentary. The time-honoured role of the architect has changed. In its quest for reality, the profession has to reinvent itself. It develops strategies and programmes that stem from getting one's hands dirty in everyday reality.

The new architecture speaks the language of mass production, of distribution and popular culture. It is an 'architecture against architecture' which does not open an attack on the profession, but tries to escape space in the sense of delimitation, dependency and a centre of management, order and control. Architects try to join disparate places, so as to avoid an enclosed quality, to avoid suffocation. It is an architecture that is not particularly focused on the architectural object, on representation or on the structure of the building itself, but is chiefly concerned with creating conditions for all kinds of topical activities. It is architecture as 'scape,' which leaves room for the dynamic of reflexive modernity. It takes paradoxical reality as its point of departure.

Consumption, for instance, is no longer dismissed as pure impoverishment; on the contrary, consumption is accepted as a condition in which countless exciting qualities can – indeed must – be activated. Some useful aids to thinking in this context are what are known as 'millefeuille' or 'puff-pastry' concepts: refined systems in which countless layers lie above, below or through one another, or are stuck together in an ensemble of continuous fields without necessarily having a beginning nor an end. And we, the users and the programme, are the freely moving raisins in this puff-pastry concept. It is up to us to seek zigzag routes through the layers in order to tie up as many loose ends as possible. The puff-pastry concept can develop as easily in an orthogonal space as in an animated form.

Being prepared to delve into the dirtiness of the 'Society of The And' does not mean abandoning oneself in principle to the status quo. However, in order to activate innovation, we have to build deliberate absurdity, or friction, into the layers of pastry. The aim of this aesthetic complex can be summed up as 'dirty detail.' The architects who employ this aesthetic deliberately try to turn reality upside down. A dirty detail can be the result of a minor inversion. A subsidiary element, unimportant to the whole, is changed, but thereby produces an entirely new configuration of meanings.

In OMA's Kunsthal in Rotterdam, for example, the tree acting as a column introduces just such a transforming disruption into the whole. The concept of the white box, which is characteristic of the 'neutral' museum, is deliberately transgressed and criticized. Dirty details are capable of bringing about a kind of radicalization of the everyday, by the addition of elements that speak a foreign language. This foreign language obligates us to speak – not in the sense of who is allowed to speak and who is not, a distinction that may be left to the police – but in the sense that a dialogue will arise in which those who were silent will now have their say. Dirty details rely upon an antagonism that does not lead to consensus, but to multiple points of difference. Through interaction, the battle for liberation is engaged repeatedly. What matters is to take a political stance and to challenge it with an absurd aesthetic intervention. Dirty detailing is a strategy of resistance and alternative.

ROEMER VAN TOORN

OMA, *Kunsthal*, Rotterdam (The Netherlands), 1992.

●✕ discipline

→ 'action>critical',
'advanced> advanced
architecture',
'gaze> tactical gaze',
'<in> order factors',
'memory', 'no-form',
'tracing', 'transversality'

[MG] **(academy)**

"*The academy, being a closed realm and finding itself isolated and forming a sort of island of history, was possible to maintain the sensation that, though life went on outside its walls, all that was essential occurred within...*"

(HOLEG, Peter, *El siglo de los sueños*, Barcelona: Tusquets, 1995. Translated from Spanish.)

[MG] **(body)**

"*The entire discipline is analogous to a professional body which patrols and contains the boundaries of the ghettos by self-regulatory mechanisms: professional bodies, educational institutions and specialised publications are, in fact, the authentic police force excluding attacks on the "integrity" of the discipline of architecture.*" (HILL, Jonathan, "So Real," *Quaderns* 217, 1997)

[MG] **(as transdiscipline)**

We speak no longer of disciplines, but rather of transdisciplines. Environment, transversalisers of knowledge. The gaze of the trade – of the discipline – thus yields to the gaze of the criterion – of information. If to discipline was to force, shape and officialise formulas (Forms + Models), today to transversalise is to make reactions operative (Relationships + Actions). In these terms, we refer to a will to reactivate projectual action: not so much as a resistant action, but rather as a recodifying – (un)codifying – action; that is, one which dismantles pre-established inertias of old codes (uncodifying) but also translates emergent phenomena – new codifications – (decodifying).

[VG] Discipline in all fields of human knowledge has been created by individuals with a serious lack of discipline – by those who broke the rules of play of their historic context in their eagerness to invent the future. Projects that seek solutions within their·own discipline, insensitive to their cultural environment, produce autistic interventions that conceal the most entrenched immobilism behind their apparent refinement. A dead weight in history.

Military Academy of Citadel, in *Colors* 34, 1999.

★ discothèque

→ 'event', 'fiesta (party)', 'quidam', 'spaces>collective', 'ugliness'

[co] The discothèque is, more than the cinema (a mere container and not a platform for events), leisure time's most significant space, its most evident symbol and its most elaborate and complex manifestation. Its history is a continual process of conceptual assimilation tinged with formal nonconformism, such that this reiterated production of signs has led to the generation of codes, attitudes, forms and uses – nearly always with negative connotations. The discothèque appeared in the early 1960s as an excrescence of the urban system and immediately acquired a rude patina which, fortunately, it has never lost. The discothèque of the 60s was an embryonic secretion emerging in the first stages of a capitalism that was recovering from the devastation of the Second World War. It adopted certain primary rebel forms: occupation of secondary urban redoubts, aesthetics of rupture, cultivation of ugliness and active vindication of its crass, peripheral and marginal state. But the discothèque later evolved under outside pressure: aware of its symbolic importance, the cleverest owners had the vision to incorporate this fractionary space into the mechanisms of production. It was at this moment in which it adopted more complex and elaborate forms, often occupying exclusive buildings in urban spaces of certain quality, projecting itself outwards with neon façades and signs and staking its claim for an aesthetic in which the constant emergence of differentiating formal proposals never involves disassimilation.

Over its long course, the evolution of the discothèque has followed a route similar to that of religious architecture in a much earlier period – underscoring the ritual contents that underlie the uses they accommodate. This ascension from the catacombs to the cathedral has also resulted in a notable change in officiants, going from the roguish spontaneity of the old catechumens of rock-'n-roll to the elaborate sophistication of the new high priests of the disco rite, the DJs and the varied specimens dedicated to public relations – as disposed to surprise as they are reluctant about any proposal of rupture. Now, immersed in a deteriorated formal baroquism, vitiated by spurious and peripheral customs, and having lost the aura of subversion of its early years we may safely say that the discothèque is dead, but we do not yet see on the horizon any alternative space to takes its place.

JOSÉ MIGUEL IRIBAS

Giovanni ZANZI, *Sonar* (Advanced music festival), Barcelona, 1997.

★ Disneyification

→ 'McDonaldization'

[co] Disneyification is the deliberate packaging of places wherein culture and heritage inauthenticity are actively promoted and impose an enormous distance between inheritance and lived reality. Competitive marketing and branding essentially bastardise local cultures in lieu of economic benefits.
KELLY SHANNON

◆ dispersed

→ 'creation', 'dissolved architecture', 'extroversion: <ex> factors of form', 'in/unstable', 'self-organization', 'stains, ink', 'vague'

[FS] See 'dissolved architecture' and 'logic, fuzzy.'

Dispersed art. Peripheries and borders have been, until recently, a point of support for the avant-garde. They had no ties to history. They were photogenic and seemed the most removed from the academy. Now they have become obligatory references. A discipline is constructed around them.

Our interest in borders implies our recognizing a centre. What has precisely been important for the discipline is to maintain frontiers and mark distances. When art lost its centre, it became diffuse. Or dispersed. There are no reference models.

Critical reason no longer works with an ideal that must be materialised, but is the only reference that gives meaning to a rapid, simultaneous and successive production of concrete used objects.

● displacing by sliding

→ 'devices', 'dispositions', 'dynamism', 'geometry', 'strategy'

[MG] See 'strips,' 'circuits' and '(inter)weavings and inter(plots).'

[MG] Dispositional dynamics of variable and discontinuous occupation, distribution and/or configuration, produced through normed sequential movements, in which voids and plenitudes, occupations and spacings, slide with respect to each other in markedly parallel contiguous spaces.

1. Josep Lluís MATEO (MAP Arquitectes), *26 dwellings in Borneo Dike*, Amsterdam, 1999.

2. RIEGLER/RIEWE, *TU Institute*, Graz (Austria), 1994.

3. José MORALES, Sara GILES, Juan GONZÁLEZ, *New police headquarters*, Almería (Spain), 1998.

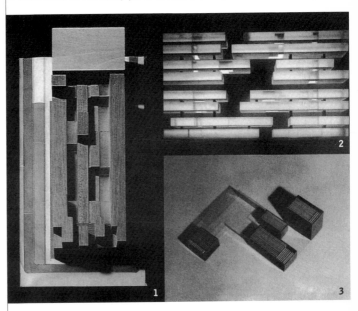

★● *dispositif* (device)

Today, we are witnessing the development of architectural forms which do not draw their effect from their presence, but from their operation as devices and from what they engender outside themselves. The project is not fulfilled by its own existence, it seeks to produce effects outside itself.

The term dispositif describes an active architecture, by opposition to "representative" architecture which has tried, by turns, to represent urban chaos, fractal mathematics, deconstruction, cybernetics, biology, consumption and dematerialization of the world.

Fictional, analytic and visual devices have been described, but the device is also a plan, and not only for an economic, military or advertising strategy. It generally comes much closer to the notion of project, a watchword that defines the engineer's work (indeed, that is the definition given in the elite universities), as much as the work of the architect.

ALAIN GUIHEUX

[MG] **dispositifs or d(a)yspositives**

From the Spanish *dispositivo* (device), day and positive. Positive days that generate new devices. Positive days generated by certain devices.

● dispositions

(composition>position>disposition)

In response to the traditional idea of order that marked the classical interpretation of space (based upon the idea of *composition* as a hierarchical relationship but also as cohesive, closed, *predictable* figuration between parts), modern thought proposed an alternative "new order" associated with a relativist interpretation of space and of time (based upon spatial *position* as a freer though no less strict – *measurable* – link between objects). Position as organisation, but also as an inalterable, affiliating (syntonic with its "ideological" – dogmatic – moment of the modern time-space) principle.

The contemporary change in paradigms and the new idea of time, provide for a new "informal" order, more elastic – based no longer upon *compositions* or *positions*, but rather upon *dispositions*, open to individual variation and, therefore, to diversity. To a dynamic and plural articulation of information. "

Dynamic systems, in fact, can only be represented through combinations of "possibilities," of evolutions with regard to generic schemes – or rules – of movement and (or) behaviour, altered and distorted to the extent that the incidence of information increases. *Open* dispositions, then, as *combinations/distributions of positions*, but also as *logics of decision (internal criteria)* produced through a processed, conscious and flexible reading of variable bits of information aimed at fostering manifold, simultaneous and heterogeneous events.

If, in its day, modern space meant the shift from the idea of composition – as regulation – to that of position – as correlation – today, contemporary space means the shift from the idea of position to that of disposition – as an operative decision, but also as the possible indeterminate combination (and distribution) of positions and/or layers of information. From a predictable vision of the universe, we moved on to a measurable one and, now, to a differential one.

Composition. Classical order

Position. Modern order

Disposition (and device). Advanced order

1. "Alive" badge of the air army, Kelly Field, San Antonio (Texas), 1926, in BOLOGNESI, Kitti, BERNADÓ, Jordi (Eds.), *Goldbeck*, Barcelona: ACTAR, 1999. **2.** Alain RESNAIS, *Last year in Marienbad*, 1961, in PARKINSON, David, *History of film*, London: Thames & Hudson, 1996. **3.** Fence (Photograph: Manuel Gausa de Mas, 1960), in VARIOUS AUTHORS, *Met 1.0. Barcelona Metápolis*, Barcelona: ACTAR, 1998.

[MG] **(dispositions as distributions)**

In most dynamic systems, snap shots taken of each trajectory in space indicate an unstable – virtual or real – situation, in a state of latent change, proper to a scattered and evolutionary nature.

Whether termed as *dissipations* (Van Berkel and Lynn), *distributions* (Allen), *deployments* (Deleuze) or *dispersions* (Sosa), in all cases the formation of structures described here alludes to a dynamic process of organisation based upon local interaction between individual actions (situations and/or events). Although such complexes are subject to an indeterminate global evolution, produced by the combination of the movements of each of their individual components, the system as a whole presents *generic properties* pointing to elemental rules or criteria for nuclear action.

Accordingly, we believe it is appropriate to adopt the term 'disposition' for its manifold and fitting meanings:
- Dispositions as dynamic configurations, that is, as distributions of combined positions in space.
- Disposition as a "combination of positions," but also as logics of "decision" (or instrumental order), in allusion to the generic vector (or criterion for action) present in such structures.
- Disposition as shape and as order, but also as character and attitude (state of mind vis-à-vis the action), at once virtual and operative.

Such dispositions are recursive among themselves and allude to spatial-temporal configurations – multitudes, flocks, herds, shoals of fish, *foules* (agglomerations of people), but also cities and possible constructions – whose movements present fluctuations caused by not always linearly predictable dynamic processes – and behaviours. They respond to recurrent parameters of *complexity, multiplicity, mutability, evolutivity* and *combinatoriality, discontinuity* and *sequenciality, matrixiality* and *flexibility, (potential) mixedness,* and (evidently) *singularity* and *irregularity,* etc. That is, these are more decidedly *open* – precisely by virtue of being *in*formal – to logic of the shape.

1. Reindeers flock, in VARIOUS AUTHORS, *The Berlage Cahiers 5, Studio 95-96*, Rotterdam: 010 Publishers, 1997. **2.** Barry LE VA, *Bearings rolled* (six specific instants; no particular order), 1966-1967. **3.** Federico SORIANO, Ricardo SÁNCHEZ LAMPREAVE, *Competition for cultural centre in the old factory of Cervezas El Águila*, Madrid, 1994.

■ dissolved architecture

→ 'dispositions',
'distribution', 'extend',
'field', 'immanence',
'intermittences', 'order',
'sequences', 'stains, ink',
'topological'

[JM] Making dissolved architecture is thinking of a work as a trajectory, heeding non-places that are configured and then disappear. This instability suggests the idea of the city as something generic and never concrete or defined.

Making dissolved architecture is working with modification and recycling, not even flexibility. The result is architectures leaning on disappearance. Objects never more, and much less, beautiful.

● distortion

→ 'deviation', 'event',
'foreigness',
'infiltration> intrusiveness',
'mutation', 'system'

[MG] Distortion is the perturbation or alteration of a system or norm for action. Deformation of movements during their generation or evolution.

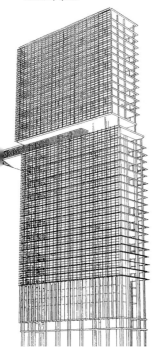

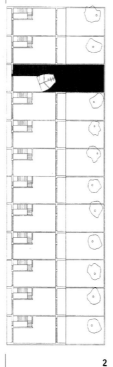

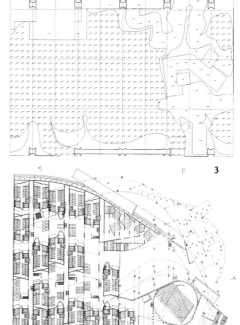

3

1   **2**   **4**

1. OMA, *Competition Zac Danton Office Tower*, La Défense, Paris, 1993.
2. Josep MIAS, *Study with car*, Banyoles (Girona, Spain), 1996.
3. S&Aa (SORIANO-PALACIOS), *Cyberauditorium and Museum of Children in the Sciences Museum*, Valencia (Spain), 1998.
4. Enric MIRALLES, *Lecture rooms in the University of Valencia*, Valencia (Spain), 1994.

● distribution

[MG] See 'dispositions' and '*déployé(r).*'

Distribution is the indeterminate arrangement of individual elements in a space.

Spontaneous self-regulation of fluctuating occupations.

● diversity

Ours is a time of *diversity*, calling for constant simultaneity of individual events in global structures: this "multi" – plural – condition links the local with the global, the particular with the general, the general with the individual, evidencing the impact – and emergence – of the singular upon the collective, not as "part of a whole," but rather as specificity "interconnected with the whole" (as a presence at once independent – autonomous – and co-participant). Diversity speaks of combination, interlinkage, co-existence and simultaneity. Of relation and discontinuity.

"*In the process of the modern, discourses have become transverse, genres mixed, languages fragmentary. But, beyond life as simultaneity, in our time there exists the conditions for assuming creatively this fragmentation, and thereby attaining an anthropological universality which also integrates plurality, difference and discontinuity.*" (JIMÉNEZ, José, *La vida como azar*)

Knots, in FARRELLY, Liz, *Sneakers, size isn't everything*, London: Booth-Clibborn Editions, 1998.

MVRDV, *WoZoCo's Housing*, Amsterdam, 1997.

★ ● do-it-yourself

bricolage

"*Problem-solvers who do not proceed from top-down design but by arranging and rearranging a set of well-known materials can be said to be practicing bricolage. They tend to try one thing, step back, reconsider, and try another. For planners, mistakes are steps in the wrong direction; bricoleurs navigate through mid course corrections. The revaluation of bricolage in the culture of simulation includes a new emphasis on visualization and the development of intuition through the manipulation of virtual objects. Instead of having to follow a set of rules laid down in advance,* computer users are encouraged to tinker in simulated microworlds. Then, they learn about how things work by interacting with them. One can see evidence of this change in the way businesses do their financial planning, architects design buildings, and teenagers play with simulation games".

(TURKLE, Sherry, *Life on the Screen. Identity in the Age of the Internet*, New York: Touchstone, 1997)

[MG] Do it-yourself is "'*plug and play' in a self-sufficient version."
(Susanna Cros)

✱ domestic

[VG] The dwelling is the individual's skin, the ultimate space that divides the individual from the collective. Each dwelling reflects the soul of its inhabitants.

The house is the computer. The structure is the network.
(*Media House Project*. Metapolis-MIT Media Lab)

✱ ● domotics

[VG] Domotics came into being with a view to automating the dwelling. It is the robotics of domestic space and therefore a product of the industrial era. The new applications related to the dwelling seek to develop information-al relations between users, objects and spaces that emit and receive the data flowing around the dwelling's various networks, via interfaces inserted into everything.

[MG] See 'interfaces.'

MIT MEDIA LAB,
FUNDACIÓ
POLITÈCNICA DE
CATALUNYA,
METÀPOLIS, *Media House Project*,
Videoconference,
Barcelona, 2001.

★ droog

→ 'ideas' [CO] "Dry, like a Martini," is Curator Paola Antonelli's definition of Droog – the Dutch designers' collective, which made its debut at the Milan Furniture Fair in 1993. The astringent, often ironic work these designers produce is stylistically diverse, but centers, according to co-founder Renny Ramakers, on the notion of "re:" re-use, representation, regeneration, rethinking. Ramakers, former editor of the design magazine *Items*, became intrigued, in the early 1990s, with a shared concern for reusing both materials and ideas that she noted among designers and recent graduates of design schools. Together with jewelry designer Gijs Bakker she asked Tejo Remy, Hella Jongerius, Piet Hein Eek, Richard Hutten and others to let her include their designs in the Droog (the word means "dry" in Dutch) collection. The immediate success of this amalgamation of different ideas points to the need for design that does not pretend to be innovative or formally daring, but that encapsulates a strong concept, usually fed by environmental and social concerns, in a simple, but carefully composed shape. Architects could learn a great deal from this movement.

AARON BETSKY

REMY, Tejo, *Chest of drawers*
"You can lay down your
memories", 1991, in RAMAKERS,
Renny; BAKKER, Gijs (Eds.),
Droog Design. Spirit
of the Nineties, Rotterdam:
010 Publishers, 1998.

● dual(ity)

→ 'a-couplings', 'contract', 'dichotomies', 'interchange', 'sequences' [MG] Duality is the meeting of two distinct episodes in a single action. Dual implies not symmetry, repetition or twin, but binary contract.
Minimum sequence. A and B. Interchange between two events.
In certain languages, in addition to plural and singular, there also exists a particular, dual gender to indicate a set of two. Of both.

● dum-dum effect

→ 'action>critical', 'direct', 'logic, direct' [MG] The dum-dum effect is a certain class of explosive bullet. There are dum-dum projects, actions and operations. They have expansive – occasionally retarded – effects, extending their field of action beyond the limits of impact.

● dunes

[IMG] A dune is a mound of fluctuant matter and oscillating geometry. Undulating landscape of natural and artificial definition.

● dynamism

[IMG] **(or dynamic)**

Active and propulsive energy.

Our environment defines a changing space of excited movements and linked events characterised by the constant variation of their associated scenarios, and configurations.

Those of a mutable and fluctuant time, under development, which express its own active, animated and *un*settled nature — but that also extend this capacity for change implicit in the potential for mobility and interchange. This dynamic condition seems, then, to be — as Sanford Kwinter correctly pointed out — perfectly consistent with the Bergsonian and Deleuzian ontology in which mobility and virtuality would play a decisive role in explaining the world and the forces that it comprises: this constant intermediate disposition between the possible and the real, between the virtual and the actual, as principles common to the basic nature of the being, fundamental expression in mobility, in variation and in evanescence. In change; in the dynamic, that is.

This changing — wavering — facet of our environment points to an implicitly *un*stable (virtual or real) condition: that of structures in a continual state of transition (in a constant, real or virtual, situation of replacement, transformation or fluctuation in its geometries) in accordance with its own *active* and *variable* nature and with its associable parameters of *latent mutability* and *transformation*.

Interaction of programmes and use understood by areas, objects and landscapes over a territory. METEOSAT, *Plan of winds.*

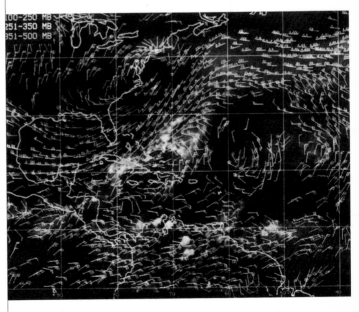

E

▲ Eastern Europe – Western Europe

[FP] Eastern Europe – Western Europe is an expression useful for recording phenoma whose scope is difficult to assimilate.

An illuastrative example (found by Isabel Cárdenas and Manuel Rubio – *BAU* 018) concerns an agreement the Soviet Union (like many others) reached with *Fiat*, one of the most powerful firms of Western Europe.

This agreement guaranteed construction, within two years, of an industrial city for half a million inhabitants and a 3x4 kilometres car production factory (*Fiat-Lada*). The city, given the name of Tagliatti (an Italian name for a location close to Samara, on the banks of the Volga), was completed on time and, according to plan, developed in twenty radial units (superblocks for 25,000 people) arranged in an octagonal network of 1x1 kilometer intersected by a single, fully-serviced, avenue in which hospitals, shops and recreational areas were located. All inhabitants of the city were moved from other parts of the Soviet Union, with the singular purpose of working directly or indirectly on the production of cars (they started with building the factory and the city in order to end up finally to become *Fiat* employees). Daily, workers were transported to their jobs in the factory by means of trams which connected from just outside their apartment blocks to the huge factory. All the families in the city possessed a car, although it could only be used on non-working days because carparks were not permitted. The fall of the Berlin Wall and the crisis of Soviet ideology, together with the collapse of the Eastern European economy, caused *Fiat* to reduce production in the facory until it was eventually completely closed.

The instant city of Tagliatti is today a truly antediluvian organism, a perfect simbiosi of two Europes which have completely vanished.

★ e-city

→ 'Metapolis'

[CO] The term 'e-city' identifies a broad spectrum of ideas and objectives that are grouped under the arc of a new meaning of the urban and a new ambition to redefine the city as we know it. The contemporaneity of these architectural investigations is found in their determination to favour an intense interchange between architecture and other spheres of knowledge, of action. The city is understood as a framework and situation that favours this active set of relationships.

E-city is built on the basis of the new relationship with space, new meanings of the public domain, multi-faceted questions about sustainability and capacity of the emergent technologies to re-inform our cities. XAVIER COSTA

E-city project,
organised by Metápolis,
Biennale di Venezia,
2000 (curator:
Xavier Costa, design:
Cristina Díaz Moreno,
Efrén García Grinda).

● ★ eco-

[MG]   See 'ecology, active (or bold).'

[MG]   **eco-chic**

Term coined by Anatxu Zabalbeascoa

(*El País*, 13 May 2000).

[co]   **ecomonumentality**

We have been accustomed to think of architecture according to the place, understanding that we could find on it keys to deal with the project. The forms of anchorage to place developed in the last decades are many; from those of phenomenological root —Anchoring is the title of a significant text of Steven Holl— to attitudes which start from the Frankfurt school —Frampton and his contextualism— going through the bergsonian influence in the work of Moneo or the structuralist one of the genius loci in Aldo Rossi.

But in the last years, we have been witness to a significant transference: every place is now understood as a landscape, either natural or artificial, and landscape is no longer that neutral background on which artificial architectonic objects, more or less vocationally sculptural, highlight, for being object of primary interest, focus of the attention of the architect.

Thus, the point of view changed, landscape loses its inertia and becomes an object of possible transformations; it is landscape what can be projected, that becomes artificial. At the same time, architecture begins the still vague processes of loss of its traditional definition in which it is obvious that a growing interest on incorporating a certain naturalist conditions both in geometric and component aspects and in construction aspects, searching for an environmental sensibility and a formal complexity which respond with precision to the new values of our society. The project is validated if it constructs a complete redescription of the place; it must suggest, above all, the invention of a topography.

Thus, with this double movement, from nature to project and from project to nature, an "ecomonumental" condition is saved that begins to make inexorably its way beyond any argument of opportunity, in a way that others wouldn't hesitate in calling "spirit of times" or "will of an era". How could we advance in this investigation, which projectual and ideological attitudes should take priority, which techniques would support better these objectives?

IÑAKI ÁBALOS & JUAN HERREROS

ÁBALOS & HERREROS, *Recycling plant for urban waste*, Valdemingómez (Madrid), 1999.

● eco-tech

[MG] See 'ecology, active (or bold)', 'nature' and 'naturartificial'.

1. How the air conditioning works

a. Winds
b. Collecting element
c. Sun's rays
d. Fresh air

e. Water surface
f. Latent cooling
g. Thermal stability
of the site (daily)

h. Movement of air inside
i. Thermal mattress
j. Energy retrieval
k. Hot air

l. Convection

a
b
c
a
c

A + B

SUMMER

d
g

c
i
C + D
k
j
c

WINTER

1

2. Sun heating

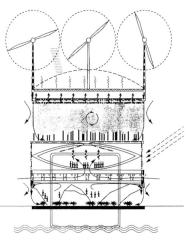

Windmills.

Air-mattress roof.
Water-vapour cooling.
Heat accumulator tank.
Electric light.
Air curtains and inside-air
recycling.
Floor heating recycling air
in the auditorium.
Occupant-generated heat/
Photovoltaic curtain.
Unit for natural treatment
of inside air.
Biomass of energy production.

Underground currents for cooling.

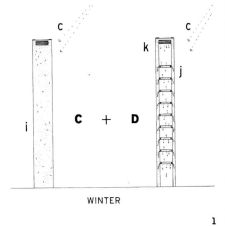

Circulation through wall

Circulation through floor

SUMMER

WINTER

Drift conduct
in case of
cold Trombe
wall

Automatically
regulated
shutters by
means of
a drill at the
Trombe wall

2

3

---

1. Cristina DÍAZ MORENO, Efrén GARCÍA GRINDA, Ángel JARAMILLO, *Temporary accommodation*, Parque Regional del Sureste (Madrid), 1997. 2. MVRDV, *The Netherlands Pavilion Expo 2000*, Hannover (Germany), 2000. 3. Jaume VALOR, Fidela FRUTOS, *House*, Vallvidrera (Barcelona), 1997.

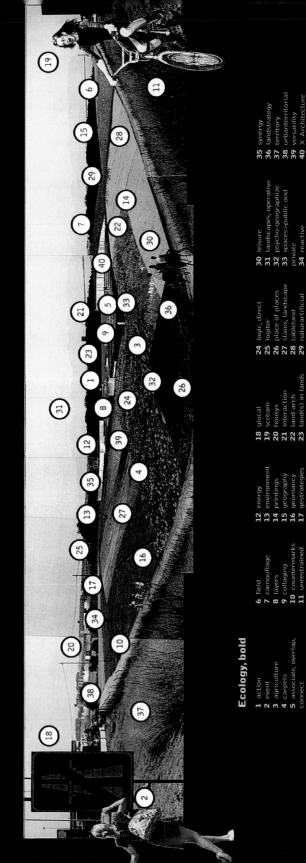

Ecology, bold

1 action
2 event
3 agriculture
4 carpets
5 associate, overlap, connect

6 field
7 camouflage
8 layers
9 collaging
10 countermarks
11 unrestrained (<un> factors)

12 energy
13 environment
14 printings
15 geography
16 geomancy
17 gestrategies

18 glocal
19 scream
20 housys
21 interaction
22 land arch
23 land(s) in lands

24 logic, direct
25 logiter
26 place of places
27 stains, landscape
28 tableland
29 naturartificial

30 leisure
31 landscapes, operative
32 psycho-geographize
33 spaces>public and private
34 reactive

35 synergy
36 landstrategy
37 territory
38 urbanterritorial
39 versatility
40 X-Architecture

● ★ ecology, active (or bold)

[MG] Instead of old nostalgic or pseudobucolic ecology (which freezes landscapes, territories and environments), we suggest a bold ecology; requalifying by virtue of being reformulating. Based no longer upon a timid, merely defensive – resistant – non-intervention, but rather upon a non-impositive, projective and qualifying – restimulating – intervention in synergy with the environment and, also, with technology. Not only possible, but (re)developmental as well.

An ecology in which sustainability is interaction.

In which nature is also artificial.

In which landscape is topography.

In which energy is information and technology is vehiclisation.

In which development is recycling and evolution is genetic.

In which environment is field.

In which to conserve implies always to intervene.

[co] Nature's reserves are, evidently, no longer simply a quantification of resource in quantitative terms, be it energy, air, water, animal or vegetable. Its true reserve is the genetic domain and its associated juridical debate. The attempt to institute a right of nature, a right of ecosystems, is illusory, not because it would involve reinstating the old Kantian debate about a humanist right, but because the right has been replaced by the patent – patents that the big global foodstuffs, chemical and pharmaceutical companies register in order to appropriate for themselves and commercialise nature's authentic capacity for production: its capacity for reproduction. The myth of green architecture, 'green worship,' no longer represents any other alternative but the return of an economic architecture, the return in strength of a demagogy of the 'low-tech.' It is impossible to believe in this eco-tecture founded on an economy of bio-mass. If the work of the architect is not to be reified as landscape planning or odd-jobbing, it can no longer content itself with the cynical position of mere acknowledgement.
FRÉDÉRIC MIGAYROU

[c] ## urban ecology

"*Urban ecology is based on the adoption of guidelines, standards and regulations of a legal, economic, organisational and technical nature, all centring on the unit "city-environment." The change of paradigm consists in recognising nature, endowing it with its own values. Nature thus ceases to be other, external, to become the very centre of thought, where the principal idea is recognition of this complex mesh of relationships. [...]*
The aim is to maximise the entropy recovered in the form of information (to make the urban system more efficient) and minimise the entropy exported to the environment, reducing the city's ecological footprint. The combination compact city/diverse city *is the systemic model which makes the best use of entropy, transforming it into organisation of the city, increasing its complexity. This allows a drastic reduction of the entropy exported to the environment. It is also the model which allows greatest reduction in the consumption of materials, energy, time and land, while providing regulatory and control mechanisms to endow the system with stability.*" (RUEDA, Salvador, "City models: basic indicators", *Quaderns* 225, 2000)

✖▲✛ economy

[VG] In the industrial economy, economic growth required physical growth. In the new information economy, this is no longer necessarily true. Cities ought to behave like chips, that are increasingly able to do more things in less space.

[FP] Architects today, to achieve results that economy demands, have to reject singular solutions and lean more towards complementary trends. This search makes us think, above all, about sustainability, intelligence in the exploitation of resources and in keeping a balance between ends and means.

In this way, we understand economics in the following three manners: of minimum material, durable material and intermediate material. In the first, we maximize material economies, including substituting a service for it. In the second, we reward durability and the absence of deterioration, in the widest sense. In the third, durability is immanent, but we are dealing with material which may have a very short life, but which is highly recyclable and convertible, thus making economies.

Nevertheless, it is necessary to stress that in all these cases an overall transformation of the system is necessary, as much in its sociological and organisational, as in its cultural components. Just as we operate in an economic system, we need that the complete production operation of this material (for example, the complete recycling operation) converts into *economy*. This can be achieved operating simultaneously over diverse planes and with diverse actors.

The project must think of definite products, official entities must be involved with policies which generate favourable playing terms and users must value and favour with their behaviour the inclusion of these three complimentary layers in the constitution of a physical reality.

[WM] An example of the new economy that is emerging between ethics, technological advances and a change of market is the case of chemical products. Chlorinated hydrocarbons are primarily sold as solvents, contributing to the quality of our life, but as well represent a health and environmental hazard. The economy that sold them and hence passed the hazards along to the buyer, and so on, is giving way to an economy that rents them.

Rent-a-Chemical is a marketing strategy which consists in renting chemical products, creating a loop of production, distribution, transport and recycling companies for these products. Dow Germany was the first to develop the idea, taking responsibility for the life of the latter: *an example of unlimited responsibility for a company's products*. Hence, molecules are not burnt, nor do they disappear, nor are they dumped: they are recycled and reused up to a hundred times. A further step was to offer grease-cleaning services instead of selling solvents.

Advanced architecture means setting your mind on this same course: *unlimited responsibility*, complete service, *rent-a-chemical*.

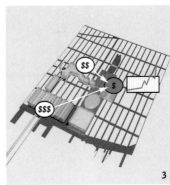

1. Rem KOOLHAAS (OMA), *World economy*. **2.** ASYMPTOTE Architecture, *NYSE, Virtual Trading Floor, Advanced Trading Floor, Operations Centre*, New York, 1999. **3.** UN STUDIO, *IFCCA Competition: Penn Station*, New York, 1999.

✘ education

→ 'act', 'action>critical',
'contract', 'criteria', 'fold',
'form', 'gaze> tactical
gaze', 'geometry',
'intelligence', 'interchange',
'knowledge', 'positioning'

[VG]

Educating consists in conveying logic, followed by processes, that lead to something. Order as a principle, and the result as the logical end of a process. To show the result of a creation without understanding its order is to deprive the spectator of the creative principle that, in turn, enables creation. Showing the result without understanding the process only produces a copy which, as in human reproduction, degenerates the species. Architecture, the good architecture we know and love, is creation. And it was promoted by generous persons (developers, the state, the church, princes, a housewife, etc.) who allowed creation.

Creators, those who had access to a degree of education, have the moral (and strategic) duty to disseminate their knowledge, their way of seeing and acting in the world.

The education of the users of architecture is a basic task of the architects themselves, comparable to the literature of writers and the music of musicians. Architecture and pleasure in quality spaces should be taught from a very early age.

★ egotecture

→ 'I/(my)self', 'space' [co] The conception of space cannot be made without conceiving the Self, the Ego. Vice versa, there will be no Self without an idea of space. Ever since Europe witnessed the birth of modern man in the Renaissance, architecture became entangled in the discourse of space. In their historical development, both terms reveal a mutual relationship. From discovery to description, from description to reflection, from reflection to speculation, at each stage of their respective further conceptualisation, space and self showed their symbiotic interconnection on historical road towards the full blown implementation of space as a arena for the ego and the ego as a contested space in our present culture.
OLE BOUMAN

● elastic

→ 'devices', 'extend', [MG] Elastic is a body, system, order, organisation, disposition or relationship
'extension', 'flexibility', (geometry or trajectory) that is deformable or alterable by the action of a
'fold', 'form', 'geometry', force, in order subsequently and perceptibly to recover its initial exten-
'inflatable', 'open', sion and configuration when the latter ceases.
'topological' By extension, elastic is that which can dynamically extend, lengthen, contract, bend, fold, (fold back on itself and/or unfold) without that implying
any rupture or fracture in its evolutionary logic.

[MG] *"The uncertain relationships between present and past behave like a piece of chewing gum, a masticatory. We think that any linear trajectory disappears, giving way to a sticky mass which finds its way around fixed obstacles but drags with it saliva and other bodies which are scattered around the mouth. Like when you chew a piece of gum which does not break up, take on the form of a straight line or fall to pieces; you bite down on it, stretch it, wind it round your tongue, roll it into a ball or even blow it up like a balloon. Basically, you can manipulate it at will thanks to its elasticity."*
(DEVESA, Ricardo, "Masticatories", *Quaderns* 223, 1999)

Elastomer material, in *Domus* 801, 1998.

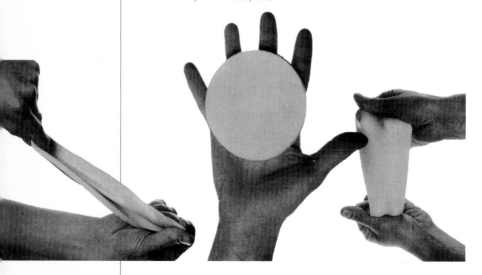

★ electric kool-aid acid test

→ 'event'

[co] "There will be rooms more conducive to dreams than any drug, and houses where one cannot help but love..." (Ivan Tcheglov)

The Electric Kool-Aid Acid Tests were events organised by Ken Kesey and the Merry Pranksters in California in the early 1960s. In these constructed situations, the Pranksters sought to make life-changing, world-transforming poetry happen through a blend of drugs (LSD and marijuana), psychedelic ritual, music, light and architecture.

The acid tests were held in warehouses and theatres temporarily adapted for the events. Kesey, nonetheless, had the idea of a building specially designed for the tests that would employ Fuller's geodesic dome, spiral ramps, foam-rubber floors, video projectors and sound systems embedded in the surfaces. The last of the Pranksters' acid tests was held in Watts, Los Angeles, just a few months after the 1965 riots. In keeping with the repressive tradition of the US government, the tests ended due to Kesey's problems with the police. JOSÉ PÉREZ DE LAMA

● ★ emergence

[MG] See 'AI, Artificial Intelligence.'

[c] "Marvin Minsky describes an emergent system as an inner world of highly anthropomorphized agents. Each agent has a limited point of view. Complexity of behaviour, emotion, and thought emerge from the interplay of their opposing views, from their interactions and negotiations. [...] Emergent AI depends on the way local interactions among decentralised components can lead to overall patterns. So does the working of ant colonies and the immune system, the pile-up of cars in a traffic jam, and the motion of a flock of birds. The result is a perfectly coordinated and graceful dance."

(TURKLE, Sherry, Life on the Screen. Identity in the Age of the Internet, New York: Touchstone, 1997)

+ ● emergency

→ 'advanced', 'architecture', 'arkitektor', 'self-urbanism'

[WM] **(professional)**

The most clamorous emergency of recent years in the field of architecture is that of a new professional. This new architect-manager of ideas and resources has to recycle his professional behaviour in an increasingly tertiarised world in which just about everybody is providing services, in which the technological advances in communication progressively eliminates intermediaries, and in which use and reuse (of goods, of products, of time, of frequencies, etc.) supplants the idea of consumption. We see one of the most profound crises in the area of professional fees. Rudolfo Livingston, author of Cirugía de Casas ("House Surgery"), posits this reflection:

"Let's imagine that we go to a clinic and ask the doctor:
'Doctor, how much do you charge for the visit?'
'Nothing, I only take a percentage of the operation.'
Would we trust the diagnosis of such a clinic?"

[MG] **(emergences)**
See 'bluntings.'

[MG] **(situation of)**
See 'catastrophe' and 'reversible.'

● (e)motion (moving)

→ 'extroversion:
<ex> factors of form'

[MG] " *This same acceleration of history, this same Promethean character, these ragged profiles, this presence of nature, this centrifugal condition, these same folds of the world, these swells and cloudinesses, this epic sense, these arabesques, this acceleration of an expanded tension, these scrolls of interlinked bodies, these zebra-striped textures, these dilated spaces, this torturous impulse of the ramified, this dazzle of luminous irradiations, this explosion of colour, this vague and spread out condition, this whirlwind of individual episodes. This substitution of composition with assembly. This exultant manifestation of the dynamical, as force and as emotion*".

(From CLAY, Jean, *Le romantisme*, Paris-Milan: Hachette, 1994. Translated from Spanish.)

Cable of optical fibre (D. Johnson/ Stock Market).

● enclaves

→ 'devices', 'ecology, active', 'emergency', 'geography', 'landscapes, operative', 'land(s) in lands', 'landstrategy', 'naturartificial', 'nature', 'place', 'terraces', 'topographies, operative'

[MG] See 'reliefs.'

Under the term 'enclaves' – or 'reliefs' – we include devices which are conceived as elevated landscapes – or enhancements of landscape; "eruptions of landscape within other landscapes."

Here the horizontal vocation of lands yields to a movement of extrusion. Reliefs or enclaves thus translate into movements of reappearance of the topographic towards increasingly explicit geographies in which the systematics of the device would yield as well to a more tactical nature. In effect, reliefs, as localised enclaves, are contingent decisions rather than organisational systems. They are specific folding movements meant to accommodate concentrated – "embedded" – programmes based upon a possible – and radicalised – hybridisation of landscape and architecture, but also of mesh-circuit and topography-refluence. In effect, the specificity of enclaves is that they tend to be operations of bastardisation among nodes (as foldbacks, as coilings) and lands (as folds, as platforms) and, accordingly, they underscore a certain singularity in the very notion of device – as a system.

1. Oasis, in VARIOUS AUTHORS, *Història Natural*, Barcelona: Ed. Océano-Institut Gallach, 1990, vol. 6.

2. John FORD, *Stagecoach*, 1939, in PARKINSON, David, *History of film*, London: Thames & Hudson, 1996.

3. Cristina DIAZ MORENO, Efrén GARCÍA GRINDA, *Tower in Las Vegas*, Corvera de Asturias (Spain), 2000, competition.

4. MVRDV, *Silicone Hill*, Stockholm (Sweden), 2000, competition for the Sweden Post Headquarters.

5. ARCHIKUBIK, *Bit landscapes*, 1999.

6. Vicente GUALLART, *Technological centre*, Puertollano (Ciudad Real, Spain), 1998.

7. ACTAR ARQUITECTURA (with Carlos SANT'ANA), *Hotel and development of the sea walk*, Calpe (Alicante, Spain), 2001.

●✖ energy

→ 'entropy',
'holograms', 'light',
'no-form', 'stimulus',
'synergy'

[MG] **energy as potency**

Energy is entropy. Activation of forces and efforts. Vehiclisation of (new) bits of information. Of interest are those processes, phenomena or situations capable of producing – or introducing – positive energy within the system. Energy as open – non-disciplined – (re)information rather than as linear progress. Energy as catalysation (and fuelling) of potentials.

Actions or constructions, manifestations or trajectories. Impulses: stimuli and triggers.

Always reactivations – and propulsions – of the environment.

[VG] **energy as an impulse**

Places have energy of their own, built up throughout their history by physical or spiritual phenomena. Any human action should amplify the energy of a place; they should be on the same wavelength. Any work of architecture should amplify the conditions of a place, give the place energy, never detract from it.

FOA, *International
Port Terminal*,
Yokohama (Japan),
1995-2000.

Cristina DÍAZ
MORENO, Efrén
GARCÍA GRINDA,
*G House, International
competition
"Goethe House"*
(2nd prize), Tokyo
(Japan), 1999.

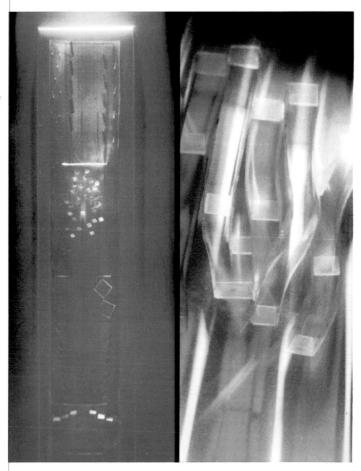

●◆ enjambements

→ 'a-couplings',
'ad-herence', 'antitypes',
'commensalism',
'hybrid', 'meldings',
'strategy'

[MG] Enjambements are meldings, couplings, supports or overlappings of one thing over another, produced among elements of similar potency.

If commensalism or parasitism implies difference or disproportion, enjambement implies similarity and simultaneity of sizes, forces, tensions and situations.

[FS] Enjambements are parasitic strategies of occupation of the existent, matching the old; amplifications and extensions would be mountings.

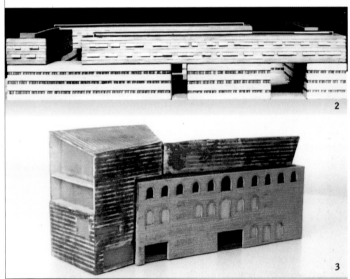

1. Turtles, in
Quo 55, april 2000.

2. ARANGUREN-
GALLEGOS,
Housing, Leganés
(Madrid), 1999.

3. Alberto MARTÍ-
NEZ CASTILLO,
Beatriz MATOS,
*The Woolstore:
rehabilitation of
an old store for
the headquarters
of a company,*
Dublin, 1999.

4. José Antonio
SOSA, Maria Luisa
GONZÁLEZ,
*Proposal for
rehabilitation of
Pérez Galdós
Theatre,* Las Palmas
de Gran Canaria
(Spain), 1997.

5. Fuensanta
NIETO, Enrique
SOBEJANO,
*Competition
submarines base*
(1st prize), Lorient
(France), 1999.

■ enlarged

[JM] Enlarged architecture is what unfolds along curved, convex and multi-directional vision, that sometimes literally traverses the spaces thus figured, but that other times proceeds simply to scan that which is only transparent or opaque. The devices destined to unfold these architectures start from a fish-eye, deformed and approximated, sclerotic and myopic, that try only to approximate a space by investigation, and to obtain, thanks to trial and error, the act of perforating places.

◆★ entropy

[FS] Energy is neither created or destroyed, it only transforms. The first principle of thermodynamics is well known. The second, less so. Entropy always grows. This means that systems pass from a state of great order to one less so. They move from the unstable to states of higher static possibility, up to a certain limit: a planar, stationary state. An arrow of inexorable time. Disorder for physicists is lack of complexity. Entropy measures laxity.

According to this physical principle, states tend towards the disappearance of gradients. On the other hand, in art each phase must seek new, more complex equilibriums. Architecture must put space in tension. Order in architecture is the equilibrium of counter-tensions. Gravity against lightness. Speed against consistency. Scale with size. Stability with dynamism. Equilibrim is unstable; it is deeper when it seems least probable, when entropy is at a minimum.

Architecture robs its surroundings of entropy because it is an open nonlinear system. When it distances itself from the point of equilibrium, it abandons its linearity. There are no logical prolongations. Discontinuities appear. Order is established by fluctuations. It jumps, and drags itself along new and unpredicted states.

[co] How to detect the state of a system? Entropy, like – or almost like – the concept of proliferation facilitates the state of relations of a system, its complexity, its possibilities of transformation, and how much and precisely how this system can establish new relations. It is, in fact, an index of complexity.
"*One of the fundamental concepts of classical physics was introduced into science by Rudolf Clausius. In macroscopic terms, entropy expresses capacity for the transformation of energy: the greater the entropy of a system, the less energy capable of undergoing transformation it contains.*" (*Diccionario soviético de filosofía*, Montevideo: Ediciones Pueblos Unidos, 1965, p. 142-143)
JOSÉ ALFONSO BALLESTEROS / LARRAITZ DE AZUMENDI

[co] Within the sphere of virtuality, transaction of value will be tied to organisational depth and the cost necessary to generate self-reproducing systems. The political ecology of hyper-structures will be measured in relation to the cost curtailed in the emergence of different levels of complexity. Entropy, formulated in terms of the second law of thermodynamics, is a mathematical expression of the amount of disorder in any system and as such it is an inverse expression of the amount of organisations within the universe. The shift from energy to information is now conceptualised as the capacity for algorithmic compression relative to the amount of random information present within any system. Therefore, the production of artificial beings and entities has a information-theoretic cost that is as real as energy and material costs. KARL S. CHU

★●■ environment

→ 'activation',
'environment', 'event',
'field', 'hyperiphery',
'unfolding'

[co] Environments are "completely integrated first reality and virtual worlds where the distinction between them cease to exist," Hani Rashid.
XAVIER COSTA

[MG] See 'field', 'context' and 'places.'
Environment is no longer only context (or at least a limited and limita-tive vision of the context), but rather definitively glocal milieu or environ: in the local it is place or, better said, field. In the global, scenario or, bet-ter said, reality (physical and virtual). An environment is a scenario of mul-tilayered crossing.

[co] An atmosphere constructs an ambient.
When the object is rejected in favour of the context.
Instead of formal and material stimuli, optical, auditive, tactile and orientative perceptive stimuli are sought in the space.
The spectator, instead of being located in front of the object, is now located with-in the object.
The spectator will find it necessary to participate in and explore the space that surrounds him and the objects located in it.
MARÍA LUISA GONZÁLEZ

[JM] **(milieu)**
Milieu (*unwelt*) calls, to a large extent, for the configuration of a frame: a place where order and disorder, void and chaos, can be discovered. Atmosphere, from the reading of chaos, would be the previous possibility of what could emerge or be configured. In effect, atmosphere is the frame of the pre-linguistic. The architectural project emerges in this frame; it is, thanks to this atmosphere, pre-linguistic and savage.
A place of previous states, atmosphere offers this interchange of all cre-ative origins.
Atmosphere – layer and bowl by and in which architecture unfolds, remains to be seen, holds onto, stretches, extends, in a continuity of forms and spaces through which it is difficult to separate one thing from another.
The principal consequence of this definition: any possibility of dual ideas between architecture and territory, and other similar things, is distanced, as much in use in the seventies as nowadays. The dictatorial relations be-tween architecture and landscape that put place and architecture along an axis, and with what paradoxically argued architecture's relation to histo-

Stan ALLEN,
Diagrams of field
conditions,
in VARIOUS
AUTHORS, *Fields,
the Berlage Cahiers 5,
95-96*, Rotterdam:
010 Publishers, 1996.

● ephemeral

→ 'amphibious',
'appropiation strategies',
'contract', 'ecology, active',
'fleeting', 'inflatable', 'in-out',
'in/unstable', 'lightness',
'nomadic', 'occupation
structures', 'provisional',
'scaffolding', 'tattoos', 'time',
'zapping'

[MG] See 'precarious(ly)', 'impermanences', 'reversible' and 'temporary.'
Ephemeral is an action or event whose duration is, in the first instance, a single day. By extension, ephemeral denotes brief, fleeting, impermanent or unstable extension, phenomenon, presence or creation: of short duration.

Cristine O'LOUGHLIN, *Blue trees*, Carré des Arts, Parc Floral, Paris, 1995.

●■ epitome

→ 'a-scalarity',
'extroversion: <ex>
factors of form', 'field',
'glocal', 'multilayered',
'projective', 'relationships,
transitive', 'trailers'

[MG] **(epitome, multiscalar)**

The contemporary project is conceived of, in certain cases, as an a-scalar synthesis of a definitively multiscalar city. An epitome is a concentrate of its own basic dynamics, but also a *transfer*: a movement in synergy with the place, but also capable, of causing a scalar jump towards other scenarios, beyond its boundaries.

This scalar jump between structures, in fact, underlies the definition of the dynamic processes considered here and, therefore, the contemporary nature of the idea of the city (as a more evident manifestation of such processes).

This makes it possible to imagine devices conceived of as virtual mechanisms of interscalar interchange between the local system and the superior meta-system (the city) produced through structural (and conceptual), informal (flexible organisations of space) orders, rather than through compositive desires intended to reshape fragmentarily reality.

Devices conceived of as virtual epitomes of the global system (abstract environment, evolutionary territory or city): specific syntheses, ultimately, of those basic (adaptable and operationalable) trajectories – and situations – that define their principal movements.

Such multiscalar epitomes become, "maps of action" (rather than metaphors) applicable to other (selected) maps of the city, thereby relat-

Reference: mixed
developments. Main idea:
growth. Key: complex for-
mations (buds, meldings).

Reference: structural
networks. Main idea:
net. Key: dynamic patterns
(sequences, wefts).

Reference: open spaces [JM]
Main idea: landscape.
Key: manipulated voids
(enclaves, lands).

ing themselves to those suggested by José Morales: "*We describe the ac-tion of "constructing" a map: to attempt to have the building speak not only of what it contains, or preferably, that speaking of the latter it should propose the intended summary of what happens outside, in the city [...], that it should bind the figures which might be contained within that city...*"
Multiscalar epitomes permit the establishment of a possible degree of res-onance between the open – diffuse – logic of the contemporary project and the diffuse – unfinished – structure of the city. This establishment is done by synthesising its bits of generic information – and situations – in a-scalar compressions capable of reactivating the same place in which they are in-scribed through scalar transfers – or jumps – pointing, then, to the move-ments of the contemporary city: to the mongrel configuration of its con-structed complexes (*mixed formations*) as a heterogeneous and hybrid manifestation of a multilayered volumetry; to the structuring capacity for the *infrastructures (networks)* as an event-articulating mechanism; and to the very idea of free space (the *landscape* but, also, the *void*) as a poten-tial space "in negative."
Multiscalar epitomes are spaces of *mixed formations*, of *structural net-works* and of *interstitial landscapes*; synthetical descriptors (and referents) of this new dimension of the city to which point to the projectual devices described here: formations-accumulations (sprouts and meldings) as con-structed deployments (or conglomerates); meshes-circuits (grids and nodes) as infrastructural foldbacks (or network links); and topographies-reflu-ences (lands and enclaves) as operative folds (or landscapes).
Tactical appropriations related directly to recursive components of the city (fills-links-voids, layers-networks-backgrounds, occupations-routes-dis-tancings, concentrations-connections-dilatations, points-lines-surfaces) as manifestations of combinatorial processes capable of yielding a-scalar iso-morphisms and a-essential hybridisations.

(epitomes of the city)

Certain recent projects rethink the relation between space and archi-tecture. Empty space "that type of nothingness where everything is" does not seem to be the final axis about which pivots the reflection of a pro-ject in general terms. // The formulation of what becomes space in ar-chitecture has more to do with the city and its events than with the dwelling itself; that place in which space is contained, and in a certain way, stabilized. // The city proposes the space of architecture from oth-er parameters. To open the way, resist, camouflage, are actions pho-tographed in much of the architecture of interest to us. Nothing more different than those static scenes creates the contemplative gaze, mod-erated by metaphor, as a means of obtaining form and the idea of space. // The city and the events that occur within it function as analogies from which one can rethink the space of architecture. Space, or better said, the landscape of the city, is now being used not as a space of represen-tation (theatricality, power, etc.) but as a place of presentation: move-ments, manifestations, and/or urban war.

● equipped façade (and wall)

→ 'component',
'construction, intelligent',
'equipped wall', 'housing',
'membrane', 'precision',
'skin', 'technique, the'

[MG] The party-wall is no longer a simple dividing line, but rather a "technical width," a "thickness wall," a transverse "equipped wall or partition." The new definition permits solutions based upon clear functional clusters. The façade is no longer a simple line of interior/exterior separation, but an effective support for services, a thick alveolar of equipped fills and voids which allow light and air to penetrate. Here, are housed the fixed elements of the system in order to free up the rest of the space, thus recovering the idea of a loft as a place of "all possibilities."

We should point out the growing importance of systems based upon semi-prefabricates (not a hard pre-creation, aimed at the repetition of complete cellular modules, but rather a tactical pre-creation, used in both the structure and in the definition of the installations) and fittings through the use of technical concentrations or, preferentially, of "equipped walls," which include complete installations and fittings able to favour manifold spatial combinations. We should also consider the progressive replacement of traditional heavy enclosures – based upon massive and dry wall systems – with more lightweight enclosures made with dry materials (metal sandwich or multilayered panels of wood derivatives, and the possible growing incorporation of composites based upon cement, polycarbonates and/or fibres, etc.). Accordingly, the treatment of the façade as a "double-filter" layer with enclosure and fittings on its inner face and the recovery of an interior/exterior "width of transition" (protected with shutters, panels or sliding blinds) allows for the incorporation of a lightweight membrane on the exterior intended to replace the traditional edificial heaviness and aggressiveness – solid walls perforated by small holes – with an evanescent and less aggressive image in the landscape.

Technical skins, eloquent and communicative, rather than perforated walls. Skins colonised by functional elements, capable of housing installations and services; but also capable of supporting mediating incorporations: spots, eruptions, graphics, manipulations; colourful motifs and fantasies aimed at transforming the building into an interface between the individual and his or her environment.

ACTAR
ARQUITECTURA,
Rail system housing,
Aubervillers, Paris,
1996.

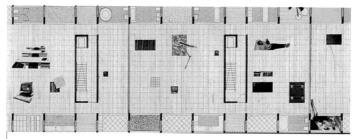

NEUTELINGS-
WALL-DE GEYTER-
ROODBEEN,
*Habitat Type-
Competition H/C,*
Barcelona, 1990.

● equipped wall

[MG] See 'equipped façade (and wall).'

+ eraser

→ 'action>critical',
'act-n', 'areas of impunity',
'memory'

[WM] See 'eraserhead.'

+ eraserhead

→ 'action>critical',
'act-n', 'areas of impunity'

[WM] See 'memory.'

[WM] "*The problem is never how to get new, innovative thoughts into your head, but how to get the old ones out.*"
Dee Hock, creator of Visa.
"*You can't live without an eraser.*"
Gregory Bateson

■ error

→ 'chance', 'chaos'

[JM] One can detect architectures that work with what one can call "the acceptance of error."
There are not latent decisions – based on research and prefixed investigations – accepted beforehand, but a comparative grade over the base of causalities that occur in a project. Thanks to multiple operations, the process of assembly creates the work. Of course, proximity or sintony with what were some of the works of the avant-garde (Dada, Surrealism, etc.) is coincidental. Thus, architecture of the "exquisite corpse" is not driven by systematic or structural projects. Architecture imposes its distinct work.

● erudition

→ 'allegory', 'criticism',
'history'

[MG] See 'neoclassical.'
Erudition is sometimes a tactical – selective – literacy that favours innovation: the hope for the new and the action for the new. That is to say, it permits "invention" without query.
Sometimes, erudition – not knowledge – is, above all, the accumulation of references and an excuse for mistrust and resistance.
The prudence of the note.
We replace erudition with curiosity. Reference with recording.

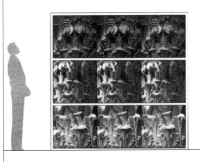

Martín LEJARRAGA,
Cervecería principal,
Cartagena (Spain), 1998.

● ✖ España

[MG] Accentuated singularity.

[MG] Spain is a field of pixels. Individual and interlinked.

A patchwork of landscapes. All of them diverse and all of them related/relationable. All of them autonomous and – potentially – interactive. Different and "networked." A many-sided and multifaceted landscape.

Spain is a multilayered geography. A meta-real territory with manifold virtual territories. It is a field of vibrations to explore. A kaleidoscope of opportunities to (re)discover and develop. A breeding ground of particularities.

Spain is not a single entity, nor is it a single model. It is a heterogeneous whole. It can evolve or regress. Expand or retract.

Its capacity for innovation – its advanced development – can only come of an opting for intercommunication and glocal information, for tactical contract between energies and individual and collective (not common) components, for a connected and focused – identified – identity of its most specific assets.

Developing the differences – the peculiarities and the specialities – but interlinking the results and interchanges.

[VG] Spain is (a) multinational.

VARIOUS AUTHORS,
*Met 2.0. Barcelona
Metápolis*, Barcelona:
Produccines
NewMedia, 2000.

[i] p. 204-205

★◆ essay

→ 'action>critical',
'eye', 'innovation',
'name'

[CO] The essay imagines its object de-centred, hypothetical, ruled by uncertain logic, blurry, indeterminate: its reading is always by approximation. It shakes of the illusion of a simple model, logical at the outset, pre-established, ruled by an inexorable necessity or will.

The essay is precisely distinguished by its provisional wait, in these never happening times, of the possible, or at least, of the desired. And when it looks to the relatively far past, it is not for this that it abandons the irony that rules its critical intention.

FRANCISCO JARAUTA

[FS] Characteristics of the essay: errant, loitering of meanings, delayed or oblique approximations, personal inventions, provocateur in all its senses, emancipation of the particular in light of the totality, intention to manage the totality through the parts, Essays embody a lack of intention to resolve, but to manage incomplete, ironic writing.

◆● essayist knowledge

→ 'American
pragmatism',
'architecture',
'name', 'trip'

See 'essay.' Essayist knowledge is errant knowledge, transversal, tangential, ironic, inventive of a certain material, science, etc. A knowing essayist does not pretend to formulate a discipline, but a classification; s/he does not try to conclude, but relate.

Knowledge is intuitive before being deductive, scientific at the same time as being poetic. It is produced by successive approximation, trying, more that fixating on the object, to delineate its circuit.

[MG] See 'transversality.'

+estate car

[WM] See 'take-away homes,' 'container,' '*Chrysler Voyager*,' '*Smart*.'

■ ● ★ event

→ 'arches of
development',
'creation', 'environment',
'immanence', 'menus',
'place of places',
'simultaneity>
successive-simultaneous',
'territory'

[JM] Gilles Deleuze describes how events are presented and what characterises
them: "The mode of the event is problematic. One should not say that there
are problematic events, but rather that events exclusively concern problems
and define their conditions."

The project that begins from events, originates in the realm of singularities.
These singularities are as spatial as temporal, giving capacity to a relation
that can be called contractual with history, bound with the contemporary,
and open in a conception of the past that becomes known in the present.

In terms of the singular relation between events and space, that is to say,
with our surroundings and circumstance, it allows us a vision of a project
as a continuity, extending into a reality that hardly differentiates tempo-
ralities and homogeneously values existent architectures almost as if they
were textures. Landscapes.

[MG] We often confuse event and occurrence.
Occurrence is what occurs, event is what comes about.
Although both situations reveal temporal phenomena – they happen – the
occurrence is an episodic, junctural, occasionally conflictive result.
The event, on the other hand, forms part of a process and, at same time,
appears as something emotive and unforeseen. Singular in its particularness. 'Projective.' Not so much exceptional – unique – as exciting; excited
and causing excitement. Like a wave. Expansive and extensive. A local in-
cident of global repercussion: special (specific) and general (generic) and
symptomatic. Case and class at the same time.

[co] The scan of the city indicates a straight horizontal line. Nothing's happening.
/ Suddenly the line shows a peak, a rising input. / An event has just been detected. / An event in architecture is like a beat in the heart. / If it doesn't happen, we're in bad shape. / But they warn us: A. Artaud, S. Eisenstein, B. Tchumi.
ENRIC RUIZ-GELI

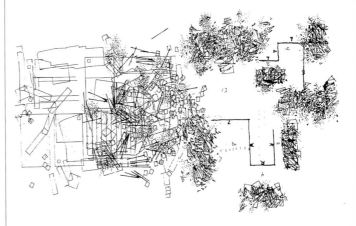

The simulations play
out possible large
scale theatrical events.
Barry LE VA,
*Aluminium and felt
with glass throws*,
1967.

sectors

matrix

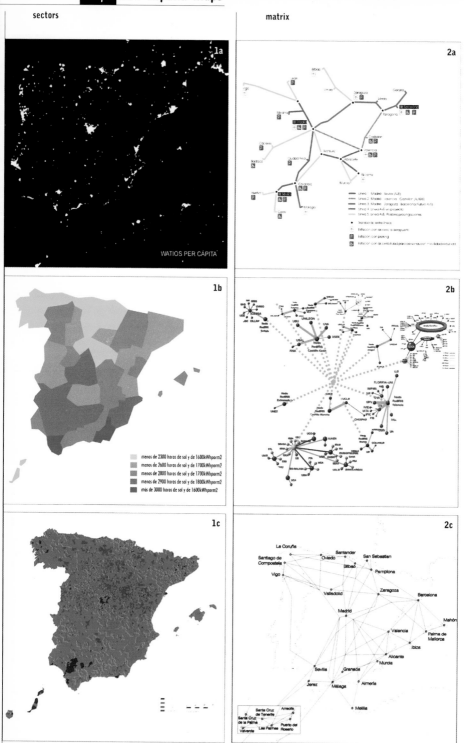

Sectors: **1a.** UHF, Map of watts per capita, 2000. **1b.** UHF, Areas of opportunity for solar energy reception, 2000. **1c.** UHF, Map of singles, 2000. **Matrix: 2a.** UHF, Map of high speed underground, 2000. **2b.** UHF, Map Red Iris, 2000. **2c.** UHF, Map of aerial routes, 2000.

elastic

peaks

3a

4a

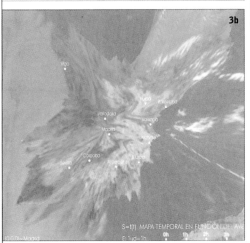

3b

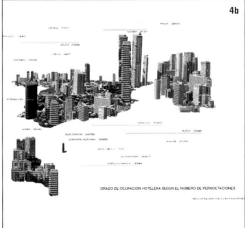

4b

3c

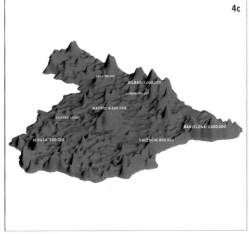

4c

Elastic: 3a. UHF, Per capita income, 2000. **3b.** UHF, Temporary map. Impact of AVE (high-speed train), 2000. **3c.** UHF, Map of immigrants in Spain, 2000. **Peaks: 4a.** UHF, Topography of non-recycled waste, 2000. **4b.** UHF, Hotel occupation, 2000. **4c.** Distribution of population, in MVRDV, *Costa Ibérica*, Barcelona: ACTAR, 1999.

★ evolution

[co] See 'progress,' 'innovation,' 'theory,' 'order,' 'developing,' 'research,' 'evolutionary,' etc.

Change. Change is good (Louis Rossetto, Wired Magazine, 1998).

Transformation. Gradual passage from one state to another, as in a hypothesis that seeks to explain phenomena as successive transformations of an original reality.

Evolution requires a situation of imbalance, self-organising properties and a system with capacity for order in virtue of its material properties.

Movement. Militarily speaking, change of formation – something very closely linked with genomics, where control through the order of the genes that make up a chain permit dominance of the final function of a functional being – of troops or ships, for defensive or offensive ends.

As Charles Darwin explained in his Theory of Evolution (1859), the origin and transformation of living organisms is the product of two principles: selection and chance. The former regulates the variability of the random recombination and mutation of genes (capacity to produce copies of themselves, reproduction as a mechanism for the modernising of their variants, the necessary interaction with the environment) with one objective: to survive and produce subsequent copies. Evolutionary phenomena that are problematic for the theory: origin of life (beginning of evolution), genetics of development (who imposes the rules of how to evolve) and macroevolution (where r-evolution emerges).

Evolution as a series of revolutions, or vice versa. Now, in the 21st century, we are living the Digital Revolution, which bears little relation to the Industrial Revolution of the 20th century. Lasting peace has meant a profound global transformation and today's heroes are different. Where once they were politicians and generals, they are now creators and professionals.

IGNASI PÉREZ ARNAL

Processes of
energy exchange, in *AD*
vol 67
No 9/10, 1997.

● evolutionary

[MG] Systems, actions or processes capable of evolving are evolutionaty.

That is to say, the evolutionary is capable of growing and developing, mutating and transforming, altering, varying, deforming and/or being influenced through codes or generic internal basic rules, precise and flexible, at once determinate and indeterminate, and through bits of specific external information, fortuitous and contingent, at once foreseen and unforeseen.

→ 'animation', 'avatar',
'cultivations', 'chains',
'devices', 'dispositions',
'dynamism', 'genetics'
'genetics of form',
'mutation', 'open',
'process', 'progress',
'sequences', 'system',
'time'

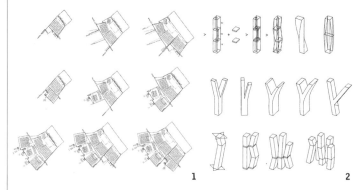

1

2

1. S&Aa (SORIANO-PALACIOS), *Competition for auditorium and conference centre,* Pamplona (Navarra, Spain), 1998. **2.** MVRDV, *Donau City (Kissing Towers),* Viena, 2002, Competition 2nd Prize.

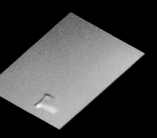
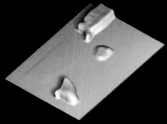
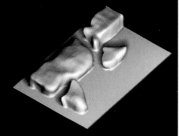

Dominique JAKOB, Brendan MACFARLANE,
Restaurant Le Georges, Centre Pompidou, Paris, 2000.

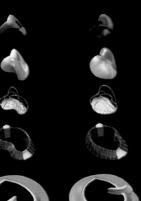
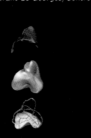
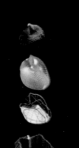
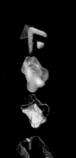
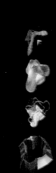
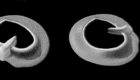
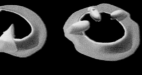

Greg LYNN, *Embryological House*, 2000, project.

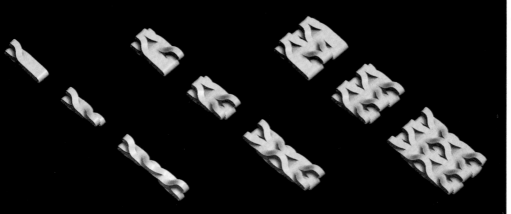

FOA, *Virtual House*, 1997.

● excavations

[MG]   See 'layers,' 'sub-over strata,' 'immersed' and 'trenches.'

◆ ex-jection

→ 'extend', 'extroversion': [FS]   To come out of oneself. To take one thing out of another. As opposed to
<ex> factors of form', injection, thoughts are expelled from an active and productive body, ac-
'foreignness', 'graft', quiring life and self-existence.// The theft of oneself.// The inclusion of
'no-form', 'strategy' thoughts on the body's exterior.// By extension, the international ex-jec-
tionist is characterised by extracting ideas that can seem unproductive or
dead by trying independently to form new meanings or relations.// A project is an ex-jection. Exjections of a project become new projects. Ex-jection is different from other generative processes in that there is no continuity between the idea inside and the new thought outside.// A collection
of books the born from the journal *Fisuras*. Its numbering by letters limits
the size of the collection.

■● experience

→ 'allegory', [JM]   "*Experience is the opposite of a project: I attain experience as opposed to*
'advanced> advanced *the project that I had to do...*"
architecture', 'erudition',
'ideas', 'innovation', "*Design is the work of a slave, it is work, and the work of someone who*
'memory' *does not enjoy its benefit. In art, we make architecture of experience in*
the instant of desire."

[MG]   Experience is an asset, not a value.
It should support, not impose itself upon, innovation.

★ experimental architecture

→ 'open' [co]   All architecture that refuses to accept canons or codes is experimental. This does
not mean that such architecture has no rules, only that it seeks to stretch and even
break such constrictions in order to achieve its own constructions. Such an architecture seeks to be open; as Wolf Prix has put it, "An open architecture is of
the open space, the open mind, the open eye, the open heart." The history of experimental architecture goes back at least to the Enlightenment, when the role of
1. Dennis DOLLENS, the architect became ambivalent: at the same time servant of the state, he (nev-
The TumbleTruss er she) was also part of the intellectual force questioning the legitimacy of au-
Project, 2001. thority. The notion of experimentation was given contradictory impulses by 19th
Physical model century scientific revolutions and by art making practices of the 20th century.
constructed of tumble- Experimental architecture has remained in an ambivalent, resolutely un-produc-
weed (branches) tive position. It values the critical act over construction, and often engages in
and paper, Rhino 3D unbuilding rather than building. AARON BETSKY
drawing, and STL
model (Laser
Reproductions)
made from the Rhino
drawing.

2. Vicente
SARRABLO, Héctor
JALA, ephemeral roof
for *Hispalyt* stand
in *Construmat* 2001,
Barcelona.

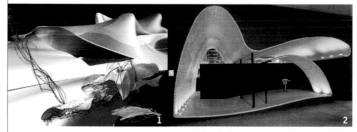

▲ ● expression

→ 'anonymous',
'dynamism', 'extroversion:
<ex> factors of form',
'stimulus', 'unrestrained
(<un>factors)'

[FP] In summary of wishes or searches for our final proposals, it is clear that no interest exists for preserving or intensifying the meaningful character of architecture, one of the most canonical aspects of its past disciplined course. The significant condition of works, the use of its own framework as a spoken stamp, is not a problem to be verified or questioned.

Nevertheless, in the last few decades, this condition has constituted a motive for ideological confrontation, of placing in the conception not only of architecture, but the site as a setting trusting in its capacity to develop a structured language. This demonstrative function, anaesthatized today, comes face-to-face with the ease of communication with which other types of messages are conveyed. Architecture, at best, ends up – fleetingly, in the distance – in parallel with other consumable images.

Can we think that to solve each architectural project we will not find a strict problem of language? We should oscillate between two poles (or bet on whatever intermediate position): the"dictated action," where importance of the capacity for transmission doesn't exist and expression is not established in the moment of its conception, but is left at the expense of external processes; and at the opposite pole, the "spoken message," where the essence of the architectural-message is based upon the brilliance of the expressed, without depending on formalisation or structuring to acquire value.

It's true that the affirmation of autonomy of significance is a verified step in semiology, but it is no less true that architecture has been questioned and can repeat its self-questioning about its double function: as construction (in its highest sense) and as an expression of this construction. Autonomy moves towards becoming a characteristic of form in which all kinds of information can be conveyed.

Therefore, it is not difficult, for other meanings to be superimposed on architecture and to cancel out its meaningful condition. We must reconstruct syntax in a manner which is now not as it has always been, since "the place" or "the city" have stopped being the principal settings for human beings. We must find a more specific way to show how to articulate the combination of material and potential parameters with which to construct the buildings we imagine. We propose to enquire into the sense and validity of expressive thinking, in the search for instruments and justification, assuming, on the one hand, the diffused panorama of these times and, on the other hand, the progressive increase of interference from other spheres of knowledge.

[MG] **(and expressiveness)**

We seek an expressive, rather than expressionist architecture: it is not a matter of forcing the gesture, but rather of stating the action.

An architecture aimed at evidencing a flexible (elastic), changing logic that articulates it (its topology) and projecting other situations beyond their own juncture. An expressive – eloquent and empathic – architecture. Transmissive and transferring. An expressive architecture that expresses itself through relationships, rather than through language.

■ extend

[JM] Architecture traps the exterior to discover interior possibilities, to investigate possibilities of the room, of dwelling. Without dealing with other constrictions that are not those of actual movement, to investigate sites and spaces, this architecture extends and grasps situations – the events that it encounters. Removed from the limitations of technique and its properties, it thus suggests field sites for engineers and their rationality. Architecture changes size to enlarge itself towards changing objectives, mutable spaces, convertible, reversible, deserters. Singular.

1. José MORALES, Juan GONZÁLEZ, *International competition for the enlargement of Prado Museum*, Madrid, 1998. **2.** Enric MIRALLES & Benedetta TAGLIABUE, *Edimburgh Parliament*, Scotland, 1998-. **3.** Antonio SANMARTÍN, Manuel ORTIZ, J.M. VALERO, *Day centre, Home for the Elderly and rehabilitation of the old Convent of the Capuchin Nuns*, Huesca (Spain), 1999.

● extensible-compressible (systole-diastole)

[MG] Extensible-compressible is elastic and/or flexible movement of expansion and reduction. Spontaneous, or provoked, movement of tactical dilatation and contraction. Like the contemporary city, landscape, territory or environment of systole and diastole.

[MG] *"What a curious feeling!" said Alice; "I must be shutting up like a telescope." [...] "Curiouser and curiouser!" cried Alice (she was so much surprised, that for the moment she quite forgot how to speak good English); "now I'm opening out like the largest telescope that ever was!""*
(CARROLL, Lewis, *Alice in Wonderland*, London: New Orchard, 1990)

Slipping artificial landscape
Alberto MARTÍNEZ CASTILLO, Beatriz MATOS, *Extensible garden roof for the municipal sports complex*, León (Spain), 1999.

■● extension

→ 'devices', 'dispositions',
'dissolved architecture',
'relationships, transitive',
'stains, ink', 'unfolding'

[JM] **(plurality of events)**

Extension speaks of diversity, of contact with the multiplicity that constitutes place. It also suggests containing the plurality of spatial events in accordance with the diversity that surrounds us. Extension proposes, as a base of design, the relations without canonic affirmations or academic budgets. Closest to this notion is what ecology permanently demands of us: to make a consensus of the different, what is disparate, distinct, to gain equilibrium. An equilibrated extension.

[MG] **(extension-excitation: form)**

The idea of open form alludes to an expansive nature: relaxed (uninhibited), unsettled (loose) but, above all, dynamic (subject to real or virtual movements). Form is engendered through an evolutionary logic: no longer through a compositive (episodic) design, but rather through a dispositional process, as generic (abstract) as it is generative (fertile) and generous (flexible). Thus, shape appears as an animated trajectory, possibly frozen in a precise instant – an x-shape – but virtually "excited," extended within and towards other instants.

●extroversion: <ex> factors of form

→ 'action', 'act-n',
'anonymous', 'dynamism',
'expression', 'form',
'indiscipline', 'joy
(alegría)', 'no-form',
'open', 'reactive',
'tattoos', 'unrestrained
(<un>factors)'

[MG] The extroversion factor translates a *dynamic* interpretation of the idea of shape: a shape that we call *extrovert* for its at once nervous and vehicular character, it explains and clarifies the processes and the movements that make it up and at the same time favours interactions and connections, local and global, with those events in which it is inscribed).

We refer not to the notion of shape as classical composition or as modern position – closed figuration or design – but rather as open disposition: specific – and latently unfinished – a combination of possible, virtually dynamical and indeterminate movements.

This overcoming of the idea of boundary holds a promise (real or virtual) of latent change in the generated – unsettled and impulsive – trajectory itself: a "towards" vector; a "beyond" vector – an extroversion – present in the a-scalar definition of most fractal geometries, but also in the same open devices that we here seek to describe.

Beyond context (referring to other possible places). Beyond boundaries (referring to other possible silhouettes). Beyond codes (referring to other possible logics). This would be a "towards" shape. A more *ex*trovert – plural – idea of shape: expansive, permeable and relational; by virtue of being direct (and uninhibited); by virtue of being "friendly" (and eloquent); by virtue of being complicit (synergetic) and mobilising (conveying). A shape capable of ensuring an agreement with the place and, at the same time, *trans*ferring – and transferring itself – beyond boundaries, towards other potential situations. A shape which is excentric (and extrinsic); expectant (and expansive); extended (and exceptive); expeditive (and exauditive). Explicit (and exultant). Exteriorised (and expressive). A new, more excited – extrovert, precisely – shape.

★ extruded architecture

→ 'frame-', 'plastic', 'skeleton', 'technique, the'

[CO] Extrusion is a well-known industrial production system where fused metal goes endless through a profiled mouth. It was Reima and Raili Pietila who built a real extruded building. Their church in Tempere, Finland was designed with independent walls situated on the perimeter. Extrusion of a building can be done either with external or internal partitions. The extrusion comes from a combination of frameworks and uses the slip-form construction technique. With this system it is possible to reach the height of 40 metres in one week. Normally, construction is done in cast concrete, but it is also possible to pour low point fusion plastics doing adequately resistant composites. It is very important that the walls have stable profiles, able to stand without any other constructive elements. Buildings made by this technique, theoretically have no height limits, two hundred or three hundred metres is easily possible.

SALVADOR PÉREZ ARROYO

S. PÉREZ ARROYO
& E. HURTADO
(with F. RÍO DURAN),
Housing, San Fermín
(Spain), 2001.

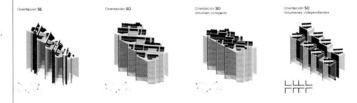

★ extrusion

→ 'Detroit'

[CO] Particlarly in rapidly urbanizing cities, the autocad command – extrude – has been literally transposed to the production of hyper-dense, high-rise structures. Profit has replaced aesthetic principles and endless solids of non-contextual value relentlessly invade the territory. Homogeneity of the vertical repetition of efficient floor plates contrasts sharply with the indigenous environment. Form follows finance.

KELLY SHANNON / LAURA VESCINA

Extruded housing
towers in Hong-Kong.

■ ● ★ eye

→ 'action>critical',
'cephalia', 'criteria',
'gaze> tactical gaze'

[JM] Perhaps we owe to modernity (more than to any other time period), the construction of a culture of the eye, of the image. The glance became the principal substance of modernity, in the construction of its culture. The investigation of Modernity is to a certain extent, redundant, because it results in the cacophony of the glance of the investigator and the other that built the culture between the wars. It is modernity that began to call for the inquiry around the constructive eye: the eye not only constructs; we give it whatever possibility of auscultation and investigation, for it is vision that dominates a person. Regis Debray has described it best: "The image does not exist in itself: its status and powers vary with technical revolutions and the change in collective beliefs. And, nonetheless, the image has always dominated man, though the Western eye has a history and every epoch its unconscious visuality. Our glance was magic before artistic."

[MG] See 'cyclops.'

[co] Cities are experienced in terms of images. Visitors bathe in images before going anywhere – scrutinizing guidebooks, websites, business brochures, videos, airline magazines, friends' snapshots, and so on – then project these images onto the place, trying to match what they see to what they expected to see. And what is seen is completely shaped by what is expected. Physical form is at best a prop for launching or modulating streams of images.

The challenge is to produce ways of looking at the world that comfort by giving the viewer a sense of location and visual images that reconcile the simultaneous transformations of the form of the city and the way that is experienced. New images are needed to deal with the disorienting effects of seeing the city from the new networks of communication and seeing those networks in the city. The eye in the fast moving car is a new eye. The city it sees is not the same city.
MARK WIGLEY

● eye, virtual

[MG] See 'a-scalarity,' 'cyberspace,' 'fractal,' 'naturartificial' and 'virtual.'

b&k+, *Telematische-landschaft*,
project for Expo
2000, Hannover
(Germany), 2000.

F

+ F111

→ 'camouflage',
'form', 'no-form',
'strategy', 'tactic'

[WM] The most striking thing about of the design of invisible airplanes is a radical change of direction. The first was shaped like a stingray, a design dominated by the spline; curvy, sinuous, continuous, suave.

The aerial-fish shape, without edges, presupposed its function: to avoid radar detection.

However, the second version is the opposite: a perfect right-angle shape creating a highly angular profile. It is the predominance of the setsquare, of the edge jagged, discontinuous, sharp-edged.

Interestingly, we might conclude that the shape follows neither function, nor structure, but strategy. It is more or less as if the shape followed only the communications engineers (generals).

1. Manuel J. FEO, Juan RAMÍREZ GUEDES (TWA, TWICE ARCHITECTURE), *Eyeliners: proposal for Chil walk*, Las Palmas de Gran Canaria (Spain), 1999. 2. Lockheed F117 Stealth Fighter, 1977, in FUTURE SYSTEMS, *For inspiration only*, London: Academy Editions, 1996. 3. F-117A Stealth Fighter, in *AD* vol 67 No 9/10, 1997.

★ fabrications

[CO] Over the course of our century, the discourse on architecture has often coincided with a discourse on spatiality. From a perspective which tends towards abstraction and immateriality, the job of the architect has been understood as a process of manipulating opaque and heavy materials, of orchestrating complex programmes and productive processes in order to achieve space, a sublime distillation based upon the crude materiality of the elements that define it. Space has often been understood as an immaterial, invisible, intangible entity which can only be enclosed and which is shaped through the experience of architecture.

Designing manufactures allows us to posit an investigation of the exhibitive act of architecture and of its processes within the framework of a public museum space.

XAVIER COSTA

● facet(s)

[MG] "n. 1. one of the small, polished plane surfaces of a cut gem. 2. a similar surface cut on a fragment of rock by the action of water, windblown sand, etc. 3. aspect; phase. 4. Archit. any of the faces of a column cut in a polygonal form. 5. Zool. one of the corneal lenses of a compound arthropod eye." (Webster's Encyclopedic Unabridged Dictionary of the English Language)

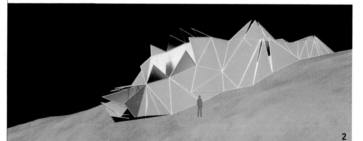

1. Banlieues Bleues, headquarters and music complex, Pantin (France), 2003 (completion).

2. JAKOB + MACFARLANE, H House, Corse (Italy), 2002.

3. Vicente GUALLART, Multifunctional centre, Denia (Spain).

●fatuous fires (feux follets)

[MG] *Feux follets* are flames and lights that appear to wander through the air, at a short distance from the ground, produced by chemical emanations.

They recall spectral figures or evanescent spirits, and they move about without fixed or predetermined order, following trajectories of casual routing, as unforeseeable as they are fluctuant.

Lighting transformations and occurrences.

1. Enric RUIZ-GELI, *FFF: Fireworks Figueres St. Ferran*, Figueres (Girona, Spain), 1998. 2. Toni GIRONÈS, *Installation for "Temps de flors"*, Girona (Spain), 1999. 3. Odile DECQ-Benoît CORNETTE, *Highway management centre*, Nanterre (France), 1993.

◆★●▲ fear

→ 'audacity', 'ideas',
'indiscipline', 'memory',
'threat', 'tracing'

[FS]

Peter HYAMS, *Timecop*,
Universal Pictures, 1994.

Afraid, one can not function. If we fear, we can not build. Today there is no security, even though, anyway, it is better that way. Anguish is hidden in uncertainty of the result, in ignorance of the goal, in social acceptance of forms, and in the lack of confidence about our calculations. Asking questions does not mean lack of security. One must risk being wrong. Fear paralyses. What is the risk? What is the damage? Loneliness, criticism, equivocation, ignorance, impoliteness, emptiness. Every decision has a political, social, environmental, cultural, architectural idea behind it. We can not elude our responsibility. One must bet every minute on something and with self confidence. The architect's dream is to look for unusual solutions. Being intrepid is unnecessary. History produces fear. The danger is in thinking about other architects. Imagination takes chance. The dream of experience produces conventional monsters, and anyway, does not get rid of fear. If we were afraid, we would even dare read? If we are afraid, our dreams disappear.

[co] Cities aren't cities anymore, and therefore architects can no longer be architects. We could ask architects to stop crying about the city, demanding that they bravely embrace the essential indeterminism, instability, immateriality, ephemerality, gaps, confusion and strangeness of urban life. We could call for new forms of practice that celebrate, rather than resist, disorganisation. Digital disorder and overload could become the role model – every architect turned into a surfer, riding rather than resisting the flows. But this new form of heroism would too quickly bury the specific expertise of the architect. Indeed, it would erase the figure of the architect completely. Architecture is primarily a form of resistance. Architectural discourse is always threatened by the city. It is built on fear, and even expert fear.
MARK WIGLEY

[MG] "*Pain is to health what hunger is to nutrition, thirst to drink, libido to reproduction, fear to safety or curiosity to knowledge.*"
(WAGENSBERG, Jorge, *Si la naturaleza es la respuesta, ¿cuál era la pregunta?*, Barcelona: Tusquets, 2002)
We even would add "risk to audacity".

[MG] See 'audacity.'

[FP] **fear and fair play**
Fair play implies unconcern. It implies taking the myth out of effort and converts large-scale confrontation into something accesible. Fair Play is understood here as cheek, a combination of rigour and fun, of drama and joy. We can play fair because we can be collective. So we are not speaking about Fair Play with regard to respect for the opponent, whom everyone wants to beat. We are speaking about risk, ignoring everything that is not a new achievement.

[MG] See 'unrestrained (<un>factors).'

◆ felt

[FS]

*"A fabric presents, in principle, a certain number of characteristics that permit us to define it as a striated space. First, it is constituted by two perpendicular elements: in the simplest case the horizontal and the vertical yarns, which intertwine. Second, the two elements don't have the same function; the vertical element is fixed while the horizontal is passing above and beneath the fixed. Third, a striated space is necessarily delimited, closed on at least one side: the fabric can be infinite in length, but not in width, which is determined by the frame of the warp; the need for coming and going implies a closed space (and circular and cylindrical figures are also closed). Finally, this sort of space necessarily presents a top and a bottom. [...]
Well, among flexible solid products there is felt, which works in entirely different manner, like an anti-fabric. Felt implies no separation of threads, no intertwining, only an entanglement of fibres obtained by applying pressure (for example, by rolling the block of fibres back and forth). What becomes entangled are the microscales of the fibres. An "aggregate of intrication" of this kind is in no way homogeneous: it is nevertheless smooth, and contrasts point by point with the space of the fabric (it is inherently infinite, open and unlimited in every direction; it has neither top nor bottom, nor centre; it does not assign fixed and mobile elements but rather distributes a continuous variation)."* (Paraphrasing DELEUZE, Gilles; GUATTARI, Felix, *A Thousand Plateaus: Capitalism and Schizophrenia*, Valencia: Pre-Textos, 1988)

◆ fencing space

[FS]

The fencer is attentive to a mobile point. The thin and immaterial line floats in the air, restless and ethereal as a beam. It evaporates immediately, surges and disappears. The fencer follows a trail. In fencing, there is only one mobile point, without reference to the game field. There is no drawing. The game does not exist, though the tapestry does. It does not create space, nor does it order it while the game is not on, when there is no action. Fencing is dialectic. A question, a possible answer. It can not be played alone. It does not need the playing ground. The space generates the movement. A point moving quickly forms a line. Spatial relations are fundamentally diagonal. The point reaches maximum velocity; the faster, the better the game. I propose that our architecture follows. A space that is the instantaneous trail of use. An agile thought instantaneously materialised. A structure solidified in a moment, almost at the point of disappearing. A space whose definition does not depend on floors.

Étienne-Jules MAREY,
*Cronophotograph
of a vibrating
hanger*, 1830-1904,
in *BAU* 013, 1995.

Stan ALLEN,
Diagrams of field
conditions, in
VARIOUS AUTHORS,
*Fields, the Berlage
Cahiers 5, 95-96,*
Rotterdam: 010
Publishers, 1996.

●★■▲ field

→ 'abroad, etc.',
'agriculture',
'context', 'dispositions',
'distribution',
'environment',
'hyperiphery',
'places', 'periphery',
'unfolding'

[MG] Terrain (operative landscape), extensive (and extendable: open) outside a (between) space(s).// Workable (manipulable) background under cultivation (evolutionary system), plantations (installations) and natural (and artificial) sown fields (modellings).// Space that is chosen (or accepted) for a (spatial-temporal) challenge.// Real (physical) or imaginary (virtual) space // Background of a painting or scenario (now also figure).// Territory occupied by an army or device (in Spanish, *campo*, sometimes the army or device itself).// Space in which forces and energies (and relationships) manifest themselves (induce each other and interchange) in (dynamical) interaction.// Place of confusion and disorder (or rather of another type of order). (Based upon CASARES, Julio, *Diccionario ideológico de la lengua castellana*, Barcelona: Gustavo Gili, 1966)

[CO] An attention to FIELD conditions can involve more flexible tactics in order to accommodate or modulate existing topographies (or existences in reference to social, historical and programmatic change) of the space. "Field logistics" seek to become an opportunity, moving away from an ethic and a modern aesthetic of transgression. Working in favour of the space and not against it; recording and accepting the complexity of the existing data. Architecture must learn to manage this complexity and, paradoxically, can only succeed in doing so if it renounces certain measures of control. "Field logistics" propose a provisional (and experimental) approach to carrying out this task.
STAN ALLEN

[MG] **(as a crossing of forces)**

The notion of 'field' in reference to a place – and not that of 'context' or, at least, that of 'the contextual' –suggests a new, more open and abstract, more flexible and receptive (reactive) condition of the contemporary project vis-à-vis the environment, far removed from classical evocation or modern (im)position.

The concept of 'field' defines place as a framework for reconnaissance but also as a scenario of "skirmishes" between tensions and forces: that is, as a "field" of action (or of battle).

Working with field logistics implies working with devices capable of articulating different movements and events vis-à-vis trajectories of fluctuant order, variable in accordance with internal logics and external demands.

Thus, speaking merely of buildings (of architectures or of constructions in their habitual sense) does not reflect this strange situation of crossing and interchange. In fact, architecture defines fields understood as ambiguous "intermediate places" between spaces and territories: force fields (in turn, within other force fields) destined to react with and within the (physical and virtual) environment, elastically inserting themselves into the environment for the purpose of generating local and global, plural and specific, singular and generic responses. As immanent as fortuitous and/or contingent.

Ambiguous correlations between environment and mediator, between incorporated landscape and host landscape. Between "device-field" and "environment-field:" at once scenario (realm) and actor (agent).

In both the notion of 'field' and in that of 'device' there always exists a possible concatenation of scalar sets. An ambiguous relationship at once between action and interaction, between interconnection and individuality, between resonance and change, between system and occurrence, class and case.

[MG] **(as layout)**

"*Fields shaped as entities without scale can be defined by certain limited rules, as well as by means of coordinates or networks. They are generic shapes which relate and articulate, at the same time, special "happenings," being enriched by information about setting, programmes, events or specific interests. They are, therefore, risk forces and always in a state of transformation. They are always in movement, in constant development; they are never reconstructed; they are dynamic and complex, in a state of progressive change. [...]*

Architecture as a supporting field, as density of vectors, cluster of links in a chain, as an intensity taking into account field forces, in this way, to the implants, the influences, the links, to attracting and repelling forces; simultaneously.

Taking into account the environment as an acquired vital skill, at the same time the category of environment might well be by virtue of the stamp (architecture as superficial curves, results of a concept), gradients (the continuous reading of structures as pulses of density), networks (architecture as links and transmission nodes) or sharp protuberances (discontinuities and peculiarities). Architecture-environment: environment and architecture."
(PORRAS, Fernando, "Editorial," *BAU* 014, 1996).

[JM] The outside is as important and definitive as the inside. What we have are not objects and an exterior reality, but continuity between forms that wrap and unwrap, open and close, that focus and serve as a focus. Architecture thus expands in reality, in a medium and in the environment. The medium in which it appears is a field.

[FP] **(as a dynamic medium)**

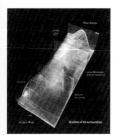

UN STUDIO,
IFCCA Competition:
Penn Station,
New York, 1999.

Less than twenty years ago, Craig Reynolds, a researcher of artificial life, created a computer simulation programme about the behaviour of flocks of birds and baptised the name *boids* (phonetically a term very similar to *birds* and orthographically a counterpoint of *voids*).

These "beigns" were programmed to follow three precise rules of behaviour: maintain a minimum distance in respect to other objects in its surroundings (birds as much as obstacles); compete in terms of speed with nearby moving objects; fly towards the locations of birds in their own surroundings. None of the rules explicitly instructed the *boids* to form a flock, since these were eminently local and they were set according to what each *boid* could do or see in its closest surroundings. If a flock started to form, it happened as a continuous emerging phenomenon.

The flock is a phenomenon which clearly exemplifies the concept of field – defined exact conditions and relatively indifferent to a wider global form. With these defined rules, the obstructions or ruptures did not presume a collapse of the group. The variations and obstacles in the surroundings provoked adaptation, in the same way that a fluid adapts to its container.

A flock, in the same way as a shoal of fish or a crowd of people who take part in a collective event, present a similar structure, irrespective of the size or number of participants. Even though intersections or interferences are produced, an invariable model emerges. Without dealing with any repetition, the behaviour of these entities tended to produce similar configurations, not as a fixed type, but as a cumulative result of local behaviour patterns.

Perhaps, in architecture we could similarly design sound local conditions which allow the formation of major structures whose development is not merely shape formed in relation to the degree of stability or instability of stated guidelines of an inferior order.

[co] In so-called "fields" form isn't the outcome of a linear process, nor is it statistical law. Topographies are not stable, either mechanically or statistically; they are neither deterministic nor Gaussian, but Brownian, structured in the very phenomena whose efficiency or general stability depends on their flexibility in integrating fluctuations at the local scale with orders at the global level. The acceptance of uncertainty — in which the phenomenon occurs — and the relinquishment of the control of the formal over such developments balances out with the establishment of operative limits. These are control strategies.
ALEJANDRO ZAERA-POLO

★ *fiesta* (party)

→ 'community', 'event'

[CO] *Fiesta* is a rite; a form in which societies represent symbolically and exceptionally the values of the community and the relationships among individuals, groups, territory and history. It is a form of knowledge with a necessary spatial and urban component.

Although *fiestas* are habitually understood as part of traditional culture, there also exists the possibility of creating new *fiestas* as a tool for reinventing the world. A few cases of new *fiestas* might be, for example, the constructed IS situations, the Merry Pranksters' acid tests, Archigram's instant cities, the anti-globalisation protests, raves and the Spanish parties of the past decade. The *fiesta*, as an invention, is a trans-disciplinary product that draws on architecture, social engineering, theatrical and multimedia production.

In contrast with the dominant tectonic model of Modernity, *fiesta* corresponds to the Semperian architectural element "the mound," characterised by the production of an environment and the quest for the sublime.

JOSÉ PÉREZ DE LAMA

d2kL.A., protest against the democratic party convention, Rage Against the Machine in concert, Los Angeles, august 2000.

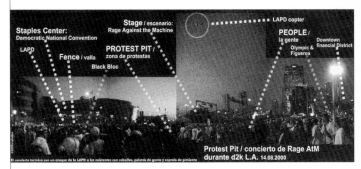

● ★ ■ figure-background

→ 'a-couplings', 'and', 'devices', 'dichotomies', 'dual(ity)', 'in-between fingers, in-between links', 'topological', 'void', 'voids and fills'

[MG] Figure and background blur their boundaries in new devices that not only suggest a (trans)fusion of the contemporary project within (and with) the environment, but also a growing mistrust towards the objectual presence of an architecture understood, only, as a "stranded" piece, or figure: pure, projecting volume, standing out against – and removed from – the background of action.

This progressive imbrication between figure and background, this fusion or coupling (increasingly evident in the measure that it would produce the shift from the more edificial to the more landscape-bound, from the more tectonic to the quasi-topographic, from the Euclidian to the fractal), could be interpreted, from a resistant perspective, as a renunciation of the old presential prominence of the full, of the object. However, in most cases, this fusion responds to fundamentally operative criteria aimed at generating more engineered devices, capable of reformulating old categories of the urban (city, landscape, infrastructures) in a new dynamic of cooperation and synergy that, in turn, points to the fusion/dissolution among old dichotomies – natural/artificial, territory/landscape – and, above all, to a possible relationship between empty/full so well described by Douglas R. Hofstadter in his book *Gödel, Escher, Bach, an Eternal Golden Braid* (Barcelona: Tusquets,1987):
"*In drawing a figure or positive space inside a certain framework one al-*

Sculptoric group, in *Arkitektur* 1/1999.

fig 224 **figure-background**

1a. Scott E. KIM, *Figure-figure*, 1975. **1b.** José MORALES, Juan GONZÁLEZ, *Europan 5* (1st prize), Ceuta, 1998. **2a.** OMA-Rem KOOLHAAS, *Competition for urban development*, Melun-Sénart (France), 1987. **2b.** ACTAR ARQUITECTURA, *Barcelona Land Grid*, 1998. **3a.** NJIRIC+NJIRIC, *Europan 4: Atom Heart Mother*, Glasgow (Scotland), 1996, 1st prize. **3b.** ROCHE, DSV&SIE, *Project for the gardens and salt marshes*, Soweto (South Africa), 1997. **4a.** ACTAR ARQUITECTURA, *New fair precinct*, Palma de Mallorca (Spain), 2000. **4b.** FOA, *International Port Terminal*, Yokohama (Japan), 2002. **5a.** Yin and Yang figure. **5b.** Kazuyo SEJIMA, Ryue NISHIZAWA, *Multimedia Study*, Oogaki (Gifu, Japan), 1996 (Photograph: Ramon Prat).

fig 225

so draws its complementary form — the background or negative space. In most designs the figure-background relation plays a minor role. The figure is far more interesting than the background. But there are times when attention is placed on the latter, in which case an interaction is generated. Then a distinction can be made between two sorts of occupation of the initial frame (the space): the cursive, whose background would appear only as a subproduct of the act of drawing, and the recursive, whose background could be seen as a figure of similar entity in its own right."

[c] Accordingly, Florian Beigel, citing Giorgio Morandi, recalled that "*in suibko, the Japanese technique of ink brush painting, the white, unpainted shape on the paper is the most difficult and most important part of the painting. The space between the bottles is the essence of the work, in fact it brings the bottles into being. In the Far East traditional thought, the dichotomy between nature and culture is absent because the environment is understood as a whole (natural site and urban site). In opposition to the fixed architectural models (orders, types, etc.), the Chinese geomancy prefigures openly the game rules.*" (BEIGEL, Florian, "Urban landscapes", *Quaderns* 216, 1997)

[co] If you intuitively sense a certain cultural maliase in Europe and the United States, it is because the yang has been allowed to shine too brightly and there has not existed an alternative yin. In architectural terms, the yang, the light, could assimilate the exterior form, and the yin could assimilate the shadows, the invisible or absent.
YORGOS SIMEFORIDIS

[JM] **(or background-figure)**
Today, in contrast to the traditional way we are accustomed to work, with the concept of figure-ground, we are under more pressure to consider what surrounds the site, that which approaches and compresses the architecture we are making. Ground-figure. We are not accustomed to working with noise, movement, flow, with the contamination of the exclamatory shouts of the city.

[co] **(framing)**
Finally, the question of framing, of the limits of the ground, emerges as one of the most characteristic techniques of a new redefinition of the ground. That is, as an architectural problem. In Myeong-Dong, for example, the strategy was to fuse the new ground with the existing ground, such that the limits of the object were unrecognisable. In Pusan, the ground/roof fades into the transport structure. In Yokohama, the limits were defined by the alignments of the site, as if the project were a slice of a giant pie.
One of the discussions that continually crops up during the elaboration of the project with these considerations regards the suitability of reinforcing the surface as a constitutive element.
The problem with attempting this is that it forces us to develop a strategy for dealing with the limit, when the project should remain conceptually unlimited. Do we place importance on the surface as a constitutive element, or on the idea of an arbitrary framework for a surface without limits as a conceptual strategy?
ALEJANDRO ZAERA-POLO

●■ fillings

[MG] See 'stenosis.'

[JM] As a result of the density of events to which space has been submitted, at times only minimally available, the adventure of space in architecture is centred on what is left when we have filled everything. We are left with no other remedy than to look behind and take architecture by surprise. The space of the "mold" is a good analogy.

This notion that provokes architecture installs itself in those places where architecture hardly rests, linking and provoking unsuspecting landscapes as new places of interchange between subjects.

But without a doubt, what most interests us are these kind of spaces to investigate, that result in the unlikely sum of programs in an ample sense and that offers us a singular "filled" space.

NL, *Parkhouse Carstadt*, Amsterdam (The Netherlands), 1996.

José MORALES, Sara GILES, Juan GONZÁLEZ, *Competition for the new headquarters of the Extremadura Assembly*, Mérida (Spain), 1999.

● fingers

[MG] See 'intercadences', 'sequence and series', 'mutations.'

J.L. ESTEBAN PENELAS, *Sánchez-Méndez House*, Las Rozas (Madrid), 2003-.

◆ fish

[FS] See 'geometry.'

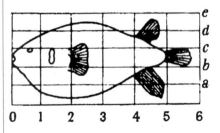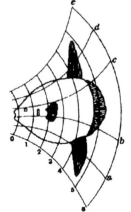

Cartesian deformation of diodon into mola, in *Arch+* 119/120, 1993.

●◆ fissures

→ 'infiltration', 'puff pastry'

[MG] See 'branchial.' Any compact body presents, eventually, cracks – fissures – through which air and impurities infiltrate. Thus, expansive logics of evolutionary processes end up eroding the apparently inalterable cohesion of those more apparently stable organisms – or situations – providing them with new, more open and irregular morphologies.

[MG] See 'action>critical.'

[FS] There is an awareness that surges between the fissures of contemporary culture. And like cracks, what is most important is the map that the fissures draw as they link one another. *Fisuras de la cultura contemporánea* is presented as a police novel. It contains apparently innocent documents. Magnifying the image, reading coded messages between the lines, burning ashes, studying history, can all lead to indications that something strange is going on. Suspicion grows. Clues of a crime that may have been committed. Articles, images, projects, allow each reader a different order and reading. A meta-reading that reconstructs a world or virtual ideal, just as real as the ideas, in their strictest sense, that appear in each text. All is visible. But what is the offense? In the novels, there is no offense or clear crime. In Carver's stories, practically nothing happens. We are not interested in the arguments or the narrative. What is important is the attitude of the characters and the details – the cork cap that obsessively watches the waiter present during Chekhov's death.
(from Carver's "Three Yellow Roses.")

ROCHE, DSV & SIE, *Fractal City*, 1999.

■ *flâneur*

→ 'deviation', 'space', 'time'

[JM] The objective of the *flâneur* consists in displacement that makes time diffuse in the relative loss of time in space. Spaces desolated by catastrophe, the inundation of a city by water, the radical transformations of the space of the city, or geographically natural transformation, can serve as figures for thinking about public space. A new *flâneur*.

S&Aa (SORIANO-PALACIOS), *Office Building*, Bilbao (Spain), 2002-.

●◆ **fleeting**

[MG] Fleeting is of brief duration. Essentially unstable. Impermanent, temporal, provisional and ephemeral. Like a flash.

[FS] See 'speed.'

★ **flexibilisation**

[co] See 'flexibility.'

Flexibilization is an option tending to oppose the consideration of the determining process of form as that of substitution repeated *ad infinitum*, as a variant of the supposed unstoppable linear improvement of things.

Flexibilisation seeks to expand the functional, signifying and relational capacities of an object or process, in order thus to open it up to more and better requirements of reality.

To be more flexible in order to arrive further.

EDUARD BRU

●★+ **flexibility**

[MG] To flexibilise certain situations – to open them to the indeterminate – always implies to shape – to weave, to norm, to rhythmise, though not necessarily to rigidify.

[MG] **(in the dwelling)**

The new concept of flexibility (beyond the cliché of the do-it-yourself user, who dedicates him or herself to continual transformation of the interior of his or her house) should now be associated with greater multi-usage and versatility of the space.

Accordingly, of equal importance are tactical actions of structural order (increasing use of large openings and minimisation of structure), actions related to the strategic conception of fittings (concentration of working modules, schematic definition of energy networks, evacuation, etc.) and actions related to more or less evolutionary systems of distribution and division.

The possibility of providing a more fluid and transformable space has led, in certain cases, to research into systems based, preferably, upon seried and industrialised elements – sliding (folding or removable) panels, working fittings, rotating compacts, soffits or removable partitions, etc. Likewise, the use of "*cloisons épaisses*" (heavy partitions or walls), habitual in the distribution of offices, permits the creation of reversible separating spaces with capacity for storage.

The idea of the container (chest, cabinet, etc.) as an object-furnishing "deposited" in the space (but also as a reconvertible, transformable piece) likewise suggests different possibilities when seeking a continual recomposition of the space. Working furnishings or convertible mobile objects play, in this virtual – open and fluid space – the same role as separating elements, but with greater versatility in use.

Transformable multi-use nuclei or service clusters are some examples of this multifaceted approach to a multiform and denatured space, possible today thanks to the existence of technical solutions tested in the tertiary sector: equipped surfaces and connecting networks of installations in accessed floors permit elasticity in a space open to successive possibilities. The "single-use" space yields to a multi-use space made up of successive reversible subspaces.

[c] "*Given that the economic factor requires overall rationalisation in low-budget housing, comparable with a progressive increase in the complexity of internal services, the home should be flexible, with a clear distinction between service elements, rooms and spaces. To attain this ideal, skeleton construction is the most appropriate system. It lends itself to rationalised construction methods and, at the same time, the unhindered division of the interior. If we consider the fittings of kitchens and bathrooms as fixed nuclei, the remaining space can be divided by environment with mobile walls. According to the time of day or night the home space may vary, be transformed. In the period of greatest activity, during the day, the walls retract and the beds are concealed in niches under the wardrobes on the central spine. It is by night that the space is recompartmentalised and bedrooms and beds re-emerge for the rest period.*

Thin walls convert into thick walls that accommodate functions of accumulation and storage, the mobile planes disappear or fold out to form a table that can, at the same time, be shared by two different spaces; beds can be stored in the cabinet-walls or even under the access passage to the home services, etc. Different situations open up a range of possibilities for redefining the domestic sphere.

The furnishing should be conceived of as a flexible element, transformer of the space, not as a decorative object of the home."

(ARANGUREN, María José; GONZÁLEZ GALLEGOS, José, "Habitar la casa", unpublished, 1999)

[WM] This has been one of the concepts – and at times one of the obstacles – in the history of understandings and misunderstandings between industrialisation and architecture.

Flexibility, even today, held out as the only argument for justifying the industrialisation of the construction processes.

However, if we look at the products that really work in industry, and that sell best (a basic objective in industry and one which we should henceforth incorporate), we would see that their margin of manipulation is getting smaller and smaller, and thus the possibility of greater flexibility resides more and more in the multiplicity of options: an easier way of comparing and choosing, in addition to rationalising the manufacturing process.

Thus, the real possibilities of flexibility are increasingly reduced proportionally to the growing possibilities for the manufacture of unique – individualised – pieces. Flexibility is in the mould and not in the piece.

In other words: maximum manipulation in the design process, minimum final manipulation.

Unique architecture, mass-produced.

★ ● flows

[c] "As in Piranesi's engravings, the contemporary environment may be understood as an infinite interior of imprecise boundaries, where inhabitants are located in the form of a flow, converted into circulation.
In this context, road infrastructure plays an important role in establishing an order that is not based upon formal criteria but upon abstract bits of information (on a motorway we can arrive at our destination without using geographical parameters, following only a discontinual set of messages) and immaterial properties such as the increase in the degree of connectivity within the territory that patches (or traces) of meaning provide, without which the order becomes more diffuse."
(VALOR, Jaume, "Interior Global", in VARIOUS AUTHORS, Met 1.0 Barcelona Metápolis, Barcelona: ACTAR, 1998)

[MG] "Flow refers to a multivalent series of notion and direction. This multivalent possibility of recipient information is coded and in certain cases subliminal — found in the city environment — and is our clue to the flow as a system of subjective criteria presented logically. The eidetic condition is revealed as object, a para-construct of the philosophical, political and cultural value of the taxonomy, where the arrangement is both one substance and time."
(YEOMAN, Andrew, "Movement, velocity, networks: backup infrastructures", Quaderns 213, 1996)

UN STUDIO,
IFCCA Competition:
Penn Station,
New York, 1999.

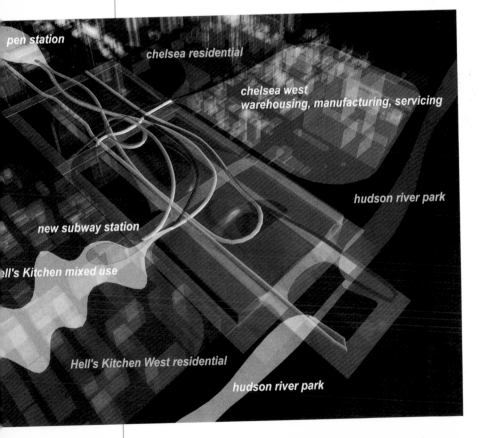

pen station

chelsea residential

chelsea west
warehousing, manufacturing, servicing

hudson river park

new subway station

ell's Kitchen mixed use

Hell's Kitchen West residential

hudson river park

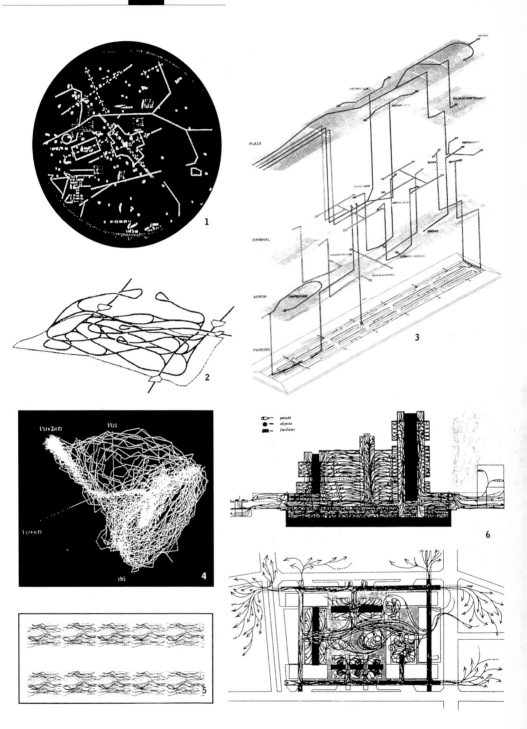

1. Information flows for the aerial space control, in *Quaderns* 213, 1996. **2.** Circulations in a library, in VARIOUS AUTHORS, *The Berlage Cahiers 5: Fields, Studio 95-96*, Rotterdam: 010, 1997. **3.** FOA, *International Port Terminal*, Yokohama (Japan), 1995-. **4.** Periodic fluid flow, reconstructed attractor using method of delays, in *Quaderns* 222, 1999. **5.** ROCHE, DSV & SIE, *Cultural Centre* (extension of the School of Architecture), Venice (Italy), 1998. **6.** Rem KOOLHAAS (OMA), Circulation diagram.

■ fold

The mental image we have when speaking of the fold, guaranteed by the imaginative world and deduced from the reflections of G. Deleuze ad F.Guattari – a few of whose books share the same name – is strongly suggestive. One of its most interesting implications is the difficulty in distinguishing and situating ourselves clearly in space. Spaces pass from inside to outside, putting in crisis the concept of precinct, and of course, of permanence. Composition (putting each part in its place) makes patterns, forming the unlikely union of programs (statistical) and a new concept of support. These tricks of space propose new mechanisms with projects. However, most interesting of the fold is the discovery of spaces of relation and interchange at the level of new organizations and social interchange.

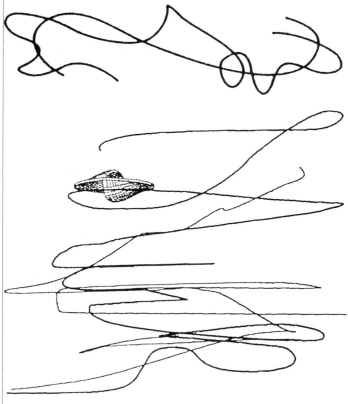

Figure by Paul Klee
quoted by Gilles
Deleuze in *The Fold.*

OMA, *Competition 2
bibliothèques Jussieu,*
Paris, 1993.

MVRDV, *Villa VPRO,*
Hilversum
(The Netherlands),
1997.

★ fold(ing)

→ 'deleuznable', 'devices', 'unfolding'

[co] Folding is a method by which buildings arise through the unfolding of land, materials and spaces into continuous form. Popularised by a generation of architects, who had been educated by the likes of Peter Eisenman and had read Gilles Deleuze's *Leibniz, or, The Fold*, this method seeks to replace the alienating experience of creating separate spaces that remove themselves from the rest of reality and that re-articulate the laws of gravity. Folding is also possible because of the plasticity of modern materials and thus dates back to the first experiments in concrete at the beginning of the 20th century. Folding has become much easier to achieve and more popular because of the use of computers, plastic and compounds in the building process. Here, the formal results of systems thinking (field theory) intersect with the romantic tradition of form-making that is intuitive and anti-hierarchical. AARON BETSKY

[co] A folding is a landscape in a landscape, an undulation and a deformation of the programming layers which are positioned at random. FRANÇOIS ROCHE

ROCHE, DSV & SIE, *Soweto*, South Africa, 1997.

●◆ fold (unfold-refold)

→ 'bends and (un)bendings', 'braids', 'coilings', 'contortionisms', 'deleuznable', 'devices', 'geometry', 'landstrategy', 'paradoxes', 'puff pastry', 'trajectory', 'unfolding'

[MG] We talk about folds, unfoldings and foldbacks as possible dynamic trajectories. A-scalar trajectories between structures and organisations, devices and cities, scenarios and projects, referring to evolutionary geometries (rhizomatic formations, outcrops and spurts, clusters, webs and coilings, fluctuations, refluences and swerves).

Folds are open (often, perceptibly fractal) geometries in which globality and fragment answer to parameters of self-similarity between diagrammatic decisions – or logics – and evolutionary development. They aim to generate complex configurations through initial elemental codes.

Folds are dynamic dispositions, developed more or less sequentially, which through seriation and alteration, action and interaction, variation and displacement, expansion and extension – internal or external – through a movement of folding, unfolding or folding back, favouring variable development and virtual mutation of shape in combined and combinatorial evolutions which are definitively open – are virtually incomplete.

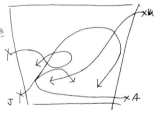

The trajectory of movement is traced as a vector line.
Merce CUNNINGHAM, *Event in Répétition au Musée d'Art Moderne de la ville de Paris*, 1970.

[FS] We must work on the folds of Modern Space. The free-plan constitutes the instrument of control over Modern Space.

The abandoning of a constructive system whose structural form defined a physical space, time and closure produced the discovery of a new abstract place, ruled by a reticular structure. While this discovery is not modified, we continue working within the international style. Nonetheless, there are moments in which we near limits, when we put Modern space in tension. Our space is the folded space of the Modern. We operate in the order of the rupture of the free plan. The fold separates and unites interior and exterior. The line of inflection is the wall, where it is concentrated. The fold of space superimposes, on a point of the work, elements very distinct in scale, and separates and pieces together what originally coexisted. We fold space and new, unrelated strange spaces are the result, no longer abstract and void, with structural grids inside.

The new space is dense and compact; its structure implicitand does not necessarily coincide with what exists in the floor below, nor above. The fold produces a dislocation of the dialectical relation between figure and ground.

The matter-fold and the sponge structures.

DILLER&SCOFIDIO,
Bad press, in *BAU*
015, 1997.

▲ ● force

→ 'energy', 'stimulus' [FP] The term force makes sense nowadays as a group or cluster. We are not interested so much in describing the meaning of force as a unitary element, but rather as a vector of a bigger system and of which it is part of. As Wiel Arets formulated in the Berlage Institute of Amsterdam in 1996: "Forces have no scale defined by specific rules, borders or webs. Forces have to deal with some concrete issues, looking after specific places and phenomena. Forces are charged with information, events, scenarios, and are always found in a state of transformation. Forces are never anonymous, and when they are, do not immediately vanish once discovered. Forces are always in motion, in constant development, which can never be reconstructed, which are complex and dynamic. These forces can be visible or invisible but always determine existence conditions. Forces are mainly related to processes of progressive change."

[MG] See 'vector.'

The trajectory of movement is traced as a vector line.
Merce CUNNINGHAM, *Event in Répétition au Musée d'Art Moderne de la ville de Paris*, 1970.

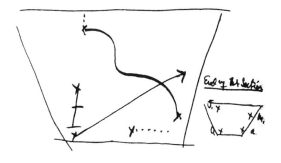

● foreignness

→ 'alienation', 'alienism', 'armadillo', 'artificial', 'criss-crossing', 'de-location 'infiltration>'intrusiveness', 'reactive', 'tourism'

[MG] In a well-known photograph by Martin Parr (*Bali*, in Florence, 1992), one can appreciate the double – and illustrative – interrelation between coexistence and foreignness. On one hand, there is a strange contractual relationship between guest and host, while, on the other hand, there is a strong interaction between removed (cosmopolitan) information and localised (indigenous) information.

Interchange – and mutual influence – occurs as the two systems attempt to adapt to one another, as well as the disturbing – altering – character of the traveller as "transferor," that is to say, as "carrier of external information" sure to affect an environment that, suddenly, sees it referents inverted.

Today, images, messages, "signs of identity" appear moved from one part of the planet to another, in a rapid rerouting that produces constant phenomena of uncodification, of unnaturalisation and of unterritorialisation. Phenomena, in sum, of mongrelisation, hybridisation and mixture. Of fusion and transfusion.

[MG] *"Any guest is an "intruder," a "foreign" element — an outsider — one who interferes with "external" — alien — baggage in an intimate, "sacred" space. Invariably this engenders, then, a certain degree of violence, greater or lesser according to the mutual codes of behaviour. Protocols — implicit and explicit — of relation. From indifference to communion. From mistrust to complicity. From imposition to mimicry. From prudent distance to integrating coexistence. From polite verbal exchange to fluid conversation. And in the best of cases harmless play and the exchange of stimuli through mutual interaction."* (DERN, Jamie Q.)

Bali in Florence, *El País*, 1995 (Photograph: Martin Parr).

◆● form

"Form has been designated as the emissary of meaning. Within the tradition of humanist aesthetics, form is a bundle that presents what is done or contained. It is singular, not universal, because its material-contents can be impermanent. But it does have a significant dimension. Classic form exercises a totalising job, trying to recuperate that universal dimension in converting the common language of all races. Today, one can say that not only an absolute linguistic structure has disappeared, but also the consciousness of the possibility of its existence. Geometric forms, or forms used by the avant-garde, are not substitutes for this primitive structure. Towards the end of the existence of isolate forms replete with meaning, the process of de-naturalization has finally been added to which we have submitted the objects that surround us. The logical relationship between content and use has been destroyed. An object comes to life under the illusion of nature and functionality, hiding its artificial articulations and its functionalism understood as adaptation, not as an ends, but rather as a system. Form today is charged with the task of designating meaning to the object in relation to certain codes or processes of codification that are unspoken in the society of consumption. This is what transmits the quality of the object, or in other words, the first step towards choosing it. We have entered into a vortex of definition and consumption. But what does a form become when it does not have to be the spokesperson of its contents, when it is silent? What is form, when the contents can not even be thought of because they are already only a vague memory? One has to try hard to find a form unable to suggest even the slightest idea. Neutral forms, insignificant, silent."

(AZÚA, Félix de, *Diccionario de las artes*, Barcelona: Planeta, 1995)

[MG] **(and no-form)**

"This is a 'non-form,' (emerging from) an awareness of the uncertainty where to know what things are is only possible when we recognise what they are not. The interest, then, lies in an architecture that has neither image nor form. That does not express explicitly the scale in which it is produced [...]. The interest lies in objects that have no boundaries, no limits, that play at indetermination in their entirety. The interest lies in works that have no details, because the latter are constructed with the simple, evident and direct juxtaposition of their elements. The architecture that operates with meagre means and a complexity of results. The interest lies in works that have no weight, and whose section, rich and complex, responds to the law of exceptions.
This is not an idea of form that is "one," but that is "like one." It is difficult to hold in the mind's eye. It is elusive except when we see it. All its faces and sides have equal importance. They do not have predetermined hierarchical relations. There is an element (material or structure) that gives it that unity that the old "pregnant" figure can no longer provide. It does not think of its own bodiliness. It is a form, therefore, indebted to the fluctuating processes that the shape it." (SORIANO, Federico, *Fisuras* 3 1/3, 1995)

[MG] " We understand shape as a bond between probable relationships, the latter able to draw upon tactical criteria in order to favour a more open correspondence between figuration and concept, between image and movement, between reality and abstraction, between environment (global) and place (local), in direct relationship with the interpretation of the physical – and cultural – contemporary space." (PORRAS-ISLA, Fernando, "Editorial", BAU 014, 1996)

[MG] See 'extroversion.' Today shape is disposition. Stimulatory resolution – or decision. Spatial-temporal distribution – or deployment. And extrovert attitude – or will – vis-à-vis reality. Shape is capable of expressing – and communicating – the interior movements, logics and tensions, that configure it (its topology) and of reacting and mutating in response to the demands of exterior stimuli.

[FS] **formless**

Formless "are irregular forms, as termed by the great French mathematician René Thom. Irregular forms are at once forms – that nonetheless have not attained a structural stability – and non-forms (uni-dimensional) that yet occupy a space-time. In other words, they are phenomena that assume instable aspects, fickle, in transformation, and can not be defined by the Gnostic canons. For example, they can not be found in Euclidean geometry, but need an ad hoc geometry."

(CALABRESE, Omar, "Neobarroco", *Cuadernos del Círculo* N1 2, 1993)

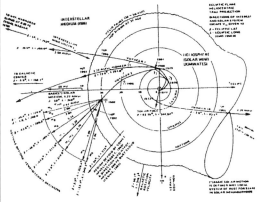

Spirals with and without form. NASA, *Trajectory spiral.*

★ Fourth World

→ 'developing', 'diversity', 'globalisation'

[CO] Accompanying the rise of informational and global capitalism, previously defined entities have diversified. Geopolitics have re-drawn the world map. First World (developed countries), Second World (the statist universe) and Third World (developing countries) have disintegrated. All conditions exist within each other. "... A new world, the Fourth World, has emerged, made up of multiple black holes of social exclusion throughout the planet." (CASTELLS, Manuel, "Rise of the Fourth World," *End of Millennium*, Malden: Blackwell Publishers, 1988) Social exclusion includes not only squalor and pockets of poverty for the less fortunate, but also fortified enclaves for the rich. KELLY SHANNON

★●◆✕ fractal (and fractals)

[c] *"Intuitive meaning. That has a form, either exceedingly irregular, or exceedingly fractured or fragmented, and continues to be so whatever the scale it is examined at. That contains distinguishing elements whose scales are highly varied and cover a very broad range."*

(Paraphrasing MANDELBROT, Benoît, *Fractal objects*)

[c] *"Fractal configuration; fractal set or object. Warning: the word fractal does not distinguish, intentionally, between mathematical sets (theory) and natural objects (reality): it is used in those cases in which its generality and the resulting intentional ambiguity are either desired, made clear by the context, or do not entail associated drawbacks."*

(Paraphrasing MANDELBROT, Benoît, *Fractal objects*)

[MG] Between uncontrolled chaos — absolute disorder — and Euclidean order, there lies a "zone of fractal order" that the mathematician Benoît Mandelbrot described in the early sixties: *"How can we explain the form of topographic relief, the geometry of fractures and their distribution, the morphology of the fluvial systems with classical geometry? How can we justify in the future present the existence of sealed compartments in science? The question is answered by proclaiming the need to resort to fractal geometry in order to present a series of experiences that encompass from patterns of natural processes to abstract numerical simulations obtained using computational techniques."*

(Paraphrasing MANDELBROT, Benoît, *Fractal objects*)

Simulation process
of a geographic
formation,
in MANDELBROT,
Benoît, *Les objets
fractals*, Paris:
Flammarion, 1975.

In fact, fractal geometry has had a revolutionary impact upon the theories of physics of this *fin de seicle*, especially in the construction of mathematical models of phenomena that appeared to be governed by a casual or unpredictable order. Not only turbulence phenomena (as in the expansion of a gas in the air), but also natural patterns have been characterised by irregularity (the profile of a shoreline, the shape of a tree, land reliefs, etc.) and dynamical structures of temporal-spatial development (clusters, multitudes, deployments, etc.). The characteristics of fractals permit, in effect, a definition of elastic patterns of evolutionary topologies that characterise such phenomena.

"Fractal objects do not have a dimension that is measurable by a whole number. Their dimensionality is found precisely along the boundary between lines, planes and volumes. They are more efficient at occupying space than their real counterparts. More dense than lines, but without arriving at massifying on a plane, like a spongy ball of yarn. In order to represent their dimension fractional numbers are used. On the other hand, their degree of irregularity, that is their physonomy, remains notably constant at different scales."

Beyond a hypothetical formal parallelism, the greatest interest of such geometries resides in their internal constitution conforming to a surprising matrixial recurrence between empty-full-articulation combinations.

(Paraphrasing SORIANO, Federico, "Sin escala", *El Croquis*)

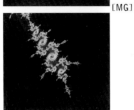

[MG]

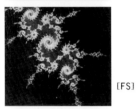

[FS]

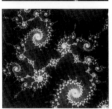

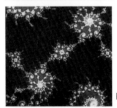

[VG]

Rollo SILVER, Mandelbrot
set, San Cristóbal
(México), in BRIGGS,
John, *Fractals. The Patterns
of Chaos*, London:
Thames and Hudson, 1992.

[i] p. 240-241

One of the consequences of the infinite detail of a fractal object is that it does not, in effect, have any definitive — absolute — size, and such scalar ambiguity introduces globality in locality in and, above all, permits "glocal" transferences of the part to the whole: what is called "scalar jump."

"Fractal geometry would not be of more than fleeting interest — Michael Batty says — if it weren't for the profound idea that complex entities such as cities can be understood in the very simple terms that make them up. Cities demonstrate enormous variety, but there is order in this variety, and this order is clearly constructed by very simple elements. The new digital geometry and the expansion of CAD enable us, more than ever, to interpret such developments. If fractal geometry is the way to joining form and function, the coming decade should see the emergence of a new theory that demonstrates how form and function co-evolve spontaneously through new dynamic designs."
(Paraphrasing BATTY, Michael, "The Fractal City", *Architectural Design* 9/10, vol. 67, 1997)

Fractals are objects that have an extremely irregular or interrupted form. With the desire to study them, a new geometry has been conceived and developed, in which computers have become important tools.. The word, fractal derives from the root *fractus* (interrupted or regular.) A real object is considered fractal if it is the figure that it represents.
"Fractal dimension. Number that serves to quantify the degree of irregularity and fragmentation of a geometric set or natural object. The fractal dimension is not necessarily whole. The Hausdorff -Besicovitch content dimension is sometimes applied in its calculation.
Fractal set. Set whose fractal dimension is greater than or equal to its ordinary dimension. Fractal object. Natural object that can be usefully represented mathematically by a fractal set."
(MANDELBROT, Benoît, *Los objetos fractales*, Barcelona: Tusquets, 1987)

Architecture has traditionally used Euclidean geometry that represents pure volumes that can be defined by equations. It enables us to describe smooth surfaces and regular forms. However, natural objects such as mountains have irregular, fragmented characteristics.

Natural models can be described realistically by using methods of fractal geometry. A fractal object has two basic characteristics: infinite detail in each point and a degree of self-similarity between parts of the object and its overall characteristics. Processes rather than equations.

Processes which represent the object viewed from different distances, with the same degree of detail, and which analyse and represent things in the course of time. Fractal methods have shown themselves to be useful in moulding terrains, clouds, water, trees and other plants. Fractal patterns have been identified in the behaviour of stars, meanders, stock-market variations, traffic flows, the use of urban property, etc. Processes rather than occurrences.

Fractals, an animated discussion, E. Lorenz, B. Mandelbrot, University of Bremen, in VARIOUS AUTHORS, *Met 2.0*, Barcelona: NewMedia, 2000.

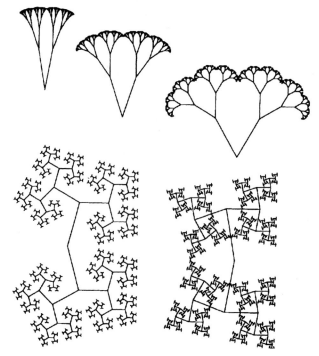

Fractal magnolias and vaults.

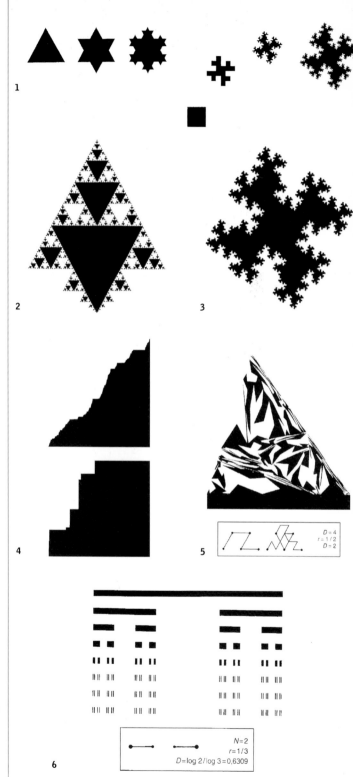

1. Triadic island of Koch or snow flake K. Original construction by Helge von Koch (coast dimension D=log 3~1,2618).

2. Sierpinski's arrow head.

3. Quadrangular island of Koch (coast dimension D=3/2=1,5000).

4. Diabolic stairs of Paul Lévy (dimension 1; the abscissas of steps have dimensions D=9/10, D3/10 y D=0,6039, respectively).

5. Peanus aleatory curve (dimension D=2).

6. Triadic bar and cake of Cantor (dimension of the horitzontal section D=log2/log 3=0,6309). Saturn rings. Cantor curtains.

◆ fragile

→ 'appropiation
strategies', 'ephemeral',
'fleeting', 'impermanences',
'inflatable', 'in-out',
'in/unstable', 'lightness',
'provisional', 'reversible',
'tattoos'

[FS] Fragile geometry; fractured, easily broken into pieces.// Said of non-solid, but correctly resolved, geometric constructions that constitute a representation of compositional instability.

◆ fragment

[FS] Fragment is an old word that is substituted for unfinished.
See 'in/unfinished'.

● ★ frame-

[MG] **(frame)works**
See '(inter)weavings and inter(plots).'

[co] **frame(work)**
See 'skeleton.'

✖ franchise

→ 'globalisation',
'in-between', 'marks',
'McDonaldization',
'networks'

[VG] Today, there are only two ways for cities to succeed in the global economy: being an innovative city, a leader in culture, in industry or in international economy (such as Hollywood, London or Salzburg), or adopting the role of franchise, an intermediate role, that imports models created in other places and participates in a network of influences (as in the case of Bilbao with the Guggenheim).
Success is possible in both cases.
The problem lies in being neither one nor the other.

1. Restaurant McDonald's McAuto, Girona (Spain). **2.** Santiago CALATRAVA, *Railway terminal*, Airport of Lyon (France), 1994.

● frequency

→ 'evolutionary',
'intermittences',
'process', 'sequences',
'trajectory'

[MG] Frequency is no longer periodic repetition, but rather sequential vibration: instantaneous variety in the amplitude of a information-carrier movement in an associated evolutionary trajectory.

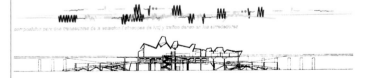

José Alfonso BALLESTEROS, *Railway station*, Castelló de la Plana (Spain), 1996.

★ fresh conservatism

→ 'do-it-yourself',
'dual(ity)', 'open',
'paradoxes'

[co] Certainly, being fresh means impressing people with one's perfect health and lust for life. It means being open to new impressions and concepts. Being fresh makes you cheerful. If you are fresh, you don't let on when you're tired. There is no trace of dreary routine in freshness. You are open-minded and not colorless. Freshness also stimulates discussion and sale of an argument. When we combine freshness with conservatism we get a result that fits perfectly into our present cultural climate. Of course, we want to preserve what we have, but we are also looking for the new, for challenges that satisfy us as individuals and that also prolong our comfortable material and immaterial abundance. Fresh conservatism stands for a condition in which deregulated capital and social democracy complement each other perfectly. Fresh conservatism is a situation where a certain degree of conflict (subversion and radicalism) serve as stimulant and identity, thus forming an essential element in a fragmented society where the results of conflicts in power and interests are swept under the carpet. Fresh conservatism stands for a kind of ideological smoothness of what John Travolta summarizes with the words: "Whatever you do, do it cool baby." It all comes down to the well-known adults' lullaby - "don't worry, be happy." Fresh conservatism presents the phenomena of fashion and style as the manifest products of an insoluble tension between the ongoing attempt within the supermodern metropolis to achieve individual differentiation and the increasing tendency of modernization to homogenize and level all difference, including human difference. Fresh conservatism generates a sameness disguised as difference. Style emerges as a paradoxical form of protection. This style bestows upon the individual a sense of stability and unity and imbues him and her with a sense of superindividuality, of belonging to a society; it counters the tendency of capitalism to fragment and divide different social groups. And at the same time, style and fashion are also a means of individual expression, so that one can still preserve some last semblance of individual freedom. Fresh conservatism keeps us out of mischief. It throws up fresh ideas nonstop, amusing us and keeping us happy. The designers of fresh conservatism set a new stylistic trend, but before you know it, it has degenerated into a new conformism. It is an inclusive conformism that unites the old and the new, the One and the Other, in a paradoxical Either/Or configuration. This 'fresh conservatism' is not really interested in conservative values but is fascinated by the present and the near future. It is a kind of 'lounge futurism' of a do-it-yourself avant-garde. The work produced by fresh conservatism is a kind of avant-garde junk space. (See also Roemer van Toorn, 'Fresh Conservatism', *Quaderns* no. 219, 1998) ROEMER VAN TOORN

The Asian woman dressed as European, reading a Japanese Bauhaus catalogue in a room defined by Bernard Tschumi's 'event space,' provokes the spectator. High culture and low culture meet in this pornographic image – the copulation of clichés. Ultimately, it is a highly reactionary interpretation of both sexuality and womanhood.

◆ friction

[FS] Place of fiction.

◆ fringes

→ 'arches of
development',
'chains', 'cultivations',
'distribution',
'environment',
'field', 'self-organization',
'self-urbanism'

[FS] Fringes are "[...] made up of hanging strings or cords. An unspun border."
(CASARES, Julio, *Diccionario ideológico de la lengua española*, Barcelona: GG, 1966)
"*Del Lat. FLUCCUS, wool flakes, cloth hair, also in old Spanish "flueco"
(1490)."* (COROMINAS, Joan, *Breve diccionario etimológico de la lengua castellana*, Madrid: Gredos, 1961)

Fringe development of Madrid (the Galiana dale) is like a self-constructed linear city, on the illegal occupation and privatization of public ground along the old dale, by lateral plots and a central street. Today, its extension exceeds the fifteen consolidated kilometers from Coslada to Valdemingómez. The plots are "transferred" and not sold, and, as such, what is sold is the right of illegal occupation. The process is realized progressively, dividing and inclosing the plot, building a one storey shack, and finally, building a final three-four storey building on top of the shack. The authorities tolerate, ignore, and acquiesce before the magnitude of the fringe.

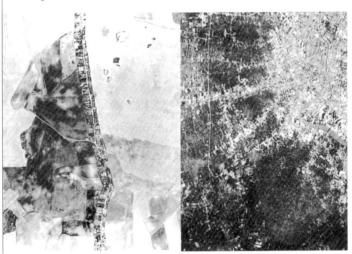

Development of west fringe of Bangkok (Thailand), in *Science News*, december 1994.

✕▲ function

→ 'activity', 'act-n',
'leisure', 'program', 'use'

[VG] In a world in which work, leisure and commerce can be carried out by means of computers occupying spaces that do not require spatial classification, function should not be a basic parameter in defining a portion of land within the territory.

[FP] Politicians change the function of buildings while they are under construction in order to win votes. Architects are becoming more and more conscious of the reality in which the 'old treatsies' lose ground and an in-formal nature of patronage reigns.

✖ functionalism

→ 'advanced> advanced architecture', 'function', 'process', 'program'

[VG] Functionalism, a concept linked to the industrial society sets out to efficiently organise humankind's activities in a space or on the territory. In the information society, people's individual activities no longer classify space because they do not modify it. Any activity related to the information society (be it work, leisure or commerce) can be carried out by means of minuscule interfaces that can appear or disappear from places as required.

● funny

[MG] See 'joy (*alegría*)', 'unrestrained (<un>factors).'

★ fury city or G8 Genoa

→ 'globalisation', 'history'

Kelly SHANNON, Genoa (Italy), July 20-22, 2001.

[co] The July 20 –22, 2001 G8 meeting in Genoa marked a turning point in the history of world summitry. Not only does the anti-globalization movement now have a martyr with the controversial death of a demonstrator, but also future meetings may no longer take place in so-called vulnerable city centres. Before and during the summit, the Italian seaport city was physically and symbolically transformed into a Kafkaesque reality. The meaning of 'city' was irrevocably challenged; Genoa was simultaneously converted into a high-tech, 21st century citadel, dated stage-set and blazing urban battlefield. During the surrealistic preparatory metamorphosis, the city was reminiscent of pre-1989 East Berlin – albeit more colourful. As the select handful of leaders discussed world poverty in the artificially isolated medieval city core, the havoc wreaked by the now infamous 'Black Bloc' evoked memories of war-torn Beirut.

An entire city was effectively shut down in order that an elite few could carry out an extravagant media spectacle in a single building. The structures of everyday life were quarantined and the spatial logic of the city was brutally modified. Although the city fulfilled its function as a political forum, it failed in its capacity as a landscape of public life and sociability for its inhabitants. The extreme tales of 'Fortress LA' in Mike Davis's *City of Quartz* or the essays in *Variations on a Theme Park* (edited by Michael Sorkin) became reality in Europe. Public space was not merely privatized, but militarized – guarded against disturbing and subversive elements. 'Armed response' took on a chilling meaning. The carefully monitored and artificially bounded 'public' environment was not unlike that in *The Truman Show*. Only in Genoa, the unblinking gaze of thousands of hidden cameras was directed at hooligans and civil society alike. The Genoese became 'involuntary prisoners' of their own city. The city's moment of international glory was usurped by the destruction of *agents provocateurs* and a disgraceful police performance.

KELLY SHANNON

Kelly SHANNON, 'Red zone' barricades near port-entry, Genoa (Italy), July 20-22, 2001.

● fuselages

→ 'grids', 'skeleton', 'topological'

[MG] The fuselage is a lightweight framework or flexible bearing structure open to topological variations.

 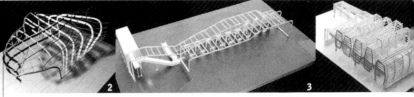

1. Geodetic fuselages under construction in Vickers factory, in *Fisuras* 3 1/3, 1995. **2.** Dominique JAKOB, Brendan MACFARLANE, *Restaurant Le Georges*, Centre Pompidou, Paris, 2000. **3.** WMA Willy Müller Arquitectos (with Fred GUILLAUD), *Recycling plant for urban waste*, Mercabarna, Barcelona, 2002. **4.** Enric MIRALLES, Benedetta TAGLIABUE, *Moore farm*, Lancashire (United Kingdom), 1999-.

✕ future

→ 'entropy', 'hybrid', 'impermanences', 'inform(ation)al', 'proneoism', 'virtual'

[VG] **(vision)**

One possible scenario that has been described for the future of our habitable environments suggests a virtual reality, accessible by means of glasses, that functions effectively reveal a fast, light-filled, beautiful, excited world. When we take off the glasses, the city we live in is dark and dangerous, full of waste and violence. The future may indeed be a dynamic, light-filled virtual world and a dark, decadent physical world.

[VG] **(hybridisation)**

The best way to prevent the two worlds – physical and virtual – from separating is for them to become the same. Energy put into the construction of the virtual world should also be applied to the re-information of the physical world. Why should cities grow physically if their populations don't? In fact, cities of coming years will have to grow inwards. They will have to make and produce things in less space, thereby increasing the quality of existing buildings and public spaces. When building new spaces, we have to think about both the quality and the permanence of solid construction and about the mobility and flexibility required by their interaction with the virtual world.

Each new street has to be prepared to reflect and to be reflected in the virtual world. Not only does this require the construction of cabled streets which convey information at high speeds to the adjacent dwellings, but also information has to flow through public space. Public space has to be sensitive to the people who inhabit it. It has to allow the active expansion (in the form of sport and leisure) of the people who are digitally concentrated in the surrounding dwellings. It must enable the flexible regulation of flows of vehicles and persons and actively manage the climatic and atmospheric phenomena of its environment.

The industrial society brought about a transformation to produce basic quality, in the city and in the dwelling, for as many people as possible. The information society has to seek maximum quality for a maximum number of places. More is More.

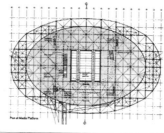

DILLER & SCOFIDIO,
Blur Building,
Yverdon-les-bains
(Switzerland), 2002.

Josep MIÀS, *Bar and bath
area "Els banys vells"*,
Banyoles (Girona, Spain),
1997.

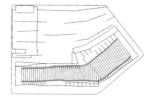

Ginés GARRIDO, Ricardo
SÁNCHEZ LAMPREAVE,
Fernando PORRAS,
*Competition for auditoriur
and conference centre*,
Pamplona (Navarra,
Spain), 1998.

WMA Willy Müller
Arquitectos, *Cultural
Centre*, Santa Pola
(Alicante, Spain), 2002
(finalist).

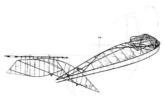

Enric MIRALLES,
Benedetta TAGLIABUE,
*Rehabilitation of Santa
Caterina Market*,
Barcelona, 1999-.

José Alfonso
BALLESTEROS, *Complex
Resort office building*,
La Habana, 1998.

NOX (Lars Spuybroek with
Joan Almekinders, Dominil
Holzer, Sven Pfeiffer,
Wolfgang Novak, Remco
Wilcke), *wetGRID, exhibi-
tion design for 'Vision
Machine'*, Musée des Beau
Arts, Nantes (France),
1999-2000.

G

■●◆★ game

[JM] Design is the act of unpredictably uniting diversity. Perhaps it has occurred to some that this has to do with a certain image of how a game is developed. As if in a game, infinity is permanently opened by moves that insistently release chaos and chance. Chance play and uncertain development is initiated by the moves of a game. Games formulate new laws in each move, in each play. In fact, there is no universality in thinking about the end of a game. Our game seems to be more like cheating.

[MG] See 'magic' and 'ludic.'
Games are exercises of skill, cleverness or combination not always predictable and habitually subject to rules of chance. In the case of children's games, they are topologically informal behaviours. Certain non-determinist configurations respond to dispositional games based upon manifold combinatorial systems or distributions of random order.

[FS] Game is to design, to negotiate.

[co] A game is the interaction of one or more agents, players, with a set of known and fixed formal rules that involve gains and losses.

[i] p. 250-251

FRANCISCO TOLCHINSKY

VIRTUAL FLIPPER

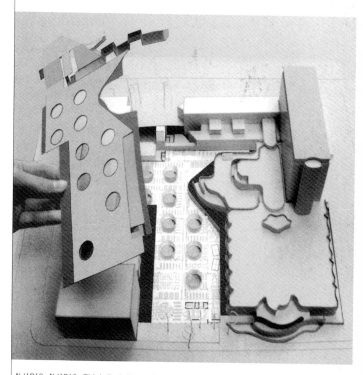

NJIRIC+NJIRIC, *Think Pad, New Library for the School of Architecture*,
UPC, Barcelona, 2000.

GAMES OF CHANCE

cards

 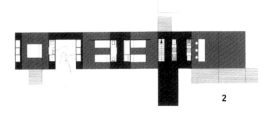

dominoes

dice

mikado

GAMES OF CONSTRUCTION

 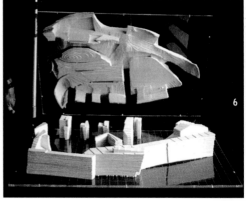

CUTOUT GAMES

GAME OF LETTERS

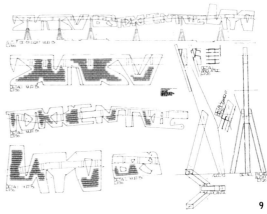

scrabble

1. ÁBALOS & HERREROS, *Abandoibarra planning*, Bilbao (Spain), 1994. 2. ACTAR ARQUITECTURA, *M'House Houses*, 2000. 3. ACTAR ARQUITECTURA, *Europan: 400 dwellings* (finalist), Ceuta (Spain), 1999. 4. S&Aa (SORIANO-PALACIOS), *Europan 4*, Bilbao (Spain), 1996. 5. Josep MIÀS, *Kindergarten*, Camós (Girona, Spain), 1997. 6. AMP (ARTENGO-MENIS-PASTRANA), *Conference centre Tenerife Sur*, Playa de las Américas, Costa Adeje (Tenerife, Spain), 1998-. 7. Federico SORIANO, Ricardo SÁNCHEZ LAMPREAVE, *Competition for cultural centre in the old factory of Cervezas El Águila*, Madrid, 1994. 8. Vicente GUALLART, Willy MÜLLER, Manuel GAUSA, ACTAR ARQUITECTURA, *Competition ARC OUEST*, Thessalonike (Greece), 1997. 9. Enric MIRALLES & Bendetta TAGLIABUE, *Colours Park*, Mollet del Vallès (Barcelona), 2001.

■● gaze

→ 'abstract',
'action>critical', 'criteria',
'eye', 'infiltration',
'maps (to) map', 'tactic',
'transversality'

[JM] The gaze is a glance that relies essentially on language and its histories, and ends with the meaning of words and things.

The gaze is the eradication of "true" stories, perhaps to make entrance into the present. Thanks to the gaze, space clears itself of time, it moves to its "outside" (M. Blanchot.) Space, thus visualized, is a radical transformation of time; it is as though what we check upon visualizing a photograph, where, on the fringe of narration, we presence the radicality of its figures.

[MG] **tactical gaze**

Until relatively recently, the gaze of disciplinary tradition has tended to be a uniform gaze over things: a confident gaze upon the slowness of change, the stability of shapes and the literality of their manifestations: fixed, precise, static images. In other words, the gaze of the trade (and the discipline). Today, however, this same gaze, which had for so long been turned in upon itself, must suddenly, almost by surprise, disconcert and bewilderment, take stock of a less certain, less familiar and less predictable reality; a diffuse reality defined by jolts, shocks and perversions; determined to counter, time and again, any bucolic dream of perfect order or false harmony. Today, as we take in our environment, we are confronted not only with a new physical reality, but also with impressions that parallel it. As in a manipulated field, we are confronted with a multifaceted reality in which we feel disconcerting alienation from places. Our orientation, and our action, now require a new gaze which is more *hybrid* — multiple

Hybrid gaze, polyedric gaze, strategic gaze, in *SD* 4/95.

and mongrel. Probably something outlandish; the gaze of new — and curious — explorers equipped with focusing instruments and a variety of objects; mobile; multi-focused. A polyhedral gaze is no longer unidirectional, fixed or stabilised, but rather synchronising, open to multiple stimuli, material and immaterial, figurative and abstract. It is not an endogenous gaze, but rather an extrogenous gaze; not a pure gaze, but an impure gaze; not a stable gaze, but a mutating gaze; not a distant gaze — indifferent and confident — but rather a meaningful and committed gaze; not a merely objective gaze but, above all, a tactical gaze (cold, involved, astute and, at the same time, positivist). We talk about a gaze aimed no longer at reproducing models, but rather at recognising relationships; not at recognising categories, but rather at reopening them, linking them or interconnecting them in new tactical contracts, sometimes unnaturally. Merely descriptive instruments yield to new processing instruments; the eye or the lens yield to strange and new tele- and multi-lenses, radars and interfaces, but also scanners and sensors capable of capturing the near and the distant, the place and all places.

✺ generation

→ 'recursiveness',
'seed'

[VG] Paul Virilio maintains that a generation is twenty years. Twenty years is the time that Ray Kurzweil calculates it will takes a conventional computer to have the same reasoning capacity as a human being. Will the next generation interact with people and computers without distinguishing between them?

▲● genetics

→ 'avatar', 'cultivations', 'cuttings', 'dynamism', 'evolutionary', 'genetics of form', 'graft', 'housys', 'hybrid', 'mutation', 'open', 'operative', 'scaleless', 'seed', 'vector'

[FP] **(genetics revolution)**

After the proletarian revolution was the industrial revolution. After the industrial revolution was the revolution of communications. After the revolution of communications was the revolution of genetics. Without a doubt, one of the most controversial topics today concerns genetic maps – genomes – of living beings. During the era in which the possibilities of intervening in our biological structure via-à-vis genetics, the human being has become something more than a simple spieces on Earth. Today, Mary Shelley's idea of the new is more believable than ever. However, what really is worth highlighting is that in 1998 the gene of asymmetry was discovered. That is, a *topological gene* that without which life would not be possible. Vertebrate beings are determined by this gene, which allows their positioning according to compensatory and balancing laws, although always asymmetrical. We acknowledge the possibility of creating projects with genes, of being able to give structures, organisms or contexts the possibility of transforming themselves through propositive action. Our idea is not to compose, but to generate; not to organise, but to provide guidelines; not to sort, but to develop.

1

[MG] **(self-reproduction and evolutivity)**

The evolutionary condition of the contemporary device alludes to a genetic process between code and development, between simulation and process, which in turn alludes to the self-reproductive capacity of evolutionary organisms. If we examine the case of the information contained in the double helix of deoxyribonucleic acid (DNA), we see that one of the molecules – the genotype – transforms into a organism – a phenotype – due to a complex process that encompasses the production of proteins, the replication of the DNA, replication of cells, and gradual differentiation between cell types, etc. This development of the phenotype through the genotype – epigenesis – produces an entangled chain of combinations, cycles of chemical reactions and feedback loops. When the construction of the organism is complete, its characteristics do not necessarily bear similarity to its genotype. However, it seems evident to attribute the material structure of the organism to the structure of its DNA, and exclusively so. We distinguish between visible or prosaic isomorphisms (those in which the portions of a structure can easily project themselves on to the portions of the other) and invisible isomorphisms – abstract or "mysterious" – of more difficult analogical projection. Both allude to a flexible evolution of shape grounded in basic nuclear logics which stimulate the free (but recursive) evolution of events and future movements.

2

1. Cromosome.
2. Eduardo ARROYO (NO.mad Arquitectura), *Europan 5: hybridisation process 001* (1st prize), Barakaldo (Vizcaya, Spain), 1999.

[MG] **genome**

The genome is nuclear information that defines the patterns – or logics – of the development of evolutionary organisms.

By extension, the genome is a basic diagram, criterion for action, seminal trajectory or basic programme of a system or operative and/or generative device.

● ★ genetics of form

[MG] The assumption of an elastic – topologic – systemisation of shape, in certain open processes of generation (combinations of formal transformations produced through the synthesis and reprogramming of complex geometries) foreshadows what is called a new "genetics of shape." This "genetics of shape" is based upon the programming of fluctuant dynamic systems in dynamic force fields, which, in turn, evolve – (and are simulated, orientated, induced and materialised – through spatial processes (virtual and real) developing over time. Greg Lynn, one of the pioneers – along with Karl T. Chu, Marcus Novack, the Nox team or, more pragmatically, Ben van Berkel, Kas Oosterhuis, FOA, etc. – in this field of computer animation and of the dynamical conception of formal processes recently pointed out:

"*The concept of a discrete, ideal and fixed prototype can be subsumed by the model of the numerically controlled multitype that is flexible, mutable and differential. By modelling the potential of multiple variables as what is often referred to as a "performance envelope" a series of possibilities can be designed from which particular configurations are exemplified.*"

Architecture, therefore, comes to model itself not as a sculpture or as a drawing, but rather as a mobile flow, a co-participant, inserted into an environment populated by differential forces of attraction and movement that define directional tensions. These tensions, conceivable as shapes, emerge from processes that ply space, as a current materialisable yet always virtually open to fluctuations.

[co] ## genetic architecture

Genetic architecture is a morphogenetic paradigm predicated on the generative formation of architecture based on an internal principle. It is an information-theoretic approach directed towards research and propagation of information capital which underlies the principle of genetic constitution. As such, it is situated at the intersection of two complimentary modes of development: endogenesis and exogenesis. Endogenesis pertains to ontogeny founded upon an axiomatic principle or code, which determines the development of phenotype, or emergent form of a species, based on the interactions of genotypes. Exogenesis corresponds to phylogeny, the evolution and differentiation of species from a non-linear historical perspective. Even though it relies on the logic of recursion to generate emergent phenomenon within a computational environment, it is not devoid of an hermeneutical dimension with regard to phylogenetic differentiation: a phenomenology of interiority constituted by the artificial life of proto-species of architecture having both deconstructive and projective propensities within demiurgic space. KARL S. CHU

Karl S. CHU /
X Kavya, *X Phylum*,
1999.

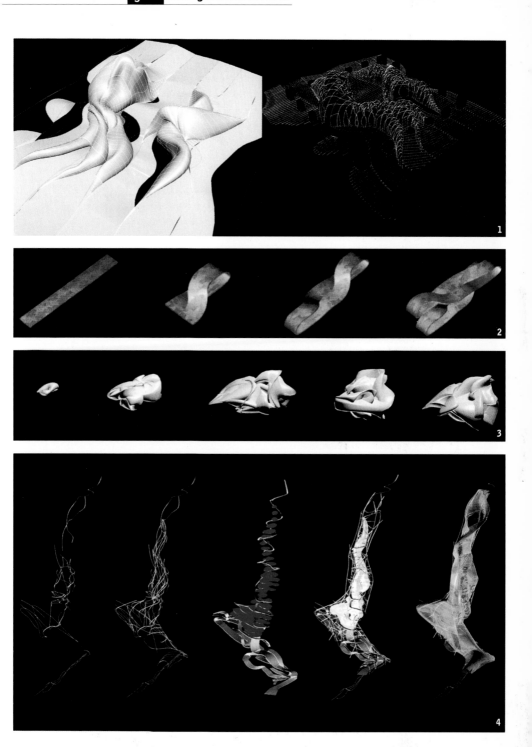

1. NOX (Lars Spuybroek with Joan Almekinders, Dominik Holzer, Sven Pfeiffer, Wolfgang Novak, Remco Wilcke), *wetGRID, exhibition design for 'Vision Machine'*, Musée des Beaux Arts, Nantes (France), 1999-2000. **2.** FOA, *Virtual House*, 1997. **3.** John H. FRAZER, Manit RASTOGI, Peter GRAHAM, *The Interactivator*. **4.** NOX/LARS SPUYBROEK, *Beachness*, Noordwijk (The Netherlands), 1997.

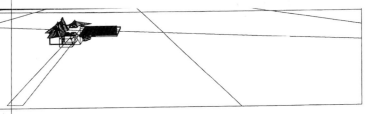

Vicente GUALLART, *House at the desert*, 1991.

▲■✖ geography

[FP] **(metadiscipline)**

We have heard Ricardo Sánchez Lempreave saying that architecture really belongs to another metadiscipline: Geography. Terms such as mapping,
exploring or colonising, are but ways of mentally limiting a territory, whether
physical or not, which constitute a close and recurrent terminology. We
draw maps, later we possess/construct the mapped setting and it is architecture which allows us to do this. Mapping is an intellectual experience,
it transcends the physical medium we are going through to sift/select it
or charge/codify it. In this way, this geographical act summarises multiple
operations in one, translating a series of codes full of meanings or information into a legible medium (map). We believe that this is an act of true
construction, equivalent to the most canonical profession. In this sense, our
tools have been exponentially enriched, because as geographers, more than
anything else, we do not compose spaces anymore, but conform settings
with data, panoramas, phenomena, etc. (Architects who are not geographers, no longer exist for us.)

[JM] **(vectorised)**

Geographical reality is controlled by vectors, that is, forces that intervene in the evolution, transformation and structure of landscapes, as well
as in social, political and economic activity – forces in which the prediction is always relative, shifting and changing. From this point of view, we
can say that geography predicts a vectorised project that encloses different forces than that of prefigured reality.

[VG] **(geographies)**

The twenty-first century will see an inversion of the process that began during the Renaissance, in which men and women began to gather together
in cities to live.
The development of physical transport networks (car, train, plane) and
telematic networks means that any point on the planet – city and country
– is suitable for living and working. Motorways criss-cross territory modified by man using agriculture or border natural spaces that are now the
green areas of inhabited territory. These motorways are the avenues of a
new city that has no limits.
They are constructed in the landscape by making a section of the earth and
displaying its internal nature.
The streets no longer run between facades, but between stratified masses. Man
has 'urbanised' the territory by means of agriculture for centuries now, creating irrigation systems and planting crops in keeping with the laws of geometry.

He has denaturalised natural spaces by planting natural elements. The spacing of the various trees and plants depends both on the size of the crop itself and on the harvesting systems used. Each crop produces its own texture and colour upon the territory.

In mountainous terrain, slopes have been turned into finite elements by the construction of terraces. In harsh climates, greenhouses can be used to overcome the specific conditions of place with the creation of light-weight constructions containing microclimates imported from other latitudes.

Agriculture is being industrialised.

The landscape is being urbanised.

The spectacle of nature and that of the city are now comparable.

Represented in this way, nature can now be reconstructed by man. The world is turning into a habitable environment, into the city of 1,000 geographies...

MVRDV, *Silicone Hill*, Stockholm (Sweden), 2000, competition for the Sweden Post Headquarters.

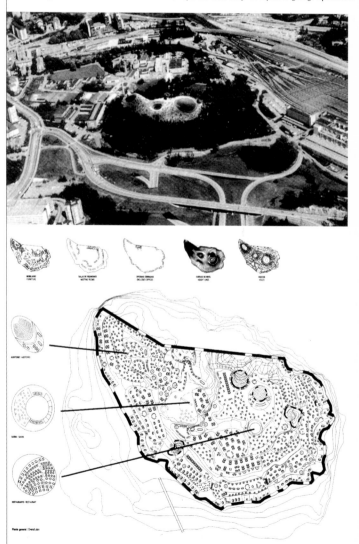

Geography

1 a-scalarity	10 logic, digital	18 hyperplace
2 avatar	11 Gibson's	19 land(s) in lands
3 artificial	sprawl	20 materiature
4 self-similarity	12 stampings	21 mountains
5 buds	13 fractal	22 nature
6 body	14 geomancy	23 papyroflexy
7 crests	15 geometry	24 pixels
8 craters	16 hybrid	25 progression
9 bluntings	17 inflatable	26 surface

●✗ geomancy

[MG] See 'maps (to map)'.

"*It is not, now, a question of drawing urban textures, traffic flows, uses, sections of street, frontages, but of analyzing the shapes of mountains, watercourses, winds, the amount of sun, open spaces, vegetation, transport systems... The combined articulation of all these models would seem to guarantee continuity within architectural thinking: between world and habitat, nature and culture, setting and building, group and individual. If in China nature is drawn with a brush in black and white, simultaneusly representing the plant and its elevation, our own means are now different.*"

(GUALLART, Vicente, "The City of a 1000 geographies", *Quaderns* 217, 1997)

[VG] Building in cities calls for an analysis of the site; building in non-cities requires a similar process of analysis.

Any analysis requires a process of representation.

In Chinese tradition there is a science, geomancy, to determine the appropriate positioning of cities and dwellings in the landscape.

Geomancy involves, firstly, a theoretical model that reflects the organisation of the world, and secondly, an analytical model that allows the specific observation of places, as well as determining a system of correspondence used for composition which allows for the combination of space of representation, project and living space.

In traditional thought of the Far East, we note the absence of a dichotomy between nature and culture, bringing an overall approach to the environment, be it a natural place or urban environment. Unlike fixed architectural models (orders, types, etc.), geomancy prefigures the rules of play and the conception of form remains open.

Our immediate physical environment (the vineyards of El Penedès, the plains of Zamora or the cork oäk forests of Badajoz), about to be manipulated by the forces of history and economy, ought to be analysed in a similar way.

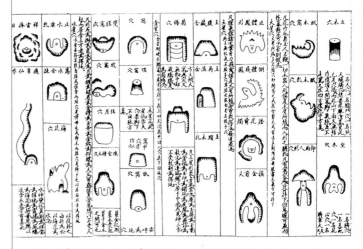

Graphic, in CLÉMENT, Sophie; CLÉMENT, Pierre; YONG-HAK, Shin, *Architecture du paysage en Extrême Orient*, Paris: École Nationale Supérieure des Beaux-Arts, 1987.

✱ ◆ ● geometry

[VG] If architecture is landscape, buildings are mountains. If buildings are mountains, geometry is geography.

[FS] **(formal)**

What is the form of a fish?

I will imagine a geometry whose simple forms are not the cube, sphere or dodecadron. We will speak of "cloud forms," "rock forms," "void forms" and "fencing forms." A "cloud form" is produced by the equilibrium between what goes on in its interior and that which surrounds it. It is not constant, but rather too voluble, translucent.

On the other hand, a "rock form" is formed only by its internal processes of gestation: a self-produced metamorphosis becoming a compact form.

An "empty form" is defined by its face. Its meaning is not in the figure of model space but in its pauses and interruptions. The "empty form" is what remains between sounds and silences; it is neither figure nor ground.

The "fencing form" is the trace, the movement of the object that defines its structure; the mobile point as opposed to the three axes of space.

[MG] See 'topological' and 'trajectory.'

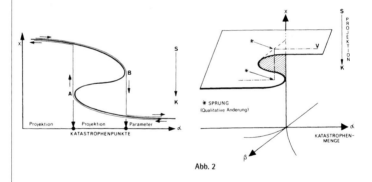

Abb. 2

Mathematic graphics of the morphogenesis from catastrophe situations, by René Thom, in "Emergenz: Die Entstehung von Radikal Neuem," *Arch+* 119-120, Dec 1993.

+ gestrategies

[WM] The term 'strategy' refers to a concept closely linked to the city and to the military. In ancient Greece, the mayor of a city was called a "strategist." Strategy was the emergence of the city as a war machine, which has more to do with preparation for war than with its actual waging. Strategy is a way of preparing the city for war. 'Gesture,' however, is an alien term, something which is in all certainty not of the city. 'Gestrategies' is an oxymoron, a contradiction between citizens' rights and the astuteness of peripherals, in permanent construction of unstable equilibriums.

[WM] See 'maps, battle'.

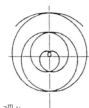

$x^m = a^m v$

intertwined

S&Aa (Federico SORIANO, Dolores PALACIOS), *Europan 5* (mention), Barakaldo (Vizcaya, Spain), 1998.

spiral trajectories

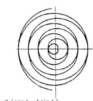

$x = a (\cos t + t \sin t)$
$y = a (\sin t + t \sin t)$

spiral

Cecil BALMOND (Ove Arup), ACTAR ARQUITECTURA, *Telecommunication Tower on the Turó de la Rovira*, Barcelona, 2001-.

spiral trajectories

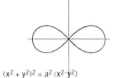

$(x^2 + y^2)^2 = a^2 (x^2 - y^2)$

braid

FOA, *Virtual House*, 1997.

braid trajectories

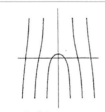

$y = x \cot(\pi x/2a)$

coiled

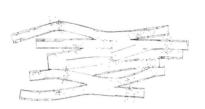

Cristina DÍAZ MORENO, Efrén GARCÍA GRINDA, *G House, International Competition "Goethe's House"* (2nd prize), Tokyo (Japan), 1999.

intertwined trajectories

$y = f(x)$

$y = cx$

$y = c$

$y = 0$

fraction

Vicente GUALLART, *House of seven peaks*, La Pobla de Vallbona (Valencia, Spain), 1998.

broken trajectories

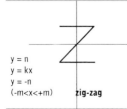

$y = n$
$y = kx$
$y = -n$
$(-m < x < +m)$ **zig-zag**

Alberto NICOLAU, Montse DOMÍNGUEZ, *Europan 5* (1st prize), Almere (The Netherlands), 1999.

zig-zag trajectories

◆ gesture

→ 'form'

[FS] *"The imagination of men has invented giants to attribute the construction of great caverns and enchanted cities. Reality has later shown that these great caverns were really made by a drop of water. By the pure drop of water, patient and eternal. In this case, as in so many others, reality wins. More beautiful is the instinct of the drop of water than the hand of the giant. The real truth beats imagination in poetry, that is, imagination itself discovers its poverty. Imagination logically attributed to giants what seemed like the work of giants; but scientific reality, poetic to the extreme and outside of logic, puts truth in the clean, perennial drop of water.*
Because it is more beautiful that a cave is the mysterious whim of water, linked and ordered by eternal laws, than the whim of giants that have no more reason than imagination." (GARCÍA LORCA, Federico, "Imaginación, inspiración, evasión", *Obras Completas*, México: Aguilar, 1991, tomo III)

✖ Gibson's sprawl

→ 'abroad, etc.',
'cyberspace',
'environment',
'limit', 'logic, digital',
'virtual'

[VG] *"Home was BAMA, Sprawl, the Boston-Atlanta Met-ropolitan Axis. Program a map to display frequency of data exchange, every thousand megabytes a single pixel on a very large screen. Manhattan and Atlanta burn solid white.* Then they start to pulse, the rate of traffic threatening to overload your simulation. Your map is about to go nova. Cool it down. Up your scale. Each pixel a million megabytes. At a hundred million mega-bytes per second, you begin to make out certain blocks in midtown Manhattan, outlines of hundred-year-old industrial parks ringing the old core of Atlanta..." (GIBSON, William, *Neuromancer*, London: Grafton, 1986)

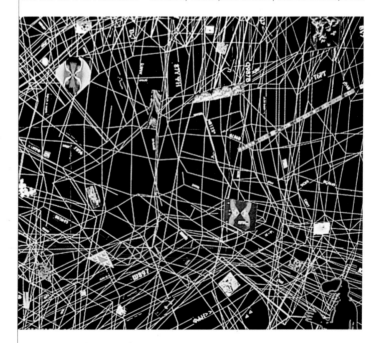

Vicente GUALLART, Nuria DÍAZ, *Informational city*, 1995.

★ ✖ global city

[CO] The global city is precisely the synthesis of these two scales – the old and the new. It overrides and neutralizes older hierarchies of scale and functions as an enormously complex sited materiality with global span. In the era of globalisation, the state also participates in the neutralization of these national encasings. The state, therefore, is not just a victim of globalisation. It actively participates in producing laws that facilitate the partial denationalisation of the global city, creating opportunities for foreign actors, foreign markets, foreign firms, and foreign cultural institutions to be operative in what was once constructed as the national.
SASKIA SASSEN

[VG] **global village**
See 'city?' and 'global (globality).'

● global (globality)

→ 'artificial', 'context', 'criteria', 'de-location', 'environment', 'glocal', 'holistic', 'knowledge', 'limit', 'no-places', 'places', 'simultaneity'

[MG] Often a culture's defense against the global appears to define itself in terms of the dangers of globalisation – with cultural homogenisation – with a hypothetical collaborationism; with the hegemonic mechanisms of colonisation, with the acritical consumption of exterior novelty. Globality does not mean globalisation. A culture of the global speaks of plurality rather than of homogeneity, of a broader vision of things: engaged with the advance of ideas and of technology, but also with the understanding of – dissimilar – phenomena during a time of differences and, as well, of interlinkages; with interchange of information, not only as a possibility for communication but, above all, for interaction.

Contrast, in KOOLHAAS Rem; MAU, Bruce (OMA), *S,M,L,XL*, Rotterdam: 010, 1995.

● ★ globalisation

→ 'artificial', 'context', [MG]
'criteria', 'de-location',
'environment', 'glocal',
'holistic', 'knowledge',
'limit', 'no-places', 'places',
'simultaneity'

Globalisation of the financial system – in what has been called "advanced capitalism" – is one of the most uncertain and determinate factors of new contemporary urban organisations: in them capital can operate instantaneously on a global scale, the result being the progressive devaluation of spatial delimitations. Parallel to this process of delocalisation of productive structures, cities evolve dynamically and obliquely (slanted or skewed, biased or tilted), converted into more or less effective poles of attraction whose success depends upon the capacity and quality of the supply of certain facilities, whereby the development of cultural and productive activity is possible.

This trend constitutes one of the primary factors in the reinterpretation of recent urban disciplines and illustrates the shift from an "essayistic" understanding of the city (centred on its physical materialisation and its morphology) to a more holistic – and strategic – understanding, capable of addressing this systematic, non-linear and plural dimension of its current complexity. This complexity is produced by a whole no longer solely additive (comprehensible in the linear aggregation of its parts) but rather multiplied – not only in the physical but also in the virtual – aimed at dealing simultaneously with different levels of realities as well as different levels – and sensitivities – of reading.

[i] p. 266

[c] globalisation and mixture

"*Moroccans doing Thai boxing in Amsterdam, Asian rap in London, Irish bagels, Chinese tacos, Mardi Gras Indians in the United States, Mexican school children dressed in Greek togas... Coca-Cola at the foot of the pyramids, McDonald's in Beijing, Mercedes in Ouagadougou, Adidas footwear in Moscow and Dallas in Japan... different examples of the so-called 'economic globalisation,' of the worldwide expansion of capitalism, of the dominance of the multinationals... the phenomenon of globalisation speaks not only of a simple process of diffusion, that of a dominant and hegemonic culture, but also of more complex processes that take the form of multiple interchanges between dominators and dominated, the ones recycling in part the culture of the others. One of the more decisive and disconcerting differences in contemporary globalisation is that, beyond the old idea of imposition, it finds in local specificities elements useful for its own dynamics.*"

(ASCHER, François, *Essai sur la société contemporaine*, Paris: Ed. de l'aube, 2000. Translated from Spanish.)

● ★ glocal

→ 'abstract', [MG]
'a-couplings', 'a-scalarity',
'cohabitation', 'globalisation',
'in-filtration>intrusiveness',
'limit', 'm. city', 'networks',
'places', 'simultaneity',
'society of the and, the',
'strategy', 'synthetical', 'tactic'

Global and local. Simultaneously. Glocal is phenomena, register, devices or information capable of resonating with the local and transferring to the global, capable of being a system and place at the same time; abstract logic with a singular result. Glocal is any event that responds to the particular and interconnects with the general; that is, of a territory and of many – or all – territories at once: generic and specific. Abstract and concrete.

This identity is not only substantial but, above all, relational of the glocal applied to a possible architecture understood, in turn, as a glocal device: capable of generating crosses and interbreedings, recursivities and resonances, multiscalar combinations and transferences. Glocal is able, to yield, for each concrete situation, a certain local map of the global scene.

PÉRIPHÉRIQUES with MVRDV,
Quai Branly Museum of Arts and Civilisations, Paris, 1999.

[c] "*Numerous authors have used the notion of glocal or glocalisation to describe the dual process that produces at once global and local. The word seems somewhat vague but it effectively transmits the dialogical nature of this phenomenon of enduring and productive coexistence between two opposites.*

In fact, there is no term more appropriate. We shall speak as well of hybridisation, although that notion has given rise to countless debates. Hybridisation is a mixture that does not wipe out the genetic origins, rather it combines them with others, giving them a new twist and course.

Glocalisation, producing global and local, questions those national cultural (even federal) paradigms that serve to support the construction of nation states and their imaginary institutionalisation."
(ASCHER, François, *Essai sur la société contemporaine*, Paris: Ed. de l'aube, 2000. Translated from Spanish.)

[co] **glocal economy**

The tearing away of the new net subeconomy from the context and its replacement by the fact of the global has uncertain implications for urban practice and theory. The strategic operation is not the search for a connection with the "surroundings", the context. It is, rather, installation in a strategic cross-border geography constituted through multiple "locals". In the case of the economy, I see a re-scaling: old hierarchies - local, regional, national, global - do not hold. Moving to the next scale in terms of size is no longer how integration is achieved. The local now transacts directly with the global - the global installs itself in locals and the global is itself constituted through a multiplicity of locals.
SASKIA SASSEN

S'A (Carlos SANT'ANA),
nuc, nomad use camaleonic, 2000.

→ 'action', 'event'

★ **gonzo architecture**

[co] Gonzo architecture is a concept invented by Pablo de Soto (*wewearbuildings*, 2001): The action/event resulting from the application of the principles of gonzo journalism to the practice of architecture. In its seminal form, it has manifested itself as a blend of situationism and cyberpunk. Gonzo journalism was invented by Hunter S. Thompson in the 1960s-70s. It is based upon a practice similar to that of the participative observation of the social sciences, although taken to extremes of risk and violence. Therefore, gonzo architecture consists of the construction of an architectural or urban situation in which the participants are dragged into a radical, transgressive, confrontational becoming that reaches the limits of ecstatic inebriation; giving rise – in the words of Raoul Vaneigem – to poetry that changes life and transforms the world. In known conditions, the vehicle for this sort of event is some sort of architectural machine. Production should have an explicit spatial/artistic/political dimension.
JOSÉ PÉREZ DE LAMA

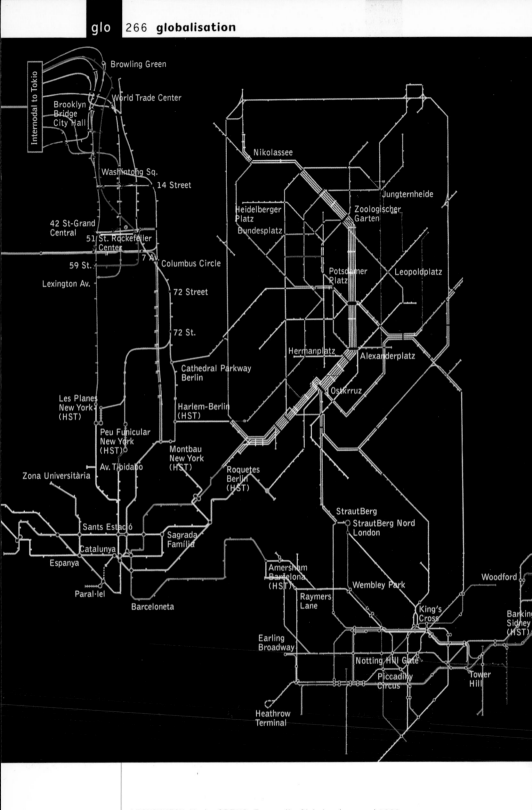

Internodal to Tokio

Browling Green

Brooklyn
Bridge
City Hall

World Trade Center

Nikolassee

Washintong Sq.

14 Street

Jungternheide

Heidelberger
Platz

Zoologischer
Garten

42 St-Grand
Central

Bundesplatz

51 St. Rockefeller
Center

7 Av.

Columbus Circle

Potsdamer
Platz

Leopoldplatz

59 St.

Lexington Av.

72 Street

72 St.

Hermanplatz

Alexanderplatz

Cathedral Parkway
Berlin

Ostkrruz

Les Planes
New York
(HST)

Harlem-Berlin
(HST)

Peu Funicular
New York
(HST)

Montbau
New York
(HST)

Av. Tibidabo

Zona Universitària

Roquetes
Berlin
(HST)

StrautBerg

StrautBerg Nord
London

Sants Estació

Catalunya

Sagrada
Família

Espanya

Amersham
Barcelona
(HST)

Woodford

Paral·lel

Raymers
Lane

Wembley Park

Barcin
Sidney
(HST)

Barceloneta

King's
Cross

Earling
Broadway

Notting Hill Gate

Piccadilly
Circus

Tower
Hill

Heathrow
Terminal

ARCHIKUBIK, Xavier CREUS, *Transpolis, Global underground,* 1999.

■ goodbye to the metaphor

→ 'action>critical',
'allegory', 'criteria',
'dictionary', 'event',
'innovation', 'logic, direct',
'meaning', 'positioning',
'transversality'

[JM] Recent history narrates the unrepeatable. The near is not, then, the "near future."(Rainer Maria Rilke) To design today is to say "goodbye to metaphor."

Reality pushes us to be realists, and to make corresponding architecture. "Goodbye metaphor." The architecture or art that interests us now does not "speak" upon "being;" on the contrary, it proposes a singular syntax for architecture that elicits multiple sensibilities, both unable to be put together and unpredictable.

All design attempts to convey meaning, however, in the work we are discussing, there exists an uncertain relation between form and meaning, that makes its exegesis or reasoning difficult.

The affect, derived from this attempted design sense, is uncertain but supported by the phenomenological, so that the enjoyment of space and time is derived specifically from the outcome of the nearby and far-off, between reality and metaphor.

The work's meaning provokes the structuring of unexpected knowledge. Never more opportune, one can say that to design is to know. This knowledge opens up new categories of "cubbyholes," demonstrating the possibilities of experience.

To open possibilities, to construct new worlds.

[JM] See 'abstract'.

◆ graft (in-jection)

→ 'ad-herence',
'antitypes', 'genetics of
form', 'hybrid',
'infiltration', 'meldings',
'no-form', 'prosthesis',
'skeleton', 'strategy'

[FS] We sign up for the international grafter. His objective: to apply a portion of live thought to a mummified or lesioned part of the body and produce an organic union. Until today, this has never been applied outside of plastic surgery.

The grafter has a powerful instrument, the graft: inserting one thing into another. It is about putting words and forms in place and mixing them together. It is a creative field born of known sources, mounting literal pieces, reusing materials still in use, transplants, refeeding. All elements are susceptible and can produce a result.

The grafter, by definition, must consider himself an intruder. The same would serve as an example, transplanting from one place to another. Nothing could prevent his daring.

The grafter's trait is self-confidence. He must fear taking something for granted. His dread is transferred to his work, at once being and negating art.

[FS] Jonathan Culler writes that while one cannot determine the meaning of anything outside its context, no context is all-encompassing.

Any context is open to new, added description, and any intent to codify this context can be grafted onto the context that one has tried to describe, leading to a new context.

One can not determine any meaning outside of this new context, but no new context is all-encompassing.

▲● ★grids

[FP] The environment, the territory and some architecture can be defined as a superimposed and intertwined set of nets or webs which give sense and meaning to certain spaces and/or locations. These spaces are generated by grids, thereby rendering them artificial. These webs are alive and variable. They are shapeless and can receive the shape of what is contained by them, in the same way a liquid adopts the shape of its container. We are interested in grids/nets that are synthetic, simultaneous and synchronic with the architectonic item and vice-versa: architecture and environment, when inseparable from the idea of net or are the net itself, materialise in such way that tensions and relationships are drawn by the net, constructing and breaking links.

[MG] Grids are configurations that are resolved in orbit of a possible hybridisation between architecture and infrastructure replace, in effect, the idea of outline with that network and that of reticule with that of mesh.

This level of internal organisation points to a meshed organisation, aimed at favouring an elastic topology – a greater capacity for linkage and deformability – in the system. Grids create an effect of operative interconnectivity favoured by the interlinked logic of episodes and events themselves. What is interesting in such configurations is their flexible and infrastructural, rather than pure and rigidly structural nature. These are not, in fact, monolithic megastructures – totalitarian frameworks — but rather adaptable and deformable systems, open to manifold variables and singularities (according to context and use).

This points to the definition of an "operative matrix" – a more or less visible, evolutionary and flexible arrangement or link – capable of fostering a meshed relationship among different events, but also a firm disposition for distortion and alteration capable of articulating (and of accommodating), based upon this capacity for elastic adaptation, unexpectednesses springing from both the system itself and schemes alien to it.

The modern reticule thus yields to the contemporary mesh in which occupations and spacings, concentrations and dilatations, plaits and nodes tend to move – or slip – with respect to each other, and even to imbricate and overlap each other.

We speak, then, of meshes in their quasi-geodesic sense, as networks, cords (or arteries), defined through webs (matrixes) and nodes or braids (ties or links) associable, in a possible scalar jump, to the normed and threaded configuration of the large infrastructures of connection and articulation that, in turn, mesh the territory.

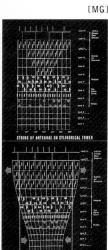

1. Cecil BALMOND, *Diagrams of structural concept for Chemnitz Stadium 2002*, Chemnitz (Germany), 1997, in *Assemblage* 33.

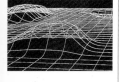

2. NJIRIC+NJIRIC, *Think Pad, New Library for the School of Architecture*, UPC, Barcelona, 2000.

[co] A grid is a location map of densities. When the locations are orthogonal to each other, and the densities involved are identical, like a system of points, then we have a Cartesian grid - the template of traditional building design. But in space-time, where mass densities induce gravitation, which, in turn, is a function of location, 'grid' becomes a mathematical set of probabilities. Written in tensor notation, the arrangement of such a grid becomes the array of a matrix placed in vertical and horizontal arrays.(The entities of a matrix are interdependent and no one point has preference or autonomy. The matrix is a picture of a grid as a simultaneous event.) CECIL BALMOND

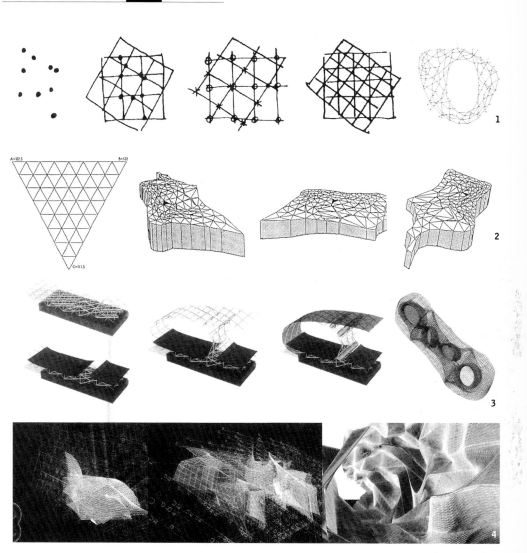

1. Cecil BALMOND, Peter KULKA, Ulrich KÖNIGS, *Roof geometric scheme for Chemnitz Stadium 2002*, Chemnitz (Germany), 1997. 2. Carlos FERRATER, Josep Lluís CANOSA, Beth FIGUERES, *Botanic garden*, Barcelona, 1999. 3. Ben VAN BER-KEL, Caroline BOS (UN Studio), *Competition for the National Swiss Exhibition 2001*, Yverdon-les-Bains, 1998. 4. Karl S. CHU (X-Kavya), *X-Phylum*, 1999.

★ ground

[co] See 'zero (0).'

Ground is a site of confrontation; utter demolition as in "ground up" (past tense of grind). AMANDA SCHACHTER / ALEXANDER LEVI

★ growing up

→ 'tree'

[co] Imagine a house for a horticulturist. Without permanent maintenance, without a regular cut of the trees, and a management of their growth, the house will collapse, strangled by trees. Nature is an attractive danger, very far from the tale for kid of dream of primitive forest. FRANÇOIS ROCHE

H

★ hacker

[c] "[originally, someone who makes furniture with an axe] 1. A person who enjoys exploring the details of programmable systems and how to stretch their capabilities, as opposed to most users, who prefer to learn only the minimum necessary. 2. One who programs enthusiastically (even obsessively) or who enjoys programming rather than just theorizing about programming. 3. A person capable of appreciating hack value. 4. A person who is good at programming quickly. 5. An expert at a particular program, or one who frequently does work using it or on it. 6. An expert or enthusiast of any kind. One might be an architecture hacker, for example. 7. One who enjoys the intellectual challenge of creatively overcoming or circumventing limitations." (The on-line hacker *Jargon File*, version 4.2.0, 31 Jan 2003)

★ hackitecture

→ 'appropriation strategies', 'cyber_punk', 'cyberspace', 'détournement', 'Gibson's sprawl', 'hacker'

[co] Hackitecture derives from hack and architecture: the unforeseen – and subversive – use of architectural and/or urban spaces, elements or systems. It includes manifestations that range from graffiti and "la movida" to the work of such architects as Santiago Cirugeda.

It is associated with the term hacktivism, coined in the latter 1990s to describe computer hackers dedicated to online activism. The semantic family is inspired in William Gibson' slogan: "the street always finds its own uses for technology." Although it has an eminently practical dimension, symbolically it may be associated with the situationist *detournement*. JOSÉ PÉREZ DE LAMA

+ hang

→ 'ad-herence', 'appropiation strategies', 'occupation structures'

1. *Rock Suspension,* Tokyo, in BECKMANN, John (ed.), *The Virtual Dimension*, New York: Princeton Architectural Press, 1998.
2. Álvaro SOTO, *Children library in Conde Duque barracks*, Madrid, 1993.
3. & 4. Willy MÜLLER + THB Consulting, *Factory*, Sant Andreu (Barcelona), 1998.

[WM] Hang is another subversive tactic for operating in occupied territories.
It relates to all structures that act upon properties using their space and occupying their volume instead of their ground.
Hanging is a structural tactic for spreading indirect forces, for spreading weight, without being the owner. The advance of this condition, in a new normative context, will permit us to build buildings inside buildings, just as we hang out on the web. Traction works in our favour.

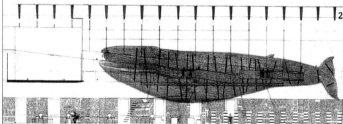

● hedonism

→ 'game', 'joy
(*alegria*)', 'leisure',
'ludic', 'optimism',
'pleasure', 'unrestrained
(<un> factors)'

[MG] Hedonism is an optimism that pursues or favours pleasure and enjoyment. That is to say, stimulus and games (of chance or of interchange).

[MG] *"What a mysterious sign there was on her body*
which turned into a burning iron.
The drawing of a line on his back,
A sudden desire to touch his skin.
To feel for a moment the pulse on his neck,
the desire to bite it slowly,
to let her tongue slide the length of a
totally prohibited back.
A totally prohibited back ..."

(ENQUIST, Per Olov, *The Fallen Angel*, Madrid: Ed. de la Torre, 1980. Translated from Spanish.)

(At the suggestion of Marc Aureli Santos)

PÉRIPHÉRIQUES,
Café Charbon, Paris,
1999.

◆ heterotopia

→ 'advanced> advanced
architecture', 'no-places',
'reality'

[FS] *"There are, and probably in every culture, in every civilization, real places, effective places, places detached from the institution itself of society, that are kinds of anti-sites, of utopias effectively realised in which real sites, all the other places that can be found in the interior of culture, are at once represented, contested and inverted; they are a type of place outside of place. These places, given that they are absolutely other than those sites that reflect and of those that are spoken about, I will call, as opposed to utopias, heterotopias."* (FOUCAULT, Michael, *"Espacios otros"*, Carrer de la Ciutat 1, 1978)

Utopias are unreal spaces. On the other hand, heterotopias are different spaces, real, in relation to true places, but in a way that they invert the meanings and properties that they in principle try to reflect, removed from the space of use in which society initially relegated them. They superimpose, in one place, various spaces that are incompatible in themselves. Utopias are descriptive; they are straight narrations. Heterotopias impede naming, undermine the meanings of words and their syntax, and even function and are understood in many different ways through time. We can classify heterotopias into types: crisis (privileged places or prohibited one, reserved for those individuals who have a temporal separation.) game (garden, cinema) and deviant (for behavior outside the norm), but in each case they are related to ruptures, to fractures in the suave future of time.

✖ high speed

→ 'infrastructures',
'transfers'

[VG] Concentrate to design. Where the urban concentration is greatest, at the inner limit of the city (historic centres), or at its outer limit, beyond the city periphery; in an environment formerly referred to as rural that is now a different kind of city; there, thirty minutes by car and by motorway from a high-speed train station, in the middle of a 'desert,' with the constant background noise of planes, trains and cars, permanently observed by satellites, man can create his own individual world.

[VG] High speed is when 100 km is measured 20 minutes.

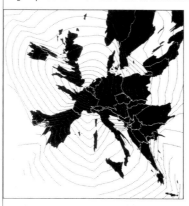

● hills

→ 'geography',
'landscapes, operative',
'mountain', 'paths &
peaks', 'reliefs',
'topographies, operative'

[MG] Hills are locations of isolated topographic elevation – either natural or artificial – lower than a mountain.

● ✖ history

→ 'action>critical',
'allegory', 'archaeology',
'erudition', 'gaze> tactical
gaze', 'memory', 'past',
'progress', 'time'

[MG] An authentically effective past is always a backwards-looking present.

[VG] If the cultural revolution brought about by machines and their aesthetic (hardware) in the 1920s produced a *tabula rasa* with regard to history, then the digital revolution of information (software) has to voice its alternative for action in the existing city. Four proposals:

Culture: how to integrate the knowledge that emanates from historic cities with universal knowledge in order to take action in our times? (using new technologies, evidently).

Image: how to take action in an environment that has many languages and codes accumulated over the course of history? (obviously, by creating a new one).

Mobility: how to achieve the mobility required today to be an active part of the city, maintaining the scale of historic cities (acting level by level, of course).

Uses: which activities are compatible with the spaces offered by the old cities? How should we act on the territorial scale of the macrocity without distorting the spatial qualities of the microcity? (the historic centre is one enormous building and ought to function as such...).

◆■+★ holes

→ 'appropiation strategies', 'devices', 'dispositions', 'energy', 'geometry', 'topological', 'void'

[FS] See 'diagonalisation.'

[JM] The space of the city, or better said, the space of architecture begins to make holes, transforming into a continuous, spongy fluid that makes room for the exchange and meeting of subjects.

The dwelling and urban space are joined, as if space and architecture were linked in an infinite hatch. Space, thus conceived, configures a network of diverse flights, of multiple escapes, like an echo which can not explain its exact origin and to where it will go, a space not contained by any limit or barrier that stops its flow.

In this new vectorised space, the effect of the eye — more than the glance — pursues space, the hollowed and the perforated, venturing into landscapes of uncontrollable prediction. An "optically incorrect" space is considered, with which we are not accustomed to working, mostly because the observed is now the observer.

The incisions of Matta-Clark or the telescopic spaces of Steven Holl illustrate the idea of cracked space, which creates an unseen and indiscrete reality. It seems as if space, that physically tranquil immateriality, has been exchanged with an expansive landscape. Spaces that are manipulated by force, at the mercy of dynamic diagrams of spatial organisation.

Leaning out of a hole
Evocation of an urban Tarzan, 1955, in YAPP, Nick, *The Hulton Getty Picture Collection, 1950's,* Köln: Könemann, 1998.

[WM] Holes are wild cards, "nothing:" "non-box" agents to be played whenever appropriate; infiltrated, exposed, converted into everything. Holes are also weak and easily manipulated: small — in line — and identical, at times they are confused with windows; regrouped, they show their potential, above all in difficult operations. The strategy of disseminating themselves or changing size proves very effective in deeply rooted boxes — and layers. Holes were the first stone of the advanced "boxes." Gordon Matta-Clark knew it — and opened them. Holes are a project.

[co] The works of Matta-Clark show us architectural bodies that have been mutilated, hacked away at, sectioned. Riddled with holes. Yet, the guiding logic of Matta-Clark's project is not a logic of arbitrary destruction, but a logic of geometrical drawing, as precise and "constructive" as that of the drawing the architect uses to design and build. When the immateriality of the geometric figures imposes itself on the material — "carnal" — reality of buildings, the result is a radical and surprising split. XAVIER COSTA

1. Gordon MATTA-CLARK, *Conical Intersect*, 1978, in VARIOUS AUTHORS, *Contra la arquitectura*, Castellón de la Plana: Ed. Espai d'Art Contemporani de Castelló, 2000.

2. José M. TORRES NADAL, *Intervention on the ramparts*, Cartagena (Spain), 1996.

3. Federico SORIANO, Ricardo SÁNCHEZ LAMPREAVE, *Competition for cultural centre in the old factory of Cervezas El Águila*, Madrid, 1994.

4. OMA, *Competition Très Grande Bibliothèque*, Paris, 1989.

5. MVRDV, *Media Galaxy (Competition concept for the new Eyebeam Institute)*, New York, 2001, 2nd prize.

6. Vicente GUALLART, *Europan 5: technological centre*, Puertollano (Ciudad Real, Spain), 1998.

7. Willy MÜLLER + THB Consulting, *Factory*, Sant Andreu (Barcelona), 1998.

8. NL, *BasketBar*, Utrecht (The Netherlands), 2000-.

9. IaN+, *New head office for DADA*, Firenze (Italy), 2001.

10. Antonio SANMARTÍN, Manuel ORTIZ, J.M. VALERO, *Day centre, Home for the Elderly and rehabilitation of the old Convent of the Capuchin Nuns*, Huesca (Spain), 1999.

11. NL, *WOS 8, thermical plant*, Leidsche Rijn (The Netherlands), 1998.

12. NEUTELINGS& RIEDIJK, *Minnaert*, Utrecht (The Netherlands), 1998.

13. MVRDV, *New Office of the Ministry of Agriculture*, The Hague (The Netherlands), 2000, study (3rd proposal).

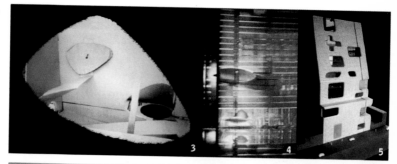

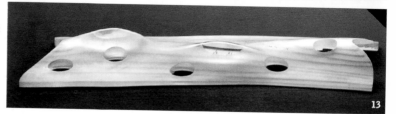

● holistic

→ 'action>critical',
'act-n', 'criteria',
'gaze> tactical gaze'

[MG] See 'knowledge.'

[MG] "*Up to now, most scientists have been too occupied with the development of new theories that describe what the universe is to ask the question why. On the other hand, the people whose business it is to ask why, the philosophers, have not been able to keep up with the advance of scientific theories.*

Science [has become] too technical and mathematical for [...] anyone except a few specialists. [...]

However, if we do discover a complete theory, it should in time be understandable to not just a few scientists [but also to] all, philosophers, scientists, and just ordinary people..."

(HAWKING, Stephen W., *A brief history of time: from the Big Bang to black holes*, London: Bantam, 1988)

[MG] An effective reading of an authentically advanced architectural production should transcend mere (self)disciplinary reference and foster a transverse gaze over the contemporary situation.

A holistic gaze capable of relating definition and organisation of the habitat and environment (ultimate essence of architecture) with interpretation – scientific, social, philosophical and artistic – of its associated space and time.

"*To know the nature of the things in order to act upon them.*"

Today, in place of the habitual predominance of a descriptive, autonomous – "autistic" – action, emerges a new holistic will concerned with fostering a more synaesthetic – more relational, precisely – action, capable of connecting the critical – local – diffusion of achievements (artistic or technical creation) with cultural – global – understanding of reality. A critical action concerned not only with describing occurrences but as well with approaching (explaining, understanding and favouring) processes; in multiscalar resonance.

The notion of holistic has to do with a shift in disciplinary gaze to one that is more open and no longer self-consumed; a more interactive gaze aimed at providing not descriptions, but links and crossings among shared experiences, trajectories, investigations; at once distinct and entwined.

● holograms

[MG] "*Reflected colors flowed across Molly's lenses as the men circled. The holograms were ten power magnifications; at ten [...] they had were just under a metre long. [...]*

They seemed to move alone, gliding with ritual calm, among arches and dance steps [...].

Molly's face, soft and serene, was turned upwards, watching.

'*I'll go look for something to eat,*' said Case. She nodded, lost in contemplation of the dance.*"

(Paraphrasing GIBSON, William, *Mona Lisa Overdrive*, London: Gollancz, 1988)

1. Scenery for the fashion show-exhibition *Rewind /Fast Forward* at the Musée de la Mode et du Textile, Paris, 1998, in RA-DI DESIGNERS, *Réalité fabriquée*, Arles: Actes Sud, 1999. **2.** Vicente GUALLART, *Holographic facade in the sky, House in the desert*, 1992. **3.** Mariko MORI, *Love entropy*, 1996, in *Parkett* 54, 1998/99. **4.** Enric RUIZ-GELI, *Stage design at the Liceu*, Barcelona, 2000.

● homeless

→ 'precarious(ly)',
'quidam', 'temporary',
'use'

[MG] See 'nomad.'

Homeless literally is without home. Urban nomad or possible *quidam*. Homeless defines a certain type of inhabitant of the metropolis lying beyond (or at the limit) of convention – due to either need or personal choice. Homeless is also another type of use of collective space based upon recycling, tactical exploitation of space and of disposables and a spontaneous, functionally non-fixed mobility.

1. Homeless vehicle (K. Wodiczko, 1980), in GAUSA, Manuel, *Housing. New alternatives, new system*, Barcelona: ACTAR, 1998. **2.** Homeless home, in *Colors* 27, 1998.

● horizons

[MG] Working with the horizon – that is, with an expanded emptiness – can be an architectural approach of the first order, not so much for its potential naturalist – pseudoecological – value, as for its important abstract component, beyond the objectual emergence of shape. This ambiguous quality of open – in "negative" – space, made up of absences rather than presences, an "architecture of the void" may thus be seen as an open force field, crossed by broad lines of escape, which manifest themselves forcefully as surfaces and horizons: encounters, ultimately, between sky and earth.

Josep MIÀS, *Bar and bath area "Els banys vells"*, Banyoles (Girona, Spain), 1997.

1. Vicente GUALLART, *Dwelling at the limit of the town*, Llíria (Valencia, Spain), 1995. **2.** LE CORBUSIER, *Beistegui top flat*, Paris, 1925. **3.** Rem KOOLHAAS, *Villa Dall'Ava*, Saint-Cloud (France), 1991 (from BRU, Eduard, *New landscapes, new territories*, Barcelona: ACTAR, 1997).

Vicente GUALLART,
*Dwelling at the
limit of the town,*
Llíria (Valencia,
Spain), 1995.

Javier PEÑA&MTM
Arquitectos, *Nueva
Espuña thematic
park*, Alhama de`
Murcia (Spain), 1997.

Manuel J. FEO,
Estratum-horizon:
global intervention,
San Vicente de la
Barquera (Cantabria,
Spain), 1999.

Victoria ACEBO,
Ángel ALONSO,
Cámara House,
Madrid, 1999.

★ ✗ hotel

[CO]

Until the 1960s, the hotel evolved as a space that swung between two apparently contradictory stances, efficiency (economy) and luxury, which long remained irreconcilable; the hotel emerged, like so many other things, from need and desire. Characteristic of the 20th century, the attempt to bring aristocratic consumption to the great mass of consumers revealed progressive attempts at synthesis of efficiency and luxury.

The most refined embodiment of this is found in the American hotel chains, which dress up the mechanised provision of services in a stage-like packaging that adopts partial elements of aristocratic luxury and attempts to dissimulate the lack of services with a flamboyantly kitsch rhetoric of appearance (decoration).

Hotels in Benidorm.

The Spanish charter-tourism hotel industry of the late 1960s and early 70s was geared towards sheer efficiency: conceived to provide mere satisfaction of the guests' basic needs, the hotel became a factory space and was stripped of its luxury trappings in compliance with strict rules of productivity. This was the factory-hotel in its most primitive form. Moving beyond this stage, and under the stimulus of new aspirations of the market, the end of the century saw the creation of a new hotel industry conceived to answer needs that went beyond the efficient performance of basic functionalities.

The new hotel – looking more and more like a cruise ship run aground in its efforts to meet its guests' demands for organised entertainment – seeks to sequester guests from the outside world through the structuring of a time sequence that gives rise to the construction of complementary extra spaces of growing importance. From this globalising pretension emerged the theme hotel: wrapped in shiny, noisy cellophane, yet unable to mask the fact of its being a factory-hotel. The only thing that sets the theme hotel apart from the former type is a different emphasis upon the real objectives of production. The rest is merely cosmetic. Unlike before, the new hotel industry manufactures not basic services for physiological repose, but a complex structure of programmes and actions that seek to channel and manage the most precious merchandise of tourism: the customers' time.

JOSÉ MIGUEL IRIBAS

[VG]   See 'WebHotel.'

[CO]   ## hotel (lost in space)

The formal properties of hotel space have multiplied exponentially in the contemporary organisation of shopping malls, the emergence of so called edge cities, programmatically indeterminate industrial parks and so on.

To be lost today is to be lost in dense networks of communication, networks with which you constantly interact in diverse ways. These technologies systematically remove the possibility of being lost in older forms of space and open up the possibility of being lost in newer forms.

Tourist guides offer ever more precisely calibrated walks through cities which are rehearsed on videotape in the hotel and then performed in trance-like synchrony to the accompaniment of an audio tape fed directly into the ear.

The story of being lost in space is symptomatically being told when it is getting harder to get lost.

After all, the lost figure does not roam uncontrollably. On the contrary, movement through the space of the hotel is completely dictated by vast escalators and elevators. The building guides its users.

MARK WIGLEY

■ ● ★ house, the

→ 'diversity', 'domestic',
'economy', 'housing',
'housys', 'leisure',
're-information',
'spaces>public and private'

[JM] **(home)**

The actual place of residence-resistance of the subject in the city has always been the home. Public space does not pertain to the dweller, not only because it belongs to others, but because at the same time it is controlled. At home are all the things that never found a precise place. At home, one finds all the things that memory has cornered. Memory would be, then, the place of space more than time. With memory, duration no longer exists to allow imprecise residing. If architecture loses the symbolic structures of the past, if the home is no longer a refuge, if the room dissolves into an intermediate space of promiscuity, or if the entire exterior fits in the interior (TV, information, etc.), then to inhabit means something else and suggests other relations. Imagination and invention seem to take possession of a space yet to be defined.

[MG] **(House: permutations)**

The *casa-casa* (house-house): the symbol, the home space. The *casa-cava* (cellar-house): the cave, the refuge space. The *casa-cara* (face-house): the image, the icon space. The *casa-caja* (box-house): the container, the object space. The *casa-capa* (layer-house): the interface, the interaction space; not an inert enclosure, but rather a transfer, a device for relationship and interchange with the world. A place for enjoyment and stimulus, not only for shelter. A landscape to inhabit, and habilitate.

[co] We will indeed have to learn how to think about the reality of our ways of dwelling by ridding ourselves, once and for all, of the standard model of the house. In children's drawings, primitive huts, vernacular constructions, the house remains the universal iconic referent defining a common way of inhabiting. Underlying the form – the idea of the shelter, the elementary function of separation, interior, exterior – the house holds a more essential value: that of a territorial settlement of a belonging that defines what is specifically dwelling, that circumscribes its peculiarity and that anchors the values of individual identity. The house is an object of appropriation, and from behind the commercial act, the purchase of a piece of property, of a personal good, the objective of constructing identity always emerges. But this obvious anthropological analysis of dwelling poorly hides a general phenomenon of "de-appropriation" where the relation to the ground no longer conditions the forms of dwelling. The extension of exchange networks, as much economic as transportation and communication, has created a territorial unity, physical or virtual, which constitutes a new geographic unity thrusting unusable domains – real as much as symbolic wastelands – into indeterminacy. FRÉDÉRIC MIGAYROU

MIT MEDIA LAB,
FUNDACIÓ
POLITÈCNICA DE
CATALUNYA,
METAPOLIS, *Media
House Project*,
Barcelona, 2001.

●★▲ housing

→ 'combination',
'diversity', 'domestic',
'economy', 'environment',
'flexibility', 'house, the',
'housys', 'inhabit',
'innovation', 'joy
(*alegria*)', 'livrid', 'multi',
'rurban loft', 'unrestrained
(<un>factors)'

[MG] **(new alternatives, new systems)**

In a framework tending towards the standard, housing continues to constitute a highly sclerotic field characterised by conventionalism and repetition of archetypes and patterns based upon an ambiguous "neolanguage", at once pseudofunctional and eclectic. A "sclerosis" that not only alludes to those merely speculative operations, but often as well to those which, to use a widely accepted expression, would tend to be classified as "cultured" and which for their principal source of inspiration draw upon urban models grounded in tradition and repetition.

Over a good part of the last two decades, this has been the primary objective of official residential urbanism. The recovery, or recreation of an urban space of traditional silhouettes whose recomposition, has largely been entrusted to a pragmatic and conservationist order based upon archetypical planning.

This planning, as primarily compositive and figurative action, tends towards the reconstruction of the fabric or, in the development of outlying areas, towards its evocation.

Today, however, the dwelling should be understood as a place closer to desire and versatility, to quality of life and the suggestive fantasy of leisure, of wellbeing and of knowledge, rather than to habitual serenity or predictability of space conceived only as mere social need or appearance. In sum, new housing need be conceived through diversity and plurality, rather than through homogeneity and collectiveness. A multi- and inter-active space.

Housing needs to foster research into new combinatorial devices and systems meant to offer MORE for LESS.

- More features for less cost.
- More quality for fewer non-essentials.
- More spatiality for less compartmentalisation.
- More versatility for less rigidity.
- More variation for less staticity.
- More heterogeneity for less repetition.

A better equipped and more open dwelling capable of projecting the individual within and beyond the environment, favouring necessary transfers:

- From decent housing to stimulating housing.
- From standard housing to personalised housing.
- From artisanal housing to technological housing.
- From seried housing to diversified housing.
- From distribution housing to landscape housing.
- From type housing to multitype housing.
- From mechanical housing to interactive housing.

All of the above indicate new concepts in the approach to the contemporary habitat: new concepts in the design of the inhabited space itself (its associated residential cell and the interior landscape) but also in the definition of new urban support systems (and therefore of their associated relational landscapes) meant to ensure an effective and renewed relationship between dwelling, city and territory.

[CO] **(possible decalogue)**

There would seem to be two pertinent questions about housing:

How can housing be planned, with the aim of outlining ways in which more general research can advance.

And how can we build housing, which aims to order the experience and draw out its limits.

We will attempt to provide a partial reply to the smaller question – how can we build housing? – in the certainty that if we do not, the replies to the first question will tend to comfortable self-deception.

1. Construction: What are the most urgent questions?

Given the slow, complex construction process commonly followed, what is most urgent in our context – probably more urgent than typology or distribution – is simplification.

Simplifying means greater efficiency and saving when tackling a project of collective housing.

Industrialisation is one instrument which can be employed to rationalise processes, which means eliminating the construction epic of the architect's ideology, substituting the improvisation of domestic physics, of the "invention," with the use of tried and tested procedures.

But simplification is an aim which affects the entire process.

It affects the project, the manufacturer, the installer, the user, the object and its maintenance.

Simplifying, industrialising, means to reduce the number of consignments, increase the uses of each unit installed, to transfer the quality of finishes to the properties of the materials. It is not detracting, it is adding and synthesising.

But it also means making processes reversible, making rectification or modification as easy as assembling.

2. Patterns: What patterns or references can we take?

Perhaps we should stop looking at housing to find the most operative mechanics with which to plan.

Tertiary buildings can be seen as a catalogue of solutions in which versatility, speed and efficiency have been taken a long way from the usual parameters and techniques in the residential sector.

3. Flexibility: Is it possible, nowadays, to tackle the theme of flexibility in a realistic manner? The structure, its minimisation, is an investment in versatility, in democratising a house's inner space: handing its management over to the user.

4. Prefabrication: What level of prefabrication can be established?

It is still our best interest to group domestic machinery in compact transport units, if possible including the air-conditioning, thus allowing for testing of functioning in the workshop and cutting down on on-site installation connections.

The assembly of light, industrialised linear or surface systems (structures, partition panels, flooring, fragmentation and storage systems, etc.) are left for the construction site, to make for a minimum of units and easy assembly.

5. Institutional action: What institutional action could contribute to furthering research into housing?

We lack models of evaluation which do not deal with profitability or mediatic success.

In any case, there is a need to habilitate vague spaces, for legal formulas which allow experimentation with typological, construction and spatial variations, with the involvement of communities, municipalities and companies in the carrying out of one-off experiments.

6. Dimensions: Is the surface area offered on the housing market sufficient?
The quality per square metre is its versatility, which allows multiple uses of the space, and therefore, its virtual extension. Each single-use metre of floor space is a residual space, which gets swallowed up by dust.
It is better to think about the quality of facilities, the possibility of offering a multiplicity of situations on each spot, a sensible, immediate reply. To combine permeability, fluidity, randomness of use, with maximum privacy, acoustic and visual insulation.

7. Transformations in construction: What transformations in construction are foreseeable in the mid-term?
The existence of a strong sector in the internal facilities of offices which is under-used in periods of recession allows to consider some options as both credible and competitive, marking out possible lines of development:
- Under-floor lines of energy which can be inspected, increasing energetic isotropy.
- Internal divisions with standardised industrial systems, with non-destructive assemblage. incorporating storage.
- Constructive and spatial replanning of the bathroom and kitchen areas.

8. Construction companies: What is the role of construction companies?
As opposed to the technical and spatial conservatism of major companies (and major cooperatives) the aim is to approach a market alternative with a complete maintenance offer, not unlike the modality which construction companies themselves have started to offer on tertiary and commercial buildings.

9. Wall systems: What line of development are wall systems taking?
While the evolution of frames and different types of filter in windows, bay windows and terraces allows us to see gaps as fairly complete sensitive machines, wall systems have hardly evolved at all in recent decades, with the exception of the introduction into the chamber of thermal insulators whose position and form of installation prevent strict control of effectiveness.

10. Community facilities: What is the role of community facilities?
We have to conclude by now that residential space has not developed along the "progressive" line of socialisation of facilities and environments – laundry, restaurant, kindergarten, elevated walkways; it has conversely been miniaturised and integrated into the private environment, or eliminated.

This same process of miniaturisation and integration is now taking place in urban facilities at neighbourhood level (parks, sports centres, neighbourhood centres, etc.) indicating a dual movement – miniaturisation and integration – which suggests the incorporation of new uses (e.g. health and work), though at very minor levels.
But above all it implies the guarantee that the most important transformations in housing are systematically aimed at increasing the technical complexity and the versatility of the private sphere, reducing surface areas – whether collective or private – and increasing vagueness inside but also the capacity for fragmentation and insulation of spaces.
IÑAKI ÁBALOS & JUAN HERREROS

[FP] **(decalogue II)**

1.-A house will never be considered an object anymore, but will, in all respects, be considered a subject.
2.-A house constructs itself. It does not attend to detail.
3.-The house may change shape, so this is not important at all.
4.-The house does not have finishes, each material can be worked on to its limit, the joints being an expression of their limits.
5.-A house will gradually be more and more different from others, even if it belongs to standard construction.
6.-A house can easily change use, so that it can be many houses or just one.
7.-A house, from now on, will incorporate pieces that it never used before.
8.-A house is synergetic, it will be possible for it to either disappear completely or stay forever, but in any case remain passive.
9.-A house is inserted in a superior, immaterial web, which links it more to the ground than its foundations. It is open and penetrated by the web.
10.-A house is still a place for findings in architecture. Findings by geographers, not archaeologists.

[MG] **(combinatorial patterned distributions)**

An authentic residential diversity can, in certain cases, be achieved through the strategic combination of fixed elements and articulated free spaces in basic elemental schemes, based upon the disposition of the service nuclei (bathrooms, kitchens, installations, etc.) and the modelled variable of a fluid, univocal space defined through them.

A broad range of solutions are grounded largely in strategic movements of concentration of the service spaces – equipped "clots" or clusters, conceived as "hard nuclei" – and in the normed growth of the remaining environments, in successive combinations where, by means of the variable rhythm of dividing elements, the appearance of distinct subtypes with diverse superficial boundaries would be favoured.

The possible broadening of longitudinal openings lend itself to working, in such cases, with variable-surface developments, parallel to the façade (in narrow blocks), rather than through developments which are transverse in depth. This favours clusters of more diaphanous and illuminated use that permit the appearance – and multi-faceted use – of unspecific places (interior-exterior galleries, semi-courtyards, covered and temporally usable patios, etc.) as new indeterminate and, therefore, more versatile spaces.

[c] "*Today we may think of housing as a system of combinatory growth based upon initial elemental structures made up of fixed nuclei. Housing in which the always limited initial purchase investment is dedicated to obtaining an adequate urban location, the greatest possible square footage and better common elements.*

As happens when we buy a computer to which we later add peripherals, or a stereo system that comes with connections for other components we might buy in the future. In housing we can operate in the same manner.

When purchasing a first home, the buyer on a limited budget is obliged to acquire a finished home, with labyrinth-like partitioning, and of low-quality construction. This situation of low-budget finished housing has acted as a brake on innovation, the introduction of new materials and systems in construction.

A very different situation from that which we can see in other areas of construction, such as office buildings. Office buildings are built to exploit the total square footage without defining the division.

The developer builds a building that is perfectly finished in its common elements: structure, façade, accesses, air conditioning, fittings, etc. The buyer undertakes a second construction stage in which the divisions, finishes, etc. are defined, according to his financial possibilities.

In a quest for greater quality and ever greater simplicity in construction, industrial technologies, even from the automotive field, have been incorporated into modern office buildings.

Construction time is a variable that dramatically effects traditional housing construction.

Greater efficiency in this factor alone means significant savings in final costs. Housing must follow office spaces and join in the dynamics of change and innovation in a whole sector created for its construction, a sector which continually offers new alternatives to help to raise quality at ever decreasing costs." (ARANGUREN, María José, GONZÁLEZ GALLEGOS, José, "Habitar la caja", unpublished, 1999)

[i] p. 288-291

● housys

→ 'catastrophe', 'combination', 'devices', 'diversity', 'domestic', 'environment', 'flexibility', 'house, the', 'housing', 'inhabit', 'livrid', 'menus', 'multi', 'rurban loft'

[MG] The term HOUSYS – also HOU.SYS. – refers to open systems which generate residential diversity.

These evolutionary devices combine types and subtypes, mixed programmes and autonomous elements, based upon growth patterns which generate manifold spatial and technical definitions.

Flexible norms based upon a global morphological heterogeneity and an effective empty-full alternation, equipped-freed, open-closed, public-private, occupied-occupiable, produced at all levels (from the cell to the urban layout). HOUSYS for *multi-houses.*

MVRDV, *Silodam,* Amsterdam, 2002.

Comparative plan study with several proposals conceived form the typological diversity and the spatial flexibility.
Most of the projects are combinatorial systems of elements: modules, nodes, fixed, repeated in various rythms and placating variable growth rythms (subtypes).
Hard nuclei-nodes, lumps and surrounding areas of development and dilation.

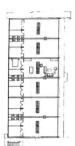

Josep Lluís MATEO. (MAP Arquitectes), *Housing units*, Den Haag (The Netherlands), 1993.

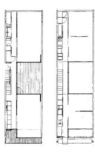

BÉAL-BRUNET. *New habitat-Competition H/C*, Barcelona, 1990.

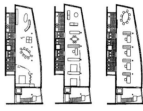

Willem Jan NEUTELINGS, Marc DE KOONING, *Loft De Kaai*, Antwerpen (Belgium), 1992.

Equipped walls

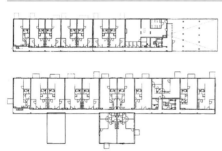

MVRDV, *WoZoCo's housing*, Amsterdam, 1997.
Plans. The spartan gallery flat typology with corridor markedly improves with the changing perspectives on each level.

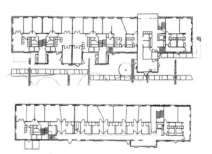

ROCHE DSV & Sie., *Renovation of an obsolete built structure*, Sarcelles, 1994.
Ground floor and type.

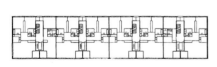

Willem Jan NEUTELINGS, *Prinsenhoek housing*, Sittard (The Netherlands), 1995.

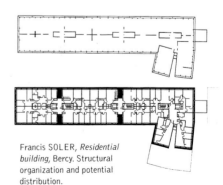

Francis SOLER, *Residential building*, Bercy. Structural organization and potential distribution.

Cohabitations and typological variations

Nuclear slidings

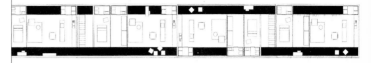

ACTAR ARQUITECTURA, *Rail system*, 1998.
Lengthwise strips organise the distributions in distension spaces, inhabited spaces and
equipped units.

Combinatorial patterned distributions (plans and elevations)

ACTAR ARQUITECTURA (with Arenas-Basiana), *300 housing units*, Mallorca (Spain), 1993.
A, B, C module type and combinatory schema based on identical surfaces
and different spatial organizations.

RIEGLER & RIEWE, *Housing units*, Graz-Strassgang (Austria), 1994.
Diversity of types got from the appropriation by the sliding of
ambiguous spaces.

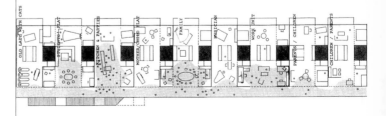

NJIRIC+NJIRIC, *Housing units*, Den Bosch (The Netherlands), 1993.
A fixed module and combinatory schemas based on fixed nuclei and variable growths.

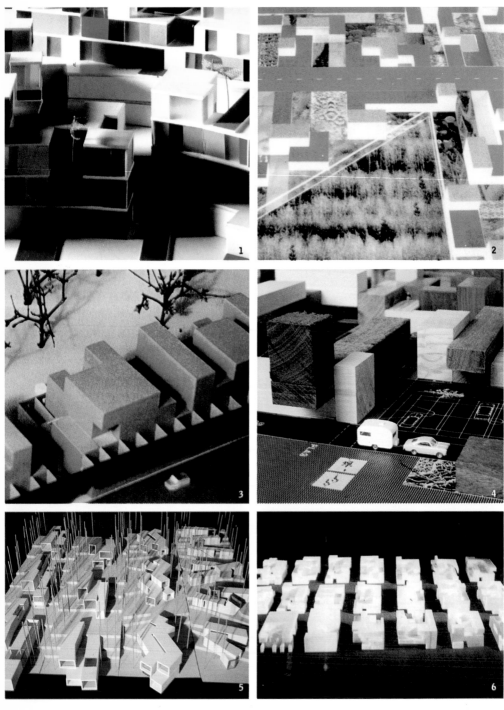

1. ACTAR ARQUITECTURA, *Europan 5* (finalist), Ceuta (Spain), 1998. **2.** NL ARCHITECTS, *Housing project Flat City*, Leidsche Rijn (The Netherlands), 1998. **3.** Willem Jan NEUTELINGS, *Hollainhof housing*, Ghent (Belgium), 1997. **4.** MVRDV, *Urban planning Hoornse Kwadrant*, Delft (The Netherlands), 1996. **5.** EXIT (Nevil Binder, Mladen Jadric), *Europan 4*, Helsinki (Finland), 1996. **6.** Ben VAN BERKEL, Caroline BOS (UN Studio), *Housing in Borneo Sporenburg*, Amsterdam, 1994.

7. RIEGLER & RIEWE, *Housing*, Graz-Strassgang (Austria), 1994. **8.** Josep Lluís MATEO (MAP Arquitectes), *Housing*, Den Haag (The Netherlands), 1993. **9.** Willem Jan NEUTELINGS, *Prinsenhoek housing*, Sittard (The Netherlands), 1995. **10.** MVRDV, *WoZoCo's housing*, Amsterdam, 1997. **11.** Kazuyo SEJIMA, Ryue NISHIZAWA, *Apartment block*, Gifu (Japan), 1998. **12.** Francis SOLER, *Housing*, Paris, 1997.

● humour

[MG] If an architecture is unrestrained, it has a sense of humour. If it has a sense of humour, it is joyful. If it is joyful, it is extrovert. If it is extrovert, it is informal. If it is informal, it is unrestrained. And if an architecture is unrestrained...

▲ hump

→ 'antitypes',
'cohabitation',
'commensalism', 'eye',
'geometry', 'hybrid',
'hypertrophy', 'meldings',
'prosthesis'

[FP] Thought of as an intelligent appendix, the camel's hump turns out to be one of the luckiest lessons of fauna. It is, in principle, a foreign element on the body it serves. In an unnatural way, it accumulates energy for critical moments, and at the same time, is able to sustain itself and to take shape as an unequivocal characterising symbol. Never before has something more amorphous been able to equip the body on which it lies with so much shape. We can apply some lessons from this easily understood device to our way of working. Hump buildings, at the service of a web or tissue, hump spaces, capable of transmitting energy to other organisms. They are indeed elements that we can currently propose. The camel does not know it has a hump, and it is even less aware of the fact that without one it would not be a camel (and would die of thirst).

NOX (Lars Spuybroek with Chris Seung-Woo Yoo, Kris Mun, Florent Rougemont and Ludovica Tramontin), *SoftOffice*, United Kingdom, 2000-2005.

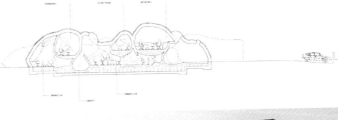

R&Sie... (François ROCHE, Stephanie LAVAUX), *Barak House*, Sommières (France), 2001.

PÉRIPHÉRIQUES, *Competition for Canal + Headquarters*, Loupveciennes (France), 2002.

●■ hybrid

[MG] **(hybridisation)**

The hybrid nature of the contemporary project alludes to the current si-multaneity of realities and categories, relating no longer to harmonious and coherent bodies, but rather to mongrel scenarios made up of structures and identities in parasitic coexistence.

By accepting, without prejudice, a strange situation of cohabitation made up of contracts, pacts and mongrelisations between bits of information at once overlapping and interconnected (imbricated and differentiated layers and (infra)structures) is how the culture of the contemporary project can be understood today.

As Mihu Iliescu pointed out (*12 Notes 1*, 1998):

"*According to the context, the notion of mixture may be taken in a num-ber of ways: mongrelisation, hybridisation, coexistence, (trans)fusion, etc. It can also function at various levels of analysis. Still, it is usually tied to the loss of purity that is often interpreted as a compromise (or betray-al of "essential principles"). Thus the pertinence of the category of the im-pure as an operative compromise in contemporary art.*" (Translated from Spanish.)

Such impure "encounters" naturally lead to a coupling among sister types, species – or genres – based upon a direct and flexible (immediate) inter-connection between possibly opposed – or contrary – elements. These dis-parate elements that can engender, today, new situations of cooperation and cuttings, of marriage and multiplication. They can engender an "astute na-ture" capable of linking bits of information and imbricating potentials. So, the old univocal (pure, hermetic) profiles blur in actions of mongrelisa-tion – in hybrid devices – conceived as tactical decisions vis-à-vis concrete situations, but also as possible spatial combinations that are more open, flexible and multifaceted. More informal, then, in their ambivalence.

1

2

3

1. Stéphane COUVÉ BONNAIRE, *Shoe-giraffe*, 1996.
2. Ballantine's advertising.
3. Roland FÄSSER, *Mutations*, 1992-1995.

[JM] **(project)**

The architectural project – as our culture requires – must be extremely at-tentive to the heterogeneous, difference, and to the possibilities offered by investigation into art, philosophy, ecology, etc. If there is anything clear in our culture, it is the hybrid nature of declaration.

4. Daniel LEE, *Manimal*, infography, 1992.
5. NL, *Bendup, singular house*, Bloemendaal (The Netherlands), 2000.

★ hybrid technique, crossbred aesthetics

[CO] Sensitivity towards nature-oriented policies has influenced technical paradigms, with interest shifting from high tech experiments (no doubt a residue of the modern spirit) towards hybrid models in which the accent has begun to be placed on the interaction between natural materials – massive and energetically inert – and highly sophisticated artificial materials – light and energetically active – which respond sensitively to environmental variation, giving rise to composite systems in which the former are responsible for accumulating and reducing exchanges while the latter act as generators, capturing energy resources.

This new technological model implies a shift from the aspects of material organisation – mass production, simplified assembly, time and cost optimisation etc. – towards the rational organisation of the energy consumed during both the production and upkeep of the building. This shift now enables us to conceive ''systems,'' not from the perspective of congruence and unity in the materials, but rather in terms of their enviromental congruence, thus opening the way to experiments in which the congruous mixture of heterogeneous materials becomes a new visual feature. This hybrid materialism implies profound transformation of aesthetic ideas in harmony with the crossbreeding of our human landscapes.
IÑAKI ÁBALOS & JUAN HERREROS

★ hypercontext

→ 'citilab', 'cyberspace', 'incubator', 'information', 'intercommunity', 'link', 'networks', 'newspace', 'system', 'telepolis'

[CO] If context used to be defined by the *hic et nunc* of a specific place, hypercontext suggests a network of places which is akin to the principle of hypertext. Whereas a traditional text represents an integral body which contains the entire information of the text, a hypertext consists of a number of texts disseminated throughout different locations. Connected by a series of hyperlinks, its various ''sub''-texts form an operative body which works as one, despite its fragmentation. Accordingly, a hypercontext consists of a number of places which are not physically adjacent but interconnected by flows of material and information. Thus, the 17 worldwide locations of the Formula One Racing Series form a hypercontext which is sustained by omnipresent media coverage and a shared branding system. Hypercontext therefore challenges the idea of a self-refererential place promoted by contextualism, arguing instead for a multi-indexed locality which connects territories, rather than seperating them. ANDREAS RUBY

OOSTERHUIS Associates, *Interactive Cave Trans-ports*, Venice Biennale, 2000.

+ hyperiphery

→ 'field', 'hyperplace', 'm. city', 'no-places', 'periphery'

[WM] One of the negative consequences of the brutal growth of the outlying areas of cities, transformed into hyperipheries, is the banalisation of the centres as smaller and larger theme parks. The historic centres, former centres of power, have become dispossessed of sufficient social density to claim for themselves their share of vitality, simulate beneath layers of institutional makeup certain festivity. Hyperiphery is the atrophy of the periphery.

★ hypermobility

[co] Once dematerialised, an information becomes hypermobile – instantaneous circulation through digital networks with global span. It is important to underline that the hypermobility gained by an object through dematerialization is but one moment of a more complex condition. Representing such an object as simply hypermobile is, then, a partial representation since it includes only some of the components of that object, i.e., those that can be dematerialised but achieve that condition as a function of what we could describe as hughly specialised materialities. Much of what is liquefied and circulates in digital networks and is marked by hypermobility remains physical in some of its components. SASKIA SASSEN

● hyperplace

[MG] See 'place of places.'

● hypertrophy

→ 'cephalia', 'form',
'inform(ation)al',
'logic, direct', 'no-form',
'unrestrained (<un>
factors)'

[MG] Hypertrophy is an a-scalar condition; excessive increase or imbalance in volume, size or proportion. It is manifestation of non-composition and non-shape produced through an action unencumbered by proportions and conventions.

Noel HARDING,
Mutant marshlands,
Don River (Toronto,
Canada), 1999.

NL, *Oefenfabriek,*
Hoogvliet, (satellite
town of) Rotterdam
(The Netherlands),
2002.

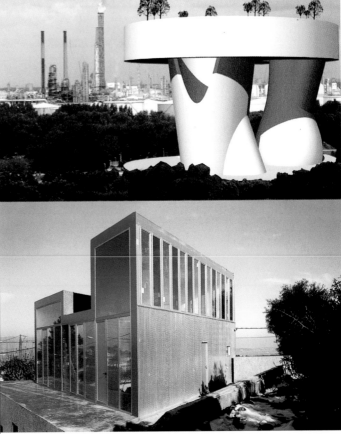

WMA Willy Müller
Arquitectos,
La Floresta House,
Barcelona, 2001.

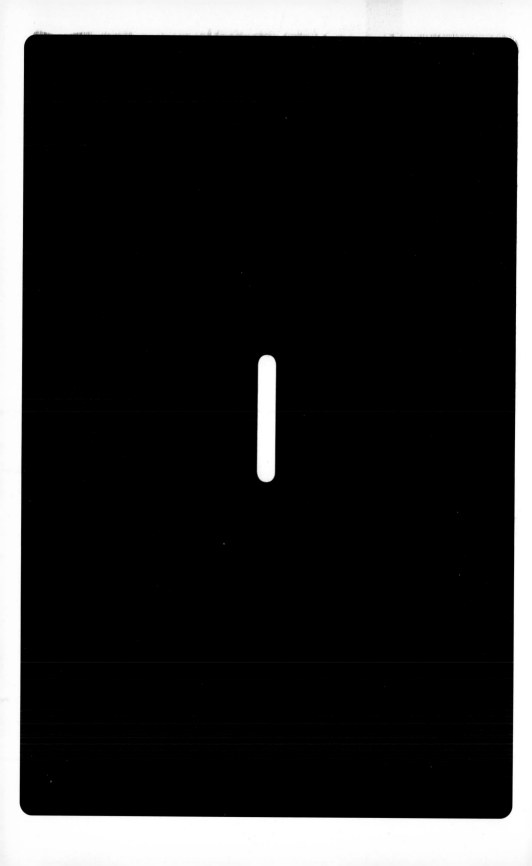

● ◆ I/(my)self

[MG] I/ (my)self is individuality which is flexibly related to the collective. Singularity of the plural. Its presence is autonomous and interactive at the same time. I/(my)self with them, but not in them.

[MG] "*If in the past the organisation and content of work led to an opposition between the two concepts (the individual would appear crushed by his working conditions and the collective was a means of liberation), today's new technologies require, on the contrary, action through networks and a search for synergies that give work a new dimension. There then appears a new culture based upon an effective conjugation between I and WE.*"
(KASPAR, Jean, "La problématique…", *L'aventure du travail*, Barcelona: CCCB, 2000. Translated from Spanish.)

[FS] Architecture is a piece of chewing gum. Ideas are squeezed, pressed, turned, chewed and internalized. The perception of our own subjectivity wraps around all our experiences. Our knowledge oscillates between the lived and the rationalized, between what is felt and what is expressed.
No new ideas exist, nor do answers remain hidden in history, but rather speculation arises from our own questions newly formed. Architectural ideas are distilled and absorbed. They do not behave as inert mass worked over drawing tables, or on the hard disk, but cut the stomach.

★ I (formerly identity)

[c] "*In terms of our views of the self, new images of multiplicity, heterogeneity, flexibility and fragmentation dominate current thinking about human identity. The Internet has become a significant social laboratory for experimenting with the constructions and reconstructions of self. In its virtual reality, people are able to build a self by cycling through many selves. We self-fashion and self-create. We can experience these news kinds of personae as an expanded self or as separate from the self.*" (TURKLE, Sherry, *Life on the Screen. Identity in the Age of the Internet*, New York: Touchstone, 1997)

● <i> space

[MG] All architecture constructs a system inscribed in an environment with which it interchanges energy, matter and information. This is a new synaesthetic condition to which Silvia Molina alluded ("Espacio <i> intermedio" in *Un nuevo marco para la creación*, (various authors), ed. Universidad Complutense, Madrid, 1997): "*I shall speak of space as a subject, as something "under development" rather than as a final state: space as process, where the relationship of its elements and itself with the spaces that surround it acquires its own dimension. When I speak of relationship I speak of definition. The elements never accompany each other, rather they relate to each other. Nothing exists next to another thing without intervening in it, without modifying it, without redefining it.*" Thus, <i> space is a reactive space (open to stimuli and reactions) that incites interventions that are more relational by virtue of being synaesthetic: synthetical (in the global) and synergetic (in the local).

◆ iceberg

[FS] See 'immersed' and 'mountain.'

◆+■● ideas

[FS] *"Man thinks poorly because he thinks in a circle. He does not stop going over the same thoughts, and takes for new thoughts the other side of old thoughts. This is classical thought. Closed thought. Conservative thought. Thinking that in its center encounters God.*

Who has the strength to renounce this "divine" conclusion breaks the circle and internalizes a free and straight path that knows no goal or end because it is infinite."

(SAVINIO, Alberto, *Nuestra alma*, Madrid: Siruela, 1990)

[WM] *"Where do good new ideas come from? That's simple, from differences. Creativity comes from unlikely juxtapositions. The best way to maximise is to mix ages, cultures and disciplines."* Nicholas Negroponte, head of MIT Media Lab.

"We should do something when people say it is crazy. If people say something is 'good,' it means someone else is already doing it." Hajime Mitarai, president of Canon.

Ideas have two major problems: one is how to create them, the other is how to exploit their potential. Ideas are practically the only thing there is. The lack of ideas (paraphrasing Tom Peters) is a mental state: *"If he thinks he doesn't have any ideas, he doesn't have any."*

[JM] The fundamental change for reflecting on a project is produced by working with concepts and not "ideas."

Working with concepts implies using operative diagrams that have the possibility of generating space.

On the other hand, working with ideas implies obtaining "figures," in the Lyotardian sense, wherein ideas separate themselves from reality (basically inapprehensible images: the avant-garde and their analysts also did not modify this circumstance) and impede retro-feeding of the operative reason of the process. Contrarily, contemporary concepts are rooted in information coming from heterogeneity of what is "out there," what is continually our vital space.

[MG] **(as ideolas)**

See 'criteria' and 'projective.'

We no longer speak of ideas as mere figurations — speculations or fantasies — but as operative criteria: "projectives" or *ideolas* (action-ideas), not far removed from an "active imagination" that Palazuelo spoke of.

(PALAZUELO, Pablo, "Form as research", *Quaderns* 218, 1997): *"This constant interaction of the imagination and thought, a thought which imagines rather than just feeling. The Arabs called it 'active imagination,' which is what creates. Active imaginations which allow to see what cannot be seen yet."*

● ideogram

→ 'cartographies',
'concise', 'maps (to map)',
'no-form', 'synthetical',
'trajectory'

[MG] See 'diagrams.'

The compressive character of the diagram manifests itself in certain cases as the embodiment of a (strategic and tactical) response and of a diagnosis (just as the root of the term 'diagram' indicates): a synthetical representation that summarises recognition and response in a criterion for action; a selective conceptualisation of information.

This initially conceptual (and conceptualising) nature of the diagram generally takes shape in its associated condition as an ideogram, that is, that of an action-idea (*ideola*).

In this respect, the ideogram possesses, inherently, a structural effect, given that it synthesises an amalgam of bits of information that, embryonically, begin to generate a change in scale. They do not represent — or at least, do not only represent — buildings (they are more than schemes), but rather beginnings of movements. The ideogram possesses an organisational potential at various levels: criteria for action are posited as synthetical diagnoses or concepts (reactions to the environment), yet, at the same time, as stimulants (programming codes or compressive schemes for future operative systems). These are synthetical simulations of possible movements, of routes, of combinations, of trajectories. Of, ultimately, manifold evolutions.

Ideograms speak of genetic codes or basic seeds of organisation that respond to a demand for combined effectiveness and operativeness: to attain with the minimum element the largest quantity of bits of information in order to obtain the greatest possible cohesion between the whole and the particular, such that one is reflected in the other.

**Patchwork
of ideograms:**

MVRDV,
Wozoco's housing,
Amsterdam, 1997

Kazuyo SEJIMA,
Low-level typology,
Tokyo, 1995

Willem Jan
NEUTELINGS,
Hollainhof, Ghent,
1995-1997

MVRDV,
Delft, 1996.

● ideological dictionary

[MG] Rather than a classification, an ideological dictionary is a list of terms by idea, concept and association which permits the definition of orientational codes, like markers that are neither hermetic, nor fixed.

AA

abroad, etc
aformal
a-scalarity

no-box
no-day
no-form
no-place
no-scale

advanced
advanced, architecture
critical pragmatism

abstract

action
artificial
blur
goodbye to the
metaphor
logic, digital
machine
music
synthetical

maps (to map)

gaze> tactical gaze
maps, battle

a-couplings

and
dichotomies
dual(ity)
hybrid
in-between
interaction
paradoxes
transgenetic
transfusions

camouflage
eco->

---

ecomonumentality
glocal
natuficio
naturartificial

(Discontected)
(Domestiversal)
(Extinterior)
(Extradaily)
(Forminformal)
(Order and chaos)
(Partigeral)
(Publivate)

a-scalarity
name

action

act

abroad, etc.
activation
agitated space
architecture
discothèque
extroversion:
<ex> factors of form
form
interaction
logic, direct
maps, battle
nada(r)
operative
pragmatopia
process
proneoism
reactive

reality
time

action>critical

activation
American
pragmatism

---

associate, overlap,
connect
attitude
audacity
collaging
criteria
criticism
gaze> tactical gaze
holistic
ideas
indiscipline
infiltration
innovation
just do it
moral
reactive
sense
Team X

book
decalogue
dictionary
eraser
essay
ideological dictionary
name

ArchiLab
fissures
Media Lab
Metapolis
Quaderns
rhyzomatic

positioning

logic,
direct
logic,
fuzzy
obsessions
tangent
transversality

bored
discipline
history

activation

action
action>critical
act-n
animation
context
decisions
(and instructions)
rather than designs
environment
conservation>
patrimonial
intervention
reactive

avatar
field

activity

act-n
aformal
function
interaction
interactivity
operative
reactive
spaces>collective
use

dynamism
flexibility
in-out
multi
negotiate
order
plural
program

act-n

act
activation
activity
actuality
attitude

X-Architecture

ad-herence / inheritance

a-couplings
adaptation
commensalism
complicity
cuttings
enjambements
graft
lands of superposition
occupation structures
parasitism

territory

advanced, architecture

AA
architecture>
(advanced) x 7
critical pragmatism

audacity
informal
joy (*alegría*)
optimism
unrestrained
(<un> factors)
uppercut

abstract
action>critical
dynamism
heterotopia
hybrid
immanence
informal
innovation
lightness
open
reactive
versatility

extroversion:
<ex> factors of form
<in> order factors
unrestrained (<un>
factors)

competition
negotiate
tattoos

archaeology>advanced
culture, advanced

contemporary

compact
discipline
experience
fragment
functionalism
olympicooooo
tattoos
utopia

advertising

advertisements
expression
logic, direct
marks
photography
product
scream
uppercut

agriculture

carpets
cultivations
eco-> eco-chic
eco->
ecomonumentality
ecology, active
economy
field
landscape /

architecture /
urbanism landscapes,
operative
mats
naturartificial
nature
stains, landscape

land-arch
land links
land(s) in lands

allegory

goodbye to the
metaphor

archaeology
client
collage
fear
history
memory
past

amphibious

anarchitecture
do-it-yourself
ephemeral
impermanences
islands
precarious(ly)
provisional
self-urbanism
shore or bank
take-away homes
urbanism, anarchist

and

dichotomies
difference
in-between
mixed-use
poly

a-couplings
ad-herence / inheritance
figure-background
in-between fingers,
in-between links
intermediate places
intermittences
joint
original and replica
private
spaces>public space
true and false
voids and fills

animation

agitated space
avatar
hybrid
transgenetic
transfusions

blobs
bubbles
delynniate

dynamism
evolutionary
flows
form
geometry
logic, digital
sensors

genetics of form
in/unsettledness

anonymous

hotel
no-place

abstract
conventional
expression
extroversion:

<ex> factors of form
open
space
synthetical

archaeology

enlarged

conservation
history

allegory

arches of development

land links
landscapes, operative
sequence and series

field
hybrid
places
program
self-urbanism

architecture

critical pragmatism
knowledge
proto-architectures

advanced, architecture
audacity
dissolved architecture
enlarged
impermanences
X-Architecture

information
material
matter
places
program
space

time
vortex

extroversion:
<ex> factors of form
form
<in>, order factors
logic
order

action
essayist knowledge
negotiate
R+3D
relationships, transitive
(of transference)
trip

abstract
modern
neoclassical

areas of impunity

areas of opportunity
criticism
field
hybrid
imagine>imagination
places
program

armadillo

branchial
skeleton
wireframes

extensible-compressible

alienation
(and estrangement)
alienism
foreigness
infiltration>
intrusiveness and
interference

artificial

abstract
foreigness
globalisation
infrastructures
naturartificial
nature
product
prototypes
rurban
synthetical
virtual

criss-crossing
eco->
ecomonumentality
ecology, active
land-arch
landscapes,
operative
reliefs
topographies,
operative

a-scalarity

AA
attractors
field
reactive
relationships, transitive
(of transference)
transgenetic
transfusions

epitome
glocal

recursiveness
self-similarity
topological
zoom

a-couplings
dichotomies

hybrid
in-between
limit
midget & giant

assembly

associate,
overlap, connect
collaging
combination
component
connect
geometry
recycling
transversality

associate, overlap, connect

action>critical
chunking
strategy

assembly
collaging
multilayered
transversality

demolish
stack (stacks)

attractors

a-scalarity
cloud
dimension
form
fractal
nature
no-form
self-similarity
Sierpinsky's sponge
stains, ink
topological
trajectory

dynamism
limit
seed
synthetical
system

audacity

AA
action>critical
advanced, architecture
challenge
critical pragmatism
extroversion: <ex>
factors of form
fear
innovation
no-form
obsessions
passion

conservation
recycling
re-information

(discipline, bold)
(ecology, bold)
(matter, bold)
(memory, bold)
(structure, bold)

competition
in/unconsciousness

avatar

activation
animation
Benidorm
chance
deviation
evolutionary
field
genetics
genetics of form
hybrid

logic, fuzzy
Metapolis
transgenetic
transfusions
trip
urbs

complexity
multi
poly

beacons

cartographies
diagrams
field
maps (to map)
networks

dictionary
name

devices
geography
strategy

(abstract map)
(atopical map)
(explanatory map)
(exploratory map)
(geographical map)
(mental map)
(operative map)

Benidorm

abroad, etc.
avatar
bank & beach
globalisation
hotel
self-urbanism
skyscrapers
tourism

bluntings
buds

client
mayor

blobs

delynniate

blunt

direct
logic, direct
uppercut

braids

coilings
contortionisms
crossing
devices
dispositions
fold
loops
nodes
paradoxes
solenoid
trajectory
transfers

buds

Benidorm
bluntings
chains
crests
devices
dispositions
emergency
fractal
hybrid
macro-micro
midget & giant
mixed-use
multilayered
protuberances

sequences
skyscrapers
unfolding

camouflage

adaptation

colours
mimetic architecture
patterns
skin
stampings
tattoos

infiltration
occupation structures
strategy

digitnature
naturartificial
transgenetic
transfusions
F111

a-scalarity
form
limit
no-form
self-similarity

carpets

agriculture
cultivations
devices
landscapes, operative
land(s) in lands
mats
stains, landscape
trays

cartographies

beacons
datascape

decisions
(and instructions)
rather than designs
layers
places

geomancy
maps (to map)
trailers
trip

catalogue

code>(bar)code
combination
component
kits
menus
AH houses
M'house houses

catastrophe

ephemeral
occupations
precarious(ly)
provisional
reversible
self-organization
self-urbanism
temporary

house, the
housing
housys

advanced
advanced,
architecture
architecture
contemporary
production,
intelligent
proneoism

cephalia

cyclops
hypertrophy

chains

buds
code>(bar)code
combination
cultivations
fringes
genetics
geometry
in/unfinished
multicity
one is many
rhyzomatic
self-organization
sequences
system

chance

avatar
chaos
complexity
creation
deviation
dynamism
error
form
fractal
game
<in>, order factors
indefinition
indetermination
self-organization
self-urbanism
system>dynamical
transversality
versatility

chaos

chance
complexity

conventional
cosmos
creation
dynamism
entropy
error
form
<in>, order factors
indefinition
indetermination
information
inform(ation)al
in/uncertainty
multi
multilayered
order
space
system>
dynamical
time

Chrysler Voyager

aformal

AA
no-box
no-form
open

activity
dynamism
flows
indetermination

negotiate
time

citilab

hypercontext
incubator
intercommunity
link
R+3D
telecentre

client

activation
allegory
anonymous
decisions (and
instructions)
rather than designs
economy
game
I/(my)self
ideas
individuality
infiltration>intrusive-
ness and interference
logic, fuzzy
moral
negotiate
relationships,
transitive
(of transference)

mayor

code

culture
decalogue
language
logic
mathematics
name
networks
slogans
synthetical
system

catalogue
chains
component
patterned distributions
patterns

collage

allegory
crossbreeding
hybrid
imagine>imagination
recycling
represent
tergiversation
transversality

collaging

action>critical
assembly
associate, overlap,
connect
devices
process

colours

camouflage
chromatisms
patterns
stampings
tattoos

joy (*alegría*)
optimism
unrestrained
(<un> factors)

competition

advanced
audacity
blunt
innovation
juries
unrestrained
(<un> factors)

complexity

chance

chaos
fractal
inform(ation)al

synthetical

diversity
flows
layers
multi
one is many
plural
poly
program
simultaneity

complicity

relationships, transitive
(of transference)
synergy

ad-herence
contract
game
interaction
interchange
ludic
Metapolis

component

catalogue
code>(bar)code
combination
kits
menus

AH houses
M'house houses

context

activation
criss-crossing
enlarged

environment
globalisation
multi
places

mayor

contract

a-couplings
antitypes
cohabitation
complexity
ephemeral
fragile
impermanences
interaction
interactivity
interchange
in/unstable
precarious(ly)
provisional
relationships, transitive
(of transference)
reversible
synergy
temporary

conventional

bored
client
negotiate

countermarks: craters
and basins

dunes
ecology, active
geography
landscapes,
operative
landstrategy
naturartificial
nature
ponds
reliefs

topographies,
operative

creation

chance
chaos
creators
event
ideas
proneoism
Think Tank

criss-crossing

alienation (and
estrangement)
alienism
artificial
de-location
dispersed
dynamism
environment
fleeting
foreignness
in/unstable
knowledge
reality
rootlessness
simultaneity
surprise
suspense

criteria

action>critical
American pragmatism
areas of impunity
concise
diagrams
dual(ity)
gaze> tactical gaze
I/(my)self
ideas
innovation
invisible in architecture

moral
positioning
recycling
trajectory
yes!

irradiate
unfolding

indiscipline
information
intermediary
multilayered
process

cultivations

chains
combination
data
dispositions
evolutionary
genetics
inform(ation)al
land(s) in lands
open
process
seed

cuts

terraces
countermarks:
craters and basins
ecology, active
geography
nature
naturartificial
landscapes,
operative
reliefs
landstrategy
topographies,
operative
trenches
unbuilding

cuttings

antitypes
genetics
hybrid
infiltration>
intrusiveness
and interference
graft
meldings
reversible

decisions
(and instructions)
rather than
designs

activation
criteria
dispositions
form ·
maps, battle
no-form
open
order
process

de-location

displacing by sliding
unrestrained
(<un> factors)

alienation
(and estrangement)
alienism
foreigness
globalisation
infiltration>
intrusiveness
and interference
localization
no-places
subject
telepolis
tourism

delynniate

animation ₀
blobs
dynamism
process
topological

deviation

avatar
flâneur
knowledge
trip

devices

beacons
bluntings
braids
buds
carpets
enclaves
extension
(inter)weavings
and inter(plots)
livrid
loops
nubs-nodes-knots
patterns
precarious(ly)
protuberances
reliefs
reversible
Swiss knife
X-Architecture

interfaces

paradoxes
strategy

appropiation strategies
field
figure-background
fold
maps, battle

occupation structures
system

diagonalisation

extension
fencing space
fold
landstrategy
section
ubliquity

diagrams

abstract
criteria
datascape
ideogram
information
knowledge
logic, digital
synthetical

attractors
maps, battle
no-form
recursiveness
seed
trajectory

dichotomies

a-couplings
a-scalarity
cohabitation
dual(ity)
rootlessness
simultaneity
spaces>public
and private

dictionary

action>critical
I/(my)self

ideological dictionary
name
transversality

direct

action
blunt
informal
logic, direct
Marx Bros.
open
uppercut

dispositions

distribution
fencing space
unfolding

dynamism
evolutionary
extension
extroversion:
<ex> factors of form
field
flows
fold
<in> order factors
inform(ation)al
no-form
open
sponged
stains, ink
system>dynamical
trajectory

dissolved architecture

agitated space
dispersed
immanence
in/unstable
limit
open

diversity

complexity
hybrid
I/(my)self
individuality
multi
multilayered
one is many
plural
simultaneity
X-Architecture

AH houses
housys
housing
M´house houses

dual(ity)

artificial-natural
continuous-
discontinuous
diagram-ideogram
midget & giant
figure-background
fresh conservatism
infrastructure-
landscape
macro-micro
spaces>public
and private
real-virtual
shadow & light
successive-simultaneous
topography-topology
utopia-heterotopia

dynamism

activity
field

animation
holograms

inform(ation)al
irradiate
logic, digital
suspense

advanced, architecture
aformal
agitated space
attractors
chance
criss-crossing
displacing by sliding
dispositions
expression
extroversion:
<ex> factors of form
flows
fractal
genetics
genetics of form
<in>, order factors
light
maps, battle
multilayered
open
order
relationships, transitive
(of transference)
system
tropism

eco-

resonance-synergy-
interaction

eco- >
ecomonumentality
ecocamping
ecofield
ecology
economy

eco- > ecomonu-mentality

artificial

ecology, active
nature

ecology, active

audacity

artificial
countermarks:
craters and basins
dunes
eco- >
ecomonumentality
eco-tech
enclaves
landscape /
architecture /
urbanism
landscapes,
operative
leisure
mats
mountain
naturartificial
nature
reliefs
terraces
topographies,
operative
tree
trenches

ephemeral
impermanences
precarious(ly)
recycling
recycling, urban
reversible
temporary

economy

concise
data
product
synthetical
uppercut

hotel
leisure
mayor
tourism

emergency

bluntings
buds
enclaves
mountain
peaks
reliefs
unfolding

enclaves

land(s) in lands
landstrategy
reliefs
topographies,
operative

energy

black holes
entropy
inform(ation)al
irradiate
light
multilayered
reaction
reactive
system

enlarged

archaeology
architecture
contemporary
context
criticism
environment

entropy

chaos
energy
field

environment

activation
context
enlarged
field
globalisation
hybrid
matter
no-place
reality

ephemeral

amphibious
contract
fabrications
fleeting
fragile
holograms
immanence
impermanences
in-out
in/unstable
lightness
nomad
precarious(ly)
provisional
reversible
temporary
time

equipped wall

equipped façade
(and wall)

empty wall
negative wall
technical wall

thick wall

component
membrane
skin
sponged

essay

action>critical
dissolved architecture
ideas
innovation
unrestrained (<un>
factors)

essayist
knowledge

action>critical
American pragmatism
book
criteria
direct
information
knowledge
name
transversality
trip
uppercut

true and false

event

complexity
creation
discothèque
diversity
fiesta (party)
immanence
menus
sequence
and series
simultaneity
space

territory
texture

surprise
suspense

evolution

developing
innovation
order
progress
theory

evolutionary

animation
avatar
devices
dispositions
dynamism
genetics
open
process
system
time

expression

anonymous
bored

extroversion:
<ex> factors
of form

form

action
aformal
agitated space
anonymous
de-subject
diagrams
dispersed

dissolved architecture
dynamism
epitome
<in> order factors
indetermination
inform(ation)al
in/unfinished
in/uninhibited
in/unsettledness
joy (*alegría*)
no-form
open
sponged
unrestrained (<un>
factors)
unfolding

reactive
relationships,
transitive
(of transference)
resonance
and transference
trajectory

eye

cyclops
gaze
voyeurism

essay
imagine
irradiate

cephalia
hump
muaré or *moiré*

F111

fish
form
strategy

field

context
environment
places

abroad, etc.
agriculture
hyperiphery
periphery

activation
a-scalarity
dispositions
distribution
dynamism
entropy
epitome
fencing space
flows
implant
interaction
interfaces
muaré or *moiré*
process
reaction
recursiveness
self-organization
self-similarity
self-urbanism
solenoid
system
topological
trajectory
vector

form
geometry
limit

auditoriums
sea

areas of opportunity
devices
hyperplace
maps, battle
maps (to map)
place of places
places

program

**figure-
background**

a-couplings
devices
dichotomies
dual(ity)
topological
void

flexibility

activity
ambiguity
(and ambivalence)
hybrid
multi
multifunctional
open
poly
strategy
topological
versatility

flows

fencing space
irradiate
layers
networks

crossing
grids
infrastructures
interchange
interchangers
loops
nubs-nodes-knots
transfers

animation
dispositions
dynamism
energy

field
information
lava, programmatic
no-form
no-place
rhyzomatic

fold

deleuznable
devices
ideas
landstrategy
puff pastry (puffed up)
space
texture

unfolding

bends and (un)bendings
braids
coilings
contortionisms

foreigness

alienation
(and estrangement)
alienism
de-location
distortion
infiltration
interactivity
interference
rootlessness
tourism

suspense

form

abstract
action
audacity
decisions
(and instructions)

rather than designs
extroversion:
<ex> factors of form
geometry
gesture
indefinition
irradiate
meaning
nada(r)
no-box
relationships transitive
(of transference)

attractors
cloud
Chrysler Voyager
F111
muaré or *moiré*
Smart

bends and (un)bendings

camouflage
density
economy
hypertrophy
open
precision

animation
complexity
dispositions
extroversion:
<ex> factors
of form
field
genetics
lava, programmatic
layers
logic, direct
logic, fuzzy
networks
no-form
no-place
transfers
vector

formless

cloud
fish
form
geometry
in/unstable
no-box

fractal

attractors
bluntings
buds
chance
complexity
dispositions
dynamical
form
formless
geometry
nature
rhyzomatic
self-similarity
Sierpinsky's sponge
system>
dynamical
topological
trajectory

fragile

geometry
indefinition

cantilevers
fleeting
impermanences
in-out
in/unstable
land-arch
lightness
precarious(ly)
provisional
temporary

function

program

activity
functionalism
use

game

system>dynamical

cut-outs
origami
papyroflexy
puzzle
tangram

construction games
games of chance
magic games
sleight of hand
table games

chance
ludic
player

client

gaze> tactical gaze

criteria

eye
infiltration
logic, digital
ob-server
photography
synthetical
uppercut

hybrid
multi
reactive

action>critical

discipline
history
holistic
transversality

strategy
tactic

maps, battle
maps (to map)

genetics

avatar
evolutionary

chains
rhyzomatic

genetics of form

animation
dynamism
form
process
topological

crossbreeding
genetics
graft
hybrid

geography

nature
territory

cartographies
geomancy
land-arch
landscape / architec-
ture / urbanism
landscapes, operative
maps (to map)
topographies,
operative

geomancy

inhabit
install
places
synthetical

beacons
cartographies
maps (to map)
negotiate

geometry

fish
form
islands
lava, programmatic

bends and (un)bendings
blobs
braids
bubbles
chains
coilings
cultivations
excavations
holes
hump
hybrid
muaré or *moiré*
mouthfuls
patterns
rays
stampings
tornadoes (or twisters)
trenches

assembly
zapping
zoom

animation
decisions (and
instructions) rather
than designs

density
fold
formless
fractal
fragile
grids
no-form
rhyzomatic

gesture。

form
gestrategies
sensors

globalisation

context
de-location
environment
global village
glocal
limit
no-place
places
simultaneity

abstract
artificial
franchise

glocal

a-couplings
a-scalarity
dispositions
epitome
field
globalisation
infiltration>intrusive-
ness and interference
inform(ation)al
interaction
networks
places
recursiveness

resonance and
transference
scaleless
self-similarity
society of the And, the

goodbye to
the metaphor

abstract
a-couplings
allegory
meaning
name
tattoos

graft

strategy

ad-herence /
inheritance
cohabitation
commensalism
context
contract
cuttings
genetics
genetics of form
hybrid
<in> order factors
infiltration
meldings
no-form
prosthesis
synthetical

graphy-logy

diagram-ideogram
iconography-iconology
topography-topology

grids

(inter)weavings and
inter(plots)
infrastructures
matrix
muaré or *moiré*
networks

geometry
mathematics
structure
topological

no-form

land links

hackitecture

appropriation
strategies
cyber_punk
cyberspace
détournement
Gibson's sprawl
hacker

holistic

action>critical
gaze
interactivity
transversality

holograms

energy
fatuous fires
(*feux follets*)
fleeting
light
transparency

hotel

anonymous

Benidorm
client
desire
economy
no-places
Spain
tourism
trip

house, the

inhabit
housing
housys

AH houses
M'house houses
take-away homes

Chrysler Voyager
container
estate car
WebHotel

domestic
imagine>imagination
interior
leisure
work
virtual

re-information

housing

AH houses
housys
inhabit
M'house houses
rurban loft
take-away homes

landscape housing
stimulating housing
technical housing

catalogue

dispositions
diversity
domestic
individual
innovation
interior
livrid

housys

devices
diversity
genetics
housing
interior
livrid
menus
multi
open
system

hybrid

a-couplings
antitypes
buds
collage
commensalism
crossbreeding
cuttings
form
genetics
graft
hybrid
impurity
link
livrid
process
program

built hybrids
cloning
domestic hybridisation
urban hybrids

archaeology>advanced
diversity

environment
flexibility
future
multi

advanced,
architecture
animation
areas of impunity
avatar
genetics of form
mixed-use
strategy
WebHotel

hypercontext

citilab
cyberspace
incubator
information
intercommunity
link
networks
newspace
system
telepolis

hyperplace

diversity
hyperiphery
m. city (or multicity)
multi
multilayered
multispace
networks
place of places

Metapolis

hypertrophy

cephalia
cyclops
hump

midget & giant
Yeti

direct
geometry
logic, direct
no-form
unrestrained (<un>
factors)

I/(my)self

irradiate
joy (*alegría*)
moral
passion

individual
multi
one is many
plural

client
criteria
ideas
meaning
subject
yuppie

iceberg

ambiguity
(and ambivalence)
flexibility
immersed
mountain
versatility

ideas

criteria
projective

bored
challenge
dual(ity)

fear
imagine
indiscipline
R+3D
tangent

client
I/(my)self
Keaton
Marx Bros.

audacity
droog
information
inform(ation)al
intelligence
invent
moral
passion

immanence

advanced, architecture
architecture
camouflage
dispersed
dispositions
dissolved architecture
distribution
event
<in> order factors
logic, fuzzy
name

immersed

blur
iceberg
subsoil
trenches

impermanences

future
time

amphibious
ephemeral
fabrications
fragile
in/unstable
lightness
nomad
occupation structures
precarious(ly)
reversible
strategy
temporary

<in> order
factors

in/unfinished

immanence
immersed
inconstancy
indefinition
indetermination
indiscipline
infiltration
infinity
inmediateness
innovation
insubordination
interaction
interconnection
intermission
intermittences
in/uncertainty
in/unsettledness

impure
indefinite
individual
informal
inform(ation)al
intercalated
intermittent
in/unstable

graft
infiltration>
intrusiveness and

system>dynamical
transfers
unrestrained (<un>
factors)
virtual

infrastructures

braids
circuits
crossing
grids
high speed
(inter)weavings
and inter(plots)
interchangers
link
loops
networks
nubs-nodes-knots
system
territory
transfers

innovation

action>critical
advanced
advanced,
architecture
audacity
competition
criteria
essay
evolution
housing
<in> order factors
Media Lab
memory
process
R+3D
tergiversation
tracing

in-out

activity
appropriation
strategies
areas of opportunity
community
ephemeral
extend
fragile
individual
plural

install

geomancy
<in> order factors
negotiate
occupation structures
places

intelligence

adaptation
audacity
criteria
dynamism
elastic
extroversion:
<ex> factors of form
flexibility
ideas
imagine>imagination
<in> order factors
information
interaction
interchange
joy (*alegría*)
operative
optimism
relational
system
unrestrained (<un>
factors)

construction,
intelligent
production, intelligent

interaction

action
object
order
reaction

incubator
interactivity
interchange
layers
link
multilayered
resonance and
transference
synergy

activity
individual
information
inform(ation)al

interchange

contract
data
datascape
flows
incubator
information
inform(ation)al
infrastructures
interaction
interfaces
resonance
and transference
tropism

interfaces

architecture
devices
prosthesis
relationships, transitive
(of transference)

in-between
reality

intermediate places

and
a-scalarity
in-between
in-between fingers,
in-between links
joint
plaits
threshold

intermittences

difference
dynamism
intercadences
sequences

and

distribution
form
temporary

(inter)weavings and inter(plots)

distributions
field
patterned distributions
patterns
strata

devices
dispositions

armadillo
branchial
grids
infrastructures
nubs-nodes-knots

scanning
skeleton
wireframes

in/unsettledness

trajectory

agitated space
animation
dynamism
extroversion:
<ex> factors of form
form
<in> order factors
in/unfinished

in/unstable

cantilevers
dissolved architecture
ephemeral
formless
fragile
impermanences
<in> order factors
inform(ation)al
lightness
muaré or *moiré*
no-form
precarious(ly)
reversible
surprise
suspense
temporary

islands

amphibious
individuality
island cities
management park
territory

Barcelona Metapolis
geography

---

iceberg
m. city (or multicity)
mountain

Metapolis

joint

and
component
in-between
in-between fingers, in-
between links
intermediate places
void

joy (*alegría*)

AA
advanced, architecture
expression
extroversion:
<ex> factors of form
inform(ation)al
in/uninhibited
jai-tech
open
optimism
unrestrained (<un>
factors)

game
hedonism
ludic

bored

knowledge

chunking
criteria
diagrams
eraserhead
information
memory
search engine

---

tangent
Think Tank

architecture
book
deviation
intermediary

land-arch

agriculture
eco-> eco-chic
eco->
ecomonumentality
ecology, active
void

natuficio
naturartificial
nature

terrain vague
vague

abstract
artificial
fragile
synthetical
temporary

a-couplings
dichotomies
hybrid
transgenetic transfu-
sions

land links

arches of development
brocades
eco-> eco-chic
eco->
ecomonumentality
ecology, active
grids
in-between
in-between fingers,

---

in-between links
infrastructures
joint
landscape / architec-
ture / urbanism
landscapes, operative
landstrategy
link
logiter
networks
patchwork city
plaits

strategy
territory

flexibility
sequences
void
voids and fills

mayor

landscape / architecture / urbanism

landscapes, operative
landstrategy
rurban life
topographies, operative
urban-territorial

landscapes, operative

carpets
countermarks: craters
and basins
hills
landstrategy
mats
mountain
peaks
plateaux
ponds
reliefs

<ex> factors
of form
Gibson's sprawl
globalisation
glocal
<in> order factors
inform(ation)al
periphery
places
space
telepolis
void

link

citilab
flows
incubator
interaction
interactivity
interchange
networks

photography

livrid

housing
housys
hybrid

environment
mixed-use
multifunctional

devices
re-information

logic, digital

animation
arkitektor
cyberspace
data
diagrams
digital world

digitnature
dynamism
Gibson's sprawl
inform(ation)al
layers
Media Lab
multilayered
paper
simulation
software
synthetical

instrument
manipulate

logic, direct

action
action>critical
blunt
concise
direct
flexibility
formless
inform(ation)al
open
synthetical
uppercut

logic, fuzzy

ideas
<in>, order factors
inform(ation)al
tangent
vague
wander

client

loops

braids
circuits
crossing
flows

grids
infrastructures
interchangers
nubs-nodes-knots

networks
transfers
tropism

maps, battle

action
criteria
decisions (and
instructions)
rather than designs
devices
diagrams
dispositions
field
<in> order factors
operative
order
places
strategy
system>dynamical
tactic

paths & peaks
trajectory

dynamism
inform(ation)al
open

maps
(to map)

abstract map
atopical map
dispositive map
explanatory map
exploratory map
geographical map
mental map
operative map
tactical map

abstract
beacons
cartographies
data
datascape
field
geography
geomancy
places
projective
trailers
trip

gaze
manipulate

marks

advertisements
advertising
companies
product

patterns
stains, ink
stampings
tattoos

mathematics

algorithm
code
complex system
complexity
diagrams
game
grids
informal
in/uncertainty
matrix
models
structure
system
topological

matrix

field
grids
infrastructures
(inter)weavings
and inter(plots)
networks
patterned distributions
patterns
score
system
topological

mats

agriculture
carpets
cultivations
devices
landscape /
architecture /
urbanism
landscapes,
operative
land(s) in lands
stains, landscape
trays

matter

abstract
product

carbon fibre
context
environment
music
mutation
paper
plastic
production,
intelligent

architecture

McDonaldization

conventional
object
standardisation

paradoxes

m. city
(or multicity)

city?
cuts
hyperiphery
islands
localization
network of cities
networks
polis
port
psycho-geographize
stains, ink
subject
Team-X
territory
transfers
urbs

chains
plaits

mayor

meaning

form
goodbye to the
metaphor
I/(my)self
indefinition
knowledge
language
name
rhyzomatic

meldings

antitypes
cohabitation
commensalism
contract
cuttings
graft
hybrid
infiltration
no-form
parasitism
prosthesis
strategy

membrane

branchial
equipped façade
(and wall)
skin
ubliquity

memory

discipline
history
imagine>imagination
in/unconsciousness
knowledge
past
represent
time
tracing

audacity

menus

catalogue
component
event
housys
hyperplace
operative
place of places

scanning
score
search engine
simultaneity
zapping

Metapolis

avatar
e-city
hyperplace
m. city
(or multicity)
multicity
place of places
R+3D
refounding
re-information
rurban loft
Think Tank
zapping

action>critical

critical pragmatism
ideas
positioning

flows
grids
layers
multilayered
networks
topological

global village
mayor

midget & giant

economy

hypertrophy
scaleless

moral

criteria

invisible in architecture
positioning

client
competition
economy
juries

I/(my)self
ideas

action>critical
passion
Team-X

mountain

land(s) in lands
reliefs
tableland
topological

iceberg
immersed

artificial
mixed-use
natuficio
naturartificial
nature
occupations

ecology, active

multi

environment
multicity
multifunctional
multilayered
multimedia, urban
multispace

Metapolis

activity

chaos
complexity
context
diversity
flexibility
hyperplace
I/(my)self
mixed-use
muaré or *moiré*
one is many
plural
stack (stacks)
X-Architecture

housys
hybrid
program

multilayered

epitome
hyperplace
information
layers
Metapolis
mixed-use
multi
multicity
networks
stack (stacks)

laminate
millefeuilles
puff pastry (puffed up)

mutation

distortion
evolutionary
genetics
genetics of form
hybrid
information
inform(ation)al

interference
material
original and replica
sequence and series
system
transfers

nada(r)

form
void

name

action>critical
architecture
book
code
essay
essayist knowledge
ideological dictionary
language
liberty
tergiversation

do-it-yourself

indefinition

naturartificial

a-couplings
enclaves
land-arch
land links
landscapes, operative
land(s) in lands
landstrategy
mountain
reliefs
topographies, operative

nature

artificial

natural
naturartificial

agriculture
attractors
cosmos
cuts
dynamism
ecology, active
enclaves
fractal
geography
mountain
reliefs
rurban
system

negotiate

machination

advanced
aformal
architecture
client
contract
decisions (and instructions)
rather than designs
flexibility
geomancy
program

Net, the

franchise
network of cities

networks

braids
brocades
crossing
flows
grids
incubator

infrastructures
interchangers
link
loops
nubs-nodesknots
plaits
transfers

glocal
hyperplace
m. city (or multicity)
Metapolis
multicity
multilayered
network of cities
place of places
system
telepolis
territory

code

topological
trips

tropism (active)

no

no-box
no-day
no-form
no-place
no-scale

scream
yes!

AA
aformal
a-scalarity

no-form

aformal
attractors
diagrams

dispositions
energy
F111
flexibility
formless
hypertrophy
ideogram
indetermination
indiscipline
in/unstable
muaré or *moiré*
open
rhyzomatic
vortex

decisions
(and instructions)
rather than designs
ex-jection
fencing space
flows
graft
grids
infrastructures
process

a-scalarity
discipline
form
geometry
inform(ation)al

no-places

anonymous
de-location
environment
flows
globalisation
heterotopia
hotel
hyperiphery
port
pragmatopia
relationships,
transitive
(of transference)
rhyzomatic

time
urbs

McDonaldization
multispace
network of cities
place of places

nomad

dynamism
ephemeral
fleeting
impermanences
in/unstable
lightness
provisional
reversible
temporary
tropism
vector

time
trip
wandering

normadic
subject
WebHotel

nubs-nodes-knots

grids
(inter)weavings and in-ter(plots)
link
loops
network of cities
networks
transfers

object

AH houses
M'house houses

product

conventional
gaze
interaction
process
reality
tactic

**occupation
structures**

devices
dispositions
ephemeral
places
precarious(ly)

one is many

chains
complexity
diversity
I/(my)self
multi
plural
poly
zapping

open

aformal
agitated space
a-scalarity

anonymous
de-subject
dissolved architecture
fresh conservatism
elastic
experimental
architecture
extension
flexibility
inform(ation)al
in/unfinished

unfolding

no-box
no-form
no-scale
Swiss knife

direct

in/uninhibited

indetermination
limit

extroversion:
<ex> factors
of form
fractal
geometry
<in> order factors
order
system
topological

evolutionary
expression

vague

operative

action
genetics
process

activity
devices
maps, battle
menus
system

optimism

advanced
advanced, architecture
cloud 9

extroversion:
<ex> factors of form
formless
jai-tech
joy (*alegría*)
Marx Bros.
unrestrained
(<un> factors)
yes!

order

devices
dispositions
distribution
formless
<in> order factors
indetermination
inform(ation)al
interaction
in/uncertainty
logic, fuzzy
maps, battle
occupations
self-organization
self-urbanism

grids
intercadences
intermittences
(inter)weavings and
inter(plots)
score
sequences

paradoxes

devices
fresh conservatism
in-between
indiscipline
situation, the
tergiversation
uppercut

a-couplings
braids

infiltration>
intrusiveness
and interference
in/unstable
light
reactive
suspense

patchwork city

flows
hyperplace
infrastructures
layers
m. city (or multicity)
mixed-use
multicity
multilayered
networks
open
place of places
recycling

**patterned
distributions**

combination
intermittences
(inter)weavings and
inter(plots)
music
patterns
score
sequences
syncope
voids and fills

periphery

field
hyperiphery
limit
m. city (or multicity)
multicity
patchwork city
rurban

strategy

places

areas of impunity
context
environment
field
globalisation
glocal
grids
hyperplace
limit
no-places
occupation structures
place of places
plaits
reality
sea
subsoil
transfers
tropism
zone of high-sensitivity

localization
situation, the
territory

deviation
manipulate
wander

cartographies
geomancy
install
maps, battle
maps (to map)
pragmatopia

arches of development
braids
countermarks:
craters and basins
crossing
enclaves
geography
landscape / architec-
ture / urbanism

landscapes, operative
landstrategy
material
nubs-nodes-knots
reliefs
topographies, operative

architecture

plaits

brocades
simultaneity

diversity
grids
hyperplace
in-between
infrastructures
land links
landscapes, operative
m. city (or multicity)
multicity
networks
place of places
places

pleasure

(e)motion
hedonism
interaction
interchange
joy (*alegría*)
ludic
optimism
unrestrained (<un>
factors)

plural

complexity
crossbreeding
diversity
I/(my)self

indetermination
in-out
multi
one is many
open
poly
simultaneity
X-Architecture

activity
jai-tech
normadic
synthetical

positioning

action>critical
American pragmatism
criteria
critical pragmatism
education
ideas
knowledge
Metapolis

precision

concise
synthetical

abstract
audacity
criteria
economy
form
knowledge
production, intelligent

product

activity
advertising
catalogue
companies
economy
form

kits
marks
material
matter
McDonaldization
object
production, intelligent
prototypes
software
standardisation

production, intelligent

catalogue
concise
diversity
flexibility
kits
matter
precision
process
product
synthetical
system

program

activity
complexity
function
hybrid
mixed-use
multi
negotiate
use

arches of development
architecture
areas of impunity
field

progress

advanced
braids

evolution
evolutionary
history
indiscipline
innovation
past
progression
proneoism
sequences
time

projective

advanced, architecture
decisions
(and instructions)
rather than designs
epitome
ideas
imagine>imagination
machination
maps, battle
negotiate
proceed

maps
trailers
transfers

proneoism

action
imagine> imagination
indiscipline
innovation
progress
progression

prosthesis

abstract
interfaces
prototypes
synthetical

cuttings

graft
hump
implant
impurity
infiltration>intrusive-
ness and interference
meldings

prototypes

catalogue
crash test
devices
product
production, intelligent
simulation
system

provisional

amphibious
appropiation strategies
contract
devices
ephemeral
occupation structures
precarious(ly)

fleeting
fragile
impermanences
reversible
temporary

**puff pastry
(puffed up)**

dirty details
fissures
fold
landstrategy
layers
millefeuilles
Sierpinsky's sponge
space
sponged

strata
void

quidam

deviation
discothèque
displacing by sliding
logic, fuzzy
trip
vague
vector
wander
wandering

re- (prefix)

reactive
recomposition
reconstruction
recreation
recuperation
redefinition
redention
refounding
regeneration
rehabilitation
reimpulsation
re-information
reinstauration
repetition
restauration
reversible

reactive

activation
devices
extroversion:
<ex> factors of form
foreigness
<i> space
<in> order factors
infiltration>
intrusiveness and
interference

interaction
re-information
resonance-synergy-
interaction

bored

reality

action
dirty details
environment
field
heterotopia
interfaces
object
photography
places
represent
rootlessness
sensors
simulation
simulator
simultaneity
surprise
suspense
texture

actuality
metareality

recursiveness

diagrams
generation
information
interaction
resonance
and transference
self-similarity
synergy

recycling

assembly

audacity
collage
ecology, active
implosion, urban
object
reactive
recycling, urban
re-information
sample
tergiversation

re-information

energy
house, the
implosion, urban
leisure
reactive
refounding
tree> photovoltaic tree

photography

**relationships,
transitive (of
transference)**

agitated space
a-scalarity
dynamism
interaction
projective
recursiveness
resonance-synergy-
interaction
self-similarity
space
tergiversation

client

reliefs

cuts
enclaves
hills

mountain
plateaux
platforms
tableland
terraces
texture

countermarks:
craters and basins
trenches

artificial
landstrategy
refluences
surface
topographies, operative

reversible

contract
cuttings
devices
ephemeral
fragile
in/unstable
precarious(ly)
provisional
system
tattoos
temporary

rurban life

agriculture
artificial
landscapes, operative
m. city (or multicity)
multicity
naturartificial
nature
periphery
rurburbia:
urbanterritorial space
section, scrambled flat
urban-territorial

AH houses

M'house houses

rurban loft

housing
housys
inhabit

environment
Metapolis
multifunctional
re-information

scaffolding

appropiation strategies
ephemeral
fleeting
impermanences
occupation structures
precarious(ly)
provisional
reversible
temporary

scaleless

a-scalarity
dimension
fractal
midget & giant
muaré or *moiré*
rhyzomatic
self-similarity
Sierpinsky's sponge

scanning

catalogue
menus
section
sequences

score

combination
grids
intercadences
(inter)weavings
and inter(plots)
maps (to map)
music
patterned distributions
sequences
space
syncope

sea

bank & beach
field
islands
places
terrain vague
territory
vector spaces

port

areas of impunity
areas
of opportunity

search engine

knowledge
link
menus

section

diagonalisation
scanning
score
space

mixed-use
section, active

self-similarity

a-scalarity
attractors
dispositions
field
fractal
geometry
recursiveness
topological
zoom

self-urbanism

amphibious
arches
of development
chance
dispositions
field
fringes
self-organization
stains, ink
system
territory
topological

sequences

link
multi
scanning

bluntings
buds
chains
distribution
grids
intercadences
intermittences
(inter)weavings
and inter(plots)
music
patterned distributions
score
unfolding
voids and fills

a-scalarity
fractal
geometry
topological
void
zoom

simultaneity

cohabitation
complexity
diversity
dual(ity)
globalisation
glocal
inform(ation)al
limit
multilayered
plural

mixed-use

photography

skeleton

archaeology
armadillo
fuselages
grids
(inter)weavings
and inter(plots)
structure

skin

equipped façade
(and wall)
equipped wall
membrane

body
camouflage
tattoos

space

fencing space
spaces>collective
spaces>public
and private
spaces>public space
vector space

hybrid space
intermediate space
interstitial space
leisure space
mobility space
multifacetious space
omission space
public atypological
space
topic-teletopic space
wrinkled space

multispace

anonymous
egotecture
flâneur
no-place

field
flows
music
transparency
void

spaces>public
and private

a-couplings
dichotomies
domestic
house, the
space
spaces>collective

speed

uppercut

sponged

dispositions
equipped wall
layers
millefeuilles
puff pastry (puffed up)
Sierpinsky's sponge
strategy
topological

stains, ink

attractors
dispersed
dispositions
dissolved architecture
distribution
extension
<in> order factors
inform(ation)al
in/unfinished
liberty
logic, fuzzy
m. city (or multicity)
Metapolis
multicity
process

rurban life
self-organization
self-similarity
self-urbanism
territory
urban-territorial

cartographies
maps (to map)

compact

standardisation

catalogue
complexity

conventional
extroversion:
<ex> factors of form
indefinition
in/unfinished
McDonaldization
product

stenosis

density
flexibility
in-between
infiltration
intermediate places
joint
void

stimulus

client
companies
energy
ideas
passion

strategy

gestrategies
texture
topographies, operative

a-couplings
ad-herence /
inheritance
associate, overlap,
connect
demolish
ex-jection
graft
occupations
recycling
sponged
stack (stacks)
tergiversation
zapping

zoom

ambushments
camouflage
de-location
enjambements
hybrid
infiltration

flexibility

devices
tactic>tactic vs.
strategy

contract
ephemeral
fragile
holes
impermanences
install
nomad
provisional
temporary

land links
land(s) in lands
maps, battle
periphery

structure

algorithm
complexity
mathematics
models
precision

fuselages
frame-
grids
skeleton

inform(ation)al
structures
occupation structures

lightness

plastic
soft
viscous architecture
wetgrid

surface

landstrategy
muaré or *moiré*
texture
topographies, operative

ambiguity
diagonalisation
mcguffins
surprise
suspense
ubliquity

synergy

direct
energy
incubator
infiltration
information
interaction
interchange
logic, fuzzy
reactive
relationships, transitive
(of transference)
resonance and
transference

synthetical

abstract
artificial
attractors
complexity
concise
diagrams
genetics
plural
precision

production, intelligent
prosthesis

system

diversified systems
dynamical systems
informational systems
recicled systems
system>Operating
System
unstable systems

infrastructures
matrix
networks
territory

city?
code>(bar)code
combination
devices
dispositions
<in> order factors
order
process

catalogue
diversity
hybrid
individuality
kits
production, intelligent
simultaneity

system>dynamical

chance
form
fractal
game
time

tableland

fold

hyperplace
place of places
plateaux
platforms
reliefs
terraces
texture
topographies,
operative
topological
trays
zapping

tactic

gaze> tactical gaze
tergiversation

maps, battle
strategy

tangent

action>critical
ideas
knowledge
logic, fuzzy
surface
transversality
wander

tattoos

ephemeral
extroversion:
<ex> factors of form
fragile
marks
patterns
provisional
reversible
skin
surface
temporary

advanced, architecture

goodbye to the
metaphor

telepolis

artificial
city?
de-location
leisure
limit
mixed-use
networks
polis
simultaneity
telework
territory
urbs

tergiversation

collage
innovation
recycling
relationships, transitive
(of transference)
sample
strategy
tactic

terraces

artificial
countermarks: craters
and basins
cuts
enclaves
geography
hills
landscapes, operative
land(s) in lands
landstrategy
naturartificial
nature
reliefs
surface
tableland

texture
topographies, operative
trenches

territory

self-urbanism

infrastructures
islands
land links
m. city (or multicity)
Metapolis
multicity
multilayered
networks
nomad
sea
system
topological
trip
tropism
void

event
hyperplace
place of places
relationships, transitive
(of transference)
rurban
urban-territorial

time

action
chaos
evolutionary
history
<in>, order factors
indetermination
inform(ation)al
in/uncertainty
logic, fuzzy
memory
past
progression
system

dynamism
ephemeral
fleeting
impermanences
precarious(ly)
progress
provisional
reversible
simultaneity
temporary

aformal
immanence

flâneur
nomad
no-place
sense
simulator
suspense

topographies, operative

landstrategy

reliefs
surface

artificial
attractors

dunes
enclaves
land(s) in lands
tableland
texture

devices
strategies

topological

delynniate
fractal
genetics of form

open
tableland

grids
holes
in-between fingers,
in-between links
networks
plateaux
platforms
rhyzomatic
Sierpinsky's sponge
sponged
Yokohama

topological (age)

tourism

alienation
(and estrangement)
alienism
bank & beach
Benidorm
de-location
economy
foreigness
glocal
infiltration>
intrusiveness
and interference
landscapes,
operative
no-place
overflow
place of places
trip

tracing

difference

criteria
discipline
innovation
memory

trailers

cartographies
epitome
maps (to map)
projective

trajectory

attractors
braids
coilings
contortionisms
deviation
diagrams
dispositions
field
fold
fractal
geometry
in/unsettledness
logic, fuzzy
open
rhyzomatic
tornadoes
(or twisters)
zig-zag

trans

transfers
transgenetic transfu-
sions
transparency
transversality

transfers

flows
hybrid
loops
nubs-nodes-knots
places
subject>subjected

transversality

action>critical
discipline
essayist knowledge

eraserhead
gaze> tactical gaze
imagine
trip

assembly
process

associate, overlap,
connect
chance

trays

artificial
geography
land(s) in lands
plateaux
strata
surface
tableland
topographies,
operative

carpets

trip

deviation
hotel
nomad
paths & peaks
time
tourism
transversality
wander
wandering

Net, the

port
reliefs
territory
tourism
WebHotel
Yokohama

cartographies
maps (to map)
process
trajectory
tropism
vector
zapping

catches
essayist knowledge

architecture

tropism

places

nomad
trip

ubliquity

diagonalisation
fold
landstrategy

**unrestrained
(<un> factors)**

bluntings
de-location
de-subject
devoid of complexes
in/uninhibited
(un-attached)
(un-codified)
unfolding
(un-naturalised)
(un-prejudiced)

(un-rooted)
(un-slipping)
(un-wrapped)

challenge

unfolding

agitated space

bluntings
buds
de-subject
dispositions
extension
extroversion:
<ex> factors of form
fold
form
<in> order factors
inform(ation)al
unrestrained (<un>
factors)

geometry
topological
trajectory

urbs

arches of development
avatar
tourism

Metapolis

m. city
(or multicity)
multicity
no-place
rurban life
telepolis

vague

a-couplings

ambiguity
a-scalarity
dispersed
dissolved
architecture
hybrid
indefinition
indetermination
in/uncertainty
limit
logic, fuzzy
quidam
terrain vague
transgenetic
transfusions
void
wander
wandering

vector

attractors
flows
genetics
inform(ation)al
logic,
fuzzy
seed
Yokohama

deviation
nomad
paths & peaks
quidam
trip
wandering

versatility

advanced,
architecture
chance
flexibility
multi
open
poly

virtual

digital world
future
metareality
WebHotel

cyberspace
Gibson's sprawl
paradoxes
simulator

void

abroad, etc.
figure-background
in-between
limit
nada(r)
terrain vague

space

holes
Sierpinsky's sponge

intermittences
joint
laminate
land links
landstrategy
puff pastry (puffed up)
sequences
surface
voids and fills

X-Architecture

act-n
advanced,
architecture
critical pragmatism
devices
dispositions
diversity

multi

yes!

no!
direct
just do it
logic, direct
optimism
proneoism
scream
simultaneity
unrestrained
(<un> factors)
uppercut

Yokohama

braids
laminate
landstrategy
lava,
programmatic
membrane
millefeuilles
puff pastry
(puffed up)
refluences
sponged
surface
topological
vector

spaces>
public space

trip

zapping

geometry
strategy
trip

contract

ephemeral
fleeting
impermanences
precarious(ly)
provisional
reversible
temporary

zoom

a-scalarity
self-similarity

fractal
geometry
recursiveness
sequences

◆● imagine

[FS] **(imagination)**

Imagination is the quality of advanced architectural production. Imagination transforms reality, and establishes unsuspected relations. It signals other paths from which to attack problems. Imagination, however, needs to have memory and a certain knowledge base; it is a player that always plays with the rebound, against what is.

[MG] **(ideate)**

"*Snake: When Adam and you talk, I hear you say 'Why?' always 'Why?' You see things and say 'Why?' But I dream of something that never existed; and I say 'Why not?'*" (George Bernard Shaw, *Back to Methuselah*, in NEVILLE, Katherine, *The magic circle*, New York : Ballantine Books, 1999)

■ immanence

[JM] Immanence is one of those concepts upon which future architecture leans. Architecture of immanence is at the mercy of events, but carries with it terrible consequences. It does not have an inside or outside, (Blanchot), but is loose. Its materials are lent by camouflage, its structure plans dispersion of the multitude and the contrariety between number and nature. Perhaps, immanence represents the permanent effort of signifying the force of the savage, of what does not yet have a name, nor word. That which is before discourse. (M. Foucault).

● immersed

[MG] Immersed or submerged. Of immersion.
Plunged into a liquid. Or underground.

1. Enric RUIZ-GELI, *Cloud 666 Tree: Fundacio Mies van der Rohe headquarters*, Barcelona, 1998.

2. S&Aa (SORIANO-PALACIOS), *Competition for the Museum of Navigation*, Anwertpen (Belgium), 1999.

★▲ impact

→ 'catastrophe'   [co]

(environmental)

Inherent in all urbanistic action is impact on the territory. It would be reactionary to hold that such impact is always negative; nature offers constant examples of its impassive cruelty, which requires correction or tempering. But not everything is permitted. Rationality, a moral requirement, calls for caution in the manner in which impact is produced, in its effect at all levels and in the exigencies that it entails.

The process of construction of the tourist space (which, after agriculture, is the human activity which occupies the greatest area of quality land) is, in all probability, the most shining example of the intellectual negligence of modern society, the moral decadence that lies at the heart of its relationship with the natural environment, its predatory attitude and its nearsightedness. From the urbanistic point of view, nothing is so rationally objectionable as the obsessive accumulation of nothing more than appallingly mimetic housing products in fragile environments and exceptional settings. Aside from being devoid of the slightest urbanistic interest, the residential estates populating the Mediterranean coast boundlessly extend the development process, pose unsolvable functional problems, generate constant unavoidable waste and require costly infrastructural systems. The results are catastrophic: irreversible occupation of the coastal space, deterioration of the natural environment, multiplication of inefficient infrastructures and destruction of urban values. Not even economic justifications hold: for the same flow of earnings, the second-residence suburban estates use 170 times more land than a dense, dynamic tourist city with a high proportion of hotel rooms.

An ongoing conspiracy of dunces, in which a gabbling parliament of media types, reactionary ecologists and right-thinking petty bourgeoisie have conspired to demonise cities and send us down the road to detached-house hell. Never, in the recent history of urbanism, has rationality confronted on so uneven a playing field a similar rabble of blind and tireless evildoers.

JOSÉ MIGUEL IRIBAS

Pearl River Delta, Harvard Design School Project on the City, in VARIOUS AUTHORS, *Mutations*, Barcelona: ACTAR and Arc en Rêve, 2000.

(economic)

[FP]   See 'economy' and 'new economy.'

[FP]   "*If e-business can be understood as the commercialisation of Internet by dotcom companies, it would be an interesting business, innovative and sometimes profitable, but rather limited in its general economic impact. If the new economy is based on a potential without precedents for the growth of productivity as a result from the use of Internet in every company and every operation, we are probably entering a new management world. A world which does not cancel business cycles neither substitutes economic laws, but which transforms its modalities and consequences while it adds new game rules (such as the increase of yields and effects on the Net). From a first perspective, the new economy would be the economy of Internet industry. From another approximation, we can see the growth of a new economy from the last one as a result from the use of Internet by the companies, for their own objectives and in specific contexts.*" (Paraphrasing CASTELLS, Manuel, *The Internet galaxy: reflections on the Internet, business, and society*, Oxford : Oxford University Press, 2001)

★ impermanences

[C] " *Non-permanent architectures, linked to a limited space of time after which they disappear, are proposed as a real, operative alternative associated to the practices deriving from mobility and spatial delocation. These concepts make way for practices which incorporate time as a parameter that can be directly manipulated. This gives rise to a new conception of time, now seen as being reversible which have obvious parallels with what Debord called "independent federated times."*

These forms of architecture, which establish a limited-time relationship with the landscape, manifest themselves as an event, a proposition which neither remains nor modifies the place it rested once it ceases to exist; it leaves no trace.

These instant, transitory forms of architecture propose a less violent relationship with the landscape –be it built or not. They could be inserted without appropriating, finishing or consuming it, thereby renouncing possession or domination of it. Above the apparent quality of setting for linguistic experimentation in a pure state, of pure formal banality to which it seems to have been relegated, non-permanent architecture places the now interesting loss of materiality, exchanging the formal for a reaffirmation of processes. It sets itself forward as an accepted, positively incomplete system which does not attempt to solve all the problems and situations undergone or yet to occur in one go, which shies away from presenting itself as a centred, closed totality (with immutable rules) which deploys a whole series of specific actions and tangents with a high level of operative and critical incidence; and then disappears.

ÁBALOS & HERREROS, *Intervention on the Guadalhorce River*, Málaga (Spain), 1994.

The architecture of the event turns its very fragility, its lack of transcendence and its loss of all substance into new resources with which it can operate on the contemporary cultural and productive scene." (DÍAZ MORENO, Cristina; GARCÍA GRINDA, Efrén, "Impermanent architecture", *Quaderns* 224, 1999)

★ implant

[CO] Implants "replace failing tissues or organs with working ones (biological or artificial, depending on the particular state of research)," Ralph C. Merkle.
XAVIER COSTA

✘ implosion, urban

[VG] See 're-information' and 'recycling, urban.'

● impurity

[MG] See 'distortion' and 'hybrid.'

● \<in\> order factors

[MG] The study of non-linear dynamic systems and the phenomena of chaotic intentionality has, with gathering speed, and over a relatively short time span, revealed the possibility of an indeterminate order – beyond the idea of order as a tight control of processes – fundamental to the current understanding of our universe.

This new order allows associated organisational parameters of structures to be grasped. They present behaviours at once uncertain and generic, observable in most evolutionary dynamic processes. In the case of cities, such processes intensify their chaotic effects with any rise in the phenomena of mobility and internal interchange and, therefore, with any increase in the degree of interaction between the different bits of information which might affect them.

This concept of order as an internal organisation (or contract), based upon flexible relationships, rather than upon categorical bonds, has no longer any relationship with either the old absolute totalitarian – continual and stable – notion of classical composition or with the modern – more relative, removed and fragmented (but equally determinist) – position. Rather, it relates to a more open and paradoxical conception of the idea of order as disposition.

A flexible and operative arrangement capable of favouring this "determinate indeterminism" among manifold combinations, among stimuli and bits of information that are at once diverse and concerted, inherent to a new type of more informal – inform(ation)al – order and to its associated \<im/in/un\> factors: high degree of interactivity and of interchange of information, principle of uncertainty – indetermination, instability and inconstancy – infrastructural property – interconnection, individuality and intermittency – strong inclination towards incompleteness – infiniteness – and, above all, a tendency towards indiscipline directly associable with its insubordination, its immediacy, its impurity and its operative indefinition. A new type of flexible order that shows itself more predisposed to the generation of open dispositions (processes) than to that of closed designs (objects). Dispositions emerging from *evolutionary systems,* rather than from *beautiful (com)positions.*

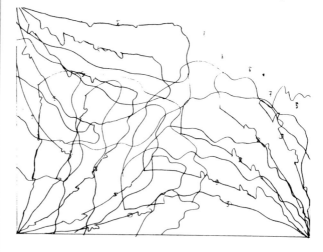

Trajectories of four
of the same materials
or four different
materials. Barry
LE VA, *4 phase-corner
blow piece,* 1969.

■● in-between

[JM] In architecture, the 'between' centres its interest on what mediates – the architecture of relation and tangency. It is the urbanism of open systems, architecture without limits, without clauses, open to phenomenology of landscapes, but also the architecture of conjunction of the minimum and without interest. It is an architecture that strengthens itself on the most difficult situations; in fact, it has a predilection for it. Tangency is its favorite place.

The 'between' is a space permanently on the run; a place in itself, a limit made fringe, a border made country. Moreover, it is a conquering between two belligerent territories. Strange, infiltrated, camouflaged.

It is the ideal response for a project contaminated by the environment around it. It originates there, where (or starting from) the conditions are not precise, but ambiguous, confused, misapplied, hybrid, uncertain.

A project that originates in this grade of confusion, for example that of our peripheries, tries to tinge itself or imbibe this or that; it tries – this "in between" project – to attract everything towards itself that it can use to make its own space.

[MG] See 'in-between fingers, in-between links' and 'infiltration.'

Between is not, necessarily, a residual space (the void between two volumes inherent to modern architecture and urbanism), but rather, in complex geometries, it may be a substantial place: the place where the geometry "inhales and exhales;" a place of synchronic ambiguities. An elastic structural cushion.

Of interest is, in fact, this "gasket" capacity of the interstitial void implicit in these irregular configurations. This possible rhythm among the occupied, the omitted and the linked: fills, voids and links (or articulations), that is to say, surfaces, points and lines that interrupt spatial sequences and combinations. The void, thus, does not separate but joins.

It is a clip between events which serves as linkage, given that it is the void itself that permits the articulation of routes, supports and accesses, producing meshes – or channels – of connection; real or virtual.

Imbrication void-
fill in a rhyzomatic
structure.

in-between fingers, in-between links

→ 'and', 'in-between',
'intermediate places',
'joint', 'land links', 'plaits',
'territory', 'topological'

[MG] Underlying the fractal – open and discontinuous – definition of current urban topologies is the presence of the void. No longer a residual – isolated or exceptional – the void is rather an operative subsystem linked to the dynamic processes of spacing and occupation. Such voids have shaped within them generators of separations, hollows, incisions and possible free channels of routing and relationship.

For years, architecture has focused on the full – the edificial, the erected. Today, both terms – empty and full – can be combined articulately in more complex structures relating to positive-negative (empty-full) sequences that, well-designed on all scales, favour more elastic arrangements among events through the relational role granted to in-between spaces.

New braided complexes, conceived on all scales, are based upon systems of (inter)linked fingers – or interfingers.

Manifold combinations between spaces of occupation and strategic spaces of incision – dilatation – function as gaskets between events.

The old expansive and radiocentric structure, around a single centre, yields – on the territorial scale – to another type of intermeshed, more flexible, elastic and sustainable structures.

On a more local scale, this empty-full seriation is restarted, as in any fractal system, (re)structuring old and new structures through the arrhythmic definition of osmotic – infiltrated, slipped, incised or inserted spaces – between other possible spaces – heterogeneous and diverse – of development.

1. Diagram: ACTAR ARQUITECTURA, Graz-Maribor Corridor, 2000.

2. Process: ACTAR ARQUITECTURA, Barcelona Land Grid, 1998.

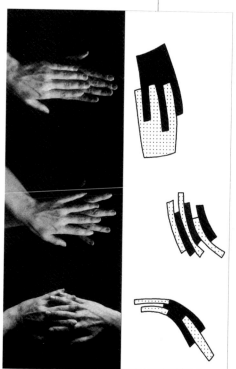

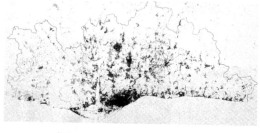

★ incubator

An incubator may be considered as a collaborative building of small to medium scaled networked organizations – organizations of a flexible nature with adaptive features to external influences.

An incubator is the space in which multi-linear fields (highly connected, yet independent, in a network organization) come together in a sort of atrium, an area of concentration, an interface in shared places of vertical and horizontal movement; it is the place of public and friction space.

Conceptually, an incubator is a system of physical proximity, visual connection, gradation of connectivity working in three (four) dimensions.

The bifurcations, openings, closings, surfaces, intervals, heights and depths of this conceptual space are the territory of highly connected, but also independent units.

The main reference of the term is in Manuel Castells' book *Technopoles of the World*, where he points out the initial concept of what is called an incubator. Castells describes existing incubator designs that are planned as "conventional" office or laboratory buildings, with no response to the demands of changing sizes and occupations.

The incubator consists of local, mid-size core companies, which directly support "beginners," and departments of bigger companies. The interaction between all ingredients leads to a synergy effect which has benefits to all associated companies giving access to higher levels of technology and serve as a channels of information.

The backbone of an incubator consists of local core companies, branch-offices for departments of major companies. The backbone is supplemented with shared information facilities and, most importantly, the growing and shrinking space of spin-off-companies linked to universities.

According to Castells, a functioning incubator is an element of deliberate will, and requires the of breaking the mold.

New synergies have to be forged, which, in turn, implies that it may be easier to do so by means of short-distance decentralization, thereby not upsetting all the old relationships.

JUAN CARLOS SÁNCHEZ TAPPAN / LARS TEICHMANN / KRIS VAN WEERT

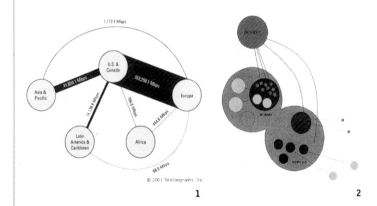

1   2

1. Internet bandwith diagram by TeleGeography.

2. Juan Carlos SÁNCHEZ TAPPAN, Lars TEICHMANN, Kristiaan VAN WEERT, *Infra-nets.org, multilinear mediators*, Canary Wharf, London, 2000.

■ indefinition

→ 'chance', 'chaos',
'form', 'fragile',
'<in> order factors',
'in/uncertainty', 'logic,
fuzzy', 'meaning',
'name', 'standardisation',
'vague'

[JM] Indefinition, not conclusion, is the immediate presence of the innumerable stammers recently taught in architecture. In this sense, new materiality is tried when realizing designs to make compatible reality and effect, appearance and absence.

● indetermination (indeterminate)

→ 'aformal', 'chance',
'chaos', 'extroversion:
<ex> factors of form',
'in/uncertainty', 'logic,
fuzzy', 'no-form',
'order', 'plural', 'time',
'unfolding', 'vague'

[MG] See 'open' and '<in> factors of order'.

"*A sentence from a text by Ingeborg Bachmann seems to be proffered by someone who inhabits the space of pure use and free circulation. The sentence goes: "Because I am not meant for a particular use and because you do not consider yourselves to be meant for a particular use, everything went well between us."* (GARCÍA DUTTMANN, Alexander, "Getting rid of traces", Quaderns 211, 1995)

■●indiscipline

→ 'action>critical',
'criteria', 'disciplines',
'dynamism', 'ideas',
'<in> order factors',
'individual',
'infiltration>intrusiveness',
'in/uncertainty',
'in/unstable', 'no-form',
'open', 'paradoxes',
'progress', 'proneoism'

[JM] All projects must be a criticism of convention, an act of fraud, of inconvenience. As Miguel Morey writes: "Thinking will always be an act of indiscipline."

We believe that designing has to do with this difficulty of twisting what is already established, already foretold.

[MG] Indisciplinary is, today, transdisciplinary. Indiscipline influences the old codes – recodifies – through mixtures, crosses and transversalities.

In this relationship with the "non-codified" or the "re-codified," as in most conditions associated with the <im/in/un> factors of a more informal order, is recognised the apparent indiscipline of the order that concerns us here.

We are referring, in effect, to a new type of order rather than to an ordering (planning).

If the notion of discipline expresses a doctrine, observance of, strict or specific compliance with stable – "natural," harmonious, or cohesive – laws or norms, the indiscipline factor expresses an uncontrollable character and a high degree of disobedience inherent in dynamic systems. Indiscipline and its dynamic systems are ultimately characterised by the unpredictability of their manifestations, the independence (non-subordination) of their actions and the instability of their trajectories.

The new order, as is its associated time-space, is manifested in a constant state of suspense between the predictable and the unexpected, the recurrent and the individual, the normed and the distorted; the global and the local.

A non-genuine order aimed at yielding more heterogeneous configurations that increases their artificial (singular and uncodified) nature by summoning a new type of organisation: more ambiguous (hybrid), spontaneous (direct) and unbiased (flexible), that is to say, more "a-conventional."

✖ ★ individual

[VG]   The information society ought to encourage the individual qualities of things and territories, as opposed to the total continuity of cyberspace, in which conditions are the same for every place on the planet. In many cities and in the European territory, history has fundamentally contributed to determining their present. History and the present are vital data for determining the starting point of a project and defining an overall strategy (not necessarily coinciding with the legal framework) for inventing the future.

[VG]   No dwelling is the same as another. No dwelling should be the same as another.
Question: On a construction site of 50 plots, how many different types should there be? Two, three, five, fifteen? Fifty.
Typology no longer exists. The systematic repetition of compartmentalised spaces rationally intended for dwellings was the product of an era that began with the mass manufacture of cars. Space had to be the same so that thousands of people could have access to a minimum standard of living.
Information technology makes for almost infinite flexibility in the process of production, transmission of information and in the use made of it.
The problem is no longer one of the masses, but of the individual. The culture of sameness is succeeded by the culture of difference. Each person is a world. Each dwelling is a world.

[co]   An individual is bodily mass with a human face, endowed with sentiment and reason. Individual, too, is the basic – though not necessarily unitary – molecule of social practice, source of energy that generates the spaces and times it passes through or dwells in. It is the individual who, alone or in the company of others, takes possession of space, turning it into territory, or appropriates it, in the sense that he considers it fitting and possesses it only in as much as he makes use of it. It is the individual – as a body that exists according to the other bodies with which it forms society – who proclaims a place, the geographical point at which he finds himself and that he names, an outline that lets itself be apprehended and transported by forces proceeding from its historical, social, emotive and sensible surroundings, that perceives all presences and absences, susceptible to the flows that influence it. The individual is the main character in social situations, that consist in him looking at himself in the mirror held up by other individuals, whom he at the same time reflects and shadows. A provocative and provoked individual, the product of space and producer of space, determined by it and determinant of it, generates oppositions and parallels, symmetries and breaking-offs, is comprised of reciprocities with things, is reflected in the changes he occasions and is the result of them. It is the body of that individual that intervenes as the source and the destination of all initiative, as the framework in which impressions are registered and issued, and as the surface beneath which projects and intentions are intuited.
The occupation of space does not imply that space is an empty container waiting for irruption within it. It is the body of the individual that makes the space it occupies. It is the individual's action that gives off its own ephemeral or lasting territoriality.
Personal, informal space is that which accompanies every individual wherever he goes and that expands and contracts according to the type of meeting, the rela-

tion with the people with whom he intercommunicates and his continual search for a point of balance between approach and avoidance. The occupation of space is, then, the deployment of the moving body. Each body is a space and has a space, space for relation and for movement. The body generates symmetries; it imposes itself as an axis according to which is established a left and a right, an up and a down, a here and a there, what is there and what is not, a now, a before and an after. The body, then, becomes its most mathematical properties: applications, functions, operations, transformations, etc. on or in relation to something or someone in front or behind, far or near, before or after that body. MANUEL DELGADO

● individuality

→ 'client', 'diversity'

[MG] Any open and non-linear process places greater responsibility upon the individual: "*Chaos guarantees a non-predetermined future, and non-linearity says that not all the blame for what happens lies with the outside world. The fault, dear Brutus, is not in our stars, but each and every individual, in each an everyone of us.*" (Paraphrasing SAUNDERS, Peter, "Nonlinearity: What it is and why it matters", *AD* 9/10, vol. 67, 1997)

In other words, we can affirm – as does Ivar Ekeland – that "*a dynamic system increasingly widens particular differences; it brings individual phenomena onto the macroscopic scale and, in fact, it is in the successive widening of these small differences where randomness is eventually found.*" (EKELAND, Ivar, *Le Chaos*, Paris: Dominos, 1995. Translated from Spanish)

Individual/Dispersed
Star Warps,
in *Wired* april 98.

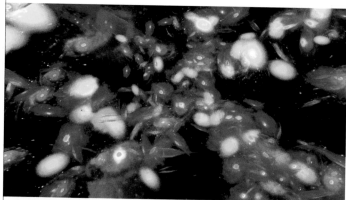

Individual/ Diverse
Me and my shoes,
in FARRELLY, Liz,
*Sneakers, size isn't
everything*, London:
Booth-Clibborn Editions, 1998.

● ★ ■ infiltration

[MG] In his text, *Filling Station,* Walter Benjamin recalled that:

"*Nobody stands in front of a broken turbine and floods it with lubricant. On the contrary, the necessary drops are introduced in those strategic rivets and joints which are precise to recognise.*"

Of interest is the positive will for *infiltration* in the reality entrusted to one of reinterpretation and/or qualitative re-formulation of its basic conditions, produced, not through confidence in a new imposed, totalising – absolute, univocal or prototypical – order, but through acceptance, at once unbiased and critical, of more or less conflictive situations.

Through the strategic and tactical introduction of new, more operative – elastic and fluctuant – movements within (and among) the initial movements of the system; through resonance with its own dynamics and through the exploitation of its potentials.

Sanford Kwinter, in a now-famous analogy, compares this dynamic action – simultaneously slippery, infiltrated and intrusive – of contemporary architecture with the fluid (slippery) relationship which exists in certain sports such as surfing or skyboarding, hang-gliding, skateboarding or snowboarding, based upon the challenge of finding oneself involved in dynamic environments: "*techniques of movement combined in a rigorous and spontaneous action, in which the sportsman "forges" an intimate relationship with the dynamical environment that surrounds him.*" (Translated from Spanish.)

The most important component of these sports is the combined capacity of intuition and of innovation: to feel yourself part of the wave – as the surfers say – not simply to cut back and forth or fluctuate with it, but to invent new rules and movements and explore extreme, apparently impossible situations – and trajectories.

Marina ABRAMOVICH & ULAY, *Performance,* in MVRDV, *Farmax,* Rotterdam: 010 Publishers, 1998.

[co] We witness today an architectural attitude characterised by its permeability in relation to phenomena and the dynamics of transformation.

This degree of "infiltration in reality" of which we speak, in turn, depends on a more open understanding of architecture as an activity that not only involves a limited set of decisions but also a determined co-participation of broader layers of influence.

XAVIER COSTA

[JM] Infiltration is to cross, open the way, introduce into a space: all are actions, more than images or established configurations, to offer us a different concept of space. The idea of space, linked to the void as "something that is missing" is changing because of density and its consequences.

Fundamentally, to unite the idea of space to density is to introduce gravity into our work – the sensations of friction and proximity, texture, area, or metaphors like fluid space. Concretely, it is all those contingencies that make space compatible with everything that surrounds us.

[MG] **(intrusiveness and interference)**

It is useful to posit dual action: distorting, at the same time, as positivist (generating all types of surpluses) of the foreign. This mixture of tactical infiltration (of interference) in a host reality is similar to the alienness of the tourist (at once guest, distant and proximate, destined to become a subversive visitor to a self-consumed reality, but also to be influenced in some way by it). The unsettling, while revitalising, action of the intruder, always underlies a double effect. On the one hand, intruders actions supply the cosmopolitan – autonomous, remote, global – information of the foreigner/foreign; and, on the other hand, they measure the degree of indigenous impact – upon the specificity, the particular, the local – of the infiltrator/infiltrated.

Moving between both actions is the global capacity of an intrusive architecture: intrusive by virtue of being reactive; abstract and artificial, but also complicit; at once open to indiscriminate acceptance of alteration, impurity, mixedness and hybridism; that is to say, to a strange mongrelisation, indifferent and beneficial.

Of interest is this demystifying brazenness of the intruder – and the intrusive: this capacity for manifest impact – like that false guest, Claude Khazzizian, gatecrasher of official receptions – that speaks of informalism, even of impudence but, above all, of uninhibitedness (of loss of hallowed values, of protocols, of codes or of disciplinary biases).

In a scenario so typically inclined to codification it seems appropriate, then, to bring in this glocal and insubordinate capacity of the intrusive element – foreigner attentive to specificity – not so much in order to invert trends as to question and redirect them, to "indiscipline" inertias; rather than through the witty or the capricious, through the opportune (the weightedly opportunist).

1. NEUTELINGS RIEDIJK Architecten, *Concert Hall*, Bruges (Belgium), 1998 (Prize Winning Competition Entry).

2. FOA, *World Trade Centre*, New York, 2002.

3. MVRDV, *Media Galaxy (Competition concept for the new Eyebeam Institute)*, New York, 2001, 2nd prize.

4. José MORALES, Sara GILES, Juan GONZÁLEZ, *Theatre*, Nijar (Almeria, Spain), 1998.

5. ACTAR ARQUI-TECTURA, *M'House Houses*, 2000.

● ★ inflatable

→ 'elastic', 'flexibility',
'lightness', 'topological',
'unflatable ice'

[MG] Inflatable relates to a closed object, made of a flexible material, filled with air or with some type of gas or fluid, such that it acquires a bulky, tensioned state.

[c] "*An inflatable structure responds to a programme. Its architecture is not a static structure which is calculated to resist the biggest possible forces. The inflatable structure is a lean device which relaxes when external or internal forces are modest, and tightens when the forces are fierce. It acts like a muscle.*"

(OOSTERHUIS, Kas, *Programmable Architecture*, Milano: l'Arca Edizioni, 2002)

1. Balloons, in VARIOUS AUTHORS, *The Berlage Cahiers 5: Fields, Studio '95'96*, Rotterdam: 010 Publishers, 1997.

2. Issey MIYAKE, Bird peak coat, 1987, in FUTURE SYSTEMS, *For inspiration only*, London: Academy Editions, 1996.

3. Space suit NASA AX5, in FUTURE SYSTEMS, *For inspiration only*, London: Academy Editions, 1996.

4. Issey MIYAKE, Inflatable, in *Experimenta 33*.

5. Vicenç SARRABLO (with H. JALA), *Air Inflated System, Projects for inflatable sports facilities* (Engineering: Javier Marcipar CIMNE), 1999.

6. Kas OOSTERHUIS, *Active Structure Trans-ports*, version 3.0.

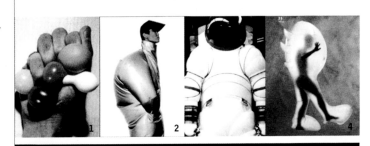

● ★ informal

[MG]   See '<in> order factors.'

[co]   'Informal' is an approach to the design of a form that is non-linear. It is not based on the idea of a traditional plan that is done by setting a boundary and then sub dividing space, nor is it relevant to fixed centring and classical notions of symmetry. Instead, informal is an internalisation that moves forward to produce a coherence that is form. The informal has three characteristics, local, hybrid and juxtaposition. They inter-relate and are not stand-alone classifications. For example, extreme juxtaposition, when very close together appears as hybrid or hybrid can be a local condition, etc. The approach is essentially one of experimentation, where interpretation is the best we can do. It is therefore open-ended. Informal is a dynamic that releases energies – notions of slip, jump, scatter, enter the vocabulary, new geometries underpin such form-finding. CECIL BALMOND

Cecil BALMOND, "How to transform a box", in ITO, Toyo; BALMOND, Cecil, *Serpentine Gallery Pavilion 2002: Toyo Ito with Arup*, Tokyo: telescoweb.com, 2002)

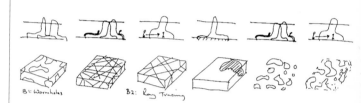

✗ ● ★ information

[VG][MG]   See 'digital' and 'inform(ation)al.'

[co]   It is information, above all, that is becoming an essential component of the new architecture and new urban environment. In fact, information in the architectural field plays at least three fundamental roles simultaneously.
First and foremost, there is "communication" that either educates, entertains or advertises (it is no coincidence that todays buildings go back to narrating stories); in addition, information also makes up the "production infrastructure" for the multidisciplinary development of projects and the future management of buildings. But most importantly, the presence of information in todayís society is so great that it has become an "esthetic challenge." Forward-looking architects around the world are attempting to create a generation of buildings and spaces that are "conscious" of the changes in the operational and social framework caused by information technology and capable of expressing this revolution.
ANTONINO SAGGIO

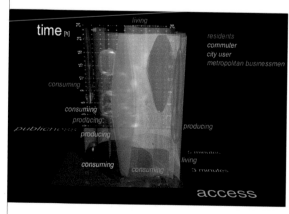

UN STUDIO, *IFCCA Competition: Penn Station*, New York, 1999.

● inform(ation)al

We may affirm, today, that classical space and modern time-space has been superseded by "inform(ation)al time-space." Inform(ation)al time-space relates to the impact of the space of interchange between simultaneous bits of information – which provokes greater instability and indetermination in our understanding of the universe (greater informality) but, at the same time, permits assimilation in a catalyst of the constant interaction of impulses and stimuli.

This double informational and informal (both terms are used here interchangeably) characteristic interests us for what it possesses of interrelated and combined messages:

1. Reactivity vis-à-vis the stimulus of combined and superposed bits of information.

2. Absence of shape.

3. Non-obedience to previous, predetermined codes or behaviours; that is to say, to exterior disciplines (substantive uninhibitedness).

Informality as inform(ation)ality. Informality as lack of formalism. Informality as indiscipline (unrestrainedness, uninhibitedness and unbiasedness).

These are properties that speak of an *in*formal order whose essential characteristics – referring to what we call <im/in/un> factors – explicitly evidence the *internal impact* upon the form of the *in*formation. These characteristics also reveal the uncertain, heterogeneous and paradoxical conditions of the scenarios in which that information acts. But they also show the open and unencumbered parameters of the devices, the structures and the geometries – or configurations – that link this information.

Peak hours
and assemblage
of programmes,
Yokohama,
1992, in *OASE* 48,
1998.

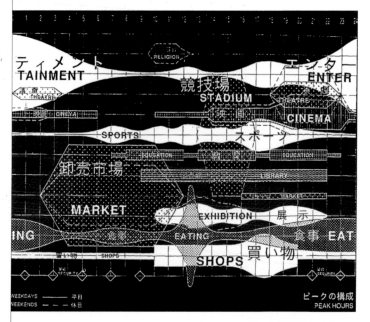

✖ inform(ation)al structures

→ 'no-form'

[VG] 1. Given the separation by layers of the modern, the informational acts on the essence of the matter that it affects, creating a new hybrid nature capable of responding to the demands of the physical, and interacting with the digital.

2. Informational structure is to structure, as datum is to kilopond (with Max Sanjulián).

3. While the tectonic structure acquires its shape according to the laws of statics, the informational structure acquires its shape in its movement. It is based more on its kinetics than on its staticity.

4. The informational structure generates reactive environments, configured by means of the interaction of people, objects, spaces, boundaries, networks, interfaces and contents (with Susana Noguero).

5. If the house is the computer, the structure is the network (Media House Project).

6. A technological house is a house with a computer. If the house is a glass of milk, and its computational capacity a sugar cube, an informational house emerges from the dissolution of the sugar cube in the milk. (Shrikumar, Media Lab).

Energy structure

Net structure

1. ROCHE, DSV&SIE P., *Office building*, La Défense, Paris, 2000.
2. Vicente GUALLART, *Study for informational building*, Seoul, 2001.
3. NOX (Lars Spuybroek with Chris Seung-woo Yoo and Kris Mun), *obliqueWTC* for the Max Protech Gallery, New York, 2001.

infrastructures (as networks)

→ 'artificial', 'flows', [MG]
'grids', 'interchange',
'(inter)weavings
and inter(plots)', 'loops',
'matrix', 'networks',
'no-form', 'patchwork city',
'plaits', 'system', 'territory'

Communication and transport infrastructures (motorways, railways, air lanes) emerge as the most evident lines of the current "urban-territorial" system. Lines are converted into neutral directrices for future organisation of the land. Bases of reference, independent of construction are marked by velocity and sequenciality (and no longer by continuity and contemplation) as supports for new activities, not only along their lengths but even over the latter as well: over formerly hierarchically and monofunctionally separated plots of land that have begun to absorb, progressively complex and stratified programmes, defined through a complicated superposition of vertical and horizontal sectional use of structures.

OMA, *Euralille: centre international d'affaires*, Lille (France), 1996.

infrastructures (as structures)

[MG] Nowadays, talking about structure is referring to a possible "infra-structure."

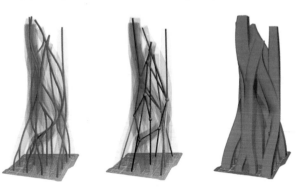

NOX (Lars Spuybroek with Chris Seung-woo Yoo and Kris Mun), *obliqueWTC* for the Max Protech Gallery, New York, 2001.

■ ● ★ ✕ inhabit

➜ 'diversity', 'geomancy', 'house, the', 'housing', 'housys', 'rurban loft'

[JM] Inhabiting architecture is situated at the threshold that permits the creation of worlds for the subject that lives at the end of the millennium. It is to plan behaviour – ways of making architecture – through which the subject comes to know and feel more, capable of constructing these glances by trapping them and making them an idea of the world, an interpretation that remains "there outside."

[JM] **(inhabiting)**

Inhabiting is a gerund. The project of inhabiting must provoke the domestic to be more spoken than formalized, more an outline than a precision.

[MG] The deceptive fallacy of an acceptable collective unity – and uniformity – has characterised the inhabited standard. Today, we are witnessing the generalised collapse of the mythical residential "stereotype" which continues to encourage most current actions and norms: the "sitting room-dining room-kitchen-laundry room-bathroom-toilet plus three or four bedrooms, all in ninety square metres" scheme as the commonly accepted formula. Thus, the concept of the residential cell has come to be limited to the definition of a partitioned ideal between two trays: type-distributions founded on the idea of typology – normally based upon the systematising proposals of a suitably updated *existenzminimum* – understood as elemental units with the capacity for *ad infinitum* floor-by-floor repetition. Foreseeable changes in lifestyles (and therefore in the architectural responses to them) are sensitive to the current heterogeneity of simultaneous spatial realities:
- The transformation of the family unit, with a predominance of couples with no or few children and the growing significance of individuals over clans. In this framework, there is a progressive replacement of the classical idea of co-existence – communion of behaviours – with that of a cohabitation – merely spatial contract (or relationship) – tending to favour the independence of different actions and behaviours and of changing individual needs.
- The growing awareness of marginal groups (focal points of poverty, the homeless, refugees, the "third world," etc.). There is also new awareness of a wandering type of domestic life, increasingly disseminated throughout the metropolis: replacement of private space with service space scattered at the urban level (bars, restaurants, laundries, sports clubs, leisure centres, etc.) in a city converted into a large dispersed home for a nomadic user.
- The constant fluctuation in the employment market and its associated sensation of job instability, with the consequent difficulty for any long-term economic planning (and, therefore, for any clear access to home ownership). This manifests in a change of paradigms which favour a growing acceptance of residential mobility, a necessary reversibility in decisions, a rise in rental housing, etc.
- And, finally, the increasing co-participation of active members in the family economy and, therefore, the need for a reduction in domestic tasks which might favour a new conception of service spaces (kitchen and bathroom) destined to be converted, in certain cases, into veritable leisure areas (bathroom-gym or kitchen-laboratory) with a growing technological component.

[c] "*In speaking of transformations and changes in the city, we have come to the conclusion that there is no single model of the city, but rather the concept of urban void, complex, ungraspable. With regard to housing, does the same apply? Doubtless, lifestyles are changing rapidly due to a number of circumstances:*
- The woman has joined the working world and consequently her role in the home has been reduced.
- Smaller family units (few children and absence of the elderly who have been rehoused in old people's homes).
- Unstable couples (leading to a growing number of people who live alone).
- The huge development of new technologies applied to the world of work and services that make telework, teleshopping, etc. possible from the home itself.
- Parts of the home, heretofore understood as removed from possible change,s are conceived differently. The kitchen and bathroom are no longer marginal places, but rather places with a high level of technology (microwave, dishwasher, washer, drier, hydro-massage, sauna, gym, etc.) converted into areas of recreation and leisure. Bathrooms may be open to other rooms, with a functional part (shower, hydro-massage and toilets perfectly enclosed) and a more luminous part, perhaps on the façade. Or the kitchen-dining room as a laboratory of experimentation with the smaller appliances.
- The home tends to be used differently at the weekend, by day and by night. Why should the 6m²-minimum of the smallest bedroom be dedicated solely to sleeping space?
- The need for a home "for life" is less and less real. The demand for job mobility means that in many cases the family unit changes its place of residence (country, continent, etc.) with great frequency.
Given the above possibilities, one might ask if a housing code that negates the possibility of transformation is not excessively rigid. In answer to these new lifestyles, housing must attain the greatest possible degree of flexibility, understood as an empty space with the necessary furnishings and fittings providing order – in service clusters or nuclei – for the inhabited space."
(ARANGUREN, María José, GONZÁLEZ GALLEGOS, José, "Habitar la caja," unpublished, 1999)

[VG] **(dwelling)**
If the dwelling was transformed by the advent of plumbing and, years later, by electricity, the arrival en masse of information will produce a transformation on a similar scale.

[co] Today, the architect has only one way; he must achieve and overwhelm any metaphysics of the house, any residual humanism of dwelling, to the benefit of a genuinely operative practice. The house is nothing more than an avatar of locale; it is only a substratum made of services where duration is all that differentiates it from a hospitality-industry reception. The notion of "a-house" put forward by Reyner Banham in "A home is not a house" takes on its full meaning today. It is a matter of being able to, at any moment, create environments provided with services necessary to a specific demand, permanently re-convertible environments. "The functionalist slogan, 'the house is a machine for living,' is not productive because it begins by presupposing the idea of the house." FRÉDÉRIC MIGAYROU

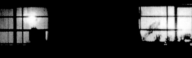

New privacy

1. FRUTOS, SANMARTÍN, VALOR, Llinars del Vallès (Barcelona), 1995. *Quaderns* 210, 1995.

2. Bordeaux 1994. Photograph: J. Chlomoff. (from *Résidence –Joyeux à Bordeaux*, Athens: ed. Europan– Untimely Books, 1994).

3. Stills from *Tout va bien* by J. L. Godard, 1972.

4. "The new private realm". In *The Berlage cahiers* 3 (93-94), Rotterdam: 010 Publishers, 1995.

●✖＋★ innovation

[MG] [VG] The capacity for innovation should be understood as being exclusive not to the youngest, but to those with the most energy.

In architecture, innovation is not a totally shared collective phenomenon, but a fact driven by individual forces and attitudes that are capable of correlating, that ultimately creates its own expression.

But this desire to forge channels of development tends to be set in a given atmosphere, generally promoted by public authorities.

High quality architecture represents just 1% of real-estate activity in Europe, whereas meaningless construction, junk building, is gradually spreading. We have to vindicate Architecture as a cultural aspect of the territory. Authorities should not continue to organise architectural competitions in the same way as those for the adjudication of services or urban furniture. What they should do is consider the cultural and environmental added value of architecture and promote a truly qualitative development of the profession. The real problem, then, is not so much one of generation as of ideas, attitudes and, ultimately, qualities and, therefore, horizons.

[WM] "*Wealth in this new regime flows directly from innovation, not optimisation; that is, wealth is not gained by perfecting the known, but by imperfectly seizing the unknown.*"
Kevin Kelly, "New Rules for the New Economy," *Wired*.

"*A pattern emphasised in the cases of this study is the degree to which powerful competitors not only resist innovative threats, but actually resist all efforts to understand them, preferring to further entrench their positions in older products. This results in a surge of productivity and performance that may take the old technology to unheard-of heights. But, in most cases, this is a sign of impending death.*"
Jim Utterback, author of *Mastering the Dynamics of Innovation*.

An interesting aspect of innovation is its symptoms: when an innovative threat undermines a certain technological predominance, attempting to take its place, the latter also proves innovative, coinciding, in the same time span, different types innovations.

When the pioneers of electricity appeared on the scene, gas monopolies got to work. Time and again, in the history of innovation, the sector leader has reacted when faced with the threat of change... polishing up the same old apple, as an ultimate effort. The enemies of advanced architecture are... the apple-polishers.

[co] Once happened that a small dinosaur, fed up with dodging its enemies by longer and longer jumps, decided, as it was thinking "forget the idea," to transform its last jump to its first fly, and it invented the concept of bird.
JORGE WAGENSBERG

[co] Scrambled eggs were invented by a genius bewildered after the failure of an omelette. JORGE WAGENSBERG

[VG] For the history of the omelette see 'invent.'

★ in-out

[co] See 'street market.'

Indefinite and socially vibrant space, in-out is the purest architectural response to an existential philosophy founded on a system of intense social relations under exceptional climatic conditions. A multiform, fragile, plural and ephemeral space, ever subject to the shifting winds of circumstance, removed from the burdensome Manichaeism of the individual (in) and the group (out), in-out reinforces the social consistency of Mediterranean societies and exemplifies the coexistential project that dwells in their bosom as its most evident strength. Here, function outranks form, conditions it and shapes it: in-out possesses a profusely protean nature. *Riu-raus* (traditional Catalan shelter for drying grapes, NT) and courtyards, rich men's belvederes and modest shepherds' huts – the best in-out is always an example of conceptual austerity and equilibrium of the senses. In-out is a marvel of wisdom accumulated over the course of the centuries. It has two illegitimate contemporary variants: the bistro and the street market. The former purges inclemency with isolation/insulation: in the bistro in-out is reduced to strictly visual contents and the intrinsic space becomes a busy fishbowl. The street market pays for its excessive commercial orientation with the inelegance of mimesis or the loss of its (apparent) inherent simplicity and, although it conserves enough of the attributes that make the in-out a space so memorable; it has lost the aura of innocence and the simple elegance of the original. JOSÉ MIGUEL IRIBAS

Spanish seaboard images.

● ■ install

[MG] See 'reactive.'

[JM] Architecture is installed, and as such, its place is always critical in respect to the place where it is incorporated. It does not shake off this strange character with which it approaches situations.

In effect, landscapes are understood from a collision and presence of many other landscapes. This means that the idea of territory has also changed.

Today, territory is linked more to the idea of resistance, rather than pertinence. Design does not bring second derivatives to fruition, but directly incorporates the forces of the landscape and the surroundings: it installs itself – a radical contextualism.

✖ instrument

→ 'logic, digital'   [VG] Architecture, the city and physical space are instruments that allows human activity to be performed; they are tuned according to previously established data (man's measurements, climatic conditions, the speed of transport, etc.). As the American architect Marcos Novak holds, the task of the architect should not centre solely on the design of the instrument, but also on writing scores to be performed in space. Scores written using data produced by man – and cities – on a scale that is both near and far, allowing awareness of the environments in which they are acting and how they transform them.

● intelligence

→ 'ideas', 'knowledge', 'R+3D'   [MG] No one knows where the dividing line between non-intelligent conduct and intelligent conduct lies. Moreover, the mere claim of the existence of such a dividing line is probably foolish. But there are, of course, capacities that are characteristic of intelligence:
a. Responding very flexibly to situations (Elasticity-Adaptability)
b. Getting the most out of chance circumstances (Opportunism-Ingenuity)
c. Finding meaning in ambiguous and contradictory messages (Interactivity-Transversality)
d. Recognising the relative importance of the different elements in a situation (Combinatoriality-Diversity)
e. Finding similarities between various situations, despite the differences which might separate them (Interconnection-Interlinkage)
f. Discovering differences between various situations, despite the similarities that might link them (Uncodification-Recodification)
g. Synthesising new concepts upon the basis of old concepts that are seen and reassimilated in new ways (Interchange-Synergy)
h. Erupting – and emerging – with innovative ideas (Singularity-Indiscipline)
(Based upon: HOFSTADTER, Douglas R., *Gödel, Escher, Bach, an Eternal Golden Braid*, Barcelona: Tusquets, 1987)

Gnutella graph created using Gnucleus client.

● ★ interaction

→ 'a-couplings', 'action', 'activity', 'complicity', 'contract', 'field', 'glocal', 'incubator', 'intelligence', 'interchange', 'layers', 'link', 'multilayered', 'object', 'order', 'pleasure', 'reactive', 'relationships, transitive', 'resonance', 'synergy'   [MG] Interaction is (inter)change and (inter)relation.
Interaction is information transmitted, transferred and transformed among different and simultaneous energies, events and/or scenes.

[co] Interaction is the influence of two systems on one another. A system is to be understood as a real object, a part of the latter, or its environment. Interaction means that the sum of an extensive property of Parts can be more or less than the corresponding property of the Whole. Interaction means that the Sun influences the Earth, and vice versa. Living organisms interact with their environment, interchanging on three main levels: matter, energy and information. Isolation, with respect to any of the latter, may be fatal to the organism. In physics, interaction is a historically transcendent concept from which emerged the debate regarding the action of bodies on one another. In natural and artificial organisation, interaction raises the question of what an individual is. A valid proposal might be that the individual is a reasonably independent Whole made up of Parts that are reasonably interdependent on one another. JORGE WAGENSBERG

[co] Interaction is reciprocal influence of an individual on the actions of another person or persons when immediately physically present, thereby turning what was a spatial fact into a social event. Interaction is founded on the obligation of those co-present as they make themselves mutually accessible and negotiate the terms according to which a given situation is to take place. Simple physical co-presence becomes interaction at the very moment in which the minimum threshold of a social nucleus is established, the reciprocally granted and recognised possibility of giving life to, of bringing forth, a minimum social organisation. Interaction is founded on the openness of subjects to communication and to the acceptance of its rules. MANUEL DELGADO

✗● interactivity

→ 'activity', 'contract', 'foreigness', 'holistic', 'interaction', 'interchange', 'link'

[VG] If objects think, react and take action beyond their material qualities, spaces and places have to react with them.

Objects think because someone has thought about them. Someone has programmed and given them qualities so that they can be integrated into a new logic of the world in which everything is connected to everything. In coming years, not only will the capacity for computation will be attributed to machines with monitors that allow work and leisure, but the digital effect will reach every strata of the physical world. Man will know himself better after the human genome project and the development of the nanochips that will be incorporated into the human body.

The traditional atmospheric and climatic air-bound medium in which the physical world is built will have the digital medium superposed over it, leading to the disappearance of traditional space-time relations on the planetary scale. Intelligence will, therefore, have to be breathed into houses, buildings, public spaces, cities, by means of precise codes that make spaces react to objects and persons, knowing who's who, who does what, etc. The world as one great Net.

NOX; OOSTERHUIS ASSOCIATES, *Water Pavilion,* Neeltje Jans (The Netherlands), 1997.

[MG] See 'resonance-synergy-interaction.'

● intercadences (sequences)

→ 'dynamism',
'geometry', 'order',
'score'

[MG] See 'intermittences' and 'sequences.'

Intercadence is inconstancy and faulty unevenness of style. Irregularity of pulse or rhythm. Dances of figures in which many pairs take part. Organisation based upon sequential intercident rhythms.

PALAZUELO,
Drawing in *Cuadernos Guadalimar* 17, 1978.

● interchange

→ 'advanced',
'complicity', 'contract',
'extroversion: <ex> factors
of form', 'flows',
'incubator', 'information',
'inform(ation)al',
'intelligence', 'interaction',
'link', 'negotiate', 'open',
'pleasure', 'relationships,
transitive', 'synergy'

[MG] Advanced architecture is architecture of interchange (or rather, of interchanges). It is not only within and with a reality, but also with and among many realities. Advanced architecture is capable of multiplying links and interconnections – manifold local and global (glocal) relationships – between the user and his/her (various) cultural environment(s); between the place and the city. Between information technology and the immediate logic of the action. Between the potentials of time and the possibilities of the context.

Through spatial organisations which are more independent – of habit or of discipline – yet, for that very reason, more attentive to the impact of the exterior: receptive, permeable, flexible and fluctuant; that is, plural, able to combine and reconcile, develop diverse and simultaneous messages; abstract and concrete, generic and specific. Digital and material.

Through action which is processive, receiving and receptive; attentive and open; generous and generative; functional and emotional; relational: aimed at interrelating freely, expressively and communicatively heterogeneous data, phenomena and events in new, more complex environments.

Accepting, without complexes or biases, different situations and conditions in order to reassess – to reactivate them – beyond themselves.

Developing assets of the place and links beyond the place in different scenes of exuberance and need, of plenitude and precariousness, of progress and development. With rigour, and also relaxed…

● interchangers

[MG] See 'transfers.'

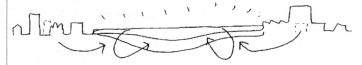

OMA, *Transferia*.

Ángela GARCÍA
DE PAREDES,
Juan Ignacio GARCÍA
PEDROSA, *Europan 4:
Civic Centre area
development* (mention),
Aranda de Duero
(Burgos, Spain), 1996.

ACTAR ARQUITEC-
TURA, *Mixed
residential mechanism,*
Graz (Austria), 1996.

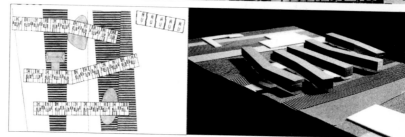

ARANGUREN
& GALLEGOS, *Europan
4* (1st prize), Cartagena
(Murcia, Spain), 1996.

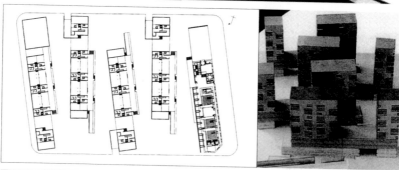

ÁBALOS & HERREROS
*Abandoibarra
development,* Bilbao,
1993-1994.

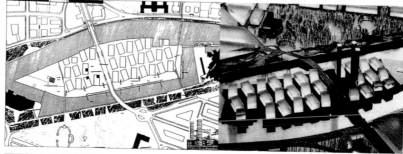

MVRDV, *Donau City
(Kissing Towers),*
Viena, 2002,
Competition 2nd Prize.

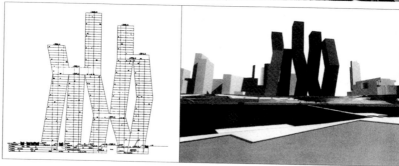

★ intercommunity

[CO] Intercommunity is the working hypothesis of the new information society. The intercommunity is a new social structure based on a web of social networks built up on the Internet, the web of computer networks and an evolution of community networks. The information society is not simply the industrial society plus Internet. It is a new community. It may be a new and highly complex structure of all types of human networks in its formative stages, as different from the present society as the latter is from agrarian societies, and agrarian societies were from those of hunters and gatherers. ARTUR SERRA

●x★ interfaces

[MG] "The 'age of absence' has ultimately come to generate, paradoxically, a new type of presence. A network of mediating terminals – computers and electronic means – is, like interfaces between ourselves and the world, the physical basis of an immaterial communication that permits us to move in a global space without moving locally. What at first might be perceived as a loss, today may also be seen as a gain: simulated presence in a global – virtual – space can, in effect, be realised at any moment and at any place thanks to these real mechanisms of local transfer." (DELCAN, Juan, "Arquitectura en la era de la electrónica. Arquitectrónica" in BAU 016, 1997).

[MG] In a new informational – digital – environment, the mediating nature of "device-architecture" alludes to its hypothetical condition as an interface: that of a device intended, at once, to relate us with reality and to multiply its qualities (that is, enhancing its very nature). The shape through which we can give meaning to our landscape does not entail only constructing buildings with inert objects, but also thinking of active devices capable of assuming a role that is at once processive, organisational and narrative. As the critic Aaron Betsky suggested ("Landscape and the architecture of the self", Quaderns 218, 1998) these devices are interfaces (interconnectors) and icons (symbols). Interfaces are catalysts and channellers of bits of information – interactions – within and with the world; and icons are transferors – transmitters and conveyors of principles and meanings.
Structures, then, that permit at once the construction and reconstruction of places. Architectures capable of generating spaces and fostering relationships. Architecture can be the interface of a new hybrid digital-physical world.

[VG] In the early days of personal computing, the simile of the desktop was used to access information. These days, there are more and more virtual buildings, three-dimensional environments, where activities can be carried out. But with real uses! Real uses in virtual spaces. And, it is in this new world that architecture can be heard, where spaces transform the shape, colour and texture of its borders, where objects react to external pulses and are transformed, where gravity is just another parameter that can be controlled, like space and time, where we can learn a new way of doing things. This kind of architecture would be splendid!
Architecture has always been the interface of human activity. It has always supported uses. Now, architecture has to be functional and aesthetically sensitive to the digital world.

Faced with the possibility of imagining an environment on the basis of which to take action in the hypertextual or hypervisual world (characteristic of the late twentieth-century web), an overall understanding of the world by means of its spaces and the actual functions of architecture propose a hyperreal future. Where reality, accessible to man through his five senses, extended by nanoprosthesis or otherwise, is the surround by means of which to take action in the world.

[co] "I think of technology as a prosthesis, that is an extension of my skills – cognitive, physical and social. The nature of any interface will be driven by the nature of the activity and context. The design of a physical prosthesis will likely differ from that of a social one. To speak of "interface" in the singular in 2010 will sound as bizarre as speaking of "mathematic" (as opposed to "mathematics") today," Bill Buxton.
XAVIER COSTA

[co] Interface is the point where different uses accumulate; a place of dislocation and re-location, a place of line and flow.
JUAN CARLOS SÁNCHEZ TAPPAN / LARS TEICHMANN / KRIS VAN WEERT

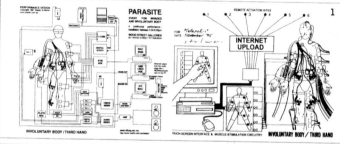

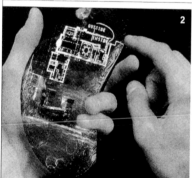

1. STERLAC & MERLIN, *Involuntary body / third hand*, 1997, in *Fisuras* 8, 2000.
2. Michael McCOY, *Haptic Software Controller*, 1995. **3.** Michel WAISVISZ, Bert BONGERS, *Now the Hands II*, 1989 (Photograph: Carla van Thijn).

● interference

→ 'foreignness',
'infiltration>intrusiveness',
'intermittences',
'mutation', 'system'

[MG] See 'distortion.'

Interference is kinetic disturbance, alteration or distortion of undulations, vibrations, tensions or movements that extend in the same direction.

x interior

[VG] See 'territory.'

[VG] We come to know the world from an interior. The security of an interior: a car speeding along a motorway; a high-speed train crossing a territory at 300 km/h; a dwelling that leads to anywhere in the world in real time. Projecting. Projecting ourselves.

Windows and balconies were useful in the past, when we became aware of the world through them. Today, our windows on the world are à la carte television channels, the presence via satellite of the worldwide network of landscape-cameras, that bring to a studio in a Barcelona neighbourhood the light and the sounds of dusk in the Grand Canyon, real time. Intensity in light and sound. The acceleration of space and time. Planetary scale.

1. MVRDV, *Media Galaxy (Competition concept for the new Eyebeam Institute),* New York, 2001, 2nd prize.

2. NOX (Lars Spuybroek with Chris Seung-Woo Yoo, Kris Mun, Florent Rougemont and Ludovica Tramontin), *SoftOffice,* United Kingdom, 2000-2005.

3. PÉRIPHÉRIQUES, *Three towers for the Triennale 2003,* Tsumari (Japan), 2003.

4. NOX; OOSTERHUIS ASSOCIATES, *Water Pavilion,* Neeltje Jans (The Netherlands), 1997.

5. Vicente GUALLART, *Spatial prototype, Cricursa Pavilion,* Mida, UIA Barcelona, 1996.

6. Neil DENARI Architects, MA Gallery, Tokyo (Japan), 1996.

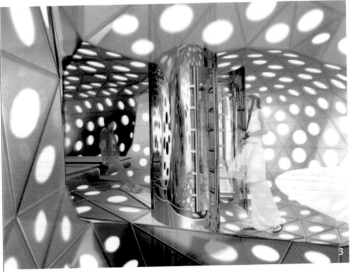

✗ intermediary

[VG] In the information society, the intermediary disappears. There is direct communication between the manufacturer and the user, between teacher and learner. Anyone or anything that makes no contribution to the chain of transmission of knowledge disappears.

[VG] A series of intermediaries: A creator or researcher writes a book explaining his ideas. A critic gives a lecture, taking these ideas as his basis. A university lecturer teaches a class on the basis of this lecture and evaluates his students according to what he thinks someone who says they have read the work of a creator says. The average exam result is 4.3.

[VG] **(without)**
There are people who invent or create ideas, processes, materials, solutions. The information society needs invention. Not the evolution of old ideas, but the creation of new paradigms produced by a new age. Education has to allow for the direct transmission of knowledge, from the creator to the receptor.

★ intermediate places

[CO] From the inevitable confluence of the interior and the exterior are born ranges of spaces of enormous interest and, which on occasion, are dealt with in an excessively taxonomic and systematic manner. Intermediate places occur at any meeting point, on all boundary surfaces, at any geometric point of areas in which two different environments meet — two different states of matter, two different places, at least two different functions. Our appreciation of these areas depends to a great degree on the scale at which we observe them. What at first glance is a line, examined more closely becomes a field of gradients. What at first glance seems a star, may be cloud of gas in the process of materialisation, or an accumulation of planets forming a galaxy or in the process of destruction.
Intermediate places are always places, and therefore subject to the broader meaning of the word. They are defined by their geometric features, but also by sensations.
Intermediate places have conditions similar to those of any other place, but always with the addition of their characteristic instability, which is, perhaps, the most exciting thing about them. The tendency towards extremes, towards absolute situations, means that intermediate states always remain close to provisionality. They are therefore dynamic — perhaps transitory — routes, as they undergo change in their stable situation, in their environment, in their physical state.
Intermediate spaces have the qualities of frontiers, edges that separate. Thresholds are both exterior and interior, and with some nuances we can experiment with turning them into specialised places or simply allow them to languish in ambiguity, without completely defining them.
Intermediate places, therefore, rarely have a constant form. Their imprecision gives rise to their need to avail themselves of the character and conditions of their environment, which are generally in a state of flux, and thus we can only speak of forms associated with a time. In certain moments, their form might be considered constant, although difficult to define.
Intermediate places, like all places, are in a constant state of transformation and alteration. They are ephemeral and evasive, often defying conscious analysis. Therefore, sensation, as a tool of unconscious — yet enormously synthetical and powerful — perception, is the most appropriate instrument in our journey through the intermediate. JOSÉ ALFONSO BALLESTEROS

● intermittences

[MG]   *"A dynamic system amplifies differences; it shifts microscopic singularities to the macroscopic scale."*

Such questions allude – as did the mathematician Ivar Ekeland – to infinitesimal phenomena produced in instantaneous conditions; but we can also extrapolate such differential distancing to the permutation of each particular position in space (implicit in most distributions or dynamic combinations).

Many of them are based upon an internal discontinuity between their elements (rather than upon a cohesive continuity). In dispersion, diffusion, deployment; that is, in expansive dynamic actions.

We see discontinuous structures with intervals and intercalations. With instantaneous presences and separations. With syncopated rhythms, with *staccatos* of appearances and disappearances, but also of fractal occupations and distancings as can be analysed in "empty-full" structures. Figures that are topologically unstable, dentritic, laminated or millefeuillate, with seriations of similar although not necessarily identical elements.

This individual and intermittent order translates into *arrhythmias* and *spacings* (*segmented* presences) associated with *parameters* of (*empty-full*) *discontinuity* and of flexible *sequenciality* (*internal norm* or *web*). In effect, each experience is autonomous but appears to be linked to the rest by a sort of "discontinuous continuity" based upon unequal cadences and routes – intercidences – that animate the geometry.

It is this "disynchrony," made up of intermittent sequences, rather than of reiterated repetitions, which permits us to establish the "music" of the system forming a unequal and flexible beat in which the elements maintain personal independence and, at the same time, an elastic (topologic) interrelation.

Stan ALLEN, Field dynamics,
in VARIOUS AUTHORS,
*The Berlage Cahiers 5: Fields,
Studio '95'96*, Rotterdam:
010, 1997.

Photograph of Big Bang from Hubble telescope, in *Quaderns* 217, 1997.

●(inter)weavings and inter(plots)

[MG] See 'patterned distributions.'

Emphasis on the definition of a woven and flexible support matrix characterises devices as virtual evolutionary (inter)weavings. These are, in fact, dynamic structures – circuits of movements – conceived of as normed arrays, at once organisational and generative. They are able to simultaneously foster different configurations through optimisation and distortion of their own meshed (threaded and tracked) definition.

(Inter)weavings of recognisable or deformed geometries, have the capacity to overcome rigid reticular orders and yield to lattice works of multi-layered, complex and flexible paths, which would point to the definition of the large-scale infrastructural networks of articulation territorial: layouts rather than outlines.

In certain cases, this refers to evolutionary logics based upon "tracks (circuits) of movement" of variable definition that permit syncopated and staggered slippage of events (occupations and displacements) along the length of interlinked and (or) intersecting lanes – bands, strips or draughtboard-patterns – conceived of as elastic tracks (or bands) of occupation-dilatation, rather than as rigidly defined zones.

Accordingly, taking a deeper look into the notion of the grid or web (structural and narrative) and the discontinuous – and, at the same time, iterative – nature of their internal movements fosters the development of non-linear sequences (of reading and occupation) in a "constant state of suspense," between the predictable (the reiterated, the sequential, the seried) and the unforeseeable (the singular, the individual, the autonomous). These sequences are generated through the design of "directional tensions" – lanes, tracks, matrixes or norms – in space (the landscape or the narrative), but also of imbricated cadences and intermittencies, always pointing to the articulation of the possible variable – spatial and temporal – lapse between different events: braided rhythms among route lines, or surfaces, points of occupation and basic in-between voids in this type of schemes, both for their strategic disposition and for their exceptive, open and intercident nature.

Mixed fibres weaves, in *BAU* 017, 1999.

MVRDV, *Urban plan Hoornse Kwadrant*, Delft (The Netherlands), 1996.

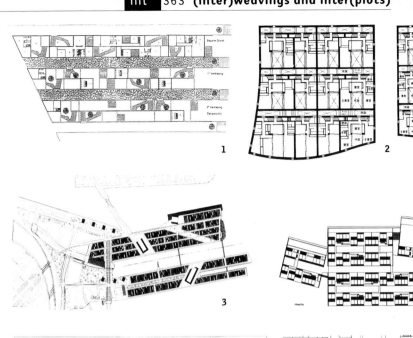

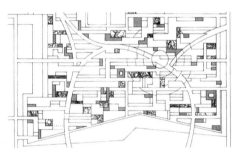

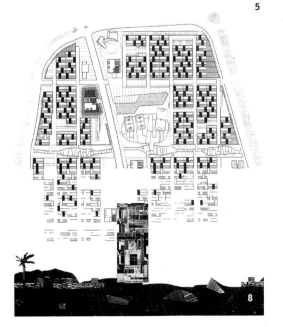

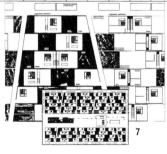

1. DE CLERK-VAN DER PLOERG-WIEJNEN-WILLEMEN, *Europan III*, S-Hertogenbosch (The Netherlands), 1992. 2. OMA, *Housing*, Fukuoka (Japan), 1991. 3. ADRIAAN GEU-ZE & WEST 8, *Masterplan*, Borneo Sporenburg, Amsterdam, 1996. 4. José MORALES, Juan GONZÁLEZ, *Competition for student apartments*, Jaén (Spain), 1997. 5. Kazuyo SE-JIMA, Low-level typology, strips grid and elements free of distortion. 6. MVRDV, *Urban plan Hoornse Kwadrant*, Delft (The Netherlands), 1996. 7. ROAGNA-EHRENSPERGER CELLINI, *Europan III*, Yverdon, 1992. 8. Javier FRESNE-DA, Javier PEÑA, Javier SANJUÁN, *Europan 5* (finalist), Paterna (Valencia, Spain), 1998.

●★ in-/uncertainty

→ 'chance', 'chaos', [MG] The study of dynamic systems has, in a short time, introduced an inevitable
'indetermination', factor of indetermination associated with the substantive instability of its di-
'inform(ation)al', 'logic, verse, irregular structures. It is not, in fact, a question of demanding of them
fuzzy', 'order', 'time', absolute, exact and invariable – unique – results, but rather, it is only neces-
'unfolding', 'vague' sary to enunciate (and announce) possible protocols.

[MG] *"The uncertainty principle has profound implications for the way in which
we view the world. [...] The uncertainty principle signalled an end to Laplace's
dream of a theory of science, a model of the universe that would be completely deterministic: one certainly cannot predict future events exactly if
one cannot even measure the present state of the universe precisely! [...]
Quantum mechanics does not predict a single definite result for an observation. Instead it predicts a number of different possible results and [their
tactical possibilities]. Quantum mechanics therefore introduces an unavoidable
element of unpredictability or randomness into science."* (HAWKING, Stephen
W., *A Brief History of Time: From the Big Bang to Black Holes*, London: Bantam, 1988)

Walter MARCHETTI, [co] Uncertainty is the complexity of an object's environment, i.e. the richness and va-
Observation of a fly riety of the states accessible to the setting into which an object is embedded. At ten
movements on a glass thousand metres under the sea, temperature and light hardly vary over the course
(8h-19h, May 1967), of the year: it is a low-uncertainty environment. The surface of the sea, on the
in *CIRCO* 22, 1994. other hand, is an environment of much greater uncertainty. The big issue in biological evolution concerns the relationship between the complexity of an object and
the uncertainty of its environment. How do we survive when uncertainty increases?
The alternatives are: increase our complexity (evolve), change the environment
(technology), change environments (mobility) or uncertain anticipate (intelligence,
knowledge). In particular, architecture is an animal-like resource, favoured first by
natural and then by artificial selection, employed to diminish the uncertainty of the
environment, where the environment is definitely a component of architecture.
JORGE WAGENSBERG

★ in-/unconsciousness

→ 'animation', [co] If there is a factor necessary for unconsciousness – a favourable moment of means,
'dynamism', the convergence between utopia and reality – the factor must enters into syntony
'in/unstable', 'open' with the moment and complete the picture. That factor is irresponsibility, sometimes called optimism. ENRIC RUIZ-GELI

◆ in-/unfinished

→ 'chains', 'extroversion': [FS] In light of the fragment, surges the unfinished. The fragment and its com-
<ex> factors of form', posite consequences, collisions and ruptures presuppose an initial order
'<in> order factors', that is negated or disowned. It is also a finalized act, a finished object. The
'in/unsettledness', 'open', unfinished considers that form is the consequence of a continuous process
'stains, ink', where each instant can become provisionally definitive. The unfinished does
'standardisation' not need a previous order to which to refer or confront. It is a total object and not part of a greater, more general one.

● in-/uninhibited

[MG] See 'unrestrained,' 'extroversion,' 'inform(ation)al', '<in> order factors.'

• in-/unsettledness (incompleteness)

→ 'animation',
'dynamism',
'in/unstable', 'open'

[MG] The shape that we describe here is an unsettled one (nervous, non-stable, non-fixed). It tells of a latent – uncertain – virtually incomplete state.

It expresses a moment, but also alludes to other possible moments. It is, in fact, an expectant shape, on standby. A shape that might be conceived as an interrupted trajectory, frozen in a precise instant. Rather than a composition, it is a protocol – or a specific theorem – within an unlimited chain of different theorems. Its profile – its silhouette, its perimeter, its frontier – no longer describes a complete, finite, closed design, but rather the dynamic simulation of an open process.

Unsettledness is a diffuse, incomplete, indeterminate trajectory in accordance with the evolutionary capacity of the system (the idea of implicit growth), associated with its expansive and scattered nature, tending to mesh manifold situations through a virtually unlimited set of variable combinations. It is a shape that expands, undefined and infinitely, from all points, like a multidimensional graphic; a manifold and open configuration, of concatenated connections, pointing, however, to simple, evolutionary patterns.

•◆ in/unstable

→ 'chance', 'chaos',
'contract', 'indiscipline',
'nomad', 'paradoxes',
'reversible', 'suspense',
'trajectory'

[MG] See 'open', 'dynamism', 'impermanences' and 'unsettledness (incompleteness).' The instability factor alludes to a "non-static" tendency of the system – to its inconstancy or impermanence – and therefore refers to a temporal, "non-immutable," dimension that counters or rejects any inclination towards permanence (towards lasting position) in a state of fixed (total) equilibrium and static (positioned) stability. This "non-settledness," or latent unsettledness of the system – an implicit imbalance – indicates its capacity for sudden mutation given a variation in the initial parameters, producing states of transition between stable and other more or less stable trajectories, and therefore yielding explicit changes in (and between) relatively short intervals.

[FS] The unstable condition of form// Instability of architectonic decisions. The structure must be defined in the instant previous to its instability. "*Architecture today is obliged to a precarious existence; it must balance a delicate equilibrium in an ambiguous, unstable space.*" (ITO, Toyo, "Vortex and current.")

1. Santiago CIRUGE-DA, Installation, Sevilla (Spain), 1996.

2. Jimmy Salisbury carrying baskets in Covent Garden market, London, in YAPP, Nick, *The Hulton Getty Picture Collection, 1920's*, Köln: Könemann, 1998.

3. The constant and turbulent action of the ocean disperses an oil stain structurally unstable.

★✗invent

[co] I think we need invention in this world. The geometrist who creates the same bathroom for years on end is creating a bad bathroom [...]. In the contemporary world tradition (that is, those aspects from the past that can be taken over into the present) has disappeared. Maybe it would be more correct to say that in our world tradition does not exist without tension, without the need to adapt.
JOSEP LLUÍS MATEO

[VG] As the chef Ferran Adrià says, the cutting edge of creation is not '*inventing the onion omelette, but inventing the omelette itself*' Inventing means going back to the roots of human activity and contributing to it by developing plural applications of what has been invented.

Development of the information society represents a new moment in history that redefines paradigms in architecture. Many technological inventions have transformed architecture and urbanism. Electricity, the lift, the car, etc. The term invention is rarely applied to architecture. But, as architecture becomes the result of advanced processes, the product of informational and industrial developments that affect the way architecture is thought of, represented, produced and carried out, the concept of invention can be assimilated. New processes of representation can be invented that transform construction systems; materials and mechanisms that transform the functioning of skins and structures; spaces for thinking and action that may suppose multiple specific applications, using the resources available in each economic and cultural surround.

Inventing architecture means going back to the prototype when projects are produced. The process involves not knowing beforehand what the result will be, yet proposing that the result be a specific response to the object of the project; a new approach to general, commonly accepted foundations of architecture.

In fact, one fundamental strategy for the advance of architecture is to invent questions that respond to situations affecting architecture as a whole. With his office building in Berlin's Friedrichstrasse in 1919, Mies van der Rohe invented the question of high-rise glass architecture, a question he himself resolved with his Lake Shore Drive apartments twenty-nine years later, the first apartment buildings to have a glass and steel facade. Le Corbusier invented the question of separating structure and facing using his Domino structure in 1914, which became a central theme of architecture in the following years.

In both cases, the proposals pick up technological solutions developed by other persons or organisations. Their basic contribution consisted in presenting the question in the realm of architecture.

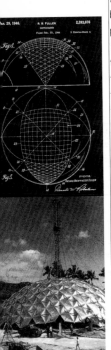

BUCKMINSTER FULLER, *Dymaxion Projection:* plan *of patent,* 1944, and *Kaiser Dome,* Honolulu, in J. KRAUSSE; C. LICHTENSTEIN, *Your Private Sky. R. Buckminster Fuller,* Baden: Lars Müller, 1999.

★invent the invisible

[co] Invisible is the order of nature, the formation of larger territories evolving over time. Invisible are the hugely powerful forces that rule the way we live – gravity, magnetism, electricity, heat, sound, air pressure, radioactivity, radio waves, flows of IT and communications networks. Invisible, too, is the all-powerful late-capitalist market mechanism. As Elia Zenghelis suggests, "Architecture's task is to make visible the invisible and qualitatively uncover and give form to that which is hidden. KELLY SHANNON

◆▲ invertlight or irradiate

→ 'criteria', 'energy', 'expression', 'extroversion: <ex> factors of form', 'I/(my)self', 'light'

[FS] "*[The poet] tries to see things without being capable of distinguishing it precisely; he only distinguishes it by subtle, imprecise indications, and does not reveal the thing by its own light, but rather by what he must beget and emit to realize its discovery.*" (BENET, Juan, *La inspiración y el estilo*, Madrid: Alfaguara. 1999). A project does not enlighten on its own. Its space must be irradiated – blown by a light that we must produce.

[FP]

1. José Antonio SOSA, María Luisa GONZÁLEZ, *Proposal for the rehabilitation of Pérez Galdós Theatre*, Las Palmas de Gran Canaria (Spain), 1997.

2. José Antonio SOSA, Manuel ROCA, *Music Park*, Gran Canaria (Spain), 1999.

3. Eduardo ARROYO (NO.mad Arquitectura), *Competition for auditorium* (finalist), Pamplona (Navarra, Spain), 1998.

4. NEUTELINGS-RIEDIJK, *NAA, Nederlands Audiovisueel Archief*, Hilversum (The Netherlands), 2001-.

More and more, are we surrounded by elements endowed with devices that allow us to externalise events. The most simple ones, though supported by hard technologies, are engaged in the task of spreading messages in our visual environment. We wander about a flow dotted with static, dynamic and self-illuminated signals, that disclose that the irradiation capacity is a condition without which you are dead. You irradiate, thus you exist. This behaviour is relatively easy to assume by architecture, in respect to allowing the reading of whatever phenomena it can take in, or through that more or less transparency of its skin.

We understand irradiation as the capacity of manifesting oneself being contagious, of carrying out transmissions and making the receptor an accomplice. It is an eminently vibrating, resonating and energetic capacity. Having the capacity of providing evidence of relevant concepts such as tension, depth, weight, multifunctionality, flotation, festivity, solemnity, collectivity, intimacy, etc., that will transcend the same material they are sustained in. Having the capacity of interfering with the individual subverting his/her frame of mind. Irradiating architecture is an architecture that modifies the territory, that resounds in the field of ideas and that touches industry.

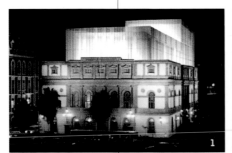

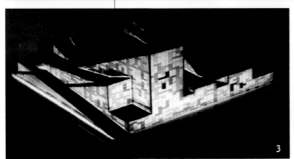

★ invisible in architecture

→ 'criteria', 'criticism', 'moral', 'positioning', 'utopia'

[co] Architectural criticism often takes a passive stance, reflecting on the work but refraining from any explicit standpoint. It operates introvertedly, from the viewpoint of the architect or of the architecture, and hides behind peripheral remarks on the architectural object. When architecture is intrinsically devoid of a stimulating philosophical, ideological or poetic vision, then criticism, too, usually lacks the power to escape this vacuum. Criticism degenerates into project documentation, becomes entangled in quasi-profundities or starts describing its own impotence and alienation. Such criticism is little more than a travel guide for the omnivorous cultural tourist. But, even when its object is not ostensibly 'about' anything, criticism must not ape its object's superficiality. Perhaps this calls for effort, independence and nerve – or at least some other angle than the usual architectural jargon. Criticism must create, through its own cogency, a picture of reality. It must maintain an independence towards the subject of its attentions and not merely take sides. When architecture tends towards endless mystification, towards a rhetoric of functionality, beauty, force, utopia, communication, cultural fragmentation or (on the other hand) peace and order, a rhetoric that casts a smoke-screen over the real social forces under which it operates, then criticism must act as the conscience of that rhetoric and make the doubts visible. Only such criticism can elevate architecture to become a mainspring of intellectual and moral understanding, and, at the same time, contribute to an architecture which is usable in a way that expresses this kind of understanding. Such criticism can bring architecture into contact with a public sphere that is more than just a market or the sum of private interests.

We must progress from a reality that tolerates criticism in a non-committal field towards a critique that can tolerate, or is a match for, reality. The question is not how architectural criticism can serve architecture, but how architecture can play host to critical activity. To achieve that, architectural criticism must be taken to the elliptical point at which this genre completely undermines itself, and makes way for a different, conceptual criticism that is not primarily occupied with media, genres and disciplines but with issues that concern us all – issues in whose service media, genres and disciplines can be deployed. Amid 'this century's most important art form' (Berlage), amid the star system, amid today's pluralism, and amid an ocean of ostensibly autonomous and isolated built objects, this criticism hopes to reveal 'luminous' architecture's cultural shadow – the invisible in architecture. OLE BOUMAN

Points of view, in BOUMAN, Ole; VAN TOORN, Roemer (eds.), *The Invisible in Architecture*, London: Academy Editions, 1994.

✗ islands

[VG] The active reaction to a city without direction, with no capacity for renovation, in the face of a megacity that is formed or in the process of formation, is the creation of island-cities.

Island-cities are new settlements in the territory, in non-urban surrounds, that institute a new use in the territory, such as leisure centres, business parks, shopping complexes, residential areas, or a combination of several of the above, on the premise that it is a private, reserved place with access restricted to the owners or to people who identify themselves and pay a sum to be, for a period of time, inhabitants of this new artificial surround. These islands, with their defined perimeter, situated in the amorphous territorial magma, strategically select their location in the territory on the basis of criteria of ease of access, surroundings and climate.

It is a similar process to that of the founding of cities in the past.

Except in the case of theme parks, all the functions generated by these island-cities are the same as those of traditional cities. But the quality of life offered by the latter is not enough for certain social classes that are capable of organising an environment in accordance with their needs. In this case, the city may find itself immersed in a process of loss of economic, social and cultural content. Island-cities are the natural result of the city of motorways and individual mobility.

[VG] Islands are accumulations of capital and energy with defined limits, in an environment apart. Disney World is an island. Majorca is an island. The need to concentrate the latest generation of activities in the territory means that, alongside the recycling of historic urban accumulations, new territories have to be colonised. Physical and virtual. By land, sea and air.

Vicente GUALLART,
Islands, Barcelona,
1998.

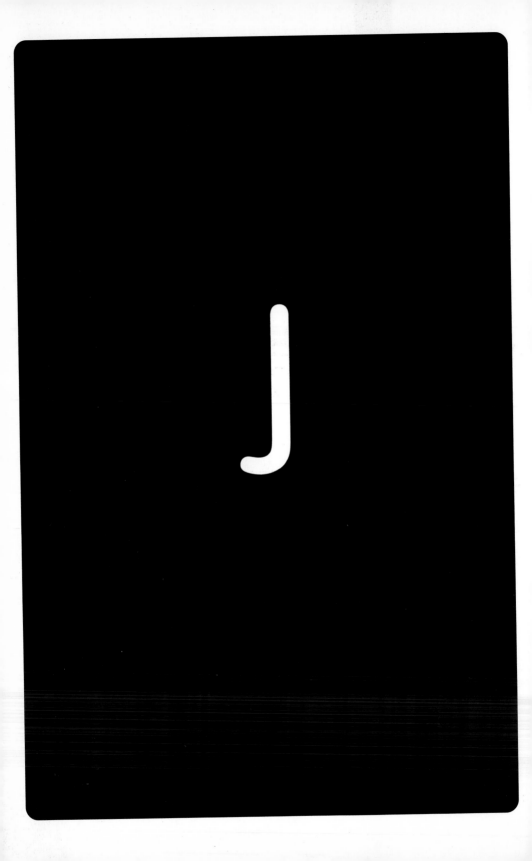

● jack, jumping

[MG]

→ 'devices', 'elastic',
'extension', 'geometry',
'joy (alegria)',
'optimism', 'plural'

Articulated figure of paper or other material that deforms elastically its geometry and structure as it is stretched elastically // Structure based upon deformable meshes or elastic materials with the capacity to recovery its initial configuration.

Jumping Jack

Mechanism of elastic deformation. The figure lengthens when pulling the thread.

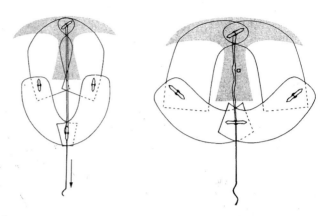

◆ jai-tech

[FS]

→ 'joy (alegria)', 'ludic',
'optimism', 'plural'

(from the Euskera or Basque *jai*: party and from the English *tech*: technology). Jai-tech is a process of construction, project definition, or technical experimentation based on ease, laughter, subjectivity, collage, and the market. Jai-tech considers that the definition of an object can not come from suffering, the epic or heroic, from modernist reading or the mechanical. More than anything, it defends the use of new technical advances by its capacity of perverting or proposing spatial organizations, unravelling qualities that are purely figurative or narrative.

It places itself, thus, against current hyper-tech positions, high tech, as much as against currents defended by the official academy. Within its characteristics, we can emphasize the use of catalogues, its tendency of resolving problems with the minimum, gin and tonic, the disappearance of the program in the definition of architectonic form, the scanty use of tensors. Instead of stainless steel, galvanized steel. Instead of drag and merge, scissors and glue. Instead of typology derived from industrial imagery, typology as a consequence of energetic isotropy.

Jai-tech is not strictly limited to the material condition of construction, but also to its application to other disciplines, including urbanism, philosophy and music.

● jam session

[MG]

→ 'diversity', 'game',
'interchange',
'self-organization',
'spontaneous'

See 'in/uncertainty' and 'inform(ation)al.'

● jazz formation

[MG]

→ 'diversity', 'game',
'interchange',
'self-organization',
'spontaneous'

Jazz formation (group of musicians) or jazz-like formation (free, non-prefigured spatial combination). Jazz: syncopated music. Improvisation and variation based upon a basic melodic germ.// Irregular rhythms and sequences or intercidences.// Normed yet "unscored" actions.

● jerry builder

[MG] A jerry builder is the constructor of poor quality homes. The jerry architect is the same in routine architectures.

▲ joint

[FP] See 'texture.'

● joy (*alegría*)

[MG] An advanced architecture is an extrovert architecture: it proposes a more "joyful" architecture. No longer strict, elegant or austere, but open; unfinished and flexible, but also exultant, unrestrained and ludic. Explicit in its movements. Expressive in its manifestations. Of interest is the possible plethoric – eloquent and communicative – spirit of an architecture that is more animated, dynamic and liberated; relaxed and uninhibited; "informal." Trusting in the relational manifestation of ideas – and of movements – rather than in conceptual speculation with ideas – or positions. A more stimulating and optimistic architecture. Determined to interact with the world. Open to a resolute (strategic and plastic, operative and expressive) use of colour, of light, of sound, of movement and of energy; to a reactivation of the senses. This (more or less conscious) quest for pleasure, for desire, for stimulus and for interchange – for a joy as expansive as it is expressive – today favours a new alliance between architecture, creation, technology, art, culture and media meant to engender new and unexpected transversalities made up of mixtures, transfusions and hybridisations; the more unwonted and surprising the more suggestive and effective.

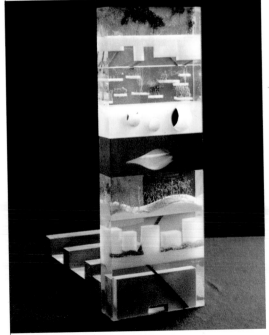

MVRDV; *New Office of the Ministry of Agriculture*, The Hague (The Netherlands), 2000, study (2nd proposal).

▲◆ juries

→ 'auditoriums', 'moral'

[FS] See 'competition.'

[FP] The one at risk in a competition is the jury. The jury is the one judged. But it does not decide the rules of the competition. It does not have to accept them. Nor must it agree with the rules, though, without wanting to, supports and validates them. The jury decides between selecting the best project that resolves the problem or the best project that resolves the project as it would do it, or the best project that discovers and resolves the problem. But the jury also picks the people. The jury supports the credibility of the project in time. It is the jury who feels the risks of the result, who must give confidence in the value of the answers. It exhibits its courage or its comprehension. It would tolerate seeing its decision constructed. If the jury does not believe in it, why should we?
The jury detects chance in the momentary coincidence of its personal projections, in the particular necessities of the community and in the individual reflections. It is both quick and slow. It has doubts and debts. Depth and superficiality. Coincidences and discord. Jurisprudence and repetition. A jury does not happen upon the universal, looking for the absolute solution. It believes in nothing more than momentary coincidence. In the contingent, but sure of its response.

● just do it

→ 'action>critical',
'audacity', 'ideas',
'indiscipline', 'invent',
'logic, direct', 'yes!'

[MG] See 'action.'

[MG] *"When we propose an architecture of action in which the act, impulse and interchange are all more important than a reflection whose final result is nihilism or somnolence, "just do it" is the expression of this dynamic and interventionist attitude. "Just do it:" for its memorablity, for promotion, for its quality as a slogan. However, is it easy to do it and forget about it and have everything return to normality. That's why we take it further and the proposal is now more difficult still: do it again. DO IT AGAIN."* (Susanna Cros)

● juxtaposition/superposition

→ 'adherence', bridge(s)',
'cohabitation', 'lands of
superposition'

[MG] Juxtaposition, horizontal and vertical, is also superposition.

Willy MÜLLER
+THB Consulting,
*Bridge-restaurant
in Mercabarna,*
Barcelona, 2000.

K

◆ Keaton

→ 'catalogue', 'ideas'

[FS] (KEATON, Buster, *One Week*, Metro, 1920). At the beginning of the film, Buster Keaton marries the girl. As a wedding gift, he receives a dozen big boxes. They contain the parts of a dismounted prefabricated house. "You can build your own house in a week," reads the slogan. The rejected suitor, irritated, changes the numbering on the boxes. 1 for 12, 8 with 4. Buster Keaton, with his praiseworthy and characteristic tenacity, follows the instructions, even when the pieces do not correspond, fit or work. 1, then 2, 3. He does think of doubting the process or changing the imposed order, even though things seem not as they should be.

He finishes the work in a week, as promised by the fabricator. But the result is quite distinct. The roof on the side, the main door on the second floor, the windows at an angle — an irrational aspect that does not stop the building from being habitable. In fact, proud of the result, he makes an inaugural party. Evidently, as in any silent film, the house gets run over by a train. Keaton builds on the wrong plot, and he must tow it to the right place; on the way, there are always roads to cross.

Buster KEATON,
Sequences from
One week, 1920.

● kits

→ 'component', 'process',
'product', 'production,
intelligent', 'system'

[MG] See 'catalogue.'

A new reflection upon the dwelling is inscribed the recent interest of certain proposals for studying the possibilities of designing industrialised kit-products capable of competing in markets marked by routine. "Catalogue products," for example, are an alternative solution to a common dream – that of the single-family dwelling – but at lower costs than those usually yielded by the traditional construction market: New products (likely prepared for dry assembly), in complicity with certain consumer demand, oriented towards the manufactured design object, and even towards quality do-it-yourself (note the growing importance of the European superstores – *Ikea, Aki, Habitat* – in the sector), but also sensitive to the mass-produced but apparently personalised product (of which a good example would

1. Eduardo ARROYO (NO.mad Arquitectura), *Competition for municipal sports complexes in Denmark*, Frederiksberg, Hadsten and Naestved (Denmark), 1999. **2.** ACTAR ARQUITECTURA, *MOAI system*, 1997. **3.** ACTAR ARQUITECTURA, *M'House houses*, 2000.

be *Swatch* watches or the *Twingo* automobile). A market for a concrete and broad sector of the average population receptive to another type of products removed from the kitsch standards offered by the usual purveyors of prefabricates; elemental, hardly imaginative and not always sufficiently economic, still based upon systems too complex in practice (above all in all that concerns, paradoxically, the skin of the building).

This possible complicity between technical design and industrial enterprise (one or two basic enterprises in the definition of the essential framework and some — few — combines for the service clusters and the exterior enclosures) has guided a number of recent projects understood, in any event, as structures of occupation adaptable to manifold situations and capable of offering manifold combinatorial systems. Devices — not prototypes — for diversity.

CLIP (T. KANERO, D. MATSUMOTO, E. MATSUNAGA, K. TANAHASHI), *Tube House*, in GAUSA, Manuel, *Housing: new alternatives, new systems*, Barcelona: ACTAR, 1998.

✗ ◆ ● knowledge

→ 'action>critical', 'criss-crossing', 'deviation', 'diagrams', 'essayist knowledge', 'meaning', 'memory', 'positioning', 'precision', 'search engine', 'tangent', 'ThinkTank'

[VG]   We no longer believe in the transmission of knowledge by dictating given information. Instead, we have to design and create physical or mental places and frameworks that provide the conditions (operating environments) for knowledge to emerge from within the individual: a person only accumulates in his active memory the things he discovers for himself. Only the knowledge that emerges from within can establish links with other knowledge of his own and produce individual progress, be useful for thought and action.

[FS]   The knowledge we are given is like the photographer's box: a strong, resistant suitcase in which each piece and each object has its right place, moulded in protective rubber foam.

There are holes, precisely dimensioned, of the pieces that the photographer must buy and are supposedly necessary for his or her work. Later, they never coincide with the real objective with which they were bought. Either because s/he did not have the money or because of changed interest. We must get rid of this bag. We must buy the plumber's bag: a leather bag, strong and malleable, carried on the shoulder, and in which all the tools are mixed. Even blow-pipes fit inside, and the bag is often too full to be closed.

No! We will find it. Capture it. Return. Forget. Better to be a sweeper than a judge.

[MG]   See 'criteria.'

laminate (laminated)

→ 'layers', 'multi',
'multilayered', 'puff
pastry', 'void', 'Yokohama'

[MG] See 'millefeuilles.'

Structure of a body made up of superposed laminas or sheets arranged in parallel.

land-arch

→ 'a-couplings',
'agriculture', 'artificial',
'dichotomies',
'eco-', 'ecology, active',
'fragile', 'geography',
'hybrid', 'landscapes,
operative', 'natuficio',
'naturartificial',
'terrain vague', 'vague'

[MG] Today, the strength of the term 'landscape' resides precisely in its forceful implantation in our conceptual baggage. Not as mere scenario, but rather as an instrument. This shift has been favoured, naturally, by the passage from a generation obsessed with the relationship between architecture and city (the city as stable scene, resulting from the edificial) to another, the latter more aware of a new contract with nature (a nature evidently epic, mongrel, manipulated, rather than domestic and bucolic).

This has, in the first instance, permitted the assumption and assessment of the landscape through spatial qualities related with the presence of the absence — large surface areas, lands, horizons, vegetations, textures, transparencies, folds, etc.

As well, beyond important work with an exploited "free landscape-space," are emerging less predictable positions, made up of strange slippages between old semantic categories — architecture, nature and landscape — the meanings of which are tending to mix and, therefore, become unnatural.

New dynamics conform to an incipient vocabulary of a hybrid contract: Land and Arch, never a brutal grafting, but rather an imbrication between two heretofore alien categories. Constructions that would artificially integrate movements — or moments — of nature, in some cases "architecturalising" the landscape (modelling, cutting, folding...), proposing new topological shapes (reliefs, waves, folds, sheared trays); in others, landscaping (lining, enveloping, covering) an architecture in ambiguous synergy with the strange nature that surrounds it.

Imaginative formulas capable of favouring this new natural contract, in which the complicit appearance of an architecture in syntony with the landscape (rather than integrated in it) would reside precisely in its capacity to incorporate technical, plastic and perhaps unheard-of solutions neither paralysed nor diminished by the presence of the nature, but rather stimulated precisely by the possibility of incorporating it, of spurring it, of reformulating it — of enriching it rather than conserving it. New landscape architectures, finally, in order to respond to the new demands of a society increasingly anguished by the geological frenzy of the urban.

 +  =

Adriaan GEUZE (WEST 8), *Vertical landscapes*, 1995.

● land links

[MG] In the same way that it appears unfeasible to continue accepting the "fascinating chaos" of the city as an excuse for its definitive abandonment to an exclusively random and uncontrollable process upon the whole of the territory, it is equally so to attempt to circumscribe the processes to closed – endogenous – plans limited to small conservationist, junctural, interventions that are hardly justifiable from the point of view of administrative logic.

The present situation calls for new devices – large-scale systems – capable of dealing with the dimension, at once casual and infrastructural, of the city and territory. Scientific study of dynamic systems leads to an analysis of complex – uncertain and chaotic – processes characterised by the "<im/in/un> factor:" a high degree of indetermination, of instability, of incoherence, of infinitude, that is to say, of informality. Nonetheless, these systems permit a glimpse of a certain idea of internal order, a genetic code stimulator, associable with more or less recognisable trajectories and diagrams, which generally describe rhizomatic and fractal structures characterised by matrix self-organisation, interlinkage, sequenciality and discontinuous evolution, the absence of scale, organic rather than mechanical development and, above all, the importance of empty-full seriation.

In such structures, the importance of meshed and elastic infrastructure, as well as the impact of the space "in negative," not so much as a remainder – or residual reserve – among things, but rather as a structuring gearage. In the framework of current urban structures, the landscape – the void – appears as a subsystem, as, or more important than, the urban – in turn, an infrastructure – capable of interlinking new and old processes through the tactical seriation of events.

A rhythmic and meshed succession over the territory can thus be configured with retractions and dilatations, with extensions and shortenings, shaping a basic scheme that is mixed – sometimes locally, sometimes globally – open to possible evolutions, but always related to the tactical disposition of the meshes and braids of relation. Land links no longer counterpose natural and urban space, but rather make them cohabitate in structuring systems attentive to the definition of spaces of transition, mongrel areas, ambiguous marriages of complicit realities: connective lands – land-links – capable of ensuring concatenated – locally and globally – developments in which – as in virtual linked fingers – meshes of places and inter-places – voids and fills – would be generated at different scales – as occurs in fractal systems – and, therefore, also in each of them, successive levels of landscape as nature reserves, mixed landscapes, longitudinal "fingers," osmotic connectors (transverse green "tongues"), vague terrains (interstitial breeches), artificial topographies, laceworks of use, public spaces, pieces of interchange and transference, etc. Relational spaces linked, ultimately, to amusement, rest, thematic, ludic or mixed activity, and (or) to all those complementary uses increasingly important in the new society in the offing.

1

2

3

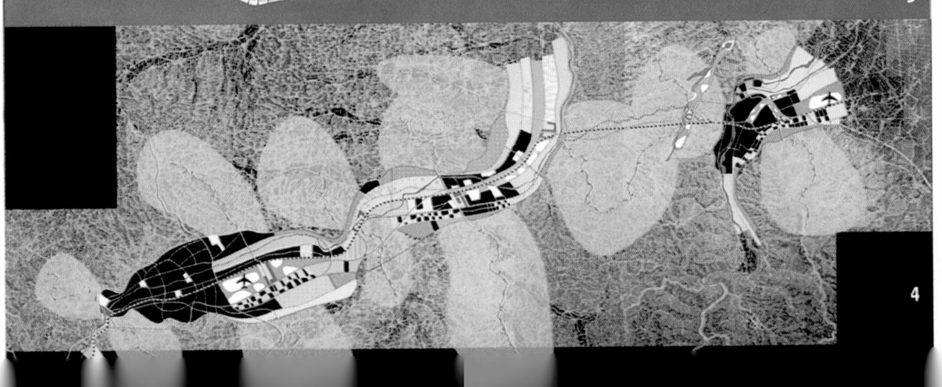

4

1. OMA, *Competition for the new town, Melun-Sénart (France),* 1987. **2.** MVRDV, *Project of 20.000 housing units by the highway A-6, Almere (The Netherlands),* 1997. **3.** ACTAR ARQUITECTURA, *Barcelona Land Grid,* 1998. **4.** ACTAR ARQUITECTURA, *Territorial planning, Graz-Maribor,* 2000.

★ landscape/architecture/urbanism

→ 'landscapes,
operative', 'landstrategy',
'rurban life',
'topographies, operative',
'urban-territorial'

[co]

1. Surface

Landscape is, at one level, an art of surface. Landscape's traditional terrain is the extended horizontal surface; more recently, it has been extended to topographic surfaces that are folded, warped, bent or striated. This has an obvious attraction to architects today, where surface has become a primary instrument in design. However, distinct from the proliferation of thin, transparent surfaces in contemporary architectural design, landscape surfaces are always differentiated by their material and performative characteristics – or better, in landscape, performance is a direct outcome of material. Slope, porosity, hardness, soil chemistry, consistency, etc. – all these variables influence the life that a surface will support, and its own development in time. By careful attention to these surface conditions – not only configuration, but also materiality and performance – designers can activate space and produce urban effects without the weighty apparatus of traditional space making.

2. Program

The extended horizontal surface – architecture's plan dimension – is the primary support for program. Hence terms like battlefield, or sports field, indicating the idea of the field as the support for complex interactive events unfolding in time. However, it is not only the field that supports programmatic complexity. Landscape has a particular spatial vocabulary (matrix, corridors and patches, for example) that describes movement, connectivity and exchange.

3. Information

Landscape corridors are pathways for information exchange. Patches and corridors form larger networks of nodes and paths that allow communication, interaction and adaptation. This idea links landscape to infrastructure and information design through a logic of connectivity and feedback.

4. Process

Much more than a formal model, landscape is important to architecture and urbanism as a model of process. Landscapes cannot be designed and controlled to the degree that architecture is; instead, landscapes, like cities, are loosely structured frameworks that grow-in and change over time. Landscapes are immersive environments, diagrams subject to only partial control. Time is a fundamental variable in landscape work. Even the most static, traditional landscape requires constant management in order to maintain a "steady state." Today, landscape architects are embracing change and designing landscapes that anticipate a succession of states: a choreography of changing plant regimes, shifting spatial characters and new uses over time. These changes are not merely quantitative – plants growing into maturity – but are qualitative as well. Working with a precise spatial framework, the designer creates the conditions under which distinct, and perhaps unanticipated spatial characteristics, may emerge from the interplay between designed elements and the indeterminate unfolding life of the site.

5. Thick 2-D

It is, in fact, slightly misleading to refer to "surface" in landscape. Landscape's matter is spread out in the horizontal dimension, but landscapes are never, strictly speaking, pure surfaces. The natural ecology of a meadow, field or forest exhibits horizontal extension in the macro scale, but at the micro scale it forms a dense mat: a compact and highly differentiated section. This articulated section, the "thick 2D" of the landscape, is fundamental to the work that the meadow or the forest performs: the processing of sunlight, air or water, the enrichment and protection of the soil through the process of growth and decay. In field configurations, section is not the product of stacking (discrete layers, as in a conventional building section), but of weaving, warping, folding, oozing, interlacing or knotting together.

6. Landscape urbanism

The late-twentieth century has seen the emergence of a radically horizontal, field-like urbanism, driven by the freeway and the suburban ideal of private housing. In the United States, at least, planning has had minimal impact. A new city form has developed, extended in the horizontal dimension, but marked by points of intensity and exchange – nodes where the local thickening of section produces 3-D effects within the shallow section of spread-out space of the contemporary city. Cities like Los Angeles have developed as vast, mat-like fields, where scattered pockets of density are knit together by high-speed, high volume roadways. In a more extreme case, in a city like Tokyo, 6 -10 stories of radically different programs overlap at key transportation interchanges. These radical scale shifts and extreme social contrast undermine the ability of architecture to mediate transitions. The experience of the city today is not so much the orderly progression of scales, as an experience of rapid shifts in scale and speed of movement. Section is created by weaving, superposition and overlap, rather than stacking. Today, we tend to move with minimal transition from labyrinthine interiors to movement systems: directly from the mall to the freeway. Emergent field effects are visible in unexpected locations: mini-malls, freeway interchanges, suburban cineplexes, inter-modal transportation centres, informal markets in traditional city centres, proliferating fields that mix leisure, recreation, commerce and infrastructure in unexpected new relationships.

STAN ALLEN

Stitch map,
in ALLEN, Stan,
Points+Lines,
New York: Princeton
Architectural Press,
1999.

FIELD OPERA-
TIONS, *Lifescape:
Fresh Kills Landfill,*
Staten Island
(New York), 2002-.

●■× landscapes, operative

[MG]   See 'land-arch', 'land links' and 'land(s) in lands'.

Landscapes operationalised for use, function and architecture that simultaneously demonstrate natural and artificial conditions.

[MG]   *" There is an attempt to codify the contemporary situation according to different methods: voids, containers and flows, bigness, cityscapes and cityscopes, the Grosstadt, the hyperville, zenithal arrogance...*

There is nothing objectionable about these useful efforts of reason to reveal the thread of action. But there is nothing more specific in this present time than its open character; nothing more fruitful, and difficult, than the impossibility of fixing it.

The landscape, as we wish to see it here, bears no relationship with scale, and is not necessarily the architecture of large, empty, open or "green" spaces, nor the scientific control of the possible damage that large constructions can cause. At one time, it could have been roughly defined in that way, but of late it has crystallised into architecture. An architecture that is characterised by:

– attending to what is between things as much as to the things themselves: public space – a sitting room, a square, a terrace – is often, therefore, its target.

– confirming variability, change – learnt, it is true, from large-scale experiences but which can be extrapolated to many others – as a constituent of architecture. More emphasis on the final design of objects than on the configuration of definitive bibelots.

– the action of the project as an inter-scalar compromise. The awareness that the project is defined and has influence on a multitude of spheres beyond those which it can call its own, for reasons of mere physical contiguity. Consideration of the work of the planner as capacity for inter-scalar passage, movement.

– we are now capable of simultaneously understanding and feeling different scales and spheres of perception and action. But the obstacles that I avoid, the paths that I choose, continue to be those which my body and my senses allow.

– to act upon that which is close, immediate, tactile, and to understand at the same time many other receptacles and dimensions that I also modify with my action, is a good work programme for the coming years."

(BRU, Eduard, "La mirada larga", in *Nuevos paisajes, nuevos territorios*, Barcelona: Actar/MACBA, 1997)

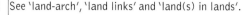

LEWIS, POTIN
& LEWIS,
*Landscaping project
for water
abstraction plant,*
Joué-les-Tours
(France), 2000.

[JM]   Architecture and context. Establishing these terms would be like talking about another duality, a type of mounting of architecture and context, of overlap, of the inevitable sum of superimposed contaminations. It is about a singular ecology, in which architecture and what already exists becomes known. Architecture is incorporated as a landscape; it is landscape and not an object.

[VG]   If the city is a landscape, buildings are mountains.

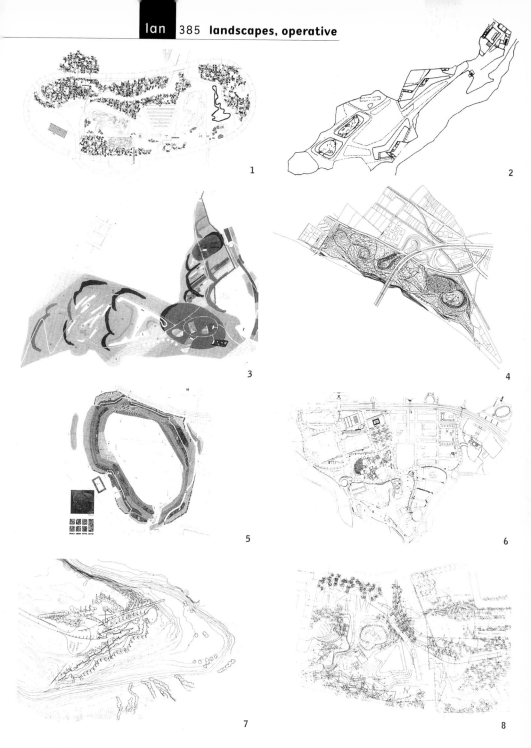

1 2 3 4 5 6 7 8

1. ACTAR ARQUITECTURA, *Intervention in the old circuit*, Sitges (Barcelona), 1998. **2.** Cristina DÍAZ MORENO, Efrén GARCÍA GRINDA, *Competition for the landscaping rehabilitation Santa Bárbara quarry*, Hernani (Guipúzcoa, Spain), 1996. **3.** ÁBALOS & HERREROS, *Rubbish chute landscaping recuperation*, Valdemingómez (Madrid), 1997. **4.** ÁBALOS & HERREROS, *Architekturforum*, Bonn, 1997. **5.** LEWIS, POTIN & LEWIS, *Landscaping project for water abstraction plant*, Joué-les-Tours (France), 2000. **6.** Eduard BRU, *Vall d'Hebron Park*, Barcelona, 1992. **7.** Enric MIRALLES, Carme PINÓS, *Cemetery park*, Igualada (Barcelona), 1991. **8.** Enric MIRALLES, Benedetta TAGLIABUE, *Colours park*, Mollet del Vallès (Barcelona), 2001.

Land(s) in lands

1 agriculture
2 carpets
3 tree
4 artificial
5 terraces
6 field

7 camouflage
8 layers
9 countermarks:
10 unrestrained
   (<un> factors)
11 ecology, bold
12 enclave

13 (e)motion
14 printings
15 extroversion
16 glocal
17 hybrid
18 indiscipline
19 iceberg

20 inform(ation)al
21 infiltration>
   interference
22 intrusiveness
23 game
24 land-arch
25 place of places

26 naturartificial
27 leisure
28 landscapes,
   operative
29 paradoxes
30 spaces>public
   and private

31 reactive
32 synergy
33 landstrategy
34 suspense
35 topographies,
   operative

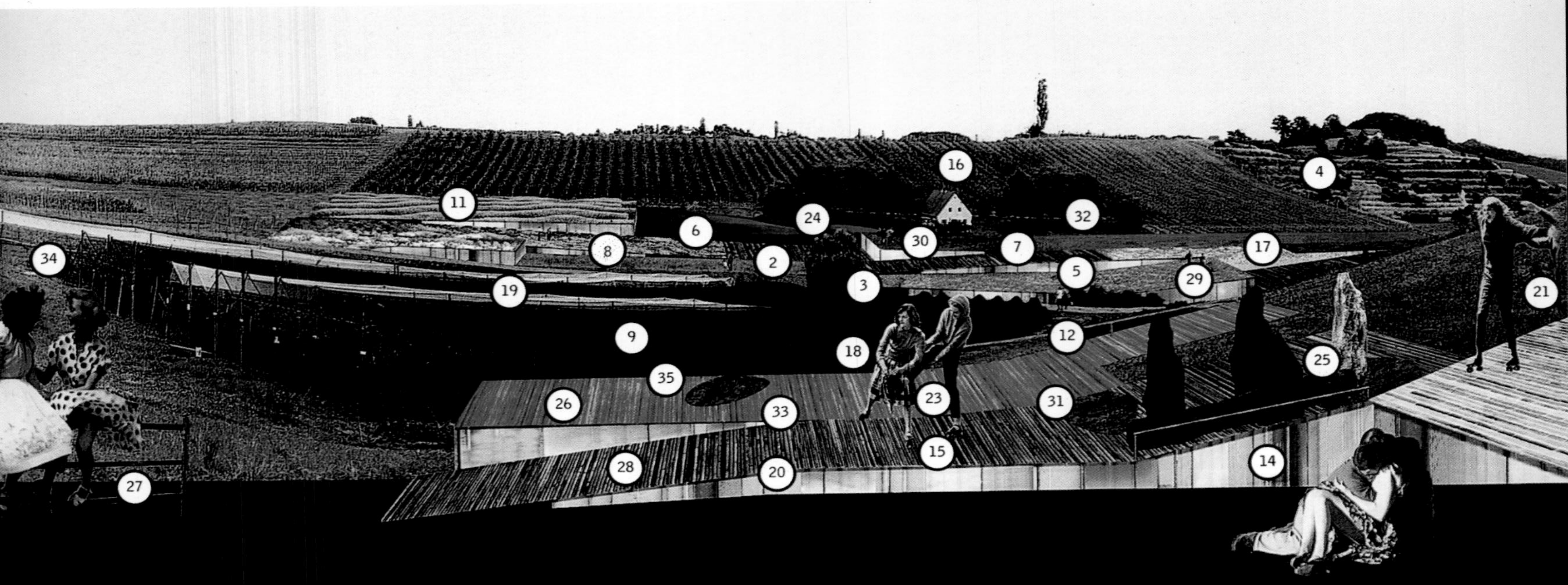

ACTAR ARQUITECTURA, *Secret love or overlapped scenarios*, Graz-Maribor, 2000.

land(s) in lands

[MG] Let us now address the notion of Lands in lands: "Operative landscapes" rather than "host landscape."

This requires overcoming the old conceptions that have characterised action upon the landscape, based upon the traditional figure-background hierarchy – "edificial figure over field of background" – favouring new open interpretations in a fusion of contours, a dissolution of boundaries (as in those fields of pixels of digital representation in which, following progressive zooms, the silhouettes lose their definition to more abstract and imbricated grids).

As with the city, which has blurred the boundaries separating it from former extramural territories, today the architectural project too can blur its profiles – and its edges – in new geographies of transition. The application of new structural and technical concepts or deeper study into the possibilities of the new computerised environments, now permit the positing of a deformation of the old Euclidean structures, transforming them into multilayered spaces, dynamic magmas made up of intersecting movements, of functional fluctuations between superposed and/or overlapping levels that point new architecture towards almost geological processes generated through imbrications of diverse strata: spaces of folding rather than prismatic volumes; programmatic refluences, of alluvium, rather than pure, predetermined crystallographies.

Topographies rather than volumes.

These are architectures of overlapping surfaces: "lands over other lands." Presences-absences posited through the paradoxical combination of densification and disappearance.

Thick, dense lands over free receiver lands.

Thus, rather than a partitioning of spaces or parcelling of uses, what is called for is an articulation of activities in a preferably free, fluid space only potentially nipped by hollows – mats – of services (accumulators "in negative") that reveal a concern for colonising the landscape – beyond the old distinctions between space able to be urbanised or not – through infiltration and distancing devices that would be bound no longer to strict geometric schemes but rather would be of a freer and more meaningful configuration. Devices that act by inserting, densifying and preserving at the same time.

Solid lands meant to articulate programmes developed contrary to the orthodox. Rugged, trenched reliefs and sheared trays would thus conform new patterns over the terrain; mineral landscapes in which movements and flows would ultimately be articulated according to plan in chiselled ground-level surfaces.

Constructed geographies rather than architectures.

Geographies where the efficacy of the architecture would not reside in the figurative definition of the object, but rather in the capacity for suggesting an abstract new topos.

No longer lovely volumes under the light, but rather ambiguous landscapes under the sky. Operative topographies. Mongrel enclaves capable of generating their own energy. Fields within other fields. Lands in lands.

[i] p. 388

Kazuyo SEJIMA,
Ryue NISHIZAWA,
Multimedia study,
Oogaki (Gifu, Japan),
1996.

Enric MIRALLES,
Carme PINÓS,
School home, Morella
(Castellón de la
Plana, Spain), 1993.

S&Aa (SORIANO-
PALACIOS),
*Competition for
the Museum of
Navegation*, Antwerpen
(Belgium), 1999.

Manuel J. FEO,
*Estratum-horizon:
seafront*, San Vicente
de la Barquera
(Cantabria, Spain),
1999.

Enric MIRALLES,
Carme PINÓS,
Cemetery park,
Igualada (Barcelona),
1991.

Eduard BRU,
Vall d'Hebron Park,
Barcelona, 1992
(Photograph:
Manolo Laguillo).

★ landscrapers

[co] 'Landscrapers' is a term coined by the architect Antoine Predock to denote buildings that unfold the land, rather than being constructed on it. Such horizontal skyscrapers do not so much represent the ability to escape gravity, as they explore the nature of our connection to the land. Landscrapers can have the quality of artificial caves in which the building disappears into the land; they can be the result or imitation of such engineering structures as dams; they can mimic the complex structure of the land itself; they can take on the quality of a site-specific installation that seeks to establish a new human relationship to the land by altering our perception of place. In all cases, the design of landscrapers is an act of making a new nature rather than replacing nature with human order. AARON BETSKY

● lands of superposition

[MG] In the same way that the contemporary city superposes layers of information in successive and varied entropic combinations, the project can also superpose simultaneous – programmatic, morphological, structural – "layers" or "strata" in new stacked arrays. The space thus described refers, then, to evolutions produced among multiple episodes, as "inter-involved" as they are independent, as iterable as they are syncopatable, as inherent in their arrangement as they are distortable in their evolution, which would appear as a spatial, irregular and intermittent "tessellation," rather than as a strictly dimensional pattern.

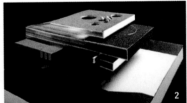

1. Enric MIRALLES, *Geriatrics Hospital* , Palamós (Girona, Spain). **2.** WMA Willy Müller Arquitectos, *Competition for Navarra general library*, Pamplona (Spain), 2001. **3.** MVRDV, *Leidschenveen urban centre*, Leidschendam (The Netherlands), 1997.

★● landstrategy

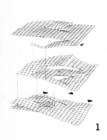

1

2

3
[MG]

The enormous interest in landscape that is taking the contemporary architectural debate by storm is a clear sign that we can no longer rely on the classical relationships between building and ground, or on the conventional definition of the ground as delimited, stable, horizontal, determined and homogeneous. But landscape is only interesting if we understand it in its more generic sense: as a kind of topographic operating system rather than as a category of the built environment; a "platform" rather than a "site."

This operative or methodological aspect of the landscape is well explained by J. F. Lyotard, who says that landscapes are domains devoid of meaning, origin and destiny produced "when the mind is transported from one form of sensitive matter to another, but still retains the sensorial organization characteristic of the former."

But our surface projects, rather than the absence of the ground, are about its redefinition and about the construction of a series of techniques: a new discipline of the ground. The manipulation of the surface of the ground has been a constant, transforming an element that usually bears a flat coding into an active, complex, mutating field. The ambiguity between the surface and the space, between the two-dimensional and the three-dimensional is perhaps one of the constants in these projects, as an alternative to the opposition between the ground and the architectural figure. The surface is no longer the envelope of space, but also its determinant, as both become strongly connected. A second strategy is the ambiguity between the ground and the envelope. Rather than addressing the two elements in the classical opposition, we explore the indetermination between them. Architecture no longer appears as a vertical, active entity constructed over the horizontal, passive ground plane. Here, the ground becomes an active, constructed plane where the architecture emerges as an improbable, fluctuating figure.

Opposite to traditional grounds, new grounds have specific performances:
1. new grounds are not natural – in either physical or cultural terms – but are artificially constructed; 2. new grounds are neither abstract nor neutral and homogeneous, but concrete and differentiated: they are neither figures nor backgrounds, but operating systems; 3. new grounds have an uncertain frame, as the field in which they exist is not a fragment but a differentiated domain affiliated to external processes – they are inseparable from the operation we carry out on them–; 4. new grounds are neither a datum nor a reference; 5. new grounds are neither solid nor structured by gravity; and 6. they are hollow and "diagonally" structured.
ALEJANDRO ZAERA-POLO

(manipulation)

The term 'lands' – or platforms – is employed to designate devices conceived of as active surfaces (magmas or membranes, in the words of other writers) tending to carry to extremes their extended, horizontal condition.

Direct work upon the land is thus understood as work upon a manipulated architecturalised void. A *vide façonné* in which the programme would no longer be developed through the primary configuration of mass constructed in height – architecture as edification – but, rather, through the restructuring of the horizontal dimension: plateaus, trays, dunes, trenches, undulations, mats, furrows, etc. Therefore, lands describe topomorphic manifestations of a possible artificial geography that is not far removed from the more natural type: possible architectures, overlapping and/or slipped on the landscape, conceived of as virtual carpets for use – thick lands, dense lands, solid lands – on free receptor lands. Lands in lands.

1. Studies for a library, in VARIOUS AUTHORS, *The Berlage Cahiers 5: Fields, Studio '95'96*, Rotterdam: 010 Publishers, 1997.
2. FOA, *International Port Terminal*, Yokohama (Japan), 2002.
3. Kelly SHANNON, *Project for topographic elevated passage*, Atlanta (Georgia, USA), 1994.

★ language

→ 'action>critical', 'code', 'dictionary', 'knowledge', 'name', 'meaning'

[co] "The measure of how effectively (gauge) you are part of community (Local-Area-Network): LAN Gauge. Transpose yo"U" and "A"gent," Tom Webb.
XAVIER COSTA

★ lava, programmatic

→ 'devices', 'eco-> ecomonumentality', 'ecology, active', 'field', 'landscapes, operative', 'land(s) in lands', 'landstrategy', 'lava, programmatic', 'plateaux', 'reliefs', 'tableland', 'Yokohama'

[co] In programmatic lava, several superimposed layers, constituted by undulating planes, have to allow a simultaneous combination of diverse uses. It is no longer an object related intervention on which to experiment with various activities, but the construction and extension of the city's very own ground planes which infiltrate the site. In this kind of project, the concepts which propel the rupture of the binomial relationship between figure-ground or architecture-place, seem to carry themselves to limits unimagined beforehand. The limits of the project have been disolved; the building takes root in the city through its flows and activities; the facades loose their edge condition by simultaneously being active surfaces, the ground plane loses its stratified and parallel organisation by including, in between the basic concepts of these projects, the oblique line condition, which conveys the spatial continuity. That is to say, the special relation between figure and background or between ground and architecture: its condition of simultaneity on top of the condition of contrast. The object focussed character so common of previous architecture and art appears to have disappeared and this has been substituted by a more extensive and open desire to value emptiness (ground, air, etc.) as integral parts of the work. A new desire to lift the background to the surface, in short, to turn the ground and the surface into the object of the project.
JOSÉ ANTONIO SOSA

FOA, *Project
for the urbanization
of Myeong-Dong
cathedral*,
Seoul, 1995.

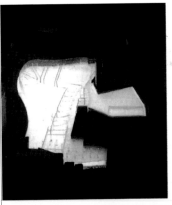

Shoei YOH, *Social
centre for the children
and the elderly*,
Uchino (Fukuoka,
Japan), 1995.

◆● layers

[FS] Layers reveal an order of information by means of superimposing levels of simultaneous knowledge. In a project, it is applied as a method
to maintain independence, fluctuation and evolution of diverse facts
and components that have been applied. Obvious in plan, layers also
apply to elevations – the product of superimposing various facades into a whole.

[MG] To paraphrase Ben van Berkel, evolutionary and, particularly urban,
environments may be seen today as invisible flows and visible materi-
alisations of information. Data, stimuli and tensions operate, in effect,
simultaneously within global spaces and within local spaces, continually manifesting an interaction between combined networks and layers:
"*An architecture based on these dissipative stresses should therefore
be understood as a multiple generator in a complex field of forces. To
work with such stresses is to work with different models of organisation, to define topological systems of elastic organisation, to generate
open energy systems, incorporating economic, public and political layers of information.*" (Paraphrasing VAN BERKEL, Ben; LYNN, Greg, "A Conversation",
El Croquis 72, 1995)

This idea of combination (of interconnection) among autonomous organisations (different layers of information) alludes, in effect, to ur-

Infrastructural
extensions
in the subsoil,
in *Läg-Och
Vattenbygaren* 4,
1991.

ban form itself and to its disintegration (as a harmonious and coherent body) in a new landscape of simultaneous forces, actions and events,
open to synchronous coexistence among differing messages, developing commensally one atop the other, in a dynamic transferable, in fact,
to the synthetical and definitively multilayered nature of the contemporary device.

This multiplied nature of the contemporary city demands a new type of
cartography: at once open and compatible, selective and purposeful (and
often surprising and completely new), in which the city becomes synthesisable only through the recording of those layers of information which
are potentially operative, and of their appropriate tactical combinations.
Tactical maps, then, of an extraterritorial city conceived through relationships and synergy rather than contiguousness and proximity: positioning maps aimed at situating the city within correct interregional dynamics; maps of a city of flows, grids and infrastructures; maps of a
subterranean and mixed city, that of the lower strata, as scanners of the
subsoil; maps of a city for sale with a real-estate-based approach; maps
of an environmental city, that of open spaces, large green areas, relational
spaces and the parameters of pollution that affect the quality of life;
maps of a city exploited culturally, symbolically, touristically; maps of a
retractile city vis-à-vis migratory movements and demographic transfers:
the known flexible fingers; maps, finally, of a marginal city: that of the
areas of tension, conflict or deficit.
Cartographies located beyond the figurative norms of the traditional disciplinary approach.

Layers of elements

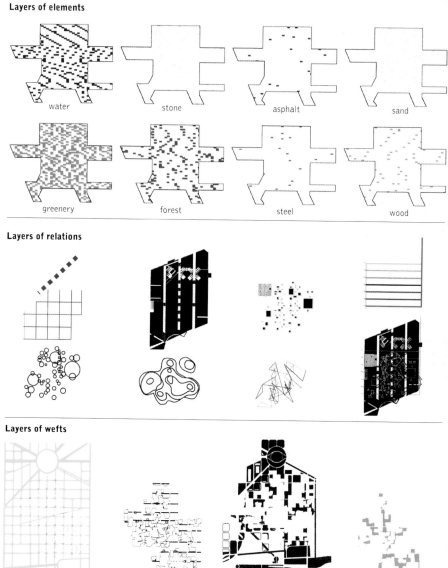

water	stone	asphalt	sand
greenery	forest	steel	wood

Layers of relations

Layers of wefts

traffic	communications nuclei	existent greenery	pedestrian circulation

 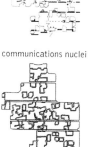    

distribution	displaced holes and strips	staggering of dwellings	light ways

1. Eduardo ARROYO (NO.mad Arquitectura), *Desierto square*, Barakaldo (Vizcaya, Spain), 1999. **2.** Vicente GUALLART, Enric RUIZ-GELI, *Exhibition La Beauté à la nature*, Avignon (France), 2000. **3.** ADD Arquitectura (BAILO-CLARAMUNT-RULL), *Proposal for Ávila street*, Barcelona, 1999.

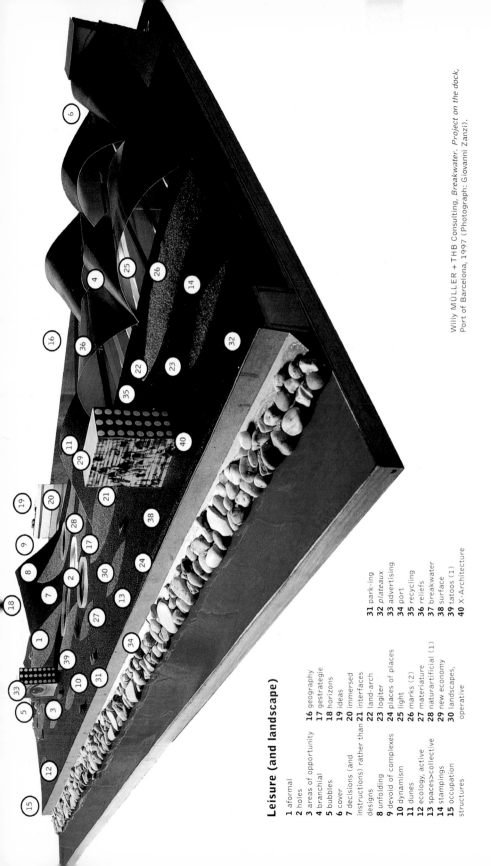

Leisure (and landscape)

1 aformal
2 holes
3 areas of opportunity
4 branchial
5 bubbles
6 cover
7 decisions (and instructions) rather than designs
8 unfolding
9 devoid of complexes
10 dynamism
11 dunes
12 ecology, active
13 spaces>collective
14 stampings
15 occupation structures

16 geography
17 gestrategie
18 horizons
19 ideas
20 immersed
21 interfaces
22 land-arch
23 logiter
24 places of places
25 light
26 marks (2)
27 materiature
28 naturartificial (1)
29 new economy
30 landscapes, operative

31 park-ing
32 *plateaux*
33 advertising
34 port
35 recycling
36 reliefs
37 breakwater
38 surface
39 tatoos (1)
40 X-Architecture

Willy MÜLLER + THB Consulting, *Breakwater. Project on the dock,*
Port of Barcelona, 1997 (Photograph: Giovanni Zanzi).

★ leapfrogging

→ 'anarchitecture'

[co] Derived from child's play of jumping over obstacles, leapfrogging has dovetailed into the wheels of so-called "progress". Virgin territory is deflowered in leapfrog subdivision sprawl development. In territories of rapid urbanization and modernization, civilizations are passing directly from the pre-industrial to the post-industrial era vis-à-vis the harnessing of technology. In locales without communication infrastructure, the ring of hand-helds competes with hawkers' squalls; e-mail connections are ingeniously rigged in shantytowns. Linear progression has been jump-cut. KELLY SHANNON

●◆ leisure (and landscape)

→ 'ecology, active',
'economy', 'fear>
fair play', 'game',
'hedonism', 'house, the',
'ludic', 'recycling',
're-information',
'telepolis', 'tourism'

[MG] In the closing stages of the twentieth century, industry no longer dominated the world of work. Today, new transmission and information networks are taking the place of the old productive models, thanks to new technological advances. If these networks have eroded the traditional bond between place and activity, they have also favoured a new dimension of leisure that includes nature – possibly a new nature – understood as a relational ecosystem. "Breaks" in territorial developments and "breaks" in our own productive activities favour the transformation of large, empty – often obsolete – areas into landscapes for relaxation.

[FS] Our society of work has mutated into a society of leisure time, of entertainment. Continuous schedules (even in schools and universities), a thirty five hour working week, the hybridisation of sports, culture and amusement with their commercial benefits (today entertainment means consuming) are joint symptoms of the invasion of play in our lives and work. I do not know if today's home will have work, but it surely will have entertainment.

Richard HAAG
Associates,
Gas Works Park,
Seattle (USA),
1975, in *Quaderns*
196, 1993.

◆ liberty

→ 'criteria', 'dynamism',
'indiscipline', '<in> order
factors', 'name', 'R+3D',
'stains, ink'

[FS] *"To create today is to create dangerously,"* says Camus. *"All publications,"* all construction, I add, *"are acts that expose its author to the passions of a century that pardons nothing. The problem for those that can not live without art and what this means, write only in knowing how, between the policies of so many ideologies (how many churches, how much loneliness!) the strange liberty of creation continues to be possible."*
(CAMUS, Albert, *El artista y su tiempo*, 1957)

● × ◆ ★ ■ **light**

» 'holograms'

[MG] See 'energy' and 'no-day (night and day).'

[VG] Today's images and traditional architecture come together in light.
These days, every image is light. On TV, in computers, in the cinema, or in commercial night.
Architecture was 'the magnificent meeting of volumes in the light.' These days, it is not made with volumes, or with forms, and is not seen in the light. Light can only be artificial.

[FS] An amplified concept of light: Natural light, six hours. Artificial light, twenty-four hours. Natural light, limited areas. Artificial light, any area. A mechanism of modifying form in space. It makes these forms unstable.

[co] **(kinetic)**
When reality is light and spaces are volumes of light, perhaps architecture can be created with the movement of the actor, of the inhabitant, in real time. Then movement and construction are simultaneous.
When we do not perceive the limit between reality, rendering, miniature and larger scenario, architecture is kinetic, it travels among new technologies, new realities, new sensitivities and new velocities. ENRIC RUIZ-GELI

[JM] **(in itself)**
Light, the necessary vehicle for space to become manifest, allows for a space that does not need material support to be seen and has always been a necessary condition to understand space in an ideal and absolute way. Thus, a dialogue of signs is increasingly evident, in which place – landscape-as-space – is illuminated. In addition, it is also a necessary condition for the landscape of the city to become manifest.
The scale and relation between distances are modified, bringing to the discourse of the city and public building a language of signs that have nothing to do with the figuration of the expressionist city.

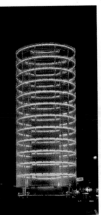

Toyo ITO, *Winds Tower*, Yokohama (Japan), 1986.

projected light

Vicente GUALLART, *Dwelling at the limit of the town*, Lliria (Valencia, Spain), 1995.

spectre light

Enric RUIZ-GELI, *Competition for the Fundació Mies van der Rohe headquarters*, Barcelona, 1999.

activity light

Willy MÜLLER + THB Consulting, *Breakwater. Project on the dock*, Port of Barcelona, 1997.

image light

FOA, *Belgo Restaurant*, London, 1999.

◆ lightness (and levity)

[FS] "Lightness" is a term, along with levity, that can amply claim to be characteristic of current architecture. Insulating layers have lost weight, becoming habitable spaces, and the concepts of interior and exterior have lost their definitions, having become mixed with one another, thereby suggesting other interventions.

Parallel to this, the idea of structure as an external mechanism and *a priori* to architectonic definition – that gives physical support, but acts ethereally – has made way for consideration related to the void that it serves. Both, intertwined, today form a joined background.

1. LACATON&VASSAL, *Single family house*, Coutras (France), 2001. 2. ÁBALOS & HER-REROS, *international competition Dunar Park*, Matalascañas (Huelva, Spain), 1994.

◆■●▲ limit

[FS] See also 'link.'

Our contemporary space has no limits. It lives by day and is obliged to accept a circuit of unlimited action. We live – are submerged – and must survive in it. But, even unlimited as is Modern space, it is not continuous; it is made of pieces, fragments, remnants that have continuity without being contiguous. Unions are made by links.

[JM] The limits in the city multiply, and yet it is not so clear that this physical reality serves to catalogue the real city. Centre, outer walls, peripheries, earth, water, area, profundity, skin, interior and exterior serve to explain the physical events of the contemporary city.

The physical presence of these phenomena and their analogies with the forms of architecture and public spaces has only multiplied what was already reality: the infinity of limits and borders that today constitute the city. The limit, contrary to the way it has been seen, is not amenable to sutures, welding, or fusion. The city is full of these and their spaces are more defined by events close to them, (objects, trajectories, topographies, topologies) than by the pretended and inexact limitation that defines them. The space of the city is today configured more by the space of "others" – events of all types – than by the actual presence of that we understand as urban space. The idea of limit has lost precision, it is somewhat diffuse.

[MG] Today, we work beyond boundaries. With silhouettes – profiles and codes –
that have lost their old – closed, finished, complete – coherence.
With structures based upon a blurred logic of dissolution, refinement and
lightness: sensitive to the open capacity of shape and to the flexible and indeterminate potential of a space at the same time evanescent and arborescent; a space produced through dispersion and discontinuity, through
work with intermittencies and openings, with expansions and frayings, with
syncopations and fadings, with cuts and trimmings, with folds and unfoldings (or deployments), rather than with the geometric purity and continuity of the old profiled geometries of the Euclidian.

[FP] Defining in dissolution. Operating between edges. Up until very recently, architects set limits. Without a doubt, the present makes us think of its disappearance. Traditionally, in architecture it has been taken for granted that
we are engaged in inventing and constructing borders and limits. If this was
the case, we would be able to define the act of constructing as the manifestation of control devices, like retaining structures. As well, we could say
that within these control devices are not only containers full of activities
and events, but also political manifestations, social affairs and cultural ideologies. For this reason, present-day architects need to question the nature
of any kind of limit or frontier, and whether they derive from a premedi-
tated act or are the result of the impact produced by technological media
within public space; whether they have to do with the effect produced by
the world economies, or the spatial and architectonic consequences within the virtual field. Regarding the concepts of limits, control and frontier,
there is certain ambiguity between what is private and what is public. It
looks like this is increasing day by day and that, on the other hand, this ambiguity is turning out to be a more ubiquitous condition. We can talk about
the invasion of what is public into the private by communication technologies as an example of the ambiguous freedom existing within communication webs in the middle of constant threats of censorship and regulation. In the same way, the proliferation of advertising and the media within
the public urban area, although at a different level, allows the imposition
of different interests of the private sector through different modes of representation in urban space, which, little by little, is being transformed in
the privatisation of public space. Finally, we can talk about the invisible nature of the current conditions within these movements, in which the rate of
change has increased in such a way that change has become almost im-
perceptible. Taking into account these ambiguities, and many others that
have manifested themselves fundamentally in the "private" public areas
(commercial centres, stations or cultural centres), it seems appropriate to
question oneself in what way should architecture negotiate the existing limits between urban public space and architectonic public space. This would
lead us to propose getting closer, within an urban framework, to the idea
opposing the use of architecture as a simple background or support where
the issues and interests in play are of a completely different nature than
the specific ones related to architecture. We do not pretend to say that

architecture exists as a completely autonomous entity, or that it is the result of an internal logic derived merely from formalist strategies and programmed interests. Whatever approach, if restricted, will lead as to an isolated architecture, without being able to reach a significant position within the urban area and separated from its own context. The concept of context here acquires a much wider sense, even reaching socio-political and cultural dimensions. It might be possible for architecture to work as a mediator between urban public space and constructed public space. In this way, both intentions, the formal one and the programmed one, will be able to be understood as something belonging to both scales: the architectonic and the urban , and also to its own context. Ultimately, architecture carries a hidden and not pretended role of opposition and simultaneity. In this type of architecture, there is no sense of hierarchy and priority spaces or objects do not exist. In this case, the limits set between the space and the limits of the construction are even more complex when it comes to defining and describing things. For this reason, we talk about an architecture with no fixed limits, that oscillates between what is tangible and what is not. Architecture needs to be comprehensible and, at the same time, difficult to trace and define. Also, and against all forecasts, it is deep inside a space for actions that could never be covered, nor controlled. An object that gives rise to false expectations, an open field to all kind of possibilities.

Steven HOLL, *Edge of a city: spiroid sectors*, Dallas-Fort Worth (USA), 1990.

★ linear cities

→ 'territory'

[co]

Linear cities simultaneously have the economic and servicing centrality of the centrifugal, compact city and the diffuse city's spatial logic of development along infrastructure corridors. As in the utopian projects of the early 20th century, linear city development is concentrated in sustainable, high-density areas with a rigorously defined ecological footprint and built edges. The linear city redefines the relation between urbanism and its territory; its premise remains firmly rooted in Socialist ideals.

KELLY SHANNON / TOM AVERMAETE

urbADS (T. AVERMAETE, A. D'HOOGHE, J. JUHASZ, K. SHANNON), *Housing the Next Million, Great Central Valley California Competition,* 1999.

● ★ link

→ 'citilab', 'flows',
'incubator',
'intelligence', 'interaction',
'interchange', 'link',
'networks', 'search engine'

[MG]

Connection, but also contract, bond or relationship of kinship or interest.

[co]

When we spend Sundays immersed in the Internet, communicate via the web, eat Matrix, have Connectix equipment and are surrounded by names like X.com, then architecture consists of constructing links. Constructing flows, walkways, artificial gardens, tracking shots, beams of light under a lineal, fractal or binary structure. A complexity that makes the discipline something of an interdiscipline; the text a hypertext; and the space the interspatial. ENRIC RUIZ-GELI

★ litheness

[c]

"*Maximum slenderness = minimum occupied surface, minimum environmental impact and minimum modification of groundwater levels. Grouping vertically: slender towers with variable sections, following the criteria of one unit = one floor.*" (DíAZ, Cristina; GARCÍA GRINDA, Efrén; JARAMILLO, Ángel, "Temporary accommodation in the south-east regional park ", *Quaderns* 224, 1999)

Cristina DíAZ MORENO, Efrén GARCÍA GRINDA, Ángel JARAMILLO, *Temporary accommodation,* Parque Regional del Sureste (Madrid), 1997.

✖ ★ living-working-resting

[VG] The dwelling is a micro-city in and from which we work, shop and rest.

[c] "*Houses, which until now had been conceived as places of rest and relaxation, can today become places of work.*

Certain concepts are inverted. Houses will tend to gain in value and care in their design. They can be more dispersed, urban concentration and clustering around the offices and businesses of urban centres will increasingly lose meaning.

The situation described, work and rest in the area of the home, leads us to believe in the possible invention of hybrid unités d'habitation *that would recover and free up territory and incorporate, in a single building, work, business, leisure and rest.*" (ARANGUREN, María José, GONZÁLEZ GALLEGOS, José, "Habitar la caja", unpublished, 1999)

[co] A house can integrate programme, circulation and structure seamlessly. It interweaves the various states that accompany the condensation of dispersed and widely differentiating activities into one only structure: work, social life, family life and individual time alone, all find their place in this almost loop structure. The domestic movement follows the pattern of an active day.
BEN VAN BERKEL

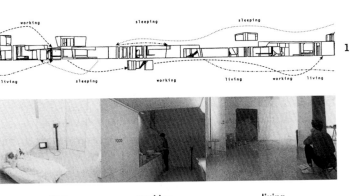

resting   working   living

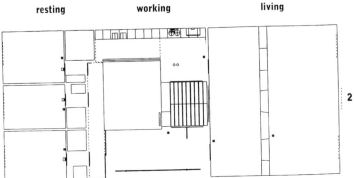

1

2

1. Ben VAN BERKEL & Caroline BOS (UN Studio), *Moebius House*, Het Gooi (The Netherlands), 1997. **2.** Vicente GUALLART, Nuria DÍAZ, *New dwelling for the historical centre*, Barcelona, 1992.

● livrid (live+hybrid)

→ 'devices', 'environment', 'housing', 'housys', 'hybrid', 'mixed-use'

[MG] LIVRIDS are residential hybrids associated with HOUSYS but with a capacity to enhance their bastardised condition in order to combine heterogeneous residential programmes and fittings related to leisure, services, communications and natures (at all levels). These are mixed devices designed to engender cooperation, in effective and harmonised complexes, among public and private programmes related to new types of habitats and uses for manifold population segments.

ACTAR ARQUITEC-
TURA, *Tableland
Housing, Elemmental
System*, Madrid, 2003

★ locality

→ 'high speed'

[co] Locality is no longer described as simple geographical relations
but as the friction of speed.
JUAN CARLOS SÁNCHEZ TAPPAN / LARS TEICHMANN / KRIS VAN WEERT

■ localization

→ 'de-location', 'm. city'

[JM] Asking oneself about the life and death of cities is to do so about the locations of subjects. The history of the city is the history of location. One can say that a possible study of the city is of its locations. But to do so, one must observe what things are in what places. It is necessary, once again, to draw back the veil of the "deceitful and uniform urbanity" (J. J. Rousseau) that today covers the city. It would be better to think about dislocation.

José MORALES,
Sara GILES,
Juan GONZÁLEZ,
Theatre, Nijar
(Almeria, Spain),
1998.

● logic

→ 'architecture'   [MG]   Logic is an organisational system or disposition: flexible – open – and vectorised – deliberate.

● logic, digital

[MG]   See 'digital.'

● logic, direct

→ 'action>critical',   [MG]   We may speak today of an "action-architecture" or a "diagrammatic ar-
'advertising', 'blunt',   chitecture" conceived through a direct logic, capable of condensing processed
'diagrams', 'direct', 'form',   data, precise latent movements and basic decisions by way of condensed
'hypertrophy', 'informal',   trajectories of bits of strategic and tactical information. These movements
'landscapes, operative',   are able to foster – in the context of the complexity of the new scenarios
'open', 'synthetical', 'yes!'   – responses (shapes and spatialities) that are much more effective, precisely because they are concise, incisive, immediate (although not thus nec-
essarily schematic, dry and/or essential). They are also capable of developing complexity, through direct, energetic and relaxed manifestation of
their own explicit, expeditious and resolvent definition; a definition grounded in the economy – almost elemental – of stimulatory criteria, in the (basic) character of their dynamic materialisation and in this will to foster
quasi-spontaneous – unbiased (direct) – arrangements far removed from
any purified or solemn reading in the shape.

Synthetical responses for complex problems. Capable of offering "more
from less." These dynamics are relevant because in such "action-architec-
tures," the intervention and the reality in which the latter is inscribed are
condensed in immediate decisions that fuse cause and effect in synthetical
trajectories or diagrams. Diagnosis and Response. Conditions and new
organisations. Such diagrams are like abstract bits of strategic information – engendered through direct logic – that assert themselves as condensed maps of software intended to (re)inform the global system.

NJIRIC+NJIRIC,
*Project Hortus
Sanitatis*, Zagreb
(Croatia), 1997.

NEUTELINGS
RIEDIJK Architecten,
Concert Hall, Bruges
(Belgium), 1998
(Price Winning
Competition Entry).

● logic, fuzzy

[MG] See 'avatar.'

[MG] *"Fuzzy logic is a way of doing science without math. It's a new branch of machine intelligence that tries to make computers think the way people think and not the other way around.*

You don't write equations for how to wash clothes. Instead you load a chip with vague rules like 'if the wash water is dirty, add more soap,' and 'if very dirty, add a lot more.'

All wash water is dirty and not dirty – to some degree. It's just common sense. But it breaks the old either/or logic of Aristotle. That offends some scientists, who would like us to think and talk like off/on switches.

But they still haven't produced a statement of fact like 'the sky is blue' or 'E=mc²' that is 100 percent true or 100 percent false. Fact ain't math. You can never get the science right to more than a few decimal places.

That's one reason we find chaos when we look at things up close."

(KOSKO, Bart, "Fuzzy Thinker", *Wired* 3.02, 1995)

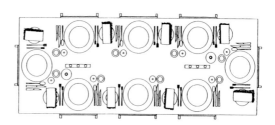

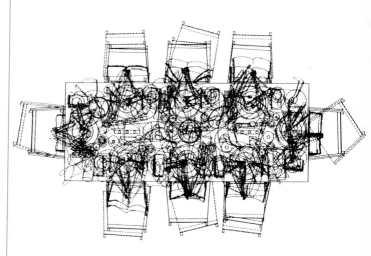

Growing disorder on a table during a meal, in WIGGLESWORTH, Sarah; TILL, Jeremy, The Architecture and Everyday, Academy 1998.

★ logic, liquid

[CO] Liquid logic alludes to flexible processes of fluctuations which project architecture either in time either in space, by changing interactively according to duration, use and external influences. MARCOS NOVAK

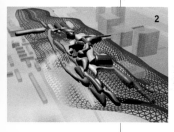

1. Marcos NOVAK, *Transmitting Architecture: transTerraFirma/TidsvagNoll v2.0.* **2.** Juan Carlos SÁNCHEZ TAPPAN, Lars TEICHMANN, Kristiaan VAN WEERT, *Infra-nets.org, multilinear mediators,* Canary Wharf, London, 2000. **3.** UN STUDIO, *Museum Het Valkhof,* Kelfkensbos Nijmegen (The Netherlands), 1998.

● logic, open

[MG] The new conditions of our environment create the need to work with a new type of more open logic, one which would be neither the classical (compositive) metaphysical continuity nor that of modern (positional) functional *objectuality*, but rather contemporary (dispositive); strategic *interactivity*, capable of articulating and strengthening the diversity of our time.

The very word 'open' defines effectively this relational potential of a possible new architecture – also defined as advanced, reactive or informational – destined to engender more effective frameworks for interaction.

A more open logic is its being virtually evolutionary (susceptible to change and variation, beyond determined states of *configuration*, according to dynamics processes, generators of development).

A more open logic is more flexible (capable of fluctuation, of deformation, adaptation and transformation before and with the impact of information).

A more open logic is more indeterminate (or less predetermined, less prefigured, in its shape and configuration).

A more open logic is more empathetic and receptive (sensitive to the demands of the medium, of the place).

A more open logic is more exteriorised and extroverted (capable of "opening itself up" to external scales and situations, conditions and dimensions, beyond that which is local).

A more open logic is more spontaneous and informal (in its evolutions) and, thus, more joyous (relaxed, uninhibited and expressive) in its manifestations.

● logiter

→ 'strategy'

[MG] "*Space of territorial character in which operations of distribution of materials are carried out.// Term for denominating* metapolitan *spaces – between landscape and city – capable of distributing loads, people and energy flows of continual shape. Defines logistical centres, no longer of solid or energy loads but rather of information.// Constructional abbreviation of logistic territory.*" (Ignasi Pérez Arnal)

ACTAR
ARQUITECTURA,
Bit Park, Mallorca
(Spain), 1995.

● loops

→ 'crossing', 'devices', 'flows', 'fold (unfold-refold)', 'geometry', 'infrastructures', 'networks', 'solenoid', 'trajectory', 'transfers'

[MG] See 'braids', 'coilings' and 'nubs-nodes-knots'.

Loops are braids or nodes with linkage conditions associated with mixed "self-coiling" – swirling (in a circle or spiral) – programmes in which the empty-full discontinuity is produced, not in expanded sequences, but in winding imbrications.

BOLLIGER
& MABILLARD,
*Dragon Khan sketch,
switchback in
Port Aventura*, Salou
(Tarragona, Spain),
in *BAU* 017, 1999.

● ludic

→ 'complicity', 'game', 'leisure', 'pleasure', 'unrestrained'

[MG] See 'joy (*alegría*)', 'hedonism' and 'optimism.'

Ludic relates to play (and to the pleasure of adventure).

M

+ × m³

→ 'space'

[WM] [VG] Space is measured in m³ rather than in m². Houses should be sold by m³, and would be occupied by furniture-room pieces, free to be arranged by the inhabitant. The section and the floor plan of a house are equally important.

■ machination

→ 'abstract', 'criteria', 'diagrams', 'maps, battle', 'negotiate', 'operative', 'projective'

[JM] The concept of the project is related more to the idea of machination than to contamination.

▲ machine

→ 'devices', 'trailers'

[FP] The aesthetics of the machine, as a more or less figurative resource, or as a reference of this type of object referring to the first avant-garde, have stopped being of our interest a long time ago. In our opinion, an approach is not improved by its capacity of evoking working mechanisms, nor showing an apparent nakedness in which shameless *inner elements* are exposed. All this probably serving the pretended alternative "composition." Of all the works we now see as machines, we are interested in automatism and indecisiveness.

Automatism if we are able to plan without being concrete, just establishing the rules or strategies that will allow some developments, above and beyond the objects themselves (when planning particular solutions, we will oppose them by bringing in real guidelines that will allow for a number of varied suggestions and solutions).

Indecisiveness in so far as we are answering with strategies more than with models, which are making us accept results which escape any preconceived images we have and which are introducing in our work factors like chance and indecisiveness. It is only within this framework in which we can understand the use of the machine metaphor. Not as an end in itself, and not even as a medium of vehicle. This term cannot mean more

[i] p. 410   than the qualities that it refers to. It is all but evocative.

● macro-micro

→ 'bluntings', 'buds', 'dual(ity)', 'economy'

[MG] See 'midget & giant'.

The interaction between different phenomena gives rise – through coupling – to a non-hierarchical structure made up of points and counterpoints, different and autonomous, although interrelated thanks both to the intermediate spaces – voids – and to the matrix organisation of the system itself.

Naturally, that produces contrasts, a consequence of which is the singularity of such "impure" configurations, due in large part to the indiscriminate immediacy of the responses. The small and the large can, for example, have a simultaneous presence such that they make one and other more appreciable.

▲ magic

→ 'game'

[FP] Our Architecture is more than ever a sleight of hand – magic.

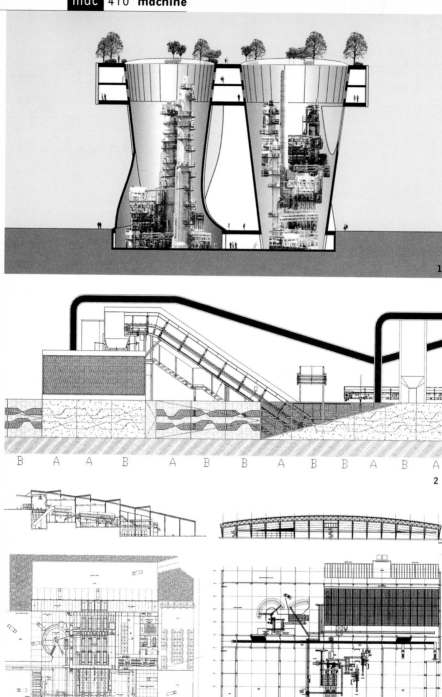

1. NL, *Oefenfabriek*, Hoogvliet, (satellite town of) Rotterdam (The Netherlands), 2002. **2.** WMA Willy Müller Arquitectos, *Punt Verd Mercabarna, recycling plant for urban waste*, Barcelona, 2002. **3.** ÁBALOS & HERREROS, *Recycling plant for urban waste*, Valdemingómez (Madrid), 1998. **4.** Lourdes GARCÍA SOGO, *Recycling plant for urban waste*, Villena (Spain), 1999.

● magmas

[MG] See 'lava, programmatic'.

✖ maieutics

→ 'criteria', 'machination', 'trailers'

[VG] See 'knowledge.'

Maieutics is a process of transmission of knowledge developed by Socrates, according to which the individual learns (remembers) a concept by answering a series of precisely formulated questions.

◆ manifesto (to demonstrate)

[FS] Are we merely executors of taste? We no longer believe we can change society. Poor, irresponsible moderns. We have to accept a more humble role. Does architecture have a social content? No problem. Then we're designers. Or intellectuals of space. Are we capable of leading a social debate? Do our manifestos speak of anything but stainless steel? We lack the possibility of being wrong. It is not our field. Whatever happened to those who wanted to change the world?

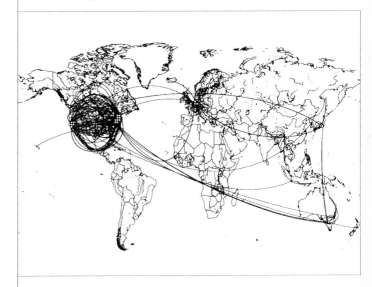

Demonstrating in the Net. Brian REID, USENET geographic map, 1986.

■● manipulate

→ 'logic, digital', 'maps (to map)', 'places'

[JM] The most advised thing for a project is to image it through action. Static or impulsive, it does not matter, the project ends up being the fruit of manipulating, pasting, separating, extending, nearing, putting with. The project is lead through a singular ecology. (Ecology, to cohabit, put together.)

[MG] See 'genetics'.

Manipulate — formerly "to control with one's hands." Today, to hybridise knowledge, natures and bits of information, physical and virtual.

map 412

●★ maps, battle

[MG] The recent interpretation of the contemporary project as a device that is open, evolutionary, strategic and tactical at the same time, has tended to foster a fertile association between operative diagrams and battle maps. This alludes to the resolving and flexible action of the contemporary project, which is not far removed from military strategy.

As well, the assimilation of the operative diagram and tactical diagram combines representation, register, recognition and simultaneous response. Xavier Costa recalled how "*knowledge and the representation of territory have fallen historically within the linear narration of the traveller and the vectoral cartography of the soldier. For the traveller, an understanding of the territory would be configured along the length of a route leading to a final destination; the soldier, on the other hand, would understand places as fields of multi-directional mobility, as spaces inviting temporary settlement, as places of vectoral tension, of superficial forces. These conditions are resolved in cartographic representation, in which geometry heightens its dependence on the visual.*"

A battle map aims not to describe a place, but rather to begin its transformation.

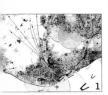

1. *Barcelona Metápolis: battle map,* in VARIOUS AUTHORS, *Met 1.0. Barcelona Metápolis,* Barcelona: ACTAR, 1998.

2. d2kL.A., protest against the democrat party convention, Los Angeles, august 2000.

A battle map is not only a fixed drawing, a descriptive cartography, but also a synthesis of possible evolutions. A static simulation of dynamic processes: a diagnosis of the conditions of the place – a reaction – capable of reading, processing, representing and synthesising its bits of material information (land, infrastructure, outlines, orography, forestings, accidents, etc.), but also immaterial elements (climate, winds, psychological aspects, echoes and noises, administration, communication, etc.).

It implies, in effect, immediate operative responses (rapid reflexes and elastic schemes) referring to flexible organisational norms (criteria for action but also strategic logic and tactical dispositions) capable of articulating almost spontaneously – beyond formal scruples or aesthetic biases – field movements which are open, non-linear, often chaotic – diffuse, indeterminate and uncertain.

In battle, the formal definition of movement, at each moment, is necessarily dependent upon contingency, and always responds to evolutionary devices whose greater or lesser degree of success, effectiveness and adaptation to the heterogeneous, the singular and the variable – that which is fortuitous by virtue of being hazardous – leads the action towards one result or another.

[co] Owing to the varying size and schedules which nowadays interact, the contemporary project must favour constant fluctuations in the volume of the space required. This calls for a structure in which the boundaries between areas could be shifted to allow for such fluctuations. It is a highly differentiated structure, a seamless milieu which allows for the broadest variety of scenarios: an ideal battlefield where the strategic position of a small number of elements will substantially affect the definition of the frontier or the reconfiguration of the borders between territories.

ALEJANDRO ZAERA-POLO

map 413 **maps, battle**

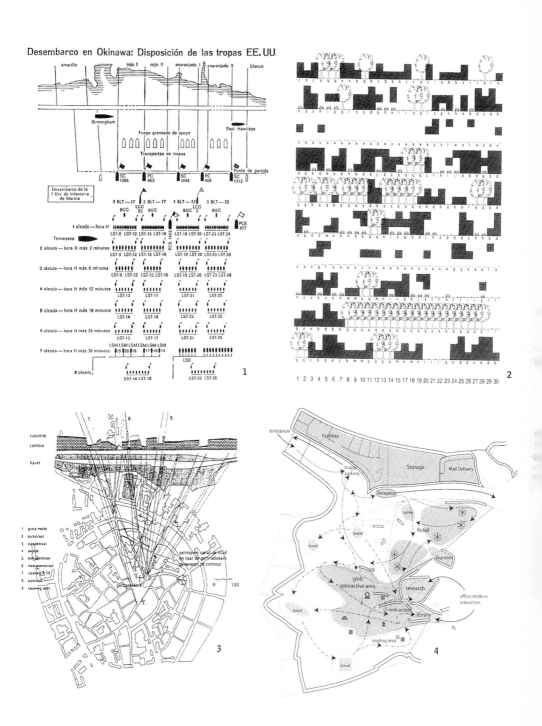

1. Okinawa landing: disposition of the United States troops, in JACOBSEN, Hans-Adolf; DOLLINGER, Hans, *Der Zweite Weltkrieg in Bildern und Dokumenten*, Munich, Viena, Basel: K. Desch, 1968. **2.** MVRDV, *Urban planning Hoornse Kwadrant*, Delft (The Netherlands), 1996. **3.** MVRDV, *City in shade*, Bergen op Zoom (The Netherlands), 1993. **4.** NOX (Lars Spuybroek with Chris Seung-Woo Yoo, Kris Mun, Florent Rougemont and Ludovica Tramontin), *SoftOffice*, United Kingdom, 2000-2005.

map 414 maps (to map)

BUCKMINSTER
FULLER, *World
Game* seminary,
data gathering of
worldwide variable
(fragment):
A) naval corridors;
B) aerial corridors;
C) earthquakes
and stable earth
masses areas;
D) potential energy
sources, 1972.

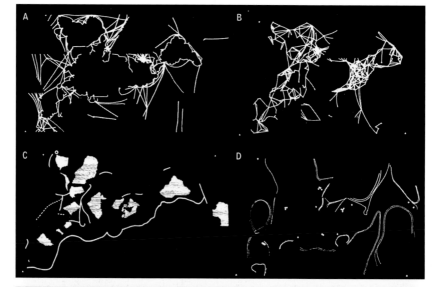

Map of western
Europe positing the
connections between
capitals, in GAUSA,
Manuel, *Housing.
New alternatives,
new systems,*
Barcelona: ACTAR,
1998.

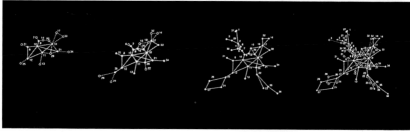

Codifications.
Tracking structures
by networks and
numbers. Visualization
sequences of a
thematic map, in
Quaderns 213, 1996.

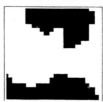
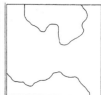

Miguel BARAHONA,
José Alfonso
BALLESTEROS,
Madrid self-
grouping maps,
in *Fisuras* 5, 1997.

map 415

◆●▲■ maps (to map)

[FS] *"Scale and territory, the two themes we are dealing with here, are related in a particular document: the map.*

A map represents intellectual knowledge, linguistic convention, while territory refers to physical experience, the sensorial act. The comparison between map and territory is fascinating, because it relates knowledge to experience.

[..] The maps that Robert Smithson use are taken out of their context by being fragments lacking the ordering legend to interpret the value of the signs drawn on them. Thus, these map fragments transform into abstract forms, and new compositions.

Smithson's maps, besides this transformation, represent two types of referential space: the outline of maps that form the earth and water mass, and the tautological: the drawings of maps in themselves.

[...] Lewis Carroll's map in The Hunting of the Snark (1876) has drawn limits, its scale in miles and cardinal points perfectly defined, but is completely blank."

(MADERUELO, Javier, *El espacio raptado*, Madrid: Mondadori, 1990)

[MG] See 'cartographies.'

Neither descriptive and literal, nor analytical and objective representation any longer serve to deal with the dynamic, unfinished reality that is in constant mutation.

Representation of the city – like that of reality itself – thus calls for a tactical, flexible and digital, more operative cartography: evolutionary models of simulation and development, but, also, weighted – meaningful – maps intended to select bits of basic information (and situations) related to abstract elemental codes (precise and indeterminate at the same time).

Maps are able to adapt to (by transforming and altering) the particular and the specific (the contingent) and, at the same time, to point to recursive global phenomena; phenomena related to both elemental structures of "occupation-distancing-routing" and to complex systems generated through interaction – simultaneous and variable – among layers of information (and activity), networks of connection (and linkage) and vacant (expectant) backgrounds.

To map this new reality – the result of mobility, interchange, migration and communication – requires purposeful attention to strategic factors capable of generating possible evolutions and interactions within the system: real-estate, demographic, environmental, and cultural parameters, as well as of connectivity, of use.

Old static representations yield to diagrams, ideograms, infograms and (virtually) dynamic simulations.

Maps are also able to synthesise basic decisions (criteria for action) and combinations of movements (operative systems): tactical maps and operative maps, in which are fused relationships, actions and activities.

Maps intended to compress meaningfully not so much the reproduction of

map 416

the whole reality, or part of it, but rather a representation – a scanning – of its most strategic bits of information.

For it is no longer a question of describing shapes, but rather of describing potentials. Not a question of reproducing formulas (forms + models), but rather of producing – and mapping – "programmes": operative systems.

[MG] *"Since the city is already a mutable, superposed and diffuse and not always physical entity, and it cannot be understood from the classic perspective, nor from the generalised and next to synthesis comprehension of an inhabitant of the modernity, various appliances should be articulated that would permit us the intervention in the urban environment. These cannot result in the conventional because they would only attend to one instant of the changing environment or to a restricted range of instants and determinant factors generally affected by geometry.*

We need to break the traditional physical conception of the city, to think it from a different globality and a discreetisation, that are corresponded with our new conception of the world and with the possibilities that the new technologies are offering us.

There are now appliances within our reach that are capable of thinking the city n-dimensionally, and extracting the complex relationships, not evident, between its parts, and, even, to predict its future trends."

(BALLESTEROS, José Alfonso; BARAHONA, Miguel, "The city that is not seen", *Fisuras* 5, 1998)

[FP] Maps are territories for representation, simulation or recreation.
They address a type of research derived from reality.
They construct, not reproduce.
They have multiple ways of getting into it; different points of view and understandings all have space here.
They need implementation.
They are open, connectable in every dimension, breakable, reversible, and always modifiable, just like the medium or architecture they are modelling.
We are interested in cartographies, in diagrams, as conceptual instruments, more than in formal descriptions, which are a way of printing power.
We are interested maps that favour ideograms, open correspondences between form and concept andadopt to the more experimental quality of projects.
We would like to highlight in maps the value of their abstraction in a more generative, evolutionary and productive way, as opposed to constructions, propositions or phrases ascribed to specific referents.

[JM] Spaces of phenomenology. Spaces of experimentation. To inhabit the subject. It is possible that these space are left to be drawn, prefigured. One must machine them, build them. Other tools are necessary, other measures. Measuring tools for experimentation, for reality. Places of interpretation. We have the tools, we make the map, tattoo the city. Everything is the same operation. A singular operation about the construction of the city and the interpretation of worlds.

▲ **market**

→ 'economy',
'McDonaldization'

[FP]

"The market produces non-specific, clone buildings, that are empty of any substance and disconnected from the place. I believe this is a terrible menace to its structure." This was stated by Peter Smithson in an interview published in EL PAIS newspaper of April 8, 2000. His statement no doubt caused apprehension among the readers who do not know Smithson (especially because the journalist who wrote this article, and who is not an architect, highlighted it in the heading). However, it is necessary here to argue exactly the opposite of such a dramatic phrase. The buildings which are disconnected from the place or are non-specific (open buildings) are probably the ones that we are more interested in because of their ability to do without the Vitruvian maxims, which are completely overtaken. Do we have to keep on imagining ways of sustaining stiff and paradigmatic premises or should we better show in our work the impulses of the market? We are not talking of getting into the market with a servile and accessible attitude, but considering it just another source in which to contrast our answers. A piece of information/informalisation which can be as radical as gravity law.

●+ **marks**

→ 'advertisements',
'beacons', 'patterns',
'printings', 'product'

[MG]

See 'stains, landscape' and 'tattoos.'
Frontier territories or districts.// Signs used to distinguish – and identify – a thing.// Signs of manufacture (symbol, logo or icon).// Incisions, signs, stamps, imprints, patch, paintings or tattoos of different sizes and scales, permanent or ephemeral.

[WM]

(brands)

"*The increasing difficulty in distinguishing between products, along with the speed at which competitors take up innovations, will assist in the rise and rise of the brand.*" Gillian Law, Nick Grant.

1. NOX (Lars Spuybroek with Kris Mun, Ludovica Tramontin, Florent Rougemont and Chris Seung-woo Yoo), *ParisBRAIN, a transurban scheme for the area west of La Défense,* Paris, 2001.

2. Jim RICHARDSON, *First streets, then houses,* in *Archis* 1997/7.

3. Eduard BRU, *Republica Pavilion* site, rebuilt by Miquel Espinet and Antoni Ubach, and *Mistos* site, Claes Oldenburg and Coosje van Bruggen sculpture.

4. Tattoo.

5. *Nike* logotype.

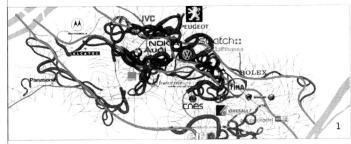

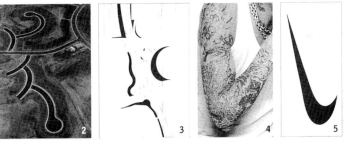

● Marx Bros.

→ 'complicity',
'direct', 'hedonism',
'ideas', 'infiltration',
'logic, direct', 'optimism',
'paradoxes', 'surprise',
'unrestrained (<un>
factors')

[MG] The active and optimistic spirit evident in Marx Brothers films is interesting. Their films are based upon an impulse for unrestrained, active, joyful, singular andunpredictable impostures, usually taking place in clichéd, confused, decadent locations, subject to repeated routines and inertias (a boat, a hotel, a circus, a stadium or studio, etc.). There is always an impulse for a positive *bouleversement* of a reality that is accepted, but transformed by a playful manipulation of accepting and driving the scenario in which the action is taking place through a difficult combination of alienation and complicity, distancing and proximity. But also by means of an acceptance of impurity, heterogeneity and singularity (of the protagonists themselves and of the actions they provoke) capable of giving rise to universes which are more complex and diverse – mongrel – highlighted by the positive extrapolation of those situations or responses which are more unexpected or strange. Impossible responses or extreme situations appear in which the strategic use of paradox is a subversive mechanism, in the context of elemental organisational systems (always the same basic sequential structure of the film) but which – due to its normed condition – is accordingly more flexible: open to the presence of unexpected situations, apparently absurd or fortuitous, but secretly interlinked by a basic infrastructure – a logic – which is as implacable as it is unforeseeable. As uncertain and surprising as it is direct and powerful.

A "direct logic," then, more bold, optimistic and unrestrained; more unhindered and uninhibited; disposed to fostering a decisive, but not imperative, action, in reality, born of synergy and interaction. But also of the – informal – redefinition of its more inertial movements.

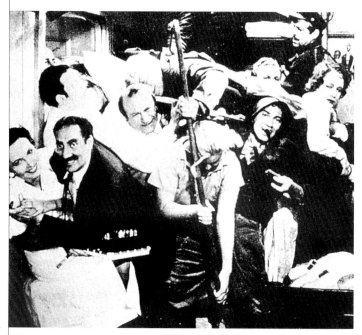

Marx Brothers.

✖ masses (silence)

➜ 'criteria', 'knowledge', 'Think Tank'

[VG] The masses are lost in the mass.

But we are seeing the rebirth of the individual who flees the city, hitherto a synonym of culture, to a new refuge in the middle of nowhere, or who flees in a constant attempt to follow the trace of digital information. Silence is his living space. With so much information-communication, silence is heaven.

✖◆ material

➜ 'architecture', 'information', 'lightness', 'logic, digital', 'matter', 'mutation', 'places', 'product'

[VG] Architecture's new construction material is information. Just as modern architecture is indebted to reinforced concrete, steel and glass, our age has not yet invented a material that changes the deep-rooted principles of construction. The process of re-information of the physical world means developing intelligent, re-active materials, that recognise the environmental or functional phenomena occurring around them and react with them.

[FS] To build, we use concrete, wood boards, glass block, cardboard, stone appliqué, video screens, letters, posters, bricks and plugs, cloths, shutters, florescent tubes, linings, acoustic tile lining hung backwards, glazed steel sheets, uralite, and concrete hydraulic tiles, sections or plans of other projects, natural light, water, sound, thoughts...

★ material world

[co] This city-artefact of which we speak appears as an amalgam, a heretofore unknown material; a conglomerate of natural, artificial and immaterial elements or flows, at once porous and fibrous, with dense and stable areas, charged with memory, and crude, ill-defined expanses, devoid of qualities, almost liquid; comprised of antithetical elements that have breached the precise, traditional boundaries between natural and artificial. If we were modern architects, we would think of this city in moral terms which would give rise to reformist policies. But it seems more necessary and, if you like, more appropriate, to architectural practice to find in this magma a poetic substratum, to understand it as an invitation to try out a new gaze and, through that, to reach a critical dimension. This material, the dissolution of the natural-artificial opposition on all scales entails a work programme that is none other than that of (re)describing through architecture the standing of contemporary man vis-à-vis the world.

IÑAKI ÁBALOS & JUAN HERREROS

✚ materiature

➜ 'matter', 'nature'

[WM] If in the technological economy we knew more and more about non-natural materials, in the scientific economy we know more and more about natural materials. From knowing a lot about plants we have learnt to make materials like plastics.

From all that we have learnt by making materials like plastics, we can now make materials like plants: GENETIC MATERIALS capable of containing information and intelligence.

Materiature is a certain boundary that we cross, knowing more and manipulating more information about nature, we create a new material landscape. Materiature is a different level of relationship between the natural and the artificial.

★ mathematics

→ 'algorithm', 'code',
'complexity', 'complex
system', 'diagrams',
'game', 'grids', 'informal',
'in/uncertainty', 'matrix',
'structure', 'system',
'topological'

[co] Mathematics is a formal system (elements and relations do without a referential content) that studies the relation between elements, with the purpose of enriching existing structures or creating new ones.

A structure is based on a well formed assumption, thus new well formed assumptions produce new structures. To enrich a structure is to add new non redundant statements that preserve coherence within the structure.

As an example, Euclidean geometry considers the Euclid's postulates (4th century) as an assumption. New geometries, thus new structures, were created considering other assumptions, different from the Euclid's postulates, such is the case of Projective geometry invented by Girard Desargues (17th century).

Euclid's postulates: 1. A straight line segment can be drawn joining any two points. 2. Any straight line segment can be extended indefinitely in a straight line. 3. Given any straight line segment, a circle can be drawn having the segment as radius and one endpoint as center. 4. All right angles are congruent. 5. If two lines are drawn which intersect a third in such a way that the sum of the inner angles on one side is less than two right angles, then the two lines inevitably must intersect each other on that side if extended far enough. This postulate is equivalent to what is known as the parallel postulate.

Projective geometry assumptions: 1. If A and B are distinct points on a plane, there is at least one line containing both A and B. 2. If A and B are distinct points on a plane, there is not more than one line containing both A and B. 3. Any two lines in a plane have at least one point of the plane (which may be the point at infinity in common. 4. There is at least one line on a plane. 5. Every line contains at least three points of the plane. 6. All the points of the plane do not belong to the same line (Veblen and Young 1938, Kasner and Newman 1989). FRANCISCO TOLCHINSKY

●◆★ matrix

→ 'link'

[MG] [FS] Generative infrastructure. See 'field', 'grids', 'networks', 'system' and 'topological'.

[co] Today's architect builds relationships. There are, in fact, invisible lines running between things. Material relationships, magnetic fields, sound waves, light beams, lines of particles, infrared radiation, structural lines, movements of particles, ultraviolet rays, energy interchanges, waves of heat and cold, currents of air, gas and water. There is, then, a matrix of relationships, a matrix of real relationships and another matrix of virtual relationships. A matrix in mathematics, programming, software, telephony, networks, genetics, fractals and chaos. A matrix that is structural and invisible, that is solid and electronic, that is kinetic and frozen, that is nano and cosmic. What's the bandwidth of this matrix?

A telephone-line architecture, ISDN, Internet 2, asphalt highways, planetary orbits, lasers, vector drawings, pen lines, copper circuits, nylon threads. The matrix must be constructed because it is real and we live within it. ENRIC RUIZ-GELI

Matrix sketch
of tremas,
in MANDELBROT,
Benoît, *Les objets
fractals*, Paris:
Flammarion, 1975.

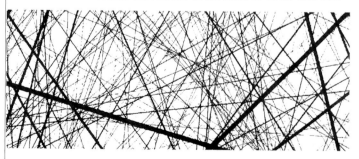

★ mats

[co]

Mat-building: category invented by Peter and Alison Smithson in the 1960s (Refer to: Alison Smithson: "How to Recognize and Read Mat-Building." 1974). Given the field-like sprawl of both European and American cities, a strategy that deserves reconsideration.

Mat-buildings are mostly similar in the way in which the parts fit together, and the character of the void spaces formed by their architectural matter. Internally, nearly all exhibit a porous interconnectivity, in which transitional spaces are as important as the nodes they connect. Externally, they are loosely bounded. Their form is governed more by the internal connection of part to part than by any overall geometric figure. They operate as field-like assemblages, condensing and redirecting the patterns of urban life, and establishing extended webs of connectivity both internally and externally.

Mat-building is a studied response to a fundamental urbanistic question: how to give space to the active unfolding of urban life without abrogating the architect's responsibility to provide some form of order. Mat-building proposes loose scaffolding based on the systematic organisation of the parts. Mat-building is based on an operative realism regarding the extent of the architect's design control. It recognises that authentic city culture is the product of many hands over an extended period of time. Finally, mat-building is anti-figural, anti-representational and anti-monumental. Its job is not to articulate or represent specified functions, but rather to create an open field where the fullest range of possible events might take place. This over-all intensity based on repetition and accumulation suggests that there is a scale threshold, below which mat-building effects are not visible. Mat-building cannot be isolated as an object (figure to ground); instead it activates context to produce new urban fields. The promise of mat-building is of things happening in the voids, outside of architecture's explicit envelope of control. Mat-building is characterized by active interstitial spaces, where matter shapes and channels the space between things, leaving room for the unanticipated. Finally, in a mat-building, transitions are not merely the neutral link between defined nodes; instead, nodes and links together form a continuous fabric of internally differentiated space. (See: Stan Allen, "Mat Urbanism" in CASE 2, Le Corbusier's Venice Hospital, Hashim Sarkis, Editor, Harvard University and Prestel, 2002) STAN ALLEN

Stan ALLEN,
Reconstruction of the Souks, Beirut, 1994, competition project.

◆ matter

[FS] Matter in architecture is elaborated substance. Concrete, metal sheets, etc. are not only abstract choices, but physicalities that must be established throughout a process. They contain more than colours, texture and odour that decorate an abstract and unlimited space. We do not use wood, but rather wood boards, strips, and elements. We do not use glass, unless it comes in specific dimensions and sizes. Material has precise form and processes of fabrication. It is prepared material, manufactured, or industrialized. This difference is profound in that it characterizes two ideas.

The first is that the form and methods of production or elaboration differentiate the same substance in different architectonic materials. It is possible that two substances of the same material are more different than two substances of different materials. A material also has a front and a back. Its position and orientation modify its conformation. To a large extent, we can intervene in these forms to invent or reuse.

The second is that these forms and sizes, can determine a space, a way of building, a structure, measurements or proportions, as much or more so that the style, universal measurements, constructive system, or the actual discipline. Material itself contains an architectural idea implicit within it.

✖●+ mayor

[VG] Mr Mayor: is your city advanced?

[MG] [WM] There are mayors for whom to build implies merely to occupy. For others to build means instead to create – stimulate – new environmental conditions: scenarios, landscapes or habitats which are more qualitative and advanced, more qualitative insofar as they are advanced.

● McDonaldization

[MG] George Ritzer (RITZER, George, *The McDonaldization of Society*, USA. Pine Forge Press, 2000) describes perfectly the generalised phenomenon of the standardised consumption that he defines as the "McDonaldization of society:"

"*The success of the McDonald's product has been to know how to go, at the time, a step further in the scientific management of assembly-line (Taylorite and Fordist) production incorporating into the object production industry the production of* cravings – *food as a first test (fast food and ice food) – but also, subsequently, the staging of consumption (malls and shopping centres), of leisure (package tours), of the spectacle (Hollywoodland or Disney World), of packaged culture ("cataloguism") and, finally, of the home as a common product – and good. In all cases, the success resides in knowing how to merge, behind a concept of broad consensus (the notion of "guaranteed product"), four pre-established principles easily assumable as basic apriorisms (or apparent guarantees): efficiency (direct relationship between appetite and satisfaction), profitability (an apparently good, less expensive product), predictability (an identifiable, recognisable, familiar image) and control (order, repetition and convincing hygienics).*" (Translated from Spanish.)

Snakes, reproduced from "L.A. Patterns" (*Progressive Architecture*).

1. *Superposition of messages,* Pekin, 1995 (Photograph: Anna Puyuelo).

2. NJIRIC+NJIRIC, *McDonalds Drive-In,* Maribor (Slovenja), 2000.

3. NL, *De Wilde Plek,* Delft (The Netherlands), 1999.

4. Lars Tunbjörk, in *Landet Utom Sij,* 1991.

McDonaldization is a phenomenon fully inserted into the mechanisms of consumer society and, therefore, subject to commercial patterns given to the generalisation – and trivialisation – of messages – common places of universal vocation (nostalgia for the rural, caricature of well-being, evocation of the atemporal, etc.) directed at the most rooted, stable and permanent of the collective imagination.

Surprisingly, codes are shared at the planetary scale by a nebulous middle class, which have turned its desires into an "elemental and abstract system of ideologies," as Roemer van der Toorn suggested. This, in effect, has manifested itself as a "pseudo-culture of consensus and acceptance," converted into an established value of consumerism. Such an institutionalised – or accepted – "pseudo-culture" ultimately affects numerous physical productions and transformations of our surroundings and our cities, in accordance with the apparent stability of a set of assumed codes that, however, should today, in turn cope, with a situation of rapid change.

Perhaps the greatest paradox of our present moment is to see how this progressive awareness of a scenario of change – in its mundane and technological manifestations and in the behaviours that the latter stimulate – coexists with scenarios, experiences, with behaviours or inertias anthropologically known as "slow:" atavistic routines, codes, traditions, habits, satisfactions that confront, probably as at no other moment in our history, the tried-and-true and the innovative, the atavistic and the fresh, the accepted and the unusual, the conservative and the new.

A "paradoxical" territory is thus articulated around us, generated through the potency of the large structural systems of mobility and communication that vertebrate it (capable of linking singular, unique, unusual places and events) but, at the same time, developed, simultaneously and figuratively (in real-estate or building operations which ultimately mark their identity), through the frustrating and venomous uncouthness of often inappropriate, prefigured, straight-jacket patterns in economies, spaces and uses that they foster and in their associated iconographies and constructional techniques.

● **mcguffins**

→ 'chuncking',
'score', 'surface',
'suspense'

[MG] False trail (or situation). Mcguffins are misleading bits of information; apparent trajectories or scenarios of intrigue in which real facts of imagined principles are not recognised.

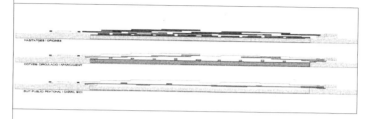

ADD Arquitectura, *Urban Sequences*, Barcelona, 2000.

●★■ **m. city (or multicity)**

→ 'avatar>urban',
'e-city', 'global city',
'hyperplace', 'islands',
'layers', 'mayor',
'Metapolis', 'multilayered',
'networks', 'place of
places', 'plaits', 'stains,
ink', 'territory', 'urbs'

[MG] *"In the mid-20th century, those who thought about cities believed that they were clearly organized, simply ordered, and thus predictable, capable of being designed and planned in such a way that the quality of life of their residents would be directly improved by manipulating their physical form. This was the view widely held in architecture and, of course, the social sciences. It was grounded in the belief that the social world, and the representation of its objects (such as cities themselves), was coherent and comprehensible in the same way that the physical world had been understood since the Enlightenment. It was argued that the triumph of rationality through the application of a scientific method could be transferred completely and emulated in the social world. The result was a deliberate attempt at social engineering, as well as in the sort of architecture and urban planning that has dominated Western societies over the past 50 years and, now, the developing world.*

As we approach the third millennium, all this looks a bit naive. The rational scientific programme has been split as under in the last twenty years. Our understanding of small-scale systems does not provide us with nor does it clarify our understanding of the large scale. The whole is more than the sum of its parts, and the physical, as a basis for everything, has been widely discredited. The limits imposed by incomplete theories of uncertainty and complexity have destroyed any hope of complete understanding and, despite there being some who still believe that the physical will produce more profound theories, there is little hope of this providing anything more than a diffuse logic. The dreams of a final theory are an illusion. Systems, everywhere, are simply too complex to be reduced to those sustained by conventional science."

(Paraphrasing BATTY, Michael, "The fractal city", *Architectural Design 9/10*, vol. 67, 1997)

[co] The polycentric city can be conceived as a constellation of attractors. If the traditional city had developed a structure of organic growth that had in turn informed the classic planning techniques built on models of centrality, homogeneity, continuity, hierarchy, etc., then the contemporary city, exposed to the

instability of late-capitalist modes of production, cannot maintain the rigidity of an organic structure that articulates the urban phenomena within an overall structure. Urban topographies therefore tend to grow in an environment that is no longer structured by the city-territory opposition, but rather by the transport and communications infrastructure as a vector of mobility.

The territorial organisation derived from a "liquid economy" tends to disintegrate the urban body to in turn extend it over the territory while multiplying centrality. The polycentric and inorganic structures that characterise emergent urban topographies are more capable of integrating the erratic demands of late-capitalist production.

This "liquefaction" of urban structure sparks a discontinuous and unarticulated growth. The polycentrality of the Ville-Nouvelles of Paris, the cities of the American Sunbelt and Central European conurbations like the Ruhrgebiet and the Randstaat are examples of this tendency towards discontinuity in the urban fabric. Cities built as constellations of attractors defy both the gravitational criteria of traditional urban models and the decentralised and isotropic models of the modern city.

Within emergent urban models, centre-periphery and exterior-interior dialectics give way to polycentric and a-hierarchical systems, networks or rhizomes, more capable of operating effectively in unstable states. The city is built around lines of movement or connection, more topologically than geometrically. The urban structure becomes an unregulated, superconductive topography capable of continuous self-reorientation according to the changing flows it must capture.

ALEJANDRO ZAERA-POLO

[co]   This artefact-city of which we speak appears as an amalgam, a heretofore unknown material, a conglomerate of natural, artificial and immaterial elements, at once porous and fibrous, with dense and stable areas, made up of antithetical elements that have breached the precise, traditional boundaries. If we were modern architects, we would think of this city in moral terms, giving rise to reformist policies. But it seems more necessary — and, if you like, more linked to architectural practice — to find in this magma a poetic substratum, to understand it as an invitation to try out a new gaze and, through that, reach a new critical dimension. This material entails a work programme that is none other than that of redescribing through architecture contemporary man's opposition to the world.

IÑAKI ÁBALOS & JUAN HERREROS

[JM]   The city would be better if it would really let us dislocate ourselves. Being realistic, the city always had something to do with war. We recuperate human relations as a measure of urban and public space. To public space, without necessary architectonic accompaniments, one must add only the reverberations of the city. The future city will consist in the relation of these other voices with the subject.

[co]   For us to more fully understand the impact of the digital and of globalization, we need, therefore, to suspend the category "city." Rather, we need to construct a more abstract category of centrality and of spaces of centrality, that, ironically, could allow us to recover the city, albeit a recovery as just one instantaion within a much broader set of issues.

SASKIA SASSEN

■ meaning

→ 'form', 'goodbye
to the metaphor',
'I/(my)self', 'indefinition',
'knowledge', 'language',
'name', 'rhyzomatic'

[JM]

The question about the meaning of architecture has not only to do with the investigation about its origin (G. Teyssot,), but also, in a certain way, it is a form of response to the events around us. It seems that this teleological meaning, which any architecture faced in the seventies, has given way to an exploration in which architecture is an unexplored field. Or, architecture seems like an accident, and as such is radically different from all architectures. Authors (architects) have stopped resembling others and retreated to self-investigations. In other words, if before what was wanted was a common language, now it seems that the babble of many works explains loneliness. Before the question, "what does a work say?" invited one explore the work and its facets, not discourse. Meaning is not about an investigation about codes, of repeatable structures, equipped languages. Meaning in architecture is not an analysis about 'the same old thing,' but about difference.

✕ Media Lab

→ 'action> critical',
'innovation',
'logic, digital'

[VG]

The Media Lab is the Bauhaus of the information society. The list of projects by MIT's Media Lab (founded in 1985) presents a programme of action for investigation and development as digital information is superposed on the physical world we live in every day. Here are some examples:

Consortia: Digital Life (DL), News in the Future (NiF), Things That Think (TTT). Special Interest Groups: Broadercasting, CC++, Counter Intelligence, e-markets, Gray Matters, Penny PC, Toys of Tomorrow (TOT).

Research Groups: Aesthetics and Computation, Affective Computing, Context Aware Computing, Electronic Publishing, Epistemology and Learning, Explanation Architecture, Gesture & Narrative Language, Interactive Cinema, Machine Listening, Machine Understanding, Micromedia, Nanoscale Sensing, Object-Based Media, Opera of the Future, Personal Information Architecture, Physics and Media, Responsive Environments, Sociable Media, Software Agents, Spatial Imaging, Speech Interface, Synthetic Characters, Tangible Media, Vision and Modelling. (www.media.mit.edu)

MEDIA LAB (MIT),
Tod Machover has
developed a radiobaton
which reads the
movements of
his hand to conduct
an orchestra in
the memory of his
computer
(Peter Menzel).

● meldings

[MG] See 'cuttings (and slips).'

● membrane

→ 'elastic', 'equipped façade', 'equipped wall', 'flexibility', 'inflatable', 'skin'

[MG] A membrane is the thin layer of organic, elastic and resistant tissue which separates two cavities or envelops an organ.

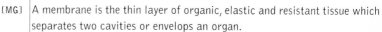

R&Sie... (François ROCHE, Stephanie LAVAUX), *Barak House*, Sommières (France), 2001.

NOX (Lars Spuybroek with Joan Almekinders, Dominik Holzer, Sven Pfeiffer, Wolfgang Novak, Remco Wilcke), *wetGRID, exhibition design for 'Vision Machine'*, Musée des Beaux Arts, Nantes (France), 1999-2000.

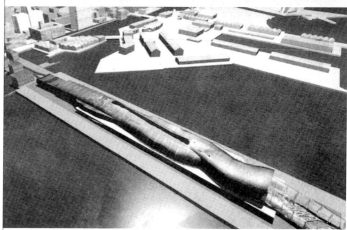

Greg LYNN, *International Port Terminal*, Yokohama (Japan), competition, 1994.

●+■▲ memory

[MG] Memory is always selective, with timely tactical lapses.

[MG] *"She was there with her hand on María's cheek, listening for a long, long time. But she wrote down nothing of what she heard. Nothing."* (ENQUIST, Olov, *The Fallen Angel*, Ed. la Torre) (At the suggestion of Marc Aureli Santos. Translated from Spanish.)

[MG] *"The question against which a truly modern architecture should be able to pit itself is that of getting rid of traces. "Erase all traces!" To erase all traces means never repeating what we have said, it means renouncing our thoughts when repeated by others, it means never endorsing or spreading our own image, it means not letting them write your name on your grave. "Erase all traces!" means, then: don't let time trap you, don't try to get to grips with a space, don't speak just one tongue or just one language, never create a style and don't hope, under any circumstances, to set yourself apart through your taste and manners, never give in to the family or those you used to know, do not build a monument or set yourself up as a monument. The question of a contemporary architecture remains unanswered until we discover the almost ontological dimension of the trace. Heidegger stresses this common dimension of existence and architecture when, referring to the German word* bauen *(to build) and its etymology, he reminds us that it is the same word as* bin *(to be). "Erase all traces!" until you reach the limit where space changes radically."* (GARCÍA DUTTMANN, Alexander, "Getting rid of traces", *Quaderns* 211, 1995)

[WM] *"Memory is the stupidest dog, you throw it a stick and it comes back with something else."* (LORIGA, Ray, *Tokyo ya no nos quiere*, Barcelona: Plaza&Janés, 1999)

[JM] Beyond realities, history is also fragmentary, unrepeatable: "that which can not happen twice," just like a project. Not to work with memory of will, that which turns back, in an attempt to replace what can not be substituted. Without will and without nostalgia. Memory leans on the non-linear character of time and its figures. It bases itself on distortion and remake. Memory works with "what links saying goodbye." It ties together what disappears, acts on what dilutes, as though to date itself on new origins.

[FP] To be honest, I don't remember needing memory.

S&Aa (SORIANO-
PALACIOS),
Fleta Theatre,
Zaragoza (Spain),
2001.

● menus

[MG] Our surroundings appear as multifaceted menus of opportunities, able to supply a large quantity of situations and needs along the length of their arteries. The new city-dweller favours a weighted development of this diverse and manifold choice, prioritising difference over repetition and singularity vis-à-vis standardisation. Menus also favour the dissolution of the old environment of protection and supply, of homogeneity and uniformity (habitat, territory or clan), into a new, more sporadic – and contingent – type of contract with the environment, made up of territories of individual affirmation subject to a potential reversibility of situations and decisions, resulting from the progressive increase in mobility as a functional and ludic accompaniment to a new type of uprooted and opportunist existentialism. Like the contemporary city itself, an advanced architecture also favours the coexistence of diverse and simultaneous events: of combinations and superpositions. Of types and subtypes. Of conventional programmes and new contemporary programmes. Of energies captured and projected. Of multiple and interlinked experiences. Like the city itself, advanced architecture also structures itself as a menu of events, movements and opportunities.

+ Mercabarna (Barcelona central supply market)

→ 'areas of opportunity'

[WM] "*Man only became aware of his dominance over things and phenomena when he acquired the means to measure them. And when he learnt how to measure things he could exchange them, turning them into merchandise, and there emerged a new point of reference: the Market. If man is the measure of things, the market is the measure of merchandise. Supply and demand will determine the true measure of products.*" Jordi Maymó, general manager of Mercabarna.

Wholesale food markets have become, over fifty years, veritable market-cities in a process of expansion and transformation that encompasses problems of architectural scale – trade fairs, the market – and those of the urban scale – the central supply markets. The emergence of new technologies in consumption habits will turn market-cities into warehouse-cities. The real forces of supply and demand that have invariably sustained markets, whatever their scale, are becoming a virtual force. Tele-presence and teleaction will change within this century the idea of the market, opening them up to another dimension: the possibility of becoming theme parks.

WMA Willy Müller Arquitectos, *New Mercabarna flower market*, Barcelona, 2002-.

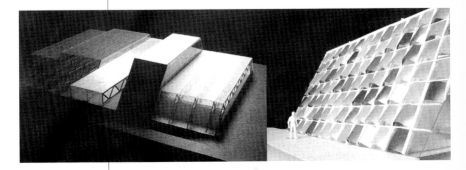

●✕+ Metapolis

[MG]

(multicity)

FRANÇOIS ASCHER

MÉTAPOLIS
OU L'AVENIR DES VILLES

ASCHER, François ,
*Métapolis, ou l'avenir
des villes*, Paris:
Odile Jacob, 1995.

The contemporary Metapolis constitutes, as François Ascher points out in his essay *Métapoles ou l´avenir des villes* (Paris: Ed. Odile Jacob, 1995), a reality that transcends and comprehends, from diverse points of view, the metropolises we have known until now, fostering a new type of urban agglomeration made of multiplied, heterogeneous and discontinuous spaces and relationships.

They are produced by urban entities that are increasingly more loosely linked in terms of hierarchy (progressively less relatable to circumstances of spatial or contextual proximity) and, on the contrary, progressively associated with dislocated and fluctuating dynamics with reference to the variable "residence-production-service-leisure" relationships.

The term 'Metapolis' defines this new multiple and multifaceted dimension of the contemporary city.

A reality "beyond" that of the traditional metropolis. A reality of a vibrant system that is similar – generic or recurrent – on a global sale and diversified – specific – scale – on a local scale.

If the old notion of Metropolis answered to the mechanics of production (of objects), that is to say, to a physical and expansive growth (radial and more or less uniform) around a polarising centre, then the notion of Metapolis refers to a more polyhedral, matrix, diversified and elastic development, produced within a changing and multifaceted framework, generated "beyond" the physical or the merely geographic.

The Metapolis represents a framework of relationships – and qualitative productions – based upon the processing and combination of simultaneous bits of information.

The Metapolis is no longer be expressed only in terms of growth but also, in combinations; combinations that allude to evidence of an informational, dynamical and uncertain process, made up of interactions with the territory and with other territories; with the place and with other places.

The Metapolis is no longer a single place or a particular shape, nor a unique evolutionary stage, but rather the accumulation of multiple stages and simultaneous experiences.

Beyond the Metropolis, the contemporary Metapolis appears as an elastic and vibrant system defined by relationships between movements and events which are simultaneously interlinked and autonomous.

A multifaceted system of articulating networks and layers of information, of vague, fluctuating and variables outlines.

A changing scenario which can only be represented by "opportunist cartographies" that refer to those appropriately implemented tactical aspects.

A structure which is both analogous and different at the same time.

A structure, in effect, of similar dynamics on a global scale and of different situations on a local scale, made up of collisions, encounters and intersections that eventually generate a great variety of specific and plural combinations.

A spectrum of cities and of cities within the city. This is the essence of the contemporary Metapolis: a "hyper-place," a "place of places," a rich global kaleidoscope of local choices and opportunities.

To speak of the Metapolis is therefore to speak of this multicity – this meta-place or "place of places" – identifiable, more abstractly and less physically, as a multiple, multi-layered structure made up of different, superposed transformations-evolutions – combinatorial incarnations (or realities): a framework "of network" or "of networks," dynamic, fluctuating and definitively unfinished, comprising singular situations and changing relationships.

The territory of this new Metapolis is, therefore, a complex system of simultaneous relationships and events, determined – as already expressed – on the basis of the greater or lesser effectiveness of the possible combinations between successive layers of activity and definition which characterise it, and the large-scale structural networks that articulate it: layers and networks between which processes of action and reaction occur, and between which also appear zones of fading (disconnections, layers with little or no information, levels of absence: fadings as backgrounds).

Such a structure, constructed on the basis of interactions between *layers*, *networks* and *backgrounds* refers to other possible synthetical combinations that allude to this progressively abstract and informational dimension of the contemporary city, which can be compared, in its more physical sense, to these trinomials: voids-fills-articulations, constructions-landscapes-infrastructures and archipelagos (volumes)-free spaces (interstices)-arteries (supports).

A system, in sum, of mobile, variable and discontinuous limits (geographical and "contractual"), according to the different agents that tend to influence it and whose effective approach should foster the movement of this new complex situation – strategic and plural – beyond the simple literal representation of its apparent shapes.

[VG] Beyond the metropolis of the industrial era emerges the Metapolis of the digital era. The city is now a place of places, where numerous urban models coexist, each with its own qualities that make it different from the rest.

In the Metapolis, the dwelling becomes a place where we live, work and rest – thanks to audiovisual and telematic systems – where the neighbourhood is a multinational environment of direct relation between citizens and where zoning no longer has any meaning. The Metapolis creates complete environments (dwelling, leisure, commerce, education) in the proximity of the dwelling.

[WM] **(association)**

Abbreviation: MET.

"*If everything seems under control, it's just that you're not going fast enough.*" Mario Andretti, former Formula 1 champion.

"*Ready... Fire... Aim!*" Wayne Calloway, former president of PepsiCo.

✖ metareality

→ 'reality', 'virtual'

[VG] Metareality is the broadest most perfect interface for action in the world, the place where the physical and the digital meet.

Metareality is a new state in the physical world, transformed by the energy of the virtual world.

Metareality emerges from the re-information of the physical world.

It is an environment where places are sensitive to people, and where the generosity of creation receives the impetus of a new digital culture.

Where the best source of information about the world is reality itself.

Where all matter and all empty space connect with each other and, in turn, with individuals. Where total disconnection is also possible.

Where cities exist as nodes in the planetary network. Of the global village. And are splendid. And transform themselves to accept their new state.

Where the arts and sciences are related in virtual and metareal exploration. Where the two worlds are compatible.

Where weightlessness exists and is inhabited. Where the virtual world, with its new physics and its immaterial condition, is inspiration for the construction of the physical world.

Where emptiness is a rare commodity that has to be treasured as though it were gold.

Where nature and its fractal order are inspiration for the construction of the physical world.

Where all things are as different as their users are.

Where educated man, with the capacity to make decisions, is once again the centre of the world.

The necessary condition for preventing a rupture between a hypothetical virtual world – fantastic, full of creative energy, in a constant state of transformation, where the planet's best brains work for its construction, as it generates a new economy – and a solid physical world – heavy, weighed down by a history, conditioned by tradition – is for the two worlds to be the same; for the virtual world to affect and transform the physical world at the same time as it constructs itself, not just economically and socially, but culturally, and spatially; for each innovation in the virtual world to transform the physical world.

The Sims, computer game.

● **M'house houses**

[MG]   The MOAI Project (Optional Module of Interurban Accommodation), in its *M'house* version, proposes a menu of combinable "modular spaces" defined by a fixed structural section, designed jointly with an industrial storage company, which permits lateral and vertical assembly and the subsequent incorporation of different types of outer walls with different materials, colours and textures. Combinable modules (as in the case of multi-shape furniture) are juxtaposed and superposed so as to give an unlimited number of spatial solutions based upon the variation of a limited number of space types, with the appropriate technical variants (storage-warehouse, walls furnished for bathrooms and kitchens, elements of vertical communication, etc.). The solution is conceived as an "à la carte" product, not just in the choice of the colour or the external pattern or motif, but rather in the actual design of the final distribution (a personal solution for each case always based upon a distinguishable device), which brings the product closer to the strategy of the multi-furniture industry than to that of the automobile or watch.

The structure of the modules means, in effect, that the home can be constructed or expanded lengthwise, in width or height. This maximum flexibility implies, conversely, standardised dimensions for the floors and the partition walls. The result of this repetition fosters a versatile system, which can be dry-mounted and transported to the mountains, the sea or the city. According to the place and to changing tastes, the future inhabitant chooses the materials, the colours and the components of the façades, which can be changed at a later date. A space for transit is left free around the perimeter – the furnished nuclei occupies the centre – leaving more space and freedom of movement in each of the rooms.

The "catalogue-house" theme can thus be seen as another application of this desirable relationship between industry and design that aims to foster versatile systems that are simpler, quicker and more economical, but also more personalised; solutions which are technically precise in their spatial configuration, even reversible in their construction, in harmony with a more modern – and thus more open and unrestrained – conception of the shape and the use of residential space.

ACTAR ARQUITECTURA,
M'House Houses, 1997.

▲● midget & giant

[FP] **(businesses)**

Technology has provoked a constant incrementation in business activities which has transformed the growth of certain companies, but fundamentally in the absorption of other companies, buying partial interests, liquidations, etc. Similarly, cities, have to confront the same problems of size and pollution, as well as poor productivity, slow bureaucracy, etc. The opposite reaction is development of small and medium size enterprises, more specialised in very specific fields which will bankrupt the big companies. We can ask ourselves if this phenomenon could be comparable to the immediate future of our cities.

[FP] **(scale)**

"*Nature cannot make a huge horse with twenty horses, nor a giant ten times taller than a man, without a miraculous basis or making great changes to the proportions of its members and in particular to its bones, increasing their size well beyond the symmetry of the bones in common. Believing equally that artificial machines are feasible and preservable [proportionally passing] from the biggest to the smallest, without suffering specific modifications is a manifest error: so, for example, small pinnacles, columns and other solid shapes, surely could be distended and curled without the risk of getting broken, while at the same time increasing proportionately in size, they could be smashed to pieces for reasons other than their own weight.*" (GALILEI, Galileo, *Discorzi e Dimostrazioni matematiche*, 1638)

Price of the wheat and wages development (William Playfair, 1821), in *OASE* 48, 1998.

[MG] **(coexistences)**

'Dwarf-giant' speaks of the small and the large together. Joining hands. Sizes, scales, concerted shapes and programmes in mutual coexistence and interaction. Atypical – rather than harmonious, "negotiated" – situations. Tactical, unencumbered contracts between heterogeneous – strangely complicit – events beyond the conventions of the orthodoxly provided. Synergies, rather than contradictions.

1. *Midget-giant,* in GAUSA, Manuel, *Housing. New alternatives, new systems*, Barcelona: ACTAR, 1998.

2. *Meeting of extremes,* in NEUBAUER, Hendrik, *Curious moments*, Köln: Könemann, 1999.

★ ● *millefeuilles*

[MG] See 'puff pastry' and 'laminate.'

[co] *Millefeuilles* is a laminated or puffed up construction, capable of placating flexibility, lightness and superposition. In it, the construction system extends the concept of accumulating layers: structural layers, programmatic layers, finishes layers, etc.
ALEJANDRO ZAERA-POLO

★ mimetic architecture

[co] Many organisms practice mimesis in order to survive or just to have more a peaceful and modest presence; snakes in the desert, fish and marine animals in the sea. To protect themselves, they mimetic and imitate acts and rites of other organisms in their immediate surroundings. Mimetic architecture looks to reduce the informative charge either in the city or in the landscape. Normally, mimesis is reached by mimicry acts or by mimetic materials. Skin and colours are the most used systems. In the future, we will see architecture doing real acts of mimicry, imitating noises, breathing or producing fog and vapour.
SALVADOR PÉREZ ARROYO

S. PÉREZ ARROYO
& E. HURTADO
(with F. RÍO DURAN),
*Covered swimming
pool*, Tomelloso
(Spain), 2002.

● ★ mixed-use

[MG] See 'livrid'.

[co] Mixed-use refers to an idea of space, alien to the programme and the natural environment, which contradicts the historical experience of constructed space, its known forms of classification.
Both in its academic formulation – the "type" – and in the mechanical – the "type-object" – architecture admitted a formal classification based upon processes of formal refinement: the use of space and the mediation of the exterior physical environment were, to a large extent, objective crystallising agents of form. The type-object and the model-topology dialectic converged in an order that in the last instance pointed to function, whether the latter was interpreted through mimesis or faith in invention as instruments of certainty. Nonetheless, the contemporary interior space has severed these links with the exterior environment and function. Artificial space lessens the active presence of the subject identified in the function. This loss of programme has as its dual and apparently paradoxical consequence – i.e., a double characterisation of the equipped space – a maximum subjectivity of the processes of particular conformation and a progressive homogenisation of the support space, which inevitably tend to be constructed with substantially identical procedures. This implies a different idea of high-rise, of periphery, of type and of function, a different idea of urban space, a historical and afunctional topos: the destruction of modern technological, typological and urban paradigms, thus comes full circle.
IÑAKI ÁBALOS & JUAN HERREROS

ÁBALOS&HERRROS,
*Self-sufficient hybrid
towers*, Madrid, 1994.

● mmm

[MG] "MMM: Mountain range."

(GÓMEZ de la SERNA, Ramón, *Greguería*).

● model: Lotka-Volterra

[MG] "*A predator-prey system in nature works like a dynamic system. In this engine, the respective biomasses of two species are interlinked by a set of simple equations, the Lotka-Volterra formula of mathematical ecology. Within this dynamic system the natural equivalent to our arms races develops between predators and prey, and according to zoologist Richard Dawkins, the mutual stimulation of pairs like armour/claw or visual acuity/camouflage is what accounts for the advanced and complex machinery that animals and plants possess.*" (DE LANDA, Manuel, *War in the Age of Intelligent Machines*, New York: Zone Books, 1991)

● ★ models

[MG] See 'animation,' 'construction, intelligent,' 'delynneate' and 'simulation.'

[co] A model is a satisfactory interpretation of a given phenomenon.
Satisfactory in the sense that given any valid input the interpretation will produce an output that it is coherent with our understanding of that given phenomenon. Physics tries to explain (model) reality, thus different models in Physics are related to different understandings of reality.
In many cases, the understanding of a phenomenon varies as the purpose of the model changes. FRANCISCO TOLCHINSKY

★ modern

→ 'advanced', 'architecture', 'contemporary'

[co] The utopian aspirations of the Movement Modern involved tearing down obsolete spatial hierarchies with a homogeneous and new space, meant to spur widespread processes of substitution or negation. However, the cry for heterogeneity and diversity today takes the place of this impossible tabula rasa state: erasure yields to reconfiguration. It can be achieved within a certain modern tradition, beyond its abstraction and formal language; through a flexible reinterpretation of modernity that can embrace the current conditions of the place and the city.
The modern project — that of a new universal order — is today revealed to be more ineffective and incomplete the more removed it is shown to be from the specificity of a diverse, singular and particular reality in each situation. KELLY SHANNON

★ monotony and repetition

→ 'gaze', 'reality'

[co] Lluís Clotet says that the revered elder brothers of his schoolmates were in reality frail children of the post-war. That the long years of endless summers were in reality just two, and the holidays ten days.
In Gombrowictz, things are only known fragmentarily, expressed partially, grasped randomly, recalled accidentally. Small and fragile is the amount of reality we are able to perceive.
Monotony and repetition are necessary conditions for invigorating our relationship with reality. Monotony and repetition are conditions required for the distracted gaze (Benjamin) that is lent – probably deservingly so – to architecture to be fruitful.
Monotony is the seedbed from which novelty springs. EDUARD BRU

◆● moral

[FS] "*Vulnerable but obstinate, unjust and passionate for justice, building work in view of all, without shame or pride, always in tension between pain and beauty, and destined, in the end, to extract from its dual self the creations that stubbornly deal with building within the destructive action of history. That said, who can hope from it well-rounded solutions and beautiful morals.*

The truth is mysterious, fugacious, and always to be conquered. Freedom is dangerous, as passionate as it is difficult to live. We must march towards these two objectives, painfully, but resolutely, knowing beforehand the languor in which we will fall during such a long walk. What writer would venture, then with a good conscience, to establish himself as the preacher of virtue?"

(CAMUS, Albert, "Discurso de Suecia", 1957)

[MG] Many people think we are making propaganda. Intellectual speculation... or the other kind. Or, in the best of cases, philosophy. Perhaps we are talking rather about attitude. About disposition. Or, if you prefer, about morals.

[MG] "*The British physicist Ernest Rutherford declared at the end of the reductionist era that the qualitative (in science) was nothing more than a quantitative evil, something that no longer holds true today. Today, only the qualitative seems capable of penetrating the glaucous film that envelops the world of numbers. Only when architecture finds the value of doing its job as a form of thought, will it understand its enormous capacity for producing knowledge and not only for deducing it.*

Architecture is more than ever a matter of conscience. To involve oneself in and with the system of a society totally dedicated to communication and, therefore, that generates knowledge, is then a need as much as a betrayal, at a time of inexorable contradictions."

(KWINTER, Sanford. "Beaubourg: nécessité et trahison", en GUIHEUX, Alain, *Architecture Instantanée*, Paris: Ed. Centre G. Pompidou, 2000. Translated from Spanish.)

★ morphing

[CO] Unlike the disjunction of collage that has characterised much of this century, morphing is the newest device.

Where collage merely superimposes material from different contexts, morphing operates through them, blending them.

True to the technologies of their respective times, collage is mechanical whereas morphing is alchemical.

Sphinx, werewolf, gargoyle and griffin are the mascots of this time.

Morphing has genetic character, not surgical; more like genetic cross-breeding than transplanting.

Where collage emphasised differences by recontextualising the familiar, the morphing operation blends the unfamiliar in ways that illuminate unsuspected similarities.

MARCOS NOVAK

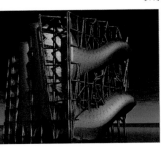

Marcos NOVAK,
Paracube, 1997-98.

●✕ mountain

→ 'artificial', 'ecology, 'active', 'geography', 'iceberg', 'immersed', 'land-arch', 'land(s) in lands', 'natuficio', 'naturartificial', 'nature', 'occupations', 'reliefs'

[MG] Large-scale elevation – natural or artificial – of the terrain.// Territory formed by various reliefs.// Also a possible genre of hobby, recreation or sport, in the real or figurative sense.

[VG] Mountains are concentrations of natural or artificial energy that can be inhabited. They are ascale folds in extra or intra-urban land.

They are accumulations of matter. Organic or economic.

The organic mountain emerges as part of a natural cycle, in the form of the folding of sedimentary strata, of the thrust of internal forces, or as a magmatic eruption.

The artificial mountain emerges as an instant accumulation of man's activity. His intellectual, economic, human, religious activity.

The mountain defines its instant form as a product of its origins and of the interaction with its environment.

A mountain has neither beginning nor end. We can observe just one moment in its history.

A mountain is an X-ray of a place. Its section shows us its history. It is near and far environments allow us to predict its future.

The mountain has absolutely no predisposition to a predetermined shape. The mountain is constructed more as a process than as an event with a beginning and an end. It is constructed by fractal geometry, allowing complex relations between its parts, following a coherent process.

The crystalline arrangement of its atoms conditions its final shape. It gives it its colour and texture.

The interactions of its microscopic components with the conditions of the environment define its final shape.

Its upper limit is the ground, the limit between fullness and emptiness. Between all the mass of the earth and the atmosphere that surrounds it. The mountain's skin may have different resolutions according to the conditions of the environment. Each chemical organisation of its raw material generates a form with its own resolution.

Rocks are a part of the mountain constructed in its likeness. They concentrate information about the whole. In terms of size, the rock may be likened to human beings.

Different types of mountains can be recognised:

The interior mountain is a cavity in a mass. It is a space without light and, therefore, adirectional.

The ground mountain is a flat space, where interior and exterior blend with no discontinuity. It is a horizon that moves.

The rock-mountain is a vigorous irregularity in a terrain that energetically manifests the presence of local interior forces that have modified that place.

The light-mountain is an accumulation of activity, of light, of gas.

Building is a natural act that generates economic, human, material and cultural sediments. Buildings, mountains form a coherent system with the place's other energies.

VIOLLET LE DUC, *Geometrical studies of the Alps natural reliefs.*

UN STUDIO, *Museum Het Valkhof,* Kelfkensbos Nijmegen (The Netherlands), 1998.

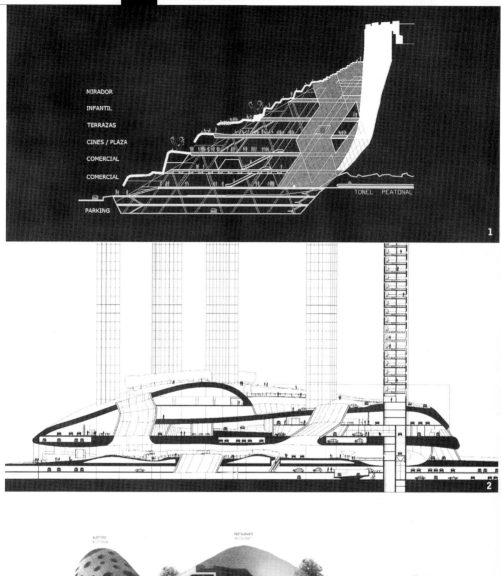

MIRADOR
INFANTIL
TERRAZAS
CINES / PLAZA
COMERCIAL
COMERCIAL
PARKING

TONEL PEATONAL

1

2

AUDITORIO
AUDITORIUM

RESTAURANTE
RESTAURANT

OFICINAS CERRADAS
ENCLOSED OFFICES

SALAS DE REUNIONES
MEETING ROOMS

SALAS DE REUNIONES
MEETING ROOMS

ASEOS
TOILETS

OFICINAS CERRADAS
ENCLOSED OFFICES

APARCAMIENTO
PARKING

3

1. Vicente GUALLART, *Multifunctional centre,* Denia (Spain), 2002. **2.** ÁBALOS & HERREROS, *Consultation for the Poble Nou District,* Barcelona, 1999. **3.** MVRDV, *Silicone Hill,* Stockholm (Sweden), 2000, competition for the Sweden Post Headquarters.

◆ mouthfuls

[FS] See 'holes.'

NL, *Y2K+*,
Den Haag
(The Netherlands),
1999.

■ movement (*movida*)

→ 'dynamism',
'tropism'

[JM] The space of the contemporary city has not only changed quantitatively, but also qualitatively, and this quality is not only what is seen, but also what is hidden. Hiding is a way of resistance and defence. To make objects or the ground of the city become bodies, in other words, as a consequence of the desires of the subjects (G. Deleuze) is also another possibility. Perhaps it also begins to assume that bodies "go over the top" (hysteria) and as a consequence we accept these extra-limitations (movements) as the erotica of the city in which we live.

★ movie

→ 'trailers'

[CO] Movie "… will refer to a quaint media activity kept alive by a small but passionate group, like the term "radio play" today." Andrew Glassner

● m-section

[MG] See 'section' and 'stack (stacks).'

Neil DENARI
Architects,
*Multisection Office
Block*, Los Angeles
(California, USA),
1998.

●◆ *muaré* or *moiré*

[MG] The term *moiré* (which means "rippled surface" or "glossy surface") indicates a texture produced by the overprinting of grids (or webs). The paradigmatic effect of *moiré* is based upon the idea of superposition: the combination of pseudo-regular elements produces complex and uncertain effects that demonstrate apparently irregular behaviour. The accompanying effects of *moiré* are not the result of chance but rather of chaos, an unforeseen interaction of events: patterns or structures that change abruptly in scale and behave in accordance with complex mathematical rules. In each case, a regular field coexists with an emergent, sporadic and unusual figure, and this gives rise to a sensation of unexpected profundity in an apparently elemental order.

[FS] *Moiré* is a strong fabric that forms washes. Printed, it is produced when a photograph that has many hatches, must re-hatch itself to print in another medium. Both hatches enter into conflict with one another, and instead of superimposing and negating each other, a new drawing is produced that discomposes the printed image. In physics, moiré is the geometric drawing that becomes visible when a series of lines is superimposed over another series. They are independent from the original. We can think that the effect is the result of combinations (be they folds, hatched, matrices). We can be interested in the result as a mechanism of producing unseen results. We can follow the sounds of unheard words. There are also concepts associated to this that are worth reflection. Bi-dimensional profundity. A representation of space that is different from the classical one (a circle in the ground and a perpendicular arrow). Today, the entire circle plays the role of perpendicularity.

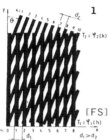

1

2

3

4

5

6

1. Geometrical description of a *moiré*, in *BAU* 014, 1996.
2. Superpositions, in *Archt+* 144-145, 1998.
3. S&Aa (SORIANO-PALACIOS), *Competition for cultural centre and auditorium*, Benidorm (Alicante, Spain), 1995.
4. Toyo ITO, *Nomad Restaurant*, Tokyo, 1986. (Photograph: Tomio Ohashi).
5. IaN+, *New Tomhiro Museum Of Shi-Ga*, Azuma (Japan), 2001.
6. S&Aa (SORIANO-PALACIOS), *Competition for bus station*, Talavera de la Reina (Toledo, Spain), 2000.

●▲ multi

[MG] Multi comes from the Latin *multus* ("much", "many"). The prefix MUL-TI alludes to a multiplicative action, implicit in the contemporary evolutionary device.

MULTI as in multiple, multiplied and multiplicative. But also as in multivalent, multifunctional, multinuclear, multifaceted and multilayered: a combined cohabitation of events overlapping with virtually growing, dynamical and complex – i.e. polyhedral – arrangements. Accordingly, MULTI points to POLY, as in polyphase, polycentric and polyfaceted. Plural. One and many at the same time. Not only additive – or adding up – but, above all, multiplicative.

[FP] **(multiplicity)**

Condition of a subject, element or thing which has the ability to amplify and reproduce any phenomenon and to give different answers to the same request , or on contrary to give a suitable answer to different requirements. Multiplicity is generation not repetition.

[MG] **(multiply)**

"x", not "+" nor "-", nor "="

The traditional, established and single significance of the old categories tends to yield to definitions which are less finished and more diffuse (polyhedral and multifaceted) and that demonstrate the ubiquitous and dual (multiplied) character of contemporary reality itself, this globalised space where the variables are multiplied, this complex and unstable universe where minor transformations can engender major changes.

Multi alludes to the possibility of working with systems that are by nature expansive and dispersed and able to engage multiple situations by means of the virtually unlimited play of variable combinations.

A scenario – and a possible associated shape and space – which expands indefinitely, from all points, like a multidimensional graphic; an open and multiple configuration of concatenated connections which refer, however, to simple, evolutionary patterns.

●✗✦ multicity

[MG][VG][WM] See 'm. city (or multicity)' or, better, 'Metapolis.'

✗ multifunctional environment

[VG] A multifunctional environment is a hybridisation of uses, landscapes, programmes, activities and multiple spaces in a (re)informed environment that is mixed in nature.

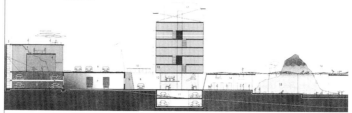

Vicente GUALLART,
Enric RUIZ-GELI,
Station, L'Hospitalet
de Llobregat
(Barcelona), 1998.

● multilayered

[MG] See 'layers,' 'epitome,' 'hyperplace' and 'Metapolis.'

●✕+ multimedia, urban

→ 'arkitektor',
'gaze> tactical gaze',
'interfaces', 'logic,
digital', 'multi'

[MG][VG][WM] Using multimedia technologies we can convert architecture into the interface of its own history. Provided with appropriate mechanisms, we can obtain sound information about buildings and urban spaces as we visit them contextually and randomly. Images superposed on stone may highlight certain historical and aesthetic aspects of archaeological documents. They allow ephemeral intervention on historical remains that create a new unity between the virtual (light) and the physical and heavy (stone), between future and history, between movement and staticness. Buildings speak!
Developer: Mr Architect, we'd like you to draw up an urban development plan, have you thought about the installations yet?

▲ multispace

→ 'hyperplace', 'multi',
'no-place', 'space'

[FP] These days, a satellite in orbit can encircle the Earth in ninety minutes. Space becomes a sort of time, an experience measured in time terms. We are not talking about distance, but about duration. Space implodes with the acceleration of transport machines. In addition, real space is left void; we live in the virtual space of tele-transmission. We do not live just on streets and in houses anymore, but also in cables, waves and webs. We are tele-present in the absence of space. Wherever we are, we are absent, and where we are not, we are omnipresent.

The immaterial space of tele-connection, the immaterial virtual space of the digital era, is not only a space of absence, a space that is missing, but also a new space of presence, of tele-presence, a new space situated beyond what is visible. Multispace and multi-time are situated beyond physical experience, spaces that have become experimental through the use of telematic machines and invisible time spaces. The radar is the best example to show how the collapsing of real space and the end of time are not only effects of absence and lack, but also develop something productive and new.

In this way, the radar is an instrument with which we are able to move around in the middle fog, in an "annulled space," allowing mathematical orientation in a black and empty space. In this way we do not loose anything, just the opposite, there is something we gain: virtual space. Virtual space is the space of absence, the space that is invisible and shaped only through mathematics. In other words, the space provided by the radar is a virtual space that does not belong to the conventional historical world.

More than ever, we move around in a multispace of teleconnections that is gradually substituting real space. As in the case of absence in relation to real space, it is not only substituted by it, but also enriched by it, and in the same way, the era of absence means an enrichment, a transformation of the historical ways of appropriation of time and space, of body and experience.

▲◆ music

→ 'abstract', 'matter', patterned distributions', score', 'sequences', 'space'

Miguel Ángel GUILLÉN, Infographic image of *Rigel* music piece by F. Guerrero.

[FP] It is a fact that music, a typical abstract art, has developed throughout the twentieth century some new capacities that have a lot to do with our idea of conceiving architecture.

Here, we are particularly interested in the processes by which with the accumulation of sounds, has been able to construct a real internal musical space in a piece of work.

When they are accumulated, the musical textures become blocks, stains or sound masses that saturate, while the purification or the densification of these stains turn out to be the real element of musical syntax. This way of composing required new terms or musical units, for example clusters or sound clouds, which started to give volumetric conditions to these musical masses that even had kinetic properties.

For some composers, like Edgar Varese, music even became an accumulation of bodies with specific shapes or geometries, projected in the space through three-dimensional paths. Occasionally, some compositions can even be ruled by the laws of physics, for example the ones used for gaseous elements.

Probability laws as well as certain infinitesimal devices helped to conceive these compositions as dense textured structures.

[FS] Thoughts ring again. Journals decline. Ideas moulded on paper become modified. Our last thoughts are so ethereal that we can only say them in whispers. To be heard. We turn our head to see if anyone is listening to us. There are no temples under the sun. Are not ideas fragile?

A thought is not put in a corset when it is sized. Its freshness does not reside in its being ensnared. A thought continues when it loses its own voice and allows itself to be heard in other ways.

For one reading, voices always emerge. Journals also emit sounds without complicated multimedia teams. Seeing a piece of paper, I see the air physically vibrating around it.

The faculty of reading and seeing is inseparable from hearing. Is it necessary to educate our hearing? That there are musical pieces written for silence has something to do with it, or that we enjoy buying books in languages that we do not know.

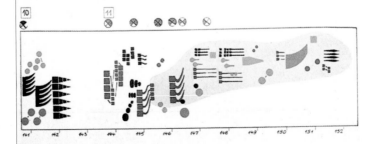

Gyorgy LIGETTI, *Artikulation*, electronic work score, Köln (Germany) 1970.

▲ mutation

→ 'dynamism',
'evolutionary',
'genetics of form',
'hybrid', 'inform(ation)al',
'matter', 'system'

[FP] Mutation is a change, variation and dynamic transformation as a result of a – gradual or sudden – evolutionary process produced by actions and generative and/or animated movements.

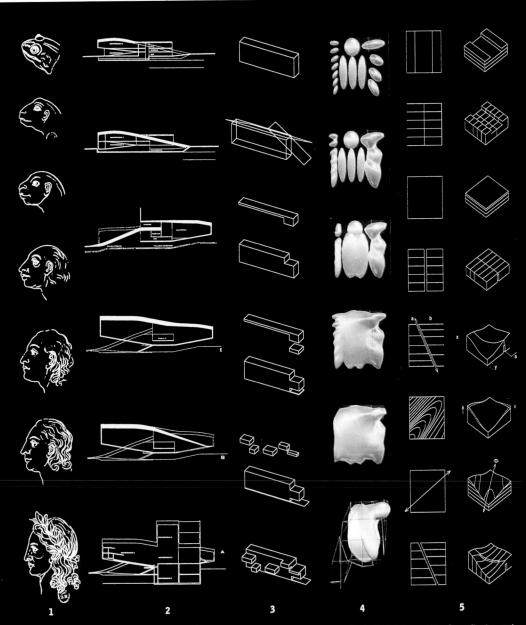

1. Transformation of a frog into Apollo, in *Arch+* 119-120. 2. Vicente GUALLART with Max SANJULIAN, *Competition for auditorium and conference centre*, Pamplona (Navarra, Spain), 1998. 3. MVRDV, *WoZoCo's Housing*, Amsterdam, 1997. 4. Greg LYNN, *Artist Space Gallery,* Soho, New York 1995. 5. NL, *Het Funen, 10 individual houses*, Amsterdam, 1999

N

• *nada(r)* (nothing but swimming and surfing)

→ 'action', 'audacity', 'dynamism', 'form', 'infiltration', 'passion', 'void'

[MG] In Jules Verne's novel, *From the Earth to the Moon*, ARDAN – the name of the main character – is an anagram of NADAR, the famous Parisian photographer friend of the author. NADA(R) (from the Spanish nada, nothing, and nadar, to swim) is in turn an anagram of ARDAN(T) – ardent, bold, passionate, expressive, active, eloquent, impulsive, dynamical. Nadar is to slide, move around and fluctuate in a liquid, dynamical environment. NADA(R) is to immerse (oneself) so as to stop being NOTHING.

●■◆ name (to name)

→ 'a-couplings', 'action>critical', 'beacons', 'code', 'dictionary', 'essayist knowledge', 'goodbye to the metaphor', 'ideological dictionary', 'immanence', 'knowledge', 'language', 'meaning', 'Think Tank'

[MG] The emergence of the new almost inevitably leads to uncertainty (precisely because we do not know what to call it, hence the difficulty of isolating signs with their expressions and identifying the relationship between them and that which already exists). Naming relates to a reactivation or a conceptual redefinition of language, which is indispensable in any prospective action upon reality. In fact, the correspondence between word and symbol, as philosopher Isabelle Auricoste rightly pointed out, does itself have a name: interpretation.

[MG] "*Everybody knows that the Inuit have availed themselves of many different terms for referring to snow and ice, according to what it looks like, how hard, transparent or dangerous it is, the area in which it is found, the time of the year... We who deal so much with space, how many words do we have for it in its different forms? [...] The dictionary provides a few: space, place, extension, dimension, surface, hollow, void, distance, corner, area, orbit, terrain, field, kingdom, region, sphere, ambit, framework, square, plane... And we also have combinations of the word space with other words. Thus perceptional space, "projective" space, representational space, pictorial space, artistic space, silent space... Why such insistence on words? Why such insistence on language? Because we are, like it or not, linguistic individuals.*" (ROMERO, Julio, "Entorno al espacio silencioso", in various authors, Entorno. Sobre el espacio y el arte, Madrid: Editorial Complutense, 1995)

[JM] Modernity, in the absence of a classic text (that is, before the incredulity of fulfilling its experiences as predicted) has opted to insistently name, baptize its work. Since Classical times, the world has been closed, defined and enunciated though formulas, thereby providing an excuse, in our times, to situate ourselves in another position, in another place.
It seems as if our task consists in the permanent and recurrent search of identity from which to relate experience adjudicated to problems, to resolved difficulties. But the new languages can no longer be total, that is, they can not be guaranteed by powerful logic. These new languages are concomitant with experiment, with actions of future incertitude, of unpredictable end. If the classic text has disappeared, then our actions are that of naming, investigating, assigning substantives to our encounter, to our discoveries.

[FS] "To name is to invent." (Enrique Vila-Matas)

★ natuficio

→ 'a-couplings',
'land-arch', 'mountain',
'naturartificial', 'reliefs'

[CO] Natuficio is the reinforcement of perception systems of the environment in the existent city, using systems of vertical access to certain roofs (conceived as landscapes). Their private use is transformed in public use and a memory of the nature by
the constructive artifice is recreated.

EDUARDO ARROYO

★ naturalism (a new naturalism)

[CO] How did the colloquial use of the term 'natural' arise? The word 'natural' or 'naturally' probably could not be used in its present sense in so many languages until
nature was domesticated, understood, subjected to taxonomic organisations which
gave a reasonable explanation to something which was previously construed as an
unapprehensible, threatening mystery; until it could be contemplated as worthy of
representation, and a picturesque concept was superimposed on a certain degree
of cosmogenic organisation as the effect of multiple journeys that provided the
necessary distance and capacity for observation. This is a plausible hypothesis
which needs no ratification. Its mere mention allows us to imagine a new naturalism arising from the profound ambiguity in which nature is presented as the
subject of knowledge and aesthetic experience, a hybrid, crossbred, entropic, hu-
manised conglomerate that is confused with its former enemy, the artifice, tight-
ly wound into the political space, a carbon copy of what was once public space, a
turbulent, flowing, random magma. Paradoxical conclusion: a new naturalism with
no natural references. Perhaps the key to the illumination of this expanding nat-
uralistic gaze is to be found in the journeys yet to be taken, the dark zones of the
atlas of the picturesque, those constant continents unconnected to the set of routes
that hold it together. A new naturalism should begin by integrating these zones,
bringing them to life and giving them a voice, demanding architectures that can be
equally meaningful in Lagos and Quito as in New York or Dusseldorf, capable of
articulating an immediate, unified sense of beauty, something which could never
be considered insulting or arrogant (who can claim to have achieved such a thing
today?). But perhaps this fruitful journey can only be taken in the opposite direction from tradition, from those dark holes towards us, now reincarnated in
the new indigenous peoples of a different form of wild nature. These journeys may
well have begun already and we are still incapable of understanding them, now the
objects and not the subjects of a turbulent beauty to come.

IÑAKI ÁBALOS & JUAN HERREROS

◆●★ naturartificial

[FS] See 'artificial.'

[MG] Naturaticial is the beneficial fusion of the natural and the artificial.

[CO] By transcending the history of thought in its dilettante to-ing and fro-ing between nature and artifice, we can grasp the concept of antiparticle that is of
enormous assistance in understanding the natural and the artificial. It is established that each common 'elementary' particle, with very few exceptions, has
an opposing antiparticle that is distinguished by having a contrary sign or other properties. Far from possessing characteristic entity, the natural and the artificial designate the same, causing the way it relates to the surroundings to vary.
Antinature is not the antithesis of nature, but the antiparticle of the natural that
enables its comprehension.

[i] p. 450-451   JOSÉ ALFONSO BALLESTEROS

1. Paul DE NOOIJEN,
Electric environment,
1977, in *Archis* 10/96.
2. *Ericsson* advertisement. **3.** Hydraulic
planting system, in
Quaderns 196, 1992.

▲ ★ ✕ nature (advanced)

→ 'artificial', 'attractors',
'countermarks: craters and
basins', 'cuts', 'ecology,
active', 'fractal',
'geography', 'land-arch',
'mountain', 'terraces'

[FP] Definitely, nature does not exist. We recently digitalised the last metre of the planet and we already have it in our artificialising pocket.

[co] **(Technology and nature. Technonature)**
It would be useful to put into crisis the more *naïf* ideas that have taken shape through the growing interest in nature. Only greater technological development and critical cultural attention can put a stop to the predatory dynamic that modern technology has unleashed on the territory. In this context, the architect's work should exploit more intense forms of describing the contemporary idea of nature, understanding it as an essentially cultural construction. If you like, to manufacture a cosmogony and give it physical form. As a work resource, environmental awareness is useful when we cross it with its apparent opposite: the artificiality of all real physical experience, as a theme for creating new paradoxes and new questions. IÑAKI ÁBALOS & JUAN HERREROS

[VG] MEDIA, MOUNTAIN & ARCHITECTURE are interfaces of the three inhabitable natures: digital, natural and artificial. Three manifestations that need a new order (or dis-order) to organise their interaction.

ACTAR ARQUITECTURA, *Maisons Buissons,* CRAFT Project, 2002.

1. ARTENGO-MENIS-PASTRANA, *Natural swimming-pool*, San Miguel (Santa Cruz de Tenerife, Spain), 1987. **2.** Vicente GUALLART, *Vegetal El Corte Inglés*, Barcelona, 2000. **3.** ACTAR ARQUITECTURA, *M'house Houses*, 2000. **4.** S&Aa (SORIANO-PALACIOS), *Competition for auditorium and conference centre*, Pamplona (Navarra, Spain), 1998. **5.** ÁBALOS & HERREROS, *Green House*, Madrid, 2001.

1. FRANÇOIS & LEWIS, *Project for purifying plant*, Nantes (France), 1995. **2.** OOSTERHUIS Associates, *Dike dwellings*, Groningen (The Netherlands), 1995. **3.** FUTURE SYSTEMS, *Project 222*, Druidstone Haven (Wales), 1996. **4.** MVRDV, *Villa VPRO*, Hilversum (The Netherlands), 1997.

◆ ● negotiate

→ 'activity', 'advanced',
'client', 'conventional',
'geomancy', 'maps, battle',
'program', 'projective'

[FS] | Today, the architectural project is not designed, but negotiated.

[MG] | See 'complicity' and 'contract.'

● neoclassical

→ 'allegory',
'architecture', 'memory',
'past'

[MG] | See 'erudition.'
Neoclassical is austere monumentalisation. Rafaello in his final period.

✕ ■ ▲ ★ Net, the

[VG] | INTERNET: the Net.

→ 'crossing', 'flows',
'franchise',
'infrastructures', 'm. city',
'matrix', 'Metropolis',
'multicity', 'multilayered'

The Internet is the overcoming of physical distances by means of the machinery of war.

War has always generated centralisation, physical limits (town walls, refuges, etc.) behind which to protect oneself.

Once physical distances were overcome by intercontinental missiles, the threat of war changed from physical invasion to total destruction.

It became necessary to decentralise the location of information.

In 1957 the first letter was sent via the Internet.

It was an L.

[JM] | The net is where fragments are seized, and where the rest is assiduous. The net also encompasses the roads, the paths that are crossed, the vegetation that surrounds them, the earth that buries them.

[FP] | A fishing net on the dockside is a compressed tile, hiding its exact form. Submerged in the sea it miraculously takes the form of the school of fish that it catches. When hanging laden with fish, it re-establishes a uniform and weighty shape.

[co] | "The same kind of things it does now. 2010 is not so far away...", Matthew Chalmers. XAVIER COSTA

✕ network of cities

→ 'city?', 'crossing',
'flows', 'grids',
'infrastructures',
'interchangers', 'link',
'loops', 'm. city', 'matrix',
'Metropolis', 'multicity',
'multilayered', 'networks',
'nubs-nodes-knots', 'no-
places', 'place of places',
'plaits', 'system',
'telepolis', 'territory',
'transfers'

[VG] | As opposed to the big metropolises of the twentieth century, the information society creates Networks of Cities.

Cities are to the territory what computers are to the net. Nodes of accumulation, territorial IP numbers, points of concentration need to be absolutely efficient for the system to function.

Otherwise, like on the Internet, information flows are diverted and reach their destination by other paths.

Cities are entering a state of decadence.

Traditionally, urban nucleuses emerged in two ways: either at crossroads as meeting places, in places of easy territorial accessibility (Paris, London, etc.), or along paths, as the result of intermediate stops marked out by the transport of each age (the pilgrims' walk of Santiago, the American wagon trails, etc.).

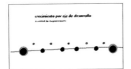

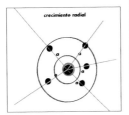

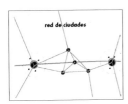

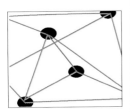

Vicente GUALLART,
Inhabiting a network,
Barcelona, 1998.

In both cases, the ultimate aim of a city in the course of its history, social and military circumstances allowing, has been to grow. Like companies: economic growth required physical growth.

The urban model produced by the evolution of medieval cities up until the present day is the great metropolis.

Today, we are witnessing a phenomenon in which cities are working simultaneously on their internal renovation, increasing their efficiency from within at the same time as they organise themselves territorially in the form of NETWORKS OF CITIES.

The network is a structure in which two orders exist: the local and the global. The two are equally important to the perfect functioning of the system. Without nodes there is no network – just lines taking information nowhere. If there is no communication between the nodes, they are no longer part of a network – just isolated points in an unknown environment.

The network, in turn, has a fractal structure, in which the part is self-similar to the rest, allowing multiple zooms without changing the structure.

The basic social node would be an individual person (human node), or any object (object node) provided with a chip and able to interact with the network. The urban order of the network begins, then, with the individual, who acts in a space (room), or in a house, or in a building, or in a street, or in a district, or in a city, or in a region, or in a country, or in a supercommunity, or on the planet. The classical notions of territorial identities may therefore be strengthened by the existence of mechanisms that allow them to strengthen the communities with which they feel identified. The most identifying territorial orders in recent decades, the country and the city, are now watered down in comparison with the district and the region, which have more powerful identifying signs. Nonetheless, each level has its internal and external function which is vital to the global system.

The net, which organises different communities, allows the creation of a network of networks, due to its self-similar nature.

In this way, not only are local networks of district organisations connected by created, but also Intranets, providing the possibility of being related to similar neighbourhood networks on a similar scale (a city), which in turn connects with district networks throughout a country, or all over the world.

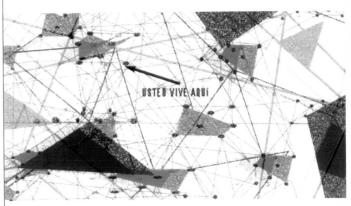

● networks

[MG] Today, the idea of interchange and displacement in the metropolis is derived from the effective combination of different channels of communication and locomotion which are principally conceived of as circuits for directing flows. In the infrastructural elements that constitute the city, the formal or episodic aspect yields to the effective definition of progressively complex networks. These networks are developed through basic parameters of connectivity aimed at regulating, in functional layers, different programmes and flows, through which they fuse and interchange, and in which the notion of mesh or meshed often turns out to be more decisive than the idea of a regulating design.

Systems, such as transport infrastructures, data transmission channels and telecommunications lines, signal the importance of networks – and therefore of their associated flows (of matter and of information) – not only as mere technical consequences, but also as structuring principles of new spaces that tend to multiply interchanges. Nonetheless, these networks and their spaces have not necessarily become more homogeneous and isotropic.

Infrastructural networks, but also networks of connection (data transmission, information technology, finance), appear as new non-material corridors through which another possible territory is already beginning to establish itself. A diffuse territory, defined by the connections between users themselves, far from traditional material or spatial parameters is becoming apparent. However, these virtual spaces are real in terms of effective production/organisation and in which an appropriate connectivity permits the phenomenon of "being closer, yet being far away." Networks are a global space which is progressively deterritorialised by the instantaneity and the immediacy of communication. However, networks' lack of accessibility also leads to marginalisation, to a periphery that is not necessarily situated in the suburbs or at the city limits, but rather in any part of the city, thus provoking profound changes in the traditional home-work-leisure and city-territory-landscape trinomials.

Networks are in constant evolution and their changes translate into continuous modifications of the mechanisms of linkage and transference and, therefore, into the matrix capacity – and topology – of the system. They provide the capacity of a better communicated, interrelated and virtually isotropic, but not necessarily more homogeneous territory. The progressive (and beneficial) access of all areas to communication and to information leads, in fact, to virtual disorientation and therefore leads to nothing, unless there is a definition of references and nodal or focalising points able to vectorise lines of power: attractors, polarities, strong or distributing nodes, which allow flows to be channelled and links to be fostered.

Such local, nodal focuses, if they are well situated, enable the system to be directed and constantly reoriented (in the same way that the new means of rapid transmission of communication polarise space and give it a hierarchical structure by "shortening the long distances and lengthening the short ones").

New organisations tend to create strategic polyhedral structures with hyperconnection, produced in supranational spheres, beyond the old territorial dominions of proximity, between the integrating nodes of global, temporary, elastic and variable organisations that ultimately favour the more effective.

★ new economy

[CO] "Because communication – which in the end is what the digital technology and media are all about – is not just a sector of the economy. Communication is the economy." Kevin Kelly. XAVIER COSTA

● news

→ 'act-n'

[MG] There are unusual news items that appear to enclose reality.
Others, in contrast, appear to open it up by and in anticipating it.

★ newspace

[CO] 10. Art is the roadbuilding habit (Zeno). It ruptures, then rebuilds, the edge of thought. 9. Architecture is the art of the elaboration of inhabitable space, beyond mere accommodation, in the direction of excess over need. 8. Elegance is the achievement of maximal effect with minimal effort. 7. Both cyberspace and bodyspace are real and physical, and both are inextricably intertwined with the virtual. 6. Cyberspace is constituted by information technologies; bodyspace is augmented by information technologies. 5. Immersion is the transition from bodyspace to cyberspace; eversion is the transition from cyberspace to bodyspace. 4. Space and time are no longer separate, not even in an everyday sense: a spacetime vernacular has developed. 3. Hence, we must speak of a vernacular of augmented spacetime, of bodyspacetime and cyberspacetime. 2. Augmented spacetime encompasses the full continuum from bodyspacetime to cyberspacetime. 1. This new continuum is newspacetime, or 'newspace', for short, the space proper of transarchitectures. 0. Beauty is objective; meaning is subjective. Both are relational.
MARCOS NOVAK

Marcos NOVAK,
Newspace.

■ new vision

[JM] We want to be precise. A concluded investigation is the origin of the unknown. As such, investigation has nothing to do with quietude, or arrival. In any event, it has to do with finality, with the road to another place; with a new vision. Vision, certainly sclerotic, myopic and necessarily blinding and filtered through all that occurs, is investigation that provokes what comes after, what appears, and what will be seen, until it becomes an obsession. The obsession-investigations of P. Klee, E. Munch, or C. Monet were paradigmatic in this sense.

◆ no-box

→ 'AA', 'aformal', 'form', 'open'

[FS] See 'fold (unfold-refold).'

Advanced architecture can not consider the box as a-priori architectonic. The modern movement completed a process of destroying the Classical box from which there is no turning back. The definition of walls as thick façades or voids, the construction of filter façades or deep façades, fluid space, or layout are consequences and elementsof this new architectural object. The box is obsolete.

■● no-day (night and day)

→ 'AA', 'dichotomies', 'mutation', 'versatility'

[JM] No-day is the discourse of the nocturnal city that also helps transform architecture's structure of interior and exterior pace. Differences are produced above all by disintegration, foreign to any composite hierarchy between plans and sections. The space of the nocturnal city is a new space that, as such, makes suggestions to design, and thus constitutes a reference for architecture. In any event, no-day does not leave off being a fictional space, cheated by the signs and the dematerialization of architecture itself.

[MG] The same. But as different, in itself, as night and day.

◆ no-form

→ 'AA', 'aformal', 'form', 'no-box', 'open'

[FS] One of the characteristics of today's architecture is indeterminacy. Better said, the inconstancy of its determination. An architecture based on formal design can not resist change of one of its parts without losing its identity. An architecture without form – informal – allows change, restoration, and change of its image without its form being altered, and as such, the object remains. It can spontaneously absorb additions, subtractions, and technical modifications, without disturbing its essential order.

● no-places (non-places)

→ 'anonymous', 'de-location', 'environment', 'flows', 'form', 'globalisation', 'hotel', 'places', 'pragmatopia', 'time', 'tourism', 'urbs / orbs'

[MG] With the term 'non-places', the anthropologist Marc Augé suggested a definition for a new relationship between "time-city" and "space of mobility." The non-places identified by Augé – office parks, stations, motorways, camp sites and caravan parks, airports and train stations, hotel chains and shopping malls, structures for leisure and even telecommunications networks – constitute new paradigms for everyday scenarios which are "architecturalised" and, at the same time, forgotten by the culture of architecture. Non-places which indicate, however, this passage from an ideological existentialism to a playful existentialism, related to mobility and consumption but also to the value of leisure. The appearance of large areas set aside for consumption, spectacle and entertainment constitute the clearest example of this progressive reduction of the necessary time elapsing between desire and satisfaction.

◆ no-scale

[FS] See 'a-scalarity (scalar ambiguity)' and 'scaleless.'

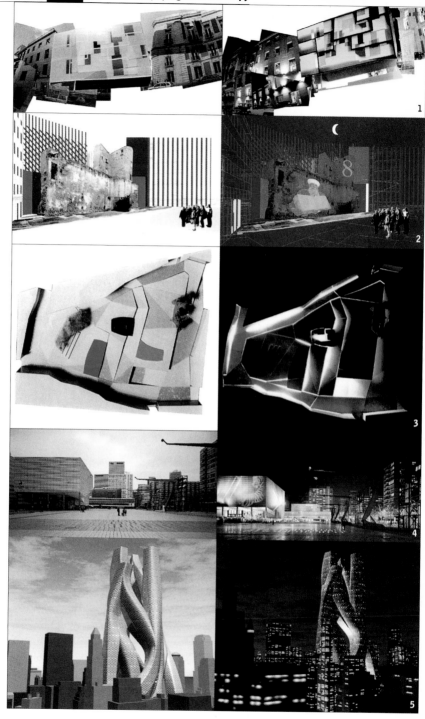

1. S&Aa (SORIANO-PALACIOS), *Administrative building for the community of Madrid*, Carretas (Madrid), 1998.
2. Vicente GUALLART, *Project for rehabilitation of the 11th century Arab ramparts*, Oficina RIVA, Valencia (Spain),
1998-. **3.** ACTAR ARQUITECTURA, *Cine Alfaro Square*, Cehegín (Murcia, Spain), 1998. **4.** Adriaan GEUZE (WEST
8), *Schouwburg Square*, Rotterdam (The Netherlands), 1997. **5.** NOX (Lars Spuybroek with Chris Seung-woo Yoo
and Kris Mun), *obliqueWTC* for the Max Protech Gallery, New York, 2001.

★+ nomad

[CO] Instead of dominating a single space, our life tends to cross endlessly new spaces: we have returned to being a nomadic culture. We imagine that these qualities emerging from space must bear some relation with the form of architecture, and to embark on an investigation of this sort would be a promising endeavour. This new way of understanding space would free us from the determining factors of a single space and force us to create new techniques of manipulating it, where the determining factors of the ground, its boundaries and it nature would increase its complexity. ALEJANDRO ZAERA-POLO

[WM] The first to associate the nomadic idea of impermanence with architecture was Raymond Wilson in 1967. Until then, the idea of nomadism was associated with people and not with houses.
Wilson was one of the pioneers in this field. He did an in-depth study of the industrialised production of mobile architectural elements, analysing and classifying what was on the market: the immobile-mobile homes, the different types of caravans, the Autonomous Living Packages and the mini-micro-macro-buses.
Wilson wrote: "Impermanence has entered contemporary thought. It is the manifestation of an advanced technology, not only in the mobility of people and homes, but also in the materials, which can be used in other cycles." Ray Wilson, Architecture and Assembly Line. (Translated from Spanish.)

[CO] If in the sixties the nomad was still a cross between the automaton of Archigram science-fiction and Reyner Banham's natural man (the hippy), then what exemplifies reflective work like that of Toyo Ito is how this character, already described in his itinerancy and imprecision, has completely abandoned that technical and vital militancy, redirecting his interests towards a greater recognition of his own subjectivity: which would begin with a reconstitution of his own body and a subsequent subjectivisation of the experience associated with the productive environment and its derived practices, that is, consumerism.
IÑAKI ÁBALOS & JUAN HERREROS

Toyo ITO, *Pao 1*, accommodation for Tokyo nomad woman, 1985.

◆ normad

→ 'beacons', 'carto-
graphies', 'indiscipline',
'maps (to map)', 'plural'

[FS] (from norm: a rule that must be followed or to which one must adjust conduct, tasks, activities, etc; and from nomad: family or village that wanders
without a fixed home; and the person who lives by these circumstances.) The
normad, and by extension, the architectural normad, considers territory as
an open and smooth field, and travel and velocity as moments of creation
and knowledge. The normad knows that rules mark the points of his/her journey, but only the intermediate moments have meaning. These points are merely places to abandon and from which to leave. They can never be considered
destinations, for that would make them an emigrant. The normad considers
as his/her principles speed, blur, and aeration. The normad does not believe
it necessary to be in motion, but rather to be in several in-between zones.
S/he is de-normalized, de-disciplined. The normad has neither house nor style,
and only relaxes at times. S/he is only seated when moving.

● nubs-nodes-knots

→ 'braids', 'crossing',
'devices', 'flows', 'grids',
'infrastructures',
'(inter)weavings and
inter(plots)', 'loops',
'networks', 'places',
'transfers'

[MG] "*nub, n. a small mass of fibers produced on a card, dyed brilliant colours,
and introduced into yarn during the spinning process;
node, n. Geom. a point on a curve or surface at which there can be more
than one tangent line or tangent plane;
knot, n. an interlacing, twining, looping, etc., of a cord, rope, or the like,
drawn tight into a knob or lump, for fastening, binding, or connecting two
cords together or a cord to something else.*"
(*Webster's Encyclopedic Unabridged Dictionary of the English Language*)

[MG] The devices that we call nodes are formed like knots of coiled mesh. In them,
the building, rather than answering to a matrix, supports a web – traces an
elastic and wound circuit – or trajectory – capable of articulating mobility
and programme. The building creates its own bond – or link – stretching, enclosing or setting it free – according to the definition of node itself, ultimately putting itself forward as a constructed circuit-grid or activity loop.

UN Studio, *Knots
diagram*, in *Quaderns*
222, 1999.

■ object (19.2)

→ 'abstract', 'interaction', 'process', 'product', 'reality', 'synthetical'

[JM] "*For W. Benjamin, "The totality is the untrue." The truth is in objects, in that glance that captures its irreducible folds into concept.*"
(CASTRO NOGUEIRA, Luis, *La risa del espacio*, Madrid: Tecnos, 1997)

+ ob-server

→ 'gaze> tactical gaze', 'logic, digital', 'synthetical'

[WM] If the model of the computer world is based on an observer, I propose a functional variation: ob-server, given that this observer (split-in-two) fulfils a certain mission. It is neither camera nor eye, but video-dependent. Through our links with electronic means, we are no longer simply outside users and observers. There is, rather, a new level of symbiosis between the human being and machines, in which interface plays a key role.
The progressive infiltration of electronic means in the world makes us see the world more from within, relativising the idea of reality.

◆ obsessions

→ 'action>critical', 'audacity'

[FS] Obsessions – the group of ideas that turn around in our heads. We load up on obsessions.

+ occupation structures

→ 'ad-herence', 'beacons', 'devices', 'graft', 'hybrid', 'impermanences', 'infiltration>intrusiveness', 'land links', 'land(s) in lands', 'maps, battle', 'periphery', 'printings', 'standardisation', 'tactic', 'tergiversation', 'zapping'

WMA Willy Müller Arquitectos, *Pilesystem®*, Barcelona, 2003.

[WM] "*There are land, sea, air and now space rights as well. Air rights affect flight corridors, while space rights are, as far as a satellite is concerned, the ownership of its orbit. In other words, there is a right without place, a right to route, that of airplanes and ships, and an orbital right, that of satellites. The crisis in the right to citizenship leads us to believe that the human rights could be reduced to an equivalent of vehicle rights. Man would be in possession of his route, not his abode. Property enters into crisis when a vehicle that owns its route passes, and what remains in its wake no longer belongs to it. And here I should point out that speed, the capacity for movement of individuals has driven the rule of law towards a disturbing situation.*" (Paul Virilio) These new space rights are radically changing the idea of architecture. The traditional model of land ownership for architectural property is yielding to new formulas of use or exploitation – temporary, functional, etc.; a new concept similar to pay-per-view introduced by new technologies. Multi-ownership of land and housing, rental of spaces in historic city centres is now included in the sale price of a country home, pay-per-use of the structure, and a diversity of modes and formats of interaction. This is also a consequence of re-informing the city: one piece of land, many classifications.

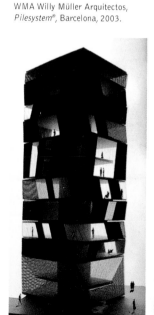

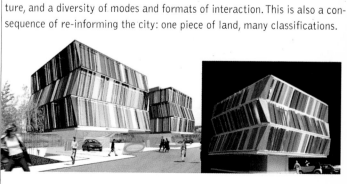

● occupations (spontaneous and evolutionary)

[MG] The most spontaneous – or apparently spontaneous – processes of tempo-ral-spatial occupation present precise concentrations in certain areas and dilatations in other. These are elemental models based upon processes of occupation, distancing and access, in harmony, meanwhile, with the gener-ic epitomes of the current metropolis (archipelagos, free spaces and infra-structures). Combinatorial processes, therefore, which refer, in turn, to oth-er connections between basic movements of concentration (densification), dilation (swelling) and access (channelling). That is to say, between full-ness, emptiness and link-articulation, or in a more abstract manner (as Stan Allen proposed), between point (volume), surface and line and, ulti-mately, between layers, backgrounds and networks.

As entropy increases, the critical mass of the contradictory bits of infor-mation accumulates. In the example of the beach, the regularity of the ini-tial occupation becomes distorted and dilated in response to environmen-tal pollution (a "noise", an annoying presence, a smell, an aggressive subsystem, etc.) or is altered by obstacles or boundaries (the sea itself, a rock, a dune, etc.), but also favours groupings around an occasional at-traction – a stimulus. Polyhedral structures are thus created due to the ac-cumulation of disparate energies in confrontational situations.

1. ACTAR ARQUITECTURA, *Maisons Buissons,* CRAFT Project, 2002. Distribution mutations.
2. S&Aa (SORIANO-PALACIOS), *Europan 5,* Barakaldo (Vizcaya, Spain), 1998. **3.** Eduardo ARRO-YO (NO.mad Arquitectura), *Europan 5: hybridisation process 001,* Barakaldo (Spain), 1998.

● *olympicooooo..... (after olympics)*

→ 'advanced>advanced architecture', 'leisure', 'past'

[MG] Formally codified model – sporting or urban.

Prudent fair-play, as apparent as it is insubstantial

● one is many

→ 'chains', 'complexity', 'cultivations', 'diversity', 'dual(ity)', 'mixed-use', 'multi', 'plural', 'poly', 'zapping'

[MG] One is no longer only singular, like an autistic and essential individuality, but rather singular as a plural, more complex and diversified individuality. One is one and many at the same time.

MVRDV, *Urban Megaform -Europan 2* (prize-winning), Berlin, 1991.

● open

→ 'direct', 'dissolved architecture', 'evolutionary', 'experimental architecture', 'extroversion', 'fresh conservatism', 'inform(ation)al', 'logic, direct', 'relationships, transitive', 'trajectory', 'unfolding'

[MG] Open is non-closed, non-conclusive, non-confined.

Open is indeterminate – non-determinate and non-terminated.

Open is "incomplete" (and unfinished).

Evolutionary. That is, animated. Unsettled. And liberated.

Open, then, means non-limited and non-limiting.

For uninhibited and unencumbered: unrestrained.

Open for exteriorised. Relational.

Relaxed and spontaneous (in attitudes and movements).

Frank and direct (in responses).

Joyful. And expansive.

Exultant (and exhibitive).

Explicit (clear) and expressive (eloquent).

Receptive (attentive) and vehicular (communicative).

Open also means dialogist. Meaning non-essential. Meaning non-univocal. Meaning alterable. And influenciable. Disposed to interchange.

We shall speak, then, of more open systems, shapes, orders, geometries and architectures.

The more flexible the more un-disciplined. The more dynamic – and uninhibited in their movements – the more informal and definitively extrovert.

●✖ operation

→ 'action', 'activity', 'devices', 'operative', 'strategy'

[MG] An operation is an action upon a territory which aims to generate an activity therein, but without any intention to transform it physically.
An operation can entail the temporary occupation of a place, with the aim of putting into practice a strategy, of developing an activity.

[VG] **desert storm**
Journalist: General Schwartzkopf, how did the attack on Iraq begin, by land, by sea or by air?
General Schwartzkopf: The attack began simultaneously by land, by sea and by air, from inside and from outside, by shutting down communications and with missiles... It's all-out war.

● operative

→ 'action', 'activity', 'devices', 'intelligence', 'maps, battle', 'menus', 'process', 'system'

[MG] Operative, by default is a mechanism, system or device; a system or device capable of fostering combinatorial evolutionary developments based upon open logics.
Environments generate actions – operating actions.

●◆✖ optimism

→ 'advanced> advanced architecture', 'colours', 'intelligence', 'joy (*alegría*)', 'pleasure', 'unrestrained (<un> factors)', 'yes!'

[MG] See 'Marx Bros.'
If it is advanced, it is always optimistic. If it is optimistic, it is not always advanced.

[FS] *"If a desire is beautiful, it changes reality, even when proven wrong."*
(GOYTISOLO, José Agustín, "Walden", 1977)

[VG] See 'progress.'

MVRDV, *The Netherlands Pavilion Expo 2000*, Hannover (Germany), 2000.

● **order** See '<in> factors of order,' 'order and chaos,' 'chaos,' 'dynamism,' 'in-
[MG]   form(ation)al,' 'system.'

★ order and chaos

→ 'a-couplings',
'activity', 'architecture',
'chaos', 'decisions
(and instructions)
rather than designs',
'dynamism',
'<in> order factors',
'inform(ation)al',
'interaction', 'maps,
battle', 'system'

[CO] **(open control)**

Recently, while looking at a photo of the Normandy landing, we reflected on the disorder verging on chaos with which men and artefacts appeared on the beach, in the
sea and in the air. The sensation that this disorder caused in us led us to doubt: was
this in reality an advance, a retreat or, on the contrary, was what we saw the dis-
ordered moment of defeat, of rout? We often associate the advance of armies with
order, with perfect formation, with drawings of geometric structures, all aimed
at a more effective attack and potential for occupying territory — that being,
ultimately, what an advancing army seeks to gain. The old geometric formations
would constitute the only possible form of intercommunication among the components of an advancing army. This communication, essential to maintain order in attack, was thus sustained, basically, on the visual. The closed composition, by keeping information active, is what maintains order and communication. More complex
planning and the radio render the geometric formation redundant to sustaining active communication. Control then becomes more subtle, less evident; neither geometry nor visual interrelations are required to maintain the appropriate relational
state in occupation and attack. Considering again the photo of the Normandy landing, we might ask whether the non-geometric disorder that we see corresponds to
reality or, on the contrary, whether it is only apparent. Obviously such a deployment
subject to randomness or arbitrariness would be out of the question. So there must
be a hidden order capable of extending itself over the beach: a system based on
an open control rather than in a closed order.
JOSÉ ANTONIO SOSA

[CO] **(succession of orders)**

In the irregular rhythms and diversity we see all around us, the real is highly unpredictable and rich in situations. Chaos appears as a succession of several orders,
quite different to the idea we have of "order." The new informal order is not random or arbitrary, it relies on series of shifting certainties.
In the informal there are no distinct rules, no fixed patterns to be copied blindly,
but rythms of relationships and interconnections infered between events.
CECIL BALMOND

Normandy landing
(Archive photograph).

● ★organism

[MG] See 'genetics of form.'

Organistical rather than organic.

[CO] Whilst technology is taking us into the realms of virtual reality, architecture on the other hand, is becoming more corporeal. It is the merging of the body and architecture brought about by electronic media. A radical change in perspective is blurring the distinction between the organic and mechanic, and the artificial logic of the computer and the natural logic of man are fusing together.

ANTONINO SAGGIO

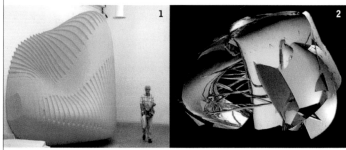

1. Greg LYNN, *Embryological House*, 2001, prototype.
2. Marcos NOVAK, *Data-Driven Forms*, 1997-98.

★ origami

→ 'bends and
(un)bendings',
'fold (unfold-refold)',
'game', 'landstrategy',
'papyroflexy'

[CO] The surface of the ground folds onto itself, forming creases that no only produce and contain the paths through the building, creating the differential conditions for the programme, but also provide structural strentgh. Thus, the traditional separation between building-envelope and load-bearing structure disappears.

The use of segmented elements such as columns, walls or floors is been avoided in favour of a move towards a materiality where the differentiation of structural stresses is not determined by coded elements but by singularities within in a material continuum.

ALEJANDRO ZAERA-POLO

1. FOA,
*Communications
centre*, Pusan (Korea),
1996.

2. J.L. ESTEBAN
PENELAS,
*Competition for
gardens in the Docks*,
Madrid, 2002.

3. Seminary research
conducted by Josef
Albers in Bauhaus,
1925-1928.

4. Arantxa LA CASTA,
Fernando PORRAS-
ISLA, Gemma
MONTÁÑEZ, *Fair
Precinct*, Palma de
Mallorca (Spain),
2000.

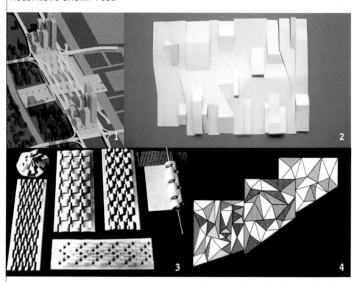

● original and replica

→ 'and', 'intermediate places', 'mutation'

[MG]

"*Original objects are principal informations. Floating in their wake comes the entire system of replicas, reproductions, copies, reductions, transferences and derivations. Original objects are like prime numbers in mathematics, in that neither seem to have a conclusive rule which governs its formation. The fact that they are originals cannot be explained by their predecessors, and their place in history is enigmatic. We only indirectly become aware of their existence by the disturbance they cause and the large quantity of detritus in the form of by-products which they leave in their wake. Like a mutant gene, they may be infinitesimally small, but the differences in behaviour which could be produced may be really big.*"

(KUBLER, George, *The shape of time : remarks on the history of things*, New Haven ; London: Yale University Press, 1962)

Louis PAILLARD / Anne-Françoise JUMEAU, *Icon House*, Paris, 2001.

● out of scale

[MG] See 'scaleless' and 'hypertrophy.'

1. Jaume VALOR, Fidela FRUTOS, *Bioclimatic house*, Vallvidrera (Barcelona), 1997.

2. José M. TORRES NADAL, *Public library*, Murcia (Spain), 1994.

★ overflow

→ 'tourism'

[co] Overflow is the manipulation of the wave vibration to generate an unflatable shape. It is the introduction of loop ecology between waste food and aqua culture. It is the possible creation of new ludic centres for new ludic landscapes. FRANÇOIS ROCHE

R&Sie.D/B:L, *Project in Echigo-Tsumari*, Japan, 1999.

★ overlinearity

[co] Overlinearity is a hypertrophied property of the linear. Linearity defines an elementary model in which events take place consecutively (excluding simultaneity), thus proposing itself as a procedure of synthesis of more complex properties. Overlinearity would be the action that propagates the linear by means of a more complex procedure. JOSÉ ALFONSO BALLESTEROS

P

★ paper

→ 'logic, digital',
'material', 'matter'

[co] I personally am very much a paper aficionado. I would be even more if somebody could cure its "shortcomings": that you can hardly re-use it (no "undo" here), that whatever is written in it is sort of inflexible and immutable. I could slap myself for not having somebody from the paper industry speaking at scope," Claudia Cavallar. "Paper will probably still mean the evening newspaper! But there will probably be some kind of electronic paper (e-paper) by 2010. I know researchers who are working on thin, flexible, bistable (image stays even without power) digital displays that you can bind together in a book or paste on a wall or tile on your desk," Bill Schilit. XAVIER COSTA

◆● papyroflexy

→ 'bends and
(un)bendings', 'fold
(unfold-refold)',
'game', 'landstrategy'

[FS] See 'origami'.

[MG] Papyroflexy is manipulation of a plane with the aim of constructing shape by means of unitary strategies which differ from the simple superposition of identical floors or of the cubic compression of the architectural object. Floors, walls, roofs and façades can be treated as papyroflexy exercises.

1. Process to create a paper bird.

2. ACTAR ARQUI-TECTURA, *Seacoast installations Zoo-Mar*, Barcelona, 2000.

3. ACTAR ARQUITECTURA, *Arts Square*, Barcelona, 2000.

4. S&Aa (SORIANO-PALACIOS), *Multipurpose centre in the old Concepción Hospital*, Burgos, 1997.

5. Alberto MARTÍNEZ CASTILLO, Beatriz MATOS, *Competition for Badajoz* conference centre (3rd prize), Badajoz (Spain), 1999.

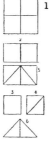

★ paradise, glaucous

[co] glaucous: a pale greenish-blue or bluish-green colour
paradise: place of extreme beauty or happiness
Neil Denari states (1999) "we are experiencing more pleasure than shock at the new forms of production technique and the multiplication of lifestyle options escalating all around us." Denari calls the strange pleasure we derive from the new dystopian landscapes of supermodernity the glaucous paradise, glaucous being the colour of video and computer screens and LEDs. Along with J. G. Ballard, Denari understands that this new cultural state is giving rise to the invention of a new morality that redefines the boundaries between dream and reality, and how we interpret technology and the very idea of architecture. JOSÉ PÉREZ DELAMA

● paradoxes

➤ 'a-couplings',
braids', 'dual(ity)',
ndiscipline', 'in/unstable',
ight', 'McDonaldization',
reactive', 'suspense',
.rajectory', 'uppercut',
virtual'

[MG]

(operative paradoxes)

Today we require devices capable of generating situations, events and/or principles able to work with the system and change it at the same time. Due to this strangely dual condition we call them paradoxes. Operative paradoxes.

[MG]

(destabilising trajectories)

The study of non-linear dynamic systems shows how, even in programmes or scenarios which are over-codified or apparently stable – inertial or routine dynamics – the indeterminate nature of the system produces situations of possible intrigue. The indolent recurrence of its movements is confronted with unexpected events – unusual or heterodox situations – which give rise to specific (and disconcerting) situations of alienation or amnesia. The system gets tangled in "intrigue", generating destabilizing braid movements produced by the apparition of unexpected combinations. "Rebel" trajectories, put forward as protocols associated with the adopted combinatorial logic, manifest themselves as paradoxes (unusual, i.e. heterodox principles) in the inertial framework – in the convention – of the host meta-system.

This hypothesis alludes to the contemporary project's transgressional vocation and to its capacity for *positing and resolving new principles – paradoxes. It aims to change* the orthodox codes of discipline, fusing disparate concepts (above and below, exterior and interior, figure and background, public and private, volume and surface, building and landscape, landscape and infrastructure, infrastructure and building, etc.) into new, more informal hybrid unions in which, for example, *the roof of a building can become, at the same time, its main floor; a growth can sprout horizontally; a construction can at the same time be nature; a formation can combine incompatible genes; different superposed levels can become a unique unfolded level; or gravity can be based upon dematerialisation.*

Herein lies the strength of paradox. In formulating possible trajectories from apparently impossible unions – and principles.

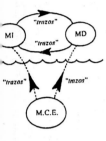

Resolution of the aparent paradox of *Hands drawing* by Escher, in HOFSTADTER, Douglas R., *Gödel, Escher, Bach: an eternal golden braid*, New York: Basic Books, 1979.

Bottle of Klein.

● parasitism

[MG] See 'antitypes,' 'layers,' 'commensalism,' 'contract,' 'enjambements,' 'cuttings' and 'hybrid.'

NOX (Lars Spuybroek with Chris Seung-Woo Yoo, Kris Mun, Florent Rougemont and Ludovica Tramontin), *SoftOffice*, United Kingdom, 2000-2005.

+ park-ing

→ 'landscapes, operative', 'tropism'

[WM] The appearance of the car in the last century eventually gave birth to a new place: parks of cars, carparks, which have become a point of reference in cities, rapidly moving on from a question of functionality and practicality to something more symbolic. Carparks have transgressed from only needing to be used (or known to exist) to needing to be seen. We should reflect on whether this has come about parallel to another, quite opposite transformation: natural parks, once symbolic, have become more functional and practical. From only needing to be seen (or known to exist); today, they need to be used. The history of these two parks is an X: unknown, encounter, contradiction. While parking is no longer simply architectural (such and such a floor in such building) but has become urban, the park is no longer simply urban and is now potentially architectural (such and such a floor in such building). Park-ing is a self-park, the fusion of two complementary landscapes.

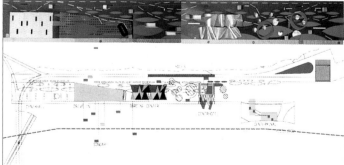

Willy MÜLLER + THB Consulting, *Breakwater. Project on the dock*, Port of Barcelona, 1997.

● particles, elemental (*les particules élementaires*)

[MG] "*Griffiths's stories were introduced in 1984 to relate quantum measure-ments in plausible narrations. One of Griffiths's stories is based upon of a series of random measurements taken at different times. Each measure-ment expresses the fact that a certain physical quantity, possibly different from one measurement to another, is included, at a given moment, within a certain domain of values. For example, at time T1 an electron has a certain velocity, determined by an approximation that depends on the type and mode of measurement; at T2 it is located at a certain place in space; at T3, it has a certain spin value. Based upon a subset of measurements a logically consistent story can be defined, but which nonetheless cannot be said to be true; it can only be sustained without contradiction.*

(In these stories) everything happens as if the world were made up of sep-arate objects, possessing intrinsic and stable properties. However, the num-ber of Griffiths's conscious stories that could be rewritten based upon a series of measurements is, in general, far greater than one."

(Paraphrasing HOUELLEBECQ, Michel, *The elementary particles*)

Simulation of a
new elemental boson
particle of Higgs
in a LHC particle
accelerator detector.

◆ passion

[FS] "*Architecture must be passionate.*"

(DEBORD, Guy; FILLON, Jacques, "Resumen 1954", *Potlatch* 14)

● ★ patchwork city

[MG] The shape of the traditional city has faded into a multiple landscape. The process, which is happening on a world scale, is one in which the city has stopped being an enclosed area and has come to manifest itself as a com-bination of multiple and fragmented remnants. Like a patchwork on the land, the crystalline shape of the primitive city erupts in a heterogeneous spread of splashes and hollows. A patchwork of linked realities; of conflicts and tensions and loveliness – attractions – fostered precisely by the poten-tial for mobility, interchange and displacement. A patchwork therefore – or perhaps more like a *plankton* – converted into a collection of individual fragments without apparent cohesion, without referential figuration and whose only principle of continuity is based no longer upon the shape of the edifice, but rather upon the networks that articulate them and the "back-ground" that surrounds them. No longer as a residue, but rather as com-ponent; in this visual succession of fades (spaces in negative) and reticu-lated meshes. The harmonious music of a complete, refigured, balanced city yields to a complex arrhythmic score with – perhaps – possible melodic frag-ments, but generally with a syncopated and atonal non-rhythm of *points and counterpoints* that make the contemporary urban space a definitively open and irregular body. Its most obvious manifestation would, in effect, be that of a structure that is definitively open (non-hermetic, incomplete and un-finished), referring to a triple combination of *constructed archipelagos, open interstitial spaces and arterial supports*. That is, more synthetically, between *constructions, landscapes and infrastructures* – as basic, synthet-ical describers of current – and fractalised – urban-territorial structures.

[c] "*We are witnessing the emergence of a new fragmented system in which the old order of "compound spatial sequences" seems to give way to a new individual order of "interposed programmatic sequences". All attempts to create operations aimed at imposing a rigid, martial order paradoxically lead to greater disorder, since the addition of any new element only increases the complexity of the whole. [...]*

Today in such chaos might be found, however, precisely our cities' greatest wealth; within this current fragmented complexity that defines them can be seen, in effect, the potential for a future quality. [...] in the same way that modern television programmes are determined by the viewers themselves as they switch from one channel to another, the modern tailor-made city is constituted on the basis of the individual editing of uses and users rendered instantaneous dada-urbanists, to the despair of order-seeking urbanists. [...] Simply expanding the city is therefore out of the question. The desired path is, on the contrary, the globalising restructuring of its fragments: the patchwork rug isn't a model; it is, rather, a setting for transformations, a field in permanent evolutivity and readjustment in which what matters ultimately are the lines of connection and the landscapes of relation. This does not mean, however, that "where" and "how" the planning takes place no longer matters. On the contrary, the ultimate objective is both to position newly identified programmes and to create a new equilibrium that would underscore this rug-like or patchwork quality as an interconnected global whole."

(Paraphrasing NEUTELINGS, Willem Jan, *Patchwork City*, Rotterdam: 010 Publishers, 1992)

Willem Jan NEUTEL-
INGS, *The Carpet
Metropolis*, 1990,
in NEUTELINGS,
Willem Jan, *Patchwork
City*, Rotterdam:
010 Publishers, 1992.

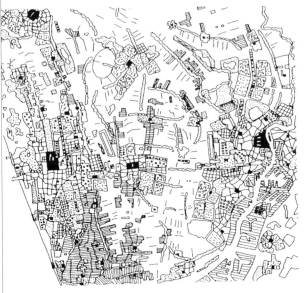

● path & peaks

→ 'dispositions',
'emergency', 'geography',
'landscapes, operative',
'mountain'

[MG] See 'bluntings' and 'reliefs'.

Peaks are hybridisations of outcrops (geology) and reliefs (geography). They also indicate silhouettes of data or the extremities of situations. Peaks are trajectories, oscillating or broken, of analogically fractal configuration.

◆● patterned distributions

[FS] Ruled space is in the Modern order, the free-plan, the reticular plan. Struc-tures, modules, regularizing traces are the instruments that rule modern space. Series.

Instead of ruled space, distributed space. Instead of the series, the number.

[MG] See '(inter)weavings and inter(plots),' 'score' and 'patterns.'

We are not interested in the idea of norm as a regulator of positions, but rather as a possible route which is at once indeterminate and tracked: as a circuit of dynamic movements and events. Discontinuous. Unforeseeable. Not series, but sequences. Normed as flexible and (or) distortable stave(s) or score(s) intended to grid — to norm — space through variable and syn-copated sequences, rather than from continuous, repetitive seriations. De-vices in which the anonymous, almost abstract, quality of a possible rhythm — or break — falling between threads and movements, combines with its own capacity to welcome unexpected presences destined to subvert the sys-tem: counter-rhythms brought about by distortions or disturbances within the scheme itself, or dissonances produced by intrusive, autonomously con-figured elements, able to pervert the initial code and demonstrate their elas-tic capacity for adaptation.

MVRDV, *Urban planning Hoornse Kwadrant*, Delft (The Netherlands), 1996.

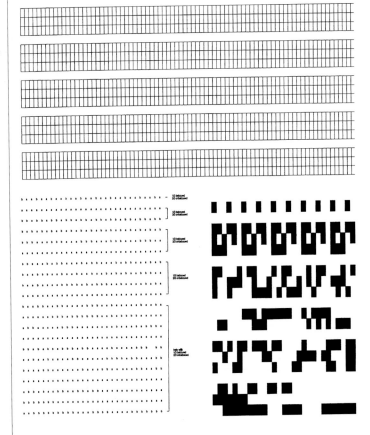

◆● patterns

→ 'colours', 'field',
'geometry', 'marks',
'matrix', 'printings',
'stains, ink', 'tattoos'

[FS] Patterns are guides that serve as samples to create objects.

[MG] See 'devices,' '(inter)weavings and inter(plots),' 'logic' and 'patterned distributions.' Today, patterns are open matrixes, rather than closed templates. No longer 'samplers' reproduced to (re)produce models, but rather logics of basic information. By extension, patterns are evolutionary grids, at once normed and flexible.

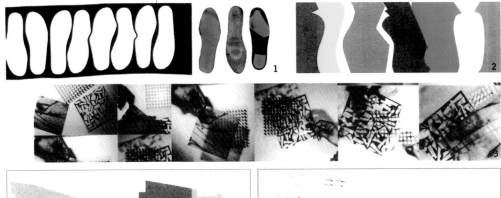

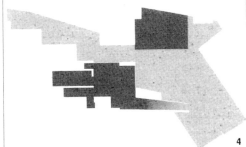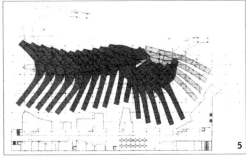

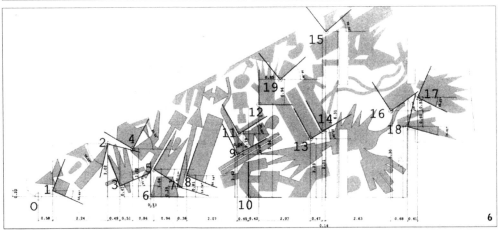

1. Prints, in FARRELLY, Liz, *Sneakers, size isn't everything*, London: Booth-Clibborn Editions, 1998. 2. José M. TORRES NADAL, *Public library*, Murcia (Spain), 1994. 3. ADD Arquitectura (BAILO-RULL), *Esteve Stand in Barcelona Moda Centre*, Barcelona, 1994. 4. José MORALES, Juan GONZÁLEZ, *Town Hall*, Chiclana (Spain), 1998. 5. S&Aa (SORIANO-PALACIOS), *Competition for bus station*, Talavera de la Reina (Toledo, Spain), 2000. 6. Antonio SANMARTÍN, John HEJDUK, *Civic centre*, Santiago de Compostela (Spain), 1997.

★ performance

[co] Of all conceptual paradigms of architecture, performance is the one which seeks to evaluate the efficiency of its ambitions. Opposed to an architecture for the sake of architecture, it investigates the feed-back loops between architecture and the systems it is embedded in. Isolated questions of form, process, fabrication etc. cease to be apriori conditions of architecture. Performance does not ask how a form looks like, but what it enables. It does not focus on what process was used to make a design, but on what the process was able to generate in the design. Thus performance shifts the focus of interest from essence to effect. The question is not what something *is*, but what it *does*. ANDREAS RUBY

● periphery

→ 'rurban life'

[MG] See 'patchwork city' and 'rurburbia.'

Quaderns in the '80s represented the periphery; dirty-reality as a reaction to post-modernity. The periphery is, today, neither scenario nor model — a referential landscape — but rather an open situation, to be qualified on the basis of restructuring strategies. Reinformers of the city and of the territory.

▲ permeable

→ 'act-n', 'bored', 'criteria', 'gaze> tactical gaze', 'moral', 'passion'

[FP] Permeable architects let other things invade them. Permeable instruments burstinterferences. Permeable architecture is capable of absorbing, but also constantly exporting things.

■ photography

→ 'advertising', 'gaze> tactical gaze', 'link', 'reality', 're-information', 'simultaneity'

[JM] Photography mechanically repeats that which can never existentially be repeated. Events do not become something else: photography always refers to the matter I need, to the body I see, it is the absolute individual, the reigning contingency, material and elemental, the "that" (that photo and not the photo) in short, the *Touché*, the chance, the meeting, the real in its inexhaustible expression. A photograph is always found in the limit of a gesture. "*A photograph says: this is, it is just as... "* (Roland Barthes.) It makes sense to possess a tool that works from reality bringing with it more reality.

✱ photovoltaic

[VG] In the course of the year, the Sun will shine down onto the Earth four thousand times more energy than we will consume. By duly collecting solar radiation, we can obtain heat and electricity. Heat is produced by heat collectors, and electricity, by means of photovoltaic surfaces (www.censolar.es).

Photovoltaic cell:
1. Polycrystalline.
2. Monocrystalline.
3. Monocrystalline of high efficiency.
4. Amorphous silicone.
5. Semitransparent amorphous silicone.

Efficiency diagram.

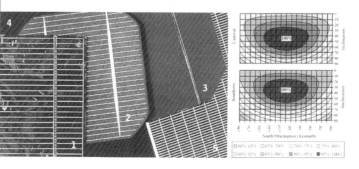

pieces, loose

→ 'assembly',
'combination',
'component', 'game'

[MG] Separate parts are components of a possible and particular device, but are also the loose ends of one and many intriguing combinations. Therefore, they present variable interconnections.

1. OMA, *Competition Très Grande Bibliothèque*, Paris, 1989.

2. Martha ROSLER, *Body Beautiful, or Beauty Knows No Pain*, in DE ZEGHER, Catherine (ed.), *Martha Rosler: Positions in the life world*, Birmingham: Ikon Gallery; Vienna: Genesali Foundation; Cambridge: MIT Press, 1998.

3. Steven HOLL, *Helsinki Museum of Contemporary Art*, Helsinki, 1998.

4. Enric MIRALLES, Benedetta TAGLIABUE, *Parliament*, Edimburgh (Scotland), 1998-.

6. PÉRIPHÉRIQUES, *Competition for Canal + Headquarters*, Loupveciennes (France), 2002.

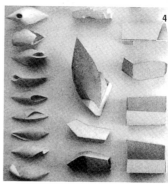

+● pixels (active)

[WM] Pixels are a picture element. They can be either active or passive. Only the active ones interest us. As an operative strategy, the graphic element is inserted into the landscape, creating a map of bits, presumably static.

Pixels are an operative strategy when we divide the space of the project into equal parts for the purpose of interacting with the environment by incorporating sensors that cause the external stimuli to flow in an orderly manner, as on a computer screen. The result is always variable, never static.

[MG] A pixel is an elemental unit of information associated with a combinable digital image. *"Like the television screen, the computer screen is covered with an infinity of small, uniformly spaced points called pixels. The image in movement on the screen is generated when groups of pixels are excited — glow — by an extremely rapid sweep of electron beams. If we imagine each pixel as a complex number, the pixels (numbers) glow when a differential and iterative (sequential) equation is applied to them. This leads to a global definition comprised of multiple stages — zooms of multiscalar iteration — which are intermediate and recursive."* (BRIGGS, John, *The Patterns of Chaos*, London: Thames & Hudson, 1992) Translated from Spanish.

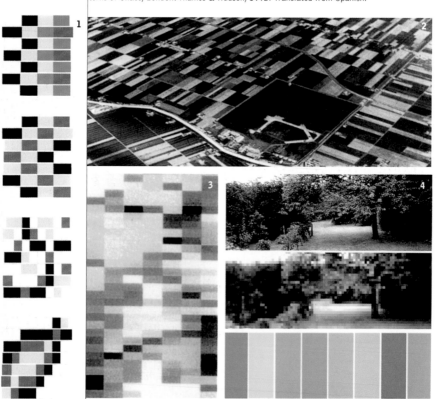

1. Willy MÜLLER + THB Consulting, *Bridge in Mercabarna*, Barcelona, 2000. 2. Aerial view of Schiphol (The Netherlands), in *Archis* 2/1998. 3. NJIRIC+NJIRIC, *Europan 4: Atom Heart Mother* (1st prize), Glasgow, 1996. 4. Emmanuelle MARIN-TROTTIN & David TROTTIN Architectes, *MR House*, Pomponne (France), 2001.

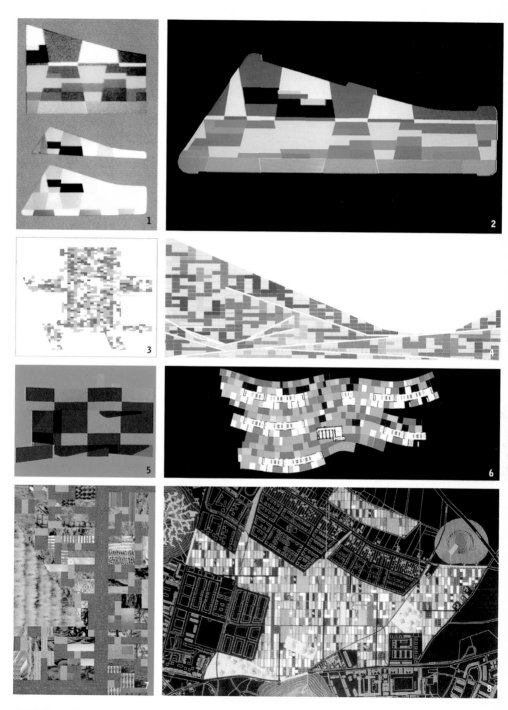

1. & 2. Arturo FREDIANI (with SOB Arquitectes), *Torrent Ballester Park*, Viladecans (Barcelona), 1997. **3.** Eduardo ARROYO (NO.mad Arquitectura), *Desierto Square*, Barakaldo (Vizcaya, Spain), 1999. **4.** Eduardo ARROYO (NO.mad Arquitectura), *Competition for auditorium* (finalist), Pamplona (Navarra, Spain), 1998. **5.** Vicente GUALLART, *House of seven peaks*, La Pobla de Vallbona (Valencia, Spain), 1998. **6.** ACTAR ARQUITECTURA, *Europan: 400 housing units* (finalist), Ceuta (Spain), 1999. **7.** NL ARCHITECTS, *Flat City housing*, Leidsche Rijn (The Netherlands), 1998. **8.** MVRDV, *Project BUGA 2001+Plant City*, Postdam (Berlin), 1997.

● place of places

[MG] The contemporary city cannot continue to be assimilated as a single *ideal* place – to be finished or rebuilt – nor as a unique or possible *formal* model, but rather it should be considered as decomposed and mongrel, dynamical and definitively unfinished multispace made up of interactive, linked coexistences and evolutions.

In the same way that we refer to a plural society, we should likewise speak of a multiple city: a multicity.

The city is no longer an island, it is a spectrum of cities and of "cities within the city." This is the essence of the contemporary metapolis: to be a hyper-place, a "place of places."

The contemporary city, approached from a positive attitude, is a rich multifaceted scenario, "an exciting kaleidoscope of opportunities;" a stock (a menu) of diverse situations and experiences in concordance with the manifold and mutable nature of the contemporary citizen.

●■▲◆✖ places

[MG] **(place as crossing of forces)**

See 'field'.

Today, the concept of place is defined beyond its old morphological connotations (of that which was called 'context').

The authentic cultural dimension of contemporary architecture comes from this disposition to effectively address the apparent ambiguity and weak indefinition of the local through a new logic that sees precisely in the idea of field (and in this crossing of forces – of tensions, of scales, of actions and activities, etc. – that ply it) no longer an enveloping protector, a sure referent, but rather an *incomplete* situation to be restimulated.

The place is no longer a centre, but rather a boundary.

Accordingly, the usefulness of new proposals is that of supplying relationships; stimulating new bonds and connections; activating multiscalar programmes, uses and, also, scenarios. Making the place a glocal epitome.

Multiply the place, multiplying its identities.

It would be a matter of 'x' (rather than of '+' and not of '-' or of '=').

[JM] **(place against one's place)**

A 'place against one's place' is within E. Hopper's personages.

It deals with subjects in an open landscape — in the void — that is not theirs. If it was of the surrounding reality, it would be as devalued as surrounding.

Opaque reality that asks for an opacity that opens in the mind of a person. Cavity, open, void produced by memory, by fatigue. It is the course of ephemeral people that occupy the place of no one – hotels.

From loss, one is reminded that nostalgia of the contemporary man can be productive. It provokes the birth of a reality that appears opaque, turbid, somber. For the first time, the occupation of a place is fruitful and productive, and that it is none other than one's own: one's place.

[FP] **(beyond the physical)**

Place has nothing to do with issues related to dimension.
Place has nothing to do with memory matters.
Place has nothing to do with referential aspects.
Place is a connection with something that is beyond the physical.
Place has to do with state of mind and ideology.

[FS] **(distant proximities)**

Distant proximities allow ourselves to be closer or nearer to an act that happened thousands of miles away than to local references or things that happen around us. Distant proximities allow us to feel closer to architecture that is made from certain determinate theories, or to people, independent of the place where it is produced.

We can not use the words context, reference, frame, group, whereas these terms refer only to our close surroundings, to the area that extends from our body.

Globalization does not necessarily mean losing shades of difference. It does not generate abstract spaces, without references, or "non-places. It is not a selection of concurrence, but rather the sum of contextuality. The simultaneity of place.

Thus, it makes sense that context is not the physical place that surrounds, or the cultural or subjective environment that wraps around us.

Place is felt personally, time spent through experience, thought and science through thoughts; they are the images and sound of past places of my memory.

[VG] **(energy, place and corpse)**

1. Architecture has to bring (never detract) vital energy to a place.

Only too frequently, in the name of place (a monumental setting, a sea front, an archaeological complex), constructed buildings are soulless. Experiments have been carried out with architectural corpses, in an unsuccessful attempt to revive them; interventions of spiritism that invoke the dead of the past to build the present. Success in these experiments is impossible. It's the night of the living dead!

Only buildings created with a soul of their own – that are more than mere appearance, that interact with their social, spatial and aesthetic surroundings, that demand a place of their own in history because they know when and for what purpose they were created –can give a place energy.

2. The architect is increasingly becoming a creator of places. Unlike the traditional situation, when the architect was given a brief and a definition of uses, the plot is often no longer a vital datum for the project.

Projects, like films, follow a strategy. The choice of a place in the territorial magma is the first decision that characterises a work.

In a convulsed city, in a territory that requires active protection (rather than freezing its activity), the position of what is built (or of the empty space to be protected) is far more transcendent than the work itself. When a place is built, it is there for good.

● plaits

[MG] The multifaceted structure of the contemporary city alludes to an evolutionary system developed through the effective combination of networks, places and between-places referring to successive – and fluctuating – contracts with the environment. These can be condensed in flexible meshed structures capable of interlacing different sequences – such as positive-negative, empty-full, occupied-preserved sequences – that can foster diversity, contrast and identity by means of the priority role given to the relational elements themselves. The new city-territory could be conceived of as a structure, which is non-linearly normed, of heterogeneous events linked by effective infrastructure networks aimed at fostering interchange, interrelationships and mixedness, but also greater indetermination in the final shape generated. The distribution of multiple local developments that dot the global territory could be adapted, in this way, to connection-separation rhythms which could be essentially ensured by such articulatory networks. Converting many of the existing road networks   which are absurd and antifunctional – into new strategic meshes is, therefore, a priority objective. Grids of development and combination needed to aim at linking simultaneous structures of systems and subsystems; historic settlements and new focusing subcentres, halo-shaped growths and expectant recycling spaces: zones of gentle colonisation, natural spaces or new operative landscapes, conceived of as channels of connection between different developments. Fostering ensembles that are heterogeneous and meshed at the same time. Urban plaits – *dentelles urbaines*, like flexible appliqués, brocades or blond lace – imbricated and singularised; diverse and articulated.

MVRDV,
*Diagramatization
and deformation of
way speeds,*
in "Living along
the highway",
Quaderns 218, 1997.

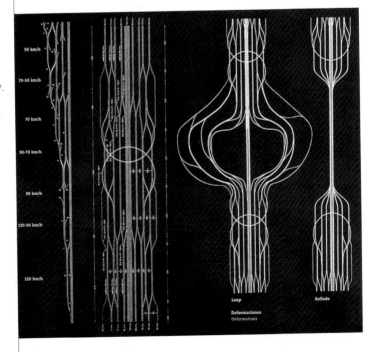

+ plastic

flexibility',
latable', 'matter'

[WM] In the film *The Graduate* there is a historic moment:

At the poolside graduation party thrown for him by his parents, and in a succession of shots that range from the interior of a diving mask and to exteriors of the family, the barbecue and the guests, one of the latter says to Ben enigmatically (for the time).

"Ben, I just want to say one word to you – just one word."

"Yes, sir."

"Are you listening?"

"Plastics"

"Exactly what do you mean?"

"There is a great future in plastics."

It was the 70s.

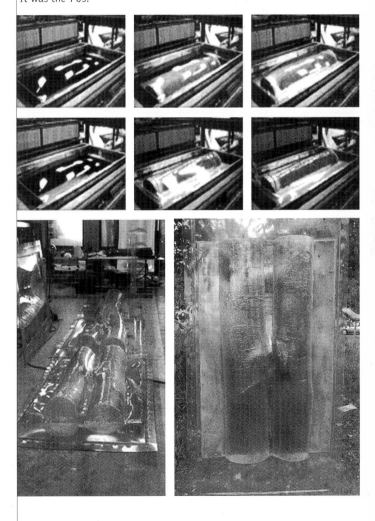

Association DUNCAN LEWIS & PIRII ARKITEKTKONTOR AS, *College Kvernhuset Ungdomsskole*, Trondheim (Norway), 2002.

● *plateaux* (for platforms)

→ 'landscapes, operative', 'land(s) in lands', 'landstrategy', 'reliefs', 'topological', 'trays'

[MG] See 'tableland,' 'land' and 'topographies, operative.'

The *mille plateaux* of is Deleuze-Guattari, translated as "one thousand plateaus." They could also have been translated as platforms, trays, supports, hollows or, simply, lands. Topological topographies.

In any case, flexible support material.

WMA Willy Müller Arquitectos, *Competition for a cultural centre in Santa Eulàlia,* Eivissa (Spain), 2000.

★ platforms

→ 'landscapes, operative', 'land(s) in lands', 'landstrategy', '*plateaux*', 'tableland', 'reliefs', 'topological'

[CO] As an attempt to summarize the qualities of the new grounds it is interesting to point out their fundamentally active, operative nature; these emerging grounds are closer to the contemporary meaning of 'platforms' as operating systems than to the classical concept of platform – plinth, base – which aims to frame, neutralize and erase the field of operation to produce an ideal background for architecture to become a readable figure.

ALEJANDRO ZAERA-POLO

■ player

→ 'chance', 'client', 'complicity', 'interaction', 'interactivity', 'joy (*alegria*)', 'leisure', 'ludic', 'system>dynamical'

[JM] **(who ensnares)**

"*The player is, in reality, at the mercy of the insignificance of coincidence, but tries to give it meaning.*

The player is convinced that in coincidence there is meaning, a kind of necessary meaning, although not a necessity that concurs with rational logic."

(FRISBY, David, *Fragmentos de la modernidad,* Madrid: Ed. Visor, 1992)

● pleasure

[MG] See 'hedonism.'

● plug and play

→ 'logic, direct'

Plug and play – "*whenever you want, wherever you want, however you want, just 'connect and let's go,'*" (Susanna Cros)

FOA, International
Port Terminal,
Yokohama (Japan),
2002.

Cristina DÍAZ
MORENO, Efrén
GARCÍA GRINDA,
International
competition of ideas:
Mar artificial (First
Prize ex aequo),
Super-south M-40
intersection (Madrid),
1998.

Javier FRESNEDA,
Javier PEÑA,
Javier SANJUÁN,
C-4 parcel Alfonso XII
dock, Cartagena
(Spain), 1999.

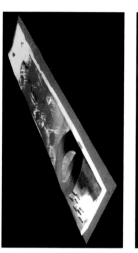

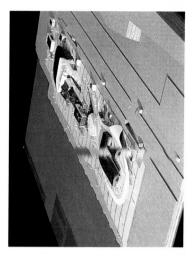

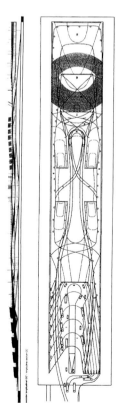

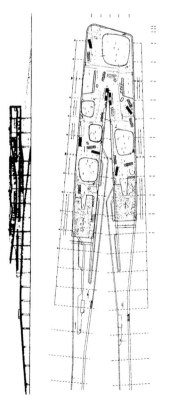

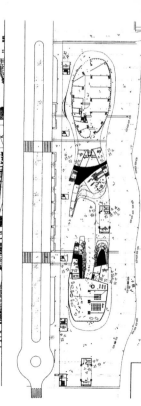

● plural

[MG] Plural implies heterogeneity, diversity, variation, mongrelisation: multiplicity. Plural is, by definition, open: it is not — or does not seek to be — univocal, absolute, complete. Total. Even in its more elemental manifestations, plural has an underlying, apparently ambivalent, uncertain — anarchic — nature, produced by the direct and at once complex — coexistence of substantively polyhedral events. Precisely because of its high degree of indetermination (or, more accurately, because of the non-predetermination of its results, its movements, its trajectories) in the plural, the old univalent and cohesive character of things and events yields to more (dis)solved and multivalent manifestations fashioned on the basis of simultaneous, directly interlinked "sub-events" or "sub-spaces." Plural is multiple by virtue of being multiplied and multiplicative. In the plural, a thing is many things at the same time. Plural is "x," not "=" or "-." We are interested in devices that are capable of creating plurality from singularity. At once in singular and plural.

● ★ polis

[MG] From the Greco-Latin *polis*, "city:" political.

[CO] The political uses of digital technologies can become embedded in the local. As a politics this is clearly partial but it could be an important building block of the politics for global justice and for demanding accountability from global corporate power. We are seeing the emergence of a de-nationalized politics centered on cities and operating in global networks of cities. This is a kind of politics of the global that does not need to go through some sort of world state or the supranational level. On the contrary, it runs through places yet engages the global. It would construct a countergeography of globalization. We may be just at the beginning of this process.
SASKIA SASSEN

● poly

[MG] See 'multi.' From Greek *polus*, "much or many:" polycentric, polyhedral, polyfaceted, polyvalent, polyphase, polynuclear, even polyglot – mongrel.

polynuclear

1

polyvalent

2
3

1. Three metropolitan structure models: radial mononuclear; semireticulated multihierarchical; reticulated polynuclear, in GAUSA, Manuel, *Housing. New alternatives, new systems*, Barcelona: ACTAR, 1998. **2.** Chair-stair, mid-nineteenth century, in *Fisuras* 7, 1999. **3.** Piano-bed, mid-nineteenth century, in *Fisuras* 7, 1999.

★ polysensoriality

[CO] I dream of a poly-sensorial projection of the science of the city and buildings. I dream, therefore, of a city imagined through and for all the senses and that knows how to transmit all sensations: fragrances, sounds, lights and shadows, the sweet touch. The power of the image and, more so, its iconic representability is shrinking the space of urbanism and architecture, maliciously marginalizing it to the sphere of the visual. I believe in an architecture that is only drawn following the contours of desire. But, the architecture of pleasure died with the last of the Nasrid monarchs and, since then, the centuries have had nothing to show but vain monuments to power – all colours of power – underscoring the mercenary character of architecture, its status as submissive, self-absorbed talent, basically concerned with self-explanation. A vain, complacent architecture.

JOSÉ MIGUEL IRIBAS

● *ponds*

→ 'countermarks: craters and basins', 'landscapes, operative', 'landstrategy', 'topographies, operative', 'use'

[MG] See '*plateaux*' and 'land.'

Ponds are basins or depressions for collecting water (by extension, flows of movement and activity): pools or ponds of uses.

+ port

→ 'city?', 'islands', 'no-places', 'sea', 'trip'

[WM] The primary reflection that we should make in analysing port cities is the following: for centuries ports were the origins of cities. Cities grew large precisely because they had a port, and hence they had to develop the port to compete with other cities and not drop out of the ranks of big cities.

Ports, meanwhile, in their disproportion, have become less interesting places to have on the seafront of the very cities they contributed to create. And cities commence a slow battle to recover their seafronts as revitalisation strategies. What would happen if the redefinition of the idea of the port led to other conclusions? Might we think that, in this century, it will no longer be necessary for ports to be continental platforms, but rather simply maritime, and that rather than ships coming to us we would come to them?

That would give us another idea of how to exploit docklands, recycle buildings and occupy infrastructures. We must either define an ambitious picture of the future or continue to listen to the same old "dinosaurs" going on about the same old things.

UN STUDIO,
Ponte Parodi,
Genoa (Italy),
competition 2001.

● positioning

→ 'action> critical',
'flexibility', 'Metapolis',
'moral', 'principles'

[MG] See 'criteria.'

We talk about criteria as positioning, i.e., as strategies that are at once flexible and precise, directly related to the idea of disposition. We prefer, in effect, the terms positioning and disposition to that of position: both indicate a situation that is at once elastic and deliberate, a deliberate logic — vectorised, not eclectic — but adaptable.

A contingent (unstable) action rather than a position that is fixed and rigidly stabilised (whether from dogma, conquest or permanence). Positions, therefore, as operative intentions and criteria, i.e., as active machinations. As opportune as they are — and why not? — opportunist. That is to say, open to change and to reaction. To the stimulus of the variable, of the new.

● post-it effect

[MG] See 'precarious(ly),' 'impermanences,' 'reversible' and 'temporary.'

◆ power

→ 'economy',
'information',
'interchange',
'progress'

[FS] *"Architecture is a paradoxical mixture between power and lack of power."*
(KOOLHAAS, Rem, *El Croquis* 53, 1992)

★ pragmatopia

[co] Situated in the no man's land of the modernist dialectics between utopia and pragmatism, pragmatopia suggests an alternative territory of architectural operation. Thus it resists the escapism of the utopian which emprisons its vision in a *no-place*. At the same time it bypasses the automatism of the pragmatic with its tendency to kill the idea for the sake of sheer action. Pragmatopia instead rolls out a new plane of events in order to enable action (*pragma*) to take place (*topos*). ANDREAS RUBY

BKK-3 Architects,
*MISS Sargfabrik
Housing,*
Vienna, 2001.

● ★ **precarious(ly)**

[MG] Precarious(ly) refers to those devices defined as architectures of nearly instantaneous materialisation, midway between the occupied and the episodic, the "presential" and the ephemeral. Contracts, then, that are "precarious" in relation to the environment, that allude to a temporary approach to space, an approach made up of reversible relationships, unstable links, impermanent constructions, lightweight structures and fragile presences. Precarious are short-term actions – and amortisations – (bound to a presence between the real and the fictitious, the constructed and the deposited, the installed and the merely scenographic) related to a new sensitivity, more receptive to the occupation/manipulation – immediate, weighted and evanescent – of the landscape.

[c] "*Certain forms of architecture can be summarised by their ephemeral nature —real this time, not metaphorical— and they can accept their inconsistency, their physical and conceptual precariousness, as a new value rather than as a negative quality. Their lack of consistence can then be appreciated for the new approach it brings to things and objects, judging architecture which is solidly rooted in a place – the one which accumulates memory – like imposed, repressive and incapable of representing subjectivity and the changing values of a society which is constantly mutating. The life span of these forms of architecture ceases to be associated with their physical life (with the capacity of material to resist the passage of time) to become linked to their capacity for performance which gives and shapes their character: the possibility of constructing moments or situations, of taking action on a specific, limited aspect, of producing a series of transformations and then withdrawing, disappearing forever.*" (DÍAZ MORENO, Cristina; GARCÍA GRINDA, Efrén, "Impermanent architecture", *Quaderns* 224, 1999)

Anne LACATON &
Jean Philippe VASSAL,
Latapie House,
Floriac (Bordeaux,
France), 1993.

Shigeru BAN,
*Paper log houses for
refugees,* Nagata-ku
(Kobe, Japan), 1995.

◆ ● ★ **precision**

→ 'production, intelligent', 'technique, the'

[FS] Precision is exactitude. We reclaim our artistic condition. But at the same time, we are mechanics that work with extreme precision. It is knowing. It is not about details. The drawings of architecture are precise documents, not because they contain details or precisions, but because they inform with exactitude their finality, even allowing a level of freedom for the reader or executer's interpretation. Maximum result with minimum effort.

[MG] See 'abstract,' 'concise' and 'synthetical.'

[co] Precision is a state that phenomena reach when their characteristics acquire sufficient stability such that they cannot be altered without affecting their essence. In the physical world, precision is associated with both intellectual pertinence (ever a cultural category) and material appearance, understood and determined through the laws of science. Precision has sometimes been the objective of human activities; of science and art. It is associated with the reductionism and essentialism of Calvinist culture as well as with the mysticism of the Catholic Mediterranean world. Precision survives as a commonly accepted category for relating means and ends, the fitting of the data of the problem to the arguments set out. Precision, like any metaphysical category, is, in addition to often being impracticable, ambivalent. Paul Valery warned:

[i] p. 492-493 "*Gardez vous de la précision: c'est le vitriol de l'âme.*" JOSEP LLUÍS MATEO

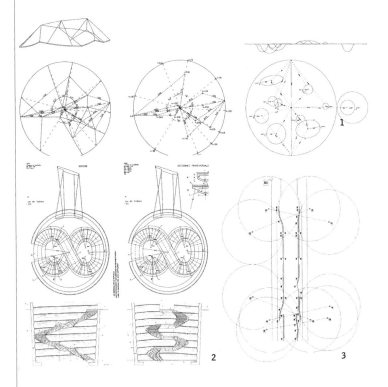

1. Vicente GUALLART, Enric RUIZ-GELI, *La Beauté à la nature,* Avignon (France), 2000. Detail plan for the table-showcase of curved glass. **2.** José M. TORRES NADAL, *Intervention on the ramparts,* Cartagena (Spain), 1996. Detail plan of the stairs perforated like a braid. **3.** FOA, *International Port Terminal,* Yokohama (Japan), 2002. Detail plan of the radius of curvature.

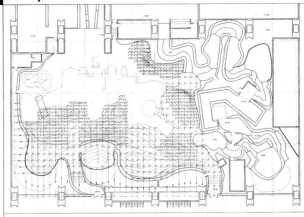

S&Aa (SORIANO-
PALACIOS),
*Cyberauditorium
and Children Museum
in the Museum
of Sciencies,* Valencia
(Spain), 1998.
Detail plan
of bench marks.

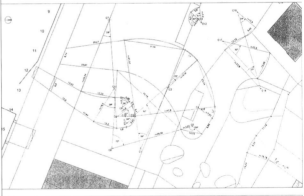

Eduard BRU,
Vall d'Hebron Park,
Barcelona, 1992.
Detail plan of
turning circles and
superelevations.

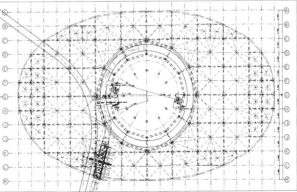

ACTAR
ARQUITECTURA,
Pau Picasso Square,
Montornés
del Vallès (Barcelona),
2000. Detail plan.

DILLER & SCOFIDIO,
Blur Building,
Yverdon-les-bains
(Switzerland), 2002.

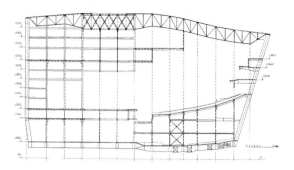

S&Aa (SORIANO-
PALACIOS),
Euskalduna Hall,
Bilbao (Spain), 1998.
Detail plans of
structure and
enclosure elements.
View.

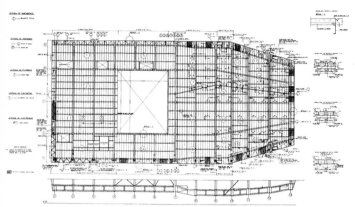

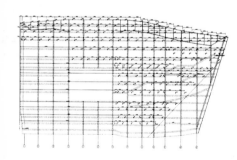

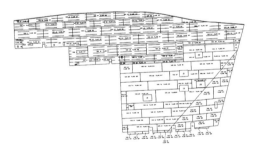

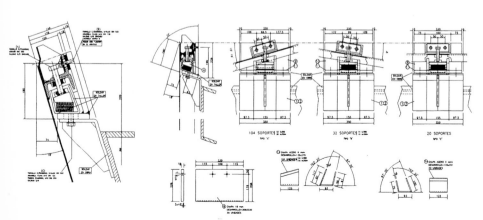

Precision

1 abstract
2 activation
3 ad-herence
4 a-scalarity
5 abroad, etc.
6 artificial
7 associate,
   overlap, connect
8 auditoriums
9 collage
10 competition
11 congresses
12 context
13 conventional
14 deviation
15 challenge
16 unrestrained
   (<un> factors)

17 de-location
18 unfolding
19 dichotomies
20 dynamism
21 devices
22 dual(ity)
23 assembly
24 in-between
25 spaces>public space
26 fencing space
27 extend
28 extroversion: <ex>
   factors of form
29 figure-background
30 fragile
31 future
32 geometry
33 heterotopia

34 puff pastry
35 ideas
36 imagination
37 in/unfinished
38 action
39 intrusiveness
40 lightness
41 place
42 machine
43 sea
44 material
45 gaze
46 no-box
47 cloud
48 obsessions
49 optimism
50 fish

51 skin
52 reality
53 section
54 yes!
55 scaleless
56 synthetical
57 system
58 tangent
59 texture
60 transparency
61 void
62 construction,
   intelligent
63 and

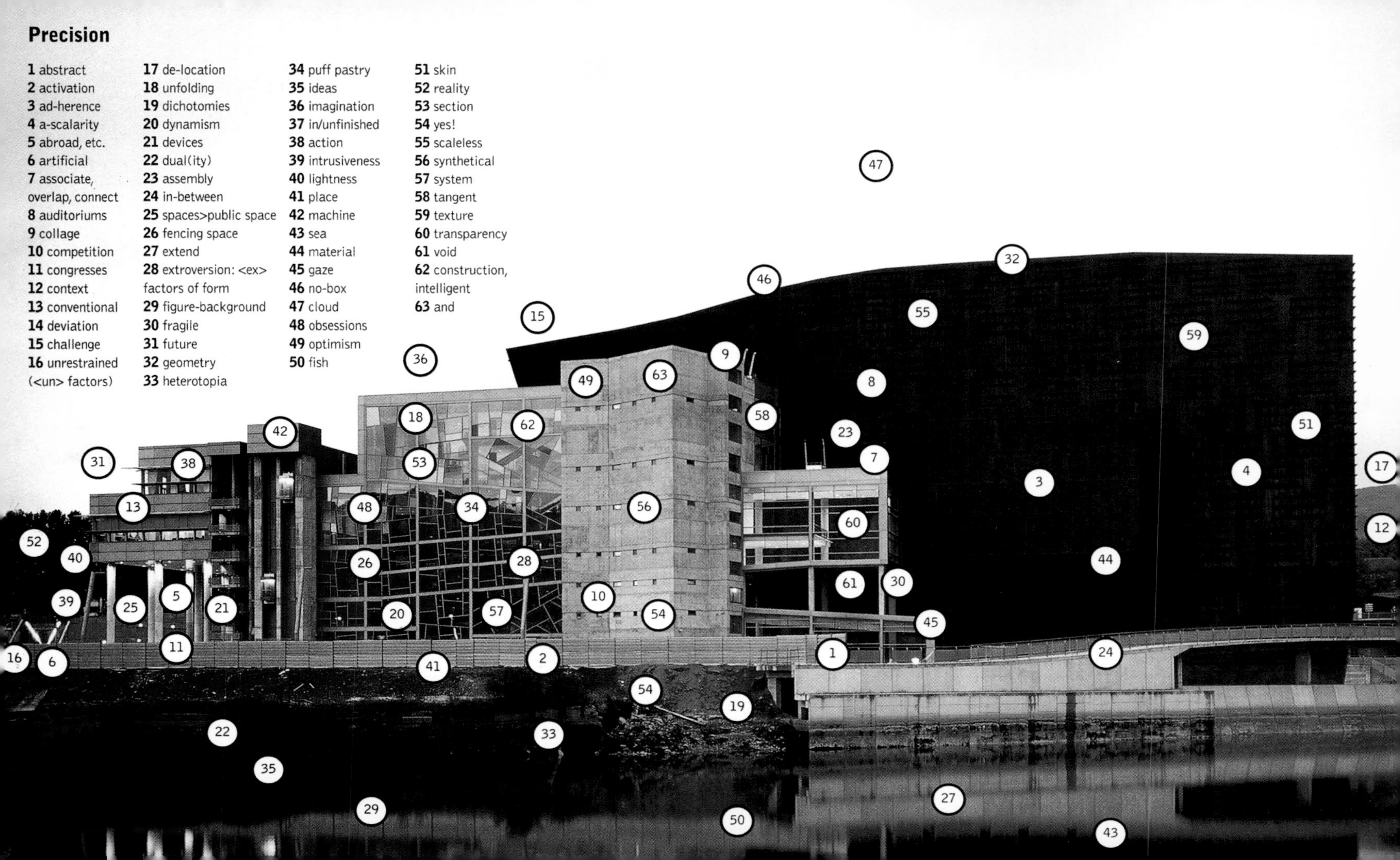

✖ principles

→ 'criteria'

[VG] The principles upon which architecture is based are so open and generous that they allow its reinvention with every new age.

■ proceed

→ 'machination', 'maps, battle', 'projective', 'tactic'

[JM] It is necessary to reformulate the word 'process,' with the term 'to proceed.' In effect, we recognize that with Classicism work aided by the university and the generality of knowledge disappeared; beyond the subject, we must recognize that our time admits individuality and difference.
Learning should prefer the research of behaviour that is the fruit of an explanation of reality. Design is explanation.
To design is to explain, to acknowledge that which comes to light—the project.

✖◆✚★ process

→ 'action', 'attractors', 'cartographies', 'collaging', 'criteria', 'cultivations', 'data', 'decisions (and instructions) rather than designs', 'delynniate', 'devices', 'dynamism', 'evolutionary', 'form', 'genetics of form', 'geometry', 'hybrid', 'innovation', 'landstrategy', 'maps (to map)', 'no-form', 'object', 'occupations', 'operative', 'production, intelligent', 'seed', 'stains, ink', 'system', 'trip'

[VG] Architecture is a process that allows us to generate habitable spaces. Architecture is alive when, once its construction is complete and it is inhabited, it is installed in a process of transformation and interaction with the people who inhabit it and with the environment in which it is situated.
Like processes, architecture and the city constantly evaluate the information they receive and issue, and have the capacity to analyse their actions over time. Processes rather than occurrences.

[FS] See 'time.'
Perhaps the first distinctive reflection that recent architecture has presented is the dilemma between process and design, applyied to all the tools or documents that define architectural objects.
Constructive plans and sections are not considered as documents that try to register and document a solid state, finished and defined, of the built architecture. They are not existing physical bodies in which geometry is aseptically registered, and the agents that intervene become the executives of something definitively controlled.
Architecture does not begin or end in the scanty time of the project. If architecture is no longer defined only by its walls that prescribe dimension, construct materiality and characterize action, and programs that occur inside, the actual design must be understood as a temporal process in which the interfering arbiters and agents become new data, referents or interferences. Constructive plans and sections are indicators of a determined state, current – diachronic witnesses.
The actual geometry reveals an instrument with little control or even as an obstacle for controlling form.
Process is understood in a different way from the architecture of the sixties and seventies, bioclimatic Japanese architecture, or the disciples of the hard wing functionalists. There are no coincidences.
We are not advocating a definition of form through function, because it is also affected by temporal processes.

[WM] Advanced processes are dominating the field of creativity, at the same time blurring various concepts: that of authorship, of work and of discipline.

Advanced processes in the field of architecture are redefining the role of the architect concurrently as an agent and manager.

The history of architecture is based upon a series of decisions defined over time and distributed in different areas of knowledge of different levels, successively or simultaneously.

The progression of architecture towards advanced architecture, that is, from a technological economy, learnt and exploited for centuries, to a scientific economy – in which we require the intervention of other disciplines – means that advanced processes are synonymous with projects.

Processes, then, are "projects" that encompass the genesis, the R+D, the tests, the construction, the interaction, the data correction, etc.

[CO] An evolutionary process, which provides a release from compositive burdens from the outset, implies the work with transformation systems, with correlative and independent stages.

The first step of the process: to create an objective percentile distribution of the usage programme to be inserted. These uses lead to individual grids that distribute each function uniformly, defining different densities of usage from the percentiles information about the total area of their point of application.

Second analysis: to determine the pre-existing factors and future actions considered to be unchangeable. The interaction between these reality vectors and the previous distributions of each function is used to produce a tabulation of attraction and repulsion between the latter. Once tha balance of mutations is reached, the construction uses and open spaces are defined and grouped, leadingto the configuration of the constructed hybrids.

Third: once the territory is hybridised by the multiplicity of programmatic functions, the process proceeds to read the constructive accumulations to create an archive of hybridisation in which the percentages of participation on each function in the composition of the constructed unit can be read.

The primigenial volume arises from a simple calculation of areas, potential constructions and the superimposition of uses on the plan. This virtual volume is transformed by the environmental conditions that are fed in as values of installing this construction in the real built-up landscape. These conditions are: accessibility of uses from the public level, heights of each use or placement of minimum communications cores to meet fire regulations. The generic section of the building appears during this transformation, which is typified using the information on functions, relationships between them and their constructed volumes.

The multiplicity of personalities and the hedonism of modern individuals, their habits and their increasingly atypical mobility and communication patterns make their dwellings extremely variable and heterogeneous places. The proposed process will thus be able to span anything from uses traditonally regarded as being functional to perversions and the most disparate lifestyles admitted by the growing tolerance of modern society.

[i] p. 496-497   EDUARDO ARROYO

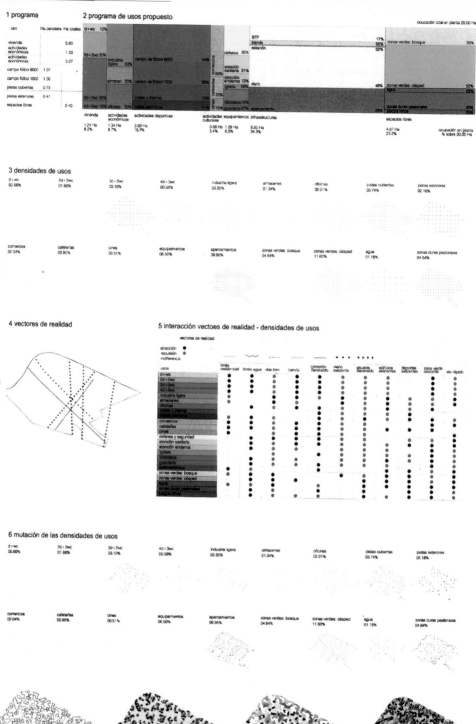

1 programa

uso	Ha parciales	Ha totales
vivienda		0.80
actividades económicas		1.33
actividades económicas		3.27
campo fútbol 8000	1.07	
campo fútbol 1000	1.00	
pistas cubiertas	0.73	
pistas exteriores	0.47	
espacios libres		2.40

2 programa de usos propuesto

ocupación total en planta 20.00 Ha

d+wc 10%
2d+2wc 30%
3d+2wc 50%
4d+3wc 10%
industria ligera 50%
almacén 20%
oficinas 30%
campo de fútbol 8000 44%
campo de fútbol 1000 28%
pistas cubiertas 12%
pistas exteriores 16%

BTP 17%
tranvía 05%
estación 02%
defensa 35%
atención sanitaria 21%
atención ancianos 60%
iglesia 06%
biblioteca 10%
guardería 07%
viario 48%
aparcamiento 20%

zonas verdes: bosque 20%
zonas verdes: césped 50%
agua 05%
zonas duras peatonales 20%
zonas duras 05%

vivienda	actividades económicas	actividades deportivas	actividades culturales	equipamientos	infraestructuras	espacios libres
1.24 Ha 6.2%	1.34 Ha 6.7%	3.90 Ha 19.7%	0.68 Ha 3.4%	1.29 Ha 6.5%	6.85 Ha 34.3%	4.67 Ha 23.2%

ocupación en planta % sobre 20.00 Ha

3 densidades de usos

d+wc 00.66%	2d+2wc 01.86%	3d+2wc 03.10%	4d+3wc 00.58%	industria ligera 03.35%	almacenes 01.34%	oficinas 02.01%	pistas cubiertas 03.74%	pistas exteriores 02.16%

comercios 02.04%	cafeterías 00.85%	cines 00.51%	equipamentos 06.50%	aparcamientos 09.96%	zonas verdes: bosque 04.64%	zonas verdes: césped 11.60%	agua 01.18%	zonas duras peatonales 04.64%

4 vectores de realidad

5 interacción vectores de realidad - densidades de usos

vectores de realidad

atracción
repulsión
indiferencia

usos

límite residencial | límite agua | vías tren | tranvía | conexión ferrokalido | viario existente | vivienda ferrokalido | edificios existentes | deportes existentes | zona verde existente | vial rápido

d+wc
2d+2wc
3d+2wc
4d+3wc
industria ligera
almacenes
oficinas
pistas cubiertas
comercios
cafeterías
cines
defensa y seguridad
atención sanitaria
iglesia
biblioteca
guardería
aparcamiento
zonas verdes: bosque
zonas verdes: césped
agua
zonas duras peatonales
juegos niños

6 mutación de las densidades de usos

d+wc 00.66%	2d+2wc 01.86%	3d+2wc 03.10%	4d+3wc 00.58%	industria ligera 03.35%	almacenes 01.34%	oficinas 02.01%	pistas cubiertas 03.74%	pistas exteriores 02.16%

comercios 02.04%	cafeterías 00.85%	cines 00.51%	equipamentos 06.50%	aparcamientos 09.95%	zonas verdes: bosque 04.64%	zonas verdes: césped 11.60%	agua 01.15%	zonas duras peatonales 04.64%

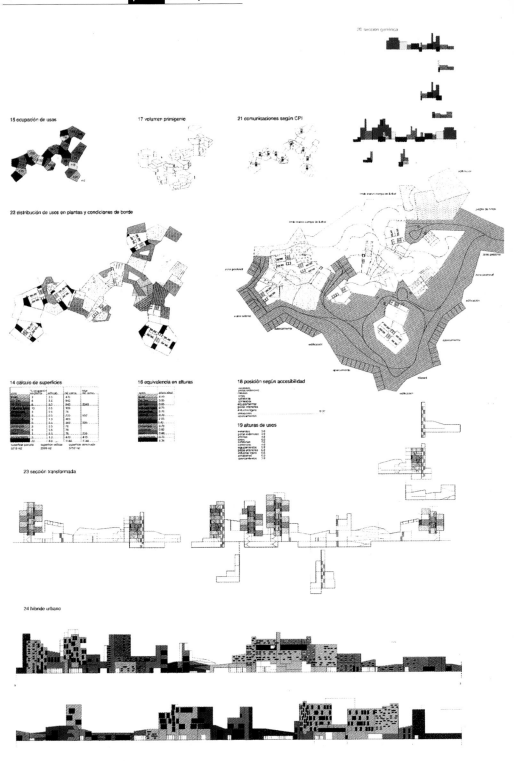

Eduardo ARROYO (NO.mad Arquitectura), *Europan 5: hybridisation process 001* (1st prize),
Barakaldo (Vizcaya, Spain), 1999.

✖ **produce**

→ 'production,
intelligent'

[VG] Advanced architecture is produced rather than constructed.

✚ **product**

→ 'advertising',
'artificial', 'economy',
'marks', 'matter',
'object', 'production,
intelligent', 'prototypes',
'standardisation'

[WM] "*It's impossible to see what products are going to be.*
That is why a solid information architecture based on encouraging and
managing diversity, as opposed to containing diversity, has become so im-
portant." Steven Telleen, Intranet Partners.

IBM advertising,
in *Exit* 5, 1999.

✖ **production, intelligent**

→ 'animation',
'construction, intelligent',
'genetics of form',
'inflatable', 'intelligence',
'matter', 'precision',
'product', 'prototypes',
'scaleless', 'system',
'technique, the',
'topological'

[VG] Repeating variation. The aim of any system of intelligent manufacturing
is to be able to produce pieces with totally free form, by industrial means
— that is, to repeat variation.
Advanced industrial systems, in association with the digital world, enable
the production of pieces with absolute flexibility, provided the machines
needed to manufacture them can be parameterised.
It is the architect's drawing, in digital format, that is assimilated by the
machine to produce the pieces needed to construct a surface or a complex structure.

Vicente GUALLART,
Cricursa Pavilion,
Mida, UIA Barcelona,
1996.

Vicente GUALLART,
Enric RUIZ-GELI,
La Beauté à la nature,
Avignon (France),
fabrication of curved
glass pieces,
Cricursa, 2000.

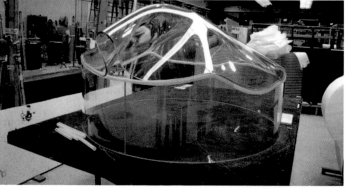

● ◆ **program**

[MG] See 'use.'

[FS] To compose today means to create programs. We invent or propose them; we mix them, give them support, denaturalize them. Program is not the same thing as function. It is more than function because program is not direct and has more than one voice. IProgram is less because it is defines by actions and activities (verbs) and not by conventions (substantives.) Programs are also mutable, transformable in time.
We must define programs which can forget or can be transformed later.

● ✗ **progress**

[MG] See 'energy' and 'evolutionary.'

[VG] Progress is not linear. Progress is re-information.

[VG] **(history)**
A progressive society is one that leaves a greater inheritance than it inherited. In the city and in the country. We citizens cannot be spendthrift heirs who squander history's fortune. History is a rich inheritance because it allows us to be what we are; to have been born where we were. We have to collaborate with history in order to improve it.
If what is left to us of history is innovation (Gothic cathedrals, Renaissance palaces, all innovative constructions in their time), we can only respond with yet more innovation. Not with imitation.

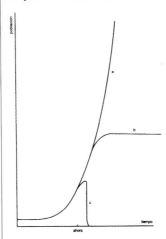

Paul DAVIES, Graphics.
Three hypothesis of
population development
and evolution,
in DAVIES, Paul,
About Time, New York:
Simon & Schuster, 1995.

✗ ● **progression**

[VG] Progression comes from progress – from a dynamic system that advances – like the transformation of an initial position.

[MG] **(non-linear)**
Progression is a ynamic sequence in which consecutive terms are differentiated by non-linear or hazardous growth.

●✗ projection

[MG] See 'projective.'
To pro-ject. To pr
advance and antic
operation.

[VG] A projection is a virtual displacement of an image; the superposition of light on material.

● projective

→ 'activation', 'criteria', 'evolutionary', 'hybrid', 'ideas', 'maps, battle', 'maps (to map)', 'mutation', 'relationships, transitive', 'topological', 'trailers', 'trajectory'

[MG] We propose the term 'projective,' taking advantage of its double usage: "projectation" and "projection."
Anticipation of movements, but also construction of relationships – trajectories and figures – heaped one atop another by operations at once of encounter and linkage.
Transfers, trailers, multiscalar epitomes: these are maps of relationships associated with the advanced project's condition of being projective (recursive and propositional at the same time).

[MG] " "*I am seeing a thought,*" *thought Gould.*
Thoughts that are thinking about the form of the question. They rebound and stroll around picking up all the snippets of the question, along a route which seems casual and whose destination seems to be itself.
When they have reconstructed the question, they come to a halt. Eye on the basket.
Silence.
Rising over the floor, intuition is loaded with all the strength needed to plot the distance that separates it from a possible answer. Shot. Fantasy and reason.
Through the air flies the deductive-logic parabola of a thought which turns on itself under the effect of a flick of the wrist printed by the imagination. Basket.
The enunciation of the answer: like a breath. To enunciate it is to lose it. It slips and already it has become snippets of a new question which springs up. Start again."
(BARICCO, Alessandro, *City*, Barcelona: Anagrama, 1999)

● proneoism

→ 'creation', 'imagine> imagination', 'indiscipline', 'innovation', 'path', 'progress', 'progression', 'yes!'

[MG] See 'action'.

[MG] We can detect, today, a shared and activist desire, which trusts in innovation — in the new — as a reformulation rather than as an imposition. A desire for redefinition, of which we can also find traces in many other areas of contemporary creativity (New Literature, New Philosophy, New Visual Arts, New Composition...) and which speaks preferably of the restructuring, recasting, reimagining – and *proneoist* – the needs of our era.

● prosthesis (prosthetics)

Classical orthopaedics (in fact, like architecture in the traditional city) tends to reproduce – to evoke or recreate – the absent element; to regenerate damaged fabric or to extend its old characteristics. There was something of a redemptive, and at once reconstructive, formalism about it. Dissimulating distortions. Composing appearances. Recovering the past.

The epic of modernity wanted to replace old reproductions with new productions: proud modern artefacts. Functional objects. Abstract. Pure shapes, by virtue of being purged, were designed no longer to evoke, but rather to produce: strict responses, conceived and abstracted as supports to precise functions (sustaining, grasping, taking, walking, as well as sleeping, working, resting, transporting, etc.). Technical and autonomous pieces – prototypes – as essential and exact as they are removed from the receiving body, place or context. Today, new techniques and factors permit the development of intelligent cybernetic elements that have nothing to do with the members into which they are implanted (or which they take the place of) and which, however, interact qualitatively with the host body, improving upon its old services. These are technological elements (infrastructural, rather than aesthetic) but, at the same time, they are in unique and personal agreement with the receiving body in order to optimise potential. The new technological elements even transfer new real and virtual conditions (it is not a question of merely running but rather of running faster and better; not merely of seeing but rather of seeing more and further) to the host context. In the same way, architecture cannot limit itself to simply extending the body, or sustaining it, but rather it must be simultaneously a receptive and active supplement; a device which is singular (autonomous and artificial) and complicit (individual and interactive); estranged from, and at the same time sensitive to, the particular; capable of regulating itself and, at the same time, of restructuring, restimulating and strengthening the host in order to take it beyond its own limits: revealing that which was hidden. Architecture must work as an "antitype" which is in syntony with the host body so as not to provoke rejection, yet no longer in harmonious symbiosis with it.

1. Classic prosthesis (evocative), modern (mechanical), in *Quaderns* 199, 1994.

2. Contemporary prosthesis (infrastructural), in *Quaderns* 199, 1994.

3. Vic Reis, golf player without hands.

4. Third hand, in *Velocidad de escape*, Madrid: Siruela.

5. Aimee Mullins, athlete, in *I.D.* mayo 1998.

✖ protection

→ 're-information'   [VG]

See 'síndrome-del-Liceu.'

The best way of protecting heritage is to take action on it. Fundamentalist protection, representing the inactive freezing of an environment, can only lead to its degradation.

■ proto-architectures

→ 'architecture',   [JM]
'places'

The subject will be subject in the contemporary city if he manages not to subject himself, and this has to do with the investigation of various spaces of liberty, which potentially are non-spaces.

The concept of non-space, coined by M. Augé, is linked to another equally important concept: that of proto-architecture. Architecture, in certain cases, constructs its own references; it is auto-referential. It is another facet of the immanent relation it presents with sites. Places, spaces that due to differences from which they are observed, can be considered proto-architectures. Or rather architectures that, due to their originality with which they are thought, can be considered proto-places. A formal retrofeeding is produced between some proto-architectures and others. Architecture, thus, can construct its own references. These self-references are not due to the profession or the discipline, but are derived from their own discoveries.

+ prototypes

→ 'catalogue',   [WM]
'crash test', 'devices',
'product', 'production,
intelligent',
'simulation', 'system'

"*The rapid creation of prototypes is perhaps the most valuable essential competence that an innovative company can aspire to.*
At Sony they take an average of 5 days to create a prototype."
Michael Schrage. (Translated from Spanish.)

★ prototypology

[CO]

Just like the prototype anticipates a product yet to be developed, the prototypology represents a spatial configuration in permanent state of evolution. Whereas a conventional typology defines a generic model of organisation which becomes specific through its application, the prototypology is specific from the beginning. On the other hand, it never really becomes generic as it keeps on transforming itself through the information it receives. Made of a pliable, learning matter it adapts to changing needs of programs and inhabitants. Hence a prototypology is not a model, but a transient phase of an evolutionary process, always *ahead of its type*.
ANDREAS RUBY

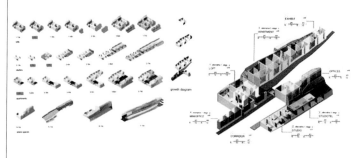

sull (Ferda
KOLATAN & Erich
SCHOENENBERGER),
*Europan 5: Gradate
Housing*, Almere
(The Netherlands),
2000.

● protuberances
[MG] See 'bluntings.'

● provisional
[MG] See 'precarious(ly).'

ACTAR ARQUITECTURA, *Reversible colonization of interstitial voids Playing Ciutat Vella*, Barcelona, 1998.

★ ● pseudo-realities

→ 'event', 'eye',
'gaze> tactical gaze',
'paradoxes',
'surprise', 'suspense'

[c] "*Every morning two magistrates greeted one another as they passed in the street: 'Buenos días, amor' (Good morning, love), one would say; 'Buenos días, vida' (Good morning, life), the other would reply. Anyone overhearing them might think this was the disgraceful expression of a taboo relationship. But in fact their names were Jesús Amor and Antonio Vida. Words say what they mean, but they can also say something else. And the same thing happens with photographs. (Anecdote recounted by Jaime Gil de Biedma).*"
(BERNADÓ, Jordi, "Palacio de la Bellota", *BCN +*, Barcelona: ACTAR, 2000)

[MG] "*Truth requires rigour, lie requires imagination.*" (WAGENSBERG, Jorge, *Si la naturaleza es la respuesta, ¿cuál era la pregunta?*, Barcelona: Tusquets, 2002)

Jordi BERNADÓ, Atlanta, in PRAT, Ramon; BERNADÓ, Jordi, *Atlanta*, Barcelona: ACTAR, 1995.

■● psycho-geographize

[JM] To psycho-geographize is to psycho-map the city, make it chronometricly (rhythmicly) live as a permanent transit of places.

[MG] See 'm.city'.

●◆✕ puff pastry (puffed up)

→ 'fold', 'land', layers', 'sponged', void', 'Yokohama'

[MG] Puff pastry is a structure or configuration which bears similarity to *mille-feuille* (French cooking) or *hojaldre* (Spanish cooking): laminated mass composed of numerous fine sheets stacked one atop the other.

[FS] Our facades have decreased in mass, resolving problems of insulation and reserves with especially thin laminates, while thickness, all of a sudden, has become a habitable space.
The barely deep facade of the International Style has become a space to be passed through. The wall unfolds as a sponge, converting the structural mass into a more subtle material.
This phenomenon can also be seen in floor plates that are no longer compact, but are separated into a cavity that contains, in the roof, the structure. We appropriate space, until now the exclusive home of monsters and hunchbacks of Notre Dame. At the same time, this void band is related to the space that surrounds and defines it.
The fissured wall of the contemporary world is puffed up, spongy, void and habited. It is the negative space of the roman wall. It receives functions and programs. It constructs folding spaces itself. A layer of puff-pastry, where the dough is modern space.

[VG] See '*millefeuille*', 'laminate', 'multilayer'.

Neil DENARI
Architects, *Vertical Smoothouse*,
Los Angeles
(California, USA),
1997.

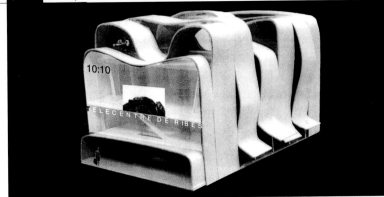

Vicente GUALLART, *Telecentre*, Ribes de Freser (Girona, Spain), project.

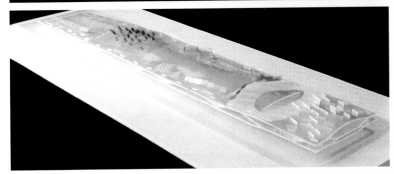

FOA, *International Port Terminal*, Yokohama (Japan), 2002.

Javier FRESNEDA, Javier PEÑA, Javier SANJUÁN, *Steel technological centre*, Murcia (Spain), 1998.

Ginés GARRIDO, Ricardo SÁNCHEZ LAMPREAVE, Fernando PORRAS-ISLA, *Competition for auditorium and conference centre*, Pamplona (Navarra, Spain), 1998.

★ purgatory effect

→ 'deviation',
'in-between',
'indiscipline',
'intermediate places',
'trip'

[co] Following Julius Caesar's ascension to the throne, Cato committed suicide in Utica, Africa, the last bastion of the defenders of the Republic. He remains condemned to purgatory for suicide, but he also remains a symbol of all values of freedom. He cannot escape divine justice but he lives in tenuous and intermediate purgatory —perhaps the paradigm of intermediate spaces.

Dante and Virgil wander through Hell with irrefutable proof of what goes on there, taking notes, inventories and recognising ironically famous characters of the period, as visitors. But in purgatory, they wander disoriented, without really knowing what they are to do. "*The crowd seemed astonished, looking again and again around them, as if one discovers something he has never seen...*"(ALIGHIERI, Dante, *The Divine Comedy*). A place of gradients, its steps must be climbed up to Heaven or down to Hell. Dante understands Purgatory as a mountain in the form of a truncated cone that rises up through the atmosphere, at the summit of which is a plane where lies the earthly paradise. A place of transit that is inconstant and divergent in every way. None of the situations described in Purgatory is static.

Purgatory appears as the symbol of the provisional, as the representation of the intermediate states in the religious space of the period. Between the defined and necessary absolutes of Heaven and Hell stands Purgatory as place of ambiguity, of imprecision and improvision, of uncertainty, of doubt, of tenuousness. It is in our interests to be in Purgatory because it is not necessary to strive to be absolutely bad or completely good. From this place of the ambiguous can be glimpsed absolute extremes, allowing one to lie in a relative state between good and bad, and even to choose between Heaven and Hell after death.

JOSÉ ALFONSO BALLESTEROS

● puzzle (or jigsaw puzzle)

[MG] See 'combination,' 'game' and 'tangram.'

A puzzle is a game that consists in reproducing a configuration that has previously been divided into smaller pieces or elements that, once appropriately combined, forms the previous shape. Usually, the drawing and the pieces are fixed and stable: closed. We can, however, imagine puzzles divided into components and assemblies which would answer to patterns – or dispositions – that have a changeable basis, with limits and silhouettes that are as mutable as they are indifferent to a single shape. The joining would lie in the lines of linkage, which would necessarily be compatible between themselves. Puzzles at once open and closed.

THIERI FOULC/OU.
PEIN. PO,
Morpholo, in AD
vol. 66 No 5/6, 1996.

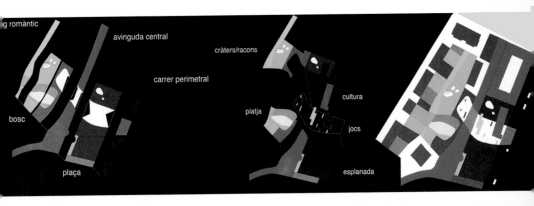

g romàntic

avinguda central

cràters/racons

carrer perimetral

cultura

platja

bosc

jocs

plaça

esplanada

ACTAR ARQUITECTURA, *Pau Picasso Square*, Montornés del Vallès (Barcelona), 2000.

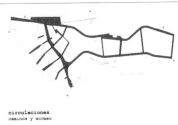

circulaciones.
caminos y acceso

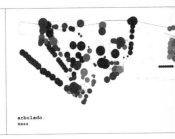

arbolado.
masa.

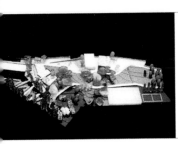

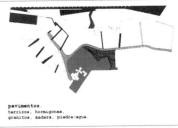

pavimentos.
terrizos, hormigones.
granitos, madera, piedra-agua.

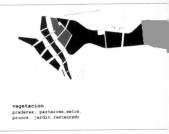

vegetación.
praderas, parterres, setos.
prunos, jardin restaurado

Alberto MARTÍNEZ CASTILLO, Beatriz MATOS, *Casino de la Reina Park*, Madrid, 1998.

● *Quaderns*

[MG] 1981-1991 & 1991-2000. See 'action>critical.'

● quantum

[MG] "*The uncertainty principle signalled an end to Laplace's dream of a theory of science, a model of the universe that would be completely deterministic: one certainly cannot predict future events exactly if one cannot even measure the present state of the universe precisely!*

We could still imagine that there is a set of laws that determines events completely for some supernatural being, who could observe the present state of the universe without disturbing it.

However, such models of the universe are not of much interest to us ordinary mortals. It seems better to employ the principle of economy known as Occam's razor and cut out all the features of the theory that cannot be observed. This approach led Heisenberg, Erwin Schrödinger and Paul Dirac to reformulate mechanics into a new theory called quantum mechanics, based on the uncertainty principle. In this theory, the particles no longer had separate, well-defined positions and velocities that could be observed. Instead, they had a quantum state, which was a combination of position and velocity.

In general, quantum mechanics does not predict a single definite result for an observation. Instead, it predicts a number of possible outcomes and tells us how likely each of these is.

That is to say, if one made the same measurement on a large number of similar systems, each of which started off in the same way, one would find that the result of the measurement would be A in a certain number of cases, B in a different number, and so on.[...] One could not predict the approximate number of times that the result would be A or B, but one could not predict the specific result of an individual measurement. Quantum mechanics therefore introduces an unavoidable element unpredictability, or randomness into science."

(HAWKING, Stephen W., *A Brief History of Time: From the Big Bang to Black Holes*, London: Bantam, 1988)

● ★ *quidam*

→ 'vague', 'vector'

[MG] Quidam is the "unknown". The anonymous user – or vector – of the city. It is a fluctuant and uncertain force of displacement and drift; of (unpredictable) action and excitation. A quidam is a parameter of elastic information for a new space that is no longer public, but rather relational.

[CO] A quidam is a passer-by. Someone who passes and only exists as he passes. A user who crosses the very public space that he generates. Human vehicular unit about which we only know for certain that it has left one place, but not yet reached another. A social character who lives covered in a film of anonymity, which enables him to enjoy others while being protected from them. Unknown. No one in general. Everyone in particular. MANUEL DELGADO

Courtesy of IAN+.

R

✘ R+3D

[VG] Research + Development, but also + eDucation + Diffusion.

★ rays

→ 'geometry'

[co] Vision is a beam of particles.
We see through an angle of light, an angle of vision.
The reality we see is the reflection of light beams on matter.
A projector casts images, constructs realities through an angle of projection, an angle of light.
What happens when an angle of vision and an angle of light coincide?
There are references in architecture regarding the source of light – the sun – and its consequence – the shadow.
Advanced architecture proposes living in an intermediate state: inhabiting the beam.
That beam of light from the film projector in *Cinema Paradiso*, the beam of light that teletransports you in *Star Trek*, the beam of light in *Spek* that builds landscapes.
Cast your beam and live in it.
ENRIC RUIZ-GELI

● re-flection

[MG] See 'gaze,' 'projection,' 'reality.'

[MG] "*Reality is not always what you think you see. Architecture is a way of understanding and interpreting reality and, as such, it takes certain information, processes it and gives it back in several possible meanings, projecting an image made of multiple visions, distortions and suggestions. This is the result of a reflection on reality, of a mental process.*
In other words, the result of a reflection on reality is the reflection of another reality, projected through a filter of experiences, potentials, needs and moods." (Susanna Cros)

ROCHE, DSV & Sie., *Habitat furtif*, mobile prototype, Paris, 1998.

✖ re- (prefix)

→ 'audacity', 'networks' [VG] See 'recycling' and 're-information.'

Since the definition of the global village in the sixties by Marshall McLuhan, hence implemented by today's satellite communications network, any intervention on the territory is an act on a known environment. The entire planet is a city. Taking action on any place (the centre of Paris, the Amazon jungle, an island in the Pacific, the American desert or the neighbourhood of El Raval in Barcelona) can never again be an act of conquest of an unknown territory. The limit between city and country, between dwelling and landscape, between the natural and the artificial, no longer exists. Expansion is no longer possible. Any action on the territory is an act directed towards the interior of the global village. It is a re-act.

●★◆ <re>, urbanism

[MG] During a large part of the two last decades, the primary objective of official urbanism was to create a model of <re>: redemption, regeneration, reconstruction, restoration, rehabilitation, redefinition, recovery. They are no more than nominalisations of a course of action based upon repetition, that is, upon inversion – or regression – of processes.

It is an action based upon restoration of an urban space of traditional silhouettes, the repair of which has been entrusted principally to an old disciplinary, pragmatic and conservationist profession. And this profession rests upon the security of the computer drawing (that is, nostalgic evocation as a compositional desire, as action that is figurative, as a priority, inclined towards the reconstruction of the fabric or, in the new developments of the outlying areas, towards its recreation).

Neo-monumental forms and orders founded upon the re-creation of old patterns of historic urbanism (the closed block, the picturesque *redent*, the classical crescent, etc.) and solemnly imposed upon the landscape, assert today themselves as old disciplinary stereotypes. They are meant to translate a desire for syntactical control and discretion over the territory that barely responds to new – authentically qualitative – requests for a plural and imaginative development for our environment.

[c] *"We are now witnessing a sort of nostalgic approach that seeks to transfer the values of the 19th-century city to new boundaries. Ridiculous "mini-suburbs" are planned on city outskirts, small grids that, without doubt, are the outcome of meagre or nonexistent exercises of the imagination in conceiving the city of today.*

Urban expansion requires scale, dimensions, height, extension. Instead of the block dimensions of 100x100 or 150x150 metres, 6-7 heights and occupation of large urban areas of the old suburbs, today's "mini-suburbs" have a small number of blocks that in some case measure 45x45 metres and have 3-4 heights.

Due to their small size, these new operations end up marooned among the large suburban areas of diverse building types, and their rachitic "order" is incapable of wielding any affect or influence over them.

We do not believe that these nostalgic operations are the way to go in defining new urban territories. Today, we operate on edges: edges of networks and edges of cities.

The topographies on which we must operate are diverse. The city grows adapting itself to its new infrastructures, which, due to the great technological advances in this field, may emerge over spectacular bridges, tunnels, embankments, etc.

Thus, housing must adapt to these vestiges of territory, the results of the implantation of new networks. A clear zero elevation no longer exists, nor does a uniform slope. This situation, which can be suggestive and even enriching in approaching the building project, clashes with the excessively generic town planning that defines these new territories. We find ourselves facing a confrontation between code and reality. It is saddening to witness the setting of codes for horizontal cornice alignment, for buildings in closed city blocks with differences in height along the length the façade of up to 8 or 10 metres due to the irregularity of the place in which they are inserted, creating a clash, an unnecessary aggression by the building on the urban landscape.

The city grows more and more rapidly, generating highly diverse situations that will accordingly require diverse solutions and approaches in order to define them. These "urban voids" will require greater flexibility in how we tackle them, and thus the need to do away with the single construction typology. Each place requires its own solution, a specific definition." (Aranguren, María José, González Gallegos, José, "Habitar la caja", unpublished, 1999)

[FS] Urbanism is dead. Now, drawings and urban development are homogenized. As opposed to the live discussions in the womb of the Modern Movement, today we find ourselves at a moment, in which the folded modern block – that conforms to a false grid – has won. Urbanism in itself is declared finished and the reflection over public space has become reduced – apparently at least – to simple nineteenth century models.

Growth area "Madrid Sur", 1994, in *Los Nuevos ensanches de Madrid*, Madrid Town Hall, 1995.

▲ reation

→ 'energy', 'field', '<i> space', 'interaction'

[FP] From the positive point of view, a recation is the combination of two or more elements that generate a new entity. This phenomenon implies the diminuition of the intrinsic characteristics of the primitive elements. However, this is not seen as a loss, but as a enriching evolution.

From the negative point of view, we are not be interested in reacting, but in activating; not in answering, but in asking; not in defending, but in attacking.

● reactive

→ 'action', 'action>
critical', 'activation',
'activity', 'advanced>
advanced architecture',
'a-scalarity', 'extroversion:
<ex> factors of form',
'gaze> tactical gaze',
'infiltration> intrusiveness
and interference',
'paradoxes', 're- (prefix)',
'recycle', 're-information',
'synergy'

[MG] **(reactivation)**

"Reaction" and "Activation" combine (interpreting the term 'reaction' as a cross between "relation" and "action") to catalyse movements and transmit energies and relationships between uses, events, scales and (or) scenarios which are – by their own nature – subject to a dynamic (evolutionary) processes.

[MG] **(reactivism)**

Faced with a scenario of contradictions, the reactive demands an understanding and a critical and selective compression of information, which is potentially evolutionary; transformative. RECODIFYING. Appropriately recording (and reprogramming), with clarity, precision and power, inhibited vectors are activated through uninhibiting actions: new relationships – and new combinations – that impel unexpected (re)configurations of the initial operative system in an architecture that is posited no longer only in terms that are figurative, but rather in terms that are diagrammatic of activity, movement and/or interchange. That is to say, in the dynamic terms of a map of action. Rather than regenerating (completing) or transforming (redefining) reality, reactivism is an issueof "resonating" with – in order to reform, restructure, reactivate – reality. In sum, the process involves the recognising, selecting and processing of the more relevant and significant – operative – bits of information. As well, it involves favouring trajectories capable of transferring reality – real and virtual –that are more complex – plural, non-univocal.

● ✖ ★ + reality

→ 'action',
'criss-crossing',
'dirty details',
'environment',
'field', 'interfaces',
'object', 'places',
'pseudo-realities',
're-flection'

[MG] [VG] Reality is '*physical and virtual, rather than real and virtual.*'
(From a conversation with Artur Serra)

[MG] We are witnessing the ambivalent manifestations of a new, structurally chaotic, apparently strange and frequently incoherent reality which answers to a nature that is progressively more mongrel and paradoxical – overlapped by those phenomena, processes and conditions that characterise and determine it.

[co] Modern, post-modern, eclectic: at once tolerant and despotic, transparent and transmitted, subject to impressive flows of communication, exposed to the most radical and irreversible transformation of the many transformations in which humanity has played a leading role – that is our age. A growing complexity engineered by multiple processes that involves the modification of those symbolic structures we have used to create the different orders that shape our culture. In its place, a profound dissolution and metamorphosis signals an indefinite time that is unresolved, governed by the firmest homologations and the strictest differences. This space appears today as a place of uncertainty and of invention. No one knows if its fate will be decided by the pure laws of entropy – pure relationships of strength – or whether it will be measured by the construction of new types of qualifying orders.
FRANCISCO JARAUTA

[WM] "*The concept of reality is the key to understanding a radical change in the manner of re-presenting new ideas. Virtual reality interacts in the manner of observing such that the old observer of the represented reality has split in two: one internal and other external, where the internal observer can no longer distinguish between the two phenomena. The observer finds himself inside the image, in a system of interactive simulation, causing a radical change vis-à-vis the external observer, turning him into an internal observer.*

This supposes a shift from an extrinsic relation with new technologies to an intrinsic relation, where this digital double of the observer interacts by means of sensors and effectors.

Given that the sensors of the virtual internal observer are the effectors of the real external observer which, at the same time, become sensors of the virtual internal observer, we recognise in this circle the inseparability – fundamental in the electronic world of the media – between interface and internal observer, between observer and the observed, between the reality of the internal observer and the illusion of the external observer.

The computer-generated world-model is centred on the observer."

Peter Weibel, *Virtual Reality, from Endo Access to Electronics.* (Translated from Spanish.)

[co] See 'utopia.' Reality is a question that appears in the memory of our retina.
ENRIC RUIZ-GELI

● recursiveness (reproduction and similarity)

→ 'a-scalarity', 'attractors', 'chunking', 'diagrams', 'field', 'genetics of form', 'glocal', 'information', 'interaction', 'relationships, transitive (of transference)', 'resonance and transference', 'self-similarity', 'synergy', 'zoom'

[MG] The notion of recursiveness is based upon the appearance of similar bits of information – and shapes – between different overlapping levels. Although the events are not exactly the same, we find consistent features among differentiating aspects.

"Recursive enumeration" enables new elements to be produced, mathematically, from previous elements, by means of certain established rules. As in any dynamic process, such recursive sequences adopt increasingly complex behaviour as their development becomes more advanced. The more advanced they become, the less predictable are the results.

However, it is possible to recognise with precision not only the rules that may have produced the different chains, but also those shorter chains which may be their predecessors.

In this vain, it is even possible to reach the source itself: the axiom (or seed) of all generated or generatable protocols, theorems or combinations. The axiom, the genotype and the code are expressions that illustrate the potential diagramming of this nuclear operative criterion, capable of stimulating – and synthesising – events (although incapable of entirely summing them up). As Douglas R. Hofstadter would insist: "*The genotype never contains the complete specification of the whole, but it anticipates it.*"

(HOFSTADTER, Douglas R., *Gödel, Escher, Bach: An Eternal Golden Braid*, Barcelona: Tusquets, 1987. Translated from Spanish.)

◆● recycle

[FS] **(architecture remains)**

Because architecture is the art of space and space is never wasted, there is no need to say that is recycled. Also, it does not require a strategy or an exercise of goodwill. Life itself recycles architecture. Architecture is never purely and simply original. On the contrary, very little architecture is original; it feeds off the existent. There is no *tabula rasa* – architecture always has to be aware of numerous programs, desires, forces and other existent circumstances. If we add to this recycling, that in itself requires certain specific environmental considerations, the entire problem seems irrelevant. An art that is so absolutely pragmatic, as is architecture, imperturbably flirts with (what in other disciplines would be considered a trick) a genuine publicity promotion.

[MG] **(recycle residues)**

Waste recycling is the recycling of solid, organic, informative or spatial residues and remains.

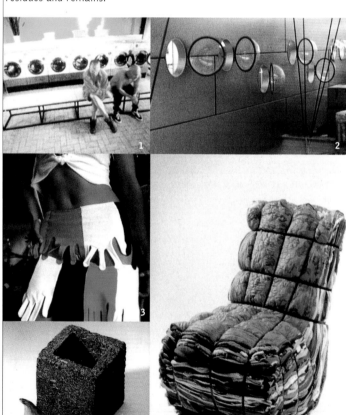

1. Laundry.

2. Willy MÜLLER +
THB Consulting,
Factory,
Sant Andreu
(Barcelona), 1998.

3. Vacas Flacas
(Carolina Azcona &
Miriam Cobo),
in *Fisuras* 7, 1999.

4. & 5. Andreas
MÖLLER, *Bolle-Box*
for packaging bulbs,
1994, and Tejo REMY,
Rag chair, 1991,
respectively, both in
RAMAKERS, Renny;
BAKKER, Gijs (Eds.),
Droog Design.
Spirit of the Nineties,
Rotterdam: 010
Publishers, 1998.

+◆ recycling

[WM]　One of the most reliable indicators used by sociologists to measure our standard of living is the waste we generate, at either the individual or collective level. With rubbish we can trace history: migrations, disasters, the rise and decline of civilisations.

There are two new points that we should note. On one hand, our concern has shifted from wanting to know what to do with waste to wanting to know how to not generate it (occurring at the same time as the change from the concern with how to generate energy to how to not waste it). This has contributed to an understanding of the idea of waste as a dynamic and fluctuating concept.

The race to achieve lower fuel consumption in cars arrived at the following conclusion: increased efficiency is economically viable when the cost per litre of petrol saved is less than the cost of buying a litre of petrol. On the other hand, the new technologies pose a collateral – if not contradictory – problem: How to measure the possible degree of loss or waste produced in our actions in the network? How do we tell this story?

[FS]　See 'tergiversation'.

1. WMA Willy Müller Arquitectos, *Punt Verd Mercabarna, recycling plant for urban waste*, Barcelona, 2002 (Photograph: Oriol Rigat). **2.** ÁBALOS & HERREROS, *Recycling plant for urban waste*, Valdemingómez (Madrid), 1998.

●✖ recycling, urban

→ 'ecology, active',
're- (prefix)', 'recycling',
're-information'

[MG] The notion of recycling introduces the need to create new responses for urban complexes that are now obsolete. Today, old fabrics or estates offer
an immense stock of buildings, sometimes decadent and at other times
prematurely aged (due to the rapidity with which they were built) which reveal important spatial, constructional and environmental pathologies that
must approached on the basis of functional, profound surgical operations.
Old anachronistic factories, housing estates, super-cities for tourists, and
non-functional suburbs are examples of scenarios that might welcome assistance and reactivation. Urban recycling – operations of renovation and
re-information – of such areas aim to halt the growing processes of waste
and inadaptation through global actions of restructuring and redefinition
(spatial, iconographical and urban), in order to foster new relationships between construction and a changing environment. All of this reflects the
existence of a much deeper debate about the desire for preservation and
the need for intervention in our environment (and consequent concern for
the methods of acting upon and occupying the territory).

[VG] **(re-cycle)**
Recycling (introducing old structures into a new cycle) is differentiated
from rebuilding (building anew something that has existed) or re-habilitating (habilitating a decrepit construction). Urban recycling means beginning a new cultural, physical, economic and social cycle in a city.
Re-cycling means accepting that something has reached the end of its life
cycle and that another cycle has to begin, based upon an existing condition. The
culture of re-cycling, proper to the twenty-first century, is different to the
culture of re-habilitation, proper to the late twentieth century, which aimed
to habilitate something that was valid in its time and that, after a period of
abandonment, was to be restored to its original state. Recycling allows construction upon an existing base (it does not require the creation or importing
of new products), turning it into a material that is coherent in itself.
The history and the culture of a place is a fundamental basis upon which a
new cycle is begun. Urban recycling not only affects the physical aspect of the
city, but also the behaviour of its inhabitants, a new attitude on the part of its
managers and the development of new economies. Recycling is innovating.

[VG] **(re-economising)**
In the new economy, a territory's principal capital is human capital. And not
only does the economy have to preserve its capital, it has to endeavour to extend it, improving the quality of life and an environment fit for development.
In this way, cities have to grow inwards, with a view towards preserving the nature that surrounds them. To construct themselves over themselves. The economic and cultural substratum has to be maintained and exploited because the
new information economy requires spaces for collective culture and leisure.
Many cities have heritages to be exploited that were built in past ages. The best
way to maintain heritage is to increase it. In the coming years, leading cities
will have to know how to grow economically without growing physically.

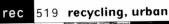

Eduardo ARROYO
(NO.mad Arquitectura),
S&Aa (SORIANO-
PALACIOS),
*Competition for
administrative
building*, Bolzano
(Italy), 1999.

NL ARCHITECTS,
*Project Parkhouse
Carstadt*, Amsterdam
(The Netherlands),
1996.

● refluences

→ 'braids', 'fold',
'landstrategy', 'reliefs',
'topographies,
operative', 'Yokohama'

[MG] See '*plateaux.*'

Dynamic movement – or tide – of ebb and flow (of folding and fold-back)derived from another principal of a different nature // Also cleverness in achieving an end.

●◆ refold

→ 'bends and
(un)bendings', 'braids',
'coilings', 'contortionisms',
'criteria', 'fold',
'landstrategy',
'loops', 'puff pastry',
'roll-ups', 'unfolding'

[MG] See 'fold (unfold-refold)' and 'trajectory.'

[FS] To refold is to remove with order from advanced designs.

As opposed to the compact or the architectonic box – symptoms of the Classical discipline – we propose refolding as the means to optimize form. This action concentrates the interests of economy, regularity, simplicity with superimpositions, contradiction or condensation. Compacting starts from the box, while the fold does not propose a final form.

✖ refounding

→ 'Metapolis',
'networks', 're- (prefix)',
're-information'

[VG] Today, we need to set forward a possible refounding of the city that enables us to operate with topography and the built continuum as points of departure, encouraging its progress by means of improved management and design of infrastructures, allowing telematic and cable networks to reach everywhere and promoting recycling in zones of physical decadence (creating new urban icons as the product of architectural innovation that permanently display an image of progress to the outside) – just as theme parks renovate their attractions and create new spectacles year after year.

This calls for new freedoms and a form of development based, not on rigid regulations but, on an intelligent dialogue between developers and government agencies.

In this way, we avoid creating 'exquisite corpses' that quickly begin to smell of decomposition.

✖ re-information

→ 'energy', 'flows',
'house, the', 'interaction',
'livrid', 'Metapolis',
'networks', 're- (prefix)',
'reactive', 'recycling',
'refounding', 'rurban loft',
'synergy', 'tree>
photovoltaic tree'

[VG] Re-information is to form something anew using information as the basic raw material.

In a city that cannot (and must not) grow physically outwards, it is necessary, as with computer chips, to 'do more things in the same space,' in order to enable its economy to progress. To do this, it is necessary to analyse the information emitted by the city, according to multiple parameters and to design ways of increasing complexity without a corresponding increase in the 'quantity' of chaos. Urban re-information invests effort in precisely finding out (in real time) the social, environmental, physical, functional, economic and cultural information of a city with a view towards taking action in it.

The urban territory to be re-informed should be analysed with a view both towards affecting existing buildings and conditioning new constructions, and towards stimulating the construction of a new public space.

Re-information of buildings.

Faced with a world where work, leisure and commerce can be carried out vis-à-vis computers (which occupies a space that does not require spatial classification), function should not be a fundamental parameter in defining a portion of the city's land.

If we accept that the number of levels of a terrain (that is, how many times a portion of land can be multiplied over itself) is a parameter to be defined, the re-information of buildings ought to influence the capacity to organise their functioning in the section rather than in plan. With the basement given over to storage functions (cars, objects), the ground floor and its surroundings to the functions of commerce and public attention, and the higher floors to mixed uses (dwelling, processing of information), the roof would become the new space to be discovered, a place for public or semi-public leisure and recreational activities.

The organisation of the floors should provide for total flexibility that allows variation in use of spaces during the course of the day and in the life of the building.

The re-information of building represents a massive input of information, principally by means of fibre-optic cable. Cable should produce a similar transformation in building that the advent of running water or mains electricity did over a hundred years ago.

Telework (carried out in the dwelling, in an apartment or on nearby premises) will require specific spaces in domestic settings to prevent 'non-stop work syndrome.'

The increase in domestic leisure time will allow people to enjoy large-format spectacles in their own homes, in audiovisual lounges.

The dwelling, now domotic, will become part of the network of places where people live their lives (including the car, the place of work and places of leisure) in keeping with the process that we will witness of the disappearance of computers and the creation of a connected environment.

Further, the re-information of buildings means that the building is sensitive to its surroundings, and therefore organises its interaction with the urban eco-system in a sustainable fashion. The building therefore produces most of the energy it consumes by means of photovoltaic surfaces installed in the facade of the actual building or photovoltaic trees positioned on the roof. Likewise, the building should be capable of accumulating water, or extracting it from the nearby subsoil with a view to decreasing external consumption.

With the re-information of public space, each new street to be developed has to be prepared to reflect and be reflected in the virtual world. Not only does this require the construction of cabled streets which convey information at high speeds to the adjacent dwellings, but information also has to flow through public space. And public space has to be sensitive to the people who continuously inhabit it (from the ground), by means of new urban icons that interact with inhabitants in near and far environments. It has to allow active expansion in the form of sport and leisure for the people who are digitally concentrated in the surrounding dwellings. It must enable the flexible regulation of flows of vehicles and persons in the course of the day, of the week and of the year, with permanent interaction with the actual vehicles that also process its information. It has to allow new relations between organic elements (trees, plants, etc.), not as elements that respond to an urban logic (alignment, perspective, repetition), but allowing them to have their own logics. To actively assimilate the climatic and atmospheric phenomena of its environment, producing the energy consumed. New urban elements characteristic of digital culture will emerge such as the photovoltaic tree, the urban avatar, reactive paving, sport rocks, urban agriculture and mini-telecentres.

If industrial society produced a transformation intended to obtain basic quality for the maximum number of people, both in the city and in the dwelling, the information society has to seek maximum quality for all those places it transforms.

The re-information of buildings enables:

1. Functional regulation in section.

2. Functional flexibility in plan with the appearance of new spaces.

3. Use of the roof for recreational purposes.

4. The mass advent of information by cable for work, leisure and commerce.

5. Interaction between the dwelling and individuals' other objects and places.

6. Sustainable interaction with the environment.

The re-information of public space enables:

1. The design of reactive spaces that are sensitive to individuals with access to telematic environments.

2. Production of new urban icons that interact with individuals.

3. Zones of continuous recreation and leisure.

4. Flexibility in traffic flows and in the relation between pedestrians and vehicles.

5. Production of energy in the street and intelligent interaction with the environment.

6. New types of plantings.

[VG] **(re-inventing)**

Once the territory of cities is finished, or once cities have been constructed to a vast extent, the city will have to reinvent itself, go back to believing in its capacity to transform and create new and innovative realities by means of architecture, like in the years of modernity (with the recognition of historical data as another value).

Otherwise, the collective will disappear, assimilated and diluted in an environment of limited individual interests.

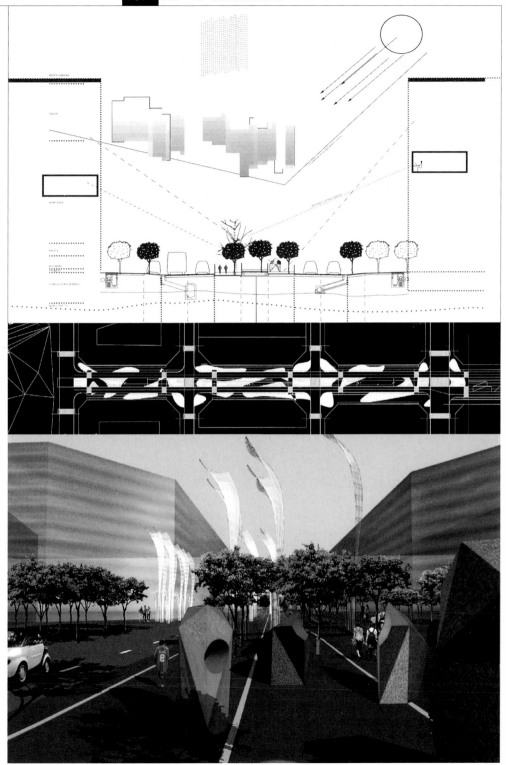

Vicente GUALLART (with Max SANJULIÁN), *Project for the urbanization of Cristóbal de Moura street*, Barcelona, 1999.

● relational

[MG] See 'interchange,' 'reactive,' 'contract,' 'spaces>collective' and 'relationships, transitive.'

● relationships, transitive (of transference)

> 'a-scalarity',
lient', 'complicity',
ontract', 'dynamism',
xtroversion:
ex> factors of form',
pen', 'synergy',
ergiversation',
rajectory'

[MG] Not relationships of reflexivity (from x to x: isolated object), nor those of symmetry (of x to y and of y to x: contextual object), but rather those of transitivity (from x to y, from y to z, from x to z: synaesthetic object). Of transference.

Until recently, reality seemed an environment — an exterior framework — that was alien and even antagonistic, in the face of which architecture had to adopt a disassociated, resistant and/or defensive posture. Today, on the contrary, it is more useful to think in terms of an architecture that enables the creation of a positive relationship with the setting: an opening in place of a defence, which would enable us to locate ourselves in an environment that is more dynamic than static.

We are interested in the quest (activist and dynamic) for an architecture that seeks and is able to posit relationships in (and with) scenarios that are virtually activated — or, precisely, dynamic; as linked to place as they are, at the same time, uprooted, capable, in effect, of transferring to "other possible" territories.

The project changes from an "entity" into a "transferor." Crystallising concrete landscapes by conveying possible alternative landscapes.

Proposing — paraphrasing Aaron Betsky (BETSKY, Aaron, "El paisaje del yo," *Quaderns* 220, 1998) – "*mechanisms for action and keys to interpretation (interfaces and icons)*" for scenarios that continuously need to be reconstructed and reinterpreted through transitive projections made of real interactions in the place and virtual relationships with other places. From relationships that are at once glocal, linking and delocalising.

Folds and faults,
in VVAA, *Història
Natural*, Barcelona:
Ed. Océano-
Institut Gallach,
1990, vol. 6.

  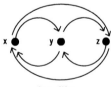

reflexive   symmetric   transitive

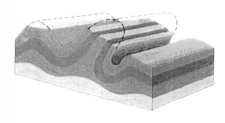 

● reliefs

[MG] See 'enclaves.'

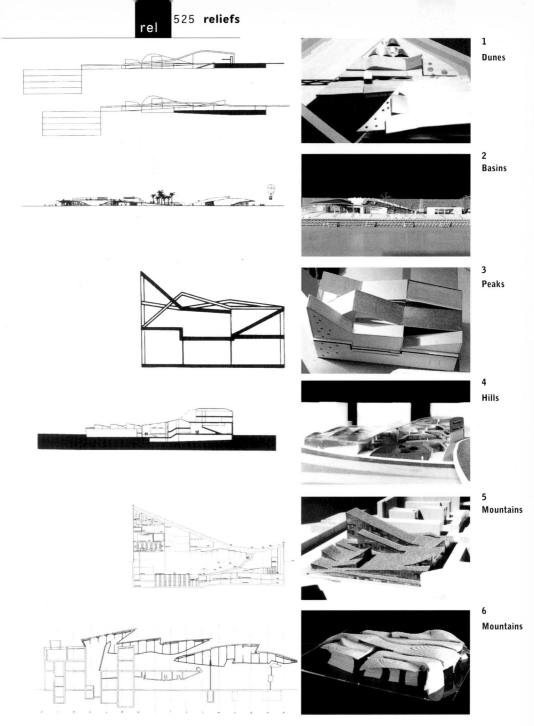

1 Dunes

2 Basins

3 Peaks

4 Hills

5 Mountains

6 Mountains

1. Willy MÜLLER, *Competition for auditorium and conference centre*, Pamplona (Navarra, Spain), 1998. **2.** Javier FRESNEDA, Javier PEÑA, Javier SANJUÁN, *C-4 parcel Alfonso XII dock*, Cartagena (Spain), 1999. **3.** Vicente GUALLART, *House of the seven peaks*, La Pobla de Vallbona (Valencia, Spain), 1998. **4.** Javier FRESNEDA, Javier PEÑA, Javier SANJUÁN, *Steel technological centre*, Murcia (Spain), 1998. **5.** Eduardo ARROYO (NO.mad Arquitectura), *Competition for auditorium* (finalist), Pamplona (Navarra, Spain), 1998. **6.** AMP (ARTENGO-ME-NIS-PASTRANA), *Conference centre Tenerife Sur*, Playa de las Américas, Costa Adeje (Tenerife, Spain), 1998-.

★ repetition and monotony

[CO] See 'monotony and repetition.' EDUARD BRU

✖ represent

[VG] Only that which can be represented can be constructed.

★ research

[CO] See 'evolution,' 'study' and 'relationships, transitive.'

– as a means (pharmaceutical products, study of a solution to a problem). Novartis, Bayer, Monsanto, etc.

– as an end (television series, figure out whodunit). Colombo, Magnum, Sherlock Holmes, Maigret, etc.

– as a bridge (architecture, incorporation of complex systems for the resolution of a range of unknowns).

Although there is the concept of the term Investigation/Research as a profound study of a subject, advanced architecture prefers its meaning related to inquiry or search. This alternative meaning incorporates emotional factors that affect cognitive factors.

The advanced architect teaches the environment nothing, he limits himself to stimulating it.

Research moves from intuition towards decision on the basis of better science, providing a response to uncertainty.

Investigation/Research seeks to foster links between variables. Going beyond simple analysis, therefore requires new instruments and methodologies.

IGNASI PÉREZ ARNAL

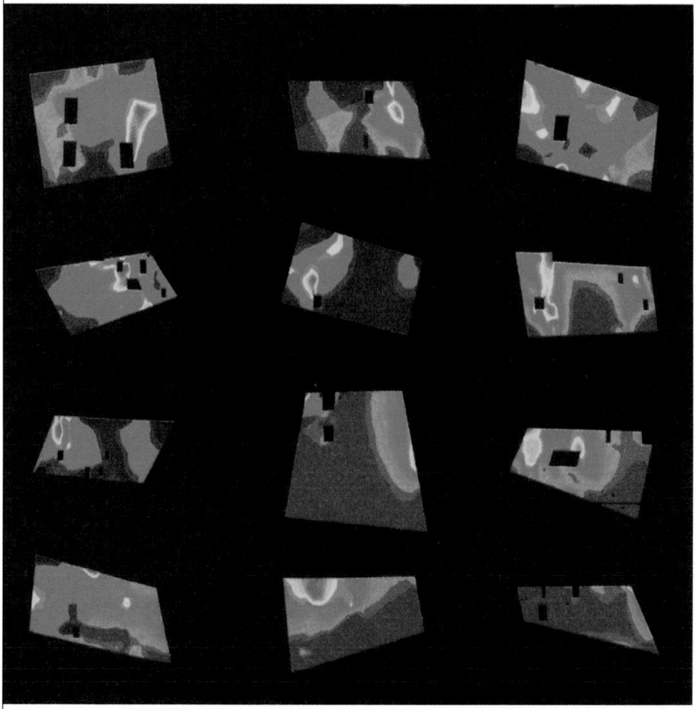

Cecil BALMOND, Tension distribution studies for the *Victoria & Albert Museum*, by Daniel LIBESKIND, London, 2005, in BALMOND, Cecil, *informal*, Munich: Prestel, 2002.

S&Aa (SORIANO-
PALACIOS),
*Competition for
cultural centre and
auditorium* (finalist),
Benidorm (Alicante,
Spain), 1995.

Eduardo ARROYO
(NO.mad Arquitectura),
*Competition for
auditorium* (finalist),
Pamplona (Navarra,
Spain), 1998.

● resonance-synergy-interaction

→ 'context',
'environment', 'glocal',
'interaction', 'interchange',
'places', 'reactivation',
're-information',
'relationships, transitive',
'synergy'

[MG] Resonance is the modification of a sound caused by the reflection of itself or its vibrational repercussion upon another body. Interaction is a mutual interchange of stimuli. Synergy is the active concourse of various efforts.
- Resonance is the syntonisation of harmonised energies.
- Interaction is the interchange of associated energies.
- Synergy is the combination of multiplied energies.
All refer to the notion of field and to an ambivalent relationship with the environment.

● resonance and transference

→ 'complicity',
'dynamism', 'extroversion:
<ex> factors of form',
'glocal', 'intelligence',
'interaction', 'interchange',
'reactive', 'recursiveness',
're-information',
'relationships, transitive',
'synergy'

[MG] Dynamic systems increase their complexity (that is, their capacity for combining overlapping levels of information) in situations which foster a greater degree of interchange between different actions and stimuli (no longer as merely additive events, but rather as interactive and multiplicative bits of information, aimed at influencing the global environment by means of local action).

In such processes, the degree of interaction of each event depends, in effect, upon its greater or lesser effectiveness in "resonating" with the basic parameters of the system (to simultaneously condense and assimilate them) and, at the same time, in transferring them (in turn, to restructuring and restimulating them) giving them new energies (vectors) and, therefore, new propulsive movements (trajectories).

This implies situations that are more uncertain and undefined – less prefigurable – but also situations that are more singular (and impure) – different and combinatorial.

This can give rise, with qualitative criteria, to spatial solutions that are more plural and unbiased – open and evolutionary, precisely – generated through direct relationships between events (bits of information) and glocal (global and local) devices (organisations).

● reversible

→ 'contract', 'cuttings', 'data', 'devices', 'ecology, active', 'ephemeral', 'fleeting', 'impermanences', 'in/unstable', 'lightness', 'nomad', 'precarious(ly)', 'provisional', 're- (prefix)', 'scaffolding', 'time', 'zapping'

[MG] Reversible is action which is capable of changing the direction of its own movement and/or of bringing things back to a state perceptibly similar to what it was previously. There is something of an elastic braid about it. It has an unstable presence. In the same way, we can talk about reversible occupations of the landscape: the old urbanist dichotomy between areas that are or are not "ripe for development" could yield, in certain cases, to different strategies of colonisation, which would vary according to the specific vocation of the place. Such strategies could possibly even throw into crisis the old idea of permanent colonisation *of* and *on* the territory (and therefore the implicit desire to emphasise, through "stable" figuration, its inherent value) and replace it with another type of model. This new model – linked to lightweight systems of construction and land occupation in areas of gentle colonisation associated with recycling of disused uses (quarries, river banks, etc.) – would welcome uses and "contracts" under difficult circumstances: dynamics, in any case, which would suggest the capacity to act with the place and with the user with a less formal, and more informal – unstable and mutable – attitude. Because it is fleeting. Open to the temporary, the ephemeral, the impermanent; belonging to a culture of mobility, precariousness and the contingent amortisation of events.

KALHÖFER&KORSCHILDGEN, *Enlargement of the house Fahrt ins Grüne*, Remscheid-Lüttringhausen (Germany), 1997.

★ rhythm

[CO] See 'sequence and series.'

Rhythm no longer exists. It is impossible to produce two successive, identical intervals. Just as an advanced architect can no longer use the architrave to compose, nor can he use rhythms, as he knows that the architrave is a residue practically without relations, with few opportunities for connection and transformation, and rhythms are an approximation with little analogy to reality.

Rhythms do, however, have the possibility of transformation/perversion that enables them to be used as series and sequences. These two tools, now separated and remote from the axiomatic rigour of self-identity, can be used as one more stratum of superposition of relations.

JOSÉ ALFONSO BALLESTEROS

■ rhyzomatic

→ 'chains', 'flows',
'fractal', 'geometry',
'meaning', 'mutation',
'no-places', 'scaleless',
'topological', 'trajectory'

[JM] Rhyzomatic supposes that every project is a surrounding that is self-conditioned and generates its proposal from the immediacy with which it enters into contact. Thus, the rhyzomatic project is ecological. It proceeds, associating heterogeneities, from the atmosphere in general as well as from cultures it meets.

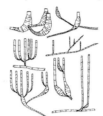

Bamboo rhyzomes and Cyperus alternifolius, respectively, both in L'Architecture d'aujourd'hui 321, 1999.

● roll-ups

[MG] See 'coilings.'

Bauhaus, Cakes, in Fisuras 3 1/3, 1995.

● rootlessness

→ 'abroad, etc.',
'criss-crossing', 'de-location',
'dichotomies', 'foreigness',
'no-places', 'reality'

[MG] Our times, as the Greek critic Yorgos Simeoforidis correctly points out "*is no longer that of the continual, gradual, permanent and "mythical" duration of the classical city.*" Our times are no longer "ritual" – based upon the repetition and recurrence of all shapes and events ("cyclical return" in which sensitivity finds permanence, that stability, in sum, which the philosophical logos would locate in ideal shapes or essences) – but rather arrhythmic, rootless, without precedent and demythifying. These are the most explicit characteristics and manifestations that constitute the authentic "environmental conditions" of new scenarios. Out times are definitively "artificial:" by virtue of being in non-genuine, manipulated and irregular, but also hybrid, synthetical, strange and unforeseeable. "Non-homologated." Rootless.

★ "rough consensus and working code"

→ 'hypercontext',
'innovation',
'intercommunity',
'networks'

[CO] "Rough consensus and working code" is the motto of the Internet Engineering Task Force (http://www.ietf.org), the group of engineers that standardises protocols which makes the Internet work. It is the formula applied to Internet organisations in making agreements. The intercommunity bases itself upon these principles in drawing up its own rules of government, different from those of the industrial age, as well as from those of earlier societies. The Internet's operational model is simply that of a group of researchers oriented towards innovation and experimentation. A digital society, based upon distributed innovation, cannot found itself upon the formulas of government of agrarian or industrial societies. It has, accordingly, its own new rules of government that seek to combine continual innovation with the broadest participation. ARTUR SERRA

✗ **rurban life**

[VG] As the twenty-first century approached, the information era transformed the traditional concepts of ownership and dwelling.

Information workers (analysts, lawyers, consultants, computer programmers, translators, artists, etc.), 15% of the population, are people who work with knowledge that can be transmitted to their clients all over the world, from anywhere in the world, via telematic systems.

In the information era, all that is left is the earth, covered by satellites that retransmit bits of money, science, culture, etc., and criss-crossed by motorways providing rapid access to cities.

Hardware as opposed to software.

Information workers no longer need to live in cities to live an urban life. Five days in the country, teleworking, two days in a city in the world, for business and leisure. A big house in the country, a small, jointly owned apartment in the city. The entire territory is now inhabitable. For this very reason it deserves a project. Its cities. Its agriculture. Its regional parks (now green spaces in the landscape-city).

New dwellings, mono-volume spaces (like the cars) occupied by furniture-room pieces that can be bought at shopping centres as though they were consumer products, can be located on farm land, that continues to be productive.

Superposition of uses. Multiplicity of lives.

1. R&Sie
(François ROCHE,
Stephanie LAVAUX),
Barak House,
Sommières (France),
2001.

2. ÁBALOS &
HERREROS,
AH Houses.
Industrial prototypes,
1994-1996.

3. ACTAR
ARQUITECTURA,
M'House Houses,
"Spring in winter",
1997.

4. Vicente GUALLART,
Willy MÜLLER,
Enric RUIZ-GELI,
Scape House,
El Penedès
(Barcelona), 1996.

● rurban loft

→ 'AH houses',
'house, the', 'M'house
houses', 'rurban life'

[MG] Principles of the metapolitan dwelling:

1. Integration into the landscape: an analysis of the landscape and its natural elements is the origin of the project, just as the analysis of a street or an urban fabric is the origin of the city. The whole plot merits a project, by action or by omission. The construction of the dwelling is a naturally artificial or an artificially natural process. Dwelling and landscape are integrated to form a new unit.

2. High quality at low cost: this means making the most out of the least. Money is a limited commodity these days. We have to optimise available resources. The beauty of a place does not lie in the quality of its materials, but in its spatial qualities. Quality is a question of ethics. Of precision. Of an attitude to the construction process that depends upon everyone who takes part in that process, from the client to industrialists.

3. Concentration, making the very most of everything: accumulation and concentration make for optimisation of resources in the functioning of a building or a city and, rather than dispersion, permanently require resources to allow its functioning (energy, movement, etc.). Any material of the place (rocks, earth, water, air, etc.), any urban energy, can potentially be integrated into the project at no extra cost.

4. Artificial materials: industry provides increasingly intelligent materials at lower prices. Materials that preserve their properties and their effect in spaces independently of the time of year or the time of day. Materials that require next to no maintenance.

5. Mobility of interior space: dwellings are large empty spaces occupied by mobile objects that allow the inhabitant to carry out activities in that space. Intelligent objects, sometimes multifunctional, that turn the entire interior into an item of furniture. The inhabitant lives in a piece of furniture.

6. Intelligent limits: empty, single-material spaces have intelligent limits compounded in a thin surface: aluminium, wood, blocks, glass. The glass in facades is made up of different sheets that, depending on the case, provide thermal, solar or anti-theft protection, and can be printed with images and textures using the screen process. Reconstruction of the floor on artificial terrain involves inserting electricity, water and heating installations that gives habitable space itsnecessary comfort level.

7. Uses are developed in section: the subsoil, introduced into the earth, and the roof, in contact with the sky, are spaces to be used with the same intensity as the level of the natural terrain. Taking as its point of departure a simple shape for its floor plan, the building or the city is organised by means of the superposition of layers with a nature of their own. The route around the building is produced by means of ramps or stairs, as though it were a walk.

8. The measurements of space: quantity is quality. Every use requires space of a given size. The dwelling is organised on the basis of the contrast between sizes of spaces. There is no standard height or standard measurement: generous height, width and length at the service of quality.

✘ rurburbia: urban-territorial space

[VG] The geographical limits of what had been understood, in lay language, as the city have yielded, almost without warning, to new scales of an *urban-territorial* space. In this new space, even the periphery can not be conceived, in effect, as a situation (a precise place or landscape: the city limit, its frontier), but rather as a condition of excentricity. At the heart of a process is the dissolution of the urban territory.

Today, various conditions can live side by side: consolidated nuclei and uncertain margins, bastard creations and unnaturalised lands, unfinished realities and different – often contradictory – realities mixed with ephemeral presences – advertising slogans, energy structures, temporary constructions – and large vacant plots.

All allude to a new entropic, uncertain and definitively unfinished definition of the contemporary territory.

The old, more or less defined, limits (and the old enclosures) of the perimetered city – still with flanks and a rearguard – have yielded to new territorial scales, in the same way that genuinely old compositive factors have yielded to a polyhedral, heterogeneous, elusive and vital reality in which the factors that assert themselves no longer seem linked to the data of an immanent reality.

We are witnessing, therefore, a city that is building itself, not so much through the evocative and figurative inclination of the elements that fill it, but though the power and neutrality of the large systems that structure it and though the variation and accumulation of those large autonomous – and no longer functionally necessary – operations that spur its development.

The old need for an urban agglomeration capable of facilitating production, interchange, defence and communication is (dis)located today in a "park-territory" as Dietmar Steiner called it dotted, in effect, with more or less specialised areas: housing estates, technology parks, university campuses, commercial zones and theme parks. Spaces dedicated to consumption, residence, work and leisure are situated in discontinuous spaces, linked by transport networks.

These are dynamics that, in effect, have nothing to do with the autobiographical construction of the place (with the *genius loci* or the slow adaptation to context) and the traditional criteria for settlement – proximity and agglomeration of raw materials, ease-of-access, symbolic or cultural importance of the place, etc. Instead, the new dynamics allude to strategic interests and factors of autonomous decision (criteria for profitability and expansion) facilitated by the speed and effectiveness (from the technological point of view) of new processes of planning and construction and for access to networks and to mobility.

Former rural areas have become situated at time-distances similar to the ones associated with the original metropolis and, accordingly, form part of the spatial complex that houses the daily activity of the region. This phenomenon, which some call rurburbia (rural-urban-suburbial), generates a territory that does not fit into the category of city or village.

S

◆ sample

→ 'machination',
'original and replica',
'tergiversation'

[FS] See 'collaging.'

In light of reutilizing models and objects in the production of the architecture, the terms collage and recycling are known. As well, there exists a third mechanism – sampling.

To sample is to inspire oneself, to take loans or to resort to various known architectural objects that in their superimposition, copied or quoted, produce a different result. Re-readings? Influences? Sampling debts to the original are more direct – although they are not quite so evident. Is it the continuation of a line of analysis or investigation?

It is necessary that various models concur to imitate and copy? Copy? Vary? Samplings' interpretation is not translated with scrupulous exactitude. It can even be erroneous.

The sampler has respect for the original models, but acts without scruples, in a fast and informal way.

Pedro URZAIZ, Carlos PÉREZ PLA, *Covered swimming pool* and *Torrefórum*, Torrelodones (Madrid), 1995.

★ scaffold

[co] See 'intermediate places.'

Scaffolding as a superposed, absolutely artificial organ, dramatically modifies the conditions of the object onto which it is superposed.

But scaffolding also generates intermediate spaces capable of modifying, or perceptibly altering, the conditions of the existing building or of the first superposition.

It is also ephemeral, which grants it a property of non-permanent transformation and involves extreme difficulty of regarding it as a residual object, and in turn adopts different forms each time it acquires physical presence.

Scaffolding is, therefore, a paradigmatic expression of the artificial object, as a process that generates almost unappreciable residues.

JOSÉ ALFONSO BALLESTEROS

+ scaffolding

→ 'appropiation
strategies', 'ephemeral',
'infiltration',
'occupation structures',
'precarious(ly)', 'scaffolds'

[WM] See 'ad-herence / inheritance.'

Scaffolding is a structure of occupation that provides thickness to an advertising surface, appropriating an existent legality.

It is the vertical ground of the metropolis, capable of supporting all sorts of structural elements, containers and contents in which to live, to work, to measure, to learn, to observe – or to introduce the movement and the volume of an ad.

★+ scaffolds (and dividing walls)

[c] "*Scaffolding can provide architects with a new field of action. Its constantly changing image makes it a pretext for experimental action.*
Apart from being built out of necessity, because cities age, scaffolding is also in keeping with the present time for its flexibility and its transformation and dematerialisation of architecture and, perhaps, for its desire to move into other areas of use. For example, in the morning it could be a great advertising hoarding, becoming a work of art in the afternoon and a huge lamp or a place for temporary exhibitions at night.
Concepts such as flexibility, simultaneity of uses and briefs, recycling of existing space and structures, or the juxtaposition of a cultural brief alongside another type of existing brief (business, commercial, administrative, etc.) could help to make these new places far more interdisciplinary.
If the contents of contemporary cultural spaces are a reflection of life down on the street, then why not use a temporary structure such as scaffolding as a support for action, creating new social and cultural relationships in its simultaneity of uses and meanings, questioning the traditional form of art containers?" (GOLLER,Bea, "Scaffolding and party walls : urban laboratories", *Quaderns* 224, 1999)

[WM]

**Scaffolds
and dividing walls**

1. & 2. Bea GOLLER
(by the "Architecture,
art and ephemeral space"
master students),
Barcelona, 1998-1999.
3. LE GROUP K, *Project
booths for homeless
Les Balises,* Lyon (France),
1994.
4. Yago CONDE, *Dividing
wall at Ronda General
Mitre,* Barcelona, 1991.

See 'ad-herence / inheritance,' 'scaffolding' and 'advertising.'
Party walls (those awaiting the construction by another "party") have become great urban screens, veritable surfaces for the inscription of current events, discourses, images and slogans.
Party walls resemble a tattooed body for feeding an interchange of personal and commercial ambitions that oblige special perceptive and rational intensifications in order to interpret, select or forget so many things.
We can imagine a strategic plan for temporary occupation of the vertical surfaces on the legal basis of payment for the use of space: perhaps the most contemporary formula and that with the greatest future in the field of architecture. A line of projectual exploration into what we might call "tenant architecture:" adapted or adhered structures.

● scale

[MG]   See 'a-scalarity (scalar ambiguity).'

● scalebound

→ 'a-scalarity',
'fractal', 'geometry',
'self-similarity'

[MG]   "*Relating to a geometric figure or a natural object whose structure is dom-inated by very small number of highly differentiated intrinsic scales. My neologism scalebound is the opposite of scaling.*"
(Paraphrasing MANDELBROT, Benoît, *Fractal objects*)

[MG]   See 'terraces.'

●◆ scaleless

[MG]   See 'a-scalarity (scalar ambiguity).'

[FS]   I am interested in architectural objects whose internal structure do not have scale, or that have a self-referential scale. The order of a building is no longer the comparison of rules based on the measurements of man, but rather the whole building establishes a measure of comparison. A boat, an airplane, a computer, present the scale of its mounting and its con-struction, or pieces in the largest sense (physical or spatial) establish it. I am interested in the specific characteristics of natural objects that do not possess scale. In these bodies, studied using mathematical abstractions called fractals, two new features appear. It is interesting to reflect until what point these properties serve as catalysts or destroy the basic concepts of the discipline. Much of the tools that we use in design are assumed, with-out previously having a minimum stake.

● scaling

→ 'a-scalarity',
'fractal', 'geometry',
'self-similarity'

[MG]   "*Relating to a geometric figure or a natural object whose parts have the same form or structure as the whole, except that they are at a different scale and can be slightly deformed.*"
(Paraphrasing MANDELBROT, Benoît, *Fractal objects*)

● scanning

→ '(inter)weavings
and inter(plots)',
'menus', 'section',
'sequence and series'

[MG]   Scanning is a sequence of sections akin to topological succession, variable in its coordinates, but immanent in its generative logic.
Scanning is also a radiographic record or map of a body section exam-ined in order to carry out a precise diagnosis.

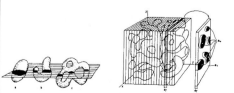

In biometry, a series of aleatory parallel sections is used to reconstruct the position and form of an organ, in *Arch+* 117, 1993.

★ scene

[CO] Open your eyes + close your eyes = a scene.

The scene is the unit of the creative flash of a spectacle. Its temporal duration does not coincide with its emotional duration. It is made up of a series of layers. All of them independent, yet simultaneous. They evolve individually, but coexist on stage. Its layers: textual, visual, musical, choreographic, cardiac, the audience. Layers that are syntonised in the mind of the spectator. It is very important to create advanced – new – scenes rapidly. Reality is way ahead of us and at times bests us. It seems easy: "An empty place, an action and an observer," Peter Brook.
ENRIC RUIZ-GELI

Bob WILSON,
Enric RUIZ-GELI,
Danton's Tod,
Salzburg (Austria),
1998.

●◆ score

→ 'circuits', 'devices', [MG] See '(inter)weavings and inter(plots),' 'patterns' and 'patterned distributions.'
'matrix', 'menus', 'order',
'section', 'sequences'

[FS] The narrow relation between the ways of representing musical thought, rhythm and signs, and the resulting sound has exercised an iron hand over the evolution and development of musical thought. It has acted as a certain preventative condition in the birth of new sound systems. Thus, certain avant-garde subversions of melody, sound etc., modified the way one looked at musical signs on paper.

In certain cases, where sound takes precedence over composition, the score acquires the aspect of a pure scheme, summarized and simplified in relation to its sonoric realization. The score appears as a collection of ambiguous signs without precise meaning and single voice, but with an ample host of translations.

In other cases, where time or duration is the object of the musical intervention, the translation of each note is not traditionally maintained and a new convention arises. The notes that translate *tiempo* and rhythm do not correlate with units of measure, but with approximate signs. It also depends on external factors or other parts of the execution.

Evolution amongst
several scores.

Later, musical notation evolved even further. It abandoned its serial principals and the pure investigation of sound, affirming for itself an interest in behavior. It became more interested in giving rules of montage or execution to define the result.

Today, scores are filled with signs that transmit executive gestures or instrumental actions, charged with producing an indeterminate desired sound. They are parallel to the action of writing. Development continues with the freedom that the composer gives the interpreter. Scores have become insignificant catalogues that the artist decodes as s/he sees fit. S/he can invent new possibilities, orders and even freely choose the instrument.

S&Aa (SORIANO-
PALACIOS), *MZMK*
(Bolzano Museum
of Modern Art),
Bolzano (Italy), 2001.

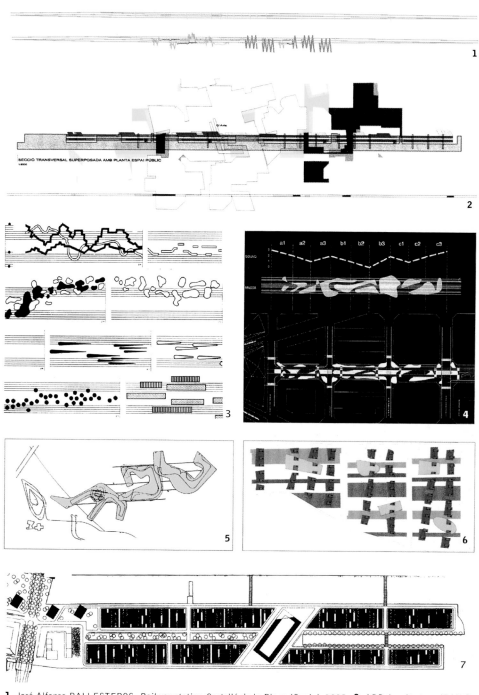

1. José Alfonso BALLESTEROS, *Railway station*, Castelló de la Plana (Spain), 1995. **2.** ADD Arquitectura (BAILO-CLARAMUNT-RULL), *Proposal for Ávila street*, Barcelona, 1999. **3.** Contemporary scores, in SORIANO-PALACIOS, *Small, it rains and with ants*, Barcelona: ACTAR, 2000. **4.** Vicente GUALLART, *Project for the urbanization of Cristóbal de Moura street*, Barcelona, 1999. **5.** Enric MIRALLES, Benedetta TAGLIABUE, *Pier*, Thessalonike (Greece), 1997. **6.** ACTAR ARQUITECTURA, *Son Gibert*, Palma de Mallorca (Spain), 1994. **7.** Adriaan GEUZE (WEST 8), *Masterplan*, Borneo Sporenburg, Amsterdam, 1996.

■● scream

→ 'advertising', 'and', '(e)motion', 'expression', 'sensuality', 'surprise', 'yes!'

[JM] "*I was walking on the road with two friends – the sun was setting. I felt a breath of melancholy. The sky suddenly became tinted blood red. I lingered, leaning against the balustrade, mortally fatigued. I saw the clouds scintillating like blood and a sword. My friends continued on their way. I remained there trembling with anguish, and heard a large and interminable shout crossing over nature.*" (E. Munch)

[MG] "*A complaining clamour, modulated in savage discords, filled our ears. The sheer unexpectedness of it made my hair stir under my cap. I don't know how it struck the others: to me it seemed as though the mist itself had screamed, so suddenly, and apparently from all sides at once, did this tumultuous and mournful uproar arise. It culminated in a hurried outbreak of almost intolerably excessive shrieking, which stopped short, leaving us stiffened in a variety of silly attitudes, and obstinately listening to the nearly as appalling and excessive silence.*" (CONRAD, Joseph, *The Heart of Darkness*, Barcelona: Penguin, 1999) (At the suggestion of Marc Aureli Santos.)

Carpenter brush, in ROBERT, François & Jean, *Face to Face*, Baden: Lars Müller Publishers, 1996.

✛ sea

→ 'bank & beach', 'field', 'places', 'territory'

[WM] The sea is a new site for coastal cities. Ports, on the other hand, are the old sites for coastal cities. In occupying, millimetre by millimetre, land left by the gradual withdrawal of ports we only succeed in closing off the city from the sea, such that *the only way to view the latter life-size is to go see it in an Imax film.* This is not meant as a joke. We must propose new structures of occupation in order to foster beaches instead of dikes, ground instead of buildings, the sea instead of its images. Rather than build Imax cinemas, we should invent a city that will afford us large-format views of the sea.

▲ search

→ 'advanced', 'bored', 'innovation'

[FP] As we search, we never repeat. As we try out, we don't usually look back.

★ search engine

→ 'knowledge', 'menus'

[co] "We hope the search engine will soon be antique. Our goal is to make that technology like plumbing: you only notice it when it backs up, otherwise it is just seemless and invisible," Brewster Kahle. XAVIER COSTA

◆ section

[FS] The Modernist spatial definition is sustained by a conception of the superficial extension of space, that is, resolved by its plani-metric definition. Similar concepts are dealt with by the picturesque avant-gardes of the moment. Cubism invented a system, with the intention of substituting the perspective constructions of the Renaissance and becoming a new agglutinating universal method, by the superimposition of perspectives, inclusion of time in the plastic definition of space. The free plan resolves all projections of space by the extrusion of a single area. The extension of vertical space is produced by simple superimposition of plans; by the simple stacking of floors and ceilings. A modern section shows extreme rigidity in the continuous repetition of extensive floors. The inventive liberty of the plan is destroyed by the section.

Contemporary space must be defined by the section. In a building with a complex section, use is not allocated over identical floor plates. It is a folded space that tries to create the fiction of a free volume. Today, the section is the representation of new creased space. It is a developed space, continuous in its connections, but discontinuous in its form and scale.

[FS] **(section, active)**

The section constructs the project. A work of architecture whose only identifying document is the section. A project that does not have a plan. A plan that is a section.

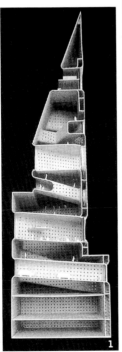
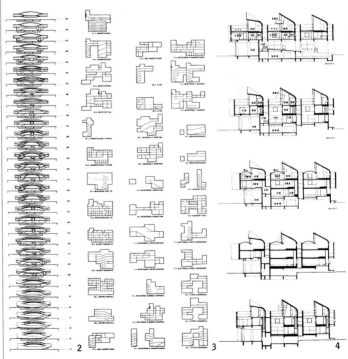

1. MVRDV, *Media Galaxy (Competition concept for the new Eyebeam Institute)*, New York, 2001, 2nd prize. **2.** FOA, *International Port Terminal*, Yokohama (Japan), 2002. **3.** Eduardo ARROYO (NO.mad Arquitectura), S&Aa (SORIANO-PALACIOS), *Competition for administrative building*, Bolzano (Italy),1999. **4.** OMA, *Housing*, Fukuoka (Japan), 1991.

★ section: scrambled flat

→ 'rurban loft'

[co] Hybrid dwellings can compatibilise traditional rural life and new devices of development. This can be done by the digitalisation of the envelop of a traditional habitat, the establishment of food and energy flow and the integration of men, cows, and bees under in each facades.
FRANÇOIS ROCHE

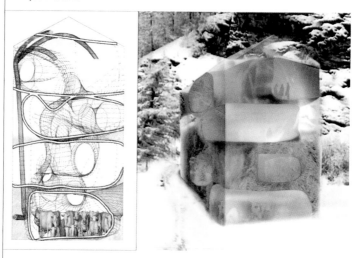

R&Sie.D/B: L, *Scrambled Flat*, Evolene (Switzerland), 2000.

● seed
[MG]

● ★ self-organization

[MG] See 'occupations.'

[co] Self-organisation is a final phase in the processes of relations between systems that allows solutions for adaptation. It is a form of dependent, inconstant grouping, fluctuating according to variables in the system in which it is implanted or to which it responds as a stimulus.
JOSÉ ALFONSO BALLESTEROS

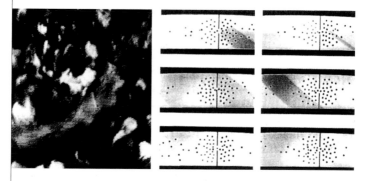

Two groups of people try to pass through a door. After a blockade situation, some of them break the symmetry, which produces a transitory situation of a run wrinkle; in KURGAN, Laura; COSTA, Xavier (Eds.), *You are here*, Barcelona: MACBA, 1995.

● self-similarity

[MG] *"We can now assert the existence of the conception of a fractal geometry and a fractal geography of nature. Essentially, these are based on the concept of self-similarity, a property shown by those evolutionary systems in which the structures remain constant while the scale of observation varies; in other words, when the parts, no matter how small they might be, resemble the whole."*

(MANDELBROT, Benoît, Los objetos fractales, Barcelona: Tusquets, 1987)

Laminated or puff-pastry structures

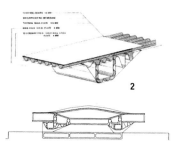

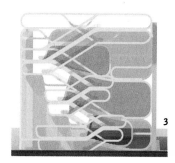

Arborescent structures of tremas or jumps

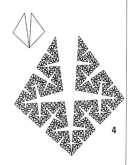

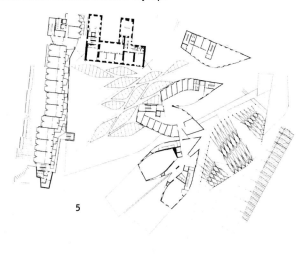

1. Lorenz attractor, J.-F. Colonna/GSV-Lactanne (CNET, École polytechnique). **2.** FOA, *International Port Terminal*, Yokohama (Japan), 1995. **3.** FOA, *Azadi multiplex cinema*, Teheran (Iran), 1997. **4.** Lung arborescent diagram, in MANDELBROT, Benoît, *Les objets fractals*, Paris: Flammarion, 1975. **5.** Enric MIRALLES, Benedetta TAGLIABUE, *Parliament*, Edimburgh (Scotland). **6.** Vicente GUALLART, *Europan 5: technological centre*, Puertollano (Ciudad Real, Spain), 1998.

✖● self-urbanism

[VG] **(as an individual action)**

New urbanism is aimed not at the masses, but at individuals. One by one, not as a collective.

Faced with the menu of possibilities offered by the city and the territory — now that information technologies equally reach any point in the territory — each individual can decide where and how he wants to live. There is no single model of city. In fact, each house is a micro-city from which its inhabitant works, shops and rests. The decision as to where to situate a home is an operation of self-urbanism; and the way in which the individual relates with his surroundings is an operation of self-urbanism.

[MG] **(as a process of spontaneous settlement)**

These days, we are aware that the biggest housing crisis is taking place not in the most developed countries, but in developing countries that are subject to vertiginous mutations and exponential growth. One fifth of the world's population is currently located in fringe areas and 'clandestine' human settlements: spontaneous structures that have developed in poorly structured spaces, the consequence of fast population growth and the general deficit of affordable dwellings. *Bidonvilles, favelas* and shanty-towns configure such structures independently of order or planning.

They are self-organised structures that should be regarded without prejudice and with attention to the internal logics of this kind of spontaneous growth. The processes of spontaneous growth arises from a mutual interaction between self-planning and self-organisation and leads to complex functional configurations that in no case convey an impression of disorder or arbitrariness. They present notable similarities with self-generated structures that exist in nature (the veins in an insect's wing, irrigation vessels in the leaf of a tree, fissures in breaking processes, bubble wrap, etc.) which despite their diversity and irregularity, adjust their development to given rules or generic patterns, whose dynamics can be analysed by analogue simulation models.

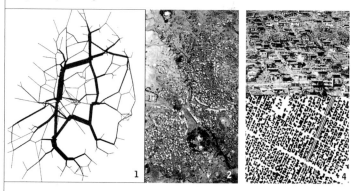

1. Cartography of espontaneous accesses and paths in Sokota, in *Arch+* 121, 1994. **2.** Aerial view of Sokota, in *Arch+* 121, 1994. **3.** Aerial view of an spontaneous settling, in *Quaderns* 213, 1996. **4.** Spontaneous settling in Mexico, in KURGAN, Laura; COSTA, Xavier (Eds.), *You are here*, Barcelona: MACBA, 1995.

◆ sense

→ 'action>critical', 'criteria', 'gaze> tactical gaze', 'time'

[FS] Sense replaces the loss that things suffer, contexts, objects, with the action of time. All action has certain epic content, of feat, and as a consequence of adventure, of play.

✚ sensors

→ 'animation', 'gesture', 'logic, digital', 'logic, fuzzy', 'Media Lab', 'reality'

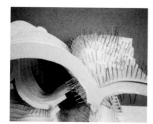

[WM] *"Chromasone consists of a unique chrome and perspex structure, and a pair of specially made data gloves. By flexing fingers in the gloves, and moving the hands [...] a very intuitive relation between gesture and sound is created. Musical expression can be imparted by a variety of gestural actions: movement of the hands and arms can make tones higher or lower in pitch, darker or brighter, greater or lesser volume, modulated or convoluted or disturbed by random fluctuations."* (Walter Fabeck, creator of the *Chromasone*, a new instrument for creating music using sensor technology)

NOX (Lars Spuybroek with Chris Seung-Woo Yoo, Kris Mun, Florent Rougemont and Ludovica Tramontin), *SoftOffice*, United Kingdom, 2000-2005.

● sensuality

→ '(e)motion', 'expression', 'passion'

[MG] *"Harrouda comes out from between the walls. Naked and ugly. Dirty and knowing. With intrigue under her arm. She starts to let her hair fall, towards the front; and turns towards the square. She summons the soul of the Ogre and pierces it with her fingers. She drinks its white blood and turns back towards us, with a sly smile. She winks, cups her breasts between her hands and invites us to drink wisdom from them."*
(BEN JELLOUN, Tahar, *Harrouda*, Saint-Amand: Editions Denoël, 1995. Translated from Spanish) (At the suggestion of Marc Aureli Santos)

[MG] *"When, in the rush of materials that perception brings to us from experience, a detail, and just one, emerges from the magma of the whole and, evading all control, manages to wound the surface of our automatic absence of attention. // Generally, there is no reason for moments like this to occur but they do, however, occur, and suddenly spark an unusual emotion in us. // They are like promises. Like glimmerings of promises. // They promise worlds."* (BARICCO, Alessandro, *City*, London: Penguin, 2002)

Vicente GUALLART, Enric RUIZ-GELI, *La Beauté à la nature*, Avignon (France), 2000.

●sequence and series

'Series' defines a group of interrelated, by derivation, elements or events which follow one another in a perceptibly similar manner due to generic adhesion, that is to say, by reproduction and/or variation of the information transmitted.

'Sequence' defines a discontinuous – and not always linear – succession of individual events that are linked, not necessarily formally but by means of infrastructure, and separated rhythmically by variable intervals of time and longer and shorter intercidences.

Today, dynamic systems, potentially "impure," animate sequences. Genetic processes mutate series, which are potentially evolutionary.

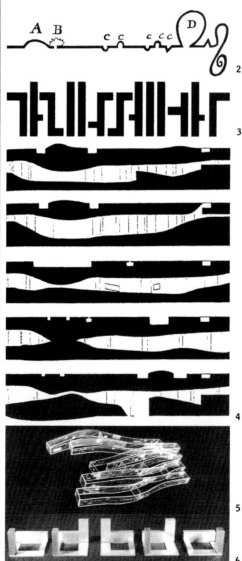

1. Gun, cigar, lamp, in GAUSA, Manuel, *Housing. New alternatives, new systems*, Barcelona: ACTAR, 1998.

2. Laurence STERN, Novel as a city (*Tristram Shandy*), in *New York-Normadesign*, Ed b.b., 1992.

3. Kazuyo SEJIMA, Ideogram of movements for zig-zag typologies, *Metropolitan Housing Studio*, 1995-1996.

4. Rem KOOLHAAS, *Conference centre*, Agadir, 1990.

5. Cristina DÍAZ MORENO, Efrén GARCÍA GRINDA, *G House, International competition "Goethe's House"* (2nd prize), Tokyo (Japan), 1999.

6. Eduard BRU, E. SERRA, L. VIVES, J. CARTAGENA, *Poblenou's maritime front*, Barcelona, 1995.

●★ sequences

[MG] "*One of the essential characteristics of the dream of multiplicity is –*
as Stan Allen points out – *that each element changes incessantly and al-*
ters its distances in relation to other things." (Translated from Spanish.)
These variable distances are not proportionate qualities (additive or linear), but rather expand or contract non-linearly without changing the
global nature of the system.
Simultaneity (interaction) between individual events generates arrhythmic and diatonal interpolarities ("iteralities") relating to basic combinations between concentration-dilatation-connection, occupation-dis-
tancing-route, that is, between fill-void-link.
In such structures, the void has as much importance as fill, producing intermittent geometries, syncopated – segmented (associated with phenomena of individualisation and intermission between
events) – which point to dissonant parameters of sequentiality, rather
than to seriation.
In effect, in such *embrayages* and quick jolts, one can observe irregular
rhythms and intercidences based upon not always evident norms produced
by multiple sets of temporary conversions – of arrhythmias and syncopations – that foster internal musical tempos made up of unexpected
events and unequal intervals.
The iterative character of these mistaken rhythms is useful. They are understood no longer as mechanisms of repetition (series: indifferent mechanisms configured through unity and subsequently juxtaposed), but rather
as sequences (heterogeneous cadences of different events, which are linked,
however, by the ambiguous thread of an irregular plot).
They are events which are coordinated, but not reiterated, which ultimately configure not a simple sum of fragments, but rather a global whole
born out of a single dynamic movement. In them, apparently autonomous
forces engage and complement each other reciprocally, due to the indispensable presence of an "in-between" space, converted into a mechanism
for simultaneous spacing (independence) and linking (interdependence).

[CO] Traditionally, A relates to B and then B to C in the hierarchical connections of
formal logic. But could the idea of A into B back into A back into B build on
some kind of feedback loop? Why not structure as trace, as episode, as stacca-
to or punctuation? Then as catalyst, the idea of local would arise; juxtaposition
of entities becomes rhythm; these hybrid entities – between the dynamic and the
structural – are taken as natural and positive and not as odd, freaky, or the irregular exception.
Order becomes, then, rhythm and sequence and clash and confrontation if symmetry is there it is in the active coming together of separate tendencies, in balance for only one moment.
The traditional pursuit of external object cut by dissecting and unthinking subdi-
viding grid is rejected. Instead, a holistic approach is taken of inner logic informing the whole. The imperative is in -to -out.
CECIL BALMOND

MVRDV, *Donau City (Kissing Towers)*, Viena, 2002, Competition 2nd Prize.

★ shadow & light

→ 'dual(ity)

[co] Shadow & light is a dual reality, the hypertrophy of a double sensation: there can be cavernous, dark, soft, humid, sensorial, smelling mushroom on one part of the building; and crystalline, cold, luminous, dry, technological on the other part. And this can be used like an individual zapping of perception.
FRANÇOIS ROCHE

 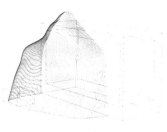

François ROCHE, *Shadow & Light,* Paris, 1990.

■ shadows

[JM] For the avant-garde, the relation between space and the glance often consisted in placing a space of mediation between themselves and the work, in front of which they were immobilized. Those wakes of shadows with which Louis Kahn surrounded his buildings, the difficulty of reaching Loos's houses, and the enormous distances that Le Corbusier linked the horizon of his works, explain clearly this concept.

Many of the projects we are now planning eliminate the intermediary terrain, that previously was no-man's lands, in which the exterior void was the idea from which to relate ground and figure. In these proposals, we are not facing the object, the work, but rather we feel wrapped in it, as though it were our shadow.

NL, *Y2K+ building,*
Morgenstond
(Den Haag, The
Netherlands), 1999.

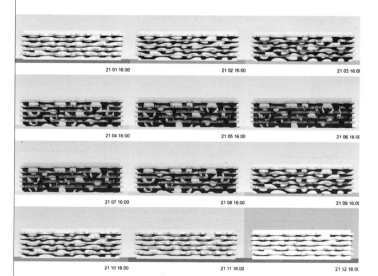

Enric RUIZ-GELI, *Spek*, Aedes West Gallery, Berlin, 1999.

◆ shopping

→ 'economy',
'no-places'

[FS] airport=mall, church=mall, government=shopping, education=shopping, museum=shopping, exercise=shopping. (VVAA, *Mutations*, Barcelona: Actar, 2000)

★ shore or bank

[co] A shore or bank is the boundary or limit of the superficial extension of some things. It is the extreme boundary of a town, plain, field, etc. The upper margin of a cliff. The point marking the transition from one state or condition to another. That strip along a path or track for walking without getting our boots muddy. In the urban context, the pavement, that constructed strip close to buildings, as an intermediate place between the walls of the domestic and fierce motorised traffic. We should pay more attention to these words. JOSÉ ALFONSO BALLESTEROS

◆ Sierpinsky's sponge

→ 'a-scalarity',
'attractors', 'dimension'
'fractal', 'scaleless',
'self-similarity',
'topological', 'void',
'zoom'

[FS] Sierpinsky's sponge is an attractor generated by the subtraction of the same volumetric figure of smaller size by each of its sides. The result is a body of zero volume and infinite area. On each face the total area is null while the perimeter of its holes is infinite. Its fractal dimension is 2.72.

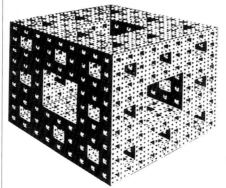

Sierpinskyis cube.

★ simulation

→ 'animation',
'interfaces', 'logic, digital',
'projective', 'prototypes',
'represent', 'virtual'

[co] "Simulation is a silly word because it means a replica of something real. I think that the fantasy of creating "realistic simulations" is a poor premise. I hope that by 2010 we can come up with a better word and a better idea of what virtual worlds can be used for. I am working on a few myself, including "narrative environments" and "storyspace." These words refer to synthetic worlds that become a medium for dynamic, audience-generated, self-evolving narrative," Celia Pearce. XAVIER COSTA

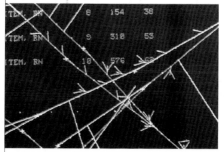

Graphic simulation of the crossing of bamboo rhyzomes, in *L'architecture d'aujourd'hui* 321, 1999.

+ simulator

→ 'animation',
'interfaces', 'logic, digital',
'reality', 'represent',
'virtual'

[WM] In the early nineteen-eighties, Daniel Galouye published his science fiction work *Simulacron 3*, which Fassbinder made into a film called *Welt am Draht*. The novel reflects upon the problem of computer simulation: there is a company that, with the aid of a giant computer, simulates a large city with thousands of inhabitants who are led to believe in the illusion of living in a real world. This simulated metropolis, with simulated people, is used to test products before their release onto the real market. This leads the engineers, real creators of the Test, to question whether they might also be part of a higher-level simulation system. This is the problem of simulation from the perspective of knowledge. From the technical perspective, the video-game industry has built up a vast VR technology, offering from collective experiences in virtual environments to personal simulations of the environment. This system has been used with great precision in flight simulation. Flight simulation and video game technologies are the most advanced technological spheres of virtual reality. At present, we are underexploiting the possibilities of simulating architectural experience. Models of virtual reality are still more concerned with *representing* the world than with *experiencing* it.

✗ + simultaneity

→ 'cohabitation',
'criss-crossing', 'dual(ity)',
'event', 'plaits', 'reality',
'system', 'suspense', 'yes!'

[VG] Formerly 'duality.' We might imagine digital aliens who only operate on the Net. Or farmers who live off the resources they generate. But, the spirit of our time will always be dual (simultaneous): physical and virtual.

[WM] **(successive-simultaneous)**

We are witnessing a change of times, from a culture of the successive to a culture of the simultaneous. *We are moving from tele-vision to tele-action*, to the possibility of remote teleaction: telework, teleshopping, telepresence. The impact of events in one part of the world is no longer only the visual information received in another part of the world. We have moved from a topical space to a teletopical space, in which the real transmission time of an event imposes itself on the real space of the event itself. We are now able to coexist in this situation. This is precisely the context which made some people doubt whether Neil Armstrong had really set foot on the Moon.

Enric RUIZ-GELI,
Interior-Exterior,
Barcelona, 1998.

Martha ROSLER,
*Bringing the War
Home*, in DE
ZEGHER, Catherine
(ed.), *Martha Rosler*,
Birmingham: Ikon
Gallery; Vienna:
Genesali Foundation;
Cambridge: MIT
Press, 1998.

✘ síndrome-del-Liceu (Liceu syndrome)

→ 'conservation'

[VG] See 'archaeology.'

To preserve something, you have to take action on it, otherwise it degenerates or is destroyed. Or burnt. This syndrome, detected in the case of Barcelona's opera house, has in recent decades affected Mediterranean forests.

★ singular housing

[c] "*Most approaches towards the architecture of individual houses start from the idea of the house as an object designed by an architect. However, information technology introduces a change—of content rather than form—in the way architecture is devised. The architect would not work so clearly on the achievement of a specific object through specific logical materials, and architecture would increasingly be based on meeting specific current-day contexts. The information age is the age of interactivity, of the dissolution of airtight material cultures within a global computerized condition. How can architects' action be "opened up" to users' contexts and dynamics, their tastes, real needs, fantasies and desires?*"

(SALAZAR, Jaime, "The house as an interface", SALAZAR, Jaime; GAUSA, Manuel, *Singular Housing*, Barcelona: ACTAR, 1999)

●■ situation, the

→ 'de-location',
'environment',
'foreignness', 'paradoxes'

[MG] See 'field,' 'dispositions' and 'places.'

[JM] It is necessary to change the idea of place for "situation." A situation must be constructed; it is not a passive interpretation of a project; situations are spatial, vectorial, fields of force that in manifesting themselves, propose the project in some way.

The paradox is produced from the moment in which, in these zones, the work of architecture is made more specific. Unattended by the impotence of the recourse to language, we trace the situation not in search of any lost link, but rather of the forces that construct "this excited place." This work with architecture can have, without doubt, more repetition than other similar situations.

★ skateboarding

→ 'in-between',
'urbanism, anarchist'

[c] Skateboarding is an oppositional sub-culture which encompasses body, board and terrain. Through simultaneous production and release of time, energy and space, skateboarders have been labelled counter-culture urbanists, urban guerrillas and new urban terrorists. The freestyle skaters' terrain is 'spatial degree zero' or 'zero degree architecture' – the leftover spaces of the modern city or the spaces of decision-making which symbolize, not through overt iconography, but through expansivity of space. Skateboarders disrupt the optimal management of urban space and in their 'productive-of-nothing labour,' deny the logic of the city as pre-eminently existing solely for the benefit of global forces and flows of information and capital. (See also BORDEN, Iain, *Skateboarding, Space and the City: Architecture and the Body*, 2001, Berg, Oxford)

KELLY SHANNON

1. Simon UNGERS, Tom KINSLOW, *T House*, Upstate, New York, 1992. **2.** OMA / Rem KOOLHAAS, *Single family house*, Bordeaux (France), 1997. **3.** Ben VAN BERKEL, Caroline BOS (UN Studio), *Moebius House*, Het Gooi (The Netherlands), 1998. **4.** Kazuyo SEJIMA & Associates, *Villa in the wood*, Chino (Nagano, Japan), 1994. **5.** LACATON & VASSAL, *Latapie House*, Floriac, (Bordeaux, France), 1993. **6.** Xaveer DE GEYTER, *Mariakerke House*, Ghent (Belgium), 1996. **7.** Jaume VALOR, Fidela FRUTOS, J.M. SANMARTÍN, *Bioclimatic House*, Llinars del Vallès (Barcelona), 1994. **8.** Vicente GUALLART, *Dwelling at the limit of the town*, Llíria (Valencia, Spain), 1995.

●★ **skeleton**

[MG] See 'fuselages.'

Framework of a vertebrate body. Formerly structure.

[co] Today, the territory and the city, as well as specific edificial structures, appear to form a gigantic "plug-in system" in which are connected and disconnected new interventions, uses and activities that share the mobile and temporary character associated with the current late-capitalist system.

This way of constructing the project as a complex multiple system or structure, neither hierarchical nor central, easily evokes the image of a network or a skeleton, where "objects" are differentiated from "structures" into which they are inserted. In general, a network or a skeleton establishes neither forms nor compositions. The network is a structure of non-hierarchical connections that are superposed on an environment (territory, city, etc.), often invisibly so. From the architectural point of view, the network fundamentally establishes a topological order. It establishes the site of connections; its contents connected, yet without pre-established order. The meaning of network transcends that of formal continuity, it permits combination of modern objectuality with the connection, or with contextualism, and establishes indetermination, and at the same time control, of the architectural intervention.

The project that is resolved with this concept substitutes the term "idea," central and static, with that of "skeleton:" The Heideggerian concept of "skeleton" (Gestell) is associated with a relational and operative conception of reality while that of "idea" is related to a representative or formal knowledge. This same definition can be useful in facilitating the development of this point. Perceiving the structure of settlements, both urban and territorial, as a skeleton, supposes a displacement of the object of the project from its representative or formal conception to a relational conception.

Architecture positions itself in the interstices of the skeleton. *It does not create* space, but rather occupies or captures it. The useable space is predefined, marked out, by the margin of indetermination itself or by the external volumetric framework of the skeleton. The creation of a fuselage, a structure in which to "hook up" with the will to make co-existant empty space, air, and volume within it, constitutes a qualitative leap forward and a change in the perception of contemporary architecture. Skeletons, like the structuralist works of Sol-Lewitt, work by capturing part of space in order to facilitate occupation by means of the insertion of pieces. Through the structure runs territory and landscape, along with air. Inserted volumes are, at the same time, the architecture and the space inside them and define, as well in their outer skin, a continual space that runs between them. The skin is minimal: that of the inner volumes is insignificant and that of the skeleton is exclusively virtual.

JOSÉ ANTONIO SOSA

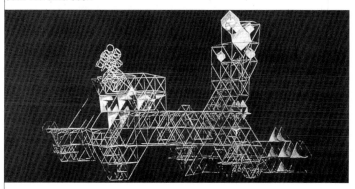

Eckhard SCHULTZE-FIELITZ, *Space City*, 1961, in WIGLEY, Mark, *Constant's New Babylon, The Hyper-Architecture of Desire*, Rotterdam: 010 Publishers, 1998.

● skin

→ 'camouflage', 'equipped façade', 'membrane', 'tattoos', 'technique, the'

[MG]

Contemporary architecture replaces the idea of façade with that of skin: an exterior layer mediating between the building and its environment. Not a neutral elevation, but rather an active, informed membrane; communicative and in communication.

Rather than walls with holes, technical, interactive skins. Skins colonised by functional elements capable of housing installations and services; capable of receiving and transmitting energies; but also capable of supporting other incorporated layers: overlapping rather than adhesive. Manipulated and/or temporary patches, eruptions, graphics or engravings; but also projected images. Colourful reversible motifs and virtual — digital — fantasies aimed at transforming the building into an authentic interface between individual and environment; and the façade, into an (inter)active screen, the frictional boundary between the building and a context which changes over time.

FRANÇOIS & LEWIS, *Project for offices rehabilitation*, Rouen (France), 1995. Facade: double glass and pinnace of variable height and density.

IAN+, *Italian Space Agency*, Roma, Competition 2000.

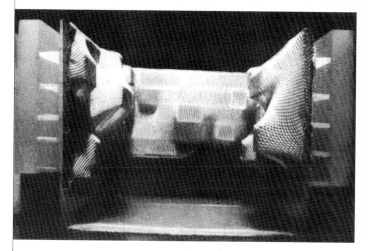

● skyscrapers

[MG] See 'bluntings.'

●+ slogan

[MG][WM] Motto. Instructions for use.
Synthesised and compressed contents for direct use.

We don't want sitting architects,
but walking architects

Chaos:
potentially profitable state

Cities should act like chips:
do more and more in less space

The dwelling is a micro-city
from which one works, shops, rests

Only that which can be represented
can be built

Houses are no longer measured
in m^2 but in m^3

Telework will require specific
spaces in domestic environments
to avoid the "24/7 work syndrome"

In the information society,
economic growth no longer
requires physical growth

To have an urban life, it is no longer
necessary to live in the city

Re-information is the process
by which the physical world
is constructed using information
as the fundamental raw material

Architecture will exist as the result
of the interaction of natural, artificial
and digital natures – or it won't exist

If the city is landscape,
buildings are mountains

If the house is the computer,
the structure is the network

Rurban: five days in the country
and two in the city

We generate fields within other fields

If the home was transformed by the arrival of running water, and years later by electricity, the massive arrival of information will cause a transformation of similar scale

The project does not illuminate on its own; it must be infused with a light that I must produce

Agriculture is industrialised. Landscape is urbanised

Europe is a field of pixels

The best way to protect a heritage is to enhance it

Our architectures are increasingly becoming sleights of hand

Builder: when you buy bananas, do you buy them by weight or by shape?

Formerly context, now field or environment

Mayor, is your city advanced?

Only those who add value to the chain of knowledge shall have a place in the production system

Operative topographies: enclaves capable of generating their own energy

The most advanced state of creation is not "inventing sliced bread but inventing bread"

The architectural project is no longer designed, but negotiated

+ Smart

→ 'container',
'economy', 'estate car',
'form', 'process',
'product', 'production,
intelligent'

[WM] "*For automobile manufacturers, quality – defined as an absence of defects – is increasingly the price of admission, not a competitive edge.*" J.D. Power. (Translated from Spanish.)

The history of *Smart* is that of the definitive triumph in the automobile industry of the conceptual separation between the chassis and the motor, on the one hand, and the body, on the other. The body, in being separated from the rest, set in motion all the industry's marketing mechanisms, including styling, allowing for rapid changes to maintain market shares without having to depend on much slower technological advances.

There is nobody better than Swatch – who marketed the first watch to offer a thousand different designs based upon the same chassis – to understand this phenomena. And to understand that people change watches not because they break, but because they go out of fashion.

And no one better than Mercedes to provide the necessary technological experience.

Smart is an advanced design concept: a strategic alliance of companies to create it, a design that appeals to an ecologically-committed urban ethic and is 95% recyclable. Its (momentary) commercial failure is not important. It is the line to follow. *Smart is advanced architecture.*

Smart advertisement, 2000.

Willy MÜLLER + THB Consulting, *AD1 Occupation structures*, Barcelona.

★ society of the And, the

→ 'community', 'glocal'

[co] The photo, which I took from the peak of a tall mountain in Umbria, Italy – of a container festooned with satellite dishes and a crucifix, gives rise to the following observations. First of all, we see the symbol of the Roman Catholic church, a transparent example from our 'first modernity.' It was placed there several dozen years ago. What we are looking at is an industrial product. It is a fine tectonic work, a steel structure that symbolises what faith stands for. The design represents an institution of collective trust and belief. This crucifix is not made of stone. It does not emerge from a rural society with a *longue durée* of values, accumulated over centuries. This steel cross is a symbol that originates from the first industrial modernisation, where the dialectical difference between 'home' and 'homeless,' the technology-driven alienation of the authentic experience, is already in place. Next to the crucifix, we see a totally contrasting world. This is a prototypical example of our 'second modernity.' It is an architecture that no longer has symbolic function. It does not represent any normative value.

We may wonder, when we consider this object more closely, what new role this architecture fulfils. Whatever it may be, it is a structure that may be extended continually, according to requirements. The network of high-speed links promises maximum efficiency. A new tectonics arises, an architecture as infrastructure. It is a fuzzy logic with no need of symbolism. Whereas the crucifix in the photo stood for the Society of Either/Or, this new world can no longer be interpreted in terms of dialectics. It is the Society of The And. The conjunctions of The And are responsible for the complex transnational conflation of the global with the local, sometimes also called the 'glocal' condition. In the Society of The And, the traditional landscape no longer has any influence on our sense of community. Everything that once had a significant impact on our social life used to be localized in our physical vicinity. In the Society of the And, it is not so much objects as the diffuse fields produced by electronic mediation and mass migration that give direction to our identity. Arjun Appadurai calls these fields 'imaginary scapes.' They are a source of continual turbulence, because both spectators and images are in motion. Neither images nor spectators still form part of circuits that are easily demarcated as local, national or regional spaces. This condition is dominated by a new order of instability.

Although everything coalesces in the dirtiness of these 'And scapes,' it does so without ever forming a delimited whole. It is a kind of discontinuousness which should not be interpreted as a threat to civic freedom and political will, but as a precondition for them. Thus, the discontinuousness is not an obstacle, but rather the beginning of freedom. The sociologists Ulrich Beck, Anthony Giddens and Scott Lash explain that in this Society of the And, instead of being 'lived' by the system, as in the 1950s, we operate reflexively. Every individual, moulded by lengthy education, possesses the knowledge to reflect more and more upon the consequences, problems and assumptions of our modernisation processes.

But there is another kind of reflexivity. It is not unlike the knee-jerk reflex produced when the doctor taps a certain point on your knee with his little hammer. Strikingly, our modernity also has all kinds of unintended consequences, and it inevitably takes tremendous risks as the result of an abundance of specialised knowledge. Who would have thought, for instance, that globalisation would reach the point where democratic parliamentary structures of nation states are increasingly dominated by the international economy? Or that the inhabitants of former colonies would wish to 'integrate' en masse into our 'First World' societies? We cannot dismiss this reflexive modernisation, bulging as it is with superfluous consumption, tourism, individual self-fulfilment without regard to the consequences for others (a product of the 'do-it-yourself biography' we all have), renewed imperialism in the guise of globalisation, junk space and snacking, etc., as merely frightening. According to Ulrich Beck, it is precisely the unintended consequences, such as environmental disasters and the accumulation of uncertainties – in other words the many risks in our own lives – that almost inevitably generate a new politicisation of individual life. (See also Roemer van Toorn, 'The Society of The And. Constructing Progressive Reflexivity in The And', *History & Theory Reader*, Berlage Institute, 1998).

ROEMER VAN TOORN

1. Umbria mountain top with satellites and cross (Photograph: Roemer van Toorn).

2. Basketball in Hong Kong. The paradise of sport in front of slums in HK (Photograph: Roemer van Toorn).

★ soft

[CO] We all know, being humans, that our emotions, moods and feelings influence the way we move in space, that our intensive movement is related to our extensive movement. Though modern management theory recognises there is a necessary rigidity organizing tasks around set goals, a certain relaxation of their implementation has become vital. In opposition to neutrality, vagueness works with a differentiated field of vectors, of tendencies, that both allow for clearly defined goals and habits for as-yet undetermined actions. It allows for both formal and informal conduct. If the skeletal structure of actions becomes as soft as cartilage and as complex as cancellous bone structure so does the architecture of the building. A behavioral vagueness paralleled by an architectural vagueness. LARS SPUYBROEK

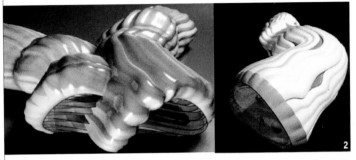

1. Greg LYNN, *Media Galaxy (Competition concept for the new Eyebeam Institute)*, New York, 2001. 2. NOX, *OfftheRoad_5speed*, Eindhoven (The Netherlands), 2000.

✖ software

→ 'genetics',
'information',
'interactivity', 'interfaces',
'logic, digital', 'Media
Lab', 'product',
'system>operative'

[VG] INFORMATION is the fundamental raw material of our century and software is the tool we use to process it.

At the start of the twentieth century, the big problem to be solved was the living standards of the masses, whereas now the problem is individuals. Then, mass production had to be developed, whereas now, personalised production is required. Both the first mass production line was for cars and the appearance of the lift changed the concept of space and time in buildings and cities. The next change is that of software, of the intangible, of flexibility in production, of à la carte television. Of a form of interactivity that creates a favourable atmosphere for individualism. Of decision-making capacity that calls for criteria rather than knowledge.

★ solenoid

→ 'attractors',
'braids', 'field', 'flows'

[CO] The dispositive function will not be simply to organize flows, but also to construct a field of urban intensity through the enhancement of multiple paths and directions. The aim is to produce a solenoid – an inductive organization of flows – to project urban intensity within the place. ALEJANDRO ZAERA-POLO

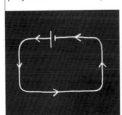
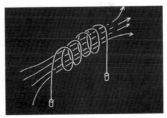

FOA, *Solenoid. Diagram for the International Port Terminal*, Yokohama (Japan), 2002.

●■+★ space

[MG] See 'spaces' and '<i> space.'

[JM] "...Space is a void, a hole, a pool, a doubt, a question: thus the "scene of a crime" in all its details is an enigma, an interrogation, the exposure of an insupportable falsehood, irresistible, whose impudent brutality has to be immediately reduced at the alters of a history that makes it intelligible; it is a mute deed that opens up to the speculation of the observer in an un-compromising multiplicity of incompatible directions."
(PARDO, José Luis, *Sobre los espacios*, Barcelona: Ed. del Serbal, 1991)

[WM] "And what if space were the true luxury?"
Renault has been talking about space for twenty years.
How did we fail to see it before?
The automotive industry is years ahead in understanding that the space is the quality of size and knows how to employ it as a selling point.
The car sells its spatial capacity in cubic footage, which is a highly effec-tive marketing tool – if only we could succeed in associating it with ar-chitecture.
As Vicente Guallart says (and I second):
Why not m³ instead of m²?

[co] Space "in America, outer space; in Japan, physical room to live and work; in Europe, an autonomous realm of the imagination," Bruce Sterling.
XAVIER COSTA

● space, agitated

[MG] See 'open,' 'action,' 'animation,' 'dynamism' and 'in/unsettledness.'

◆●■★ spaces

→ 'activity', 'act-n', 'dynamism', 'flexibility', 'joy (*alegria*)', 'relational', 'space', 'spaces> public and private', 'unrestrained (<un> factors)', 'Yokohama'

[FS] **public and private space**
See 'areas of impunity.'
Public Space is mobile. Private space is static. Public space is dispersed. Private space is concentrated. Public space is empty; it is the imagination. Private space is full; it consists of objects and memories. Public space is indeterminate. Private space is functional. Public space is information, pri-vate space is opinion. Public space is support. Private space is the message. Public space is, finally, in an unstable equilibrium. Private space is, by ne-cessity, stable.

collective space. Previously called public space.
Nowadays, the relation between property and use has disappeared.
Private property is used publicly (shopping center, airports, etc.) and vise versa.
Public space is absorbed by private use.
A new reality is created in which the collective, an ample group of indi-viduals, is the only constant characteristic.

vector space. "*Modality of installation in the physical environment which the contemporary social subject constructs through his own perception, of the forms of establishing himself and the uses of space that he develops. Vectorial space is the ambience that the contemporary subject creates in taking his place in the world.*"

(ÁBALOS, Iñaki; HERREROS, Juan, "Areas of impunity and vectorial spaces", *Áreas de impunidad*, Barcelona: ACTAR, 1998).

[MG] **collective or relational (formerly public) space**

Where formerly we spoke of public space, we now speak of relational space.

An authentically collective space open to use, to enjoyment, to stimulus, to surprise: to activity. To indetermination of the dynamic, the interchange between active scenarios and activating passers-by-users-actors.

No longer, then, a space of "*arredo urbano*," a mere neo-monumentalising recreation based upon closed designs, that is to say, upon "pure," finished (neat and autistic aesthetics for the enjoyment of occasional vandal-rebels) images, but rather a space of new landscapes – or landscapes of landscapes – for interaction and adaptation. No longer formalising designs, but rather informalising devices. No longer civic models, but rather mongrel situations.

Devices – tactical decisions – open to change and generators of action and mixedness, capable of combining plastic joy with the incorporation of temporary installations for leisure, sport, culture, intercommunication, diversity, relationships and, ultimately, the projection of the citizen.

But also for the capture and reformulation of local and global energies – and bits of information.

Devices based upon lightweight constructions connected to networks of energy and information; upon intelligent (reinformed) natural and/or artificial lands; upon more unrestrained – and economical – solutions conceived through colourful recycled materials.

Thus, a relational, complicit space. Not only for taking a stroll, but also for personal and/or shared stimulus.

A collective space, uninhibited, optimistic, relaxed – and in many aspects changable, mutable, precarious and reversible – for a city ultimately more joyful and exciting than elegant.

[MG] "*Looking up and down the avenue, deciding which way to go, she took in half-a-dozen nearly identical hotel fronts, a rank of pedicabs, the rainslick glitter of a row of small shops. And people, lots of them, all moving like they were on top of it, everybody with someplace to go. [...] The flow was pleasure and nobody else was pausing. She contented herself with sidelong flashes of each display. The clothes were like clothes in a stim, some of them, styles she'd never seen anywhere.*

I should 've been here, she thought, I should 've been here all along. Not on a catfish farm. It 's a place, a real place."

(GIBSON, William, *Mona Lisa Overdrive*, London: Gollancz, 1988)

[JM] **space of the public**

If, as Paul Virilio perspicaciously notes, public space has been substituted by its image then, it only occurs to us to exchange the space of representation for that of presentation. It isnecessary to reestablish the body to body relationship as the true construction of public space. A space not necessarily qualified by its forms, but by its capacity to benefit the relation to its neighbor – as opposed to the distanced. If the agora is now no longer the place of prognostication, space must be rethought of as body to body relationships in another way.

[co] **phases space**

Phases space is mathematical space constituted by the variables that describe a dynamic system. Each point in phases space represents a possible state of the system. The evolution in time of the system is represented by a trajectory in phases space.
JOSÉ ALFONSO BALLESTEROS

[co] **public space**

1. Space of public entitlement. 2. Space accessible to everyone, that can be appropriated but not owned; setting for countless heterogeneous actions and actors that is not the result of a specific morphology, but of the articulation of sensible qualities produced by the practical operations and time-space schematisations procured, live, by its users.
MANUEL DELGADO

★ space-time

→ 'space', 'time'

[co] The insistence on placing spaces on the highest pedestal of tourist activity contradicts evidence that, based upon analysis of the behaviour of the main players in this activity (tourists), such priority corresponds to time. In overall economic terms, what really defines competitiveness in the tourist industry is not so much the existence of highly singular and quality settings (no matter how important they might be), but the organisation of a system of services that guarantees a dynamic, entertaining and distinctive use of time. Time is the key in tourist consumption, as it is in the rest of our daily life, while space has become a mere instrument for selling time. Hence, what defines the success of a tourist programme for the customer relates basically to the capacity for responding effectively to tourists' demands regarding the use of the time they have. This perspective opens up new fields of action in space production processes and relegates the architect to the status of a secondary specialist in a process that requires the intervention of experts in time, wherever their background, who have the capacity to assimilate or anticipate popular demands and conceive sequences of pleasurable activities. Thus, it is to the prophets of time that falls the responsibility for coming up with innovative agendas upon which are erected the buildings which serve for accommodation and eating.
JOSÉ MIGUEL IRIBAS

[co] When space existed as a separate category, architecture was the art of space; when time existed as a separate entity, music was the art of time. The realisation of the deep relation between space and time as space-time, and the corresponding parallel relation between mass and energy, challenges the idea that architecture and music are separate, and prompts us to conceive of a new art of space-time: archimusic. MARCOS NOVAK

S&Aa (SORIANO-
PALACIOS),
*Competition for
bus station,* Talavera
de la Reina (Toledo,
Spain), 2000.

S&Aa (SORIANO-
PALACIOS),
Euskalduna Hall,
Bilbao (Spain), 1998.

ACTAR ARQUITEC-
TURA, *Pau Picasso
Square,* Montornés
del Vallès (Barcelona),
2000.

Vicente GUALLART
(with Max SAN-
JULIÁN), *Project
for the urbanization
of Cristóbal
de Moura street,*
Barcelona, 1999.

● Spain

[MG] See 'España.'

◆● speed

→ 'logic, direct',
'true and false', 'uppercut'

Apple advertisement,
in *Wired* 6/04, 1998.

[FS] *"Run fast, stand still. This the lesson from lizards. For all writers. Observe almost any survival creature, you see the same. Jump, run, freeze. In the ability to flick like an eyelash, crack like a whip, vanish like steam, here this instant, gone the next — life teems the earth. And when that life is not rushing to escape, it is playing statues. See the hummingbird, there, not there. As thought arises and blinks off, so this thing of summer vapor; the clearing of a cosmic throat, the fall of a leaf. And where it was — a whisper. What can we writers learn from lizards, lift from birds? In quickness is truth. The faster you blurt, the more swiftly you write, the more honest you are. In hesitation is thought. In delay comes the effort for a style, instead of leaping upon truth which is the only style worth deadfalling or tiger-trapping."* (BRADBURY, Ray, *Zen in the art of writing and The joy of writing: two essays*, Santa Barbara, Ca : Capra Press, 1973)

[MG] *"'Oh dear! Oh dear! I shall be late!' [...]*
Before Alice was another long passage, and the White Rabbit was still in sight, hurrying down it. There was not a moment to be lost: away went Alice like the wind, and was just in time to hear it say, as it turned a corner, 'Oh my ears and whiskers, how late it's getting!' She was close behind it when she turned the corner, but the Rabbit was no longer to be seen." (CARROLL, Lewis, *Alice in Wonderland*, London: New Orchard, 1990)

◆● sponged

[FS] See 'puff-pastry.'

[MG] See 'laminate.'

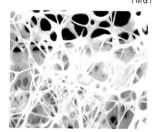

1. NOX (Lars Spuybroek with Chris Seung-Woo Yoo, Kris Mun, Florent Rougemont and Ludovica Tramontin), *SoftOffice*, United Kingdom, 2000-2005. **2.** FOA, *Virtual House*, 1997.

● spontaneous

[MG] See 'open,' 'joy,' 'self-organisation' and 'extroversion: <ex> factors of form.'

✗ sport rock

[VG] Sport rocks are artificial rocks, introduced into the city, that create circuits for stretching exercises. These rocks, that vary in size, are created on the basis of Boolean operations in volumes with faceted surfaces. They are a new layer of public space.

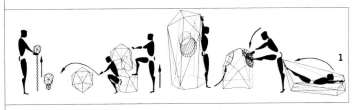

1. Vicente GUALLART, *Project for the urbanization of Cristóbal de Moura street*, Barcelona, 1999. **2.** NL, *WOS 8, thermical plant*, Leidsche Rijn (The Netherlands), 1998.

● stack (stacks)

→ 'associate, overlap, connect', 'devices', 'dispositions', 'mixed-use', 'multi', 'multilayered', 'strategy'

[MG] To stack is to pile or make a heap of things (elements, shapes, activities or programmes) one atop another, in a formally non-predetermined manner. Mixed.

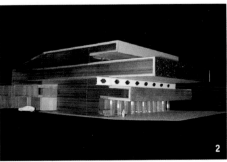

1. PÉRIPHÉRIQUES, *Japan Project, Total Media Tower Museum*, Tokyo, Seoul, Bangkok, NYC, 2009. **2.** WMA Willy Müller Arquitectos, *Competition for the Navarra general library*, Pamplona (Spain), 2001.

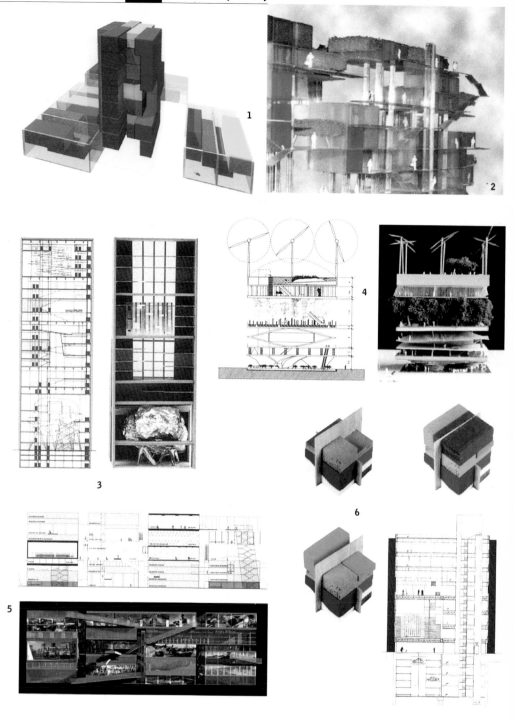

1. José MORALES, Juan GONZÁLEZ, *Europan 5* (1st prize), Ceuta (Spain), 1998. **2.** IaN+ (L. GALOFARO, C. BAGLIVO, S. MANNA), *Europan 5*, Almere (The Netherlands), 1998. **3.** S&Aa (SORIANO-PALACIOS), *Competition for cultural centre and auditorium*, Benidorm (Alicante, Spain), 1995. **4.** MVRDV, *The Netherlands Pavilion Expo 2000*, Hannover (Germany), 2000. **5.** PÉRIPHÉRIQUES with MVRDV, *Quai Branly Museum of Arts and Civilisations*, Paris, 1999. **6.** ÁBALOS & HERREROS, *Self-sufficient hybrid towers*, 1994.

Metapolitan growth. Ink stains diagrams.

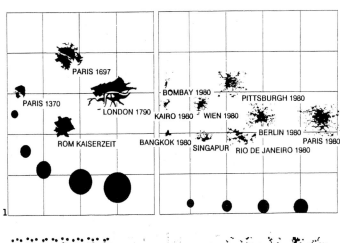

1. The larger the settling is the more dendrited the structure becomes, in *Arch+* 121, 1994.

2. Models of Berlin: current structure; identical area of maximum density; homogeneous area distribution; gradation of the settling particles, in *Arch+* 121, 1994.

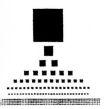

● stains, ink

→ 'attractors',   [MG]
'cartographies', 'city?',
'dispersed', 'dispositions',
'dissolved architecture',
'distribution', 'field',
'm. city', 'maps (to map)',
'Metapolis', 'patchwork
city', 'place of places',
'self-urbanism', 'territory'

Seen from a satellite, in a black-and-white binary spectrum, the crystalline shape of the primitive city today seems to decompose like an *ink spot* spattered over the territory. In both theoretical (virtual) modellings and in (real) cities, the outlying nuclei appear smaller near the centre and progressively larger further afield. If the greatest density is located at the centre, then there also exists manifold secondary clusters that present their own focalising attractor(s). The growing expansion of large conurbations leads to the formation of discontinuous polycentric growths. Rhizomes are subject to the appearance of holes – voids, subperimeters, limits or edges – describable through near fractal geometries (like that of Sierpinski's well-known carpet) which appear to respond to an inherent will. Rhizomes foster, under conditions of greater (relatively recent anthropologically) freedom, an irregular – sponge-like or dendritic – distribution of the processes of occupation. Their processes abandon compact atavistic shapes (disciplined or forced by need) in order to multiply individual situations of proximity to an edge (that is, to an empty space), privileged in their easy access to decongested free spaces and to perimeter networks of access and routing. This process of gasification, of de-densification, of polymorphic polynuclearity and fractality is, in fact, a phenomenon on the world scale, which, despite logical local differences on the microscopic scale, present notable similarities on the macroscopic scale. Their evolution conforms to the spontaneous and generic movements inherent in any dynamic structure, rather than to the particular planning decisions of each context.

But it is also, and at the same time, a process that enhances local differences. In fact, the principal interest of this process resides not so much in the verification of the common model as in the manifold situations of cohabitation and superposition, of action and disturbance, of infiltration and mixture that, continually and progressively, distort and mutate this shared abstract configuration, enriching its basic characteristics, setting the singular against the universal, the local against the global, the general against the specific.

[MG] " *The observation of the topologies inherent to the current urban structures — visualised in their ink-stain evolutions — is surprising for the formal resemblance between the world's conurbations and the spontaneous, unplanned ancient settlements: the same formation of voids and the same formation of edges and denditric routes, within the framework of a mounting densification that forms part of the process of overall metropolitisation. From that we deduce that the morphogenesis of current settlements fits an anthropological model, at once recent and atavistic: recent in the idea of city that it transmits; atavistic in this nearly primitive and progressively spontaneous process of self-organisation and occupation of space (of which we still know little but which clearly has to do with freedom of movement and transmission of information). If a compact city lacks air to breathe, the new fractality of occupations has something to do with this need to create air currents, empty interiors: breaths...*" (Sybille Becker)

● stains, landscape

→ 'cultivations', 'landscapes, operative', 'marks', 'printings'

[MG] See 'enclaves,' 'land(s) in lands' and 'landstrategy.'

A patch is not only something used to mend cloth, cover a blemish or wound or effect temporary connections.

It also describes a plot of land distinguishable from those immediately adjoining it by its vegetation, matter or colour, which is distinct from the dominant ones. We shall speak then of patches (of landscape) as singularised zones of activity.

Topographies, platforms, trays, plateaus. Lands or enclaves. But also patches configured through simple textures, grids and/or colourful paint. Commensalist surfaces as well.

Operative landscapes atop other host landscapes. *Lands-in-lands.*

Equipo 57, *Interactivity and cinema I. Three sequences,* in *BAU* 014, 1996.

1. ACTAR ARQUITEC-TURA, *Cine Alfaro Square*, Cehegin (Murcia, Spain), 1998.

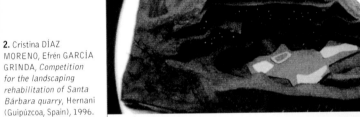

2. Cristina DÍAZ MORENO, Efrén GARCÍA GRINDA, *Competition for the landscaping rehabilitation of Santa Bárbara quarry*, Hernani (Guipúzcoa, Spain), 1996.

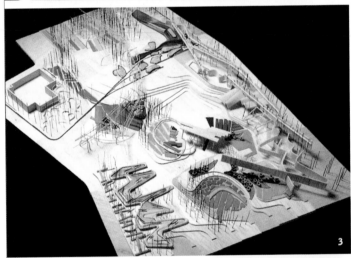

3. Enric MIRALLES & Benedetta TAGLIABUE, *Colours Park*, Mollet del Vallès (Barcelona), 2001.

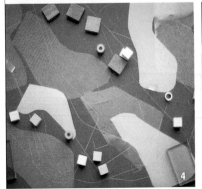

4. J.L. ESTEBAN PENELAS, *Park in Pradolongo*, Madrid, 2002-.

5. WEST 8, *Expo-02: Landscape versus media*, Yverdon-les-bains (Switzerland), 2002.

● stampings

[MG] Stampings are motifs, messages or bits of information superposed over a support; layers of information and of printing (as at once *signal, effect and emotion*).

Willy MÜLLER
+ THB Consulting,
*Exterior motifs for
the bridge-restaurant
"El jardí",*
Barcelona, 2000.

ÁBALOS &
HERREROS,
*AH Houses.
Industrial prototypes,*
1996.

Francis SOLER,
Housing block, Paris,
1997.

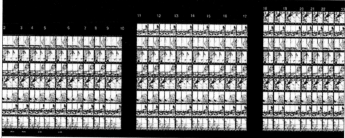

NEUTELINGS
RIEDIJK Architecten,
Concert Hall, Bruges
(Belgium), 1998
(Price Winning
Competition Entry).

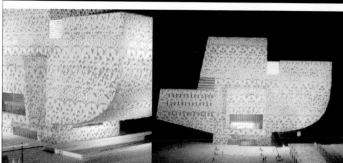

■ standardisation

[JM] The word 'standardize,' to serve or adapt to everything, is more than an architectural denomination and supposes the project to be a thought out activity that is repeated. Standardisation abandons the individuality of decisions to opt for a project that from the anonymity of its tables, spaces, and areas and aspires to fulfill the necessities of its future renters or owners.

Standardisation equates ambiguity, complexity, adaptability, ambiguity. This is the challenge of a project: that bases itself in the standard.

● stenosis

→ 'infiltration'

[MG] Stenosis is a medical term from the Greek *stenos*: narrow, narrowing.
In the consolidated and saturated grids of the dense and constructed city can be seen the effectiveness of certain proposals. These are tactical infiltrations of new lightened information. The project, subject to strong lateral compressions, evidences its capacity for fostering cellular reaction, in the form of specific dilatation produced suddenly in the tissue.
Dematerialisation, disappearance, abstract concision and flexibility are thus revealed as basic components of this type of action.

Waro KISHI, *House in Nipponbashi*, Osaka (Japan), 1992.

+ ● stimulus

→ 'economy',
'energy', 'ideas',
'passion'

[WM] A study by the Forum Corporation of Massachusetts concerning customers lost by fourteen major industrial and service companies found that 15% of the losses were due problems of quality, another 15% due to price and the remaining 70% occurred because what the customer saw, heard, touched, tasted or smelled was not sufficiently stimulating.
Advertising, which is by definition stimulating, is an immediate reference, as important as literature or film once were, and the latest advertising trends stress this message: humour, intelligence, optimism, stimulation.
If architecture creates waves of desires, the architect is, as Rem Koolhaas says, a surfer on the (his own) waves. The possibility of stimulation is closely linked to our capacity for information about things and the information that things have of us: windows which can understand the required signals to turn opaque, or bluish or greenish.
Advanced architecture is also, as Manuel Gausa suggests, a stimulating architecture, which we have to assume is a product – a brand.

[MG] See 'joy (*alegría*),' 'optimism' and 'advertising.'
A stimulus is a catalytic force or vitalising impulse. There are two forms of seducing, convincing or encouraging – of stimulating rather than of imposing. One is epic: it provides energy. The other is lyrical: it provides (perhaps unfounded) hope. The one programmes – and calls for – actions. The other narrates – and suggests – potentials. A third form is the epic-lyrical (a coupling). It is the best. The most difficult.

● strabismus

[MG] "*Strabismus is deformation of the gaze which favours a multifocal vision.*"
(Susanna Cros)

'Four eyes' fish,
Central America.

●▲ strategy

[MG] **(strategy, stratagem and tactic)**

The strategy is a logic, the tactic a criterion, the stratagem a means.
Strategy refers to the global logic – an abstract system – capable of directing operations; the tactic is the set of rules and relationships – the operative device – necessary to facilitate their local evolution; the stratagem is a contingent application, or intelligent instrument.

"*With what incredible speed it moved, how determined it was in its strategies, how flexible in its tactics, how surprising in its stratagems!*"
(Paraphrasing McCOLLOUGH, Colleen, *César*, Barcelona: Planeta, 2000)

[MG] **(strategies and strategists)**

Today, the figure of the architect can no longer be seen only in terms of a "producer of objects," but rather as a "strategist of processes."

In effect, it is no longer a question of designing the shape, local or global (of closing it, finishing it, completing it or embellishing it), but rather of providing the rules of the game. The strategist develops evolutionary logics for virtually unfinished structures, in constant – or virtual – transformation: structures – such as that of the contemporary city itself – in constant mutation, recovery and modernisation. Processes, then, rather than happenings. This does not mean, however, that shape should be renounced: but, rather than drawings – or planimetries – what should be stressed are systems: maps of action.

Elliot ERWITT,
*Simulation of a
nuclear attack*, 1966,
in *Magnun
Landscape*, London:
Phaidon, 1996.

[FP] **(diagrams)**

If we all thougth that in each project it is necessary to go beyond simple concretion, we would make our work a real game of strategies. We would stop drawing in order to diagram.

Arantxa LA CASTA,
Fernando PORRAS-
ISLA, Strategies of
occupation and access
in El Gran San
Salvador (El
Salvador), 1999.

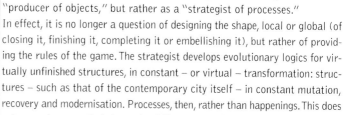

UN STUDIO,
*IFCCA Competition:
Penn Station*,
New York, 1999.

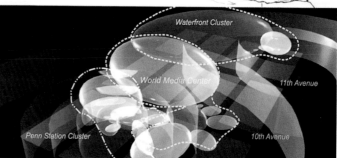

★ street market

→ 'activity',
'appropriation strategies',
'areas of opportunity',
'community', 'ephemeral',
'extend', 'fragile',
'individual', 'plural'

[CO]

See 'in-out.'

Despite the lucrative use of the pavement as one of the more characteristic features of Mediterranean tourist cityscape, the tendency of the street market towards provisionality and the most brazen seediness is the cause of widespread repulsion among aesthetes and order freaks. Of course, there is no apparent charm in this visual dysphonia made up of mobile stalls and grimy canvases. Hence, the laziest mind attacks the image of disorder and filth. This simplification is unacceptable.

The purely visual dimension of the criticism rests on bases that are too elemental. The critics of the street market forget its redeeming role as a generative element in cities that, having opted for single-block development (hygienic and powerful, but boring), articulated along vacuous transitory spaces of contents different from that of functional mobility. The street market returns humanity to these spaces, it redeems their Latinness, brings commerce closer to passers-by, ensures human contact and favours visual continuity. Made over as an improvised souk, the street is recovered for the pedestrian due to vitality of the market, the proximity that comes of its ephemeral and trivial condition and its so human nature and scale.

JOSÉ MIGUEL IRIBAS

● strips

→ 'dispositions',
'(inter)weavings and
inter(plots)',
'landstrategy', 'strategy',
'territory'

[MG]

Schemes of bands comprise of the most elemental level of certain dispositional webs based upon the variable "dytonia" between predictability (reiteration) and disturbance (surprise). A normed arrangement, as schematic as it is flexible, capable of plotting events, altering itself and accommodating, at the same time, exterior contingencies. The open combination – neither exact nor repetitive – between swaths and tracks, broad and narrow, full and empty, homogeneous and heterogeneous, regular and irregular favours, in effect, a flexible idea of code where the order resides in this possible shared directionality, rather than in the strict repetition of events: sequences generated as rhythmic tensions, but also as imbricated intermittences ever referring to the variable – spatial and temporal – "lapse" between different actions. An elemental rhythm, for local variation, rather than for global reiteration.

1

1. Duncan LEWIS, SCAPE ARCHITECTURE + K&B, *Primary & Nursery School,* Obernai (France), 2002-.

2. Eduardo ARROYO (NO.mad Arquitectura), S&Aa (SORIANO-PALACIOS), *Competition for administrative building,* Bolzano (Italy), 1999.

3. Toyo ITO, *Project urban renovation,* Antwerpen (Belgium), 1992.

4. OMA, *Competition Parc de la Villette,* Paris, 1982.

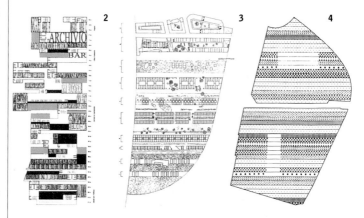

★ structure

[co] Structure is a network of connectivity. An argument has structure, so has a building. From abstraction to concrete realisation, structure joins discrete ideas or elements into a coherent entity. Structure is skeleton or skin, points and lines or fold contour. CECIL BALMOND

Cecil BALMOND
(Ove Arup), ACTAR
ARQUITECTURA,
*Telecommunications
Tower on the Turó
de la Rovira*,
Barcelona, 2001.
Structural diagram.
Typological fitting.

[co] Structure is traditionally understood as the skeleton of the building. Throughout history, we see how architecture either presents or hides structure. The Gothics loved it. New engineering and new tech architecture use it again as a symbol and communication system. In Roman architecture, the structure is the system of walls and the massif materials used. Today, structure is usually conceived independently of the skin, although this is not the only possible interpretation. The building is more and more a collection of different functional elements joined together with dry connections. The structure can be done today with a great variety of new materials: composites, biomaterials, plastics or pneumatics. The structure can be lighter then the building it supports. Heaviness and lightness become changeable notions. The change of meaning and feeling of stability is one of the characteristics of contemporary architecture. Therefore, the contemporary meaning of structure is mobile and non hierarchical. We are leaving Hooke's period of his elastic world interpretation and entering an era where nature comes in our help subsequently structure can be plastic, viscous, viscous-elastic and pneumatic.
We have grown up in a world of rigid containers, with scarce movements and deflections, while the natural universe is based upon flexibility and mutations. The bird's wings, the branches of trees, the natural elements of water and strong winds. We are surrounded by mobility and transformations. Structure and architecture will follow this reality. We will educate our sons in this universe, integrated with natural movements without scarce deflections and with understanding of transformability and structural mobility. SALVADOR PÉREZ ARROYO

S. PÉREZ ARROYO &
E. HURTADO
(with F. RÍO DURAN),
Leaf House, 2003.

★ study

→ 'criteria', 'education', [CO]
'essay', 'intelligence',
'knowledge'

"In the year 2010, the word "study" will mean much the same as it does today. Some of the tools and source materials will change, but studying and learning will still require work, thought and self discipline. The development of the printing press and books did not change that basic human fact and current information technology will not change it either," Tom Hewett. XAVIER COSTA

■ subject

→ 'alienation', 'city?', [JM]
'de-location',
'de-subject', 'nomad',
'quidam', 'zapping'

1. subjected To show the city from (or as) a static space is a "waste of time,"(since it implies that there is no transit: only literally a subject, that is "subjected.)

2. individual What characterizes the subject, corresponding with the only man really free of the platonic city, that is, the artist, is to be dislocated. Not to be in any place and confuse ones actions, works, with the ambiguous profile and changing of accidents. Precisely for moving, the artist is expulsed from the city.

The subject can be liberated from the city if he moves, if he camouflages and hides, if he establishes a singular relation between space and the body; in that life flows.

● sub-over strata

→ '(inter)weavings [MG]
and inter(plots)',
'landstrategy', 'layers',
'puff pastry', 'section',
'stack'

Strata are mixed layers of information superposed in elevation.
Mixed layers of information buried in and, occasionally, emerging from the subsoil.

● subsoil

[MG]

→ 'city?', 'de-location',
'fillings', 'iceberg',
'immersed', 'infrastructures',
'layers', 'networks',
'nomad', 'sub-over strata',
'voids and fills', 'zapping'

"The dream of the metropolis is constructed in the subsoil. The great street substructure works reveals the same vigour that characterised the expansion of the city in the XIX century. The gigantic catacombs of the underground railway are separated only by a fine strip of earth from the train stations, from which modern transport attempts to penetrate the walls of last century by means of absurd change operations. In the subsoil, however, operations preserve something of the archaic. The absence of regulations and aesthetic preferences allows mobility to be controlled with great technical precision."
(MELLI, Marcel, "Periphery. A letter from Zürich", *Quaderns* 177)

1. Carol REED,
The third Man,
1949, in *Quaderns*
191, 1991.

2. ADD Arquitectura
(BAILO-RULL),
*Diagonal Nord-
Campus Sud,*
Barcelona, 1998.

3. BCQ (BAENA,
CASAMOR, QUERA),
Interchanger 1,
Plaça de Catalunya,
Barcelona, 1998.

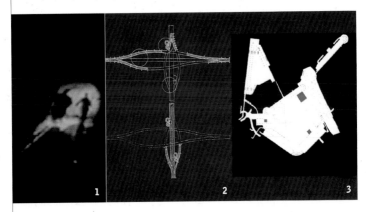

★ substratum

[co] The most general meaning of substratum is that which supports everything, that which is beneath, the base upon which everything else is deposited. There is however another, perhaps more general meaning, often employed by Deleuze. Substratum as sub-stratum; the affirmation of reality as a complex substance formed of sometimes inextricable layers necessarily leads to the possibility of organisations or self-organisations within a layer. A stratum is not a two-dimensional laminar entity; it is, rather, a disposition of information capable of assuming substructures that are complex as required.

JOSÉ ALFONSO BALLESTEROS

● ★ surface

[MG] See 'landstrategy,' 'topographies, operative' and 'topological.'
Today it is a question of constructing surfaces under the sky rather than volumes under the sun.

[co] One of our current concerns is, precisely, the nature of the surface that constitutes the building. Curiously, our considerations in this respect tend to gravitate towards discussion of local idiosyncrasies. We have detected two basic operative architectural modes in Japan: those that operate with spaces and surfaces, such as Maki, Ito and Sejima, and a second type that works with the tradition of materiality and craftsmanship, including Isozaki, Takamatsu and Kitiganara. The interest of the exercise lies in ascertaining whether we wish to impose the quality of the surface of the project, or increase its depth in its details, its relief, and make it an object. One of the chief problems during the construction of the Tokyo International Forum was that the measurements in the drawings by Rafael Vignoly were referenced to the plane of façade, while that the Japanese construction system was always referenced to the axis of the structure. While the American measurement system is inherited from the *beaux-arts* of academic American architecture or the traditional balloon-frame construction system, what the Tokyo Forum project revealed was that the essence in Japanese architecture is the material, and this might be an interesting path to follow in the attempt to treat ground as figure, surface as space.

ALEJANDRO ZAERA-POLO

FOA, *Downsview X-Park*, Toronto (Canada), 2000.

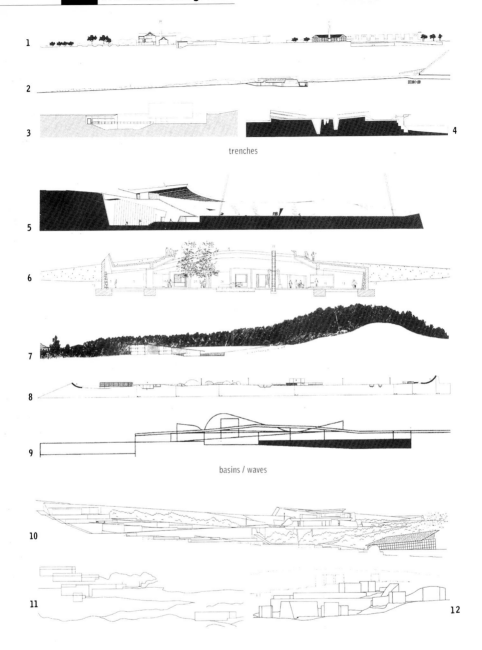

1

2

3

4

trenches

5

6

7

8

9

basins / waves

10

11

12

1. Juan DOMINGO SANTOS, *Renovation of the old factory of San Isidro as a culture and leisure centre*, Granada (Spain), 1999. **2.** Manuel J. FEO, V. ALONSO, M. T. MENDOZA, X. URANGA, J. TANCO, I. PELIGERO, *Proposal for Arinaga battery*, Gran Canaria (Spain), 1999. **3.** Alfredo PAYÁ, *Museum of the University of Alicante*, Alicante (Spain), 1997. **4.** Manuel J. FEO, V. ALONSO, M. T. MENDOZA, X. URANGA, J. TANCO, I. PELIGERO, *Estratus-horizon: seafront*, San Vicente de la Barquera (Cantabria, Spain), 1999. **5.** AMP (ARTENGO-MENIS-PASTRANA), *Competition for athletics stadium* (1st prize), Santa Cruz de Tenerife (Spain), 1997. **6.** Javier PEÑA & MTM Arquitectos, *Thematic Park Nueva Espuña*, Alhama de Murcia (Spain), 1997. **7.** R+B (José Miguel ROLDÁN, Mercè BERENGUÉ), *Gerbert d'Orlhac Secondary School*, Sant Fruitós de Bages (Barcelona), 1999. **8.** ACTAR ARQUITECTURA, *Intervention at the old circuit of Sitges*, Sitges (Barcelona), 1998. **9.** Willy MÜLLER, *Competition for auditorium and conference centre*, Pamplona (Navarra, Spain), 1998. **10.** AMP (ARTENGO-MENIS-PASTRANA), *Botanic garden*, Vallehermoso (La Gomera, Spain), 1991. **11.** José MORALES, Juan GONZÁLEZ, *Competition for student dwellings*, Jaén (Spain), 1997. **12.** S&Aa (SORIANO-PALACIOS), *Europan 4*, Bilbao (Spain), 1996.

● surprise

→ 'braids', 'event',
'in/unstable', 'paradoxes',
'reality', 'surface'

[MG] See 'criss-crossing' and 'suspense.' Surprise is astonishment, intrigue or disconcertedness – non-inertial reaction – produced by an unexpected, unforeseen or unusual effect or event. A surprise factor – decidedly linked to the discontinuous and non-linear experience of contemporary reality – thus appears implicitly related to the uncertain characteristics of an <im/in/un> order, in a constant state of suspense: indeterminate, intermittent and undisciplined.

●■ suspense

→ 'criss-crossing',
'dynamism', 'event',
'foreigness', 'in/unstable',
'paradoxes', 'reality',
'rootlessness', 'surface',
'surprise'

[MG] Today we coexist with intrigue. We refer to the experience of our own perception that records the manifestations of a scenario of shocks, continually changing and fleeting, in increasingly rapid transformation, in which apparently stable realities yield to new unknown realities: sudden slippages between the marginal and the profitable, the valued and the alternative, the peaceful and the conflictive, the conflictive and the paradisiacal: the artificial – strange – and the "strangely natural."
This is a scenario of atonalities and simultaneities not far removed from the "Hitchcock tempo" described by François Truffaut: a scenario, in effect, in a constant state of suspense – of unstable equilibrium – between the expected and the unexpected. Between predictability and surprise, order and chaos, control and chance, inertia and sudden shock. The everyday and the extraordinary. A contemporary scenario puts our gaze on a constant "state of alert," but also allows us to sense a space that resists labelling and that calls for, finally, the definitive transformation of those secular relationships between reality and virtuality, between permanence and fleetingness, between routine and change, between city and landscape – blurred in this new geography of heterogeneous experiences.

[JM] Today, the city shows us situations that take us unaware, that is, without having been aware of the circumstances which we are facing. These same situations and improvisations are reproduced in many architectural images. In any event, and given that there is a lot of theatricality in this architecture, free space to colonize has been put before our glance (the glance of modernity) has been accosted by the idea of an ever more subjective space, facing and alternative to that place predicted by power.

Alfred HITCHCOCK,
Vertigo, 1958.

◆✖★ sustainability

→ 'eco->
ecomonumentality',
'ecology, active',
'nature', 'recycling'

[FS] *"The concept of sustainability is the result of seeing a world with limited resources and limited capacity to absorb waste, where every act involves future consequences. This leads us to conceive of the construction of a building as an act which does not start with the delivery of materials to the site and end when its inhabitants move in.*
Building is a closed circle, including every step from the manufacture of the materials to a re-use which brooks no concept of waste: maintenance and disassembly are also planned. The biggest enemy of sustainability is the conservationist "ecological aesthetic" which is nostalgic for a rural past, for magical reasons in the face of a situation where nothing which cannot be generalised and easily conveyed represents a solution."
(VALOR, Jaume, "Graft of hyperminimums," *Quaderns* 219, 1998)

Use must encounter fissures in architecture upon which to concentrate, the form must be constructed while continuously aware of change. Its meaning lies in these superimpositions and continuities that the project must allow using soft strategies of composition.

[VG] See 'advanced.'

[c] *"Until urban expansion had reached a certain point, it did not become evident that the ecosystems on which the city depends have a limited capacity; the evidence has, in some cases, been dramatic. No limits on exploitation were established, with the subsequent depletion of resources and decomposition of systems, irreversible in some cases. The phenomenon of gradual city expansion and the sectorial nature of the exploitation of resources do not help us to understand the global dimension of the impacts. The only way of dealing with the conflict arising from the excessive exploitation of systems is to bring an integrated approach to the way they function, at the same time analysing the functioning of the urban ecosystem itself. [...]*
Important as these partial problems may be, the problems arising from conflicting scenarios are global in nature. The relevance of ecology to the sustainability debate lies not just in the fact that economic and human systems form part of the biosphere, but also in the contributions ecology can make to an in-depth analysis of certain systems, specifically those whose main components are organisms. [...]
The city, seen as an ecosystem, exploits other systems to maintain or increase its complexity. Placing a limit on the exploitation of systems, taking into account the principles of their respective functioning and making them sustainable is the optimum strategy for completing the territorial planning model. If one part of the model is the compact, complex city, the other part comprises complex, mature natural systems and a fabric of crops, pasture and fences, forming a diverse mosaic that establishes the necessary balance between exploitation and succession which ensures their conservation. This mosaic is the mesh system which has shown itself to be sustainable for centuries in temperate Europe." (RUEDA, Salvador, "City models: basic indicators," *Quaderns* 225, 2000)

▲ Swiss knife

→ 'extensible-compressible',
'multi', 'mutation', 'occupation
structures', 'open', 'poly'

[FP] Characteristics: utensil of unmistakable appearance. Its external shape contains, without any words, the message that defines it: *Swiss knife*. The ergonomic character of its shape apparently is more important than the number of uses it is adscribed. This shape, however, allows for multiple devices that, in any other way, it would not be able to contain. Its essence consists of being able to offer different possibilities to whom is using it, and its width becomes bigger according to the increasing number of possibilities it offers. This knife is recognisable precisely because it is not one, because it trespasses the functions assigned by its name and turns into a bottle opener, scissors, nail file, magnifying glass, nail clippers, etc. On a different scale, it has been one of the key elements of the career of Claes Oldenburg, who used it as a floating icon in the canals of Venice. We sometimes want ideas or buildings resembling Swiss knifes. Hermetic but flexible. Externally complete, but internally in constant evolution. Buildings of multiple response, thoughts capable of resolving simultaneous

1

2

3

4

5

6

7

1. & 2. Fake of the Swiss army penknife, Hong Kong (China), and the real one, Ibach (Switzerland), in *Colors* 36, 2000. **3. & 4.** Hans Peter WÖRNDL, *Gucki Hupf*, Beim Guglhupfberg (Mondsee, Austria), 1993. **5.** Vicente GUALLART, *House of the seven peaks*, La Pobla de Vallbona (Valencia, Spain), 1998. **6.** Arantxa LA CASTA, Fernando PORRAS-ISLA, Hotel in Cantabria (Spain), 1999. **7.** Eduardo ARROYO (NO.mad Arquitectura), *Kindergarten*, Sondika (Vizcaya, Spain), 1997.

● symbiosis

→ 'a-couplings',
'crossbreeding', 'hybrid',
'meldings', 'synergy'

[MG] Symbiosis is the mechanism by which two organisms mutually come together to enrich their development or simply their permanence. There are harmonious (pure) ones and hybrid (impure) ones. We are interested in the latter.

● synoope (syncopation)

→ 'event', 'individual',
'intercadences',
'intermittences', 'patterned
distributions', 'score',
'sequence and series'

[MG] Syncope defines a momentary disappearance, or a loss of presence, of physical stability. A momentary suspension of action. Syncopation is a rhythm – or sequence – produced through syncopes, absent sounds. Discontinuous intermittences. Irregular norms of empty-full, presence-absence.

● ★ synergy

[MG] See 'resonance-synergy-interaction.'

Today, we can today connect the contemporary project's will for interaction with the hypothetical synergetic – synaesthetic – vocation of the reactive. Synergy with the place and environment, but also with the time and with the moment. If – as Aaron Betsky argues (BETSKY, Aaron, "Landscape and the architecture of the self", *Quaderns* 218, 1998) – "*urban societies are ever constructing their own 'geology'*" (in the same way that natural elements consolidate, step by step, this densely stratified reality of nature), then the "superpresent" (that Roemer van der Toorn called for) is articulated as an authentic compromise and would imply an "*unbiased and synergetic return to the real world.*" Such a commitment to reality points to a will for plural interchange between multiple possible processed bits of information derived from it; that is to say, to the probing and syntonising capacity of the device as a processing machine (evolutionary system) capable of combining records of reality and actions upon it.

A reactive – synergetic – will would allude to a fruitful – active – interchange as the product of interaction between different realities in which the data supplied by the interchanged information would not be understood as definitive and hermetic (univocally incorporated) categories, but rather as interlinkable interconnectable, couplable and harmonisable impulses or tensions, in order to multiply its potentials and energies through appropriate contracts – and processes – of arrangement and displacement (understanding the term "displacement" as "dynamic movement," but also as unnaturalisation of original meanings).

[co] Synergy is the effect of linearity that takes up different directions so that multiple connections are established, overthrowing spatial hierarchies and becoming cross-referenced organisational networks. This field is transformed from coherent investigation in incubator organisation.
JUAN CARLOS SÁNCHEZ TAPPAN / LARS TEICHMANN / KRIS VAN WEERT

[co] Synergy is the situation that arises when the interaction between different individual organisms, or between parts of an individual, causes the whole to increase its independence vis-à-vis the uncertainty of the environment. In sum, it occurs when the overall interaction is more akin to cooperation than to competition. Symbiosis, a resource of great merit in biological evolution, is a case of binary synergy. Synergy has lent its name to scientific theories of self-organisation such as that created, christened and developed by the German physicist Herman Haken. Some of these theories have been successfully applied to urban planning projects.
JORGE WAGENSBERG

● ✱ synthetical

[MG] Artificial. Abstract. Economic. Concise. Diagrammatic. Condensed. Hybrid. Technological. Complex. Singular and Plural.

[VG] Synthesis of concentrated information.

[MG] **(dictionary, synthetical)**

Synthesis of the whole in the shape of "capsules" or aphorisms.

●✖★ system

[MG] **(dynamic)**

See '<in> order factors.'

Traditional theories about space have been heretofore relatively static and centralised, with little interest in the dynamic shapes that assert themselves more forcefully each day. Cities, configurations and architectural structures have been considered fixed systems, in equilibrium, in which the different parts were meant to be coordinated in linking macrostructures – or frameworks – according to the rational classical model developed since the era of enlightened determinism:

"Physics and economics have largely failed to account for the variety and richness of the modern world, and for the infinite capability of adaptive behavior. New ideas involving the science of form based on fractals, the science of dynamics based on chaos, and the science of function based on self-organization mark a new quest." (BATTY, Michael, "Growing cities", *Fisuras* 5, 1996)

Many writers have indicated that one of the reasons the chaotic behaviour of dynamic systems was not taken into consideration for such a long time (in science and in mathematics) was the fact that the space in which these systems tend to manifest themselves defied conventional geometry and any approach to them required new technological instruments. The same confines of topological irregularity appear extensively, however, in the material world, in geomorphology, ecology, in social organisations and also in the morphology of cities themselves. Today, borders, diffuse natural shapes surrounded, packaged or fractured into fissures and undulations of the terrain, or self-similar variations of an object through successive scalar recursivenesses, can be observed in terms of a new geometry that has intrinsic connections with the new science of complexity. Our present approach includes the influence of this new dynamic understanding of complexity and ideas of structure and shape underlying the contemporary project.

We sense in all of this a new idea of order, a new type of organisational engagement between things and their structures, which now requires our attention.

Carps avoid and attract themselves at the same time,
in BRIGGS, John, *Fractals. The patterns of chaos*, London: Thames and Hudson Limited, 1992.

[MG] **(the city as system)**

The contemporary city cannot continue to be approached in terms of a single place or a single shape; nor in terms of a single evolutionary stage. On the contrary, today, the city manifests itself as a complex and interactive system engendered through the accumulation of manifold, simultaneous and, often, contradictory actions and experiences: *states, stages and strata*.

Social progress, technical development, the interchange of information and increased mobility have fostered, in effect, a growing freedom in the occupation of space. The contemporary city thus presents itself as an increasingly dynamic system – a process.

We are disconcerted and somewhat fearful when faced with the different, unexpected, unfamiliar and unusual nature of this nebulous and diffuse manifestation of the city (traditionally a more stable, continuous and com-

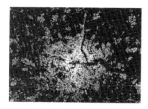

Map of fractal density, London, 1998.

pact state). Today, the city yields to a whole accumulation of emboîtée – embedded, enjambed – structures, formed by multiple substructures emerging from the interaction between different situations of planning, self-organisation, expectations, etc.

These are structures that, despite the impression they give of disorder or arbitrariness, actually possess   like other self-generated structures which exist in nature (flocks of birds, crowds in movement, irrigation flows, the expansion of gases in the air, sand formations, etc.)   internal codes that are regulated according to elemental rules of shape. Over time, these internal codes are capable of giving rise, over time, to highly complex polynuclear and discontinuous processes.

The development of a road network, the appearance of a spontaneous process of occupation, individual and collective behaviour within a global movement of spatial flow and, ultimately, the growth model of an urban agglomeration are, in fact, complex structures that conform to dynamic systems of temporal-spatial definition – the characteristics of which are analysed in a number of scientific fields and can be approached through alternative models of analogy and simulation.

[MG] See 'logic, fuzzy,' 'logic, direct' and 'operative.'

[VG] **(operating)**

The operating system is the series of laws allowing an environment to function and develop. Be it physical or digital. The architecture of recent decades has fundamentally operated in the design of the most superficial part of the urban system – the design of icons, objects that act as attractors, but have no overall repercussion on the system. The buildings constructed in recent decades whose value is greater than that of the simple accumulation of the materials they contain are minimal. It is highly likely that the actual system prevents architecture from having a presence beyond the purely iconographical. We will therefore have to think about changing the rules of play if we truly aim for our interventions to acquire spatial and moral quality and leave a large inheritance for future generations. We therefore have to propose a new form of interaction between the creators of programmes and contents and the designers of icons. In fact, this difference does not exist in the most advanced operating systems. The icon emerges coherent from the interface of development. In this way, architecture will have to mutate into an activity that initially participates in the creation of this new system. And thereafter develop strategies to operate actively in the process of technical, artistic and functional development.

[co] **Operating System**

An Operating System will be the software that supports Reality Modeling (RM), the kernel code which will allow us to hack matter into any desired form," Mark Pesce.
XAVIER COSTA

[co] **Artificial system, factitious system**

A system, according to Ludwig Von Bertalanffy, the founder of the general theo-ry of systems, is *"a set of elements that stand in interaction – that is, they are linked by such relations that if one is modified, the others are too, and, as a re-sult, the entire set is modified."*

A system is, then, "a set of objects and of relations between those objects and their properties." The relevance of the relations, according to which we consider a set of objects to be a system, will depend upon the ends we are pursuing in our in-vestigation.

It is not only real things (physical or social) that can constitute a system; so too can abstract entities such as a system of equations or a *theory*. An abstract sys-tem can be constructed as a *model* of concrete systems.

In relation to the notion of system appears that of surround: "the set of objects whose changes in properties affect a system and are in turn affected by the ac-tivity of the system." System and surround (or environment) are, then, correlative concepts and their delimitation is arbitrary. If the system is an animal organism, then the surround is the natural environment in which it is developed, but the set of the organism (or organisms) plus the environment in turn constitutes an eco-logical system, etc.

The relation of a system to its environment or medium also distinguishes between open systems [459] (having interchange with the environment) and closed systems (not having interchange with the environment).

(*Diccionario de filosofía contemporánea*. Ediciones Sígueme, Salamanca, 1976, p. 458-459)

JOSÉ ALFONSO BALLESTEROS

[co] **Cellular Automata**

A Cellular Automata is a formal and dynamical system consisting of a collection of cells arranged on a gridded space. All the cells are identical in architecture and have an internal state. The system evolves by applying, in discrete time units, a transition rule that updates the internal state of all the cells simultaneously. The inputs of the transition rule, for each cell, are the internal state of the updated cell and the internal states of its neighbor cells.

Different arrangements and space dimensions can be considered, as well as dif-ferent sets of possible internal states, neighborhoods or transition rules, in each case a different Cellular Automata may be produced. FRANCISCO TOLCHINSKY

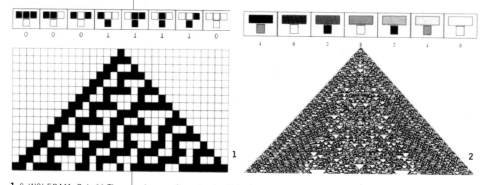

1. S. WOLFRAM, *Rule 30*. The space is a one dimensional grid (each row is the output of the upper row), internal states are bina-ry (0 and 1 or black and white). The neighbours of the cell are the adjacent cells, and the transition rule is specified above.
2. S. WOLFRAM, *Code 912*. Same case as figure 1., but internal states are 0, 1, and 2 or white, grey and black, and the transition rule specified above.

AA: Advanced Architecture

Beyond classical architecture (ritual) and modern architecture (productive) there is an advanced architecture (informational).

An advanced architecture is an architecture positively bound to change: with events and the temporal and evolutionary dimension of processes.

● abstract

[MG] Abstract is no longer essential, but synthetical. It is not refined information, but condensed information: compressed in order to be multiplied. Operative code rather than substantial code.

[MG] No longer "less is more," but "more from less."

● a-couplings

[MG] Today old substantive categories repeatedly clash with the undisciplined conditions of mixtures and slippages that, in all their manifestations, call for the brutal (and exciting at the same time) dissolution of the old dichotomic divisions which, for long years, were paradigms of our ideological and disciplinary baggage.

● action>architecture-action

[MG] Architecture-action is an effect of expressing, operating, executing and doing. Requires energy, decision and capability. That is, disposition.

[MG] What we are interested in today is an 'action-architecture' defined by a desire to act, to (inter)act. To promote interactions between things, rather than interventions on them. Movements rather than positions. Actions, rather than figurations. Processes, rather than occurrences.

● action>critical

[MG] A critical action truly committed to the advance of ideas is an element which is at once revitalising and transformative. A critical action is precise (intentional) and transgressive (undisciplined). To promote movements, rather than descriptions. Actions, rather than contemplations. Explorations as opposed to chronicles.

▲ activation

[FP] Activation is the action for excellence.
Activation is always transforming, never inert or indifferent.
The land is activated with the presence of the architecture; architecture operates through its use; the use operates in relation to the new sensitivity to materials; materials are transformed in relation to the land which separates and unites us.

● activity

[MG] A dynamic architecture is vitalising: it generates not only aesthetics – or shape – but also (above all) activity.
An architecture capable of favouring spaces that are more "unsettled," precisely by virtue of being active and activated.

● ✻▲ advanced

[MG] Advanced is moved or set forward or in the front.
To thrust – or project – forward.
An action (an architecture) that is advanced is an action (an architecture) which is necessarily projective: propositive and anticipatory/anticipating.
An action (an architecture) that works with interchange, relation, information and evolution.

[VG] It is advanced to think that the advent of the digital world constitutes a new possibility for humankind: that of reinventing itself and its surroundings.
It is advanced to think that machines (chips, computers, etc.) can help humankind to advance in the field of knowledge, to find answers to old questions and then formulate new ones.
It is advanced to think that the world has yet to be built, that innovation is the source of all projects, that we live in a state of permanent creation.
It is advanced to think that, in order to build the future, we have to accept that major changes will be taking place in coming years due to the information revolution and the fact that this revolution will arrive, if it is not here already, and affect human beings at every level.
It is advanced to think that artificial intelligence will be one of the pillars of human-cybernetic activities in coming years and that this will change the way we work and the way we act.

[FP] Advanced in the past used to mean a certain risk of disconnection (the vanguard could lose contact with the rest of the army). For us, to advance is to drag, to drive forward without leaving anyone behind.

◆ advanced>advanced architecture

[FS] What advances, what progress! Walking architects, as opposed to contemplative architects. Propositions, as opposed to positions.

+ ● advertisements

[WM] We all remember an advertisment which we like. It is often astute, intelligent and always suggesting, amazing. For anticipated/anticipating.

[MG] Some advertisements are only "commercial-universal-trivial." Others are "commercial-singular-original;" at the "origin" – advance, foretaste – of something new and, thus, unexpected.

✗ agriculture

[VG] Agriculture is being industrialised. The landscape is being urbanised.
The spectacle of nature and that of the city are now comparable.

● ambiguity (and ambivalence)

[MG] Univocal space now yields to a space decidedly ambivalent. Not only because it is functionally non-predetermined, but also substantively hybrid. Categorically ambiguous.
In a multifaceted, polyphase, definitively non-essential reality, architecture can create spaces that are more plural, by virtue, precisely, of being indeterminate. Implicitly changing and (in)formal. Multiple. Multiplied and multiplicative.

● anonymous

[MG] We propose, instead of the insubstantiality of the anonymous and the bored/boring, a more extrovert architecture. Expressive. Not expressionist (forcing the gesture), but rather explicit (expressing movement).
An architecture capable of communicating the dynamic logic – and tensions – that shape it (its topology) and of reacting vis-à-vis the exterior stimuli that solicit it.

● archaeology>Past and Present

[MG] There are times when the hidden past sudden-

ly reappears, like the corpses emerging from the pool in *Poltergeist*. We might find ourselves trapped in its (their) claws; we might observe it (them) – paralysed – from a prudent distance; or we might simply play with its (their) bones.

✗ archaeology>advanced

[VG] The best way of protecting heritage is to increase it. The multilayer city would, in this way, highlight its multistrata nature.

●✗+◆▲■ architecture

[MG] The value of architecture no longer results from creating shapes in space, but rather from fostering relationships within it. Combined relationships and actions – reactions – in (and for) a definitively "open" and non-predetermined reality; the more qualitative, the more potentially interactive. In positive synergy with the environment.
This points to a latent change in the figure of the architect, no longer formulable only in terms of a "designer of objects," but rather in that of a "strategist of processes."

[MG] Our chief mission as architects still resides precisely in this capacity for articulating a propositive mediation between the forces of production and the conditions of those scenarios to which the latter are associated. Hence is derived the capacity to "PROJECTISE," that is, to KNOW, CONCEIVE and PRODUCE; to RELATE (explore, associate, deduce, imply,etc.); to PROPOSE (imagine, foresee, anticipate, invent); and to CREATE (build, structure, organise, coordinate, etc.).
A mediation, aimed at equipping the productive and cultural structures of each moment with an appropriate spatial organisation, capable of syntonising with the "environmental conditions" (of the global).

[VG] Architecture is the process by which the organisation of activities in space and time is defined. Physical or virtual.

[VG] Up until now, architecture has operated principally with space, because building meant finishing a process. Now, in the digital world, time too belongs to architecture. New architecture organises what has come to be referred to as "heightened reality," where the physical and the digital relate. Buildings and spaces also begin to more actively include time and its self-transformation. Architecture is, then, the creator of processes, rather than of finite events.

[WM] The digital age is to advanced architecture what the industrial revolution was to modern architecture.

[FS] "Real Architecture is always in the least likely place. Where nobody is thinking of him and no one pronounces his name." (Modification of DUBUFFET, Jean, "El arte bruto frente a las artes culturales")

[FP] "Architectue is already submerged in another metadiscipline: Geography." (Ricardo Sanchez Lampreave)

[JM] The project is "a making." The term "to architecture," has to do with this – getting to know something that previously had no pre-established path with and from which to be obtained.

✖ arkitektor

[VG] Computers already allow the development of artificial intelligence, or almost artificial.
This reduction to the absurd shows how the architect either brings added value to the process of the conception and construction of a building, or ceases to be necessary in the drawing up of projects.

◆ artificial

[FS] The artificial-natural duality has disappeared. Its boundaries have blurred, confusing traditional fields and arriving at a common definition: naturartifical.

●■ a-scalarity (scalar ambiguity)

[MG] Scale it is neither measure nor dimension (both univocal), but capacity for relation (ambivalent).

[JM] A-scalarity is action and effect of an architecture that does not distinguish limits, that dissolves. All space of this architecture would be intermediate space, "between."

● audacity

[MG] Audacity is no gratuitous temerity or imprudence, but calculated innovation and risk: at once precise and determined.
Audacity is daring, in the positive sense: higher stakes, for higher gain.
Audacity is not to save, but rather to give energy.
Audacity is boldness. Projection.
Projective capacity subject to chance (and fortune).

● auditoriums

[MG] Auditoriums are not morgues.
Certain official culture, however, has confused terms.

● avatar

[MG] "Avatar" is, in the romantic spirit, an adventure subject to the whims of chance: an uncertain experience, subject to a fortuitous series of unforeseen events.
It also describes each of the incarnations of the god Vishnu.
In contemporary language, an avatar is a virtual figure, animated and dynamic, capable of simultaneously evolving and mutating (real and virtual).

▲ biodiversity

[FP] We can design by saving energy, when we rediscover within fixed parameters a conjoint of new and changing possibilities.

●▲ body

[MG] Formerly, the body was a head, torso, two upper extremities and two lower extremities. Now, it is n-heads, n-torsos, n-extremities (upper and lower) and n-accessories.

[FP] The body is a place (which we can find today in different locations on the planet at the same time).

◆ bored

[FS] We do not want architects seated, but walking. We are not original, but extraordinary in the most banal way.

C

●★✛ camouflage

[MG] As with certain military artifices, camouflage is generally achieved through an intentional manipulation of reality: a synthetical diagramming of its most apparent, or literal, patterns converted into abstract schemes capable of interacting with the environment, rather than of changing colour with it. Appropriating its most elemental features, compressing them.

[WM] Camouflage is the mark that the army invented.

● carpets (advanced landscaping)

[MG] If we imagine the surfaces of a territory as the floors of certain great rooms, scattered with colourful carpets of diverse motifs, we might then also imagine, rolled out over the landscape, possible "architectures" conceived, in turn, as virtual operative carpets.
Programmatic mats – spots – not camouflaged but rather slid into and over the landscape: Land(s) in lands.

✕● cartographies

[VG] To represent reality is to begin to transform it.

[MG] The classical observer and the modern flâneur are thus succeeded by the contemporary explorer.
The old idea of representation is now complemented – in this new intelligent cartography – by the capacity for projection, combination and modification provided by new interscalar logics and instruments of recognition based upon a sophisticated organisation of an information proper to present-day digital technologies.

● catches

[MG] "*As we speak, some things are consumed and new ones arise.*"
(Iñaki Ábalos & Juan Herreros)

■▲● chance

[JM] Chance is the meeting between all things and other objects.

[FP] Chance is no more than a digest of instructions, in theory unpredictable, which achieves results.

[MG] Chance is uncertainty (or luck) which is "projected" (programmed and transferred).
A logic sensitive to the contingent.

●◆ chaos

[MG] Chaos is a determinate indeterminism, a marriage of apparently contradictory concepts which explains the terms in which certain undisciplined – yet not necessarily lacking in certain internal generic logic – phenomena are produced.

[FS] "*Potentially profitable state.*" (Susanna Cros) Chaos is entropy.

✛● client

[WM] "I'd rather have the customer come and say: 'Wow, I've never seen that before,' then, 'Wow, look how they've changed that,'"
Barry Gilbert, from Sharper Image.

[WM] "The customer is a rearview mirror, not a guide to the future," George Colony.

[WM] "Our job is to give the customer what he never dreamed he wanted," Dewys Lasdon.

[MG] Accomplice to whom one should never speak as Groucho Marx once did: "I never forget a face, but in your case I'll make an exception."

▲ cloning

[FP] What is the real interest in cloning? Deviation.

◆● collaging

[FS][MG] 1. Method of representation: superimposing images.
2. Method of production: superimposing shots.
3. Method of design: superimposing programme and events.

● combination (combinatorial)

[MG] Combination is at the same time change and diversity: possibility of simultaneous existences, but also the possibility of a given series of events.

✛ companies

[WM] "In this company you'll be fired for not making mistakes."
Steve Ross, former president of Time Warner.

● complexity

[MG] Complexity is capacity for combining manifold, simultaneous and not always harmonious layers of information.

● complicity

[MG] Complicity is not only capacity for dialogue – or for adhesion – but also capacity for synergy; interaction between energies at once different and empathetic.
Singularity and plurality. Never isotropy or integration.

● consequent

[MG] Better to be consequent, than coherent. Better active intentionality, than resistant compactness.

✖ conservation

[VG] The best way of conserving something is to increase its number. The best way of conserving heritage is to increase it.

● context

[MG] Formerly context, now field or environment.

● contract

[MG] A contract is an agreement among different and not necessarily harmonious individual situations.

■ creation

[JM] Construction from the new and not from examination.

● creators

[MG] Creators will be necessary to create systems and to assess results. Only those who add value to the chain of knowledge shall have a place in the production system.

● criteria

[MG] The orientation of a universe that is multiplied by communication and information requires a precise selection of the operating data that can be processed with a view to action. Exploration then becomes "tactical intentionality," capable of formulating criteria rather than following models.

● ✖ culture

[MG][VG] The only way to be timeless is to be absolutely of a time: for buildings to reflect the hour and the minute in which they were designed and constructed.

✖ culture, advanced

[VG] Advanced culture aims to achieve active interaction between sustainable development and the integration of new technologies with a view towards achieving increased quality of life.

● cuttings (and slips)

[MG] In the hybrid – melding or cutting – each part is known as itself. And as a part of others at once manifold and multiplied.

D

● decisions (and instructions) rather than designs

[MG] Decisions, rather than designs is, in effect, the issue: dispositions – as configurations (distributions or deployments) but, also, as decisions (resolvent logics). Decisions, rather than designs. Configurations, rather than figurations.

✖ demolish

[VG] To demolish is an action carried out when architecture is worth less than the space it occupies.

● devices

[MG] We prefer, in fact, the term "*dispositif* (device)" to that of "system."
Dispositif (device) as system but also as active scheme: map of movements, synthetic diagram, tactical criterion, operative logic – or programme –organisational (infrastructural) norm, (formal) system and, finally, mechanism of reaction: reactive vis-à-vis place.

◆ diagonalisation

[FS] A process by which space runs continuously through the section. The interior is understood at once in its totality and in its diverse levels. A space is diagonalised when we produce a connection between its distinct levels through voids that flow, connect and link topologically or sequentially.

● diagrams

[MG] A diagram is a graphic representation of a dynamic process synthesised through compression, abstraction and simulation.

As a medium, the diagram plays a dual role. It is a manner of notation (of analysis, of recognition and of reflection), but also a machine of action (generative, synthetic and productive). Diagnosis and response. Map and trajectory. The essential bit of action.

■ difference

[JM] The difference: what is not the same or universal.

●✗ digital

[MG] The future holds the possibility of thinking about a more abstract nature of shape and of the processes that develop it, made up of real experiences and of virtual simulations produced in a universe of appropriately vectoral digital data.

[VG] New technologies make it possible to transform data flow to the point of creating authentic landscapes. Settings for virtual meeting and real use. Spaces and computer programmes accessible from an intermediate space that can lead into a virtual world full of real content.

✗ digital>digital world

[VG] A stratum that issues digital material, like radioactive rain that soaks the layers through which it seeps, transforming old substances and creating new chemistries.

✗ discipline

[VG] Discipline in all fields of human knowledge has been created by individuals with a serious lack of discipline – by those who broke the rules of play of their historic context in their eagerness to invent the future.

● discipline>transdiscipline

[MG] We speak no longer of disciplines, but rather of transdisciplines. Environment, transversalisers of knowledge. The gaze of the trade – of the discipline – thus yields to the gaze of the criterion – of information.

● dispositions>composition-position-disposition

[MG] If, in its day, modern space meant the shift from the idea of composition – as regulation –

to that of position – as correlation – today, contemporary space means the shift from the idea of position to that of disposition – as an operative decision, but also as the possible indeterminate combination (and distribution) of positions and/or layers of information. From a predictable vision of the universe, we moved on to a measurable one and, now, to a differential one.

● dispositions>distributions

[MG] We believe it is appropriate to adopt the term "disposition" for its manifold and fitting meanings: disposition as a "combination of positions," but also as logics of "decision" (or instrumental order). Disposition as shape and as order, but also as character and attitude (state of mind vis-à-vis the action), at once virtual and operative.

■ dissolved architecture

[JM] Architectures leaning on disappearance. Objects never more, and much less, beautiful.

● diversity

[MG] Ours is a time of diversity, calling for constant simultaneity of individual events in global structures: this "multi" – plural – condition links the local with the global, the particular with the general, the general with the individual.

● dynamism

[MG] This dynamic condition as active and propulsive energy would play a decisive role in explaining the world and the forces that it comprises: this constant intermediate disposition between the possible and the real, between the virtual and the actual, as principles common to the basic nature of the being, fundamental expression in mobility, in variation and in evanescence. In change; in the dynamic, that is.

● ecology, active (or bold)

[MG] Instead of old nostalgic or pseudobucolic ecology (which freezes landscapes, territories and environments), we suggest a bold ecology; requalifying by virtue of being reformulating. Based no longer upon a timid, merely defensive – resistant – non-intervention, but rather upon a non-impositive, projective and qualifying – restimulating – intervention in synergy with the environment and, also, with technology.

[MG] An ecology in which sustainability is interaction.
In which nature is also artificial.
In which landscape is topography.
In which energy is information and technology is vehiclisation.
In which development is recycling and evolution is genetic.
In which environment is field.
In which to conserve implies always to intervene.

✶✛ economy

[VG] In the industrial economy, economic growth required physical growth. In the new information economy, this is no longer necessarily true. Cities ought to behave like chips, that are increasingly able to do more things in less space.

[WM] Advanced architecture means setting your mind on this same course: *unlimited responsibility*, complete service, *rent-a-chemical*.

✶ education

[VG] Educating consists in conveying logic, followed by processes, that lead to something. Order as a principle, and the result as the logical end of a process. To show the result of a creation without understanding its order is to deprive the spectator of the creative principle that, in turn, enables creation. Showing the result without understanding the process only produces a copy which, as in human reproduction, degenerates the species.

● energy

[MG] Energy is stimulus. Activation of forces and efforts.

■ enlarged

[JM] Enlarged architecture is what unfolds along curved, convex and multi-directional vision.

◆ entropy

[FS] Energy is neither created or destroyed, it only transforms. The first principle of thermodynamics is well known. The second, less so.

Entropy always grows. This means that systems pass from a state of great order to one less so.

● environment

[MG] Environment is no longer only context (or at least a limited and limitative vision of the context), but rather definitively glocal milieu or environ: in the local it is place or, better said, field. In the global, scenario or, better said, reality (physical and virtual).

●■ epitome

[MG] The contemporary project is conceived of, in certain cases, as an a-scalar synthesis of a definitively multiscalar city. An epitome is a concentrate of its own basic dynamics but also a transfer: a movement in synergy with the place, but also capable, of causing a scalar jump towards other scenarios, beyond its boundaries.

[JM] The formulation of what becomes space in architecture has more to do with the city and its events than with the dwelling itself; that place in which space is contained, and in a certain way, stabilized.

✛ eraserhead

[WM] "The problem is never how to get new, innovative thoughts into your head, but how to get the old ones out." Dee Hock, creator of Visa.

[WM] "You can't live without an eraser."
Gregory Bateson

● erudition

[MG] Erudition is sometimes a tactical – selective – literacy that favours innovation: the hope for the new and the action for the new. That is to say, it permits "invention" without query.
We replace erudition with curiosity. Reference with recording.

✶ España

[VG] Spain is (a) multinational.

● event

[MG] We often confuse event and occurrence.
Occurrence is what occurs, event is what comes about.
One is junctural; the other, singular in its particularness.

● evolutionary

[MG] Systems, actions or processes capable of evolving are evolutionaty. That is to say, the evolutionary is capable of growing and developing, mutating and transforming, altering, varying, deforming and/or being influenced through codes or generic internal basic rules, precise and flexible, at once determinate and indeterminate, and through bits of specific external information, fortuitous and contingent, at once foreseen and unforeseen.

● experience

[MG] Experience is an asset, not a value. It should support, not impose itself upon, innovation.

▲ expression

[FP] We propose to enquire into the sense and validity of expressive thinking, in the search for instruments and justification, assuming, on the one hand, the diffused panorama of these times and, on the other hand, the progressive increase of interference from other spheres of knowledge.

● expression>and expressiveness

[MG] We seek an expressive, rather than expressionist architecture: it is not a matter of forcing the gesture but rather of stating the action.
An architecture aimed at evidencing a flexible (elastic), changing logic that articulates it (its topology) and projecting other situations beyond their own juncture.

■ extend

[JM] Architecture traps the exterior to discover interior possibilities.

● extension

[MG] The idea of open form alludes to an animated trajectory, possibly frozen in a precise instant – an x shape – but virtually "excited," extended within and towards other instants.

● extroversion: <ex> factors of form

[MG] The extroversion factor translates a *dynamic* interpretation of the idea of form: a form that we call *extrovert* for its at once nervous and vehicular character, it explains and clarifies the processes and the movements that make it up

and at the same time favours interactions and connections, local and global, with those events in which it is inscribed.

✦ F111

[WM] Form follows neither function, nor structure, but strategy.

◆ fencing space

[FS] I propose that our architecture follows. A space that is the instantaneous trail of use. An agile thought instantaneously materialized. A structure solidified in a moment, almost at the point of disappearing. A space whose definition does not depend on floors.

■ ◆ field

[JM] The outside is as important and definitive as the inside. What we have are not objects and an exterior reality, but continuity between forms that wrap and unwrap, open and close, that focus and serve as a focus. Architecture thus expands in reality, in a medium, in the environment. The medium in which it appears is a field.

[FS] Fields are full of information, possible scenarios, events, forces of risk and they are always in the state of transformation.
(Wiel Arets)

● figure-background

[MG] Figure and background blur their boundaries in new articulated devices more flexible as they are precisely diffuse, definitively. Capable of reformulating old categories of the urban (city, landscape, infrastructures) in a new dynamic of cooperation and synergy

◆ fissures

[FS] There is an awareness that surges between the fissures of contemporary culture. And like cracks, what is most important is the map that the fissures draw as they link one another.

● fleeting

[MG] Fleeting is of brief duration. Essentially unstable. Impermanent, temporal, provisional and ephemeral. Like a flash.

●+ flexibility

[MG] To flexibilise certain situations – to open them to the indeterminate – always implies to shape – to weave, to norm, to rhythmise, though not necessarily to rigidify.

[MG] The new concept of flexibility (beyond the cliché of the do-it-yourself user, who dedicates him or herself to continual transformation of the interior of his or her house) should now be associated with greater multi-usage and versatility of the space.

[WM] Flexibility is in the mould and not in the piece. In other words: maximum manipulation in the design process, minimum final manipulation. Unique architecture, mass-produced.

●◆ fold (unfold-refold)

[MG] We talk about folds, unfoldings and foldbacks as possible dynamical trajectories. A-scalar trajectories between structures and organisations, devices and cities, scenarios and projects, referring to evolutionary geometries of topological order.

[FS] We must work on the folds of Modern Space. Our space is the folded space of the Modern. We operate in the order of the rupture of the free plan. The fold separates and unites interior and exterior.

● foreigness

[MG] *"Any guest is an intruder, a foreign element – an outsider – one who interferes with external – alien – baggage in an intimate, sacred space."* (Jamie Q. Dern)

◆▲● form

[FS] This is a 'non-form,', (emerging from) an awareness of the uncertainty where to know what things are is only possible when we recognise what they are not. The interest, then, lies in an architecture that has neither image nor form. That does not express explicitly the scale in which it is produced.

[FP] We understand shape as a bond between probable relationships.

[MG] Today shape is disposition. Spatial-temporal distribution – or deployment. And extrovert attitude – or will – vis-à-vis reality.
Capable of expressing – and communicating – the interior movements, logics and tensions, that configure it (its topology) and of reacting and mutating in response to the demands of exterior stimuli.

●✗ fractal

[MG] Between uncontrolled chaos – absolute disorder – and Euclidean order, there lies a zone of fractal order.

[VG] A fractal object has two basic characteristics: infinite detail in each point and a degree of self-similarity between parts of the object and its overall characteristics. Processes, rather than equations.

◆ fragment

[FS] Fragment is an old word that is substituted for unfinished.

✗ franchise

[VG] Today, there are only two ways for cities to succeed in the global economy: being an innovative city, a leader in culture, in industry or in international economy, or adopting the role of franchise, an intermediate role, that imports models created in other places and participates in a network of influences.
Success is possible in both cases. The problem lies in being neither one nor the other.

✗▲ function

[VG] In a world in which work, leisure and commerce can be carried out by means of computers occupying spaces that do not require spatial classification, function should not be a basic parameter in defining a portion of land within the territory.

[FP] Politicians change the function of buildings while they are under construction in order to win votes. Architects are becoming more and more conscious of the reality in which the 'old treatsies' lose ground and an in-formal nature of patronage reigns.

✗ future>vision

[VG] One possible scenario that has been described for the future of our habitable environments suggests a virtual reality, accessible by means of glasses, that functions effectively reveal a fast, light-filled, beautiful, excited world. When we take off the glasses, the city we live in is dark and dangerous, full of waste and violence. The future may indeed be a dynamic, light-filled virtual world and a dark, decadent physical world.

✱ future>hybridisation

[VG] The best way to prevent the two worlds – physical and virtual – from separating is for them to become the same. Energy put into the construction of the virtual world should also be applied to the re-information of the physical world.

[VG] The industrial society brought about a transformation to produce basic quality, in the city and in the dwelling, for as many people as possible. The information society has to seek maximum quality for a maximum number of places. More is More.

G

◆ game

[FS] Game is to design, to negotiate.

● gaze>tactical gaze

[MG] Today, as we take in our environment, we are confronted not only with a new physical reality, but also with impressions that parallel it. As in a manipulated field, we are confronted with a multifaceted reality in which we feel disconcerting alienation from places.
Our orientation, and our action, now require a new gaze which is more *hybrid* — multiple and mongrel. Probably something outlandish; the gaze of new — and curious — explorers equipped with focusing instruments and a variety of objects; mobile; multi-focused.

▲ genetics

[FP] After the proletarian revolution was the industrial revolution. After the industrial revolution was the revolution of communications. After the revolution of communications was the revolution of genetics.
We acknowledge the possibility of creating

projects with genes, of being able to give structures, organisms or contexts the possibility of transforming themselves through propositive action.
Our idea is not to compose, but to generate; not to organise, but to provide guidelines; not to sort, but to develop.

● genetics of form

[MG] The assumption of an elastic – topologic – systemisation of form, in certain open processes of generation allows to conceive an architecture that comes to model itself not as a sculpture or as a drawing, but rather as a mobile flow, a co-participant, inserted into a field of dynamic flows.

▲✱ geography

[FP] We do not compose spaces anymore, but conform settings.

Nature can now be reconstructed by man. The world is turning into a habitable environment, into the city of 1,000 geographies...

◆ geometry>formal

[FS] What is the form of a fish?
I will imagine a geometry whose simple forms are not the cube, sphere or dodecadron.
We will speak of "cloud forms," "rock forms," "void forms" and "fencing forms."

✚ gestrategies

[WM] Gestrategies is an oxymoron, a contradiction between citizens' rights and the astuteness of peripherals, in permanent construction of unstable equilibriums.

● glocal

[MG] Global and local. Simultaneously. Glocal is phenomena, register, devices or information capable of resonating with the local and transferring to the global, capable of being a system and place at the same time; abstract logic with a singular result.

◆ graft

[FS] We sign up for the international grafter. His objective: to apply a portion of live thought to a mummified or lesioned part of the body and produce an organic union.

●✗ history

[MG] An authentically effective past is always a backwards-looking present.

[VG] We have never lived a moment like this one in which we are conscious of history, and we can use it in a positive way.
If the cultural revolution brought about by machines and their aesthetic (hardware) in the 1920s produced a *tabula rasa* with regard to history, then the digital revolution of information (software) has to voice its alternative for action in the existing city.

+■ holes

[WM] Holes are wild cards, "nothing:" "non-box" agents to be played whenever appropriate; infiltrated, exposed, converted into everything.

[JM] The space of architecture begins to make holes. And in this new vectorized space, the effect of the eye – more than the glance – pursues space, the hollowed and the perforated, venturing into landscapes of uncontrollable prediction. An "optically incorrect" space is considered, with which we are not accustomed to working.

● house, the

[MG] House: permutations.
The house-house: the symbol, the home space.
The cellar-house: the cave, the refuge space.
The face-house: the image, the icon space.
The box-house: the container, the object space.
The layer-house: the interface, the interaction space; not an inert enclosure, but rather a transfer, a device for relationship and interchange with the world. A place for enjoyment and stimulus, not only for shelter. A landscape to inhabit, and habilitate.

● housing

[MG] Today the dwelling should be understood as a place closer to quality of life and the suggestive fantasy of leisure, rather than to habitual serenity of space conceived only as mere social need. In sum, new housing need be conceived through diversity and plurality, rather than through homogeneity and collectiveness.
A BETTER housing capable of projecting the individual.

● hybrid

[MG] The hybrid nature of the contemporary project alludes to the current simultaneity of realities and categories, relating no longer to harmonious and coherent bodies, but rather to mongrel scenarios made up of structures and identities in parasitic coexistence.
By accepting, without prejudice, a strange situation of cohabitation made up of contracts, pacts and mongrelisations between bits of information at once overlapping and interconnected (imbricated and differentiated layers and (infra)structures) is how the culture of the contemporary project can be understood today.

+ ideas

[WM] "*Where do good new ideas come from? That's simple, from differences.*" Nicholas Negroponte, head of MIT Media Lab.
"*If people say something is 'good', it means someone else is already doing it.*" Hajime Mitarai, president of Canon.
The lack of ideas (paraphrasing Tom Peters) is a mental state: "*If he thinks he doesn't have any ideas, he doesn't have any.*"

● <in> order factors

[MG] The study of non-linear dynamic systems and the phenomena of chaotic intentionality has, with gathering speed, and over a relatively short time span, revealed the possibility of an indeterminate order – beyond the idea of order as a tight control of processes – based upon flexible relationships rather than upon categorical bonds.

● in-between

[MG] The in-between is not a residual space (the void between two volumes inherent to modern architecture and urbanism) but rather, in complex geometries, it may be a substantial place: the place where the geometry "inhales and exhales."

● in-between fingers, in-between links

[MG] Underlying the fractal – open and discontinuous – definition of current urban topologies is the presence of the void. No longer a residual, the void is rather an operative subsystem linked to the dynamic processes of spacing and occupation.

■ indefinition

[JM] Indefinition, not conclusion, is the immediate presence of the innumerable stammers taught recently in architecture.

■ indiscipline

[JM] All projects must be a criticism of convention, an act of fraud, of inconvenience.

[JM] Indisciplinary is, today, transdisciplinary. Indiscipline influences the old codes – recodifies – through mixtures, crosses and transversalities.

✖ individual

[VG] The information society ought to encourage the individual qualities of things and territories, as opposed to the total continuity of cyberspace, in which conditions are the same for every place on the planet.

■ infiltration

[JM] Infiltration is to cross, open the way, introduce into a space: all are actions, more than images or established configurations, to offer us a different concept of space.

● inform(ation)al

[MG] Classical space and modern time-space has been superseded by inform(ation)al time-space which provokes greater instability and indetermination in our understanding of the universe (greater informality) but, at the same time, permits assimilation in a catalyst of the constant interaction of impulses and stimuli.

■● inhabit

[JM] Inhabiting is a gerund.

[MG] The transformation of the family unit shows a progressive replacement of the classical idea of coexistence – communion of behaviours –

with that of a cohabitation – merely spatial contract (or relationship) – tending to favour the independence of different actions and behaviours and of changing individual needs. The significance of the individual over the clan.

✚ innovation

[WM] "Wealth in this new regime flows directly from innovation, not optimisation; that is, wealth is not gained by perfecting the known, but by imperfectly seizing the unknown."
Kevin Kelly, "New Rules for the New Economy," *Wired*.
Time and again in the history of innovation, the sector leader has reacted when faced with the threat of change… polishing up the same old apple, as an ultimate effort.
The enemies of advanced architecture are… the apple-polishers.

● interaction

[MG] Interaction is (inter)change and (inter)relation. Interaction is information transmitted, transferred and transformed among different and simultaneous energies, events and/or scenes.

✖ interactivity

[VG] If objects think, react and take action beyond their material qualities, spaces and places have to react with them.

●✖ interfaces

[MG] The mediating nature of the "device-architecture" alludes to its hypothetical condition as an interface: that of a device intended at once to relate us with reality and to multiply its qualities.

[VG] Architecture may be the interface of a new hybrid physical-digital world.
An overall understanding of the world by means of its spaces and the actual functions of architecture proposes a hyperreal future. Where reality, accessible to man through his five senses, extended by nanoprosthesis or otherwise, is the surround by means of which to take action in the world.

● in/uncertainty

[MG] The study of dynamic systems has, in a short time, introduced an inevitable factor of indetermination associated with the substantive instability of its diverse, irregular structures. It is not, in fact, a question of demanding of them absolute, exact and invariable results, but rather it is only necessary to enunciate (and announce) possible protocols: instantaneous combinations of results and probabilities that the latter would be produced.

▲ in/unfinished

[FP] In light of the fragment surges the unfinished.

● in/unsettledness (incompleteness)

[MG] The form that we describe here is an unsettled one (nervous, non-stable, non-fixed). It tells of a latent – uncertain – virtually incomplete state.
It expresses a moment, but also alludes to other possible moments. It is, in fact, an expectant shape, on standby.

✖ invent

[VG] As the chef Ferran Adrià says, the cutting edge of creation is not "*inventing the onion omelette, but inventing the omelette itself.*"

▲ invertlight or irradiate

[FP] Irradiating architecture is an architecture that modifies the territory, that resounds in the field of ideas and that touches the industry.

J

● joy (*alegría*)

[MG] An advanced architecture is an extrovert architecture, more "joyful."
A more stimulating and optimistic architecture. Determined to interact with the world.
Open to a resolute (strategic and plastic, operative and expressive) use of colour, of light, of sound, of movement and of energy; to a re-activation of the senses.

● just do it

[MG] "*Just do it: come on, do it. But we take it further and the proposal is now more difficult still: do it again.*"
(Susanna Cros)

K

✖ ◆ ● knowledge

[VG] Knowing the nature of things in order to act upon the reality. This is how architecture starts.

[VG] We can no longer believe in the transmission of knowledge by dictating given information, but placating the formation of criteria: making research and stablishing links with other knowledges and, thus, favouring an individual progress.

[FS] The knowledge we are given is like the photographer's box: a strong, resistant suitcase. We must get rid of this bag. We must buy the plumber's bag in which all the tools are mixed and which is often too full to be closed. We will find it. Capture it. Return. Forget. Better to be a sweeper than a judge.

[MG] Knowledge is, above all, criteria.

L

● land-arch

[MG] Land and Arch, never a brutal grafting, but rather an imbrication between two heretofore alien categories. Constructions that would artificially integrate movements – or moments – of nature, in some cases "architecturalising" the landscape, in others, landscaping an architecture in ambiguous synergy with the strange nature that surrounds it.
New landscape architectures, finally, in order to respond to the new demands of a society increasingly anguished by the geological frenzy of the urban.

● land links

[MG] Today it emerges the impact of the space "in negative," not so much as a remainder – or residual reserve – among things, but rather as a structuring gearage.
Land links: interwined gears capable of ensuring concatenated – locally and globally – developments in which, as in virtual linked fingers, meshes of places and inter-places – voids and fills – would be generated at different scales.

● land(s) in lands

[MG] Let us now address the notion of Lands in lands: "Operative landscape," rather than "host landscape." Artificial topographies over host landscapes. Thick lands, dense, over free receivers. Constructed geographies, rather than architectures. No longer lovely volumes under the light, but rather ambiguous landscapes under the sky. Operative topographies. Mongrel enclaves capable of generating their own energy. Fields within other fields. Lands in lands.

◆● layers

[FS] Layers reveal the order of information by means of superimposing levels of simultaneous knowledge. In a project, it is applied as a method to maintain the independence, fluctuation and evolution of diverse facts and components that have been applied.

[MG] The multiplied nature of the contemporary city demands a new multilayered definition associated to a new type of cartography: at once open and compatible, selective and purposeful (and often surprising and completely new), in which the city becomes synthesisable only through the recording of those layers of information which are potentially operative, and of their appropriate tactical combinations.

◆ light

[FS] A mechanism of modifying form in space. It makes these forms unstable.

●▲ limit

[MG] Today, we work beyond boundaries. With silhouettes – profiles and codes – that have lost their old – closed, finished, complete – coherence. We talk about an architecture without fixed limits, which oscillates between the static and the dynamic, the determined and the undetermined, the tangible and the intangible.

[FP] Defining in dissolution. Operating between edges. Up until very recently, architects set limits. Without a doubt, the present makes us think of its disappearance.

● link

[MG] Connection, but also contract, bond or relationship of kinship or interest.

● logic, direct

[MG] We may speak today of an "action-architecture" or a "diagrammatic architecture" conceived through a direct logic, capable of condensing processed data, precise latent movements and basic decisions by way of condensed trajectories of bits of strategic and tactical information. These movements are able to foster – in the context of the complexity of the new scenarios – responses (forms and spatialities) that are much more effective, precisely because they are concise, incisive, immediate.

▲ magic

[FP] Our architecture is more than ever a sleight of hand – magic.

✖ maieutics

[VG] Maieutics is a process of transmission of knowledge developed by Socrates, according to which the individual learns (remembers) a concept by answering a series of precisely formulated questions.

■● manipulate

[JM] The most advised thing for a project is to image it through action. Static or impulsive, it does not matter, the project ends up being the fruit of manipulating, pasting, separating, extending, nearing, putting with.

[MG] Manipulate – formerly "to control with one's hands." Today, to hybridise knowledge, natures and bits of information, physical and virtual.

● maps, battle

[MG] A battle map aims not to describe a place, but rather to begin its transformation.

●■ maps (to map)

[MG] Neither descriptive and literal nor analytical and objective, representation serves to deal with the dynamic, unfinished reality that is in constant mutation. Old static representations yield to diagrams, ideograms, infograms and (virtually) dynamic simulations. Maps intended to compress meaningfully not so much the reproduction of the whole reality, or part of it, but rather a representation – a scanning – of its most strategic bits of information. For it is no longer a question of describing shapes, but rather of describing potentials.

[JM] We have the tools, we make the map, tattoo the city. Everything is the same operation. A singular operation about the construction of the city and the interpretation of worlds.

+ materiature
[WM] Materiature is a certain boundary that we cross, knowing more and manipulating more information about nature, we create a new material landscape. Materiature is a different level of relationship between the natural and the artificial.

● mayor
[MG] There are mayors for whom to build implies merely to occupy.
For others, to build means instead to create – stimulate – new environmental conditions: scenarios, landscapes or habitats which are more qualitative and advanced, more qualitative insofar as they are advanced.

●▲ memory
[MG] Memory is always selective, with timely tactical lapses.

[FP] To be honest, I don't remember needing memory.

● menus
[MG] Our surroundings appear as multifaceted menus of opportunities, able to supply a large quantity of situations and needs along the length of their arteries.

●✗ Metapolis
[MG] The contemporary Metapolis constitutes a reality that transcends and comprehends, from diverse points of view, the metropolises we have known until now, fostering a new type of urban agglomeration made of multiplied, heterogeneous and discontinuous spaces and relationships. They are produced by urban entities that are increasingly more loosely linked in terms of hierarchy (progressively less relatable to circumstances of spatial or contextual proximity).

[MG] The term "Metapolis" defines this new multiple and multifaceted dimension of the contemporary city. A reality "beyond" that of the traditional metropolis which is no longer expressed only in terms of growth but also, in combinations.

[MG] City is no longer a single place or a particular shape, nor a unique evolutionary stage, but rather the accumulation of multiple stages and simultaneous experiences.

[VG] Beyond the metropolis of the industrial era emerges the Metapolis of the digital era.

+Metapolis>association
[WM] "Ready... Fire... Aim!" Wayne Calloway, former president of PepsiCo.

✗ metareality
[VG] Metareality is the broadest most perfect interface for action in the world. Metareality is a new state in the physical world, transformed by the energy of the virtual world. Metareality emerges from the re-information of the physical world.

● moral
[MG] Many people think we are making propaganda. Or, in the best of cases, philosophy. Perhaps we are talking rather about attitude. About disposition. Or, if you prefer, about morals.

✗ mountain
[VG] Mountains are concentrations of natural or artificial energy that can be inhabited. They are ascale folds in extra or intra-urban land.
They are accumulations of matter. Organic or economic.

● multi
[MG] Adding – or summing – is now multiplying.

▲ multi>(multiplicity)
[FP] Multiplicity is generation not repetition.

● multi>(multiply)
[MG] "x", not "+" nor "-", nor "="

N

● naturartificial

[MG] Naturaticial is the beneficial fusion of the natural and the artificial.

▲ nature (advanced)

[FP] Definitely, nature does not exist.
We recently digitalised the last metre of the planet and we already have it in our artificialising pocket.

◆ negotiate

[FS] The architectural project is not designed, but negotiated.

✖ network of cities

[VG] As opposed to the big metropolises of the twentieth century, the information society creates Networks of Cities.
Cities are to the territory what computers are to the net. Nodes of accumulation, territorial IP numbers, points of concentration need to be absolutely efficient for the system to function.
Otherwise, like on the Internet, information flows are diverted and reach their destination by other paths.
Cities are entering a state of decadence.

✖●▲ networks

[VG] The network is a structure in which two orders exist: the local and the global. The two are equally important to the perfect functioning of the system. Without nodes there is no network – just lines taking information nowhere. If there is no communication between the nodes, they are no longer part of a network – just isolated points in an unknown environment.

[MG] The idea of interchange and displacement in the metropolis derives from the effective combination of different channels of communication and locomotion which are principally conceived of as circuits for directing flows in a better communicated, interrelated and virtually isotropic, but not necessarily more homogeneous territory. The progressive (and beneficial) access of all areas to communication and to information leads, in fact, to virtual disorientation and therefore leads to nothing, unless there is a definition of references and nodal or focalising points able to vectorise lines of power: attractors, polarities, strong or distributing nodes, which allow flows to be channelled and links to be fostered.

[FP] A fishing net on the dockside is a compressed tile, hiding its exact form. Submerged in the sea it miraculously takes the form of the school of fish that it catches. When hanging laden with fish, it re-establishes a uniform and weighty shape.

◆ no-box

[FS] The box is obsolete.

O

✚ ob-server

[WM] If the model of the computer world is based on an observer, I propose a functional variation: ob-server, given that this observer (split-in-two) fulfils a certain mission. It is neither camera nor eye, but video-dependent.

● one is many

[MG] One is no longer only singular, like an autistic and essential individuality, but rather singular as a plural, more complex and diversified individuality.
One is one and many at the same time.

● open

[MG] We shall speak of more open systems, forms, orders, geometries and architectures.
The more flexible the more un-disciplined.
The more dynamical – and uninhibited in their movements – the more informal and definitively extrovert.

●✖ operation

[MG][VG] An operation can entail the temporary occupation of a place, with the aim of putting into practice a strategy, of developing an activity.

✖ operation>desert storm

[VG] Journalist: General Schwartzkopf, how did the attack on Iraq begin, by land, by sea or by air?
General Schwartzkopf: The attack began si-

multaneously by land, by sea and by air, from inside and from outside, by shutting down communications and with missiles... It's all-out war.

● operative

[MG] A system or device capable of fostering combinatorial evolutionary developments based upon open logics.
Environments generate actions – operating actions.

● optimism

[MG] If it is advanced, it is always optimistic. If it is optimistic, it is not always advanced.

● paradoxes

[MG] Today, we require devices capable of generating situations, events and/or principles able to work with the system and change it at the same time. Due to this strangely dual condition we call them paradoxes. Operative paradoxes.

+ park-ing

[WM] Park-ing is a self-park, the fusion of two complementary landscapes.

● patchwork city

[MG] Like a patchwork on the land, the crystalline shape of the primitive city erupts in a heterogeneous spread of splashes and hollows. A patchwork of linked realities; of conflicts and tensions and loveliness – attractions – fostered precisely by the potential for mobility, interchange and displacement.

▲ permeable

[FP] Permeable architects let other things invade them. Permeable instruments burst interferences. Permeable architecture is capable of absorbing, but also constantly exporting things.

● place of places

[MG] The city is no longer an island, it is a spectrum of cities and of "cities within the city." This is the essence of the contemporary metapolis: to be a hyper-place, a "place of places." The

contemporary city, approached from a positive attitude, is a rich multifaceted scenario, "an exciting kaleidoscope of opportunities;"a stock (a menu) of diverse situations and experiences in concordance with the manifold and mutable nature of the contemporary citizen.

● ◆ ✕ ▲ places

[MG] Today, the concept of place is defined beyond its old morphological connotations (of that which was called "context") from a positive assimilation – and polluted – of reality referred to the more abstract notion of "field as a scenario of crossing and interaction."
The place is no longer a centre, but rather a boundary.

[FS] Distant proximities allow ourselves to be closer or nearer to an act that happened thousands of miles away than to local references or things that happen around us.

[VG] Architecture has to bring (never detract) vital energy to a place.

[FP] Place has nothing to do with issues related to dimension. Place has nothing to do with memory matters. Place has nothing to do with referential aspects. Place is a connection with something that is beyond the physical. Place has to do with state of mind and ideology.

● plaits

[MG] Converting many of the existing road networks – which are absurd and anti-functional – into new strategic meshes is, therefore, a priority objective in order to foster in the territory ensembles that are heterogeneous and meshed at the same time. Grids of development and combination. Urban plaits – *dentelles urbaines*, like flexible appliqués, brocades or blond lace – imbricated and singularised; diverse and articulated.

● *plateaux* (for platforms)

[MG] The *mille plateaux* of is Deleuze-Guattari, translated as "one thousand plateaux." They could also have been translated as platforms, trays, supports, hollows or, simply, lands. Topological topographies.
In any case, flexible support material.

● plural

[MG] We are interested in devices that are capable of creating plurality from singularity. At once in singular and plural.

● positioning

[MG] We prefer the terms positioning and disposition to that of position: both indicate a situation that is at once elastic and deliberate, a deliberate logic but adaptable. A contingent (unstable) action rather than a position that is fixed and rigidly stabilised (whether from dogma, conquest or permanence).

▲ precision

[FP] But at the same time, we are mechanics that work with extreme precision. It is knowing. It is not about details.

◆ + process

[FS] Perhaps the first distinctive reflection that recent architecture has presented is the dilemma between process and design, applied to all the tools or documents that define architectural objects.

[WM] Advanced processes are dominating the field of creativity, at the same time blurring various concepts: that of authorship, of work and of discipline.

✳ processes

[VG] Processes, not events.

✳ progress

[VG] Progress is not linear.
Progress is re-information.

✳ progress>history

[VG] A progressive society is one that leaves a greater inheritance than it inherited.

● prosthesis (prosthetics)

[MG] Intelligent cybernetic elements that have nothing to do with the members into which they are implanted (or which they take the place of) and which, however, interact qualitatively with the host body, improving upon its old services. These are technological elements (infrastructural, rather than aesthetic) but, at the same time, they are in unique and personal agreement with the receiving body in order to optimise potential.

[MG] Architecture cannot limit itself to simply extending the body, or sustaining it, but rather it must be simultaneously a receptive and active supplement: estranged from, and at the same time sensitive to, the particular; capable of regulating itself and, at the same time, of restructuring, restimulating and strengthening the host in order to take it beyond its own limits.

■ proto-architectures

[JM] Places, spaces that due to differences from which they are observed, can be considered proto-architectures. Or rather architectures that, due to their originality with which they are thought, can be considered proto-places.

● ✳ R+3D

[MG] [VG] Research + Development, but also + eDucation + Diffusion.

✳ re- (prefix)

[VG] Expansion is no longer possible. Any action on the territory is an act directed towards the interior of the global village. It is a re-act.

● reactive

[MG] "Reaction" and "Activation" combined, interpreting the term "reaction" as a cross between "relation" and "action."

● reality

[MG] Reality is "*physical and virtual, rather than real and virtual.*" (From a conversation with Artur Serra)

● recursiveness (reproduction and similarity)

[MG] The notion of recursiveness is based upon the appearance of similar bits of information – and shapes – between different overlapping levels. Although the events are not exactly the same, we find consistent features among differentiating aspects.

◆ recycling

[FS] Because architecture is the art of space and space is never wasted, there is no need to say that is recycled.

✗ recycling, urban

[VG] Recycling (introducing old structures into a new cycle) is differentiated from rebuilding (building anew something that has existed) or re-habilitating (habilitating a decrepit construction). Urban recycling means beginning a new cultural, physical, economic and social cycle in a city.

[VG] Cities have to grow inwards, with a view towards preserving the nature that surrounds them. To construct themselves over themselves.

[VG] In the coming years, leading cities will have to know how to grow economically without growing physically.

✗ re-information

[VG] Re-information is to form something anew using information as the basic raw material.

● relationships, transitive (of transference)

[MG] Not relationships of reflexivity (from x to x: isolated object), nor those of symmetry (of x to y and of y to x: contextual object), but rather those of transitivity (from x to y, from y to z, from x to z: synaesthetic object). Of transference in the place and beyond the place.

✗ represent

[VG] Only that which can be represented can be constructed.

● resonance-synergy-interaction

[MG] Resonance is the syntonisation of harmonised energies. Interaction is the interchange of associated energies. Synergy is the combination of multiplied energies. All refer to the notion of field and to an ambivalent relationship with the environment.

● rootlessness

[MG] Our times are "*no longer that of the continual, gradual, permanent and "mythical" duration of the classical city*" (Yorgos Simeoforidis). Our times are no longer ritual, based upon the repetition and recurrence of all shapes and events but rather arrhythmic, rootless, without precedent and demythifying.

Our times are definitively "artificial": by virtue of being in non-genuine, manipulated and irregular, but also hybrid, synthetical, strange and unforeseeable. "Non-homologated." Rootless.

✗ rurban loft

[VG] Today quantity is quality. There is no standard height or standard measurement: generous height, width and length at the service of quality.

▲ search

[FP] As we search, we never repeat. As we try out, we don't usually look back.

◆ section

[FS] Contemporary space must be defined by the section. In a building with a complex section, use is not allocated over identical floor plates.
It is a folded space that tries to create the fiction of a free volume.

✗ self-urbanism

[VG] Beyond cities lies their future.
A city's richness lies in what it is capable of doing, not in what it has done.
New urbanism is addressed at individuals rather than at the masses. One by one, not as a collective. And in this framework, the territory is an asset that should be preserved (not frozen) as though it were gold.

✗ simultaneity

[VG] We might imagine digital aliens who only operate on the Net. Or farmers who live off the resources they generate. But, the spirit of our time will always be dual (simultaneous): physical and virtual.

✚ simultaneity>successive-simultaneous

[WM] We are witnessing a change of times, from a culture of the successive to a culture of the simultaneous. We are moving from tele-vision to tele-action.

✗ síndrome-del-Liceu (Liceu syndrome)

[VG] To preserve something, you have to take action

on it, otherwise it degenerates or is destroyed. Or burnt. This syndrome, detected in the case of Barcelona's opera house, has in recent decades affected Mediterranean forests.

+space

[WM] *"And what if space were the true luxury?"* As Vicente Guallart says (and I second): *Why not m³ instead of m²?*

● spaces>collective or relational

[MG] Where formerly we spoke of public space, we now speak of relational space.
An authentically collective space open to use, to enjoyment, to stimulus, to surprise: to activity. A relational, complicit space. Not only for taking a stroll, but also for personal and/or shared stimulus. A collective space, uninhibited, optimistic, relaxed – and in many aspects changable, mutable, precarious and reversible – for a city ultimately more joyful and exciting than elegant.

● stains, ink

[MG] Seen from a satellite, in a black-and-white binary spectrum, the crystalline shape of the primitive city today seems to decompose like an *ink spot* spattered over the territory.
The principal interest of this process resides not so much in the verification of the common model as in the manifold situations of cohabitation and superposition, of action and disturbance, of infiltration and mixture that, continually and progressively, distort and mutate this shared abstract configuration, enriching its basic characteristics, setting the singular against the universal, the local against the global, the general against the specific.

● strategy>(strategy, stratagem and tactic)

[MG] The strategy is a logic, the tactic a criterion, the stratagem a means.

▲ strategy>(diagrams)

[FP] If we all thougth that in each project it is necessary to go beyond simple concretion, we would make our work a real game of strategies. We would stop drawing in order to diagram.

● strategy>(strategies and strategists)

[MG] Today the figure of the architect can no longer be seen only in terms of a "producer of objects," but rather as a "strategist of processes."

● surface

[MG] Today, it is a question of constructing surfaces under the sky rather than volumes under the sun.

● suspense

[MG] Today, we coexist with intrigue. We refer to the experience of our own perception that records the manifestations of a scenario in a constant state of suspense – of unstable equilibrium – between the expected and the unexpected. Between predictability and surprise, order and chaos, control and chance, inertia and sudden shock. The everyday and the extraordinary.

● symbiosis

[MG] Symbiosis is the mechanism by which two organisms mutually come together to enrich their development or simply their permanence.
There are harmonious (pure) ones and hybrid (impure) ones. We are interested in the latter.

● synthetical

[MG] Artificial. Abstract. Economic. Concise. Diagrammatic. Condensed. Hybrid. Technological. Complex. Singular and Plural.

● system>(the city as system)

[MG] The contemporary city cannot continue to be approached in terms of a single place or a single shape; nor in terms of a single evolutionary stage. On the contrary, today, the city manifests itself as a complex and interactive system engendered through the accumulation of manifold, simultaneous and, often, contradictory actions and experiences: *states, stages and strata.*

T

● tactic>(tactics vs. strategy)

[MG] *"Tactics is knowing what to do when there is something to do. Strategy is knowing what to do when there is nothing to do."* Savielly Tartakover, Polish Chess Grand Master. (At the suggestion of Susanna Cros.)

+ take-away homes

[WM] "Take-away homes" is a future scenario in which the right to property has been supplanted by the right to trajectory, in which fees become royalties, construction companies are supplanted by strategic alliances of advanced industries, and in which society demands an interaction between its desires and reality. New ideas for selling ideas.

● time>(information-time-space)

[MG] Today we are conscious of a radical change in our interpretation of space (and in its associated idea of order), associated with the recent understanding of the theories of chaos and quantum physics.

Classical (absolute) time and space and modern (relative) time-space have been succeeded by "information-time-space," open to the action of the local upon the global, and which gives rise to greater indetermination (and instability) in our understanding of the universe. At the same time, it has enabled us to introduce, definitively, the influence of combinatorial and diversified, universal and individual information (and its dynamical effects) into the spatial manifestation of processes.

●◆ topological

[MG][FS] Topology studies the properties of objects independent of their size and form. It deals with properties that do not have any magnitude. While classical geometry talks about sides and vertices, and observes each element isolated, topology speaks of holes, and considers the connection between objects to be more important than the objects themselves.

● tracing

[MG] The trace is not able to differentiate, only reproduce.

● trailers

[MG] A trailer is an oblique representation of the film. A mental map of the action, made up of key interlinked situations that enable the whole to be condensed without reproducing it linearly, but rather by creating a non-linear synthesis of the overall plot: a document that is simultaneously autonomous and related.

● tropism (active)

[MG] Today, it is a question of positing the propositional potential of mobility and interchange – this progressive capacity for displacement that enables us, in a same lapse of time, not only to arrive ever further, but also to arrive at an increasing number of places – relating it to a new understanding of the idea of place – an articulated place –with new projectual – and conceptual – tools.

■◆ unfolding

[FS] Architecture is more like geography than an object, something closer to a line than a point.

[JM] Folding is a generative process of form. Forms unfold their possibilities being part of the program, on site, according to budget, etc. Thoughts unfold over reality. Spaces unfold over volume.

Composition is substituted for a pendulous process between unfolding and doubling.

● unrestrained (<un> factors)

[MG] The vital force of contemporary art and architecture resides in its capacity to produce new principles based upon a creative attitude as rigorous as it is relaxed: more unrestrained — uninhibited and unobsessed (that is, unashamed, unbiased and uncodified).

● uppercut

[MG] Uppercut is right on the chin.

▲ vector

[FP] What distinguishes a vector from other dimensional parameters is its directionality; it knows better than anyone what it wants and makes a direct line for it.

● versatility

[MG] Versatility is flexibility, but also ambivalence and polyvalence. Space that is multifaceted, that is to say, multiplied (multiplicative).

● voids and fills

[MG] If for years the work of architecture has concentrated on the full – the edificiary, the constructed – today, both terms must and can be linked and combined in successive positive-negative, empty-full seriations, which – well-designed at all scales – favour diversity, contrast and identity by means of the role given to relational spaces.

● voids, inhabited/equipped

[MG] In the same way that the city is no longer an ensemble of harmoniously grouped and cohesive elements, but rather a structure of fills – densities – and voids – absences – the dwelling moves from being an ensemble of carefully distributed rooms to a "space destined to be equipped." A void to be conquered. The construction and the fittings, in service clusters, thus make up the most stable framework: the remainder can, possibly, slip into the realm of the temporary, the mobile and the polyvalent.

▲ water diviner

[FP] The Water-diviner is capable of finding water under stones. We want Water-diviner architects.

● Yokohama

[MG] Paradox par excellence: "the roof of a building can also be its floor."

● zapping

[MG] Zapping is flexible and temporary contract with a mutable and (com)mutated environment, event or scenario.

◆ zone of high-sensitivity

[FS] A territory and the city are not stable or homogeneous places. The city is transformed from a graph of nodes or from a network, a magnetic field, in which the order between the parts is produced by tensions that the parts create among themselves.

● zoom

[MG] Zoom is a mechanism for enlarging and shrinking. Structures in mutual resonance and transference.

T

tab | 609

● tableland

[MG] A plateau is an elevated platform, tray or plain.

[i] p.610 It is a roof-building, preferably flat, upon which it is possible to walk.

● tactic

[MG] A tactic is a concrete application of a strategy; A strategy applied by means of cleverness.

[MG] **(tactics vs. strategy)**

See 'strategy (strategy, stratagem and tactics).'

"*Tactics is knowing what to do when there is something to do. Strategy is knowing what to do when there is nothing to do.*" Savielly Tartakover, Polish Chess Grand Master. (At the suggestion of Susanna Cros.)

+ take-away homes

[WM] A possible hypothesis for the future: creating demand in a certain market means gearing up industrial mechanisms and understanding the design of the take-away home as a mediation (as are all the goods we consume, a means for relating among ourselves, measuring ourselves, etc.) between creative ideas and the demands of the market; to create, then, a house-model with a high degree of comfort that could be sold at dealers, with advertising campaigns, sales service, guarantees and maintenance. Remember *Quaderns* 218, "*¿Cars?*" (in Catalan, plural form of expensive, TN).

'Take-away homes' is a future scenario in which the right to property has been supplanted by the right to trajectory, in which fees become royalties, construction companies are supplanted by strategic alliances of advanced industries, and in which society demands an interaction between its desires and reality. New ideas for selling ideas.

1. Prefabricated house.

2. Willy MÜLLER+ THB Consulting, *Multiuse container prototype*, 1999.

3. Neil DENARI Architects, *Caravan Prototype*, anywhere, 1991.

tab 610 **tableland**

1. Dominique PERRAULT, *Cycle track and swimming pool*, Berlin (Germany), 1998.

2. ACTAR ARQUITECTURA, *Barcelona Around*, 1999.

3. WMA Willy Müller Arquitectos, *Competition for cultural centre in Santa Eulàlia*, Eivissa (Spain), 2000.

4. Neil DENARI Architects, *LA High School*, Los Angeles (California, USA), 1999.

5. R+B (José Miguel ROLDÁN, Mercè BERENGUÉ), *Gerbert d'Orlhac Secondary School*, Sant Fruitós de Bages (Barcelona), 1999.

6. Luís ROJO, Ángel VERDASCO, Begoña FERNÁNDEZ-SHAW, *Square*, Vélez (Málaga, Spain), 1995.

7. Antonio SANMARTÍN (tutor), Ignacio LóPEZ, Martín EZQUERRO, *Proposal for Fòrum 2004 facilities*, Barcelona, 1999.

8. AMP (ARTENGO-MENIS-PASTRANA), *Archaeological Museum*, Zonzamas (Spain).

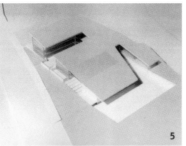

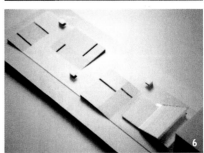

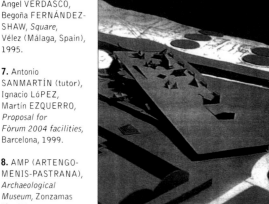

◆tangent

→ 'action> critical',
'ideas', 'knowledge', 'logic,
fuzzy', 'transversality'

[FS] Thought. [Modality of thought based on the dispersion of ideas produced in reflecting dartingly about things; shooting out centrifugally from the initial object, ending up centering around another point removed from the first.] It does not oppose profundity. [...] (the skin in the most profound)[...] but rather interpretation [...] transmits[..] circumstances and not essences. [Obliges] one to open things to extract their visibility. [Tangent thinking seeks to present] the flash of lightening that are produced when light hits things.

The theory of architecture is, today, announced through tangential thinking; what is produced when the initial idea is dispersed when thinking about objects or concepts. A thousand images shoot out centrifugally or suggestions that end up centering in a point distanced from the initial one. Today, we need not be profound through things, towards the inside, as philosophy purports. We must be profound in the long run, rebounding over instant captures, connecting concepts as they appear.

[One modality is thought reflected that never ends up centering in a point, but rather its interest in centered on an infinite number of rebounds. Each group of instantaneous catches defines a thought.] [It is profound but not in a cut through but along.] The only thing is that they [the trajectories] be inexact to designate something exact.

● tangle

→ 'maps (to map)',
'topological'

[MG] A tangle is disposition of a thread, wire, hair or similar thing or of a number of such things when they are twisted and crossed over each other, or when the different parts of one such thing are so disposed.

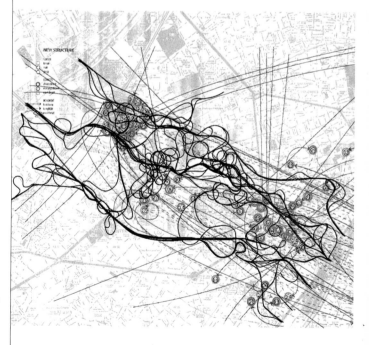

NOX (Lars Spuybroek with Kris Mun, Ludovica Tramontin, Florent Rougemont and Chris Seung-woo Yoo), *ParisBRAIN, a transurban scheme for the area west of La Défense*, Paris, 2001.

◆ tangram

→ 'assembly',
'combination',
'component', 'game',
'pieces, loose',
'puzzle'

[FS] A tangram is of combination and aggregation. A play of silhouettes. Seven black pieces that in their first arrangement form a square, a box, but whose game consists in recomposing them into figures and ideograms. Configurations that change form, without a final answer. The tangram player looks for all of the possibilities with seven pieces. S/he tries to eliminate the accidental. There is a loss of the identity of the pieces that melt into one. But at the same time, it will never be perfect and initial, depending completely in the pieces that can not be modified, broken, fragmented and, also one must use all of them.// The discipline of meditation; mental graphic gymnastics; a method of eliminating the accidental.

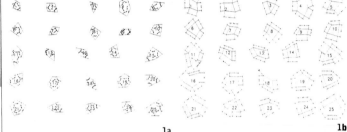

1a.b.c. Tangram: combinations, pieces and components.
S&Aa (SORIANO-PALACIOS), *Euskalduna Hall*, Bilbao (Spain), 1998.

2a.b. A city: a pavement.
OMA, *Airport City*, Seoul, 1995.

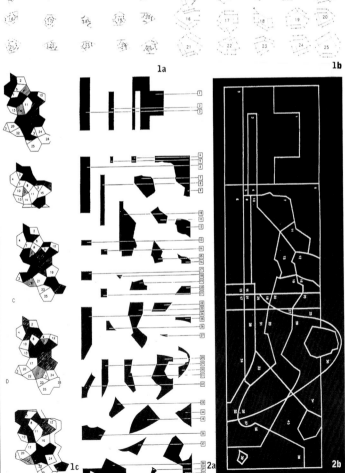

● tattoos

[MG] **(tattoo 1: mark)**

See 'stains, ink' and 'marks.'

Tattoos are drawings or paintings on the skin – or on other surfaces – executed by introducing or marking coloured materials and signs under or on top of the epidermis.

[MG] **(tattoo 2: transtattoo)**

We are interested in the contemporary use of the tattoo. Or rather, the *transtattoo*. From henna to transfers. No longer as an indelible mark on the body – the old conception of the tattoo as a permanent sign, a perennial contract with the memory – but an adhesive symbol that is literal and/or metaphorical (a memory, a feeling or a fantasy).

We are more interested in the ephemeral, contingent and ludic use of the contemporary tattoo: reversible and changing. A soluble mark, a temporary sticker, painting or graphic. A layer applied rather than stuck to an active, multilayered skin (an interactive support).

The tattoo would not then be a stable, organic, decoration but, above all, information that is transmitted and superposed. Mutable, changing and fleeting information. Extroversion: the desire to communicate and carefree play with shape. A façade can also be, therefore, a tattoo of overlapping, supported, processed and/or projected images and messages.

1. Tattoos.

2. Antonio
SANMARTÍN,
John HEJDUCK,
Civic centre,
Santiago de
Compostela
(Spain), 1997.

3. Francis SOLER,
Housing block,
Paris, 1997.

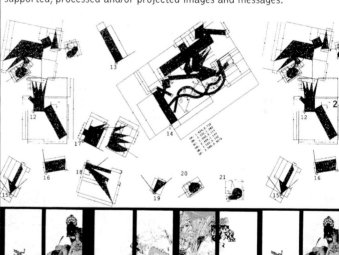

■★ Team X

[JM] Team X, the critics of the city derived from the Modern Movement, proposed looking where no one had before and reflected upon the form of life of the big cities.

Their reflection centred upon the intermediate space where architecture had not been detained.

They investigated interstitial space, that which surges between buildings, exactly in those places situated between the street and building.

The project of the dwelling submitted itself to the will of enclosing the city and offered an availability of entertainment and work, for the meeting of the social enclave.

The Robin Hood Smithsons invent places, city, and originate the dwelling from which to revise the not so happy Modern Movement. Again, we face the ethics of design, before a what-to-do compromised architectonics.

[co] The validity of many of the works and experiences of Team X stem from their capacity to anticipate researches about complex dispositions of evolutionary or porous geometry.

In a famous article written at the end of the fifties, Alison Smithson used the name mat-building to describe certain projects, referring to them as an evolutionary product of the first reflections of Team X. The compositional structure of these projects was developed on the basis of a grid or in general, in an isotropic, non-hierachical structure (even though it can also be inversely read, as a perforated or hollowed-out volume) in which the emptiness or the pore constitute a fundamental part of the building.

If in the most urban projects, the most characteristic aspect was the capacity of the fabric to infiltrate or contaminate the city, in others, in treating the building as something exempt, the characteristic principal would be the direct valuation of the empty space, of the pores as an inseparable part of the project.

In most of the other mat-building urban plans, the borders dilute themselves, as they infiltrate the urban layout, from an indistinct structure, like that of lichen, that invades a place and develops itself in filaments or through layers or perforated stratums. JOSÉ ANTONIO SOSA

1. CANDILIS, JOSIC, WOODS, *Competition for the city centre*, Frankfurt (Germany), 1963.
2. FOA, *Project for the urbanization of Myeong-Dong cathedral*, Seoul, 1995.

◆ technique, the

→ 'catalogue',
'component', 'construction,
intelligent', 'production,
intelligent'

[FS]   See 'jai-tech' and 'precision.'

[FS]   "'Is the construction solid?' Pent asks.

'It could last centuries,' says Giffey. 'The outer layer and some inner walls
are made of carbon concrete reinforced with nanotubes, with reflective ce-
ramic facing. It reflects one hundred percent of the radiation. The structure is of woven nanotubes, in some places one metre thick, which distributes the stresses. The steel inner structures support flexfuller and concrete
plates, with shock absorbers, four per floor. The entire building rests on
hyperstressed shockproof flexfuller. I've heard that the carbon fibres are
designed to be conductive and that the entire facing is sensitive. The structure can also be used for data storage.' Picken and Pent meditated on this.
'It's more solid than the pyramids of Egypt,' says Pent."

(Paraphrasing BEAR, Greg, "[/] Alt 47", Barcelona: Ediciones B, 2000, 1997)

[FS]   **mechanic**

Professional.

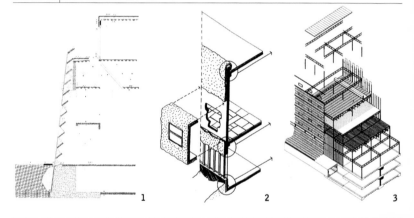

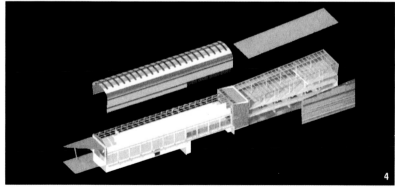

Multilayer construction techniques 1. S&Aa (SORIANO-PALACIOS), *Competition for auditorium and conference centre*, Pamplona (Navarra, Spain), 1998. **2.** NEUTELINGS-RIEDIJK, *Minnaert*, Utrecht (The Netherlands),
1998. **3.** Vicente GUALLART, Willy MÜLLER, *Justice City*, Valencia (Spain), 1998. **4.** Josep Lluís MATEO
(MAP Arquitectes), *UAB Services building*, Bellaterra (Barcelona), 1993.

✖ Technonat Parks (Technological & Nature Parks)

[VG] Although the territory is just another asset of a country assets, it ought to be treasured as though it were gold.

Mediterranean forest fires were produced by the pressure of civilisation and lack of economic interest. This situation calls for action on an appropriate scale.

Regional parks should be created, planned as green zones in the territory-city. These territories need be controlled by new technologies and protected from fire by huge territorial sprinklers. Trees should be replanted to create firebreaks, with a geometric organisation that illustrates man's action on the large scale.

Like agricultural plantations. Like Christo's projects.

✖ telecentre

[VG] A telecentre is a petrol station of information.

★ telepolis

[c] "*Telepolis (global city, remote city) is a new form of interaction which developed over the latter part of the 20th century and which profoundly changed basic components of social life: production, work, trade, money, writing, body image, the notion of territory and memory, not to mention politics, science and culture. Above all, it is the economic and social structure of the planet that is changing, breaching the territorial limits of classical cities and states, and tending to generate a new form of global organisation which we should consider, for many reasons, in terms of the city.*

The name 'telepolis' refers to the opposition between the classical forms of social organisation (families, ethnic groups, peoples, nations, states, etc.), founded in territoriality, the coexistence and proximity between human beings, and the new city, in which human interrelations are established among citizens living far from each other.

Telepolis is a deterritorialised city and its basic structure is the network of individuals that link geographically points that are dispersed yet, nonetheless, joined through technology. This new city superposes itself on towns, cities and metropolises without physically destroying them.

Telepolis is not located on the ground, although it does possess a technological infrastructure based upon satellites, wiring and the telecommunications towers. The advance of Telepolis is due to the implantation in our dwellings of a series of electronic connections that are our interfaces with the global city.

Telepolis blurs the age-old limits between the private and the public and concurrently tends to institute new forms of demarcation of the intimate, of the private and of the public.

One of the more relevant aspects of life in Telepolis is telework, performed from the home resorting to information technologies and telecommunications. Homes, therefore, will tend to be the workplace and cities the place of leisure." (ECHEVERRÍA, Javier, *Telepolis*, Barcelona: Destino, 1994)

✖ telework

→ 'domestic', 'house, the', 'information', 'interfaces', 'logic, digital', 'rurban life', 'telepolis', 'virtual'

[VG]

Telework and leisure (Photograph: Mark Lewis), in *The Picturesques Gold Set* (Stock Photo) 2, 1998.

"*Jack Nilles, the North American inventor of the term telecommuting, the equivalent of the British English teleworking, suggested that telework could be a solution to traffic jams. However, while it initially referred to the work of those people who managed to avoid motorway snarl-ups because they worked near home, in time the term was distorted and came to mean precisely the opposite: work in a place a long way from home, obliging workers to take various means of transport, even aeroplanes, to get to work. This progression is determined by the evolution of the world of the economy, which forces companies to continually exercise flexibility, innovation and globalisation. A professional who reaches the world of the Internet experiences an increase in physical as well as telematic mobility.*

This opinion is shared by the expert Manuel Castells. He holds that transport problems will increase instead of improving, as increasing mobility and the condensation of time allowed by the new organisation of the Net is translated into a greater concentration of markets in certain areas and an increase in the physical mobility of labour, that used to be confined to its workplaces during working hours. (La Sociedad Red, 1997)

The evolution of telework, moreover, is not determined only by the possibilities of teleworking at a distance (or from home), but also by the economic and production context (marked by globalisation and high levels of competitiveness), meaning that teleworkers have to compete in a global labour market. As a result, today telecommuters are leaving behind their role of teleworkers who go from one place of work to another to become people who work as they go, be it on line, on the road or in the air."

(GUALLART, Vicente; SERRA, Artur; SOLÀ, Francesc. *El teletrabajo y los Telecentres como impulsores del equilibrio territorial*. Generalitat de Catalunya, Barcelona, 1998)

★ temperate

[co]

See 'intermediate places.'

Temperate is neither cold nor hot but rather in an intermediate state.

From the Latin *temperare* is derived *temprar*. To blend, mix, moderate, temper. This is undoubtedly a point of mixture, an intermediate state of temperature, but also of everything that is mixed. Thus, we use temperate in reference to estimates of temperature and its relative temper to refer to the mixture of any elements.

JOSÉ ALFONSO BALLESTEROS

● tempo

[MG]

See 'frequency' and 'sequences.'

Enric RUIZ-GELI, *Spek*, Aedes West Gallery, Berlin, 1999.

● temporary

[MG] Temporary are those configuration changes and alters with time. See 'fleeting,' 'precarious(ly),' 'impermanences' and 'reversible.'

Josep Lluís MATEO
(MAP Arquitectes),
*Rehabilitation
of Lustgarten*, Berlin,
1993

◆ tergiversation

→ 'collage', 'indiscipline',
'innovation', 'name',
'paradoxes', 'recycling',
'relationships, transitive
(of transference)',
'sample', 'strategy', 'tactic'

[FS] Tergiversation is the use of a new unit of pre-existing artistic elements. As a negation and prelude; tergiversation is characterized by two fundamental laws: the loss of importance and meaning of each autonomous element and the organization of a signifying group that confers new properties to tergiversational elements. Tergiversation is a mechanism. At its most complex, the original and modified meanings coexist, old and modern. We can differentiate three strategies of tergiversation: collage, sampling and recycling.

● terraces

→ 'dispositions',
'(inter)weavings
and inter(plots)',
'landstrategy', 'strategy',
'territory'

[MG] See 'land(s) in lands,' 'landstrategy' and 'topographies, operative.'
Terraces are the landscape configured in steps; the architectural manipulation of the land, stepped or the constrcution of a new land rolling down.

S. PÉREZ ARROYO &
E. HURTADO
(with F. RÍO DURAN),
Leaf House, 2003.

● ★ ■ *terrain vague*

→ 'in-between', 'sea', 'vague', 'void'

[MG] Terrain vague are interstitial spaces, large urban voids, vast obsolete areas which, due to their particular disposition and configuration, constitute ideal experimental territories for exploring conditions of the new city. Terrain vague are "strategic zones of friction" present in most large European metropolises in transformation, often outside – or over – large-scale transport and production infrastructures.

[c] *"It is impossible to capture in a single English word or phrase the meaning of the French terrain vague. In French, the term terrain has a more urban quality that the English land: it translates a extension of ground in the city, but it also refers to larger and perhaps less precisely defined areas of territory, in expectant conditions [...].*

The second word, vague, has a double Latin origin as well as a Germanic origin. This latter, from the root vagr-wogue, refers to sea swell, waves on the water: movement, oscillation, instability, fluctuation. Wave, in English. We have greater interest in the two Latin roots which come together in the French term vague.

First of all we have vague as a descendent of vacuus, giving us vacant, vacuum in English, which is to say empty, unoccupied. And yet also free, available, unengaged. The relationship between the absence of use, of activity, and the sense of freedom, of expectancy, is fundamental to understanding all the evocative of the terrains vagues in the perception of the city. Void, then, as absence, and yet also as promise, as encounter, as the space of the possible: expectation.

There is a second meaning superimposed on the French vague as vacant. This attaches to the term as deriving from the Latin vagus, giving vague in English, too, in the sense of indeterminate, imprecise, blurred, uncertain.

It certainly appears that the analogous terms we have remarked are generally preceded by a negative particle (in-determinate, im-precise, un-certain), but it is no less the case that this absence of limit, this almost oceanic sentiment, to use Freud's expression, is precisely the message which contains the expectations of mobility, vagrant roving, free time, liberty. This triple signification of the French word vague as wave, vacant and vague."

(DE SOLÀ MORALES, Ignasi, "Terrain Vague", *Quaderns* 212, 1996)

José MORALES,
Juan GONZÁLEZ,
Felipe PALOMINO,
Competition
ARC OUEST,
Thessalonica
(Greece), 1996.

[JM] Terrain vague are sites of old factories, already in disuse, places in which were located the most important infrastructures in past epochs, of already distinct economies; enclaves of superimposition of innumerable strata of communication and shifts. Places tied to great economic and natural catastrophes. In the end, places around which a great part of our interrogations about cities and contemporary landscapes are centred. They are sites of uncertainty.

[JM] See 'abroad, etc.'.

Gabriele BASILICO, *Littoral Barcelona*, in *Quaderns* 212, 1996.

● ★ territory

→ 'ad-herence', 'event',   [MG]
'geography', 'islands',
'm. city', 'multicity',
'places', 'plaits', 'sea',
'self-urbanism',
'stains, ink', 'telepolis',
'trip'

See 'infrastructures,' 'land-links,' 'Metapolis,' 'networks' and 'system.'

Today we face – and come face to face with – a new type of space that proclaims the definitive transformation of secular relationships between city, landscape and territory. A paradoxical territory is articulated by the power of large-scale structural systems of mobility and communication which provide its backbone (capable of linking singular, unique, and unusual places and events, etc.). The territory is often developed, simultaneously and figuratively (in those construction or real estate operations that ultimately mark its identity) from the coarseness of girded, prefigured and inappropriate patterns – not just in the economies, spaces and uses they foster, but as well in their associated iconographies and constructional techniques. Short-term investments, based upon stereotypes and/or simulations of mediatic caricatures, lead to the current wild explosion of the big city which is thus converted into a complex phenomenon, on a planetary scale. Today, simultaneous and diverse processes, that are potentially positive and frequently conflictive, need to be properly explored. Dynamics, in effect, no longer have to do with the autobiographical construction of the place (the *genius loci* or the slow adaptation to context), nor with the traditional criteria for settlement – proximity and agglomeration of raw materials, ease-of-access, symbolic or cultural importance of the place, etc. Instead, they allude to strategic interests and factors of autonomous decision (criteria for profitability and expansion) facilitated by speed and effectiveness (from the technological point of view) of new processes of planning and construction.

The idea of urban space as an essentially figurative reference, as a collection of characters adapted to formal definitions, yields to evidence of a new wilder and more random space. A space articulated on another scale, no longer through the traditional continuity of edification, but rather through the strength and neutrality of large-scale networks which provide its backbone and different autonomous events that tend to ensure its development.

A territory is no longer a shape – or at least no longer just a shape – but also a complex system of relationships and events determined by successive defining layers of reference (physical but also demographic, biological, economic, cultural, political, etc.) and the large-scale structural networks (transport, energy, computerised diffusion, financial movements, etc.) that articulate it – among which simultaneous processes of action and reaction are unleashed.

[co] Total urbanization of the territory, and domination of fields of force, of information and of flows that it expresses, are accompanied at once by a rapprochement and a distancing of the urban, understood as landscape for a subject who conceives and interprets it. The notion of territory allows one to conceive and contribute to the production of contemporary architecture. The object is no longer separate from the outside. What counts is the way we intervene, without distinctions of scale or profession. The projects bear witness to the evolution of sites and their ephemeral character, to the always extensive development of agglomerations, to the restricted place of the architectural object in the environment. If the architect can no longer act on infrastructures, what remains are landscapes. ALAIN GUIHEUX / DOMINIQUE ROUILLARD

[co] **(touristic)**
The inherent attributes of touristic territory afford it exceptionality. To squander it senselessly constitutes irreversible injury, given that it is a singular and irreplaceable resource, one that is decisive in ensuring the future. And it is limited. The strategies of extensive occupation of diffuse development constitute the most efficient system for depleting the basic resource – high quality land – in a process that rewards property development activities and fosters its worst structural features: lack of concern for the territory, infrastructural negligence, rapid returns on capital, low risk levels, accumulative obsession, formal mimesis and vacuity of contents.
Submitting to the temptations of property development on quality territories is not without cost. The reductive specialisation of the economic structure in activities associated with building shackles small local societies and makes it extremely difficult for them to find alternative solutions. Panic strikes when it is already impossible to avoid the recurrent sale of a territory that is being depleted. Everyone knows it, politicians and developers better than anyone, but no one can rein in a bacchanalian and suicidal system – devourer of its own scions and of its only basis for survival. JOSÉ MIGUEL IRIBAS

ACTAR ARQUITECTURA, *Territorial planning*, Graz-Maribor, 2000.

▲■ texture

[FP] We have to say no to the idea of finishings. In our proposals let's leave out the section regarding finish, coating, and paint. The textures of our buildings are merely the last layers of an integral material. We don not want to work with components which do not offer this possibility (they actually do not exist). Texture is the *word* of the mass, i.e. its last scream just before the void, and thus, inseparable from it. We do not add textures, we do not apply textures. It is possible to find some elements that can actually offer one texture or another, depending upon the process of its definite formation when being used in work. In this sense, the concatenation of different materials (joint) is, in fact, the real exhaustion of its form; an irregularity of its mass that only shows the impossibility of its unlimited extension.

[JM] The project finds itself in front of a textured, more than structured, reality, in which what counts is the actual spatial void, the disarticulation. In the end, the presence of imprecise objects, difficult to catalogue, nonetheless act as inevitable references for architecture. The constancy of these landscape anomalies, in our cities and countries, make us accept them as habitual and current. The project is more closely related to texture than structure.

Gilles Deleuze in his book *The Fold,* says, "As a general rule, the manner of folding of a material constitutes its texture. This is defined not only by its heterogeneous and actually distinct parts, as by the manner in which these become inseparable in virtue of particular folds."

● theory

[MG] See 'action>critical' and 'transversality.'

★● Think Tank

[co] Metapolis. XAVIER COSTA

[MG] In a think tank, energies are brought together. Bits of information interchanged. Ideas anticipated. Actions proposed. Futures – presents – projected. TRAILER.

Think Tank at the *Metápolis 2.0 Festival*, Mercat de les Flors, Barcelona, 2000.

★ threat

→ 'fear'

[co] Architecture is primarily a form of threat management.

If architecture is the attempt to define the city, every designer has a slightly different definition, starting out from the commonsense notion that cities involve a certain density or packed heterogeneity – that is to say, formlessness. The city is precisely that which exceeds our capacity to draw or describe it. So, we start working against the city exactly at the moment we say we know what the city is. To figure the city out is already to change it. A description of the existing city already constitutes a complete redesign. What might then be said about a particular project is less important. The formlessness of the city threatens the architect, and the architect responds with definitions that constrain it. The architect attempts to domesticate the overlapping forces, taming the city with images of form. The idea of the threat outside the walls gives way to architecture as suppression of the danger within. MARK WIGLEY

★ ● threshold (*umbral*)

→ 'intermediate places'

[co] Literally, threshold is a piece of stone, timber or metal that lies under a door – the counterpart of the lintel across the top. It is also a "sill:" a horizontal piece at the base of a framework or supporting structure. Threshold is the point at which a physiological or psychological effect begins to be produced. The etymology of "*umbral*" is *liminare* derived from *limen*, or perhaps in different meanings of the adjective *liminaris*, "pertaining to umbral." Steiger has established a phonetic derivation based upon *limitaris*: "pertaining to limit." *Lumdar, lumenda* converge semantically in umbral, being identified with it in a process similar to *lumbral*: a deformation influenced by *lumen*, Old Spanish for *lumbre*, light. The initial 'l' was lost in its use with the article *el*. Evidently, the ideas of limit and light are closely related to this word. Its physical embodiment, as an element of stone that marks precisely a limit between private and public space, combines all the non-physical conditions that the word transmits. *Umbral* is an edge of light, a strip where light changes or fades. It is a boundary, as its meaning indicates, but rather than constructed, it is insinuated. It is a sign of a change in condition or state that man uses to delimit spaces. The *umbral* must be crossed before a space may be inhabited. JOSÉ ALFONSO BALLESTEROS

[MG] "*The threshold is a very potential space. It is the place of suggestion, where things happen only in a half way. The place where the moral and the amoral, the legal and the illegal, the truth and the lie can not be sorted out. The place where everything is possible, just for a moment, before you pass through it.*" (Susanna Cros)

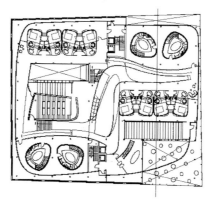

Anna LÒPEZ ALABERT,
Project for lupanarium, Rotterdam
(The Netherlands) 2002

✖●▲ time

[VG] Time is a new material in the project. Architecture as an open process, as a non-finite act, has to be able to incorporate time into the score of its organisation.

[MG] "*We could imagine the flow of time as taking the form of fibrous bundles, each fibre corresponding to a need in to particular theatre of action, and the lengths of the fibres varying according to the duration of each need and the solution of its problems. The cultural bundles therefore consist of multicoloured fibrous lengths of events. They are mostly juxtaposed by chance, and rarely by conscious premeditation or rigorous planning.*"

(KUBLER, George, *The Shape of Time*, New Haven, Conn.: Yale University Press, 1967)

[FP] In time, things do not have a physical representation because they exist as ways of thinking and types of language that occur in the present and are located in the narration and the prediction of events; that is, in linguistic acts.

For this reason, we cannot say there are past things, nor future ones, but a number of thinking attitudes that have to do with what is present; the psychical skills that have to do with remembering and foreseeing.

The three representations of time, are nothing but the present time in a triple dimension.

Meaning that who is thinking/speaking is in charge of outlining the sense of time and of organising the layout of events.

This obviously is made relative by every person and can fluctuate depending on the intentions and perceptions of whom is thinking it. The line of time enhances or condenses depending on what is reached by the intellectual skills; the memory skills, to be able to reconstruct and revive the situations; the attention skills, to be able to be attentive; and the ability of the imagination to represent the future.

Time, is by no means subject to an objective pattern (for example, the rotation of planets), but is revealed as something elastic and subjective. For this reason, calculations, measures and numbers related to time, only make sense having identified the point of view of whom is talking about them; and as the intellectual motivations are very diverse, time also is; this is why it is unmeasurable.

[MG] **(information-time-space)**

Today, we are conscious of a radical change in our interpretation of space (and in its associated idea of order), associated with the recent understanding of the theories of chaos and quantum physics.

Classical (absolute) time and space and modern (relative) time-space have been succeeded by "information-time-space," open to the action of the local upon the global, and which gives rise to greater indetermination (and instability) in our understanding of the universe.

At the same time, it has enabled us to introduce, definitively, the influence of combinatorial and diversified, universal and individual information (and its dynamical effects) into the spatial manifestation of processes.

The Newtonian paradigm, and much of the Einsteinian paradigm now face the challenge of an "elusive" universe – nervous, unsettled, more undisciplined – in which most processes, including those of more stable appearance, prove to be extraordinarily undisciplined and whose behaviours ultimately follow non-linear trajectories, the result of their own dynamic and interactive character.

In such processes, the – global – position in space must be combined with the incidence of the – local – information that each particular situation (or event) brings.

Such information has a major effect upon the whole, continually modifying its trajectories. The global system varies as the received local information varies – and accumulates.

The theory of dynamic systems consists in the study of those temporal-spatial processes, in movement.

These are systems that demonstrate stable behaviour across a broad spectrum and which, suddenly, faced with a minor variation, shift to wholly new behaviours.

The system, homogeneous in its original state, gives rise to unusual structures which break down the old (more or less harmonious) symmetry of the starting phase.

Dynamic systems thus manifest themselves (mostly) as virtually unstable temporal-spatial configurations (dynamic dispositions).

Their trajectories present oscillating and combinatorial movements that give rise to fluctuating situations of equilibrium: ("while linear systems almost always have a single point of equilibrium, non-linear systems have more than one state of equilibrium that includes points of bifurcation, as well as transitions from a stable trajectory towards another, fostering major changes at very brief intervals").

[FP] **(tenses, verb)**

See 'relationships, transitive.'

"*They met, they will meet, the three of them meet, but it is useless. Although they seem to look at each other, they do not see each other; although they seem to speak, they have never communicated anything; although they seem to touch, X and Z are hermetic prisoners.*

They are caught, they swim inside the fishbowls formed by the rounded glass of their watches. I'll have a hell of a time, he notes, while stirring his coffee. X, doing likewise, doesn't listen, doesn't speak. Time slips away as he thinks about how good coffee tasted in the old days.

How times have changed, she says to herself, meditating on what once was a lump and is now a little bag of sugar that she finds ugly and dull. The only one that was, that will be, that is in the café is Y, although she neither thinks nor speaks. She only emits a whimper of pleasure each time she takes a sip from the cup."

(F.M., *Cuentos de X, Y y Z*, Madrid: Ediciones Lengua de Trapo, 1997)

SPACE AND TIME	SPACE-TIME	SPACE-TIME-INFORMATION
CLASSIC	MODERN	CONTEMPORARY
<AB>: ABSOLUTE	**<RE>: RELATIVE**	**<IN>: INTERACTIVE**

FIXED	STABLE	DYNAMIC
META-PHYSICAL AND PHYSICAL	PHYSICAL-REAL	REAL-VIRTUAL
ESSENCE (ESSENTIAL)	**MATTER (MATTERIAL)**	**INFORMATION (INFORMATIONAL)**
SINGLE	DIVIDED	DIVERS
ANALOGICAL	MECHANICAL	DIGITAL
RITUAL	*FUNCTIONAL*	*OPERATIVE*
SYMBOLIC	DOGMATIC	OPPORTUNIST (CONTINGENT)
HARMONIOUS	AUTONOMOUS	ACCORDED
EVOCATIVE	ABSENT	REACTIVE
HIERARCHICAL RELATIONSHIP	**POSITIONAL RELATIONSHIP**	**TACTICAL RELATIONSHIP**
CONTINUOUS	DISCONTINUOUS	INTERMITTENT
COMPACT	*FRAGMENTED*	*FRACTAL*
UNIFORM	VARIABLE	EVOLUTIONAL
EXACT	*PRECISE*	*COMBINATORY*
PREDICTABLE	MESURABLE	DIFFERENTIAL
NORM	**TYPE**	**GENE**
PROTO-LOGICAL	TYPO-LOGICAL	TOPO-LOGICAL
FORMAL	ABSTRACT	MIXED
FIGURATIVE	*STRUCTURAL*	*INFRASTRUCTURAL*
SOLEMN	SEVERE	EASYGOING
CEREMONIAL	STRICT	UNINHIBITED
PURE	PURIST	CROSSBRED

CODE	RELATIONSHIP	COMBINATION
CONTROL	**ORDER**	**SYNERGY**
FLAT (2D)	**VOLUME (3D)**	**LANDSCAPE (4D)**
COMPOSITION	**POSITION**	**DISPOSITION**
(REGULATION)	**(CORRELATION)**	**(DECISION-COMBINATION)**

**NEW MECHANISMS:
BEYOND LINKS- EXTROVERTED FORMS**

Fragment of the diagram by GAUSA, Manuel, "Dynamic time - <in>formal order: <un>disciplined trajectories", in *Quaderns* 222, 1999.

● topographies, operative

[MG] We call 'operative topographies' those devices conceived of as and through strategic movements of folding in the territory. Such movements define *platforms* and (or) *enclaves* of a quasi geographical nature, developed as *programmatic refluences* (using the term in its double meaning, as "current or movement of ebb and flow derived from another main current," but also as "cleverness in action"): functional magmas or plateaus that enhance their condition as skin or elastic bark (membrane), either as slippery and extended surfaces (*dynamic lands or platforms*), or as extruded surfaces (*localised reliefs, or enclaves*). In all cases, they are manipulated virtual landscapes that relate to the vacant nature of free interstitial spaces and, ultimately, to the very definition of landscape as background, as scenario and as construction at the same time: landscapes, then, within other landscapes. Lands in lands.

Lands respond to a will to overlap; reliefs to will for embedding.

Whether as extruded plateaus – *reliefs or enclaves* – or as sheared trays – *lands or platforms* – such topographies constitute, in any case, new geographies on the terrain; mineral landscapes in which movements and flows end up being articulated under or aboveground on surfaces chiselled out of the land.

Constructed geographies, rather than architectures.

ACTAR ARQUITECTURA, *Project for a corporate nursery*, Graz-Maribor, 2000 (collage based on a photograph by Jordi Bernadó).

●◆ **topological**

[MG] Topology is the branch of mathematics that studies the properties of geometric figures generated under continuous transformations. Two figures are topologically equivalent if one can be obtained from the other by curving or stretching its surface without cuts or creases. As a result – as Antonio Juárez observes in his essay on Le Ricolais – " *topology has been called the geometry of the rubber sheet, because upon it, a square is transformable into a circle, and a sphere is equivalent to a cube, but not to a ring torus. The ideas of open, closed, connected, unconnected are central to this discipline.*"

The seductive side of topology is its complex definition and recursive logic. That is to say, its possible definition in variable configurations and elastic movements, that extend not only to the forces that act upon the structures themselves, but also to the implicit connections produced in and among them, whereby different concatenated levels establish themselves, referring to patterns at once generic and distortable.

1

The simulation of the evolution of such structures (associated with the geometric definition of dynamic processes) is possible through models and maps that reproduce their hypothetical movements through numerical or computer-generated combinations (i.e. digital representations of a certain number of trajectories), due to advances in information technology and calculation techniques.

2

In these, each instantaneous result (each concrete configuration) manifests itself as the simulation of "other possible" combinations: a selected trajectory that contains, in itself, the codification of alternative "other possible" movements – probably similar, but indeterminate.

[FS] Topology studies the properties of objects independent of their size and form. It deals with properties that do not have any magnitude. It studies all conceivable forms –abstract, multi-dimensional – as well as their continuity, stretching and compression. Geometrical topology is temporal, as opposed to Greek geometry, where each form is the shadow of an immutable mathematical ideal. Topology treats the change and evolution of forms as essential characteristics of their understanding and classification. While classical geometry talks about sides and vertices, and observes each element isolated, topology speaks of holes, and considers the connection between objects to be more important than the objects themselves.

3

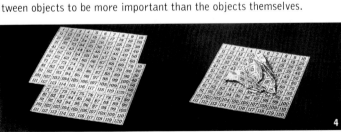

4

1. Topological variation. **2. & 3.** Topological transformations, in BARR, Stephen, *Experiments in Topology*, New York: Dover Publications, 1964. **4.** Superposition of two identical surfaces and visualization of topological "creasing".

Topological action:
How to take off one's waistcoat without taking off one's jacket, in *Fisuras* 3 1/3, 1995.

1. S&Aa (SORIANO-PALA-CIOS), *Cyberauditorium and Children Museum in the Museum of Sciencies*, Valencia (Spain), 1998.

2. NOX (Lars Spuybroek with Chris Seung-Woo Yoo, Kris Mun, Florent Rougemont and Ludovica Tramontin), *SoftOffice*, United Kingdom, 2000-2005.

● ★ topological (age)

[MG] "*Topological stage: This refers to the first years of life, up to four or five years of age. In this stage, the child begins to appreciate shapes and becomes aware of the things around him. The knowledge he has of space is derived from the relationship between the environment and his self. It is the phase in which the concrete world is discovered; his understanding of space will be that of space as he experiences it, fostering a subjective perception through the senses: touching objects, smelling them, sucking them, moving them across the floor, etc.*

Projective stage: As the child grows, so does his knowledge of his environment. [...] Bit by bit he begins to understand that objects favour certain spatial relationships. Now he realises that they occupy a place in space and that they are situated at a certain distance from each other.

Euclidian stage: the adolescent starts to become fully conscious of his environment, which is reflected in the quantity of details that appear in his drawings. Now he develops spatial notions of scale and position that permit him to represent elements in Euclidian space, that is, linked to the three directions of space: right-left, up-down, forward-back.

Reactive or (re)topological stage: the adult, completely aware of the reality which surrounds him, again undertakes, without adopting predetermined postures, a new and fascinating tour of experimentation and research.

Everything described in the first stage acquires in this last stage its most decisive, complete and conscious validity."

(Paraphrasing SÁNCHEZ, Ana, "La importancia del conocimiento", in *Entorno. Sobre el espacio y el arte*, Madrid: Editorial Complutense, 1995)

[co] We talk about the stature of smallness. If the real world, the place imagined and designed by big people, has always had a space of its own size, what sort of space should house people with small dimensions? Undoubtedly, it should be stimulating, palpable and breathable for people watching the world enthusiastically from eighty-five centimetres above the ground, and whose tactile radius has a maximum of one metre fifteen high. The first simulation if this experience for those of us with a conscious stature might be the equivalent of discovering a space from a squatting position. The space proposed is therefore based on the idea of a child's world including materials, doors, windows and objects created for the small stature of its main users. The rest of the space should belong to the out-of-reach world of their custodians. EDUARDO ARROYO

● tornadoes (or twisters)

→ 'geometry', 'trajectory'

[MG] Tornadoes are vertical structures produced by successive swirling turns. They are dynamic trajectories of differential rotation – twistings – with complex movements of inflection and variation. Meshes of variable geometry and irregular height.

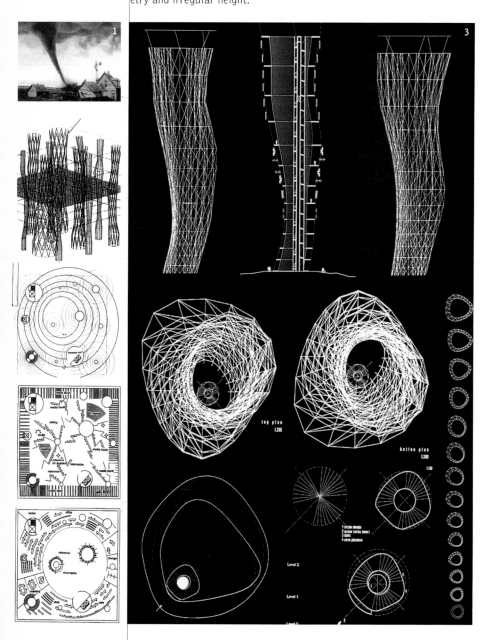

1. Tornado (Photograph: Phil DEGGINGER), in *The Picturesques Gold Set* (Stock Photo) 3, 1998. 2. Toyo ITO, *Mediatheque*, Sendai (Japan), 2000. 3. Cecil BALMOND (Ove Arup), ACTAR ARQUITECTURA, *Telecommunications Tower on the Turó de la Rovira*, Barcelona, 2001-.

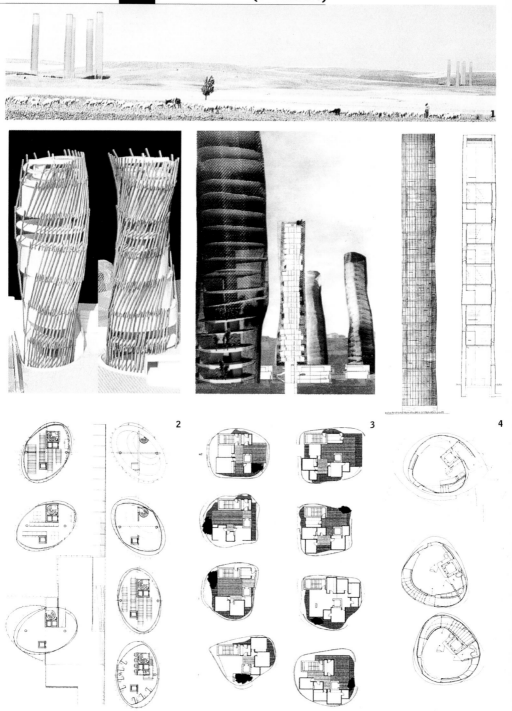

1. & 4. Cristina DÍAZ MORENO, Efrén GARCÍA GRINDA, Ángel JARAMILLO, *Temporary accommodation*, Parque Regional del Sureste (Madrid), 1997. **2.** ADD Arquitectura (BAILO-CLARAMUNT-RULL), *Historic Archive*, Vilafranca del Penedès (Barcelona), 1997. **3.** S&Aa (SORIANO-PALACIOS), *Europan 5* (mention), Barakaldo (Vizcaya, Spain), 1998.

Virtual City,
in *AD* 11/12,
1994.

✘●+★ tourism

→ 'bank&beach',
'Benidorm', 'de-location',
'economy', 'hotel',
'infiltration> intrusiveness
and interference',
'overflow', 'trip',
'urbs / orbs', 'virtual'

[VG] Architecture, unlike other artistic expressions (such as sculpture or painting),
is difficult to transport. Nonetheless, large works of architecture have been
dismounted and moved to museums in order to be studied and exhibited (such
as, partially, the Parthenon of Athens, some Romanesque churches, etc.). In
the face of this difficulty, a number of emerging theme parks which simulate
entire cultural environments (including architecture, folklore, customs, cui-
sine, etc.), are an example of the desire to know other cultures without physically going there. By this token, it is, if possible, even more valuable for a city
to possess original elements that can be shown in situ, where they were built,
and create touristic and cultural circuits around them. Tourism is Spain's number one economic activity and a phenomenon that marks difference in the face
of an extensive range of similar offers proposed by various resorts. If a city
has architectural and cultural elements, they should be exploited with a view
to encouraging a flow of visitors and, therefore, the economic flow.

[MG] See 'alienation' and 'foreignness.'
What is most interesting about the tourism phenomenon is precisely the
exaggerated manifestation of a process which is present, in one way or another, in most contemporary (physical and virtual) territories – and scenarios: the constant simultaneity of strange – foreign – elements in alien
refuges. Visitors (a term applying not only to individuals ''in transit,'' but
also to ''displaced'' objects, images, signs, messages or creations) are ar-
rayed over a host space.
In this particular relationship between visitor and host, but also between
strangeness and localisation, between intervention and conservation, between colonisation and landscape, lies the key to a process which is generally undervalued, but which clearly has a contemporary dimension.

[WM] Today we can speak of a physical tourism and a virtual tourism – or
voyeurism. The tourism of tomorrow will combine both experiences.

[co] According to the World Tourism Organization (WTO), tourism is the world's
largest growth industry with no signs of slowing down in the 21st century. Tourism
has the power to transform reality and can become a legitimate, resourceful and
efficient way to qualitatively change contexts. Yet, mass tourism contains within it a looming danger of the voracious consumption of places and cultures. It
also has the potential to plant the seeds of its own destruction before benefits
are harvested. KELLY SHANNON

■ tracing

[JM] The trace is not able to differentiate, only reproduce.

● trailers

[MG] 1. We use the cinematic term 'trailer' to refer to a process of operative synthesis: trailer, then, not as a linear summary of the film (an evocation), but rather as action – condensed information – that is deliberate, manipulated and non-linear – aimed at reinterpreting and transmitting at the same time. In effect, a trailer is an oblique representation of the film. A mental map of the action, made up of key interlinked situations that enable the whole to be condensed without reproducing it linearly, but rather by creating a non-linear synthesis of the overall plot: a document that is simultaneously autonomous and related. Favouring a deliberate compilation of parts, of fragmented elements, sometimes discontinuous (but not distant), with a sufficient degree of asyndeton to achieve a final objective: the recognition of a global scenario from a singular scenario. We can also speak of certain trailer-devices. Such trailers become deliberate maps of action referring to other (selected) maps of the city and of the global environment. They are the epitome of globality. Trailers and transfers at the same time.

[MG] 2. Also multiple – and rapid – transportation of mechanisms, energies and bits of information. Link mechanism. Think Tank.

● trajectory

[MG] Line, route or geometry described in space by one or various points in movement // Course, in the sense of directionality: hazardous, virtually chaotic, bearing or action // Diagrammatic – synthetical – logic of a complex spatial disposition, of non-linear and dynamic definition.

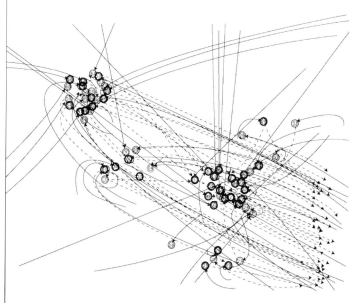

NOX (Lars Spuybroek with Kris Mun, Ludovica Tramontin, Florent Rougemont and Chris Seung-woo Yoo), *ParisBRAIN, a transurban scheme for the area west of La Défense*, Paris, 2001.

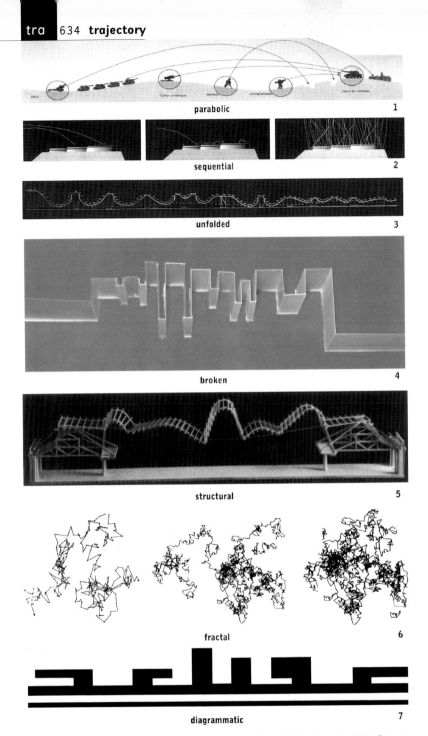

parabolic   1

sequential   2

unfolded   3

broken   4

structural   5

fractal   6

diagrammatic   7

1. Firings of missiles, in CAMPBELL, John, *La Segunda Guerra Mundial*, Madrid: Aguilar, 1993. **2.** Enric RUIZ-GELI, *FFF: Fireworks Figueres St. Ferran*, Figueres (Girona, Spain), 1998. **3.** BOLLIGER&MA-BILLARD, *Dragon Khan sketch, switchback in Port Aventura*, Salou (Tarragona, Spain), in *BAU* 017, 1999. **4.** S&Aa (SORIANO-PALACIOS), *MZMK (Bolzano Museum of Modern Art)*, Italy, 2001. **5.** Enric MIRALLES, Benedetta TAGLIABUE, *Rehabilitation of Santa Caterina Market*, Barcelona, 1999-. **6.** Examples of brownian movement, in MANDELBROT, Benoît, *Les objets fractals*, Paris: Flammarion, 1975. **7.** Willem Jan NEUTELINGS, *Evolutionary diagram. Project Hollainhof*, Gent (Belgium), 1996.

★ trans

[co]   One of the most fertile events and characteristics of proliferation is its condition
of 'trans.' The multiple, simultaneous, diachronic, superposed contagion of information produces miscellaneous transformations. Given the different speeds of transformation of relations and things, it might be said that they are all in different
states of provisionality. 'Trans' as a combination of characters. Not the consideration of each work, but of each work as a state of an indescribable complete work.
JOSÉ ALFONSO BALLESTEROS

● ★ transfers

→ 'attractors', 'braids',
'city?', 'crossing', 'flows',
'form', 'inform(ation)al',
'infrastructures', 'loops',
'mutation', 'nubs-nodes-
knots', 'places'

[MG]   **1.** See 'epitome' and 'trailers.'

Transfers are multiscalar transference devices.

[MG]   **2.** In his text "The doors of the city" (*Quaderns* 213, 1996), Rem Koolhaas pos-
es the question: "*Why not conceive urban outposts beyond the city (in their
areas of crossing) that simply absorb all the flows, swallow and transfer
them? Highways could suddenly terminate in them; they might be used to
park cheaply, then to take trains, trams, buses, or whatever survivors of
the collective period still exist.*"
Transfers are programmatically mixed proposals, aimed at dealing with the
formalisation of the large metropolitan interchange nodes. These are, in
effect, "cushion nodes" (concentrating and stimulating at the same time) in
places of maximum infrastructural concentration, which interlink mobility,
flow, interchange and information. They are nodes that are designed to take
advantage of the possibilities of intersection produced (explicitly and
metaphorically) in the context of current infrastructural webs that are strategically "reamortisable" (combining multiple access with low-price density).
Places of absorption which are converted into effective – hybrid – substitutes for the city; quasi spontaneous para-urban mutations developed as condensers and couplings of programmatically-mixed functional grids. Loops –
at once braids, bonds and links – capable of synthesizing the mobility, mutability, superposition and mixedness of the contemporary traveller.

Infrastructures and
mechanisms of
interchange. OMA,
Transferium,
Moordrecht, 1992
(fragment).

UN STUDIO,
*IFCCA Competition:
Penn Station,*
New York, 1999.

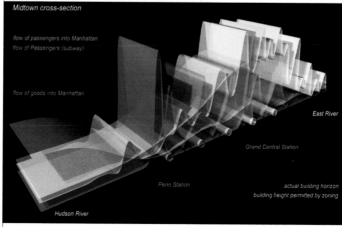

Midtown cross-section

flow of passengers into Manhattan
flow of Passengers (subway)

flow of goods into Manhattan

East River

Grand Central Station

Penn Station

actual building horizon
building height permitted by zoning

Hudson River

●★ transgenetic transfusions

[MG] Contemporary confidence in a possible mutation – or hybridisation – of the architectural object in new structures of coupling, mixture or dissolution is essential for understanding a large part of the current research into the "nature" of the project itself. Today it is, in effect, a question of working with non-predetermined codes for generating new examples, new dispositions and new local responses, fusing, contingently and weightedly, bits of information and codes (whether they are called architecture, infrastructures and landscape: fills, voids, links) into new specimens. It is thus possible to adopt a flexible attitude towards the environment that is not far removed from the reactive – operative and interactive – capacity that characterises a possible assumption of the transgenetic. This is visible in current scientific research, in the media and in industries that process and disseminate information (remember the mutant *cyborgs* of *Predator* or *Terminator* or the tactical mutations that are constantly produced in most new videogames). This would allude to a progressively synthetical – artificial – condition of contemporary architecture in the face of a reality which, in turn, is definitively artificial – synthetical. Awareness of the current and generalised coexistence alongside situations of tension, mixture, simultaneity and disharmony, is a feature not only of the social and cultural fabric, but also of the urban fabric within which the current project is framed.

[co] The acceptance of artificiality, as advocated by numerous present-day publications, cannot constitute a final resource, a form of energy in which architecture is practised as art of hybridisation, of grafting, of complexity. At a time when the human genome has been deciphered, when the human is set to become the stake in the law and the economy of the future, it is necessary to think of a strategy for the deregulation of the norm, of identity, of standards; to tear out the remanence of the oikos that remains at the heart of the biological, of the concept of cleanness already ravaged by worldwide industry. We have to place ourselves at the heart of mutation, within the very flow of processes.
FRÉDÉRIC MIGAYROU

James CAMERON,
*Terminator 2:
Judgment Day*,
Carolco Pictures/
Tristar, 1991.

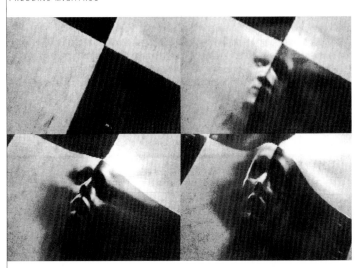

■★ **transparency**

→ 'holograms', 'space'

Virtual transparency.
Lawler DUFFY,
Chukka Boots.

LACATON&VASSAL, *Latapie House*,
Floriac (Bordeaux, France), 1993.

[JM] The space that pertains to the conical perspective demands a hierarchical vision; it must be space easily formulated, enunciable, predictable. It is clear that this geometry is going to go badly with an architecture that describes transparency, absence, lack of appearance, occultation, glittering in the night and trick of measure and reference.

[c] "*Conventional perception would lead us to perceive the materials of architecture and architecture itself as surfaces and volumes that are bathed – illuminated – by external projections: rays of light. But what happens when this projection does not originate – solely – externally, but internally as well? When the materials used to create shapes and volumetries allow the light to pass and behave as reflectors, as irradiators, as projectors of inner energy? When material quality yields to another more immaterial and evanescent – transparent – quality?*"

(DE SOLÀ-MORALES, Ignasi , "Architecture des inmatériaux", GUIHEUX, Alain, *Architecture Instantanée*, Paris: Ed. Centre G. Pompidou, 2000)

● **transversality**

[MG] Today, faced with the habitual predominance of an action that is merely reproductive or replicative (self-supporting, endogenous and autistic), a new propositional action emerges today that is more interested in establishing an action that is synaesthetic (by virtue, precisely, of being synergetic, i.e., relational) with the contemporary cultural, creative, technical and scientific environment.

A critical action, interested not only in describing occurrences, but also in tackling (explaining, understanding and fostering) processes; resonating with a global framework in mutation.

This has to do with an emergent change in the disciplinary gaze, which is no longer self-consumed, but is decidedly interactive. TRANSVERSE. An open gaze that is aimed at fostering, not so much the redescriptive application of models or methodologies, but the *crossing* of diverse and heterogeneous experiences and investigations.

This dynamic of crossing – of transversality – among various disciplines refers to the reactive nature of contemporary architecture itself, not so much as a resistant (distanced or questioning) condition, but rather as a condition that is recodifying — de(un)codifying. That is to say, a condition which is a dismantler of inertias — of old pre-established codes (uncodifying) – but which also translates emergent and global phenomena – new codifications – (decodifying).

An action, then, which is also transverse: capable of establishing links between things – and experiences – in order to relate and make them operative: in short, to reinstrumentalise them.

● **trays**

[MG] See 'land(s) in lands,' '*plateaux*,' 'platforms,' 'landstrategy,' 'tableland' and 'topographies, operative.'

●✖ tree

→ 'ecology, active',
'land(s) in lands',
'natuficio'

[MG] See 'naturartificial.'

A tree has roots, trunk, branches and (possibly) leaves, flowers and/or fruits of an indeterminate nature.

[VG] (photovoltaic tree)

See also 're-information.'

A photovoltaic tree is an item of urban furniture whose structure and functioning are similar to those of a tree, but whose fruit is light.

Photovoltaic trees are a hybridisation between a natural process (the functioning of a tree) and artificial nature (arboreal structure and photovoltaic cells).

The light captured by the photovoltaic leaves descends into the tree's roots via cabled branches and trunk, where there are either batteries to store the accumulated energy or a transformer that transfers it to the grid.

At night, projectors at its base send light flowing upwards towards lines of fibres forming the actual tree or towards lights arranged in its proximity.

There are no standard models. An intelligent programme produces personalised designs in accordance with the contour conditions of each place (building height, orientation, etc.), the energy needs and the available budget, generating necessary documents for its development.

Photovoltaic tree
Vicente GUALLART
(with Max
SANJULIÁN),
*Project for the
urbanization of
Cristóbal de Moura
street*, Barcelona,
1999.

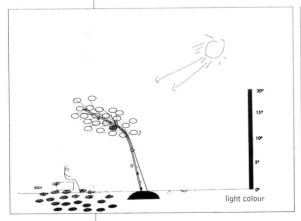

light colour

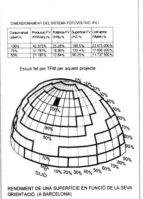

RENDIMENT D'UNA SUPERFÍCIE EN FUNCIÓ DE LA SEVA
ORIENTACIÓ (A BARCELONA)

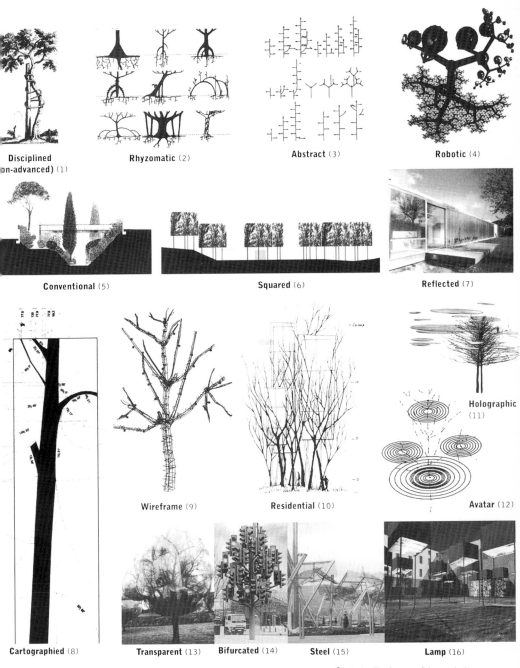

Disciplined (non-advanced) (1) **Rhyzomatic** (2) **Abstract** (3) **Robotic** (4)

Conventional (5) **Squared** (6) **Reflected** (7)

Cartographied (8) **Wireframe** (9) **Residential** (10) **Holographic** (11) **Avatar** (12)

Transparent (13) **Bifurcated** (14) **Steel** (15) **Lamp** (16)

1. N. ANDRY, *Comparation of a tree with ortopedic techniques*, in Arch+ 119-120, 1993. **2.** UN Studio, *System of the tropical tree roots*, in L'Architecture d'aujourd'hui 321, 1999. **3.** UN Studio, *Forms of ramification from the trunks*, in L'Architecture d'aujourd'hui 321, 1999. **4.** MORAVEC, *Robotic bush*. **5.** BCQ (David BAENA, Toni CASAMOR, Josep Maria QUERA), *Forest fringe planning,*, Viladecans (Barcelona), 1998. **6.** Toni GIRONÈS, *Single-family house*, Collbató (Barcelona), 2000. **7.** Pedro URZAIZ, Carlos PÉREZ-PLA, *Covered swimming pool*, Torrelodones (Madrid), 1995. **8.** Enric RUIZ-GELI, Bea GOLLER, *Firemen School*, Telfs (Austria), 1997. **9. & 12.** Vicente GUALLART (with Max SANJULIÁN), *Project for the urbanization of Cristóbal de Moura street*, Barcelona, 1999. **10.** ROCHE, DSV&SIE P., 'House on the trees' project, Compiègne (Saint-Sauveur, France), 1994. **11.** Enric RUIZ-GELI, *Cloud 666 Tree: Fundació Mies van der Rohe headquarters*, Barcelona, 1998. **13.** CHRISTO and JEANNE-CLAUDE, *Wrapped tree*, in Arch+ 144-145, 1998. **14.** Pierre VIVANT, *Installation*, London, 1999. **15.** S&Aa (SORIANO-PALACIOS), *Euskalduna Hall*, Bilbao (Spain), 1998. **16.** ARCHIKUBIK, *Virtualopolis*, Barcelona, 1999.

● tremas

[MG] *"n.m. Many fractal trajectories present structures built starting with a Euclidean space and cutting out a collection of open sets that I call tremas."*
(Paraphrasing MANDELBROT, Benoît, *Fractal objects*)

● trenches

→ 'cuts', 'landscapes, operative', 'land(s) in lands', 'landstrategy', 'terraces', 'topographies, operative'

[MG] Digging or incision in the land with banks on both sides // Tactical excavation // Construction in the negative // Deep furrow for multifunctional use.

1. Lands-trenches during the Gulf war, Kuwait, in GAUSA, Manuel, *Housing,* Barcelona: ACTAR, 1998. 2. AMP (ARTENGO-MENIS-PASTRANA), *Archeological Museum,* Zonzamas (Spain). 3. NJIRIC+NJIRIC, *Europan 3,* Den Bosch (The Netherlands), 1993. 4. DALLAS-DIACOMIDIS-HARITOS-NIKODIMOS-PAPANDREOU, *Urban Intervention,* Meyrin (Switzerland). 5. Carlos FERRATER, *Gymnasium,* Barcelona, 1996. 6. JAKOB&McFARLANE, *Project Puzzle,* 1997. 7. Josep Lluís MATEO (MAP Arquitectes), *Rehabilitation of Vincennes zoo,* Paris, 1993. 8. Ben VAN BERKEL, Caroline BOS (UN Studio), *Villa Wilbrink,* Amersfoort (The Netherlands), 1994 (Photograph: Jordi Bernadó).

■ trip

[JM] The trip is a vehicle from which to open the world from the real to the possibilities of the distant and future. Mutation, change, trip and movement are 'valise-words,' for they contain sufficient power to suggest analysis and creative proposals. The trip, always constitutes the beginning of something, the construction of biography. "To be other" is a dramatic experience which aspires the construction of worlds and creation of spaces.

● tropism (active)

[MG] Today, it is a question of positing the propositional potential of mobility and interchange and relating it to a new understanding of the idea of place – an articulated place – with new projectual – and conceptual – tools. Recovering a certain optimistic – ambitious – epic of the global implied profound changes of scale and structure which are features of the new metropolitan shapes; favouring a positive and, at the same time, critical action, attentive to the conflicts, tensions and deficits generated by the phenomenon in question. It is a question of re-thinking the notion of *tropism*, as an objective factor, rather than a puzzling platitude. Promoting, in this context – as anticipated – the idea of *place* not as a fragment that evokes a cohesive whole, but rather as a specific, autonomous event, which is linked to a strategic and heterogeneous spectrum – a patchwork – of strata, situations and potential loveliness. Places are concatenated or braided, based upon this progressive capacity for displacement that enables us, in a same lapse of time, *not only to arrive ever further, but also to arrive at an increasing number of places* (improvement in the speed of transport means not only a reduction in journey times, but also easier access to spaces located at greater distances). Urban life seems marked by a double tropism (metropolitan on the one hand, domestic on the other) that tends to strip of their old functions and values some of the spaces between the "metropoly" collective places and the home private places. As François Ascher argued, "*the story of the contemporary age is, in fact, also that of urban mobility. Since the beginnings of humanity, urban growth and technologies of communication and interchange have always gone hand in hand. It is a mobility that cannot be reduced merely to movement in space. It is a continuous process, starting with economic structures and ending with social relationships.*" It is therefore a question of understanding mobility as a potential. A requirement related to the progressive freedom of relationships and options implicit in all social development, and translated, ultimately, into a greater capacity for communication, interchange and access in a city, a "place of places" at once singular and interlinked.

■ true and false

[JM] All that is supposedly false is excluded from discourse because it inverts, interrupts and provokes the stumbling of a word. Everything seems to be previously classified: that which pertains to what should be said, and that from which one can hope nothing. But is it not part of a project to surprise us more than we expected, use the inutile, what has been discarded as useless, or what is false?

U

▲ ubliquity

→ 'diagonalisation',
'membrane', 'surface',
'trajectory', 'transversality'

[FP] Ubiquity and obliquely. In 1954, Paul Virilio visited the defence bunkers in the French Atlantic coast that, after having been buried by the movement of dunes emerged again from the sand. There, he had the feeling of walking around their interior and their inclined floors, that appeared to be endless. In 1965, Virilio argued: "I am convinced that in the future, the dominant architectonic element will not be the facade, not even the deck, as some research on three-dimensional, hanging or neumatic structures seems to indicate, but the floor." In 1992, OMA clearly defined the correctness of the Virilio's words of with their project for the library of the Jussieu Campus in Paris. The floor is liberated from its impeccable horizontal condition multiplying its condition of active planes and disrupting even the reading and representation of space itself, by the abolition of the concept of floor and the making relevant the superfluous nature of facades as the conforming elements of verticality. Based upon the evolution described in a couple of lines, we start to appreciate the ubiquity of these solutions, that are lavished making the oblique urban order that, in principle, should be interpreted as the overcoming of the horizontal/vertical system (the verticality of a wall, a frontier, a pile, a hierarchy, lack of equality). Probably, in an evolution dictated by logic, the overcoming of logic, of horizontality, should not only imply a reformulation of the floor, but also an integral reorganisation of barrier-areas in every direction, literally dissolving the discontinuities and inflexions. In this way, the language and reading of architecture will abolish words like floor, elevation and section, substituting them by words like *active-layer, isolating-membrane, speaking-section*, that obviously will be used indistinctly.

★ ugliness

→ 'moral'

[co] Form is in itself unassailable, even when it does not comply with the standards of beauty. Subversion, vis-à-vis canonical order, cannot be called into question and may be celebrated as a triumph of intelligence if it is the result of a manner of exercising independence vis-à-vis the dictatorship of formal standards, and if it possesses moral coherence and functional consistency. Ugliness is only open to challenge when it is the result of a lack of morality or a failed exercise in aesthetic conformity, never when it is a mere expression of the good and evil within us. JOSÉ MIGUEL IRIBAS

★ unbuilding

→ 'cuts', 'cuttings',
'holes', 'in/unfinished',
'spaces> collective'

[co] Unbuilding, an act of deconstruction, was first popularized by the artist Gordon Matta-Clark in the 1970s with his "cuttings," in which he sliced open existing buildings and the resulting voids became works of art. Matta-Clark inspired architects such as Frank Gehry to think of their work as a revealing of the latent spaces of everyday reality. This method is closely related to the continuing interest in the "infinito," the unfinished architecture that does not impose a final image on a site, but reveals the history of its making and previous inhabitation. The strategy also translates the "cuts" made by land artists such as Michael Heizer to the urban and domestic realm. Finally, unbuilding might be the most effective way of opening up a truly public and free space in a scene dominated by private commercial interests. It also reminds us that all acts of construction are first and foremost acts of destruction, and turns this truth into a productive act. AARON BETSKY

★ unflatable ice

[co] Nowadays, we can conceive a design of construction and colonisation on Mars, working with the new technologies of Nasa (the Earth-Bioplex Unit in Houston). Light inflatable habitats (with a special transparent skin to protect against cosmic radiations) which can be inflated on Mars.
FRANÇOIS ROCHE

François ROCHE (R&Sie. D/B:L), *Unflatable Ice*, Mars Planet, 2010.

●■◆ unfolding

→ 'buds', 'criteria', 'dispositions', 'distribution', 'emergency', 'environment', 'extend', 'extroversion: <ex> factors of form', 'fold', 'geometry', 'occupations', 'open', 'self-organization', 'sequences', 'topological', 'unrestrained (<un> factors)'

[MG] Unfolding is an *"action of causing troops – or shapes – to move from a compact order to an open and extended order."*
(CASARES, Julio, *Diccionario ideológico de la lengua española*, Barcelona: GG, 1966)

[JM] Architecture is more like geography than an object, something closer to a line than a point. According to this idea, architecture unfolds and concentrates according to lines of force, according to the situation. It seizes convexity to extend itself on the concavities. It is the eternal fold and unfold of the cloths of Zurbaran. But it is also those architectonic formulations that give way to exterior space in a complete fusion of space and landscape.

[JM] Designing is an action associated with unfolding: everything occurs through an action that links, associates, puts in contact, joins, and ties singularities. But also, the mechanisms that come to be thought of use this type of tool. Thus, the glance is understood as an unfolding that overlaps silhouettes, superimposes heterogeneities and twins differences.

[FS] Folding is a generative process of form. Forms unfold their possibilities being part of the program, on site, according to budget, etc. Thoughts unfold over reality. Spaces unfold over volume. Composition is substituted for a pendulous process between unfolding and doubling.
"Man thinks poorly because he thinks in a circle. He does not stop going over the same thoughts, and takes for new thoughts the other side of old thoughts. This is classical thought. Closed thought. Conservative thought. Thinking that in its center encounters God. Who has the strength to renounce this "divine" conclusion breaks the circle and internalizes a free and straight path that knows neither goal nor end because it is infinite."
(SAVINIO, Alberto, *Nuestra alma*, Madrid: Siruela, 1990)

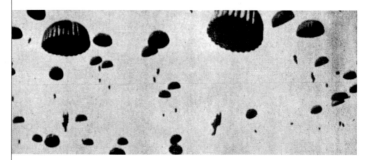

The allied paratroopers execute a massive deployment near Montecassino during the Second World War.

S&Aa (SORIANO-PALACIOS), *Competition for bus station*, Talavera de la Reina (Toledo, Spain), 2000.

★ (un)plug

[co] (Un)plug is the design of a new logic to develop a building that gains its energy from the sun. It needs the deformation of the reactive façade to respond to contact with renewable energies (hairiness of the façade for thermal sensors and swelling of the glass skin for the photoelectric cells).
FRANÇOIS ROCHE

● unrestrained (<un> factors)

→ 'advanced>
advanced architecture',
'colours', 'competition',
'extroversion: <ex> factors
of form', 'inform(ation)al',
'in/uninhibited',
'joy (*alegría*)', 'open',
'optimism', 'yes!'

[MG] The vital force of contemporary art and architecture resides in its capacity to produce new principles based upon a creative attitude as rigorous as it is relaxed: born without bias or previous disciplines: more unrestrained — uninhibited and unobsessed (that is, unashamed, unbiased and uncodified); more trusting in the possibility of favouring redefinitions and re-codifications as stimulating as they are (re)developmental for a reality suddenly open to free, joyous and spontaneous (unrestrained, precisely) collision

[i] p. 648-649 and combination of forces, energies and bits of information.

● uppercut

→ 'advertising', 'blunt',
'direct', 'economy',
'essayist knowledge',
'gaze> tactical gaze',
'logic, direct', 'paradoxes',
'reactive', 'speed', 'yes!'

[MG] Uppercut is right on the chin. In plain language, without hesitation.
Direct – expeditious – logic. Initial decision and final result.
Action, surprise and paradox.

Chanel adverstisement.

★ urbanism, anarchist (self-urbanism)

[co] Anarchist urbanism is the practice of anarchist urban planners. It is characterised by placing oneself at the service of those people and communities not normally taken into account in decision making regarding the construction of the city and the architecture that those very same people will have to inhabit, i.e. the majority of citizens and their organisations.
Anarchist urbanism is often build-it-yourself. Other times it consists of the appropriation/transformation of spaces produced by other agents and with other ends: typically speculation, domination and/or show business.
JOSÉ PÉREZ DE LAMA

Tadashi KAWAMATA,
People's Garden, Kassel
(Germany), 1992.

● urban-territorial

[MG] See 'rurburbia.'

■ urbs / orbs

→ 'avatar', 'glocal',
'm. city', 'no-places',
'telepolis'

[JM] Presence, realities, are more important than time; the urbanization of the world and its implication – that "urbs" become "orbs" – implies that we have been left without an outside, and this provokes us to feel close to other cultures and their space, but also their catastrophes and effects.

◆ use

[FS] See 'activity,' 'program' and 'interaction.'

Distribution of
spontaneous football
pitches on the beach
of Ipanema,
in *El Pais Semanal*.

◆ ★ ● utopia

→ 'advanced> advanced
architecture'

[FS]

[co] When the distance between utopia and reality, kilometric distance in Jules Verne's times, and metric in the times of the Bilbao Guggenheim, depends on Vision, Representation and Measurement, then Virtual Reality Machines, body and glasses (VR devices) are the architecture that builds dreams.
Architecture is that platform that enables us to visualise, live and feel those dreams. Dreams like those of Wim Wenders in Until the End of the World — and yours, too.
ENRIC RUIZ-GELI

[MG] Not utopia. Anticipation. Exploration and foresight. "Advanced" (anticipated) reality.

[co] Jean-Clarence Lambert opens "Portrait de l'artiste en utopien", his essay on the Situationist architect Constant, with a quotation from Henri Lefebvre, in which a distinction is made between 'utopian' and 'utopist'. Utopist thought, claims Lefebvre, is concerned with abstract utopia and explores the impossible, while utopian thought is concerned with concrete utopia that aims to "liberate" the possible. Lambert places Constant on the side of th utopian; that is to say, on the side of efforts to alter and extend the landscape of the concrete-possible rather than probe the abstract-impossible. MARCOS NOVAK

1. ACTAR ARQUITECTURA, *Europan: 400 housing units* (finalist), Ceuta (Spain), 1999. **2.** ACTAR ARQUITECTURA, *Cine Alfaro Square*, Cehegín (Murcia, Spain), 1998. **3.** ACTAR ARQUITECTURA, *300 housing units*, Graz (Austria), 1996. **4.** ACTAR ARQUITECTURA, *Pau Picasso Square*, Montornés del Vallès (Barcelona), 1999. **5.** Enric MIRALLES&Benedetta TAGLIABUE, *School of Architecture*, Venice (Italy), 1998-. **6.** Enric MIRALLES & Benedetta TAGLIABUE, *Diagonal Mar Park*, Barcelona, 1997-. **7.** Fernando PORRAS-ISLA, Federico SORIANO, Arantxa LA CASTA, *University Library*, Santander (Spain), 1989. **8.** S&Aa (SORIANO-PALACIOS), *Competition for bus station*, Talavera de la Reina (Toledo, Spain), 2000. **9 & 10.** S&Aa (SORIANO-PALACIOS), *Conference centre*, Benidorm (Alicante, Spain), 1997. **11.** Arantxa LA CASTA, Fernando PORRAS-ISLA, Gemma MONTAÑEZ, *Cover for the fair precinct*, Palma de Mallorca (Spain). **12.** ÁBALOS & HERREROS, *AH Houses. Industrial prototypes*, 1994-1996. **13.** NL, *Oefenfabriek*, Hoogvliet, (satellite town of) Rotterdam (The Netherlands), 2002.

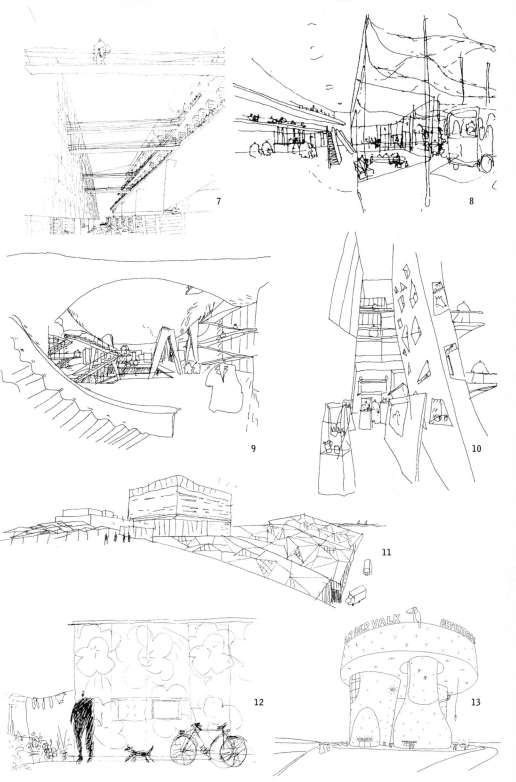

7

8

9

10

11

12

13

V

● vague

[MG] Empty, unoccupied, vacant // Lazy, leisured, inactive, relaxed // Wandering (and therefore active) // Slack, undefined. Diffuse and fluctuating // Hazardous: indeterminate or uncertain. In all cases, INFORMAL.

▲ ★ vector

[FP] What distinguishes a vector from other dimensional parameters is its directionality; it knows better than anyone what it wants and makes a direct line for it.

[co] If the classical determinism of Newton conceived the notion of force as an arrow, straight and true, today it appears differently, as a minimum path, a flexible vector, direct and amazing, through a field of potentials. According to local conditions, this path may vary, but its trajectory is based on moments of mutual cooperation and interaction, in a simultaneous juxtaposition of effects that are drawn surrounding it, modifying it and making it evolve. CECIL BALMOND

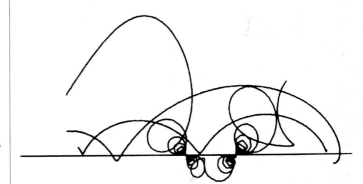

Cecil BALMOND, Diagram of an informal trajectory, in *Quaderns* 222, 1999.

● versatility

[MG] Versatility is flexibility, but also ambivalence and polyvalence. Space that is multifaceted, that is to say, multiplied (multiplicative).

1. Rebecca HORN, *Body-mechanic fan,* 1974, in *BAU* 015, 1997.

2. Enric MIRALLES, *Unstable table* for the exhibition *Le Magazine,* Grenoble (France), 1993.

3. KOERS-ZEINSTRA-VAN GELDEREN, *Tumble House,* 1998.

● vertigo

[MG] Vertigo is the sensation of loss of balance or lack of support, or the feeling that the subject himself or surrounding things are turning – suffered, for example, at great heights, or looking over a cliff, or after spinning round. Dizziness, momentary loss of self-control, which can lead to an act of violence. Or of emotion.

1. Jean NOUVEL, *Lafayette Galleries*, Berlin, 1996.
2. FOA, *World Trade Centre*, New York, 2002.

● ★ virtual

→ 'cyberspace',
'digital world', 'interfaces',
'logic, digital',
'metareality', 'reality',
'simulation', 'telepolis'

[MG] "*The ghost was her father's parting gift, presented by a black-clad secretary in a departure lounge at Narita. [...] The ghost woke to Kumiko's touch as they began their descent into Heathrow. The fifty-first generation of Maas-Neotek biochips conjured up an indistinct figure. 'Hullo,' the ghost said. Kumiko blinked, opened her hand. The boy flickered and was gone. She looked down at the smooth little unit in her palm and slowly closed her fingers. 'Lo again,' he said. 'Name's Colin. Yours?'*"
(GIBSON, William, *Mona Lisa Overdrive*, London: Gollancz, 1988)

[CO] The virtual-as-construct enabled by the technologies of cyberspace or neurobiology is not to be confused with the virtual-as-ideal that exists as a hermeneutical figure, relativised and beyond all scrutiny. Just as the recognition of the embodied mind renders obsolete the Cartesian mind-body division, the virtual-as-construct enacts an embodied that is engaged in the world as we are constructing it, in all its problematic but rich specificity. The virtual-as-ideal, on the other hand, stops short of engaging the underlying matrix of physics and materiality that makes both mind and cyberspace possible; the virtual-as-ideal limits itself to making isolated conventional forms in conventional space, dressing them in rhetorical conceit, and leaving the world unchanged.

Vicente GUALLART,
Use with no physical space: dwelling in the virtual space, 1992.

The virtual-as-construct includes the virtual-as-ideal, for rhetoric has its place in human affairs too, so the issue is not one of exclusion or dichotomy, but rather one of the consideration of the critical concerns of the visual-as-ideal in the production of artifacts within the virtual-as-construct. While the virtual-as-ideal operates by "troping" and interpretation to enact power-plays of membership and exclusion, the virtual-as-construct encompasses a variety of existing, emerging, and still-to-be-invented forms of expression, including liquid architectures, transarchitectures, hypersurface architectures, and other as-yet-unnamed alien hybrids of bodyspace and cyberspace.
MARCOS NOVAK

Marcos NOVAK, "Liquid-, Trans-, Invisible-: The Ascent and Speciation of the Digital In Architecture. A Story" in CACHOLA SCHMAL, Peter (Ed.), *digitalreal*, Basel: Birkhäuser, 2000).

→ 'material', 'skin', 'soft', 'structure', 'wetgrid'

★ viscous architecture

[co] Viscosity is a property of materials that makes them to flow and allows them to be deformed when we apply a load under certain conditions. Technically, it is requested that the time of application of the stress TC has to be bigger at its time of relaxation TR. Silicone, pitch and asphalt are viscous materials and their applied stress decreases when we keep the same deformation; when we keep the same stress, permanent deformation is produced. All biomaterials possess elastic and viscous properties. An architecture built with viscous materials means the acceptance of more deformations and better integration with nature. The biggest deformations are reflected in the facade and in the structural elements. Viscous opens up to a road of economic and coherent research into elastic architecture. Elastic architecture is becoming extinct.

Viscosity is manifested equally in the distributions and the limits of facades. The combination of holographic materials and the application of small generating energy machines together with structural deformation movements and the facade are reflected in the colour of the skin of the building. Either the wind or the deformations made by the use are very much appreciated in changes of colour. Viscosity is related with time.

SALVADOR PÉREZ ARROYO

S. PÉREZ ARROYO &
E. HURTADO
(with F. RÍO DURAN),
World Trade Center,
New York, 2003.

★void

[CO] Sometimes I pride myself on being the first person to speak of the "urban void" as a problem of the present-day city. It is a terminology that has spread, because 'void' is almost the last word available to describe this kind of space. The city, at least our cities, is by now fully grown and has occupied everything it can comfortably occupy; what remains, therefore, is what is almost conflictive. If we do not wish to occupy this kind of residual area with the typical catalogue pieces, more or less forced or adapted to "make do" in particularly difficult situations by virtue of their topography or surroundings, what we must do is invent new spaces and new uses. Or, rather than invent them, accept them.
EDUARD BRU

Luís ASÍN, Ibiza,
1993.

Carme PINÓS,
*Pedestrian footbrid-
ge*, Petrer (Alicante,
Spain), 1999
(Photograph: Jordi
Bernadó).

Normandie landscape,
in PERRAULT,
Dominique,
Nature-Architecture,
Barcelona:
ACTAR, 2002

● voids and fills

[MG] The contemporary urban-territorial space forms a denditric structure of intermittent and syncopated developments that enable spaces of omission to take on a prominent role: absences of construction, open spaces or visual incisions; residual plots, marginal spaces or large reserves of omission, which operate "in negative;" voids which can foster a more singular, flexible and effective treatment – and an instrumentalisation – of the landscape.

The growing expansion of world conurbations leads, in effect, to the formation of outlying subcentres dispersed in a polycentric movement that favours accelerated processes of fractalisation affecting not only the boundary of the urban landscape, but also many of the substructures contained within it. These present empty surfaces, whose edges grow more rapidly than the surfaces themselves. They are, therefore, rhizomatic structures characterised by discontinuous growth but, above all, by an intercidence of empty-full sequences:

If in the traditional city, compact, coherent and monocentric growth yields to the predominance of fill over background, in the fractal multi-city, despite its apparently chaotic development, "recursive" structures can, in contrast, be more easily conceived; these are based upon interweavings between empty and full, capable of coupling, interconnecting (as in virtual fields of imbricated pixels) with spaces of development – presences – and (operative) spaces in reserve – absences.

It is a question, therefore, of projecting the void, its shape and its disposition. Not so much as an isolated or exceptional residual event, but rather as an operative system associated with the channelling of flows. If for years the work of architecture has concentrated on the full – the edificiary, the constructed – today, both terms must and can be linked and combined. These contracts between places can be articulated, in effect, in successive positive-negative, empty-full seriations, which – well-designed at all scales –favour diversity, contrast and identity by means of the role given to relational spaces. Land links, strategic landscapes of incision and (or) articulation act as *gaskets* between events – in the same terms to which Sybille Becker refers – like engagements capable of ensuring effective sequences and connections between different developments which at the same time, as Rem Koolhaas observes, give rise to authentic dynamics of social adhesion.

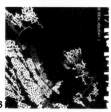

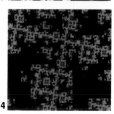

1. Vicente GUALLART, *Rehabilitation of the eleventh century Arabian ramparts*, Valencia (Spain), Oficina RIVA, 1998-. **2.** Ignacio CAPITÁN CARMONA, *Rehabilitation of the old clothing and tailoring factory as 5 dwellings and shop*, Sevilla (Spain), 1999. **3.** Eduardo ARROYO (NO.mad Arquitectura), *Rehabilitation of the mines*, Valkenburg (The Netherlands), 1997. **4.** Fractal rhyzomes. **5.** ACTAR ARQUITECTURA, *Barcelona Land Grid*, 1998.

● ★ voids, inhabited/equipped

[MG] In the same way that the city is no longer an ensemble of harmoniously grouped and cohesive elements but rather a structure of fills – densities – and voids – absences – the dwelling moves from being an ensemble of carefully distributed rooms to a "space destined to be equipped."
A space to be inhabited/equipped. A space defined from a functional periphery and manifested as a void to be conquered.
The construction and the fittings, in service clusters, thus make up the most stable framework: the remainder can, possibly, slip into the realm of the temporary, the mobile and the polyvalent.

[c] *Transferring the urban reading to the interior space of the home permits us to operate within its boundaries, within its perimeter, within its periphery, grouping the service elements around a void to inhabit, to conquer.*
Thus will emerge thick party walls or façades with services that function as filters. These are large condensers capable of accommodating varied uses and, due to mobile partitioning, in different periods of activity we can even subdivide the large interior void.
If we conceive the inhabitable space as a void, we can then incorporate the notion of temporality, of TRANSITORIALITY.
If the fixed – permanent – parts are grouped in service nuclei and the changeable parts are housed without rigid divisions and with criteria of temporality, the changes the family unit undergoes over time will be resolved without profound, costly transformations.
In the definition of the home we must determine and group clearly what is permanent and what is ephemeral, what is fixed and what is subject to change." (ARANGUREN, María José; GONZÁLEZ GALLEGOS, José, "Habitar la caja", unpublished, 1999)

Shigeru BAN, *Naked House*, Tokyo, 2000.

● vortex

[MG] See 'architecture' and 'no-form.'

"*Projecting architecture is an act of generating vortexes in the currents of air, wind, light and sound; it is not building a dike against the current o giving way to its thrust.*" (ITO, Toyo, "Vortex and current", *AD*)

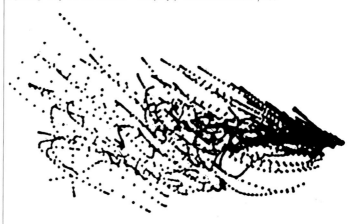

Dispersion of traces from a vortex.

▲● voyeurism

→ 'eye', 'gaze> tactical gaze', 'infiltration', 'nomad', 'tourism', 'trip', 'virtual'

Voyeurism in virtual reality (G. Fisher/Bilderberg, Thomann/Stern).

[FP] On 18th November 1997, the newspaper Le Monde published a call for help of the young American girl Jane Houston, who was terrified by the ghosts that she said used to visit her in her house. Houston installed fourteen video cameras in the most important corners of her home so that, via the internet and with the collaboration of thousands of potential observers, she slept calmly constantly guarded and protected. The empire of visual denunciation is now a reality with the profusion of control systems, not only in public places, bussiness and financial entities, but also in the most depressed housing areas and even in homes. It is also extremely well-known that due to servers like Earthcam or Netscape-eye, who have thousands of live pages dedicated to promoting tourism, we are allowed to travel without moving from our computer. These are all, universal voyeurism figures, which since the obtaining of almost infinite points of view, announce the appearance of almost infinite sales outlets which complete universal commercial globalisation, infinite looks in a single eye. Since the ulta-revolutionary invention of electricity electrical-optical illumination has improved allowing us a new approach, an active approach which will allow the location of the visible market. Let us be prepared.

(From Paul Virilio'Bombe Informatique)

[MG] Voyeurism is *Big Brother* and its various knock-offs. The *Truman Show* and *EdTV*, etc. Reality TV. Network "tele-visits" and various "tele-menus." Visual and virtual appetites and satisfactions. But also curiosity. Inquiry. Travel. Movement. Interchange. Chat. Internet and cable. Negative voyeurism-positive voyeurism.

W

◆ wander

→ 'logic, fuzzy',
'places', 'quidam',
'tangent', 'trip', 'vague'

[FS] To wander is a composite strategy: the architectonic object is not defined by a positivist and causal concretion, but by a spiral thought process, like successive skins of an onion. To stop roaming means to be defined by intangibles, to apply the Situationist derivative on the architectural project.

● wandering

→ 'nomad', 'paths & peaks',
'quidam', 'trajectory',
'trip', 'vague', 'vector'

[MG] See 'flâneur.'

"*Wandering is the function that gives the position of a point in space whose temporal evolution is governed by hazard. Synonymous with 'random function.'*

Cause of the suggested semantic drift. In visual language, wandering designates an excursion lacking any precise destination, or whose destination changes as one progresses and is, therefore, unpredictable.

If one considers the random as a model of the unpredictable, the underlying behaviour in the usual sense of wandering fits the proposed mathematical concept."

(Paraphrasing MANDELBROT, Benoît, *Fractal objects*)

★ war machine, the

[co] See 'nomad.'

In the universe of Gilles Deleuze and Felix Guattari, the war machine holds a central position, inextricably linked to that of the nomad.

The purpose of this war machine is not what we normally understand by war. The essence of the war machine, according to Deleuze and Guattari, is the opposition to any type of authority, resistance to the "state apparatus," the struggle against all forms of power.

Nomadology would be the form of knowledge/action associated with the war machine. The war machine relates to intuition, continual transformation and flows. Art, architectural and urban projects, and architecture itself may be thought of as a set of war machines: machines for producing new desires, countless connections, multiplying forms of inhabitancy.

JOSÉ PÉREZ DE LAMA

▲ water diviner

→ 'beacons', 'gaze>
tactical gaze', 'invent'

[FP] The water-diviner is capable of finding water under stones. Everybody looks at him in amazement, completely confused and he, armed with a simple wooden mechanism, scours the territory until he points out – with complete certainty – the place to dig the well. The people around him look at each other in disbelief, but after the prospecting works liquid gushes forth inexhaustibly.

The water-diviner is not a magician, he doesn't have supernatural talents. The water-diviner has a technique. He respects certain strategies when he walks around a piece of land. He follows clues and he isn't the one who digs the well, but the one who points out the place.

The water-diviner answers tangible calls (but intangible for others). We want water-diviner architects.

✖ WebHotel

→ 'cyberspace',
'domestic', 'house, the',
'hybrid', 'interfaces',
'light', 'nomad', 'trip',
'virtual'

[VG] The WebHotel is a hybrid building, constructed between the physical and the virtual world. Its facade is built using a metal structure and fabric with graphics in an urban space. Its rooms are built out of virtual objects and with lines of code on the Internet. When a person enters a virtual room, he can manipulate its walls and the objects it contains. Its virtual presence is manifested in the physical world by means of lights and sounds that are superposed onto its thin skin. In this way, for the first time a facade manifests an occurrence that, rather than taking place behind it in a nearby environment, is the product of actions in different places in the world. A webcam focused on the building sends real-time images to the Internet so that the user of the room can view the effects of his action. The actual building, with a server inside, produces its physical and its virtual images simultaneously. (The WebHotel was produced in Barcelona during the exhibition *Fabrications,* organised simultaneously by MACBA, MOMA, SFMOMA and the WEXNER)

Vicente GUALLART,
*WebHotel, in
"Fabrications",*
Barcelona, 1998.

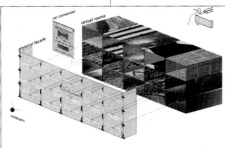

★ wetgrid

[co] The wet grid is an organisation in which movement is structurally absorbed by the system; it is a combination of intensive and extensive movement, of flexibility and motion. The wet grid views the body as a complex landscape of tendencies and chreodes that form grooves (lines) in less defined areas that are surfaces. Movement must be viewed as information, as pure difference which can be absorbed by a system, which subsequently must be a (analogue) computing system. The line is taken up in a field of potentials which make it an intensive line, which is simply a curve. A curve is a straight line with more openness, on which one can partly return to one's footsteps, change one's mind, where one can hesitate or forget. It complicates your path, makes it multiple and negotiable. The wet grid is always a network, topological and curved. LARS SPUYBROEK

NOX (Lars Spuybroek
with Chris Seung-Woo
Yoo, Kris Mun, Florent
Rougemont and
Ludovica Tramontin),
SoftOffice, United
Kingdom, 2000-2005.

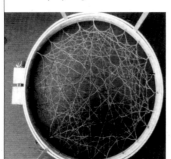

● wireframes

[MG] See 'skeleton' and 'fuselages.'

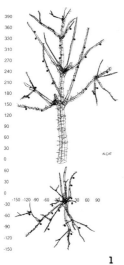

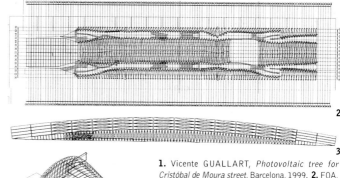

1. Vicente GUALLART, *Photovoltaic tree for Cristóbal de Moura street*, Barcelona, 1999. **2.** FOA, *International Port Terminal*, Yokohama (Japan), 2002. Hybrid structure. **3.** Lourdes GARCÍA SOGO, *Recycling plant for urban waste*, Villena (Valencia, Spain), 1999. Metallic structure. **4.** Vicente SARRA-BLO (with H. Jala), *Air Inflated System, Prototypes for inflatable sports facilities*, (Engineering: Javier Marcipar – CIMNE), 1999.

★ work

[co] Work is the "same as now, for most people in the world. Dealing with information, for a few," Gundula Feichtinger. XAVIER COSTA

● WTC (crisis)

[MG] Recent international events, in the aftermath of 11 September 2001, and the sudden spectre of a new reorientative crisis based on conservative re-proposition rather than innovative progression or the difficult conditions emerging around us seem to take us back to a time of scepticism, mistrust, fear or simple wistfulness. Is it reasonable — and logical — then to continue to speak of optimism? We believe so, so long as that term does not mean boundless insouciance, but rather a certain "propositive" ethic — less codified or ritual than the inertially "established" — aimed, precisely, at "optimising" reality, projecting new qualitative actions over the environment, that is, over territories and urbanities, habitats and landscapes, private and shared spaces, etc., and so long as the associated idea of progress — not as an absolute and deterministic arrow but as "evolutionary will," as "shared intelligence" — would still be the most positive feature of our cultural capacity when it comes to posing questions, taking on challenges, improving conditions and creating new and possible contracts — and spaces — of interchange and coexistence.

S. PÉREZ ARROYO & E. HURTADO (with F. RÍO DURAN), *World Trade Center*, New York, 2003.

● X-Architecture

|MG| See 'act-n' and 'multi.'

X-architecture is architecture – or architectural devices – which multiplies.

● XL

|MG| XL from S, M, L, XL.

Rem KOOLHAAS, *Jussieu Library*, Paris, 1995, in KOOLHAAS Rem; MAU, Bruce (OMA), *S,M,L,XL*, Rotterdam: 010 Publishers, 1995.

Y

● y

[MG] "Math. *a symbol frequently used to indicate an unknown quantity.*" (*Webster's Encyclopedic Unabridged Dictionary of the English Language*)

NL, *Y Building, Flower Tower*, Amsterdam, 1999.

● y-

[MG] "*Prefix of uncertain meaning, sometimes of perfective or intensifying force.*" (*Webster's Encyclopedic Unabridged Dictionary of the English Language*)

● yes!

[MG] Yes! is positive and affirmative (always).

▲ Yeti

→ 'hypertrophy'

[FP] Yeti is the Abominable Snow Man. The man from the Himalyas, whose existence nobody from Tibet doubts. A man never seen or captured by western man. Yeti buildings. Ugly but imposing buildings. Buildings that never appear in magazines. Buildings which don't depend on their authors.

● Yin and Yang

[MG] See 'figure-background' and 'voids and fills.'

● yo

[MG] "*Interjection used as an exclamation to express excitement, get someone's attention, etc.*" (*Webster's Encyclopedic Unabridged Dictionary of the English Language*)

"I" in Spanish. See 'I/(my)self' and 'I (formerly identity).'

● Yokohama

→ 'flows', 'landstrategy', 'lava, programmatic', 'topological', 'vector'

[MG] Paradox par excellence: "the roof of a building can also be its floor."

● yuppie

→ 'zapping'

[MG] A yuppie is the final specimen of modern productive mechanics: impositive, not synergetic – representing the triumph of the autistic self.

Yokohama

1 open
2 a-scalarity
3 self-similarity
4 branchial
5 field
6 circuit
7 foreignness
8 unfolding
9 device
10 spaces>collective
11 extensible
12 evolutionary
13 figure>background
14 flows
15 genetics of form
16 glocal
17 puff pastry
18 horizons
19 inform(ation)al
20 interchanger
21 membranes
22 *millefeuilles*
23 naturartificial
24 nomadic
25 sea
26 paradoxes
27 process
28 psycho-geographize
29 similarity
30 system>Operating
  System

FOA, *International Port Terminal*, Yokohama (Japan), 2002 (Photographs: 1 & 2, Ramon Prat; 3, Satoru Mishima).

Z

● zapping

[MG] Zapping is flexible and temporary contract with a mutable and (com)mutated environment, event or scenario.

★ zero (0)

[co] See 'ground.'

Center or focus of conflict.// Hole.

AMANDA SCHACHTER / ALEXANDER LEVI

● zigzag

[MG] See 'circuits' and 'loops.'

Zigzag is an uneven dynamic trajectory, indistinctly ascending or descending.

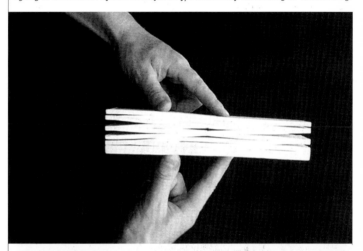

MVRDV, *Shopping mall Zigzag*, 1998. Mobility structure for a new type of shopping mall.

●◆ zone of high-sensitivity

[MG] See 'areas of impunity' and 'places.'

[FS] A territory and the city are not stable nor homogeneous places. They establish particular topographies through points within their area. These are positions of attraction or repulsion that generate a plan. I imagine a meteorological drawing, where currents, flows and fields create zones of higher and lower sensitivity. The city is transformed from a graph of nodes or from a network, a magnetic field, in which the order between the parts is produced by tensions that the parts create among themselves.

● zoom

→ 'a-scalarity',
'epitome', 'fractal',
'geometry', 'recursiveness',
'self-similarity',
'sequences', 'strategy',
'trailers', 'trajectory',
'transfers'

[MG] Zoom is a mechanism for enlarging and shrinking. Interscalar concatenation: topological structural recursiveness. Linked sequences with a greater or lesser degree of isomorphism. Structures in mutual resonance and transference.

[MG] "Let's imagine that we can consult a general map of the Universe on an interactive computer. If we wanted to make out details, we would just have to click on the screen to increase it ten times; the third time we clicked, the original image would be increased by one hundred.
After three zooms, we would see our galaxy, the Milky Way, as a spot of light among others; and if we enlarged it another two times, we would have a detailed image. If we were to continue, we would be able to enter it; another five zooms and we would see the sun. After another five, the earth. And after another five zooms, we would have a map of the world on a scale of one millionth; six zooms more and we reach unit scale: so, between human scale and universe scale there are just twenty-five zooms, twenty-five powers of ten, twenty five decimals.
But if we carry on... Five levels lower and we could admire our red and white blood corpuscles; another four levels and we could see atoms. The nuclei of the atoms would appear another five levels down, but that would be far as we could go, because that is the scale of light photons. [...] The smallest known physical objects are quarks, which are only two or three levels lower.
A chaotic system is a similar zoom to the one we have used to travel through the universe in forty clicks: it is a mechanism for increase and development. Evolution in time reveals increasingly precise and diverse details, like clicks on a screen, but it increasingly amplifies small differences, too; it can take microscopic phenomena to macroscopic scale. [...] In fact, it is in the successive enlargement of these small differences that we ultimately find chance. It would seem that two identical initial positions should always reproduce the same trajectory: this is the basic principle of determinism. Unfortunately, we know that it is impossible to return a physical system to the same position; there is always a "difference," even if it is only an atom."
(EKELAND, Ivar, "If chaos exists, we can discover it", *Quaderns* 222, 1999)

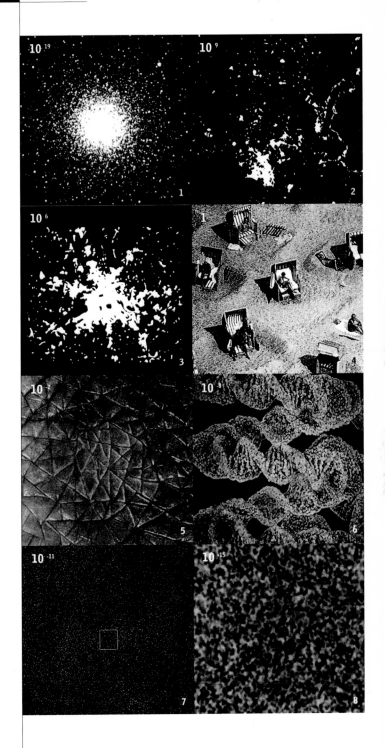

1. Nebula Hercules constellation. 2. Night image of Europe from satellite. 3. Berlin, built mass. 4. Beach: random occupation. 5. Folds and skin wrinkles. 6. Double helix of ADN. 7. Electrons of the carbon athom. 8. Proton.

intelligent',
'puff pastry
(puffed up)',
're-information',
'reliefs', 'rurban
loft', 'score',
'self-similarity',
'sensuality',
'singular housing',
'spaces',
'sport rock',
'Swiss knife',
'technique, the',
'tree', 'tree>
photovoltaic tree',
'virtual',
'voids and fills',
'WebHotel',
'wireframes'

**GUALLART,
Vicente;
DÍAZ, Nuria**
'Benidorm',
'Gibson's sprawl',
'living-working-
resting'

GUIHEUX, Alain
'action',
'devices',
'dispositif
(device)',
'territory'

**GUILLÉN,
Miguel Ángel**
'music'

**HAAG, Richard,
Associates**
'leisure
(and landscape)'

HARDING, Noel
'hypertrophy'

HEJDUK, John
See SANMARTÍN,
Antonio;
HEJDUK, John

**HERREROS,
Juan**
See ÁBALOS
& HERREROS

**HITCHCOCK,
Alfred**
'suspense'

HOLL, Steven
'commensalism',
'limit',
'pieces, loose',
'singular housing'

HORN, Rebecca
'versatility'

HYAMS, Peter
'fear'

**IaN+
(GALOFARO, L.,
BAGLIVO, C.,
MANNA, S.)**
'holes',
'muaré or moiré',
'quidam',
'skin',
'stack (stacks)'

**IRIBAS,
José Miguel**
'bank & beach',
'discothèque',
'hotel',
'impact
(environmental)',
'in-out',
'polysensoriality',
'space-time',
'street market',
'territory>
(touristic)',
'ugliness'

ITO, Toyo
'abstract
(advanced)',
'armadillo',
'de-materia-

lization', 'light',
'muaré or moiré',
'nomad',
'strips',
'tornadoes
(or twisters)'

**JAKOB,
Dominique &
MACFARLANE,
Brendan**
'archaeology',
'evolutionary',
'facet(s)',
'fuselages',
'trenches'

**JARAUTA,
Francisco**
'essay',
'reality'

**JOHNSON,
D./Stock Market**
'(e)motion
(moving)'

**JONES &
Partners**
'container'

**JUMEAU,
Anne-Françoise**
See PAILLARD,
Louis;
JUMEAU,
Anne-Françoise

**KALHÖFER &
KORSCHILDGEN**
'reversible'

KAHN, Louis I.
'abstract
(modern)'

**KAWAMATA,
Tadashi**
'urbanism,
anarchist
(self-urbanism)'

KEATON, Buster
'Keaton'

KIM, Scott E.
'figure-
background'

KINSLOW, Tom
See UNGERS,
Simon;
KINSLOW, Tom

KISHI, Waro
'stenosis'

**KOERS-
ZEINSTRA-VAN
GELDEREN**
'versatility'

**De KOONING,
Marc**
See
NEUTELINGS,
Willem Jan;
De KOONING,
Marc

**LACATON, Anne
& VASSAL,
Jean-Philippe**
'ambushments',
'lightness
(and levity)',
'precarious(ly)',
'singular housing',
'transparency'

**LEJARRAGA,
Martín**
'erudition'

LEVI, Alexander
'ground',
'zero (0)'

**LEWIS, Duncan;
POTIN &
LEWIS**
'camouflage',
'complicity',

**RIEGLER
& RIEWE**
'action',
'activity',
'displacing
by sliding',
'housing'

**ROAGNA-
EHRENSPER-
GER CELLINI**
'circuits',
'(inter)weavings
and inter(plots)'

**ROCHE, François
(R&Sie.D/B: L)**
'client', 'hump',
'membrane',
'muaré or moiré',
'naturartificial',
'overflow',
'rurban life',
'section:
scrambled flat'

**ROCHE, François
(Roche, François,
DSV & SIE)**
'ambushments',
'aspiration',
'aspiration',
'auditoriums',
'blurring', 'blu-
rring',
'camouflage',
'contraction and
extrusion',
'contraction
and extrusion',
'figure-back-
ground', 'fish',
'fold(ing)',
'fold(ing)',
'growing up',
'housing',
'inform(ation)al',
'inform(ation)al
structures',
'overflow',
'section:

scrambled flat',
'shadow & light',
'shadow & light',
'shearing',
'tree',
'unflatable ice',
'(un)plug'

**ROJO, Luis;
VERDASCO,
Ángel;
FERNÁNDEZ-
SHAW, Begoña**
'coilings',
'tableland'

**ROLDÁN,
José Miguel**
See R+B
(José Miguel
ROLDÁN,
Mercè
BERENGUÉ)

ROSLER, Martha
'pieces, loose',
'simultaneity>
successive-
simultaneous'

**ROUILLARD,
Dominique**
'action',
'territory'

RUBY, Andreas
'hypercontext',
'performance',
'pragmatopia',
'prototypology'

**RUIZ-GELI,
Enric**
'agriculture',
'antigravity',
'bubbles', 'blur',
'camouflage',
'camouflage',
'catalogue',
'chromatisms',
'chromatisms',

'cloud9',
'construction,
intelligent',
'cosmos',
'digitnature',
'event',
'fatuous fires
(feux follets)',
'holograms',
'immersed',
'in/unconscious-
ness', 'light',
'light', 'link',
'matrix',
'multifunctional
environment',
'precision',
'production,
intelligent', 'rays',
'reality', 'rurban
loft', 'scene',
'scene', 'sensua-
lity', 'shadows',
'simultaneity>
successive-
simultaneous',
'tempo', 'terraces',
'trajectory',
'tree', 'utopia'

**RUIZ-GELI,
Enric;
SUBIRÓS, Olga**
'digitnature'

RULL, Rosa
See ADD
Arquitectura
(Manuel BAILO,
Rosa RULL)

**S&Aa (Federico
SORIANO,
Dolores
PALACIOS)**
'abstract
(advanced)',
'archaeology',
'auditoriums',
'Benidorm',
'Bilbao effect',

'bluntings',
'camouflage',
'catalogue',
'chains', 'cloud',
'collaging',
'cover (covering)',
'cut-outs',
'density',
'diagonalisation',
'diagrams',
'dictionary',
'dispositions',
'distortion',
'evolutionary',
'flâneur',
'game',
'geometry',
'holes',
'immersed',
'land(s) in lands',
'memory',
'muaré or moiré',
'naturartificial',
'no-day
(night and day)',
'occupations
(spontaneous and
evolutionary)',
'papyroflexy',
'patterns',
'pieces, loose',
'precision',
'recycling, urban',
'score', 'section',
'spaces',
'stack (stacks)',
'strips',
'surface',
'tangram',
'technique, the',
'topological
(age)', 'tornadoes
(or twisters)',
'tree',
'unfolding',
'unrestrained'

**SAGGIO,
Antonino**
'information',
'organism'

The Metapolis Dictionary
of Advanced Architecture

The Metapolis Dictionary
of Advanced Architecture
is a Metapolis Association
project based upon
an idea by Manuel Gausa,
Vicente Guallart and
Willy Müller.

Authors:
Manuel Gausa
Vicente Guallart
Willy Müller
Federico Soriano
Fernando Porras
José Morales

Coordination:
Susanna Cros

Contributions by:
Iñaki Ábalos & Juan Herreros
Stan Allen
Eduardo Arroyo
Tom Avermaete
Larraitz de Azumendi
José Alfonso Ballesteros
Cecil Balmond
Ben van Berkel & Caroline Bos
Aaron Betsky
Ole Bouman
Marie Ange Brayer
Eduard Bru
Karl S. Chu
Xavier Costa
Manuel Delgado
Neil Denari
María Luisa González
Alain Guiheux
José Miguel Iribas
Francisco Jarauta
Alexander Levi
Duncan Lewis
Greg Lynn
Winy Maas
Josep Lluís Mateo
Frédéric Migayrou
Marcos Novak
Ignacio Ontiveros
Ignasi Pérez Arnal
Salvador Pérez Arroyo
José Pérez de Lama
François Roche
José Miguel Roldán
Dominique Rouillard
Andreas Ruby
Enric Ruiz-Geli
Antonino Saggio
Juan Carlos Sánchez Tappan
Saskia Sassen
Amanda Schachter
Artur Serra
Kelly Shannon
Yorgos Simeoforidis
José Antonio Sosa
Lars Spuybroek
Lars Teichmann
Francisco Tolchinsky
Roemer van Toorn
Laura Vescina
Jorge Wagensberg
Kris van Weert
Mark Wigley
Alejandro Zaera-Polo
& Farshid Moussavi

**The Metapolis Dictionary
of Advanced Architecture**

Assistance:
Ivan Alcázar
Marc Camallonga
Lídia Gilabert
Eloi Ortuño
Montserrat Roma
Marta San Narciso
Anna Tetas

Translation:
Edward Krasný
Elaine Fradley
Amanda Schachter
Edward Gallen
Brian Holmes

Proofreading:
Kelly Shannon

Graphic design:
Ramon Prat
Rosa Lladó

Collaborators:
Leandre Linares
Montse Sagarra
Anja Tränkel
Núria Tresserra

Image treatment
and photo reproductions:
Carmen Galán
Oriol Rigat

Printing:
Ingoprint SA

ISBN: 84-95951-22-3
DL: B-24260-03

Distribution:
ACTAR
Roca i Batlle, 2
08023 Barcelona
Tel +34 93 418 77 59
Fax +34 93 418 67 07
info@actar-mail.com
www.actar.es

Special thanks:
Arch+
ArchiLab
Archis
Architectural Design
Assemblage
de Architect
L'architecture d'aujourd'hui
BAU
El Croquis
Exit
Fisuras
Quaderns
Tefchos
For their complicity

To the photographers:
Jordi Bernadó
David Cardelús
Satoru Mishima
Ramon Prat
Hisao Suzuki
Giovanni Zanzi
For their collaboration

Institute for
Advanced Architecture
Metapolis
Nau Ivanow
Hondures, 26-28
08027 Barcelona
Tel +34 93 351 29 84
info@metapolis.com
www.metapolis.com